Harry Miner

Harry Miner's American Dramatic Directory for the Season of

1884-85

Harry Miner

Harry Miner's American Dramatic Directory for the Season of 1884-85

ISBN/EAN: 9783744791137

Printed in Europe, USA, Canada, Australia, Japan

Cover: Foto ©Andreas Hilbeck / pixelio.de

More available books at **www.hansebooks.com**

HARRY MINER'S

AMERICAN DRAMATIC

DIRECTORY

FOR THE

SEASON OF 1884-'85.

*A complete Directory of the Dramatic and Operatic
Professions and a Guide to the Opera Houses,
Theatres and Public Halls of America.*

TOGETHER WITH MUCH OTHER

INFORMATION OF VALUE TO THE AMUSEMENT PROFESSION.

HARRY MINER, EDITOR.

NEW YORK:
WOLF & PALMER DRAMATIC PUBLISHING COMPANY,
NOS. 81 AND 83 ELM STREET.
1884.

PREFACE.

IN compiling and presenting this work to the public I have endeavored to fill a hitherto vacant place in the useful department of American libraries.

The growing popularity of the Stage, and almost universal desire to become better acquainted with things theatrical, convinced me several years since that a Directory would be not only eagerly sought after, but, if accurate, greatly simplify the labors of both managers and agents. I accordingly instructed the agents and managers of my various combinations to forward from time to time correct information regarding theatres, halls, hotels, railways and steamers to the office of the People's Theatre, where I carefully revised and arranged the volumes of matter thus collected; and I take this opportunity to furnish them for the use of the public in general, and the theatrical profession in particular.

Having a regularly organized staff of traveling managers and agents constantly employed in the working of my amusement enterprises, and being in communication with the leading representatives of the Theatrical World, I enjoy advantages that enable me to make the work I have undertaken more thorough and complete than any Guide or Directory ever published in America.

The routes around the world, capacity of public buildings, distance and census tables have been gathered from reliable sources, and if they prove as useful to my readers as they have been difficult to obtain, I shall be amply repaid for my time and labor.

Very truly yours,

HARRY MINER.

People's Theatre, October, 1884.

ROUTE AROUND THE WORLD.

The following route around the world has been taken from the private diary of
MR. J. CHARLES DAVIS,
who compiled it from his actual experience in the different localities — Mr. Davis having spent seven years abroad with amusement enterprises, leaving San Francisco in June, 1877, and returning in June, 1884.

At San Francisco take Pacific Mail or Occident & Orient Line steamers. Fare on each line to Hong Kong, China, $300 for each first-class passenger. Professional rate, $250. Average time of voyage, 28 days. Cold season in China and Japan from October to June; this is also the healthy season.

JAPAN.

Yokohama. — GAIETY THEATRE — Good stage and scenery; well lighted with gas; seating capacity, 600; G. F. Davidson, proprietor; rent, $25 a night, including gas. Windsor House, best hotel; theatrical rate, $1.50 a day; Woolfe & Smith, proprietors. Newspapers (three daily) — Japan Mail, morning, J. Beal, manager; Japan Herald, evening, J. Brookes, editor; Japan Gazette, evening, Jas. R. Angelin, editor; advertising rates, 50 cents an inch by the week; extra charge of 50 cents for change. Box-office, Kelley & Co., 5 per cent.; Davidson, manager. Dr. Stuart Eldridge, professional friend. No customs duties.

Kobie, or Hiogo. — Forty-eight hours by steamer through the Inland Sea. GYMNASIUM THEATRE — Seats 300; rent, including lamps and oil, $15 a night; J. Sym, agent; also has box plan at his store. Hiogo Hotel; rate, $1.50 a day (good house). Hiogo News, daily, small paper, 50 cents an inch for advertising. Railroad to Kioto, but not worth visiting.

Nagasaki. — Forty-eight hours steam. NAGASAKI THEATRE — Seats 300; rent, $15 a night, with lamps and oil. One weekly newspaper, The Rising Sun. China and Japan Trading Co., agents of the theatre; also sell reserved seats. Belle View Hotel; rate, $1.50 a day (good). Powers & Co., American merchants and professional friends. Take Nilso Bisi steamers (Japanese line) for Shanghai, China; fare, professional rate, $55 each person; three days steam.

CHINA.

Shanghai. — Three days steam from Nagasaki. European population, 7,000. Theatre, LYCEUM — Seats 1,200; usual prices, $3 and $2, according to location; rent, including gas and electric light, $50 a night; George Corner, agent; the theatre has fine stage and plenty of good scenery; box office, Kelly & Walsh, 5 per cent. Three daily papers — North China Daily News, morning, — Greathead, Esq., manager; Shanghai Courier, evening, Geo. Thirkill, editor; Shanghai Mercury, evening, J. Clark, editor; 50 cents an inch for advertising. Hotel Des Colonies; rate, $1.50 a day; Jas. Brown, manager. Astor House, same; R. Jansen, proprietor. Sayle & Co. for furniture and properties. Town good for three months with good company. Steamers every day for the south.

Foo Chow.
Swatow. — Small towns. Only good for one night while steamer lies over.
Amoy.

Hong Kong. — Three days steam from Shanghai. THEATRE ROYAL — Seats 600; fine large stage, plenty of good scenery; rent, $50 a night. Hong Kong Hotel, Victoria Hotel and Stag Hotel; rates, $1.50 a day. Three daily newspapers — Daily Press, morning; China Mail,

evening, and Hong Kong Telegraph, evening; rates for advertising, 50 cents an inch. Critics
—Robert F. Smith, Telegraph; E. W. Watson, Press; R. J. Smith, Mail. Box-office, Kelly
& Walsh, 5 per cent. J. Moore, Hong Kong Hotel, bill-poster. Steamers leaving every day
for south and west Cochin China will not repay a visit.

PHILIPPINE ISLANDS.

Manilla.—Three days steam from Hong Kong; fare, $25 each person, by Russell &
Co.'s steamers. Theatres—THE PHILIPPINO—Seats 500; rent, $25 a night; good stage and
scenery; Sen. Cuberro, agent; Government company plays here four nights a week; TEATRO
TONDO—Seats 800; rent, $35 a night; Sen. Belvino Reys, agent; good stage and scenery
Hotel Lala; rate, $2.50 a day; Ramon Lala, proprietor, who also acts as interpreter for show-
men. Three daily newspapers—El Comercio, El Oceano and El Diario de Manilla; reasonable contract for weekly insertions. Sen. Groet, director of orchestra, furnishes men for
$1.50 a night, each person. Door-keepers, stage-hands and ushers receive 50 cents a night.
Compulsory complimentary tickets—Captain-General, two boxes each night, Intendente, one
box each night; Guardia Civil, two seats each night. Government permission necessary for
each programme, which must be printed and submitted before opening the doors.

Illo.—One day's steam. Small ball. Will not pay large troupe.

MALAYA.

Singapore.—Five days steam; fare, $50 each person. TOWN HALL THEATRE—Good
stage and scenery; seats 400; rent, $20 a night; E. Presgrave, Town Clerk, agent of theatre.
Hotel de la Paix and Hotel de Europe, three rupees a day each person. Straits Times, daily,
and Straits Intelligence, tri-weekly; cheap contracts can be made. Box plan, Sayle & Co., 5
per cent. Frank Jackson, professional friend. Steamers leave once a week for Bangkok,
the capital of Siam, where a certainty may be obtained from the King's agents. Steamers
leave every three days for Saigon, a small French town in Cochin China. Steamers every
day for India and Burmah.

Penang.—Three days steam; fare, $20. TOWN HALL THEATRE—Seats 400; rent, $20;
Town Clerk, agent; no scenery, but good stage and lights. Penang Gazette, daily, W. A.
Cullen, editor; Penang Times, Batten, editor; cheap rates for advertising. Box plan at H.
Maynard's store, 5 per cent. Piano from Penang Club, free.

Thal Ping and **Penak** on the Malay mainland, small places; will not pay large
companies. Steamers leave for India and Burmah every day.

CEYLON.

Point De Galle.—One week's steam from Penang; fare, 100 rupees. GARRISON
THEATRE—Seats 4'0; rent, 20 rupees. No lamps or scenery, but they can be obtained from
the hotels. Two good hotels—rate, 3 rupees a day.

Colombo (Capital of Ceylon).—78 miles overland, or 150 miles by steamer around the
coast; fare either way, 30 rupees. Theatres—GARRISON—Stage and scenery; seats 400; rent,
30 rupees; ASSEMBLY ROOMS—No scenery; rent, 50 rupees. Box plan at Maitland's store, 5
per cent. Hotels—British India, Grand Oriental, Galle Face; rates, 3 rupees a day. Newspapers—Ceylon Observer, morning; Ceylon Times, morning; Examiner, evening.

Kandy (Home of the Ceylon Kings).—Five hours by railroad; special car, half usual
fare. TOWN HALL—Stage and scenery; rent, 30 rupees; seats 300. Queen's Hotel; rates, 3
rupees a day. Box plan at Smythe's store, free. Town good for two nights, then back to
Colombo. Steamers leave every day for Calcutta, Bombay, Madras and Rangoon.

BRITISH BURMAH.

Rangoon (Seat of Government).—Four days steam from Colombo; fare, 50 rupees.
Theatre, ASSEMBLY ROOMS (in the cantonment)—Seats 500; rent, 25 rupees a night, with
lamps; good stage, but very little scenery; E. C. Jordan, agent of theatre. Everoend's Hotel,
Jordan's Hotel; rate, 3 rupees a day. Box plan at Paxton & Co.'s store, 5 per cent. Newspapers—Rangoon Times, Rangoon Gazette (daily); advertising rate, 25 rupees a page for one
week. J. F Reagan, professional friend for favors; Governor of Burmah for patronage.
Town good for two months. Steamers every week for India.

Moelmyne.—One day's steam from Rangoon; good only for small shows. TOWN
HALL, GARRISON THEATRE—Rent, 20 rupees a night; no scenery. Moelmyne Advertiser

(daily, cheap), J. C. Hodges, proprietor. No hotels, but can get in private bungalows. Steamer back to Rangoon.

INDIA.

Calcutta (Seat of Government).—Three days steam from Rangoon ; fare, 100 rupees each person. Theatres—CORINTHIAN—Seats 1,000 ; rent, 1,000 rupees a month; Seal Brothers, proprietors (Hindoo Babos); good stage, fine scenery and gas; bars can be rented out for 300 rupees a month. THEATRE ROYAL.—Seats 1,000 ; rent, 1,000 rupees a month; good stage and scenery, and gas ; J. Andrews, proprietor ; also proprietor Spence Hotel. OPERA HOUSE—Seats 800; rent, 1,000 rupees a month; good stage and scenery, with gas; James Brown, agent. Three large halls for concerts, etc. Newspapers—Indian Daily News; rate, 2 annas a line; J. Napier, manager; Clarke, editor; Englishman in India, daily, 2 annas a line ; Scott, manager ; Statesman and Friend of India, daily ; J. Murphy, editor; rate, 60 rupees a month for six-inch space. Native papers only good for circus advertising, which can be had for two season tickets each. Hotels—Great Eastern, Spence's and Adelphi; rate, 100 rupees a month, or 3 a day. Bill poster, Wm. Saunders; contracts for season at 25 rupees a week; good man. Job printer, Erasmus Jones, No. 5 and 6 British India street; good work; reasonable rates. Police tax, 100 rupees a month, if theatre bars open. Stage hands, etc., average 30 rupees a month ; this work is all done by coolies. Furniture and properties—Lazarus Brothers, Chowringhee Road. Ushers, ticket-sellers, door-keepers, etc., receive 1 rupee a night ; musicians, 3 rupees a night; doorman or sepoy watchman, 1 rupee a night. Any good company can play to big business for three months here if able to change programme twice a week. Comic opera, comedy, society drama, burlesque or sensational drama are all good for India. Variety, minstrelsy or melodrama will not draw, no matter how well given. Vocal and instrumental stars can get one or two good houses only if they have a good European reputation.

Bombay.—1,750 miles by rail from Calcutta; fare, 100 rupees. Theatres—GAIETY THEATRE—Capacity, 800 ; rent, 100 rupees a month; A. F. Soondy & Co., agents; good stage, scenery and gas; electric lights front of house; GRANT ROAD THEATRE—Rent, 600 rupees a month or 40 a night; seats 1,000; Hindoo Lihlb Lai, proprietor. Hotels—Watson's Hotel, Bycolla Hotel, English Hotel, Grand Central, Waverly Hotel; rates, 3 rupees a day or from 80 to 100 a month. Newspapers—Times of India (daily), Bombay Gazette (daily); rates same as Calcutta. Job printing—Kiser I. Hinel Press, Franju C. Meltia, proprietor, who will also contract to have his coolies post bills. Police tax, if bars open, 100 rupees a month. Box plan, Soondy & Co.'s music store, 5 per cent. Piano, 25 rupees a month. Help, musicians, etc., same as in Calcutta. Furniture, etc., from hotels. Town good for two months.

Poona.—Hill station or summer resort, four hours rail from Bombay; fare, 20 rupees. INSTITUTE HALL THEATRE—Seats 500; rent, 30 rupees. Good stage and scenery, lighted by lamps; Commandant of station, agent. Napier Hotel; rate, 3 rupees a day. Newspapers, two daily—Poona Observer, Deccan Herald; rates very low. Box plan at Preacher & Co.'s store, 5 per cent. Sir John Ross, K. C. B., Commander of the Post, also great friend of professionals. Town good for two weeks.

Jabbelpore.—On the line between Calcutta and Bombay. Good for two nights. THEATRE ROYAL—Rent, 30 rupees a night; stage scenery and gas. Corsajee & Co., agents. Jackson's Family Hotel; rate, 3 rupees a day. Box plan at Corsajee & Co.'s store, free. Tuge village here. Well worth a visit.

Allahabad.—Large railroad and garrison town on the line between Calcutta and Bombay. RAILWAY THEATRE—Seats 600 ; rent, 50 rupees a night ; good stage, scenery, dressing-rooms and gas; station agent, manager. The Pioneer (only daily newspaper) is one of the largest and best in India ; advertising rate, 2 annas a line. Hotels—Great Eastern, Great Northern ; rates, 3 rupees a day. Box plan at Lyell & Co's. store, free. Job print, Railway Press ; reasonable and good. Sir Alfred Lyle, K. C. B., Lieutenant-Governor ; Sir Herbert McPherson, K. C. B., Vice-Councillor, for patronage to any special night; work garrison for soldiers' patronage. Town good for two weeks in the season.

The following large East Indian cities all have garrison theatres, good hotels, and can be worked (by a small party) with success; the expenses of everything will run nearly the same as the foregoing places and the stay that can be made is one, two and three nights. They are all railroad towns :

Bhosawahl,	Mhow,	Khandwa,
Hyderabad,	Benares,	Fyzabad,
Lucknow,	Delhi,	Agra,
Cawnpore,	Dianapore,	Jamalpore,
Madras,	Simla,	Dum Dum,
Baroda,	Decca,	Secounder Abad.

The healthy season in India is from September to June. June, July, August and September are the hot, rainy months, when cholera is very bad and the European residents are away in the mountains for the Summer.

Poona, Simla and **Secounder Abad** are hill stations or sanitariums, but they are too expensive for any but small parties. The natives will not patronize anything but a circus. A Hindoo, Mohammedan or Parsee Chief will sometimes give a large sum for an English company to play at his palace on great nights. On these occasions they usually build a stage in the large hall of the palace and entertain the company as guests.

South Africa may be reached by semi-monthly steamers from Bombay, calling at Zanzibar and Delegoa Bay. Fare, 400 rupees each person.

SOUTH AFRICA.

Cape Town (Cape of Good Hope), the capital of Cape Colony—45,000 European population; 14 days steam from Liverpool, 18 days from Bombay, 7 days from Port Louis. THEATRE ROYAL, Beng street — Seats 1,000; rent, £35 a week, with gas; good stage and scenery; Darter Brothers, agents. EXHIBITION BUILDING—Seats 2,000; rent, £20. Newspapers—Cape Times, daily, J. Murray, editor; Cape Argus, daily, H. Dormer, editor; Advertiser, daily, Saul Solomen, editor; Evening Express, daily, M. Wright, editor; Lantern, weekly, M. McCombie, editor; advertising rate, 2s. 6d. an inch by the week. Hotels—Masonic, Imperial and St. George ; 6s. or $1.50 a day; £2 a week. Bill-poster, H. J. Fiedler; box plan, Thorp's Library, Adderly street. Job print, Advertiser office; cheap and good. Furniture, Lazarus Brothers. Wineburg, City Point, Sea Point and Clairmont must all be well billed, as the street cars run until after the theatres are out. City good for three months with strong company that can give new programme each week.

Paarl and Branfort, West.—Two small towns on the railroad, good for three nights each, if a success in Cape Town.

Port Elizabeth.—Two days steam from Cape Town ; fare, £5. THEATRE ROYAL, DRILL HALL and TOWN HALL—All have scenery and gas, and rent for £50 each a night. Newspapers—Herald, Star and Telegraph, all daily, with same rates as Cape Town. Hotels—Phœnix and Masonic ; £2 a week, or 6s. a day ; town good for two weeks.

Grahamstown.—Three hours rail from Port Elizabeth ; fare, 7s. Town HALL and MUTUAL HALL—Stage and scenery in each hall; rent, £2 a night, with gas. Newspapers—Eastern Star, Penny Mail and Journal, all daily ; same rates of advertising as in Cape Town. Hotels—Railway and Royal; rate, £2 a week. Take rail back to Port Elizabeth, then steamer to East London.

East London.—Two days steam from Port Elizabeth. Fare, £2. MUTUAL HALL—Stage and scenery; rent, £12 a week. Newspapers—Dispatch and Advertiser, daily; rate, 2s. 6d. an inch. Hotels—Buffalo and Masonic; rate, £2 a week. Town good for one week.

King William's Town.—Three hours rail from East London. CITY HALL—Stage and scenery; rent, £15 a week. Newspapers—Standard and Watchman; rate, 2s. 6d. an inch by the week. Hotels—Commercial and Masonic; rate, £2 a week. Town good for two weeks.

Queenstown.—Five hours rail from King William's Town. NEW TOWN HALL—Stage and scenery; rent, £15 a week. Newspapers—Free Press, Standard and Independent; rate, 2s. 6d. an inch per week. Hotels—Masonic and Oriental; rate, £2 a week. Furniture, Hood, Morris & Co. Box plan, Mendelssohn's music store. Take wagon trains here for the Diamond Fields, 600 miles from the railroad. Time usually occupied in traveling, one month.

Kimberley (the Diamond Mines).—THEATRE ROYAL—Stage and scenery; rent, £25 a week including lamps and oil. Secretary, agent. Newspapers—Independent Diamond News, Advertiser, daily; rate, 2s. 6d. an inch by the week. Hotels—Masonic, Jardines and Imperial;

rates, £5 a week. Usual prices for theatrical entertainments, 10s., 8s. and 5s. Town good for eight months—then back to the coast via Natal.

D'Urban, or Port Natal.—THEATRE ROYAL — Complete and well furnished; rent, $25 a week. TRAFALGAR—Stage and scenery; rent, $12 a week. Newspapers—Mercury and Advertiser; rate, 2s. an inch per week. Box-office, Davis & Son's book store, free. Hotels—Masonic, Victoria, Royal and Central; rate, £2 a week. Town good for two weeks.

Peter Merritt's Borg.—THEATRE ROYAL and GAIETY THEATRE. — Rent, with stage, scenery and light, £12 a week. Hotels—Crown and St. George; rate, £2 a week. Newspapers—Witness and Times; rates, 2s. an inch (weekly). Railroad back to Natal for steamer to Port Louis, Isle of France, seven days steam via Madagascar; fare, £12 each person, by the Union and French lines of steamers.

MAURITIUS, OR ISLE OF FRANCE.

Port Louis (Seat of Government).—Population, 250.000. Mauritius is now an English Crown colony, was formerly a French settlement. French is still the prevailing language. THEATRE DE PORT LOUIS—Seats 1,500; rent, £5 a night; gas, £5 a night; fine, large house with every modern improvement; scenery painted in Paris; Town Clerk, agent; Mayor's permission necessary for each programme; usual prices of admission from 1s. to £5, according to location. Six daily papers; theatrical advertising free—Cernlan (French), morning; Le Pays (French), morning; Progress (French), morning; Colonial (French), morning; Record (English), morning; Sentinel (English), morning. Critics of English papers—C. E. Leal, Sentinel; W. L. Bowers, Record. All advertising matter must be in French and English to be effective. Hotel Masse and Occidental Hotel; rates for professionals, 6 shillings a day. J. D. Prentiss, United States Consul, friend of professionals and will help clear all theatrical baggage at the Customs. The Right Hon. F. Napier Broome, C. M. G., Lieutenant-Governor, will give his patronage to all first-class entertainments. Town good for two weeks. Steamers once a week for Reunion Borbon, which is good for comic opera or concert. Steamers to India, Australia and Africa every few days.

JAVA.

Batavia—OPERA GEBOUW—Stage, 30x120; splendid scenery; rent, 5 per cent. of gross; seating capacity, 850. Address Secretary Schouwbourg, Batavia.

Buitenzorg—Forty miles from Batavia by rail. CONCORDIA CLUB THEATRE—Rent, 20 dollars (50 florins); small stage and curtain; no scenery; will seat 500; prices, 5 florins, 3 florins and 2 florins ($2, $1.20 and 80 cents).

Cheribon.—CONCORDIA CLUB HALL—Rent free; stage, 25x30; no scenery; will seat 300; admission, $2 (5 florins). Population, 5,000.

Semarang.—OPERA GEBOUW—Rent, 75 florins ($30) per night; seating 900; stage 30x80; good scenery; admission, 5 florins ($2). Address Secretary. Population, 40,000. Paper—De Locomotief.

Djockokarta.—HARMONIA CLUB HALL—Stage, 30x10; no scenery; seats 300; admission, 5 florins ($2); rent free. Paper—De Mataram. Population, 5,000.

Sourabaya.—Population, 70,000. COMEDIE GEBOUW—Stage, 25x70; good scenery; seating 800; rent, 75 florins ($30) per night. Address Secretary.

Passroan.—Population, 3,000. CLUB HARMONIA HALL—Rent free; no stage; no scenery. Address Secretary.

AUSTRALIA.

Melbourne.—VICTORIA HALL (new)—Stage, 25x15; seating 600; address Fred. Hiscocks; share. THEATRE ROYAL, PRINCESS'S THEATRE; address Williamson, Garner & Musgrove; share only. BIJOU THEATRE—Rent, £70 per week; address Mr. Lewis, seats 1,000; splendid stage and scenery. Papers—Argus, Telegraph, Herald, Age, Australasian, Bulletin, Evening News.

Adelaide.—ACADEMY OF MUSIC—Seats 800; stage, 30x50; rent, £30 per week. GARNER'S THEATRE—Seats 700; stage, 30x40; share. THEATRE ROYAL—Seats 1,000; stage, 40x70; splendid scenery; share only. Population, about 60,000.

Sydney.—THEATRE ROYAL—Stage, 30x50; seats 1,000; share; good scenery; address Williamson, Garner & Musgrove. OPERA HOUSE—Seats 900; stage, 30x40; good scenery; rent, £100 per week or share; address Wilson, proprietor. GAIETY THEATRE—Seats 800; stage, 30x35; good scenery; share.

New Castle.—THEATRE ROYAL—Rent, £50 per week ; seats 700 ; stage 35x45 ; population about 40,000.

Brisbane.—THEATRE ROYAL—Seats about 1,000 ; Hickey, manager ; share only ; stage 40x80 ; good scenery.

Gulong.—EXHIBITION HALL—Seats 1,000; rent, £8 per night; stage 30x70.

Landhurst.—PRINCESS' THEATRE—Seats 1,200 ; share ; stage 40x80. Papers—News, Independent. MASONIC HALL—No stage; seats 1,000; rent, £10 per night.

Ballarat.—MECHANICS' HALL—Rent, £5 per night; stage, 20x30; seats 600. Papers—Courier, Star, Post.

NEW ZEALAND.

Invercargill.—SLOAN'S THEATRE—Rent, £5 per night; seats 600; stage 20x25. Papers, Southland News, Times.

Dunedin.—PRINCESS' THEATRE—Seats 1,000; stage 35x80 ; good scenery ; rent, £8 per night. Papers—Times, Herald, Star, Press.

Christchurch.—GAIETY THEATRE—Seats 500; rent, £3 per night; stage, 20x40. THEATRE ROYAL—Share; seats 1,000; stage, 30x70. Papers—Times, Telegraph, Society.

Wellington.—THEATRE ROYAL—Share ; seats 1,000; stage, 30x60; good scenery. Papers—New Zealand Times, Evening Post.

Poverty Bay.—McFARLANE'S HALL—Certainty is paid all good shows. Small stage; no **scenery.**

Auckland.—ABBOTT'S OPERA HOUSE (New)—Seats 1,000; share; stage, 33x50; Abbott, manager; good scenery. THEATRE ROYAL—Seats 1,000; stage, 30x60; good scenery; share; Abbott, manager. Papers—Star, Herald, Free Lance, **Bulletin.**

TASMANIA.

Launceston.—MECHANICS' INSTITUTE—Seats 300; stage temporary; rent, £5 per night. NEW THEATRE—Seats 800; share. Papers—Telegraph and Examiner.

Hobart Town.—THEATRE ROYAL—Seats 800; stage, 30x80; share.

QUEENSLAND.

Gympie.—TOWN HALL—Seats 500; stage, 20x40; rent, £3 per night. Paper, Gympie Miner.

Maryboro.—TOWN HALL—Rent, £5; seats 700; stage, 20x30).

McKay.—SCHOOL OF ARTS—Seats 600; stage, 20x25; **rent, £4** per night. Papers—McKay Standard and Chronicle.

Townsville.—SCHOOL OF ARTS—Seats 600; rent, £5 per night; stage, 20x25. Papers—Northern Argus and Chronicle.

Charters Towers.—SCHOOL OF ARTS—Rent, **£5 per night;** seats, 700; stage, 20x30. Paper, Northern Miner.

PROFESSIONAL DIRECTORY.

ACTORS AND ACTRESSES.

— A —

Ackerman, Miss Irene, juvenile leads, Shook & Collier's Lights o' London Western Co.; dram. agts., Simmonds & Brown; permanent address, 20 W. 15th st., New York.

Acosta, Miss Marie L., juveniles and leads, dram. agt., J. Alex Brown; per. ad., Madison Square Theatre, New York.

Adrian, Walter, leading heavy or juvenile; Maude Atkinson Co.; dram. agts., Simmonds & Brown; per. ad., Rahway, N. J.

Addison, Miss Fanny, heavy lead and character, Madison Square Theatre Rajah Co.; per. ad., Madison Square Theatre, New York.

Addison, Miss Grace, singing soubrette, W. F. Mott's N. Y. Co.; dram. agts., Brooks & Dickson; per. ad., 97 S. Desplaines st., Chicago.

Adel, Miss Helene, heavy leads, Clara Morris Co.; dram. agt., J. Alex Brown; per. ad., 64 E. 14th st., New York.

Adam, A. K., old men; per. ad., 36 Carnes st., Lynn, Essex Co., Mass.

Ahrendt, Carl, old men; dram. agts., Brooks & Dickson; per. ad., 215 Bank st. Baltimore.

Aiken, Frank E., leads; dram agts., Brooks & Dickson; per. ad., 264 E. 124th st., New York.

Allen, Leslie, leads, Brooks & Dickson's La Charbonnier Co.; dram. agts., Brooks & Dickson; per. ad., 44 W. 23d st., New York.

Allen, Frank D., juveniles and heavies; dram. agts., Brooks & Dickson; per. ad., 380 Bridge st., Brooklyn.

Allen, Mrs. Octavia, old women; dram. agts., Brooks & Dickson; per. ad., Ocean Spray, Winthrop, Mass.

Allen, Miss Ada, singing soubrette; dram. agts., Brooks & Dickson; per. ad., 39 Cedar st., New Bedford, Mass.

Allen, Miss Wealthy, juveniles, C. B. Bishop Comedy Co.; dram. agts., Brooks & Dickson; per. ad., 44 W. 27th st., New York.

Allen, Harry, baritone and comedian; dram. agts., Brooks & Dickson; per. ad., 25 W. 39th st., New York.

Alliston, Miss Annie, old women, Brooks & Dickson's In the Ranks Co.; dram. agts., Brooks & Dickson; per. ad., 67 E. 12th st., New York.

Alliston, Miss Lillie, soubrettes; Brooks & Dickson, per. ad., 67 E. 12th st., New York.

Allyne, Miss Kitty, leading lady, Harry Miner's Eighth Avenue Theatre, New York.

Aldridge, James, heavies, Bertha Welby Co.; dram. agts., Brooks & Dickson; per. ad., 46 W. 26th st., New York.

Aldridge, Bristow, juvenile leads, George C. Miln Co.; dram. agt., J. J. Spies; per. ad., 12 Union Square, New York.

Alberta, Miss Laura, leading, Lillian Olcott Co.; dram. agts., Simmonds & Brown; per. ad., 20 Sutton Place, New York.

Andrews, Chas. specialty, necromancer, ventriloquist and animal trainer; per. ad., Great Bend, Kan.

Andrews, Miss Lillian, leads and light comedy; dram. agts., Brooks & Dickson; per. ad., 283 E. 18th st., New York.

Andrews, Wm. C., juvenile comedy, Barney McAuley Co.; dram. agts., Simmonds & Brown; per. ad., 108 Division st., Paterson, N. J.

Anderson, C. H., comedian and tenor; dram. agts., Brooks & Dickson; per. ad., 1161 S. Front st., Camden, N. J.

Anderson, L. S., responsible; per. ad., 33 North Russell st., Boston.

Anderson, Miss Mary, tragedy star, Dr. Hamilton Griffin, man.; London Lyceum Theatre, London, Eng.

HINES STROBRIDGE,   CLIFFORD B. WRIGHT,
President.   Secretary.

THE

STROBRIDGE

Lithographing

COMPANY,

Nos. 124, 126, 128, 130 and 132 N. Canal St.,

CINCINNATI, O.

BRANCH OFFICES:

44 West 23d Street, New York, A. A. Stewart, Agent.

89 Strand, London, Eng., Sam'l French, Representative.

THE LARGEST AND MOST SUCCESSFUL SHOW-PRINT-
ING ESTABLISHMENT IN THE WORLD.

Apjohn, C. P., comedian, Shook & Collier's
Lights o' London Co.; dram. agts., **Brooks
& Dickson**; per. ad., 117 E. 12th st., New
York.

Armory, J. R., comedian, Mlle. Rhea Co.;
dram. agts., Simmonds & Brown; **per. ad.**,
608 Lexington ave., New York.

Arnold, Miss Florence, juveniles; dram. agts.,
Brooks & Dickson; per. ad., 3 Green st.,
Fall River, Mass.

Arnold, Miss Mabel **B. (specialty), cornet**
soloist; per. ad., 183 Water st., Springfield, Mass.

Arnott, Miss Jennie, juveniles and soubrettes;
dram. agts., Brooks & Dickson; **per. ad.**,
54 W. 24th st., New York.

Arlington, Miss Maggie, leads; dram. agts.,
Brooks & Dickson; per. **ad.**, 23 E. 31st
st., New York.

Arnold, **Miss Tiny, singing soubrette and
boys; dram. agts., Brooks & Dickson;
per. ad., 240 E. 86th st., New York.**

Archer, T. M., juveniles, **Harry Miner's Silver
King Co.** No. 1; dram. agts., Simmonds &
Brown; **per.** ad., People's Theatre, New
York.

Arden, Edwin, leading juvenile, Boston Museum Stock Co.; per. ad., Vernon **ave.,**
Brooklyn.

Ashton, I. **L., character and heavies, Thorne's**
Black Flag Co.; **per. ad., 631 12th st.,**
Detroit, **Mich.**

Atkins, **Thos., old men; dram. agts., Brooks
& Dickson; per. ad., 77 Bedford st., New**
York.

Atkinson, **Miss** Maude, starring; Goodnow
& Johnston, man.; per. ad., 131 Sandusky st., Allegheny City, Pa.

Atkins, Edward (specialty), stage director and
vocalist, Globe Dime Museum, New
York.; per. ad., 2029 Emerald st., **Philadelphia.**

Ayling, Herbert, juvenile and comedy; dram.
agts., Brooks & Dickson; per. ad., 133 E.
17th st., New York.

— B —

Bachellor, **Miss Josie**, juveniles and soubrettes; dram. agts., Brooks & Dickson;
per. ad., Continental Hotel, New York.

Backus, P. T., juvenile; dram. agts., Brooks
& Dickson; per. ad., 50 E. 9th st., New
York.

Backus, Geo., juveniles, Kate Claxton Co.;
dram. agts., Brooks & Dickson; per. ad.,
39 W. 26th st., New York.

Baird, R. H., character comedian, Murphy's
Kerry Gow Co.; dram. agts., Brooks &
Dickson; per. ad., 33 Esther st., Toronto,
Can.

Bailey, **Miss Josie, juveniles and soubrettes;**
dram. agts., Brooks & Dickson; per. ad.,
955 Broadway, New York.

Bailey, Miss Bessie, juveniles and soubrettes;
dram. agts., Brooks & Dickson; per. ad.,
414 W. 34th st., New York.

Baker, Miss Emily E., leads, Bartley Campbell's White Slave Co.; dram. agts.,
Brooks & Dickson; per. ad., 528 Seventh
ave., New York.

Baker, Miss Katie, ingenues and soubrettes,
Brooks & Dickson's Romany Rye Co. B;
dram. agts., Brooks & Dickson; per. ad.,
44 W. 23d st., New York.

Balfe, Miss Louise, leads, Clara Morris Co.;
dram. agts., Simmonds & Brown, 231 W.
14th st., New York.

Bangs, F. C., leads, Harry Miner's Silver King
Co., No. 1; per. ad., People's Theatre,
New York.

Barbour, C. J., juveniles and old men, Brooks
& Dickson's In the Ranks Co.; dram.
agts., Brooks & Dickson; per. ad., 105 W.
67th st., New York.

Barton, F. C., juvenile or character, Fred.
Warde Co.; per. ad., 347½ Woodward ave.,
Detroit, Mich.

Barclay, De Lancey, character and old men,
Brooks & Dickson's In the Ranks Co.;
dram. agts., Brooks & Dickson; per. ad.,
319 W. 42d st., New York.

Barnes, J. H., leads, Union Square Theatre
Stock Co.; per. ad., Union Square Theatre, New York.

Barr, George, character, Nell Burgess' Vim
Co.; dram. agts., Simmonds & Brown; per.
ad., 486 6th st., Buffalo, N. Y.

Barr, Lottie, child parts, Nell Burgess' Vim
Co.; dram. agts., Simmonds & Brown;
per. ad., 486 6th st., Buffalo, N. Y.

Barron, J. M., light comedy and juveniles;
per. ad., Royal Oak, Md.

Bankson, Jno. W., heavies and old men;
dram. agts., Brooks & Dickson; per. ad.,
60 E. 9th st., New York.

Barrows, James O., leading comedy, Mlle.
Aimee's English Comedy Co.; dram.
agts., Simmonds & Brown; per. ad., 1165
Broadway, New York.

Barrymore, Harry (specialty), char. actor and
motto vocalist, Agnes Wallace-Villa Co.;
dram. agt., J. Alex. Brown; per. ad., 923
Green st., Philadelphia.

Barrymore, Miss Georgie Drew, leads; **dram. agts.**, Brooks & Dickson; per. ad., **Haymarket Theatre**, London, Eng.

Bartram, Ernest, eccentric com. and char., Rehan's 7-20-8; dram. agts., Simmonds & **Brown; per.** ad., 739 N. 7th st., **Philadelphia.**

Barnard, E. K., leads and heavies ; Gardner & Brown Dramatic Co.; per. ad., rooms 17 and 18 Walker Block, Detroit, Michigan.

Barney, Ariel N., advance agent, **Brooks & Dickson's Romany Rye Co. B.; dram. agts.**, Brooks & Dickson; **per. ad , 44 W.** 23d st., New York.

Barrett, Lawrence, tragedy **star, starring in** the legitimate drama; **Joseph Levy,** manager.

Barrett, Miss Florence, soubrettes; dram. agts., Brooks & Dickson; per. ad., 364 W 33d st., New York.

Barringer, Chas., heavies; dram. agts., Brooks & Dickson; per. ad., 374 Eighth ave., New York.

Barry, Miss Helen, leads; **dram. agts., Brooks & Dickson;** per ad., **4 E. 23d st., New York.**

Barney, Edwin, heavies; dram. agts , Brooks & Dickson; per. ad., 158 College st., Buffalo, New York.

Barker, Miss Eva, leads and soubrettes, Sothern Comedy Co.; dram. agts., Simmonds & Brown; per. ad , 14 Superior st., Cleveland, O.

Barfoot, Harry, character; dram. agts., Brooks & Dickson; per. ad., 126 W. Fayette st., Baltimore.

Bateman, Miss Victoria, leading juveniles, Brooks & Dickson's Romany Rye Co. A ; dram. agts., Brooks & Dickson; per. ad., 44 W. 23d st., New York.

Bauverie, Herbert, character; **dram. agts.,** Brooks & Dickson; per. ad., **223 Wash**ington st., Brooklyn.

Bayley, Edward, responsible; Tavernier Dramatic Co.; dram. agt., J. J. Spies; **per.** ad., 240 W. 14th st. New York.

Beane, George, jr., character comedian, Dan Sully's Corner Grocery Co.; per. ad , **Harry Miner's Bowery Theatre,** New **York.**

Beane, Miss Fannie, soubrettes, Chic Coterie in Collars and Cuffs; per. ad., Harry Miner's Bowery Theatre, New York.

Beanmont, John and Fanny (specialty), musical artists; per. ad., box 763, Oswego, N. Y.

Bebus, Davenport, leads; dram. agts., Brooks & Dickson; per. ad., 968 Broadway, New York.

Becks, George, light comedian and stage manager; per. ad., 42 Fulton st., New York.

Bedell, D. D., tenor in comic opera; dram. agts., Brooks & Dickson; per. ad., 1249 Broadway, New York,

Beers, Newton, starring in Only a Woman's Heart; C. R. Gardiner, man.; per. ad., 12 Union Square, New York.

Beebe, Miss Kate, old women, Bella Moore's Mountain Pink Co.; per. ad., Hawley's, Cincinnati, O.

Behrens, **Miss Charlotte.** leads, **Harry Miner's Silver King Co. No. 2; dram. agts.**, Brooks & Dickson; **per. ad., 149 E. 29th st., New** York.

Bell, Charles J., light comedy and juveniles ; dram. agts , Brooks & Dickson; per. ad., 29 W. 27th st., New York.

Benham, Mrs. Mary E., old women and heavies, C. B. Bishop's Co.; per. ad., J. J. Spies, 12 Union Square, New York.

Benn, Walter, heavies; dram. agts., Brooks **& Dickson; per ad., 290** Washington st., **Boston.**

Bernard, Mrs. Mollie, old women or heavies; per. ad., 109 E. Broadway, New York.

Bernard, Adolphe, **comedy** and character, Harry Miner's Silver King Co. No. 1; dram. agt., J. J. Spies ; People's Theatre, New York.

Bernard, **Miss** Hattie, soubrette, Peck's Bad Boy Co.; per. ad., Centre ave., Chicago.

Berkely, **Miss** Dora, soubrette; dram. agts., Skiff & **Morgan** (Chicago); **per. ad.,** 820 Charleston ave., St. Louis.

Beresford, Miss Fanny, soubrettes, Wallick's Bandit King **Co.; per. ad.,** New **York** Dramatic News.

Bergman, Henry, leading juvenile and heavies, Mme. Janauschek Co.; dram. agt., J. J. Spies; per. ad., 201 W. 14th st., New York.

Berrill, Mrs. Marial, old women; dram. agts., Brooks & Dickson; per. ad., Rockaway Beach, Long Island, N. Y.

Berlein, Miss Annie, starring in Under The Upas; dram. agts., Brooks & Dickson; per. ad., **46 S.** Washington Place, New **York.**

Beethoven (colored) Comedy Quartet, calliopes and warbles, imitations, **etc ;** Draper's Uncle Tom's Cabin Co.; per. ad., 241 Longworth st., Cincinnati, O.

Beverley, Alfred, comedian. Crimes of London Co.; per. ad., New York Dramatic News.

Billings, Miss Lillian, leading juveniles. Hanlon Bros.; dram. agts., Simmonds & Brown; per. ad., 36 W. 35th st., New York.

Bingham, Miss Marie, walking lady, Brooks & Dickson's Romany Rye Co.; dram agts., Brooks & Dickson; per. ad., 44 W. 23d st., New York.

Bingham, Wlll M., heavies, T. W. Keene Co.; dram. agts., Brooks & Dickson; per. ad., New York Mirror.

Bird, Miss Mary, soubrette, Barry and Fay Co.; dram. agts., Spies & Smart; per. ad., 60 E. 9th st., New York.

Bird, Miss Helena Bell, juvenile comedy, Clara Morris Co.; dram. agts., Brooks & Dickson; per. ad., 44 E. 10th st., New York.

Bird, Miss Edith E., juveniles, Clara Morris Co.; dram. agt., J. Alexander Brown; per. ad., 64 E. 14th st., New York.

Bird, George F., stage manager and light comedian, Clara Morris Co.; dram. agt., J. Alexander Brown; per. ad., 64 E. 14th st., New York.

Bishop, Miss Annie, leads; dram. agts., Brooks & Dickson; per. ad., 153 W. 14th st., New York.

Bishop, C. B., comedian, starring; Charles J. Bishop, manager; per. ad., 12 Union Square, New York.

Bland, L. E., character and old men; dram. agts., Brooks & Dickson; per. ad., 16 Irving Place, New York.

Black, K. L., second baritone, Wilbur Opera Co.; per ad., New York.

Blake, Orlando W., comedian; dram. agts., Brooks & Dickson; per ad., 510 Pine st., St. Louis.

Blake, Miss Ida May, juveniles, soubrettes and comedy; dram. agts, Brooks & Dickson; per. ad., New Harmony, Ind.

Blaucke, Miss Annie, soubrette; dram. agts., Brooks & Dickson; per. ad., 2347 Eighth ave., New York.

Blanchard, Miss Gertie, juveniles; dram. agts., Brooks & Dickson; per. ad., Boston Museum, Boston.

Bloch, S. S., leads, Roland Reed Co.; dram. agts., Simmonds & Brown; per. ad., 3 Astor House, New York.

Boales, Geo. R., light comedy and juveniles, Neil Burgess' Vim Co.; dram. agts., Simmonds & Brown; per. ad., 1113 Chestnut st., Philadelphia.

Blythe, Helen, starring in The Creole; Ed. Clayburg, man.; per. ad., 12 Union Square, New York.

Booth, Edwin, tragedy star, starring in the legitimate drama; R. M. Field, manager. Boston Museum, Boston, Mass.

Booth, Miss Rachel, soubrettes, Williams & Tillotson's Lynwood Co.; dram. agts., Brooks & Dickson; per ad., 359 Monroe st., Rochester, N. Y.

Booth, Miss Marion, juveniles and soubrettes; dram. agts., Brooks & Dickson; per ad., Victoria Hotel, Asbury Park, N. J.

Boswell, Mrs. Emily, old women; dram. agts., Brooks & Dickson; per ad., 11 4th st., Williamsburg, N. Y.

Bowell, Edwin, heavies; dram. agts., Brooks & Dickson; per. ad., 154 E. 10th st, New York.

Bowers, Mrs. D. P., leads; Brooks & Dickson's La Charbonnier Co.; dram. agts., Brooks & Dickson; per. ad., Victoria Hotel, New York.

Boyd, Miss Nellie, starring; G. M. Welty, man.; per ad., Fresno, Cal.

Breeenridge, Henry, responsible; Brooks & Dickson's Romany Rye Co. A.; dram. agts., Brooks & Dickson; per. ad., 44 W. 23d st., New York.

Bresn, Louis, old men; dram. agts., Brooks & Dickson; per. ad., 138 E. 22d st., New York.

Brent, Wm. H., heavies; dram. agts., Brooks & Dickson; per. ad., 57 E. 12th st., New York.

Brewer, Robt., character, Harry Miner's Silver King Co. No. 1; per. ad., People's Theatre, New York.

Brien, J. J., leads; dram. agts., Brooks & Dickson; per. ad., 1293 Broadway, New York.

Bright, Miss Jennie, singing soubrettes, Rehan's 7–20–8 Co.; dram. agts., Simmonds & Brown; per. ad., 673 N. 13th st., Philadelphia.

Bridges, Miss Winona, singing soubrette; dram agts., Brooks & Dickson; per. ad., 291 W. 7th st., Cincinnati.

Brigham, Willard, heavies, Gardiner's Only a Woman's Heart Co.; dram. agts., Brooks & Dickson; per. ad. Grand Rapids, Mich.

Brodock, Chas. S., juveniles; dram. agts., Brooks & Dickson; per. ad., 214 W. 14th st., New York.

Brooks, Miss Alice, soubrettes; dram. agts., Brooks & Dickson; per. ad., Box 6, Yonkers, N. Y.

Boyle, Miss Anna, leads; dram. agts., Brooks & Dickson; per. ad., 108 W. 17th st., New York.

Bradley, H. B., character, heavies, Stetson's Monte Cristo Co.; dram. agts., Simmonds & Brown; per. ad., Astor House, New York.

Bradley, Miss Maude, singing soubrettes; dram. agts., Brooks & Dickson; per ad., 226 E. 10th st., New York.

Braden, Findly, lecturer; per. ad., 3090 N. 5th st., Philadelphia.

Bradshaw, Charles H., leading comedian Lotta Co.; dram. agts., Brooks & Dickson; per. ad., North Scituate, Mass.

Branick, John H., comedian, Bunch of Keys Co.; dram. agt., J. J. Spies; per. ad., 204 W. 33d st., New York.

Brandon, Miss Ethel, soubrette, Kiralfy Bros. Sieba Co.; dram. agts., Brooks & Dickson; per. ad., 46 W. 24th st., or Madison Square Theatre, New York.

Brand, J. E., principal baritone, Wilbur Opera Co.; per. ad., Dramatic News, New York.

Bray, Will H., character comedian and vocalist, Morton & Bell's Strategists; per. ad., 2339 Mission st., San Francisco.

Brelsford, R. M., old men and heavies; dram. agts., Brooks & Dickson; per. ad., 6 Sixth ave., New York.

Brelsford, Miss Florence, juveniles; dram. agts., Brooks & Dickson; per. ad., 6 Sixth ave., New York.

Brennan, H. R., old men; G. A. Hill's Theatre Co.; dram. agts., Simmonds & Brown; per. ad., 148 W. Houston st., New York.

Brennan, Thomas, juveniles and heavies; dram. agts., Brooks & Dickson; per. ad., 22 E. Mechanic st., Newark, N. J.

Brooke, Craven, character comedian, Shook & Collier's Lights o' London Co.; dram. agts., Brooks & Dickson; per. ad., 139 Cedar st., New York.

Brooks, Miss Helen, soubrette; Brooks & Dickson's In the Ranks Co.; dram. agts., Brooks & Dickson; per. ad., 138 W. 29th st., New York.

Brooks, Walter J., juvenile lead; Mlle. Rhea Co.; dram. agt., Simmonds & Brown; per. ad., 1166 Broadway, New York.

Brown, Sedley, comedian; dram. agts., Brooks & Dickson; per. ad., 148 W. 14th st., New York.

Brown, W. G., juveniles and light comedy; Wood's Western Theatre Co.; per. ad., News Letter, Chicago.

Brown, Harry, heavies and old men; Phillips & Wells' Boston Theatre Co.; per. ad., 214 Lincoln avenue, Evansville, Ind.

Brown, F., old men and character; dram. agts., Brooks & Dickson; per. ad., 691 Michigan avenue, Detroit, Mich.

Brotone, Mrs. Julia, character old women; dram. agts., Brooks & Dickson; per. ad., 230 W. 24th st., New York.

Buckley, E. J., leads, Brooks & Dickson's In the Ranks Co.; dram. agts., Brooks & Dickson; per. ad., 11 W. 23d st., New York.

Buckingham, Miss Fannie Louise, melodramatic and equestrienne actress; per. ad., Long Island City, N. Y.

Buckingham, W. P., juvenile; dram. agts., Brooks & Dickson; per. ad., 229 W. 45th st., New York.

Burke, Charles, singing and eccentric comedian, Gunther's D. A. M. Co.; dram. agts., Simmonds & Brown; per. ad., 2024 Third ave., New York.

Bunnell, Geo., vocalist, Williams & Kernell Specialty Co.; dram. agt., J. A. Brown; per. ad., New York Clipper.

Bunny, John H. A., character; dram. agts., Brooks & Dickson; per. ad., 116 High st., Brooklyn.

Bunt, Miss Nellie, vocalist, soubrettes and boys; per. ad., P. O. Denver, Col.

Bunt, Mrs. Agnes, old women and heavies; per. ad., P. O. Denver, Col.

Burbidge, C. J., juveniles, Harry Miner's Silver King Co. No. 2; per. ad., People's Theatre, New York.

Burgess, Neil, starring in Vim; per. ad., Highlands, Monmouth Co., N. J.

Burgess, Mrs. Nell, juvenile, leads, Neil Burgess Vim Co.; per. ad., Highlands. Monmouth Co., N. J.

Burke, Jno T., juvenile and character; dram. agts., Brooks & Dickson; per. ad., 59 W. 24th st., New York.

Burleigh, Jno. L., leads Shook & Collier's Ruth's Devotion Co.; dram. agts., Brooks & Dickson; per. ad., Union Square Hotel, New York.

Burlingame, Miss Kate, character and ingenues, Lizzie May Ulmer Co.; dram. agts., Simmonds & Brown; per. ad., Clinton, N. Y.

Burrows, Chas. R., comedian; dram agts., Brooks & Dickson; per. ad., 110 Fourth ave., New York.

Burrows, Miss Ida., juveniles; dram. agts.,

2

Brooks & Dickson; **per. ad.**, 108 Fourth ave., New York.

Butler, Robert, comedian and pantomimist, Hanlon Bros.; per. ad., Station T., New York.

Butler, C. W., **leads,** Brooks & Dickson's Romany Rye **Co.** A.: dram. agts., Brooks & Dickson: per. ad.. 44 W. 23d st., New York.

Butler, Miss Alice, juveniles **and character,** Brooks & Dickson's **Romany Rye Co.** A.: dram. agts., Brooks & Dickson: per. ad., 44 W. 23d st., New York.

Byers, George, assistant machinist, **Hanlon Bros.'** Voyage en Suisse Co.. per. **ad ,** 519 W. 7th st., Cincinnati.

Byers, H. D., genteel or character heavies; Bella Moore Mountain Pink Co.: dram. agts., Simmonds & Brown; per. ad., 390 Clinton ave., Albany, N. Y.

Byran. W. H., old men, Chanfrau Co. dram. agts., Brooks & Dickson: per. ad., 62 Duane st., New York.

,Byrne, Miss Bessie leads; dram. agts., Brooks & Dickson: per ad., 132 E. 28th st., New **York.**

— **C** —

California Quartette—Morant, Wyatt, Holland and Wetter; per. ad 819 Broadway, New York.

Campbell, Norman comedian; dram. agts., Brooks & Dickson: per. ad., 253 Cumberland st., Brooklyn.

Campbell, **Frank G.,** leads and heavies, **Gus** Williams' Co.; dram. agts., Simmonds & Brown, per. **ad.,** 1166 Broadway, New York.

Campbell, Camille, child parts; Gus Williams' Co.; dram. agts., Simmonds & Brown; per. ad., 1166 Broadway, New York.

Carey, Miss Eleanor, leads, Harry Miner's Silver King Co. No. 1; per. ad., People's Theatre, New York.

Carhart, James L., old men and character, Shook & Collier's Lights o' London Co.; dram. agts., Simmonds & Brown; per. ad., Pontiac, Mich.

Carleton, Harry, comedian: dram. agts., Brooks & Dickson: per. ad., 148 Cambridge st., Boston.

Carleton, William, comedian; dram. agts., Brooks & Dickson; per. ad., 325 East 14th st., New York.

Carleton, Frank and Bessie (specialty), sketch artists; per. ad., 430 Spruce st., Scranton, Pa.

Carroll, Richard F., light comedy and char., Hanlon Bros.' Co.; dram. agts., Simmonds & Brown; per. ad., **1166 Broadway,** New York.

Carroll, R. M , comedy and character, Hanlon Bros.' Co ; dram. agts., **Simmonds &** Brown; **per.** ad., 1166 Broadway, **New** York.

Champney, Miss Evelyn, soubrettes; dram. **agts** , Brooks & Dickson; per. ad , 67 **E.** 10th st., New York.

Chantore, Miss Lilian, juveniles, B. McAuley **Co.:** dram. agt , **J.** J. Spies: per. ad., 117 W. 28th st , New York.

Chapman, Thomas, old **men** and character: **dram. agts.,** Brooks & Dickson: per. ad., 135 E 40th st., New York

Chaplin, **George D., leading,** Janauschek: dram. **agts., Simmonds & Brown and** Spies: per. ad., **245** W. **Eleventh st.,** New York.

Chapman, Ed , principal comedian, Wilbur Opera Co.; per. ad., New York.

Chappelle, C., leads and heavies: dram agts., Brooks & Dickson; per. ad , 126 E. 12th st., New York.

Charles, Charles, old men; dram agts. Brooks & Dickson; per. ad., 141 N. Elliott place, Brooklyn

Charles, George C., comedy and character, Bartley Campbell's White Slave Co.; **per.** ad., 53 Nassau st., Brooklyn, N. Y

Chase, Charles W., juveniles, Peck's **Bad** Boy Co.; per. ad., 613 Centre ave , **Chi**cago.

Chester, Miss Kate, juveniles and soubrettes; dram. agts., Brooks & Dickson: **per.** ad., Chicago, Ill.

Chisnell, Newton, characters and old men; Mlle. Aimée's English Comedy Co.; dram. agts., Simmonds & **Brown;** per. ad., Akron, O.

Christie, Miss Jennie, soubrettes; dram agts.: Brooks & Dickson: per ad., 52 E. 9th st., New York.

Christie, Miss Louise, juveniles and singing soubrettes; dram. agts., Brooks & Dickson; per. ad., 29 E. 18th st., New York.

Chur. Miss Emma, soubrette, Hyers' Colored Comedy Co.; per. ad., John B. Jeffery Printing House, Chicago.

Chur, John, Hyers' Colored Comedy Co.; per. ad., John B. Jeffery Printing House, **Chicago.**

Church, Miss Lottie, leads and comedy; dram agts., Brooks & Dickson; per ad., 75 **New** Utrecht, N. Y

Clarges, Verner, comedian, Barry & Fay Co.; dram. agt., J. J. Spies; per. ad., 12 Union Square, New York.

Clark, Miss Adel, soubrettes character and old women; dram. agts., Brooks & Dickson; per. ad., 39 Seventh ave., New York.

Clark, Miss Kittie, **contralto,** Fay Templeton Opera Co.; per. ad., Sohmer & Co. Warerooms, E. 14th st., New York.

Clarke, Redfield, juveniles and walking gents, Maude Atkinson Co.; per. ad., care T. D. Clarke, Midland, Mich.

Clark, Harry, comedian, **Shook & Collier's Lights o'** London Co.; **per. ad.,** New York Dramatic News.

Clarke, Miss Mae, leads, Mlle. Rhea Co.; per ad., 335 Eighth ave., New York.

Clarke, Howell, **properties,** Bartley Campbell's White Slave Co; per. ad., 60 E. 9th st., New York.

Claxton, Miss Margaret, juveniles; dram. agts., Brooke & Dickson; per ad., 239 W. 14th st., New York.

Clemens, Harry C., walking gent, Felix A. Vincent Co.; per. ad., 128 Summit st., Akron, O.

Clements, Frank, leads, Jananschek Co.; dram. agts., Simmonds & Brown; per. ad., 1166 Broadway, New York.

Clifford, Ed, heavies; dram. agts., Brooks & Dickson; per. ad., 110 Fourth ave., New York.

Clifford, Miss Maude, **soubrette,** Hanlon Bros. Co; dram., agts., Brooks & Dickson; per. ad., 234 W. 14th st., New York.

Clifton, H. D., **leads;** dram. agts., Brooks & Dickson; per. ad., 248 W. 36th st., New York

Clifton, Miss Marion P., character old women; dram. agts., Brooks & Dickson; per. ad., 101 E. 25th st., New York.

Clifton, Miss Bessie, character old women; dram. agts., Brooks & Dickson; per. ad., 60 E. 9th st., New York.

Coburn, S. K., light comedian and juveniles; dram. agts., Brooks & Dickson; per. ad. New York Clipper.

Coghlan, Miss Eily, juveniles and singing soubrettes; dram. agts., Brooks & Dickson, **per.** ad., 79 W. 57th st., New York.

Coghlan, Miss Rose, leads, Wallack's **Theatre Stock Co.; per. ad., Wallack's Theatre,** New York.

Collings, W. H., old men and character, Harrison & Gourlay Co.; dram. agts., Simmonds & Brown; per. ad., New York Mirror.

Coleman, T. L., heavies; dram. agts., Brooks & Dickson; per. ad., 205 E. 12th st., New York.

Collins, O. B., heavies; dram. agts., Brooks & Dickson; per. ad., 1319 Alidrie st., Philadelphia.

Colson, Miss Lizzie, singing soubrette; per. ad., Crawfordsville, Ind.

Colton, Harry, heavies, Harry Miner's Silver King Co.; dram. agts., Brooks & Dickson; per. ad., People's Theatre, New York.

Colville, J. M., juveniles, Joseph Murphy Co.; dram. agts., Brooks & Dickson; per. ad., 60 E. 9th st., New York.

Compston, Nelson, leading heavies, Bella Moore Co.; per. ad., 164 Vine st., Cincinnati.

Conly, J. E., principal tenor, Wilbur Opera Co.; per. ad., Boston.

Connell, Edward L., baritone; dram. agts., Brooks & Dickson; per. ad., 114 Waverly Place, New York.

Constantine, W. J., character and old men; dram. agts., Brooks & Dickson; per. ad., 34 W. 26th st., New York.

Conyers, Joseph P., comedian, Brooks & Dickson Romany Rye Co.; dram. agts., Brooks & Dickson; per. ad., 39 Clinton Place, New York.

Conway, Hart, juveniles and comedy; dram. agts., Brooks & Dickson; per. ad., box 6, Yonkers, N. Y.

Conway, George, old men and character; Harry Miner's Silver King Co.; dram. agts., Simmonds & Brown; per. ad., Actors' Order of Friendship, 7 W. 14th st., New York.

Cooke, Miss Rose, heavy and character old women; dram. agts., Brooke & Dickson; per. ad., 140 W. 26th st., New York.

Cook, Ellsworth (specialty), soprano and burlesque, Gibler's Specialty Co.; per. ad., Shelbyville, Ills.

Cooper, Archie, leads or character; dram. agts., Brooks & Dickson; per. ad., 40 E. 12th st., New York.

Cooper, Wm. H., old men and character, Crossen's Banker's Daughter Co.; dram. agt., J. J. Spies; per. ad., 355 Deane st., Philadelphia.

Cooper, Levy, heavies and character, Mlle. Rhea Co.; per. ad., 56 E. 7th st., New York.

Cooper, James, char.; dram. agts., Brooks & Dickson; per. ad., 78 Washington Place, New York.

Corbett, Alexander, old men; T. W. Keene Co; per. ad., 4 James st., Boston.

Cornell, Miss Elma juvenile leads; dram. agts., Brooks & Dickson; per. ad., 65 Dellevan st., Rochester.

Corlett, Miss Helen, juveniles and soubrettes; dram. agts., Brooks & Dickson; per. ad., 53 Irving Place, New York.

Cottrell, Miss Bessie, singing soubrettes; dram. agts., Brooks & Dickson; per. ad., 73 W. 12th st., New York.

Cottrell, F. M., leads, heavies or juveniles; dram. agt., Brooks & Dickson; per. ad., 73 W. 12th st., New York.

Couldock, C. W., leading old men and character; Madison Square Theatre Hazel Kirke Co.; per. ad., Madison Square Theatre, New York.

Courtney, H. T., juveniles; dram. agts., Brooks & Dickson; per. ad., 154 Schermerhorn st., Brooklyn.

Cowper, Will. C., leading juveniles, Brooks & Dickson's La Charbonnier Co.; dram. agts., Brooks & Dickson; per. ad., 113 Waverly Place, New York.

Creese, Miss Lizzie, leads; dram. agts., Brooks & Dickson; per. ad., 59 W. 24th st., New York.

Crocker, Miss Josephine, juvenile leads; dram. agts., Brooks & Dickson; per. ad., 60 E. 9th st., New York.

Crosbie, W. C., comedian and stage manager, Flora Moore Bunch of Keys Co.; per. ad., 319 7th st., Jersey City.

Cumming, Miss Addie, soubrettes and dialect character; dram. agts., Brooks & Dickson; per. ad., 672 Broadway. South Boston.

Currier, F. J., character; dram. agts., Brooks & Dickson; per. ad., Saltersville, Hudson County, N. Y.

Cushman, Miss Lillia, leads; dram. agts., Brooks & Dickson; per. ad., 164 W. 33d st., New York.

— D —

Dade, Chas., juvenile; dram. agts., Brooks & Dickson; per. ad., 64 E. 9th st., New York.

Daly, M. C., comedian, Bartley Campbell's Siberia Co.; per. ad., Kingsbridge, New York City.

Daly, Wm. H., stage manager, Mme. Janish Co.; dram. agts., Simmonds & Brown; per. ad., 60 W. 4th st., New York.

Danvers, Wm. H., leading heavy and character, Carrie Swain Co.; dram. agts., Brooks & Dickson; per. ad., Philadelphia.

Dagnau, W. J., comedy, Mr. and Mrs. W. Florence Co.; dram. agts., Brooks & Dickson; per. ad., 2 Christopher st., New York.

Davenport, Miss Fanny, starring in Fedora, E. H. Price, man.; per. ad., Canton, Pa

Davidson, Miss Kate, character, Draper's Uncle Tom's Cabin Co.; per. ad., Newark, O.

Davidson, Dave, character; dram. agts., Brooks & Dickson; per. ad., 18 W. 36th st., New York.

Davidson, W. H., comedian, Draper's Uncle Tom's Cabin Co.; per. ad., Newark, O.

Davis, Edwin C., utility, Mlle. Rhea Co.; dram. agt., J. J. Spies; per. ad., 56 Lake st., Cleveland, O.

Davis, Miss Christine, juvenile and soubrettes, Robert McWade Co.; per. ad., 1096 Day st., Dubuque, Ia.

Davis, Miss Emma M., juveniles; dram. agts., Brooks & Dickson; per. ad., 44 W. 23d st., New York.

Davis, Scott, old men; dram. agts., Brooks & Dickson; per. ad., Ridgewood, L. I.

Davis, Frank L., juveniles; dram. agts., Brooks & Dickson; per. ad., 24 W. 30th st., New York.

Davis, Miss Marie, old women; dram. agts., Brooks & Dickson; per. ad., 95 New Oxford st., London.

Dawson, Nathan, reader, lecturer and litterateur; per. ad., care Houghton, Mifflin & Co., Boston.

Day, Wilson, leads and light comedy, Tavernier Comedy Co.; dram. agt., J. J. Spies; per. ad., 37 Park st., Hartford, Conn.

Day, Murray E., heavies, old men and character; dram. agts., Brooks & Dickson; per. ad., 121 W. 15th st., New York.

Daymond, Joseph, old men; dram. agts., Brooks & Dickson; per. ad., 61 Fourth ave., New York.

Dayton, Frank H., comedian, Harry Miner's Silver King Co. No. 2; dram. agts., Simmonds & Brown; per. ad., People's Theatre, New York.

De Amaralds, Miss Isabella, soubrettes; dram. agts., Brooks & Dickson; per. ad., 228 W. 39th st., New York

Deal, W. C., heavy, character and old men; Nell Burgess' Vim Co.; per. ad., New York Mirror.

Deane, Mrs., old women; dram. agts., Brooks & Dickson; per. ad., 492 Eighth ave., New York.

Dean, A. G., ventriloquist. **Heywood Mastodon** Minstrels: per ad., **New York Clipper.**

Deaves, Miss Ada, walking lady, Wallack's Theatre Stock Co.; dram. agts., Brooks & Dickson; per. ad., Wallack's Theatre, New York.

Deaves, Miss Rillie, juveniles and soubrettes; dram. agts., Brooks & Dickson: per. ad., **46 W. 24th st , New York.**

De Bellville, Frederick, leads, Harry Miner's **Silver King Co. No. 1; per. ad.,** People's **Theatre, New York.**

De Bevoise, C , juveniles and comedy: **dram. agts.,** Brooks & Dickson; **per. ad., 141 E.** 19th st., New York.

De Camo, (specialty), juggler. **Andrea' Carnival** of Novelties: per. ad., **New York** Clipper.

De Forrest. Miss Gussie, leads; dram. agts., Brooks & Dickson; per. ad., 335 E. 19th st., New York.

De Forrest, M. L., properties and responsibles; **dram. agts.,** Skiff & Morgan (Chicago); **per. ad., 159** Loomis st., Chicago, Ill.

De Forrest, **Miss Irene,** juvenile **and leads;** Louis Lord Co.; per. ad., 1191 Euclid ave., Cleveland, O.

Defossez, Miss Kate, old women; **dram. agts.,** Brooks & Dickson; **per. ad., 315 W.** 26th st., New York.

Degez, John **F.,** juveniles; Rehan's 7—20—8 Co.; dram. agts., Brooks & Dickson; per. ad., 44 W. 23d st., New York.

De La Croix, V., baritone; **dram. agts.,** Brooks & Dickson, per. ad., 54 E. 9th st., New York.

De Land, Miss Annie, character old **women; dram.** agts., Brooks & Dickson ; **per.** ad., 464 W. 20th st., New York.

De Lange, Louis, comedian: dram. agts., Brooks & Dickson: per. ad., Asbury Park, N. J.

Delmanning Bros., Archie and Den, (specialty), song and dance, Agnes Wallace Villa Co.; dram. agt., Dick Fitzgerald: per. ad., 248 Six h st., Williamsburg, N. Y.

Delmore, Ralph, heavies and characters; dram. agts., Brooks & Dickson: per. ad., 238 E. 48th st., New York.

De Mond, Allen, leading heavy, Lizzie Evans' Fogg's ;Ferrry Co ; dram. agt., J. Alex. Brown: **per ad.,** 64 E. 14th st., New **York.**

De Newburne, (specialty), tight wire and trapeze: per. ad., New York Clipper.

Dennis, Walter L., heavies and character; Brooks & Dickson's Romany **Rye** Co. A: dram. agts., Brooks & Dickson; per. ad , 44 W. 23d st., New York.

Deshon, Sabra, heavies and **leads in** burlesque. Agnes Wallace Villa: **per** ad., New York Clipper.

De Vere, George F., Jr., character: Bartley Campbell's Siberia Co.; dram. agts., Simmonds & Brown; per. ad., Ronkonkoma, Long Island, N. Y.

De Vernon, Frank, juvenile leads: dram. agts., **Brooks** & **Dickson; per.** ad., 119 E. 93d **st., New York.**

Devereaux, J. P., **(specialty),** black face comedy: per. **ad., 1238** Moyamensing ave., Philadelphia.

Devere, Miss Elsie, **soubrettes: dram. agts.,** Brooks & Dickson; **per. ad., 316 E.** 57th st., New York.

Devoy, John, (specialty), topical vocalist: per. ad., New York Clipper.

Deyo, Mrs. Kate, old women; dram. agts., Brooks & Dickson; per. ad., 215 W. 36th st., New York.

Dickson, **Chas.** S., leads, Robson & Crane Co.; **per. ad.,** 134 Bowery, New York.

Dickson, Miss Belle, soubrettes and boys, Harrison & Gourlay; dram. agts., Simmonds & Brown; per. ad., New York Mirror.

Dillin, A., old men and character, Baker **&** Farron Co.; dram. agt., J. J. Spies; per. ad., 443 W. 57th st., New York.

Dixon, Wm., comedian: dram. **agts , Brooks** & Dickson; per. ad., **115 Fourth ave.,** New **York.**

Doherty, E. T., **properties and utilities,** Ethel Tucker Comedy Co ; per. ad., Opera House, Wyandotte, Kan.

Don, Miss Laura, juvenile leads, Brooks & **Dickson's La** Charbonnier Co.; dram. **agts., Brooks** & Dickson; per. ad., 44 W. 23d st., New York.

Donald, Miss Nellie, juveniles: dram. agts. Brooks & Dickson; per. ad., 152 E. 28th st., New York.

Donaldson, W. C , leading heavy, Mlle. Aimee's English Comedy Co ; per. ad., 110 Dundas st., Toronto, Canada.

Donman, Ralph, heavies: dram. agts., Brooks & Dickson; per. ad., 115 S. Sharp st., Brooklyn.

Dooley, Thos. H., master machinist, Hanlon Bros. Co.; per. ad., 31 Elliot st., Boston.

Dorlan, Miss Minnie C., soubrettes: dram. agts., Brooks & Dickson: per. ad., 81 Johnston st., Brooklyn.

Dorian, Alf. (specialty), serpent man, Gardiner & Zozo the Magic Queen Co.; dram. agt. J. Alex Brown; per. ad., 648 Broadway, New York.

Dond, Frank, heavies and characters, Brooks & Dickson's; Romany Rye Co.; dram. agts., Simmonds & Brown; per. ad., 155 2d st., New York.

Douglass, Byron, juveniles; dram. agts., Brooks & Dickson; per. ad., 54 W. 24th st. New York.

Douglass, Miss Ethel, old women; dram. agts., Brooks & Dickson; per. ad., Grand View Hotel, New York.

Douglass, Miss Belle, character old women; dram. agts., Brooks & Dickson; per. ad., 213 E. 21st st., New York.

Douglass, Miss Annie, old women; dram. agts., Brooks & Dickson; per. ad., 239 E. 79th st., New York.

Downing, Robert L., starring in Tally Ho, F. B. Murtha, manager; per. ad, Park Theatre, New York.

Downs, Miss Clara, soubrettes and boys, Bartley Campbell's White Slave Co.; dram. agts., Brooks & Dickson; per. ad., Brentwood Hotel, New York.

Downs, Miss Kate, juveniles and soubrettes, C. B. Bishop Comedy Co.; dram. agt , J. J. Spies; per. ad , 62 Barre st., Baltimore.

Drake, Chas., heavies and old men, Charlotte Thompson Co.; dram. agts., Brooks & Dickson; per. ad., 200 E. 37th st., New York.

Drayton, Frank, comedian, Harry Miner's Silver King Co. No. 2; per. ad., People's Theatre, New York.

Drew, Maurice F., juvenile leads, Romany Rye Co. B.; dram. agts., Brooks & Dickson; per. ad., 44 W. 23d st., New York.

Drew, I. N., heavies and character; Brooks & Dickson's In the Ranks Co.; dram. agts., Brooks & Dickson; per. ad., 2103 Mt. Vernon st., Philadelphia.

Drew, John, comedian, Daly's Theatre Stock Co.; per. ad., Daly's Theatre, New York.

Drmmeir, Frank, juveniles; dram. agts., Brooks & Dickson; per. ad., 1917 Carmac st., Philadelphia.

Drury, Thomas B., eccentric comedy and character, Hudson Jerrold Co.; per. ad., Lafayette, Ind.

Dudley, Miss Ella, leads, Broadway Theatre Co.; per. ad., New York Clipper.

Dudley, Miss Annabel, soubrette and character; dram. agts., Brooks & Dickson; per. ad , 60 W. 4th st., New York.

Dudley, Miss Marie, juveniles and soubrettes; dram. agts., Brooks & Dickson; per. ad., 21 W. 30th st., New York.

Dudley, Walter, comedian, Metropolitan Theatre Co.; per. ad., New York Clipper.

Dugan, Chas., baritone; dram. agts., Brooks & Dickson; per. ad., 134 E. 24th st., New York.

Duncan, W. F., old men; dram. agts., Brooks & Dickson; per. ad., 16 Russell place, Brooklyn.

Dunne, John W., leads, Patti Rosa's Co.; dram. agt., J. J. Spies; per. ad., 12 Union square, New York.

Durr de Bang, Miss Sadie, mezzo soprano and soubrette, J. H. Kean's Mrs. Partington Co.; per. ad., New York Mirror.

Du Sauld, Miss Gabrielle, leads, Union Square Theatre Stock Co.; dram. agts , Brooks & Dickson; per. ad., 54 W. 26th st., New York.

Dustan, Mrs. R. J., juveniles; dram. agts., Brooks & Dickson; per. ad., 39 W. 36th st., New York.

— E —

Eagle, O. W., juveniles and heavies; dram. agts., Brooks & Dickson; per. ad., Care New York Mirror, New York.

Eans, Frank, heavies and old men; J. G. Stuttz' Co.; per. ad., Houston, Tex., care A. Clay.

Earle, Clark, juveniles, J. K. Emmett Co.; dram. agts., Brooks & Dickson; per. ad., 318 W. Lombard st., Baltimore.

Earle, Miss Mattie, leads; dram. agts., Brooks & Dickson; per. ad., 239 W. 28th st., New York.

Earle, Miss A., singing soubrettes and boys; per. ad., 142 E. 87th st., New York.

Eldinger, Lawrence, character and old men, Bartley Campbell's Siberia Co.; dram. agts , Simmonds & Brown; per. ad., Albany, N. Y.

Edgar, Louis, character and comedy; dram. agts , Brooks & Dickson; per. ad., New York Clipper.

Edgerly, William, character, Brooks & Dickson's Romany Rye Co. A., dram. agts., Brooks & Dickson; per. ad., 44 W. 23d st., New York.

Edgington, Miss Lillian, juveniles; dram. agts. Brooks & Dickson; per. ad., 54 W. 24th st., New York.

Edmonds, Leslie, juveniles; dram. agts., Brooks & Dickson; per. ad , 138 W. 33d st., New York.

Miss Mabel Stanton,

LEADING LADY.

En tour Murphy's Kerry Gow Co.

Permanent address:

SYRACUSE, N. Y.

Charline Weidman,

SOUBRETTE AND CHARACTERS.

Aimee Comedy Co., Maurice Grau, Manager.

Season 1884-'85.

Jessie West,

SOUBRETTES,

With B. McAuley.

"Clip," in "Uncle Dan'l."

"Chubb," in "The Jerseyman."

Permanent address:
124 East 11th St., ·
New York City.

Miss Laura Wallace,

LEADING AND LIGHT COMEDY.

Aimee Comedy Co.

Maurice Grau, Manager.

Season 1884-'85.

Wm. McCready,

OLD MEN, DIALECTS AND COMEDY,

With Patti Rosa Co.

Address : J. J SPIES,
or as above, at A. O. of F.,
7 W. 14th Street,
New York.

E. S. Halstead,

COMEDIAN.

Address: care of J. J. SPIES,
12 UNION SQUARE, NEW YORK,

or 1138 S. 11th Street,
Philadelphia, Pa.

D. Gilfether,

HEAVIES and

CHARACTERS,

With B. McAuley's Company

J. J. SPIES, Agent.

Permanent address:
18 Boylston St ,
Boston, Mass.

Frank Leo,

The Popular Young

CHARACTER ACTOR & VOCALIST,

Supported by the D. S. Harold Combination.

Repertoire : "East Lynne," "Uncle Tom's Cabin," "Oliver Twist," "Two Orphans," "Felon's Bond," "Vagabond Tim,"
New Scenery, Wardrobe. Printing, etc.
Under the management of D. S. HAROLD

Permanent address: 489 BROADWAY, EAST ALBANY, N. Y.

Edmonds, Miss Anna Jean, singing soubrettes; dram agts., Brooks & Dickson;
per. ad., 13 W. 33d st., New York.

Edmunds, Chas. J., leads, Hazel Kirke Co.;
per. ad., 46 W. 24th st., New York.

Edmunds, Lee, tuba and double bass, J. E.
Stuttz Dramatic Co.; per. ad., Houston
Texas, care A Clay.

Edward, J. L., character, old men and
heavies; dram. agts., Brooks & Dickson;
per. ad., 23 Washington place, New York.

Edwards, James L., old men and heavies,
Clara Morris Co.; dram. agt., J. J. Spies;
per. ad., 12 Union Square, New York.

Edwards, Miss Amelia, juveniles, Evans &
Hoey's Meteors; dram. agt., J. J. Spies;
per. ad., 12 Union Square, New York.

Edwards, Jas. S. and Katie, (specialty,) dramatic and vocal artists; per. ad., Edward's
Theatre, St. Louis, Mo.

**Edwins, Mrs. Chas., character and comedy,
old women; dram. agts., Brooks & Dickson; per. ad., 46 W. 24th st., New York.**

Egbert, T. F., leads and heavies; dram. agts.
Brooks & Dickson; per. ad., 245 W. 37th
st., New York.

Ehrent, H., baritone; dram. agts., Brooks &
Dickson; per. ad., 71 E. 2d st., New York.

Elliott, Gilbert, leading juveniles, Salsbury's
Troubadours; dram. agt., J. J. Spies, 12
Union Square, New York.

Elliott, Miss **Nettie, walking lady and character, old women, Standard** Comedy Co.;
per. ad., Northville, **N. Y.**

Elmer, Chas. J., juveniles leads; per. ad., 719
E. 4th st., South Boston, Mass.

Elmore, Miss Florence, leads; dram. agts.,
Brooks & Dickson; per. ad., St. Stephen's
Hotel, **E.** 11th st., New York.

Elmore, Harvey E., Langley & Elmore's Comedy Co.; per. ad., News Letter, Chicago.

Eldridge, Chas. E., negro, comedy, **Pulse of
New York** Co.; dram. agts., Brooks **&
Dickson; per.** ad., 205 E. 88th st., **New**
York.

Ellis, Miss Marah, character, old **women;**
dram. agts., Brooks & Dickson; per. **ad.,**
Moulton House, Chicago.

**Elsler, Miss Annie, soubrettes; dram. agts.,
Brooks** & Dickson; per. ad., Academy of
Music, Cleveland, Ohio.

Ellsworth, Chas. (specialty), change artist and
comedian, Wilbur & Ryan's New Consolidated Minstrels; per. ad., Osage Mission,
Kansas.

Endres, J. P., juveniles and light comedy.

Tavernier Comedy Co.; dram. agt.; J. J.
Spies; per. ad., 911 Albany st., Boston.

Enos, A. G., juveniles and heavies; dram.
agts., Brooke & Dickson; per. ad., 459 W.
43d st., New York.

Enscoe, Jas., master carpenter, Brooks &
Dickson's Romany Rye Co.; dram.
agts., Brooks & Dickson; per. ad., 105 E
13th st., New York.

Erwood, Robert J., comedy and character;
dram agts., Brooks & Dickson; per ad.,
333 E. 75th st., New York.

Enlick, Miss Stella, walking lady and old
women, J. G. Stuttz Dramatic Co.; per.
ad., Temple, Texas.

Eveleth, Miss Ray, soubrettes, Neil Burgess'
Vim Co.; dram. agts., Simmonds &
Brown; per. ad., 486 Sixth st., Buffalo,
N. Y.

Evelyn, Miss Carlotta, juvenile leads; dram.
agts., Brooks & Dickson; per. ad, 143 W.
15th st., New York.

Everitt, L. H., stage manager, old men and
comedy, Frederick Warde Co.; dram.
agts., Brooks & Dickson; per. ad., 330 E.
24th st., New York.

Eyre, Miss Sophie, juvenile leads, Wallack's
Theatre Stock Co.; per. ad., Wallack's
Theatre, New York.

Eyre, Gerald, leads, Pulse of New York Co ;
dram. agts., Brooks & Dickson; per. ad.,
Lambs' Club, New York.

Eytinge, Miss Rose, starring; Cyril Searle,
man.; dram. agts., Brooks & Dickson;
per. ad., 140 E. 27th st , New York.

Eytinge, Walter, juvenile and heavies; dram.
agts., Brooks & Dickson; per. ad , 935
Broadway, New York.

F

Fanshawe, Arthur L., character and stage
manager, Heywood's Mastodon Minstrels;
per. ad., 8 N. 4th st., Troy, N. Y.

Farnham, D., juvenile, Harry Miner's Silver
King No. 2; per. ad., People's Theatre,
New York.

Farnum, Miss Adele, soubrettes; per. ad., 231
Eustis st., **Boston.**

Fairchild, Richard, responsibles; per. ad., 500
Congress st., E. Detroit, Mich.

Farron, T. J., comedy star, Baker & Farron
Co.; per. ad., 115 West ave., Buffalo, N.Y.

Farron, Mrs., old women and heavies, Clara
Morris Co.; dram. agts., Simmonds &
Brown; per. ad., 323 82d st., New York.

Farwell, C. L., leads; dram. agts., Brooks &
Dickson; per. ad., 201 E. 30th st., **New**
York.

Feeley, Al. K., stage manager, Mlle. Aimee's English Comedy Co.; dram. agts., Simmonds & Brown; per. ad., 1165 Broadway, New York.

Ferguson, W. J., comedy and character, Madison Square Theatre Called Back Co.; dram. agts., Brooks & Dickson; per. ad., 151 Adams st., Brooklyn, L. I.

Ferguson, J. F., character and heavies; Brooks & Dickson's La Charbonniere Co.; dram. agts., Brooks & Dickson; per. ad., 44 W. 23d st., New York.

Ferree, Owen, stage manager and character, Mlle. Rhea Co.; dram. agt., J. J. Spies; per. ad., 12 Union Square, New York.

Fessler, Walter W., juveniles, Gus Williams' Co.; dram. agts., Simmonds & Brown; per. ad., Greenville, Pa.

Fetter, Miss Selina, leads, Brooks & Dickson's In the Ranks Co.; dram. agts., Brooks & Dickson; per. ad., 1511 Broadway, New York.

Field, Miss Emma, juveniles and soubrettes; dram. agts., Brooks & Dickson; per ad., 59 W. 19th st., New York.

Field, Miss Frances, juveniles; Fred. Warde Co.; dram. agts., Brooks & Dickson; per. ad., 323 W. 23d st., New York.

Fillmore, Harry E., responsible; per. ad., New York Mirror.

Fisher, Alexander, old men, character and stage manager, Bertha Welby Co.; dram. agt., J. J. Spies; per. ad., Room 14, No. 7 W. 14th st., New York.

Fisher, Alf., character comedian, Daly's Theatre Stock Co.; dram. agts., Brooks & Dickson; per. ad., Daly's Theatre, New York.

Fisher, Chas. E., character comedian; dram. agts., Brooks & Dickson; per. ad , 42 St. Mark's Place.

Fisher, Geo. E., comedy and singing; dram. agts., Brooks & Dickson; per. ad., 60 E. 9th st., New York.

Fisher, Miss Jennie character dialect and singing, old women; dram. agts., Brooks & Dickson; per. ad., 60 E. 9th st., New York.

Fisher, Perkins D., comedian and character actor; Brooks & Dickson's In the Ranks, Co.; dram. agts., Simmonds & Brown; per. ad., 23 Moseley ave., Dorchester, Mass.

Fitz Allen, Miss Adelaide, juveniles; dram. agts., Brooks & Dickson; per. ad , 109 5th ave., New York.

Fitzgerald, W. H., comedian; dram. agts.,

Brooks & Dickson; per. ad., 6 E. 14th st., New York.

Fitzpatrick, J. H., heavies; Brooks & Dickson's In the Ranks Co.; dram. agts., Brooks & Dickson; per. ad., 44 W. 23d st., New York.

Fisk, Miss May, leading; per. ad., 17 W. 27th st., New York.

Fisk, Harry C., treasurer; per. ad., New Rochelle, New York.

Fitch, Carl Irving (specialty), solo concert, harmonica and baritone vocalist; dram. agt., J. Alex. Brown; per. ad., 234 E. 34th st., New York.

Flagg, Jared, comedian; dram. agts., Brooks & Dickson; per. ad., 25 E. 14th st., New York.

Flagg, Miss Clara, juveniles; dram. agts., Brooks & Dickson; per. ad., 111 E. 27th st., New York.

Fleming, Miss Marian, soubrettes, Mr. and Mrs. Geo. S. Knight Co.; dram. agts., Brooks & Dickson; per. ad., 65 Irving Place, New York.

Fletcher, Howard, Watts & Dorsey (specialty) Jubilee Quartet, Memphis Students; per. ad., cor. Broadway and 9th st., New York.

Flohr, Miss Belle, soubrettes; dram. agts., Brooks & Dickson; per. ad., 59 W. 24th st., New York.

Forrest, J. W., heavies and old men; dram. agts., Brooks & Dickson; per. ad., 446 W. 31st st., New York.

Forrester, Miss Fanny W., juveniles and singing soubrettes; dram. agts., Brooks & Dickson; per. ad., 131 Eustis st., Boston.

Forster, Miss Louise, leads; dram. agts., Brooks & Dickson; per. ad., Rockaway Beach, L. I.

Fosdick, Miss Flora M., juveniles; dram. agts., Brooks & Dickson; per. ad., 10 E. 9th st., New York.

Fostell, Albert and Lottie (specialty), musical, sketch and change artists; per. ad., 341 E. 67th st., New York.

Foster, Charles, eccentric comedy and character, Harry Miner's Silver King Co No. 1; per. ad., 201 East 116th st., cor. Third ave., New York.

Foster, F. R., leading heavies; Bartley Campbell's White Slave Co.; per. ad., 305 W. 22d st., New York.

Foster, Mrs. F. R., first old women and character; Bartley Campbell's White Slave Co.; per. ad., 305 W. 22d st., New York.

Foster, M., old men; dram. agts., Brooks & Dickson; per. ad , 216 Jay st., Brooklyn.

Foster, Miss Evelyn, leads, Stafford-Foster Co.; per. ad., New York Mirror.

Foy, Miss Bertha, juveniles; dram. agts., Brooks & Dickson; per. ad., box 1979, Bridgeport, Conn.

Fox. D. F., leads, Maud Atkinson Co.; per. ad., 364 N. Franklin st., Chicago.

Francis, Geo., char. and old men; Brooks & Dickson's Romany Rye Co.; dram. agts., Brooks & Dickson; per. ad., 44 W. 23d st., New York.

Francis, Miss Fannie, juvenile leads and soubrettes; Whiteley's Hidden Hand Co.; dram. agts., Brooks & Dickson; per. ad. New Bedford, Mass.

Frankau, Joseph, comedian; Brooks & Dickson's La Charbonnier Co.; dram. agts., Brooks & Dickson; per. ad , 44 W. 23d st., New York.

Fracklin, Lester, character, New York Co.; per. ad., St. Charles Hotel, Chicago.

Fraser, Frank, low comedy, G. A. Hill's Theatre Co.; per. ad , New York Clipper.

Frawley, T. D., juvenile, Barry & Fay Comedy Co.; dram. agt., J. J. Spies; per. ad., 12 Union sq., New York.

Freeman, Miss Ada, character, old women and soprano; Hyers' Comedy Co. per. ad. 484 State st., Chicago.

Freeman, Max, character; dram. agts., Brooks & Dickson; per. ad., 42 W. 23d st., New York.

Freeman, Maurice S., juvenile; Katie Putman Co.; dram. agts., Brooks & Dickson; per. ad , 315 E. 14th st., New York.

Freeth, Miss Nina, soubrette; dram. agts., Brooks & Dickson; per. ad., 108 E. 11th st., New York.

Frew, Chas., character and comedy, Sothern Comedy Co.; per. ad., 74 Superior st., Cleveland, O.

Frye, Miss Alice, juveniles ; dram agts., Brooks & Dickson; per. ad , 215 W. 15th st , New York

Fulmer & Perry (specialty), Dave and Ed., boy mesmerists; per. ad., 5 Mathewson st., Providence, R. I.

Fuller, Hugh, old men and character; dram. agts., Brooks & Dickson; per. ad., 54 W. 12th st., New York.

Fuller, W., heavies; dram. agts., Brooks & Dickson; per. ad., 54 W. 12th st, New York.

Furlong, J. R., comedy and character; dram. agts., Brooks & Dickson; per. ad., 141 Orchard st., New York

— G —

Gale, George, burlesque lyric artist, Barlow-Wilson Minstrels; per. ad., 76 E. Michigan st., Indianapolis, Ind.

Gallagher, Miss May, juveniles; dram. agts., Brooks & Dickson; per. ad., Piermount, New York.

Gallagher, Miss Maggie, soubrette; dram. agts., Brooks & Dickson; per. ad., 161 Sixth ave., New York.

Gallagher, M. J., comedy, Her Atonement Co.; dram. agts., Brooks & Dickson; per. ad., 13 Sixth ave., New York.

Gaugton, Miss Genie, soubrettes; dram. agts., Brooks & Dickson; per. ad., 53 S. Washington sq., New York.

Garland, Geo. S. (specialty), Dutch comedy; New York Clipper.

Garrick, Mrs. Eva, juveniles and soubrettes; dram. agts., Brooks & Dickson, New York.

Garrick, Thos. E., juveniles; dram agts., Brooks & Dickson; per. ad., 157 W. 20th st., New York.

Gardner, Miss E., heavy leads; dram. agts., Brooks & Dickson; per. ad., 268 W. 21st st., New York.

Gaylord, Dwight, responsible, T. W. Keene Co.; per. ad., 33 Ash st., Chelsea, Mass.

Gayler, Miss Grace, character old women; dram. agts., Brooks & Dickson; per. ad., 282 Putnam ave., Brooklyn.

Gerard, Miss Lillian, juveniles; dram. agts., Brooks & Dickson; per. ad., West Haven, Conn.

Germon, Miss Effie, leads; dram. agts., Brooks & Dickson; per. ad., 50 E. 10th st., New York.

Germaine, R., heavies or light comedy; dram. agts., Brooks & Dickson; per. ad., 119 Fourth ave., New York.

Gilday, Charles, comedian, Chic Coterie in Collars and Cuffs; per ad., Harry Miner's Bowery Theatre, New York.

Gillow, Wm., character comedy and old men, Duff's Standard Opera Co.; per. ad., 226 W. 35d st., New York.

Gilfether, D., heavies and characters, B. McAuley's Co.; dram. agt., J. J. Spies; per. ad , 16 Boylston st., Boston.

Gilfillan, Wm. A., leads, Gardner's Only a Farmer's Daughter; dram. agt., J. J. Spies; per. ad., New Haven, Conn.

Gibbs, Robert P., juvenile and comedy; dram. agts., Brooks & Dickson; per. ad., 46 W. 15th st., New York.

Gilbert, Lew, comedian, Hyers' Colored Comedy Co.; per. ad., Jno. B. Jeffrey Printing House, Chicago.

Gilbert, Jas. M., character comedian; dram. agts., Brooks & Dickson; per. ad., 36 W 26th st., New York.

Gilligan, H. Victor., juveniles; dram. agts., Brooks & Dickson; per. ad., 28 Chester sq., Boston.

Gilmour, J. H., juveniles; dram. agts., Brooks & Dickson; per. ad., 85 Union ave., Montreal.

Gilray, Miss Julia, soubrettes and boys, Brooks & Dickson's Romany Rye Co. A.; dram. agts., Brooks & Dickson; per. ad., 454 Second ave., New York.

Gilpin, Miss Sophia L., juveniles; dram. agts., Brooks & Dickson; per. ad., Cumberland, Md.

Girard, Frank, stage manager, Tony Pastor's Co.; per. ad., Tony Pastor's Theatre, New York.

Glassford, Kate, juveniles; dram. agts., Brooks & Dickson; per. ad., 245 W. 37th st., New York.

Gleason, A. L., trainer of animals. Tony Denier's Pantomime and Specialty Co.; per. ad., Greenwich, Washington Co., N. Y.

Glenn, Sam'l W., old men, character and comedy; dram. agts., Brooks & Dickson; per. ad., 49 Valley st., Baltimore.

Glenny, T. H., character and old men; dram. agts., Brooks & Dickson; per. ad., 154 W. 20th st., New York.

Glover, Russell S., tenor; dram. agts., Brooks & Dickson; per. ad., 183 W. 44th st., New York.

Glover, Louis M., juveniles, Brooks & Dickson's In the Ranks Co.; dram. agts., Brooks & Dickson; per. ad., 1293 Broadway, New York.

Godfrey, Miss Carrie, prima donna, Rice & Dixey's Adonis Co.; dram. agts., Brooks & Dickson; per. ad., 41 E. 10th st. New York.

Golden, Frank (specialty), banjoist and comedian, Healy's Indian Show; per. ad., 332 E. 114th st., New York.

Goldthorp, Miss Helen, juveniles; per. ad., Room 29, Wescott block, Richmond, Ind.

Goldthorp, Arthur, juveniles and light comedy, Agnes Wallace-Villa Co.; per. ad., New York Mirror.

Gonzaleze, Miss Fannie, character old women and singing soubrette, Jos. Jefferson Co.; dram. agts., Brooks & Dickson; per. ad., 225 W. 23d st., New York.

Gonzalez, Mrs. Frankie, character; dram. agts., Brooks & Dickson; per. ad., 130 Castle st., Boston, suite 2.

Goodrich, Mrs. Joan, juveniles and soubrettes, Brooks & Dickson's Romany Rye Co.; dram. agts., Brooks & Dickson; per. ad., 18 Cottage Place, New York.

Goodwin, Miss Myra (specialty), song and dance, Tony Pastor's Co.; per. ad., Boston.

Gordon, Miss Jewell, juveniles; dram. agts., Brooks & Dickson; per. ad., 815 Ninth st., Philadelphia.

Gossin, Leslie, leads; dram. agts., Brooks & Dickson; per. ad., 345 W. 29th st., New York.

Gourley, Miss Maude, juveniles; dram. agts., Brooks & Dickson; per. ad., 231 W. 2 d st., New York.

Grady, T. J., comedian, Barry & Fay Co.; dram. agt., J. J. Spies; per. ad., 12 Union sq., New York.

Graham, R. E., comedian, starring in Wanted a Partner; dram. agts., Simmonds & Brown; per. ad., 110 Fourth ave., New York.

Granger, Will F., juveniles, Devil's Auction Co.; dram. agt., J. J. Spies; per. ad., 22 N. Ninth st., Philadelphia.

Granville, R. P., old men; dram. agts., Brooks & Dickson; per. ad., 140 E. 15th st., New York.

Grandil, E. E., heavies; dram. agts., Brooks & Dickson; per. ad., Morton House, New York.

Graves, C. L., business and stage manager, Brooks & Dickson's Romany Rye Co.; dram. agts., Brooks & Dickson; per. ad., 112 Fourth ave., New York.

Gray, Neil, character and old men, Brooks & Dickson's Romany Rye Co. A; dram. agts., Brooks & Dickson; per. ad., 44 W. 23d st., New York.

Gray, Miss Mary, character and old women, Sothern Comedy Co.; dram. agt., J. J. Spies; per. ad., Box 169, Key Port, N. J.

Gray, Mme. Katherine, leading heavies and dramatic reader; per. ad., Grand Opera House, Richmond, Ind.

Gray, Miss Lizzie, character, old women; dram. agts., Brooks & Dickson; per. ad., 1121 Chestnut st., St. Louis.

Gray, Miss Alice, heavy and character, old women; dram. agts., Brooks & Dickson; per. ad., 355 W. 23d st., New York.

Gray, Miss Elsie, soubrettes and boys; dram. agts., Brooks & Dickson; per. ad., 60 E. Ninth st., New York.

Gray, Miss Ada, soubrettes; **dram. agts.,** Brooks & Dickson; per. ad., **5 E. 12th st.,** New York.

Green & Seville, James F. and Dot, specialty, character and sketch artists, Renfrow's Jolly Pathfinders; per. ad., New York Clipper.

Gregory, Nathan W., stage manager, Crossen's Banker's Daughter Co.; dram. agts., **Simmonds & Brown**; per. ad., **P. O. Box 197,** Rahway, **N. J.**

Gregory & Cransel, **Geo. L. and Frank** (specialty), **dialect comedians and pantomimists**; per. **ad., 421 W. 54th st., New York.**

Gregory, Miss Eliza L., leading. **juveniles; dram. agts.,** Simmonds & Brown; per. ad.. **P. O. Box 197,** Rahway, N. J.

Greiner. W. M., character **and eccentric comedian,** Metropolitan **Comedy Co.;** per. ad., Fairmount, Va.

Grisel, Miss Mamie, juveniles, singing soubrette; dram. agts.. Brooks & Dickson; per. ad., 270 W. 38th st., New York.

Grisel, Louis R., old men; dram agts., Brooks **& Dickson; per.** ad., 270 W. 38th st., New **York.**

Griswold, Miss Bessie. walking lady, Only a Farmer's **Daughter Co.; dram. agts.,** Brooks **& Dickson; per. ad., 111 W. 33d** st., New York.

Grosse, Benjamin, stage carpenter, Romany Rye Co. No. 1; dram. agts.. Brooks & Dickson; per. ad., 404 W. 36th **st.,** New York.

Guthrie. Miss **Francesca, prima donna; dram.** agts., Brooks & **Dickson; per. ad., New** York Dramatic **News.**

Guthrie, S. J. (specialty), ventriloquist; per. ad , **163 E. 93d st., New York.**

--- **H** ---

Hadley, Miss Lillian, soubrettes **and juveniles;** dram. agts., Brooks & Dickson; per. ad., 22 E. 13th st., New York.

Hague, J. W., old men and character; dram. agts., Brooks & Dickson; per. ad., 208 W. 22d st., New York.

Hall, Mrs. Clinton, juveniles; dram. **agts.,** Brooks & Dickson; per. ad., **Soldiers'** Home, Dayton, O.

Hall, Charles Berrien, responsibles, Milu Dramatic **Co.;** per. ad., box 242, Hyde Park, Ill.

Hall, Clinton, leads; dram. agts., Brooks & Dickson; per. ad., Soldiers' Home, Dayton.

Hall, A. E., juveniles and light **comedy,** Frazer & Cleveland's People's **Theatre Co.;** per. ad., box **82, Northville, N. Y.**

Halsted, J. G , juvenile ; **dram.** agts., Brooks & Dickson; per. ad., **75 E.** 10th st., New York.

Halstead, E. S., comedian, Patti **Rosa Co.;** dram. agt., J. J. Spies; per. ad., **1138 S** 11th st., Philadelphia, Pa.

Halloway, Miss Maggie, soubrettes and eccentric comedy; dram. agts., Brooks **&** Dickson; **per. ad., 232 E. 34th** st., New York.

Hamilton, T. C., heavies; dram. agts., Brooks **& Dickson; per. ad., 146 High** st., Brook**lyn.**

Hamilton. F. C., leading heavies or juveniles, Dickson's **Sketch Club; per. ad..** Pope's Theatre, St. Louis.

Hamilton, Theo., heavies; dram. agts.. Brooks & Dickson; per. ad., 115 E. Townsend st., Baltimore.

Hampshire, Wall, tenor; dram. agts., Brooks & Dickson; per. ad., 10 Union Square, New York.

Hanchett, David, **heavy, leading and old** men. Shook & Collier's Ruth's Devotion Co.; dram. agts., Simmonds & Brown ; **per. ad., New** York Mirror.

Handyside, Clarence A., leads, **Brooks &** Dickson's Romany Rye Co.; **per. ad.. 41** W. 23d st., New York.

Hanford, Charles **B.,** juveniles and heavies, Thos. W. Keene Co.; per. ad., 204 F st., **N. W.,** Washington, D. C.

Hanlon Bros., managers and pantomime stars; per. ad., care of Simmonds & **Brown.** 1166 **Broadway, New York.**

Hanley, Lawrence, juveniles. Harry Miner's Silver King Co.; **dram.** agts., Simmonds **& Brown; per. ad., 20 Bull st., Savannah,** Ga.

Hanna. George, character comedian, Bella Moore Co.; **per. ad.,** Carthage, O.

Hannon, Victor, juveniles; dram. agts., Brooks & Dickson; per. ad., 275 W. 125th st., New York.

Harcourt, William, heavies; dram. agts., Brooks & Dickson; per. ad., 19 Great Jones st., New York.

Hardy, Frederick, character. Brooks & Dickson's Romany Rye Co. No. 1; dram. agts., Brooks & Dickson; per. ad.. 11 Washington Place, New York.

Hardy, Vernon, juveniles or heavies; dram. agts., Brooks & Dickson ; per. ad., 217 E. 14th st., **New York.**

Hardy, Jas. H., leads; dram. agts., Brooks & Dickson; per. ad., 29 Carlton ave., Brooklyn.

Hardy, Harry, cornet soloist, Alvin Joslin Comedy Co.; per. ad., Piqua, O.

Harkins, Miss Lenora, juveniles; dram. agts., Brooks & Dickson; per. ad., 303 W. 29th st., New York.

Harkins, W. S., leads; dram. agts., Brooks & Dickson; per. ad., 303 W. 29th st., New York.

Harkins, D. H., leads; dram. agts., Brooks & Dickson; per. ad., 145 E. 17th st., New York.

Harlem, Miss Genie, juveniles and soubrettes; dram. agts., Brooks & Dickson; per. ad., 1917 Clarence st., Philadelphia.

Harley, Claude B., responsible ; per. ad., New York Mirror.

Harmoyne, Miss Lotta, soubrettes, Atkinson's Peck's Bad Boy Co.; per. ad., Box 45 East Providence, R. I.

Harmoyne, Harry, low comedy and juveniles, Atkinson's Peck's Bad Boy Co.; per. ad., 45 East Providence, R. I.

Harris, Miss Anita, singing soubrettes; dram. agts., Brooks & Dickson; per. ad., 183 Sixth ave., New York.

Harris, Frank, carpenter, Brooks & Dickson's Romany Rye Co.; dram. agts., Brooks & Dickson; per. ad., 1805 Vine st., Philadelphia

Harris, Chas. and Billy (specialty); per. ad., 306 E. 78th st., New York

Harrison, Billy, character and comedy; per. ad., New York Clipper.

Harrison, Jas., heavies and character; dram. agts., Brooks & Dickson; per. ad., E. Monument st., Baltimore.

Harrison, Miss Pertie, soubrettes and boys; dram. agts., Brooks & Dickson; per. ad., 337 E. Monument st., Baltimore.

Hart, Daniel, comedy; dram. agts., Brooks & Dickson; per. ad., 102 Sands st., Brooklyn.

Harvey, Clarence, juveniles, Rehan's 7-20-8 Co.; dram. agts., Simmonds & Brown; per. ad., 309 W. 14th st., New York.

Haskell, Harry, singing comedian; Geo. S. Knight's Comedy Co.; per. ad., Mason. N. H.

Haskell, Edwin, character; dram. agts., Brooks & Dickson; per. ad., 67 E. 10th st., New York.

Hassall, Frank (specialty), vocalist, dancer and comedian; per. ad., New York Clipper.

Hassan, E. J., comedy and character; dram. agts., Brooks & Dickson; per. ad., 13 W. 11th., New York.

Hastings, Alice, leading light comedienne, Roland Reed Co.; dram agts., Simmonds & Brown; per. ad., 50 E. 10th st., New York.

Hathaway, Miss Grace (Mrs. W. Reynolds), chambermaid and character; dram agts., Simmonds & Brown; per. ad., New York Dramatic News.

Hatter, W. H., minor baritone parts in opera, Lights o' London Co.; dram. agts., Simmonds & Brown; per. ad., 41 Marion st., New York.

Haucker, H. A., old men or heavies, Crimes of London Co.; dram. agt., J. J. Spies.

Haven, Frank P., comedian, Edwin Clifford Comedy Co.; per. ad., 695 W. Madison st., Chicago, Ill.

Haven, Miss Louise, soubrettes, Edwin Clifford Comedy Co.; per. ad., 695 W. Madison st., Chicago, Ill.

Hawke, J. W., juveniles; dram. agts., Brooks & Dickson ; per. ad., 34 E. 12th st., New York.

Hawk, Harry, comedian; dram. agts., Brooks & Dickson; per. ad., 756 Erie st., Philadelphia.

Hawkins, John, light comedy and character, Hanlon Bros.; dram. agts., Simmonds & Brown; per. ad., 1166 Broadway, New York.

Hawkins, Miss Ruth, heavies, Bella Moore Co.; per. ad., Walnut Hills, Cincinnati.

Hawley, Geoffrey, juveniles; dram. agts., Brooks & Dickson; per. ad., New York Hotel, New York.

Hayes, R. B., old men and heavies, Gardner's Only a Woman's Heart Co.; dram. agt., J. J. Spies; per. ad., Lock Haven, Pa.

Hayes, Bruce, juveniles and character, Only a Woman's Heart Co; per. ad., 12 Union sq., New York.

Haynes, Miss Marie, leading juveniles, Maude Atkinson Co.; dram agts., Skiff & Morgan (Chicago); per. ad., Chicago News-Letter.

Hazelrigg, Jno., leads, Bertha Welby Co.; dram. agts., Brooks & Dickson; per. ad., 12 Union Square, New York.

Hazleton, J. H., heavies and character; dram.

agts., Brooks & Dickson; per. ad., 46 Clinton pl , New York.

Hazleton, Mrs H., soubrettes; dram. agts.. Brooks & Dickson; per. ad., 46 Clinton pl., New York.

Heald, Frank G., trombone, Jolly Pathfinders Co.; per. ad., Grand Rapids, Mich.

Healey, Mrs. J. R., char. and old women, Milton Nobles Co.; dram. agts., Brooks & Dickson ; per. ad., 60 E. 10th st., New York.

Hegner. Mrs. Minnie, char. old women, Stuttz Co.; per. ad., Temple, Tex.

Heisey, Mart. E., character, Maude Atkinson Co ; per. ad , Burlington, Iowa.

Helmrich, Charles, property man, Harrison & Gourlay Co.; dram. agts., Simmonds & Brown; per. ad., 21 Cottage Place, New York.

Hemple, Sam, old men, character and comedy; dram. agts., Brooks & Dickson; per ad., 679 Bankson st., Philadelphia.

Henderson, Miss Carrie, soubrettes and light com.; dram. agts., Brooks & Dickson; per. ad., 36 E. 12th st., New York.

Henderson, George, juveniles; dram. agt. Brooks & Dickson; per. ad., 35 South Wilton, Conn.

Henderson, William, comedian; dram. agts. Brooks & Dickson; per. ad., 86 Horatio st., New York.

Hendricks, Louis, heavies and old men; dram agts., Brooks & Dickson; per. ad., 60 E. 69th st., New York.

Hendrie, J., old men and comedy; dram. agts., Brooks & Dickson; per. ad., Boston Museum, Boston.

Herbert, Charles, character; dram. agt , Brooks & Dickson; per. ad., 10 Putnam ave , Brooklyn.

Herbert, William, comedy, old men, character and opera bouffe, Joe Jefferson Co.; dram. agts., Simmonds & Brown; per ad., 330 W. 59th st , New York.

Heritage, Clarence, juveniles; dram. agts., Brooks & Dickson; per. ad., 48 E. 10th st., New York.

Herman, H. W., juveniles and genteel heavies, Joseph Jefferson Co ; dram. agts., Simmonds & Brown; per. ad., New York.

Herman Charles D., leads, Bartley Campbell's White Slave Co.; dram. agts., Simmonds & Brown; per. ad., 803 Poplar st., Philadelphia.

Heron, Miss Bijou, leads ; dram. agts., Brooks & Dickson ; per. ad., 74 W. 38th st., New York.

Heubner, F. C., leading. Lights o' London Co Western; dram. agts , Simmonds & Brown; per. ad., Penn Yan. N. Y.

Heywood. Miss Nellie, juveniles and soubrettes; dram. agts., Brooks & Dickson; per. ad., 60 E. 9th st., New York.

Hill, Miss Caroline, leads; Brooks & Dickson's In the Ranks Co.; dram. agts., Brooks & Dickson; per ad., Barrett House, New York.

Hill, Geo. H., comedian; dram agts., Brooks & Dickson; per ad., 505 E. Douglas st., Bloomington, Ill.

Hilforde, Miss Marie, leads, Bertha Welby Co.; dram. agts , J. J. Spies or Brooks & Dickson; per. ad , Detroit Opera House, Detroit.

Hilton, Edward P , heavies; per. ad., P. O. box 296, St. Paul, Minn.

Hines, John E, comedian; dram. agts., Brooks & Dickson; per. ad., 18 University Place, New York.

Hinkley, Miss, soubrettes; dram. agts., Brooks & Dicksons; per. ad., 29 Canal st , New York.

Hinton, Miss Lillie, starring; R. K. Hinton, manager; per. ad., 1424 S. Broad st , Philadelphia.

Hiram, Charles, utility; per. ad., 252 S. Paca st., Baltimore.

Hirshberg, H. J., character or responsible, Gardner's Only a Farmer's Daughter Co ; dram. agt., J. J. Spies; per. ad., Youngstown, O.

Hodges, D. B., business agent; Wm. Emmett's Comedy Co.; per ad., 778 Adams st., Chicago.

Hoey, D. R., juveniles; dram. agts., Brooks & Dickson; per. ad., 33 E. 21st st., New York.

Hoffman, Jay S., prompter and responsible; Rehan's 7 20-8 Co; dram. agt., J. J. Spies; per ad., 48 Unity st., Frankford, Pa.

Holland, George, character and comedy; dram. agts., Simmonds & Brown; per. ad., the Lambs' Club, 34 W. 26th st., New York.

Holland, E. M., comedian; Madison Square Theatre Rajah Co.; per. ad., Lambs' Club, 34 W. 26th st., New York.

Holland, Mrs. E. M., juveniles; dram. agts., Brooks & Dickson; per. ad., 307 E. 57th st., New York.

Holland, J. J., juveniles, heavies and character; dram. agts., Brooks & Dickson; per. ad., 34 W. 26th st., New York.

Hoiliday, Harry J., comedian; dram. agts., Brooks & Dickson; per. ad., 39 W. 19th st., New York.

Holman, William., character; d am. agts., Brooks & Dickson; per. ad., 12 Buckingham st., Adelphi, London.

Holmes, Mrs. E. B., com. and old women; dram. agts., Brooks & Dickson; per. ad., 519 W. 61st st., New York.

Homer, Gus, comedian; Sterling Comedy Co.; dram. agt., J. Alex. Brown; per. ad., 873 N. 84th st., Philadelphia.

Honning, B. T., leads and heavies; dram. agts., Brooks & Dickson; per. ad., 234 W. 38th st., New York.

Hopper, Chas. H., comedian; Harry Miner's Silver King Co. No. 1; dram. agts., Simmonds & Brown; per. ad., 175 Arlington st., Cleveland, O.

Horn, Harry, eccentric and character comedy; Bertha Welby Co.; dram. agt., J. J. Spies; per. ad., 45 Orchard st., New York.

Hotto, Harry, leading comedian; Rehan's 7-20-8 Co.; dram. agts., Simmonds & Brown; per ad., Station R., New York City.

Houston, Miss Edith, leads or juveniles; dram. agts., Simmonds & Brown; per ad., 133 E. 15th st., New York.

Howard Sisters, specialty, song and dance; Agnes, Wallace-Villa Co.; dram. agt., Dick Fitzgerald; per ad., 878 Bergen st., Brooklyn.

Howard, J. H., juveniles, Harry Miner's Silver King Co. No. 2; dram. agts., Brooks & Dickson; per ad., 152 E. 48th st., or People's Theatre, New York.

Howard, Edward C., Irish comedian; Morton & Bell's Our Strategists Co.; dram. agts., Simmonds & Brown; per ad., 106 Greenwich st., New York.

Howard, Ralph, com. and character; Maude Atkinson Co.; dram. agts., Skiff & Morgan, (Chicago); per ad., Chicago News Letter.

Howard, Miss Genevieve, char. and heavy old women; dram. agts., Brooks & Dickson; per ad., 113 E. 27th st., New York.

Howard, Charles, character; dram. agts. Brooks & Dickson; per. ad., 463 W. 23d st., New York.

Howard, Miss Ada, leads; Tucker & Bourne's Metropolitan Co., per ad, Detroit, Mich.

Howard, Harry J., specialty, tenor and motto vocalist; per. ad., New York Clipper.

Howard, Edgar A., juveniles and comedy; per. ad., 1670 3d ave., New York.

Howe, Emilu, old men and character; dram. agts., Brooks & Dickson; per ad., Morton House, New York.

Howland, J. H., responsible, Harry Miner's Silver King Co No. 1; dram. agts, Simmonds & Brown; per. ad., 41 Soley st., Charlestown, Mass.

Huber, Fred. J., comedian, Harry Miner's Eighth Avenue Theatre, New York.

Hudson, Miss Eliza S., walking ladies and boys. Maggie Mitchell Co.; dram. agts., Brooks & Dickson; per. ad., New Lisbon, Wis. P. O. Box 84.

Hrdson, Harry B., heavies or juveniles, Oliver D. Byron Co; dram. agts., Brooks & Dickson, per. ad., P. O. Box 84, New Lisbon, Wis.

Hudson, Robert C., leading heavies, Frederick Warde Co.; dram. agts., Simmonds & Brown; per. ad., 2705 Washington st., Boston.

Hughes & West, Wally and Nelly, Sketch Team; per. ad., Room 16, 33 Monroe st., New York.

Hughes, Wm. P., teacher of music and voice culture; per. ad., P. O., Brooklyn, L. I.

Hune, John H., responsible, Robert McWade Co; per. ad., 1096 Clay st., Dubuque, Ia.

Hunt, Miss Alice, juvenile and soubrette, Tavernier Co.; dram. agt, J. J. Spies; per. ad., 328 W. 20th st., New York.

Hunt, Miss Julia, leads; dram. agts., Brooks & Dickson; per. ad., 327 W. 49th st., New York.

Hunter, Miss Bessie, leading heavy; dram. agts., Brooks & Dickson; per. ad., 129th st. and 3d ave., New York.

Hunter, Miss Marie, juveniles and soubrettes; dram. agts., Brooks & Dickson; per. ad., 22 Crivion Building, New York.

Hunter, Fred, stage manager, Gardiner's Only a Farmer's Daughter Co.

Hunting, Percy, juveniles, Kate Claxton Co.; dram. agts., Brooks & Dickson; per. ad., 402 4th ave., New York.

Huntington, Jay, old men and heavies, Draper's Uncle Tom's Cabin Co.; per. ad., Blissfield, Mich.

Huntington, Miss Dott, soubrettes, Draper's Uncle Tom Co.; per. ad., Blissfield, Mich.

Huntley, Mrs. J. H., juvenile and leads; dram. agts., Brooks & Dickson; per. ad., Mobile, Ala.

Huntley, J. H., leads; dram. agts., Brooks & Dickson; per. ad., Mobile, Ala.

Hurley, W. J., heavy and character, Fanny Davenport Fedora Co.; dram. agts.,

Brooks & Dickson: per. ad., 60 E. 9th st., New York.

Hurst, Lin., juvenile; dram. agts., Brooks & Dickson; per. ad., 54 Union Square, New York.

— I —

Ingles, Miss Lizzie, character, Lizzie Evans' Fogg's Ferry Co.; dram. agt., J. A. Brown, New York.

Irving, Ed. J., low comedy and character; dram. agts., Skiff & Morgan, Chicago.

Irving, Mrs. Ed. J., old women and character; dram. agts., Skiff & Morgan, Chicago.

Irving, Miss Henrietta, heavy old women, Janauschek Co.; dram. agts., Brooks & Dickson; per. ad., 71 2d ave., New York.

Irving, Norman, juvenile; dram. agts., Brooks & Dickson; per. ad., 337 W. 32d st. New York.

Irwin, Mrs. Selden, character and old women; dram. agts., Brooks & Dickson; per. ad., 463 W. 36th st., New York.

— J —

Jack, Edwin B., juvenile, Roland Reed Co.; dram. agts., Brooks & Dickson; per. ad., 257 Chester st., Philadelphia.

Jack, John, leading comedian, Wm. Harris' Dead Heart Co.

Jackson, Miss Mary, heavy old women; dram. agts., Brooks & Dickson; per. ad., 140 W. 4th st., New York.

Jackson, Wallace, character and comedy, Mr. and Mrs. W. J. Florence Co.; dram. agts., Brooks and Dickson; per. ad., 218 E. 39th st., New York.

Jackson, Harry, comedian; dram. agts., Brooks & Dickson; per. ad., 41 Christopher st., New York.

Jackson, W. T., old men, character and comedy; Brooks & Dickson's Romany Rye Co.; dram. agts., Brooks & Dickson; per. ad., care P. O. Box 1229, New York City.

Jackson, Chas. J., character, Brooks & Dickson's Romany Rye Co A; dram. agts., Brooks & Dickson; per. ad., 312 W. 24th st., New York.

Jackson, Joseph E., old men and character; dram. agts., Brooks & Dickson; per. ad., 140 W. 4th st., New York.

James, Howard, Jr., comedian, Gardner's Only a Woman's Heart; dram. agts., J. J. Spies; per. ad., New York Mirror.

Jamison, Frank E., leads, Power of Money

Co.; d am. agts., Simmonds & Brown; per. ad., 183 South Peoria st., Chicago.

Janauschek, Mme., tragedy star; Edward Taylor, man.; per. ad., 23 E. 14th st., New York.

Janish, Mme., tragedy star; Harry Sargent, manager.

Jarbeau, Miss Vernona, singing soubrettes, Kiralfy Bros.' Sieba Co.; dram. agts., Brooks & Dickson; per. ad., 140 W. 36th st., New York.

Jeffreys, Miss Ida, leads; dram. agts., Brooks & Dickson; per ad., 109 E. 28th st., New York.

Jennings, Miss Helen, juvenile; dram agts., Brooks & Dickson; per. ad., 433 Fourth ave., New York.

Jennings, John W., old men, Harry Miner's Silver King Co. No. 1; per ad., People's Theatre, New York.

Jeremy, Miss Lizzie, juveniles; dram. agts., Brooks & Dickson; per. ad., 144 W. 21st st., New York.

Jewett, Miss Sara, leads, Union Square Theatre Stock Co.; per. ad., Union Square Theatre, New York.

Johns, Miss Effie, light comedy; dram. agts., Brooks & Dickson; per. ad., 192 S. Peoria st., Chicago.

Johnston, Wm. J., heavy leads, Wm. Stafford Co.; per. ad., Syracuse, N. Y.

Johnson, W. T., character and comedian, Brooks & Dickson's Romany Rye Co.; dram agts., Brooks & Dickson; per. ad., 1318 Second ave., New York.

Jones, J. H., singing and comedy; dram. agts., Brooks & Dickson.

Jones, Miss Nellie, character and heavies; dram. agts., Brooks & Dickson; per ad., 319 W. 42d st., New York.

Jones, Richard, character and property master, Hanlon Bros.' Co; dram. agts., Simmonds & Brown.

Jones, Mrs. W. J., character and old women, Brooks & Dickson's Romany Rye Co. A; dram. agts., Brooks & Dickson; per. ad., 44 W. 23d st., New York.

Jordan, George C., leading heavies; dram. agts., Brooks & Dickson; per. ad., 157 W. 20th st., New York.

Jordan, Charles, double bass and tuba; Rentfraw's Jolly Pathfinders Co.; per. ad., Grand Rapids, Mich.

Jordan, Miss Lulu, leads; dram. agts., Brooks & Dickson; per. ad., 51 E. 31st st., New York.

Jordan, M. J., leading heavies; Brooks &

Dickson's Romany Rye Co. A. dram. agts., Brooks & Dickson; per. ad., 44 W. 23d st., New York.

Joyce and Carroll, Edwin and Verona (specialty), vocalists, dancers and sketch artists; per. ad., New York Clipper.

— K —

Kahn, Julius, character, Joseph Jefferson Co.; dram. agts., Simmonds & Brown; per. ad., 35 Warren st., Newark, N. J.

Kahl, J. W., juvenile; dram. agts., Brooks & Dickson; per. ad., 1801 14th st., N. W., Washington.

Karsner, Miss Jenny, juveniles; Bartley Campbell's Siberia Co.; dram. agts., Simmonds & Brown; per. ad., Nashville, Tenn.

Kean, Miss Emily, vocalist and soubrette; Hanlon Bros.' Co., dram. agts., Brooks & Dickson; per. ad., 105 E. 17th st., New York.

Keane, Joseph H., comedian; starring in Mrs. Partington; **per. ad., Royalton, Berrien Co., Mich.**

Keen, Alberta, child parts; per. ad., 4 Sutton pl., New York.

Keen, Harry P., leading heavies and stage manager, Alvin Joslin Co.; per. ad., New York Dramatic News.

Keen, Miss Nellie, juveniles; per. ad., 4 Sutton pl., New York.

Keene, Thos. W., **tragedy star, starring in the legitimate drama; W. R. Hayden, man.; per. ad., care National Printing Co., Chicago**

Kelcey Herbert, leads; dram. agts., Brooks & Dickson; **per. ad., Barrett House, New York.**

Kendall, Edward, juveniles; **dram. agts., Brooks & Dickson; per. ad., 143 Court st., Boston.**

Kendell, Joseph B. (specialty), Irish comedian; per. ad., New York Clipper.

Kendrick Miss Adel, juvenile; dram. **agts., Brooks & Dickson, per. ad., Freeport, Ill.**

Kendrick, Miss F. M., character; dram. agts., Brooks & Dickson; per. ad., 250 W. 24th st., New York.

Kendrick, F. M., character and comedian; dram. agts., Brooks & Dickson; per. ad., Freeport, Ill.

Kennington, George, comedian; dram. agts., Brooks & Dickson; per. ad., 153 E. 33d st., New York.

Kent, **S. W., juvenile; dram. agts., Brooks &** Dickson; per. ad., Coleman House, New York.

Kidder, Miss Kate Mitchell, soprano, light opera; dram. agts., Simmonds & Brown; per. ad., 1166 Broadway, New York.

Kidder, Charles, light comedy, Mlle. Rhea; dram. agts., Simmonds & Brown; per. ad., 1166 Broadway, New York.

Kilbaume, J. P., comedian; dram. agts., Brooks & Dickson; per. ad., News-Letter, Chicago.

Kilday, Frank, juveniles, leads, Brooks & Dickson's In the Ranks Co.; dram. agts., Brooks & Dickson; per. ad., 44 E. 10th st., New York.

Kingsley, Harry, juveniles; dram. agts., Brooks & Dickson; per. ad., 106 E. 28th st., New York.

Kirwan and De Witt (specialty), musical artists, Tony Denier's Pantomime Co.; per. ad., 317 E. 9th st., New York, or 174 Atlantic ave., Brooklyn.

Kirwin, Miss Susie, prima donna, Wilbur Opera Co.; per. ad., Philadelphia.

Kitts, C., juveniles, Harry Miner's Silver King Co. No. 2; per. ad., People's Theatre, New York.

Klein, Charles, low comedy, Brooks & Dickson's Romany Rye Co. (A); dram. agts., Brooks & Dickson; per. ad., 409 3d ave., New York.

Kline, Miss Nellie, leads, Madison Square Theatre Esmeralda Co.; dram. agts., Brooks & Dickson; per. ad., 113 W. 42d st., New York.

Kline, Alf., comedian; dram. agts., Brooks & Dickson; **per. ad., 341 E. 76th st., New York.**

Knight, Fred. W., character; dram. agts., Brooks & Dickson; **per. ad., cor. 12th st. and 4th ave., New York.**

Knowlton, Miss Georgia, prima donna, Wilbur Opera Co.; per. ad., Brooklyn, N. Y.

Kories, Miss Emma, chambermaids, J. G. Stuttz Comedy Co.; per. ad., Temple, Tex.

Kropp Family, instrumentalists, vocal concerts, etc.; **per. ad., 64 Jones st., Newark, N. J.**

— L —

Lackey, W. A., juveniles; dram. agts., Brooks & Dickson; per. ad., Soldiers' Home, Dayton.

Lackey, Wm. A., comedian; dram. agts., Brooks & Dickson; per. ad., Soldiers' Home, Dayton, O.

La Croix, Miss **Ada**, character and comedienne; dram. agt., J. J. Spies; per. ad , 12 Union Square, N, Y.

Lake, J. Will, old men, McElroy's **Old Dominion Co.**; per. ad., Louisvilla, Ky.

Lambson, Geo. D., baritone vocalist, Gorton's New Orleans Minstrels ; per. ad., Gardner, Mass.

La Mierie, Miss **Elsie, heavy leads and old** women, Jane **Coombs Co.; dram. agts., Brooks & Dickson; per. ad., 60 E. 9th st , New York.**

Lane, Miss Eleanor, leading juveniles, Harrison & Gourlay Co.; dram. agts., Simmonds & Brown; **per. ad., 314 N. 39th st , Philadelphia.**

Lane, John A., leads; dram. agts., Brooks & Dickson; per. ad., 181 E. 16th st., New York

Lane, W. F., heavies; dram. agts., Brooks & Dickson; per. ad., 109 Fourth ave , New York.

Langdon, H. W., heavies, Mme. **Ristori** Co.; dram. agts , Brooks & Dickson; per. ad., 54 Union Square, New York.

Langdon, Miss Lena, juveniles; dram. agts., Brooks & Dickson: per. ad., 399 E. 72d st., New York.

Langley, Ed. D., heavies, first old men and character; dram. agts., Skiff & Morgan, Chicago, Ills.

Lapiere, Miss F., soubrette; dram. agts., Brooks & Dickson; per. ad., 317 W. 36th st., New York.

Larker, Miss Annie, juveniles; **dram. agts.,** Brooks & Dickson; per. ad., 365 W. **15th** st., New York.

Larkin. Chas. A., comedian, Stultz **Dramatic Co.;** per. ad., Streator, Ill.

Larrier, Miss Margaret, leads; **dram. agts., Brooks & Dickson; per. ad., 206 E. 15th st., New York.**

Lascelles, Geo. (specialty), stage manager **and** museum lecturer; per. ad., 145 Congress st., Troy, N. Y.

Lascelles, Miss Sara, soubrettes and **boys; dram. agts., Brooks & Dickson; per. ad.,** 44 E. 10th st , New York.

Lask, Geo. E., comedian and stage manager; dram. agts., Simmonds & Brown; **per. ad., 1207 Pine st., San Francisco, Cal.**

Latham, Miss Emma, leads; per. ad., **18 W.** 23d st., New York.

Laurell, Julian (specialty), gymnast; per. **ad.,** 63 Harrison st., Baltimore.

La Veer, Harry, specialty **gymnast; per. ad.,** Kansas City, Kan.

La Verde, Miss Lillie, soubrettes, Sanger's Bunch of Keys Co.

Lavelle, Wm. A., juveniles, light com. and heavies, Fred Warde Co ; dram. agts., Simmonds & Brown; per. ad., Post Office. **Pittsburg, Pa.**

Lawler, J., character, Brooks & Dickson's In **the** Ranks Co.; dram. agts., Brooks & **Dickson; per** ad., 44 W. **23d** st., New **York.**

Lawrence, Edwin F., responsibles, Frederick **Warde; dram.** agts., Brooks & Dickson; 185 Devoe st., Brooklyn.

Lawrence, Miss Josephine, leads; dram.agts., **Brooks & Dickson; per.** ad., 62 Irving **Place, New York.**

Leach, George C. (specialty), **xylophone** soloist; per. ad., **1408 Ridge ave.. Philadel**phia.

Leahert, Chas. F., character **and** old men; dram. agts , Brooks & Dickson; per. ad., 199 Delancy st., New York.

Le Baron, Miss Lizade, leading juveniles and comedienne; dram. agts., Simmonds & Brown; per. ad.. Hotel Royal, New York.

Le Clair, Harry, burlesque, Tony Pastor's **Co.; per. ad.,** Hotel Osborn, Boston.

Lee, Henry, **leads, Fanny** Davenport Fedora Co.

Lee, Miss Amy, soubrettes; dram. agts., Brooks & Dickson; **per. ad., 463 W. 23d** st., New York.

Le Gros, Miss Marie, char., old women; dram. agts., Brooks & Dickson; per. ad., 110 Fourth ave., New York.

Lennon, Lester, juveniles; dram. agts., Brooks & Dickson; **per. ad.,** 481 Berkley st., Camden, N. J.

Lennox, Walter, Jr, character, comedy and **old men**; dram. agts., Brooks & Dickson; per. ad , 62 Irving Place, New York.

Lennox, Miss Minnie C., soubrettes, Gus Williams Co.; dram. agts., Brooks & Dickson; **per. ad ,** 155 W. 14th st., New York.

Leo, B. Frank, leads, D. S. Harold Co.; per. ad., 489 Broadway. E. Albany, N. Y.

Leonard, Hubert G., juvenile leads; dram. agts., Simmonds & Brown; per. ad., 234 W, 14th st., New York.

Leonhardt, Walla, (specialty), pantaloon and gymnast, Tony Denier's Co.; dram. agt., George Castle (Chicago); per. ad., New York **Clipper.**

Leopold, Harry, (specialty), white or black face comedian, Williams and Kernell's Specialty Co.; dram. agt. J. A. Brown; per. ad., New York Clipper.

Lester & Allen (specialty), negro comedians, Tony Pastor's Co.; per. ad., Hoffman House, New York.

Lester, Miss Louise, prima donna; dram. agts., Brooks and Dickson; per. ad., 122 W. 37th st., New York.

Lewes, Miss Marie, leads; dram. agts., Brooks & Dickson; per. ad., 210 E. 10th st., New York.

Lewis, J. E., leading heavy, G. A. Hill's Theatre Co.; dram. agt., J. A. Brown; per. ad., 95 Waverly st., Yonkers, N. Y.

Lewis, Harry C., juvenile; dram. agts., Brooks & Dickson; per. ad., Phillion's Museum, Paterson, N. J.

Lewis, Miss Helen M., leads; dram. agts., Brooks & Dickson; per. ad., 108 E. 74th st., New York.

Lewis, Mrs. W. H., old women; dram. agts., Brooks & Dickson; per. ad., 61 N. 11th st., Williamsburg, N. Y.

Lewis, Evelyn, singing soubrette; per. ad., 1400 43d st., Chicago.

Lewis, Miss Ida, leads, Crossen's Banker's Daughter Co.; dram. agt., J. J. Spies; per. ad., 335 Dean st., Philadelphia.

Leydon, W. A., old men and character, Brooks & Dickson's Romany Rye Co. A; dram. agts., Brooks & Dickson; per. ad., 44 W. 23d st., New York.

Lieb, Miss Beatrice, leads, Wm. Harris Co.; dram. agts., Simmonds & Brown; per. ad., Dubuque, Ia.

Linden, Miss Laura, character and heavies; dram. agts., Brooks and Dickson; per. ad., 37 E. 10th st., New York.

Lindeman, Eugenie, leads; per. ad., 206 E. 15th st., New York.

Lindley, Miss Irene, soubrettes and character, Dominick Murray Co.; dram. agt., Boston Dramatic Agency; per. ad., New York Clipper.

Lingard, Miss Catherine, soubrette, Brooks & Dickson's In the Ranks Co.; dram. agts., Brooks & Dickson; per. ad., 309 W. 23th st., New York.

Lingard, Miss Nellie, juveniles and soubrettes, Shook & Collier's Storm Beaten Co.; dram. agts., Brooks & Dickson; per. ad., 202 E. 16th st., New York.

Lingwood, Miss Sophie, singing soubrettes; dram. agts., Brooks & Dickson; per. ad., 20 E. 9th st., New York.

Linsome, Harry, leads, Crossen's Banker's Daughter Co.; per. ad., 31 Carmine st., New York.

Lionel, Miss Amy, juveniles; dram. agts., Brooks & Dickson; per. ad., 110 W. 49th st., New York.

Lipman, A. S., leads, Kiralfy Bros'. Sieba Co.; dram. agts., Brooks & Dickson; per. ad., 235 E. 79th st., New York.

Little, Frank, light comedian and juveniles, J. McCullough Co.; dram. agts., Simmonds & Brown; per. ad., Washington Heights, New York City.

Livingston, Miss Pearl, vocalist, Wyman's Wonders Co.; per. ad., —— Fourth ave., New York.

Loane, Miss Josie, leads, Bartley Campbell's White Slave Co.; per. ad., 251 W. 23d st., New York.

Lock, E. A., comedian; per. ad., 107 S. Union st., Rochester, N. Y.

Lockhart, C. R. (specialty), illusionist; per. ad., 2700 Carson st., Pittsburg, Pa.

Logan, Miss Grace, soubrettes, Bertha Welby Co.; dram. agt., J. J. Spies; per. ad., 357 W. 59th st., New York.

Loraine, Miss Emma, soubrettes; dram. agts., Brooks & Dickson; per. ad., Morton House, New York.

Losee, Frank, leads; dram. agts., Brooks & Dickson; per. ad., 339 W. 47th st., New York.

Lotto, Fred, comedian and character, Poole & Gilmore's Seven Ravens Co.; dram. agts., Simmonds & Brown; per. ad., 68 W. 19th st., New York.

Luce, Miss Mamie, juveniles, Geo. S. Knight Co.; dram. agts., Brooks & Dickson; per. ad., 65 Irving Place, New York.

Lucette, Miss Madeline, prima donna; dram. agts., Brooks & Dickson; per. ad., 226 W. 39th st., New York.

Lynch, M. A., juveniles, F. A. Vincent Co.; per. ad., 60 Eagle st., Cleveland, O.

Lyon, Billy, soprano vocalist and female impersonator; per. ad., N. Y. Clipper.

Lyon, Miss Esther, juveniles; dram. agts., Brooks & Dickson; per. ad., 211 W. 25th st., New York.

Lyons, Miss Marie, prima donna; dram. agts., Brooks & Dickson; per. ad., 238 Sixth ave., New York.

Lyons, Fred, specialist and negro comedian, Waldick's Bandit King Co.; dram. agts., J. J. Spies; per. ad., N. Y. Clipper.

— M —

Maciery, Wallace, tenor; dram. agts., Brooks & Dickson; per. ad , 74 State st., Brooklyn.

Madara, Louis, juveniles; dram. agts., Brooks & Dickson; per. ad., 215 E. 50th st., New York.

Maddern, Miss Minnie, starring in Caprice; Chas. Frohman, manager; per. ad., 18 W. 23d st., New York.

Maddern, Miss Mary, old women; dram. agts., Brooks & Dickson; per. ad., 335 E. 10th st., New York.

Madigan, Miss Gertrude L., singing soubrette and character, Wilbur Opera Co.; per. ad., N. Y. Clipper.

Maher, John T., comedian and vocalist, Graham Bros. Co.; per. ad., New York Clipper.

Malcolm, Henry M., utility and second old men, Pence Opera House Stock Co.; per. ad., 402 1st st., South Minneapolis, Minn.

Mallon, Miss Katie, old women; dram. agts., Brooks & Dickson; per. ad., 51 E. 31st st., New York.

Mallon, A. A., character and comedy, Wallack Theatre Co.; dram. agts., Brooks & Dickson; per. ad., 436 Fourth ave., New York.

Manley, Charles, character and old men, J. S. Murphy Kerry Gow Co.; dram. agt., J. Alex. Brown; per. ad., 245 10th st. Brooklyn.

Mann, Frederick, juveniles and character, Hanlon Bros.; dram. agts., Simmonds & Brown; per. ad., 1271 Broadway, New York.

Mantell, Robt. B., leads, Madison Square Theatre Called Back Co.; per. ad., Madison Square Theatre, New York.

Manzio, Miss Marie, leading juveniles, Gardner's Only a Woman Heart Co.; dram. agt., J. J. Spies; per. ad., New York Mirror.

Marble, Miss Ella, juveniles and heavies, Nellie Boyd Co.; per. ad., New York Clipper.

Marble, Wm., comedian, Nellie Boyd Co.; per. ad., New York Clipper.

Marble, John, comedian; dram. agts., Brooks & Dickson; per. ad., 441 3d ave, New York.

Marks, Eddie, eccentric comedian, Barlow & Wilson's Minstrels; per. ad., 278 11th st., Jersey City, N. J.

Marlowe, Mrs. Owen, old women; dram agts.,

Brooks & Dickson; per. ad., 209 E. 109th st., New York.

Marlowe, Miss Virginia, soubrettes; dram. agts., Brooks & Dickson; per. ad., 209 E. 109th st., New York.

Marsden, E. R., **juveniles; dram.** agts., Brooks & Dickson; per. **ad.,** 152 E. 48th st., New York.

Marshall, Miss Albertina, juveniles; **dram.** agts., Brooks & Dickson; per. ad., 237 W. 15th st., New York.

Marshall, John, juveniles and heavies; dram. **agts.,** Brooks & Dickson; per. ad., 251 W 14th st., New York.

Martell, L. M., responsibles and props., C. B. **Bishop Comedy Co.; dram.** agt., J. J. Spies; per. **ad., 39 Clinton** Place, New York.

Marten, Harry, motto vocalist and character comedian, Draper's U. T. Cabin Co.; dram. agt., Dick Fitzgerald; per. ad., N. Y. Clipper.

Martin, A. Robert, character and juveniles; dram. agt., J. Alex. Brown; per. ad. Madison Square Theatre, New York.

Martin, Mrs. Burt (specialty), solo and variety pianist; dram agt., Ed. P. Hilton, St. Paul; per. ad., 12 Park, Concord, N. H.

Martin Burt (Specialty), descriptive lecturer and specialist; dram. agt , Ed. P. Hilton St. Paul, Minn.; per. ad., 12 Park st., Concord, N. H.

Martin, Jacques, character comedian; McKee Rankin Co.; dram. agts., Brooks & Dickson; per. ad., 85 Dearborn st., Chicago.

Martin, Reginald, character; dram. agts., Brooks & Dickson; per. ad., 226 W 39th st., New York.

Martin, Luke, comedian and character; dram. agts., Brooks & Dickson; per. ad , Hotel Brentwood, New York.

Martal, **Miss** Dasie; dram. agts., Brooks & Dickson; per. ad., 150 Castle st., suite 2, Boston.

Martinetti, Albert, pantomimist, Devil's Auction Co.; dram. agt., J. Alex. Brown; per. ad., 48 North Moore st., New York.

Martinetti, Ignacio, eccentric character comedian (singing and dancing), Denman Thompson Co.; per. ad., 488 Washington st., Boston.

Martinot, Miss Sadie, soubrette, Lyceum Theatre Stock Co., per. ad., Lyceum Theatre, New York.

Mason, William J., comedian, Devil's Auction Co.; dram. agt., R. Fitzgerald; per. ad., New Central Theatre, Philadelphia.

Mason, B. C., treasurer; per. ad , Harmony Theatre, Galveston, Tex.

Mason, Wilbur A., juveniles; Haverly's Michael Strogoff Co ; per. ad , N. Y. Mirror.

Mason, Chas., juveniles; dram. agts., Brooks & Dickson; per. ad., 257 W. 24th st., New York.

Mather, Miss Margaret, tragedy star, starring in the legitimate drama; J. M. Hill, manager; per. ad , cor. of Clark and Madison sts., Chicago.

Mathews, Harry, old men; dram. agts., Brooks & Dickson; per. ad., 451 W. 39th st., New York.

Maulray, Miss Maude, character heavy; dram. agts., Brooks & Dickson; per. ad. 156 E. 55th st., New York.

Maude, Cyril, light comedian and character, Eric Bayley Comedy Co.; dram. agts., Simmonds & Brown; per ad., New York Mirror.

Maurice, F. W., comedian, Frank Mayo Nordeck Co.; per. ad., 1635 Columbia ave., Philadelphia.

Mayer, Dustin, juveniles and heavies; dram. agts., Simmonds & Brown; per. ad., care Dr. Miller, 358 W. 42d st., New York.

Maynard, Miss Agnes, old women and character, Gardner's Only a Woman's Heart Co.; dram. agt., J. J. Spies, per. ad., New York Mirror.

Mayo, Frank, starring in Nordeck, Sheridan Corbyn, manager ; per. ad , Crockett Lodge, Canton, Pa.

Mayo, Will. H., comedian; dram. agts., Brooks & Dickson; per. ad , New York Clipper.

Mays, Edwin F , leads and juveniles; dram agts., Brooks & Dickson; per. ad., Morton House, New York.

McCabe, Thos. F., heavies; dram. agts., Brooks & Dickson; per. ad , 202 E. 20th st., New York.

McCarthey, Thos., second heavies, Bartley Campbell's White Slave Co.; per. ad., 1109 S. 3d st., Philadelphia.

McCaull, Miss Lizzie, juveniles and soubrettes; dram. agts., Brooks & Dickson; per. ad., 39 W. 16th st., New York.

McClelland, F.W., utility, Croesen's Banker's Daughter Co.; dram. agt., J. J. Spies; per. ad., care Dr. Clarke, 79th st. and Broadway.

McConnell, J. W., leading juveniles, Mattie Vickers Co.; dram. agts., King & Castle.

Chicago ; per. ad., 345 Van Buren st., Milwaukee, Wis.

McCready, Miss Addie, soubrettes; dram. agts., Brooks & Dickson; per. ad., 223 W. 10th st., New York.

McCready, Wm., old men, dialects, comedy. Patti Rosa Co.; dram. agt., J. Spies; per. ad., A. O. of F., 7 W. 14th st., New York.

McCullough, John, tragedy star, starring in the legitimate drama; William Connor, manager; per. ad , St. James Hotel, New York.

McDonald, George F., leading heavy and character, Brooks and Dickson's Romany Rye Co.; dram. agts., Simmonds & Brown; per. ad., 231 Clinton st., Brooklyn.

McDonald, J. F., old men, character and comedy; dram. agts., Brooks & Dickson; per. ad., 188 E. 22d st., New York.

McDonald, Frank, character, Harry Miner's Silver King Co. No. 2; per. ad., People's Theatre, New York.

McDowell, J. Gordon, comedian, Tucker & Bourne's Metropolitan Co.; per. ad., Detroit, Mich.

McDowell, W. M., juveniles; dram. agts., Brooks & Dickson; per. ad., 158 W. 28th st., New York.

McGinley, Benjamin, leading old men and character, Madison Square Thea re May Blossom Co.; per. ad., Madison Square Theatre, New York.

McHenry, Miss Tillie, old women; dram. agts., Brooks & Dickson; per. ad., Highlands of Navesink, N. J.

McKisson, Harry, grotesque comedian, Barlow & Wilson's Minstrels; per. ad., New York Clipper.

McKean, Miss Gabriella, character and heavies, Gus Williams Co.; per. ad., Simmonds & Brown.

McNair, Robt , comedy, old men and character; dram agts., Brooks & Dickson; per. ad., 192 S. Peoria st., Chicago.

McNavin, James, manager, Georgie Woodthorpe Co.; per. ad., N. Y. Clipper.

Meaford, Albert, light comedy; dram. agt., J. J. Spies; per. ad., 462 Henry st., Brooklyn.

Meek, Miss Kate, leading heavy, Fred. Warde Co.; dram. agts., Brooks & Dickson; per. ad., 158 W. 22d st., New York.

Meir, Miss Edith, soubrettes; dram. agts., Brooks & Dickson ; per. ad., Hamilton House, 125th st. and Eighth ave., New York.

"Our Work Our Reference."

R. H. Eichner & Co.,

THEATRICAL
LITHOGRAPHERS,

Cor. Pratt and President Sts.,
BALTIMORE, MD.
P. O. Box 298.

Correspondence solicited.

Summers & Allen,

CITY BILL POSTERS,

N. W. Cor. King and Pitt Streets,

ALEXANDRIA, VA.

C. M. Hamilton,

Owner of bill boards and dead
walls,

CITY BILL POSTER,

PRAIRIE DU CHIEN, WIS.

All orders by mail promptly attended to.

M. Breslauer,

CITY BILL POSTER,

MINNEAPOLIS, MINN.

Commercial work a specialty.

T. W. ADAMS.   WILL A. HIGBE.

Northern Michigan Circuit,

ADAMS & HIGBE, Managers,

BIG RAPIDS, MICHIGAN.

Big Rapids, Stanton, Reed City,

Cadillac, Manistee.

The Albany Calcium Light Co.,

No 26 WILLIAM STREET,
ALBANY, N. Y.

Oxygen and Hydrogen Gas in
any quantity. Operators and apparatus sent to any part of the
country at short notice.

MATT McCARTHY,
Manager.

Fraizer's

THEATRICAL EXPRESS,

12 UNION SQUARE,

New York.

Breslauer & Lawler,

CITY BILL POSTERS,

ST. PAUL, MINN.

Commercial Work a Specialty.

Address for both cities:

Box 961, Minneapolis, Minn.

Meldon, Percy, juveniles and heavies; dram.
agts., Brooks & Dickson; per. ad., 1214
Third ave., New York.

Mellon, J. A., character; dram. agts., Brooks
& Dickson; per. ad., 425 Penn ave., Pittsburg.

Melton, John V., leads and heavies, Stetson's
Monte Cristo Co.; dram. agts., Simmonds
& Brown; per. ad., 108½ E. 11th st., New
York.

Merron, Eleanor, juveniles, Shook & Collier's
Lights o' London Co.; dram. agts., Brooks
& Dickson ; per. ad., 40 E. 12th st., New
York.

Mertens, Miss Christine, soubrettes; dram.
agts., Brooks & Dickson; per. ad., 210 W.
24th st., New York.

Mestayer, Chas., leads and heavies, Louise
Sylvester Co.; dram. ag., J. J. Spies;
per. ad., 118 W. 30th st., New York.

Metkiff, Geo., juveniles; dram agts., Brooks
& Dickson; per. ad., 418 Warren st.,
Brooklyn.

Meyer, Miss Annie, juveniles, Wilbur Opera
Co.; per. ad., Baltimore.

Meyer, Fred., character, Brooks & Dickson's
Romany Rye Co. A.; dram. agts., Brooks
& Dickson ; per. ad., 44 W. 23d st., New
York.

Meyers, Miss Mary, old women, dram. agts.,
Brooks & Dickson; per. ad., 235 E. 79th
st., New York.

Meynall, Percy, treasurer and stage manager,
Hanlon Bros.; dram. agts., Simmonds &
Brown; per. ad., 1166 Broadway, New
York.

Michels, Mme. Ivan C., character and old
women; dram. agts., Brooks & Dickson;
per. ad., 330 E. 14th st., New York.

Millen, Miss Blanch, soubrettes; dram. agts.,
Brooks & Dickson; per. ad., 63 S. Washington Sqare, New York.

Miller, Mrs., juveniles and soubrettes ; dram.
agts., Brooks & Dickson; per ad., 52 E.
9th st., New York.

Miller, Leslie, juveniles, heavies and character; dram. agts., Brooks & Dickson;
per. ad., 358 W. 42d st., New York.

Miller, Henry, leads and juveniles; dram.
agts , Brooks & Dickson ; per. ad., 74 W.
38th st., New York.

Miller, J. Horace, juveniles, Bella Moore
Mountain Pink Co.; dram. agt., J. J.
Spies; per. ad. Philadelphia.

Mills, Miss Mary, ingenues and boys, Bartley
Campbell's Separation Co.; dram. agts.,
Brooks & Dickson.

Miller, Max, German comedian, O. D. Byron
Co.; per. ad., 161 E. 55th st., New York.

Mills, Harry, comedian; dram. agts., Brooks &
Dickson; per. ad., 302 Bloomfield st., Hoboken.

Mills, Miss Genevieve (Mrs. Harry Mann),
leading juveniles; per. ad., 341 W. 46th
st., New York.

Mills, J. K., old men and heavies, Dominick
Murray Co.; dram. agt., Boston Dramatic
Agency ; per. ad., New York Clipper.

Milward, Miss Jessie, leads, Madison Square
Theatre Called Back Co.; per. ad. Madison
Square Theatre, New York.

Mitchell, Mason, juvenile, leads; dram. agts.,
Brooks & Dickson; per. ad , 91 Fifth
ave., New York.

Mitchell, Lewis, character; dram. agts.,
Brooks & Dickson; per. ad., 256 Bleecker
st., New York.

Mitchell, Jas., character comedian, Shook &
Collier's Lights o' London Co.; dram. agts.,
Brooks & Dickson; per. ad., 138 W. 124th
st., New York.

Mitchell, H. W., leads, Kiralfy Bros. Excelsior
Co.; dram. agts., Brooks & Dickson; per.
ad., 129 W. Washington pl., New York.

Mitchell, W., character old men; dram. agts.,
Brooks & Dickson; per. ad., Occidental
Hotel, New York.

Mitchell, Miss Maggie, comedienne, starring;
H. L. Paddock, manager; per. ad., Long
Branch, N. J.

Moncrief and Rice (specialty), Irish and
Dutch comedians; per. ad., N. Y. Clipper.

Montague, Miss E., old women; dram. agts.,
Brooks & Dickson; per. ad., 229 High
st., Brooklyn.

Montaine, Clarence F., eccentric comedian,
Bartley Campbell's Siberia Co.; per. ad.,
222 W. 15th st., New York.

Montserrat, Geo. L., juveniles and leads, Little's World Co.; per. ad., Louisville, Ky.

Moodie, Miss Louise, dram. agts., Brooks &
Dickson ; per. ad., 201 W. 13th st., New
York.

Moore, Eugene, juveniles, T. W. Keene Co.;
per. ad., Allston, Mass.

Moore, Miss Bella, starring in A Mountain
Pink; per. ad., 311 Walnut st., Cincinnati.

Moore, Miss Elsie, juveniles; dram. agts.,
Brooks & Dickson; per. ad., 210 W. 38th
st., New York.

Moorhouse, Miss Lena, juveniles, Bertha Welby Co.; dram agts , Brooks & Dickson; per. ad., 266 W. 21st st., New York.

Morell, Miss Emily, soubrettes and char. old women; dram. agts., Brooks & Dickson; per. ad , 243 W. 14th st., New York.

Morley, Louis (specialty), ventriloquist and lecturer with stereoptical illustrations; per. ad., 229 E. 17th st., New York.

Mormon, Mrs Rilla, juveniles, J. G. Stuttz Dramatic Co.; per ad., Little Rock, Ark

Morrell, C. H., comedian; dram agts., Brooks & Dickson; per. ad., Morton House, New York.

Morris, Ed., comedian, Harrison & Gourlay Co.; per. ad , 74 Lexington st., East Boston.

Morris, Miss Isabel, leads, Bartley Campbell's White Slave Co.; per. ad., 305 W. 23d st , New York.

Morrison, Lewis, leading heavy, Wm. Harris' Dead Heart Co.; dram agts., Brooks & Dickson; per. ad., Ocean Grove, N. J.

Morrison, Mrs. Ella, leads; dram. agts., Brooks & Dickson; per ad., 261 W. 31st st., New York.

Mortimer, Miss Mabel, soubrettes and char., dialects; dram agts., Brooks & Dickson; per. ad., 28 E. 12th st., New York.

Mortimer, Mrs. Annie, old women and character, Roland Reed Co.; per. ad , Riverelde, R. I.

Morton, Tracy, **juveniles;** dram agts., Brooks & Dickson; per. **ad., 205 Henry st.,** Brooklyn.

Morton, Miss Jennie, soubrettes, **Bartley Campbell's White Slave Co.; per. ad , 22 E. 20th st., New York.**

Morton, George, leads, Hoop of Gold **Co.: d:am. agts., Simmonds & Brown; per ad., 175 Dean** st , Brooklyn.

Morton, Miss Ada, juveniles, soubrettes **and** boys, Hoop of Gold Co.; dram. agts., Simmonds & Brown; per. ad., 175 Dean st., Brooklyn.

Moses, Miss Lillie, Laura Dainty Mountain Pink Co ; dram. agts., Skiff & Morgan (Chicago); per. ad., 28 Pacific ave, Chicago.

Mountcastle, Miss Fannie, starring in Sea **of** Ice; dram. agts., Simmonds & Brown; per. ad., 111 Franklin ave., Cleveland, **O.**

Moyre, **R. J.,** Dutch comedy, Lights 'o London Co.; per. ad., Union Square Theatre, **New York.**

Muldner, Miss Louise, leads; dram. agts.,

Simmonds & Brown, per. ad , 306 **Henry** st., Brooklyn.

Murdoch, Miss Frances, leads, Patti Rosa Co.; Simmonds & Brown; dram. agts., per. ad., 2825 Cottage Grove ave., Chicago.

Murilla, Miss Edith, singing and dancing soubrette; Denman, Thompson Co.; per. ad., 488 Washington st., Boston.

Murielle, Miss **Constance, leads; dram. agts , Brooks & Dickson; per. ad., 3 Seventh ave, Asbury Park, N. J.**

Murphy, B. J. comedy and character; dram. **agts., Brooks & Dickson;** per. ad., 213 **E. 21st st., New York.**

Murphy, **B. J., old** men and character, Brooks & Dickson's **Romany Rye** Co. A; dram agts. Brooks **& Dickson; per. ad , 44** W. 23d st., New York

Murray, John, character comedian, starring in A Man Without a Country, Chas. E. Cook, manager; per. ad., Metropolitan Hotel, Boston.

Murray, Jas. C., comedian and vocalist; Kansas City, Mo.

Murray, J. Winston, heavies; Brooks & Dickson's Romany Rye Co. A; dram. agts., Brooks & Dickson; per. ad., 207 Livingston st., Brooklyn.

Murray David, M., juveniles ; dram. agts., Brooks & Dickson ; per. ad., 7 Spring Terrace, Meeker ave., Brooklyn.

Murray, T. J , juveniles; dram. agts., Brooks & Dickson; per. ad., 72 Lexington ave , New York.

— N —

Nagle, E. F., leading heavy, Hanlon Bros. Voyage en Suisse; dram. agts , Simmond's & Brown ; per. ad., 1166 Broadway, New York.

Nannery, P. A., old men and character ; dram. agts., Brown & Dickson ; per. ad , 34 E. 12th st., New York.

Nash, George F., juvenile and light comedy, Fred Ward, Co.; dram. agts., Simmonds & Brown: per. ad., 500 Market st., Philadelphia.

Nathal, Louis, baritone; dram. agts., Brooks & Dickson; per. ad , 126 W. 47th st., New York.

Neill, James, leads; dram. agts., Brooks & Dickson, per. ad., 168 Hall street, Savannah

Nelson, Miss Olive, character and soubrettes; dram. agts., Brooks & Dickson; per. ad., Orange. N. J.

Nelton, Harry, juveniles; dram. agt., J. Alex Brown; per. ad., 64 E. 14th street., New York.

Nepier, Wilson, walking gent, Stafford Foster Co.; per. ad., care John Williams, 165 Chambers st., New York.

Neuville, Mme. Rosina, old women and leading heavies; Brooks & Dickson's Romany Rye Co. B.; per. ad., 555 Atlantic ave., Brooklyn.

Neuville, Augustin E., responsibles; treasurer Lee Avenue Academy of Music, Brooklyn, E. D., per. ad., Lee Avenue Academy of Music, Brooklyn, E. D.

Neville, George Wm., old men and comedy; dram. agt., J. J. Spies; per. ad., 4 Rogers ave., Boston.

Neville, Miss Sara, leads; dram. agts., Brooks & Dickson; per. ad., Highlands, N. J.

Newborough, W. H., stage manager, Wilbur Opera Co.; per. ad., New York.

Newcomb, Theresa, leads; dram. agts., Brooks & Dickson; per. ad., P. O. Box 1229, New York.

Newhall, Miss Fanny, juveniles and soubrettes, Michael Strogoff Co.; dram. agts., Simmonds & Brown; per. ad., Creighton House, Boston.

Newman, Frank, juvenile; dram. agts., Brooks & Dickson; per. ad., Rockaway Beach, care of Mrs. Brocksmith.

Newton, Miss Alice, soubrettes; dram. agts., Brooks & Dickson; per. ad., 51 Middagh st., Brooklyn.

Nichols, C. A., tenor; dram. agts., Brooks & Dickson; per. ad., 431 r. 83d st., New York.

Nichols, C. T., leading heavies and character, Shook & Collier's Ruth's Devotion Co.; dram. agts, Simmonds & Brown; per. ad., Rockaway Beach, L. I., N. Y.

Nichols, Miss Maggie, soubrettes; dram. agts., Brooks & Dickson; per. ad., 225 Gough st., Baltimore.

Nicol, Joseph E., musical director, Mlle. Aimee's English Comedy Co.; dram. agts., Simmonds & Brown; per. ad., 24 Vananden st., Auburn, N. Y.

Nielser, Mme. Geraldine Irving, soprano, old women and eccentric character; dram. agt., J. Alex. Brown; per. ad., 234 E. 34th st., New York.

Noble, Warren, juveniles and heavies, Alvin Joslin Comedy Co.; per. ad., Chariton, Ia.

Norcross, Frank M., light comedian and juveniles; dram. agts., Brooks & Dickson; per. ad., 110 Fourth ave., New York.

Norcross, Frank M., juveniles; dram. agts., Brooks & Dickson; per. ad., 110 Fourth ave., New York.

Norman, S. P., tenor; dram. agts., Brooks & Dickson; per. ad., 105 E. 14th st., New York.

Norris, Chas., juveniles and light comedy; dram. agts., Brooks & Dickson; per. ad., 400 Fourth ave., New York.

— O. —

O'Brien, Wm. Smith, juveniles. J H Keane's Mrs. Partington Co.; per. ad., 125 N. Clark St., Chicago, Ill.

O'Byrne, Ignatius J., comedy, Bartley Campbell's White Slave Co.; per. ad., 243 E. 31st st., New York.

O'Hara, Pat, Irish comedian; per. ad., 147 Fuller st., Brooklyn.

Olcott, Miss Lillian, starring in the legitimate drama; R. L. Tayleur, manager; per. ad., Brooklyn.

Oliver, Dr.N. T. (Nevada Ned), specialty, rifle and pistol shot; per. ad., N. Y. Clipper.

Olive, Miss Bertha, juveniles and singing soubrettes; per. ad., N. Y. Clipper.

Olmi, George, principal baritone, Fay Templeton Opera Co.; per. ad., care Fay Templeton Opera Co., 182 Fulton st., New York.

O'Mara, Jas., heavies; dram agts., Brooks & Dickson; per. ad., 56 N. Market st., Chicago.

O'Neil, James, starring in Monte Cristo; John Stetson, man.; per. ad., Fifth Avenue Theatre, New York.

Osborne, Henry, eccentric comedian; per. ad., Box 115, Long Branch, N. J.

Osborne, Fanny, Irish comedian; per. ad., Box 115, Long Branch, N. J.

Osborne, Charles, character and heavies, Brooks & Dickson's Romany Rye Co. B; dram. agts., Brooks & Dickson; per. ad., 44 W. 23d st., New York.

Osmond, Walter, responsible, Fred. Warde Co.; per. ad., 20 Franklyn st., Pittsburg, Pa.

Ottelengui, Miss Helen, leading juveniles, Shook & Collier's Lights o' London Co.; dram agts., Simmonds & Brown; per. ad., 368 Livingston st., Brooklyn, N. Y.

Outram, Leonard S., juveniles and heavies; dram. agts., Brooks & Dickson; per. ad., 31 W. 26th st., New York.

Overpeck, A. J., stage machinist, Bartley Campbell's Siberia Co.; dram. agts., Simmonds & Brown; per. ad., Albany, Ill.

Owen, W. R., juveniles; dram. agts. Brooks & Dickson; per. ad., University Building, Washington Square, New York City.

Owen, Walter, character and heavies, Ivanroff Co.; dram. agts., Brooks & Dickson.

— P —

Padgett, J. C., light comedy and character; dram. agts., Brooks & Dickson; per. ad. 39 W. 16th st., New York.

Page, William H., juveniles or heavies; dram. agts., Brooks & Dickson; per. ad., 268 State st., Chicago.

Palmer, Miss Minnie, soubrette, starring in My Sweetheart; John R. Rogers, manager; per. ad., 54 W. 12th st., New York.

Palmer, Miss Nellie, juveniles; dram. agts., Brooks & Dickson; per. ad., 54 W. 12th st., New York.

Pantomimic Trio (specialty), Andy Morris, clown and comedian; Miss Ida Hussey, pantomimist and soubrette; "Young Tootsey," juvenile clown; per. ad., New York Clipper.

Parker, Harry D., comedian and character; dram. agts., Simmonds & Brown; per. ad., 94 E. 10th st., New York.

Parker, H. S., heavies and character; dram. agts., Brooks & Dickson; per. ad., 58 E. 9th st., New York.

Park, Will. A., juveniles; dram. agts., Brooks & Dickson; per. ad., 54 E. 9th st., New York.

Patterson, Charles, properties and responsible business, Roland Reed Co.; per. ad., 436 E. 14th st., New York.

Paul, Henry, Jr., leader of orchestra and band; per. ad., 1025 Oxford st., Philadelphia.

Paul, Logan, comedian; dram. agts., Brooks & Dickson; per. ad., 325 E. 14th st., New York.

Paul, Will A., juveniles; dram. agts., Brooks & Dickson; per. ad., 203 E. 69th st., New York.

Payton, Geo., leads; dram. agts., Brooks & Dickson; per. ad., 223 E. 12th st., New York.

Peissert, Edgar S., light comedy or juvenile, Bertha Welby Co.; dram. agts., Brooks & Dickson; per. ad., Bethlehem, Pa.

Pell, Miss Kate, character, old women; dram. agts., Brooks & Dickson; per. ad., 5 Elm pl., Brooklyn.

Pennoyer, Miss Alice, singing soubrettes; dram. agts., Brooks & Dickson; per. ad., 1741 Marshall st., Philadelphia.

Pennoyer, Miss Nellie, soubrettes; dram. agts., Brooks & Dickson; per. ad., 1741 Marshall st., Philadelphia.

Pepper, Mrs. M., old women; dram. agts., Brooks & Dickson; per. ad., 1741 Marshall st., Philadelphia.

Percy, Mrs. Townsend, juveniles, McCaull Opera Co., dram. agts., Brooks & Dickson; per. ad., 175 W. 45th st., New York.

Percy, Miss Marion, soubrettes, Gardiner's Only a Woman's Heart Co.; dram. agt., J. J. Spies; per. ad., Philadelphia.

Percy, R. V., old men, Brooks & Dickson's In the Ranks Co.; dram. agts., Brooks & Dickson; per. ad., 107 7th ave., New York.

Perkins, Walter, comedian; dram. agts., Brooks & Dickson; per. ad. 556 Oak st., Kansas City, Mo.

Perlman, Louis, old men and character, Gardiner's Only a Women's Heart Co.; dram. agt., J. J. Spies; per. ad., New York Mirror.

Perry, Miss Alfa, juveniles and ingenues, Bella Moore Mountain Pink Co.; dram. agts., Simmonds & Brown; per. ad., 390 Clinton ave., Albany, N. Y.

Perry, Thomas R., treasurer, Wallick's Bandit King Co.; per. ad., Bancroft House, 920 Broadway, New York.

Perry, Miss Alfa, singing soubrettes and juveniles; dram. agts., Brooks & Dickson; per. ad., 10 W. 18th st., New York.

Peters, Mrs. Chas., character and old women, Brooks & Dickson's In the Ranks Co.; dram. agts., Simmonds & Brown; per. ad., 209 E. 109th st., New York.

Peters, Fred, dialect, comedy and character; dram. agts., Brooks & Dickson; per. ad., 40 E. 10th st., New York.

Peters, Miss Maude E., juveniles; dram. agts. Simmonds & Brown; per. ad., 209 E. 109th st., New York.

Pfaff, H. C., clarinet and tenor and bass vocalist, Gorton's New Orleans Minstrels; per. ad., 25 Second ave., New York.

Phelps, Miss Minnie, light comedy and singing soubrettes; dram. agts., Brooks & Dickson; per. ad., 53 W. 12th st., New York.

Phillips, H. B., character and old men; dram. agts., Brooks & Dickson; per. ad., 266 Clinton ave., Brooklyn.

Pierce, Miss Abbie, juveniles, Harry Miner's Silver King Co. No. 2; per. ad., People's Theatre, New York.

Pierce, Miss Nellie, juveniles and soubrettes;

dram. agts, Brooks & Dickson; per. ad., 20 E. 28th st., New York.

Pierce, Miss Margaret, leads; dram. agts., Brooks & Dickson; per. ad., 58 McCullough st., Baltimore.

Pierce, Frank, juveniles and characters; dram. agts., Brooks & Dickson; per. ad., 35 Fourth ave., New York.

Pierson, Harry, juveniles, Harry Miner's Silver King Co. No. 1; dram. agts., Simmonds & Brown; per. ad., 209 Second ave., New York.

Pierson, Harry H., juvenile and heavies, Brooks & Dickson's In the Ranks Co.; dram. agents., Brooks & Dickson; per. ad., 59 W. 24th st., New York.

Pigott, J. W., comedy and character, Wallack's Theatre Co.; dram. agts., Simmonds & Brown; per. ad., Wallack's Theatre, New York.

Pike, Miss Dollie, character and old women, Madison Square Theatre Rajah Co.; dram. agts., Simmonds & Brown; per. ad., 311 W. 34th st., New York.

Pike, Maurice, comedian; dram. agts., Brooks & Dickson; per. ad., 98 Canal st., New York.

Pincus, S. Harry, comedy and character, Dion Boucicault Co.; per. ad., Colonial Exchange, 23 Union Square, New York.

Pitt, H. M., leads, Madison Square Theatre Rajah Co.; per. ad., Madison Square Theatre, New York.

Pixley, Lucy B., soubrettes and boys; dram. agts., Brooks & Dickson; per. ad., 353 Third ave., New York.

Plunkett, Miss Addie, soubrettes; dram. agts., Brooks & Dickson; per. ad., 214 W. 45th st., New York.

Plunkett, Charles, comedian, dram. agts., Brooks & Dickson; per. ad., 214 W. 45th st., New York.

Poole, Mrs. Charles, old women; dram. agts., Brooks & Dickson; per. ad., 636 Green st., Brooklyn.

Porter, Miss Julia, old women; dram. agts.; Brooks and Dickson; per. ad., 48 W. 12th st., New York.

Post, Mrs. E. M., eccentric comedy; dram. agts., Brooks & Dickson; per. ad., 249 E. 21st st., New York.

Powell, Edward, juveniles; dram. agts., Brooks and Dickson; per. ad., 154 E. 16th st., New York.

Power, John, comedy and old men; dram. agts., Brooks & Dickson; per. ad., Detroit Opera House, Detroit, Mich.

Powers Brothers (specialty), skaters and jugglers, Girard and Vokes' London Bicycle and Skating Co.; dram agt., J. Alexander Brown; per. ad., 44 Public st., Providence, R. I.

Powers, J. M., comedian; dram. agts., Brooks & Dickson; per. ad., 470 W. 43d st., New York

Praeger, Miss Adelaide, prima donna; dram. agts., Brooks & Dickson; per. ad., 162 E. 21st st., New York.

Pratt, Henry H., comedy character and stage manager; dram. agts., Simmonds & Brown; per. ad., Dramatic News.

Prescott, Miss Marie, starring; per. ad., 1214 Fourth ave., New York.

Prescott, Harry A., eccentric character and comedian; dram agts., Simmonds & Brown; per. ad., care Simmonds & Brown, 1166 Broadway.

Preston, Miss Isabella, old women; dram. agts., Brooks & Dickson; per. ad., 57 W. 11th st., New York.

Prochaska, J. C., leader band and orchestra; J. G. Stutz Dramatic Co.; per. ad., Austin, Texas.

Proury, Edward W., orchestra leader; Agnes Wallace-Villa; per. ad., P. O. Box 289, Spencer, Mass.

— Q —

Quinn, Thomas J., responsible, Harry Miner's Silver King Co. No. 2; dram. agts., Simmonds & Brown; per. ad., 656 Second ave., New York.

Quinton, Miss K., juveniles, singing soubrettes and boys; dram. agts., Brooks & Dickson; per. ad., 410 N. 5th st., Philadelphia.

— R —

Radcliff, James B., eccentric commedian; Boarding School Co.; dram. agt., R. Fitzgerald; per. ad., New York Dramatic News.

Radcliff, Miss Carrie, L., soubrettes; dram. agts., Brooks & Dickson; per. ad., 46 W. 15th st., New York.

Rainforth, Harry, character and comedy; dram. agts., Brooks & Dickson; per. ad., 364 W. 32d st., New York.

Rand, H. E., comedian; dram. agts., Brooks & Dickson; per. ad., 131 W. 42nd st., New York.

Randolph, Miss Jessie, juveniles; Gardiner's Only a Woman's Heart Co.; dram., agts.,

Eighth Annual Tour.

B. McAULEY

In his New Creation of

Gilderoy Punk, THE JERSEYMAN,

AND

UNCLE DAN'L,

A Messenger from Jarvis Section.

B. D. STEVENS, Manager.

Permanent address: 329 WEST 23D STREET, NEW YORK CITY.

Miss Fanny Addison,

(Theatres Royal, Drury Lane, Haymarket, Olympic,
Gaiety, etc., etc., London, England,)

MADISON SQUARE THEATRE,
" RAJAH " CO.

HEAVY LEAD and CHARACTER BUSINESS

Disengaged Season **1885 and 1886.**

Address :   MADISON SQUARE THEATRE.

Simmonds & Brown; per. ad., Bridgeport, Conn.

Randall, Adelaide Mrs. T. C., prima donna soprano; dram. agts., Simmonds & Brown; per. ad., Mt. Vernon, N. Y.

Randel, J. N., heavies; dram. agts., Brooks & Dickson; per. ad., 951 Gates ave., Brooklyn

Rankin, Mr. and Mrs. McKee, starring; per. ad., Third Avenue Theatre, New York.

Rattenbury, Harry E., baritone and comedian; dram. agts., Brooks & Dickson; per. ad., 1819 N. 24th st., Philadelphia.

Ray, Charles, comedian and treasurer, Wellesley & Sterling's Danites Co.; per. ad., New York Clipper.

Ray, Philip, stage manager, Earle Comb.

Raymond, John T., comedian, starring; dram. agts., Brooks & Dickson; per. ad., 44 W. 23d st., New York.

Raymond, Miss Louise, juveniles and soubrettes; dram. agts., Brooks & Dickson; per. ad., 150 E. 124th st., New York.

Raymond, John F., character and ballet master, Arthur Rehan's 7—20—8 Co., per. ad., 1212 Market st., Philadelphia.

Rea, Frank, old men; dram. agt., Brooks & Dickson; per. ad., 205 W. 13th st., New York.

Reed, Roland, comedian, starring in Cheek and Humbug.

Rees, Miss Stella, leading juveniles, Barry & Fay Co.; dram. agts., Brooks & Dickson; per. ad., New York Mirror.

Rehan, Miss Ada, leads, Daly's Theatre Stock Co.; per. ad., Daly's Theatre, New York.

Renard, Miss Rochelle, juveniles; dram. agts., Brooks & Dickson; per. ad., 126 E. 12th st., New York.

Renner, Miss Malvina, vocalist; dram. agt., R. Fitzgerald; per. ad., 103 Clinton Place, New York.

Revillo, Signor Eugene (specialty), magician, parlor legerdemain and trained canaries; Tony Denier's Pantomime and Specialty Co.; dram. agt., R. Fitzgerald, 10 Union Square; per. ad., 155 W. 128th st., New York.

Reynolds, Walter, leads and characters; dram. agts., Simmonds & Brown; per. ad., Dramatic News, New York.

Reynolds, P. J., juveniles, Harry Miner's Silver King Co. No. 2; per. ad., 52 W. 19th st., New York.

Reynolds, Miss Carrie, leads; dram. agts., Brooks & Dickson; per. ad., New York Dramatic News.

Rial, Miss Louisa, leads; dram. agts., Simmonds & Brown; per ad., Hotel Royal, cor. 6th ave., and 4th st., New York.

Rich, Henry W., singing comedian and character, Baker & Farron Co.; dram. agt., J. J. Spies; per. ad., 112 Centre st., Toronto, Ont.

Rich, J. F., vocal comedian; per. ad., 71 Monroe st., New York.

Richards, George, singing comedian, George S. Knight Co.; per. ad., New York Dramatic News.

Richmond, W. L., comedy and character, F. G. White Co.; per. ad., Crawfordsville, Ind.

Richardson, W., comedian; dram. agts., Brooks & Dickson; per. ad., Stratford, Conn.

Richardson, Miss Hattie, prima donna; dram. agts., Brooks & Dickson; per. ad., 91 Walnut st., Chelsea, N. Y.

Richford, George H., old men; dram. agts., Brooks & Dickson; per. ad., 303 W. 125th st., New York.

Ridsdale, Frank, baritone; dram. agts., Brooks & Dickson; per. ad., 55 W. 19th st., New York.

Rieffarth, Miss Jennie, juveniles and soubrettes, Rice's Adonis Co.

Roberts, Theodore, leads; Nellie Boyd Co.; per. ad., 904 Washington st., San Francisco.

Roberts, Frank, leads; Bartley Campbell's White Slave Co.; per ad., Warwick House, 28th st. and 6th avenue, New York.

Robertson, Miss Ellie B., soubrettes; dram. agts., Brooks & Dickson; per ad., 138 W. 29th st., New York.

Robertson, Donald, juveniles; dram. agts., Brooks & Dickson; per ad., 34 W. 20th st., New York.

Roble, Louis, leading juveniles and stage manager; Harry Miner's Eighth Avenue Theatre, New York.

Robinson, Geo. D., heavies; dram. agts., Brooks & Dickson; per ad., 81 W. 12th st., New York.

Robinson, Geo. S., leads, Robinson's Adventurers; per. ad., Morton House, New York.

Robinson, Miss Florence, Robinson's Adventurers; per. ad., Morton House, New York.

Robson, Miss May, singing soubrettes; dram. agts., Brooks & Dickson; per ad., 439 W. 35th st., New York.

Roche, Ray, old men and heavy character; dram. agts., Brooks & Dickson; per ad., 117 E. 12th st., New York.

Roche, O. W., property and utility; Richardson's Dramatic Co.; per ad., Bellefontaine, O.

Rochelle, Miss Minnie (specialty), bicycle rider; Girard & Vokes' London Bicycle and Skating Co.; per ad., Detroit Opera House, Detroit, Mich.

Rochelle, Miss Inez, leads; dram. agts., Brooks & Dickson; per ad., 72 E. 11th st., New York.

Rockwell, Miss Clara, soubrettes; Jno. A. Stevens' Co.; dram. agts., Brooks & Dickson; per ad., 174 E. 91st., New York.

Rodgers, Miss Jessaline, juvenile and soubrette; dram. agts., Simmonds & Brown; per ad., Hawley's, 184 Vine st., Cincinnati, O.

Rogers, Miss Katherine, leads; dram. agts., Brooks & Dickson; per ad., 856 W. 34th st., New York.

Rook, Theo. T, comedian and eccentric character, Alvin Joslin Comedy Co.; per ad., New York Clipper.

Rosa, Miss Patti, soubrette, starring in Mizpah; dram. agt., J. J. Spies; per ad., Baden, North St. Louis.

Ross, F. McCullough, character and heavies; Harry Miner's Silver King Co., No. 1; dram agts., Brooks & Dickson; per ad., 91 Seventh ave , New York.

Rouse, William A., low comedian and character old men, Shook & Collier's Lights o' London Co.; per. ad., 260 W. 22d st., New York.

Rouse, Miss Fannie Denham, old women, char. and dialect comedienne; Shook & Collier's Lights o' London Co ; per ad., 260 W. 22d st., New York.

Royston, Willie, comedian; Harry Miner's Silver King Co.; dram. agts., Brooks & Dickson; per ad., 7 W. 14th st., New York.

Russell, W. J., character comedian, Tony Pastor Co.; Hotel Osborn, Boston.

Russell, John and James, comedians, Tony Pastor Co.; dram. agt., J. Alex. Brown; per. ad., 205 W. 10th st., New York.

Russell, Harold, leading juveniles and light comedy, Minnie Maddern Co.; dram. agt., J. Alex. Brown; per. ad., cor. 14th st. and Fourth ave., New York.

Russell, Miss Susie, juveniles and soubrettes; dram. agts., Brooks & Dickson; per. ad., 52 E. 9th st., New York.

Ryan, Sam. E., old men, character and comedy; dram. agts., Brooks & Dickson; per. ad., Moulton House, Chicago.

Ryan, J. F., heavies or old men. John A. Stevens Co.; dram. agts., Brooks & Dickson; per. ad., 12 Union Square, New York.

Ryan, J. A., responsible utility, Baker & Farron Co.; dram. agt., J. J. Spies; per. ad., 136 Linden ave., Baltimore.

Ryan, J. H., comedian; dram. agts., Brooks & Dickson; per. ad., 805 First ave., New York.

Ryan, W. H., comedian; dram agts., Brooks & Dickson; per. ad., 62 Duane st., New York.

Ryno, William H., property man, Flora Moore's Bunch of Keys Co.; per. ad., 22 Jones st., New York.

S

Sackett, Frederic, juvenile; dram. agts., Brooks & Dickson; per. ad., 22 E. 20th st., New York.

Sackett, Miss Millie, juveniles; dram. agts., Brooks & Dickson; per. ad., 96 Canal st., New York.

Sage, Miss Annie, musical-glass specialist; per. ad., Walton, Huron co., Ontario, Cannada.

Sampson, Will C., eccentric and low comedy; dram. agt., J. J. Spies; per. ad., 12 Union Square, New York.

Sanders, F. W., juvenile and musical specialist; per. ad., 226 Ogden st., Newark, N. J.

Sanford, Walter S., leading heavies and character, Rich & Harris' Nobody's Claim Co.; per. ad., Ledger Job Office, Philadelphia.

Sargent, Harry S., comedy and character. Travesler Comedy Co.; per. ad., New York Clipper.

Sartelle, Miss Minnie, singing soubrette, J. H. Keane's Mrs. Partington Co.; per. ad., 306 W. Madison st., Chicago.

Saunders, John, comedian, Osborne's Oddities; dram. agt., J. Alex. Brown; per. ad., 187 Franklin st., Buffalo. N. Y.

Savage, Miss Jennie L., character and heavy; dram. agts., Brooks & Dickson; per. ad., Greenwood, Mass.

Sawtelle, J. Al., leads, Sawtelle Comedy Co.; per. ad., 65 Delevan st., Rochester, N. Y.

Sawyer, Miss Della, leads; dram agts., Brooks & Dickson; per. ad., 59 W. 24th st., New York.

Scanlan, Liz ie, soubrette, Western Light-
o' London Co.; dram. agts., Simmonds &
Brown; per. ad., Penn Yan, New York.

Scharf, Henry, old men and eccentric character; dram. agts., Brooks & Dickson;
per. ad., 110 Fourth ave., New York.

Scheparde, G. E. W., old men; dram. agt.,
Brooks & Dickson; per. ad., 125 40th st.,
Brooklyn.

Schneider, Gus (specialty), roller skater and
contortionist, Wyman's Wonders Co.;
per. ad., cor. 61st st. and 3d ave., New
York.

Schultz, Miss Emma, soubrettes, Harrison &
Gourlay Co.; dram. agts., Simmonds &
Brown; per. ad., 1196 Broadway, New
York.

Scott, Julius, leading heavies, Thos. W.
Keene; dram. agt.; J. J. Spies; per ad.,
94 Market st., Memphis, Tenn.

Scott, Miss Mattie, juveniles; dram. agts.,
Brooks & Dickson; per. ad., 25 Liberty
st., Newburyport, Mass.

Scott, M. Ainsley, old men, dram. agts.,
Brooks & Dickson; per. ad., 210 W. 24th
st., New York.

Scott, Rufus, juveniles and comedy; dram.
agts., Brooks & Dickson; per. ad., 234 W.
21st st., New York.

Scott, Cyril, comedy and characters; dram.
agts., Brooks & Dickson; per. ad., 232 E.
75th st., New York.

Scott, Miss Claire, leads; per. ad., New York
Clipper.

Seabrooke, Thomas Q., light comedy and
juveniles; dram agts., Brooks & Dickson;
per. ad., 514 Third ave., New York.

Seabrooke, Miss Elvia, soubrettes, Mr. and
Mrs. McKee Rankin's Co.; dram. agts.,
Brooks & Dickson; per. ad., 514 Third
ave., New York.

Searle, Miss Louise, prima donna; dram.
agts., Brooks & Dickson; per. ad., 403 W.
54th st., New York.

Searle, Cyril, leads; dram. agts., Brooks &
Dickson; per. ad., New Brighton, S. I.

Secor, George J., character and comedy;
dram. agts., Brooks & Dickson; per. ad.,
126 E. 12th st., New York.

Sedgewick, Miss Helen, starring in A Mountain Pink; dram. agts., Brooks & Dickson; per. ad., 50 E. 10th st., New York.

Selden, Edgar, eccentric comedian, Brooks &
Dickson's Romany Rye Co.; dram. agts.,
Brooks & Dickson; per. ad., 81 Johnson
st., Brooklyn.

Selden, Mrs. Edgar, character and old women,

Brooks & Dickson's Romany Rye Co.;
dram. agts., Brooks & Dickson; per. ad.,
81 Johnson st., Brooklyn.

Senzner, Frank H., tuba and double bass;
Gorton's New Orleans Minstrels, per. ad.,
Case City. Mich.

Seymour, Harry F., leading heavies, Simon
Comedy Co.; per. ad., 2124 South Broadway, St. Louis, Mo.

Shackford, Chas., character, Shook & Collier's Storm-Beaten Co.; per. ad., Union
Square Theatre, New York.

Shannon, Mrs. Effie M., juveniles, Harry
Miner's Silver King Co. No. 2, dram.
agts., Simmonds & Brown; per. ad.,
People's Theatre, New York.

Shannon, Minnie, child parts, Harry Miner's
Silver King Co.; dram. agts., Simmonds
& Brown; per. ad., People's Theatre. New
York.

Shannon, Miss Lavinia, juveniles, Brooks &
Dickson's La Charbonniere Co.; dram.
agts., Brooks & Dickson; per. ad., 102
4th st., S. E., Washington.

Shaw (specialty), female impersonator, Murphy & Mack's Comedy Four Co.; per.
ad., New York Dramatic News.

Sheehan, W. T., character and comedy; dram.
agts., Brooks & Dickson; per. ad., 110
Fourth ave., New York.

Sheldon, Miss Ella, character, Olympic Thea-
tre Stock Co., Chicago; dram. agt., J.
Alex. Brown; per. ad., 48 N. Moore st.,
New York.

Sheldon, Miss Julia, soubrettes, Barry & Fay
Co.; dram. agt., J. J. Spies; per. ad., 556
Leonard st., Greenpoint, Brooklyn, E. D.

Sheppard Sisters, Minnie and Julia (specialty),
sketch artists and balladists; per. ad.,
Theatre Comique, Providence, R. I.

Shepard, Miss Inez, soubrettes; dram. agts.,
Brooks & Dickson; per. ad., 10 Bank st.,
New York.

Sheridan, Charles, utility, Brooks & Dick-
son's La Charbonniere Co.; dram. agts.,
Brooks & Dickson; per. ad., 44 W. 23d st.,
New York.

Sheridan, Wm. H. (specialty), vocalist and
sketch artist; per. ad., New York Clipper.

Sherwood, Miss Florena, singing soubrette;
per. ad., New York Clipper.

Shewell, J. H., old men and comedy; dram.
agts., Brooks & Dickson; per. ad., 131 E.
16th st., New York.

Shields, Miss Tillie, old women and soubrettes; dram. agts., Brooks & Dickson;
per. ad., 325 E. 14th st., New York.

Fred. A. J. Dunwick,

BUSINESS MANAGER

and Treasurer,

Press and Advance Agent,

Glens Falls, Warren Co., N. Y.

Geo. H. Lennox,

EXPERIENCED BUSINESS AGENT,

At liberty.

Permanent address:

STAUNTON, VIRGINIA.

H. H. Haven,

AMUSEMENT MANAGER,

Joplin, Mo., and

LESSEE AND MANAGER,

Joplin (Mo.) and Columbus (Kas.)

Opera Houses.

White's Opera House,

Concord, N. H.

Population of Town, - 15,000
Seating capacity of Opera
House, - - - - - 1,000

No Better Show Town.

For dates, terms, etc., address
B. C. WHITE,
Manager.

Mrs. H. A. Richardson,

THEATRICAL COPYIST
and Type-Writer,

24 WEST 9TH ST., NEW YORK.

Thoroughly experienced in Dramatic work.
Orders by express promptly executed.

REFERENCES: New York Dramatic News.
New York Mirror.

Lake Shore House,

37 & 39 Bank St.,

Cleveland, Ohio.

Headquarters for Professionals.

Rates, $1.25 and $1.50 per day.

W. H. DEITRICK,
Proprietor.

Hotel Palace,

D. J. BLOCK, Proprietor,

N. E. Cor. 4th & Washington Sts.
Springfield, Ill.

Finest Sample Rooms in the city, on first floor.
Strictly first-class.   'Bus to all trains.

Headquarters for
Commercial Men and
First-class Theatrical Troupes.

Special Rates to the Profession.

Shine, Giles comedian, Brooks & Dickson's La Charbonniere Co.; dram. agts., Brooks & Dickson; per. ad., 102 4th st., S E., Washington, D. C.

Shine, Thad., comedian; dram. agts., Brooks & Dickson; per. ad., 42 St. Mark's Place, New York.

Siddons, Harry, comedian; **dram.** agts., Brooks & Dickson; per. ad., 286 W. **12th** st., New York.

Silvo (specialty), balancing, Tony **Pastor's** Co.; dram agt., J. Alex Brown; per. ad., 169 Bowery, New York

Simon, Hy., character and comedy; dram. agts., Brooks & Dickson; per. ad., **72** Purchase st., New Bedford, Mass.

Simmons, Henry, character; dram. **agts.,** Brooks & Dickson; per. ad., 485 **Canal st.,** New York.

Sims, Miss Lizzie, danseuse, Howard Athenæum Specialty Co.; dram. agt., J. Alex Brown; per. ad., 438 Washington Place, New York.

Sinclair, Harry, character and stage manager, J. S. Murphy's Kerry Gow Co.; dram. agts., Simmonds & Brown; per. ad., 10 Schaeffer st., Brooklyn, E. D.

Sinclair, E. V., character, Hanlon Brothers'; dram. agts., Simmonds & Brown; **per.** ad., 1166 Broadway, New York.

Singleton, Miss Agatha, **leads,** Earle Combination.

Singleton, Miss **Kate,** old **women;** dram. agts., Brooks **& Dickson;** per. ad., 311 E. 65th st., New York.

Sisson, Miss Josie, **leads** and singing soubrette; Six Peas in a Pod Co.; dram. agt., J. Alex. Brown; per. ad., Sisson's Lodge, P. O. Box 147. Madeira, O.

Skerritt, Miss Emma, heavy old women; dram. agts., Brooks & Dickson; per. **ad.,** 47 E. **9th st.,** New York.

Slade, S. I., utility, Brooks & Dickson's La Charbonniere Co.; dram. agts., Brooks & Dickson; per. ad., 44 W. 23d st., New York.

Sloane, William H., low comedy and singing parts; dram. agt., Simmonds & Brown; per.ad., 2352 Thompson st., Philadelphia.

Small, Charles T., basso and old men; S. B Hyer's Comedy Co.; per. ad., 494 State st., Chicago

Smedley, W. H., low comedy and character; Atkinson's Peck's Bad Boy Co.; per ad., Chester, Pa.

Smith, **Chris. J.,** leader of orchestra and baritone; Rentfrow's Jolly Pathfinders; per. ad., Grand Rapids, Mich.

Smith, Clarence H (specialty), bicycle rider; Girard and Vokes London Bicycle and Skating Co.; per ad Detroit Opera House, Detroit, Mich.

Smith, Harry A, heavies or character; dram. agts., Brooks & Dickson; per ad, Sheboygan. Wis.

Snader, Ed L., responsible; George C. Miln Co.; per. ad., Metropolitan Hotel, corner Fifth ave, and Randolph st., Chicago.

Snow, Matt .Wm and Thomas B. (specialty), musical artists, Graham Bros. Concert Co.; per. ad., New York Clipper.

Snyder, M. B., heavies, Brooks & Dickson's Romany Rye Co. A; dram agts., Brooks & Dickson; per ad, 11 W. 23d st. New York.

Sophmore, Charles P., leads and low comedy, Criterion Comedy Co.; per. ad., Toledo. O.

Sothern, Miss Ella, soubrettes, juveniles and boys, New York Co.; dram. agts., Brooks & Dickson; per. ad., 9 Durham Place, Brooklyn, N. Y.

Spencer, Miss Lillian, leads; dram agts, Brooks & Dickson; per. ad., 412 W. 23d st., New York.

Spencer, A. J., character, Crimes of London Co; dram agt., J. Alexander Brown; per. ad., New York Clipper.

Spencer, Earle, leading juvenile and light comedy; dram. agts., Skiff & Morgan, Chicago; per. ad., 830 Charleston ave., St. Louis.

Spence, George M., comedian and instrumental soloist, J. H. Keane's Mrs. Partington Co.; 966 W. Madison st, Chicago.

Sprague, George R. juveniles and heavies; dram. agts., Brooks & Dickson; per. ad., 207 E. 116th st., New York.

Sprague, Miss Fanny, heavies; dram. agts., Brooks & Dickson; per. ad, 207 E. 116th st., New York.

Sprague, Arthur, heavies; dram. agts., Brooks & Dickson; per. ad., 99 Durgm ave., Jersey City Heights.

Stack, Robert, property man, Brooks & Dickson's Romany Rye Co. B.; dram. agts., Brooks & Dickson; per. ad., 44 W. 23d st., New York.

Stafford, William, tragedy star, starring in the legitimate drama, Stafford-Foster Co.; per. ad., New York Mirror.

Stafford Maurice, juveniles; dram. agts.,

Brooks & Dickson; per. ad., 218 W. 25th st., New York.

Standish, Walter, juvenile leads, Shook & Collier's Lights o' London Co.; dram. agts., Simmonds & Brown; per. ad., New York Mirror.

Standish Harry, baritone and comedian; dram. agts., Brooks & Dickson; per. ad., 158 W. 29th st., New York.

Stanford, Billy (specialty), comedian, vocalist and dancer, White Elephant Theatre, Cleveland, O.

Stanhope, Miss Ada, juveniles and soubrettes; dram. agts., Brooks & Dickson; per. ad., 141 E. 15th st., New York.

Stanley, Miss Carrie, character comedienne, Alvin Joslin Comedy Co.; per. ad., New York Clipper.

Stanley, Miss Isabelle, heavy char. old women, J. K Emmet Co.; dram. agts., Brooks & Dickson; per. ad., 250 W. 22d st., New York.

Stanley, Miss Constance, starring; Manager, Edwin Clifford; per. ad , Columbus, O.

Stanley, Frank J., zoo. lecturer and **stage** manager; **per. ad** , New York Clipper.

Stanton, Miss Mabel, J. S. Murphy Kerry **Gow** Co., per. ad., Syracuse, N. Y.

Stanton, Walter (specialty), char. com., vocalist and mimic; per. ad , 285 W. Houston st., New York.

Stanwood, Harry (specialty), **banjo soloist and** comedian; per. ad., Coburg, **Can.**

Stedman, C. A., leads; dram. agts. Brooks & Dickson; per. ad., 158 E. 21d st., New York.

Steele, D. P., character and low comedy, Shook & Collier's Storm Beaten Co.; dram agts , Simmonds & Brown.

Steele, Miss May, juveniles and soubrettes, Shook & Collier's Storm Beaten **Co.;** dram. agt., Simmonds & Brown.

Stengel, Phil., comedian; dram. agts., Brooks & Dickson; per. ad., 512 Dillwyn st., Philadelphia.

Stephens, E. H., comedian; dram. agts., Brooks & Dickson; per. ad., 222 E. 57th st., New York.

Sterling, Earle, comedian, Mr. and Mrs. W. J. Florence Co.; dram. agts., Simmonds & Brown; per. ad., Lambs' Club, New York.

Sterling, Bostcoell, **tenor,** Theodore Thomas Concert Co.; **per. ad.,** 35 W. 14th st., New York.

Stern, Mrs. Ben., character old women, Brooks & Dickson's Romany Rye Co. B.;

dram. agts., Brooks & Dickson; per. ad , 44 W. 23d st , New York.

Stern, Miss Nellie, juveniles; **dram. agts., Brooks & Dickson; per. ad., 50 W. 12th st., New York.**

Stevens, Frank R., character old men and responsible, Walker Whiteside Co.; dram agt., J. J. Spies; per. ad., 18 Union Square, New York.

Stevens, Thad., comedian, Hyer's Colored Comedy Co.; per. ad., John B. Jeffery Printing House, Chicago.

St. Felix Sisters (specialty), song and dance; **dram. agt. J. Alex.** Brown; per. ad., 17 Clinton Place, New York.

St. Quintin, Miss Ruby, juveniles and singing soubrettes; dram. agts., Brooks & Dickson; per. ad., 5 E. 12th st , New York.

Stiles, John, negro comedian, Gorton's New Orleans Minstrels ; per. ad., New York Clipper.

Stoddart, Mrs. George, light comedian; per. ad., Parsonage, Highlands, Monmouth **Co., N. Y.**

Stoddart, George, old men and eccentric **com.,** Parsonage, Highlands, Monmouth **Co., N. Y.**

Stokes, **Miss Katie, juveniles and singing soubrettes; dram. agts , Brooks & Dickson; per. ad., 74 W. 49th st.,** New York.

Stokes, Miss Belle, singing soubrettes; dram. agts., Brooks & Dickson; per. ad., 74 **W.** 49th st., New York.

Stone, W. D., character and comedy; dram. agts., Simmonds & Brown. New York.

Stony, Miss Anna Warren, dram. agts., **Brooks & Dickson;** per. ad., 1921 H st., **Washington, D. C.**

Story, Miss, old women; dram. agts., Brooks & Dickson; **per. ad.,** 118 W. 20th **st.,** New York.

Stowe, Miss Emma, char. and com , old women; dram. agts., Brooks & Dickson; per. ad., Sheboygan, Wis.

Strong, Rudolph H., character; dram. agts., Brooks & Dickson; per. ad., 73 Henry st., Brooklyn.

Stuart, **Miss Julia, juveniles; dram. agts., Brooks & Dickson;** per. ad., 221 W. 23d st., **New York.**

Stuart, Miss May, character; dram. agts., Brooks & Dickson; per. ad., 39 W. 25th st., New York.

Stuttz, Miss Alma **E.,** leads; J. G. Stuttz Dramatic Co.; **per. ad.,** 107 E. Jefferson st., Louisville, **Ky.**

Sullivan, John T., leads; Mlle. Rhea Co.;
per. ad., 365 W. High st., Detroit, Mich.

Summer, Miss Frances, leads; Katie Putnam
Co.; dram. agts., Brooks & Dickson; per.
ad., 25 W. 16th st., New York.

Sutherland, Miss, singing and soubrettes;
dram. agts., Brooks & Dickson; per. ad.,
New York Clipper.

Sutherland, John, old men and character, Lil-
lian Olcott Co.; dram. agts., Simmonds &
Brown; per. ad., 20 Sutton Place, New
York.

Sutton, Charles W., juvenile leads; Harrison
and Gonrlay Co.; dram. agts., Simmonds
& Brown.

Swain, C. W., comedian, J. K. Emmett Co.;
dram. agts., Brooks & Dickson; per ad.,
60 Fourth ave., New York.

Swinburne, John, char., old men and heavies,
Mlle. Rhea Co.; dram. agts., Brooks &
Dickson; per ad., Dramatic News.

—— T ——

Tannehill, Ed., leads; dram. agts., Brooks &
Dickson; per ad., 50 W. 12th st., New
York.

Tavernier, Albert, eccentric comedy, Tavernier Dramatic Co.; dram. agt., J. J. Spies;
per ad., 12 Union Square, New York.

Taylor, J. H., heavies and old men; dram.
agts., Brooks & Dickson; per ad., 415
Pine st., Philadelphia.

Taylor, Jerry, responsible or stage manager;
T. W. Keene Co.; per ad., 702 Pine st.,
Philadelphia.

Taylor, Miss May, juvenile, Neil Burgess
Vim Co.; per ad., Parsonage Highlands,
Monmouth Co., N. J.

Taylor, Master Harry, child parts, T. W.
Keene Co.; per ad., 702 Pine st., Philadelphia.

Taylor, James, heavies, Stetson's Monte
Cristo Co.; dram. agts., Simmonds &
Brown; per ad., 42 Fulton St., New York.

Tearle, Osmond, leads, Wallack's Theatre
Stock Co.; dram. agts., Brooks & Dick-
son; per ad., 9 Queen st., Wakefield,
Eng., or Wallack's Theatre, New York

Temple, E. P., baritone; dram. agts., Brooks
& Dickson; per ad., 1348 Lexington ave.,
New York.

Templeton, Miss Fay, prima donna, Star
Opera Co.; John Templeton, manager;
per ad., Montmoor, N. Y.

Thacker, Allan J., heavies and juveniles, B.
McAuley Co.; dram. agt., J. J. Spies;

per ad., 102 Mulberry st., Fall River,
Mass.

Thomas, Edw. H., juveniles, Sterling Comedy
Co.; per ad., Sea Isle City, N. J.

Thompson, Miss Minnette, leads; dram. ag's.,
Brooks & Dickson; per. ad., 1207 Fifth
st., N. W., Washington, D. C.

Thompson, Miss Connie, soubrettes; dram.
agts., Brooks & Dick-on; per. ad., 59
Clinton Place, New York.

Thorne, Miss Blanche, leads; dram. agts.,
Brooks & Dickson; per ad., 103 W. 54th
st., New York.

Thornton, Miss Dolly, old women; dram.
agts., Brooks & Dickson; per. ad., 347 W.
28th st., New York

Thornton, Miss Isabella, juveniles; Wallack's
Theatre Co.; dram. agts., Brooks & Dickson; per. ad., 229 E. 31st st., New York.

Thornton, Charles, leading or character;
Headless Horseman Co.; dram. agt., J.
J. Spies; per. ad., 12 Union Square, New
York.

Thorpp, Mrs. Lou., char. old women; dram.
agts., Brooks & Dickson; per. ad., 251 E.
13th st., New York

Thorpp, Miss Florence, soubrettes; dram.
agts., Brooks & Dickson; per. ad., 251 E.
13th st., New York.

Tiffany, Miss Annie Ward, leads; Shadows
of a Great City Co., dram. agts., Brooks
& Dickson; per. ad., 20 E. 28th st., New
York.

Tighe, James F., stage manager and old men;
Harrison & Gonrlay; dram. agts., Sim-
monds & Brown; per. ad., 31 Eldridge st.,
New York.

Tilge, Howard, character old men; Standard
Theatre Dramatic Co., per. ad., 1216
Styles st., Phila.

Till, John and Louisa (specialty), Royal
Marionettes; Tony Pastor's Own Co.,
dram. agent., R. Fitzgerald; per. ad.,
Canton, Pa., P. O. Box 126.

Till, Howard, old men; dram. agts., Brooks &
Dickson; per. ad., 50 E. Ninth st., New
York.

Tingay, Charles F., leads; Master Whiteside
Co., dram. agt., Brooks & Dickson; per.
ad., Dramatic News, New York.

Tittel, Miss Charlotte, leads, Madison Square
Theatre Rajah Co.; dram. agts., Brooks
& Dickson; per. ad., Madison Square
Theatre, New York.

Titus, Chas. S., character old men, Strategists Co.; dram. agts., Simmonds &

Brown; per. ad., 142 E. 49th st., New York.

Tracy, Miss Genevieve, old women; dram. agts., Brooks & Dickson; per. ad., 52 E. 30th st., New York.

Tracy, Miss Helen, leads, Shadows of a Great City Co.; dram agts., Brooks & Dickson; per. ad., 71 W. 48th st., New York.

Tracy, Morton, heavies; dram. agts, Brooks & Dickson; per. ad., 205 Henry st., Brooklyn.

Travers, J. Edwin, juveniles, W. J. Comley Dramatic Co.; dram. agts., Simmonds & Brown; per. ad., 133 E. 15th st., New York.

Trimble, Miss Ada, juveniles; dram. agts., Brooks & Dickson; per. ad., 252 W. 24th st., New York.

Tucker, Miss Emma, juveniles, Draper's Uncle Tom's Cabin Co.; per. ad., New York Clipper.

Tucker, Will, comedy, Draper's Uncle Tom's Cabin Co.; per. ad., New York Clipper.

Tucker, Little Nanie, child parts, Draper's Uncle Tom's Cabin Co ; per. ad., New York Clipper.

Tufts, M. R., utility; per. ad., St. Joseph, Mo.

Turk Bros. (specialty), marionettes, Wyman's Wonders Co.; per. ad., 403 W. 48th st., New York.

Turner, John M. (specialist), banjoist; dram. agt , Dick Fitzgerald; per. ad., 1162 Broadway, New York.

Tyffe, Chas. J., old men; dram. agts., Brooks & Dickson; per ad., 203 W. 22d st., New York.

Tyler, Miss Georgia, leads, Hoop of Gold Co.; dram. agts., Simmonds & Brown; per. ad., Westfield, Mass.

Tyler, Miss Odette, leads, Kiralfy Bros.' Sieba Co.; dram. agts., Brooks & Dickson; per. ad., 337 W. 23d st., New York.

— U —

Ulmer, Miss Lizzie May, starring in Dad's Girl; G. T. Ulmer, man.; per. ad., North Scituate, Mass.

Ungerer, John L., heavies and stage manager, Wallick's Bandit King Co.; dram. agt., J. J. Spies; per. ad., New York Clipper.

Union, Frank L., heavies; dram. agts., Brooks & Dickson; per. ad., 15 Cottage st., Chelsea, Mass.

— V —

Van Cortland, Miss Ida, leads, Tavernier Dramatic Co ; dram. agt., J. J. Spies; per. ad , 8 Union Square, New York.

Van Deren, David W., character or comedy, Lyceum Theatre Stock Co., Lyceum Theatre, or 9 Washington Place, New York.

Van Dyke, Miss Justyn, juveniles or leads, Janauschek Co.; dram. agts , Simmonds & Brown; per ad., 94 E. 10th st., New York.

Van Tassell, Miss Cora, juveniles and singing soubrettes; dram. agts., Brooks & Dickson; per. ad., 308 E. 14th st , New York.

Vane, Miss Alice, comic opera, Fay Templeton Opera Co.; per. ad , care New York Clipper.

Vane, Miss Lilla, leads; dram agts , Brooks & Dickson; per. ad , 363 W. 29th st , New York.

Varney, Edwin, juveniles and character; dram. agts., Brooks & Dickson; per. ad., 159 College st., Buffalo.

Varny, Miss Alma, juveniles and serio comic, Agnes Wallace-Villa Co.; dram. agts., Simmonds & Brown; per. ad., 19 E. 124th st., New York.

Varny, Colin, leading juveniles and comedy, Agnes Wallace-Villa Co.; dram. agts., Simmonds & Brown; per. ad., 19 E. 124th st., New York.

Vaughn, Blanche, soubrettes, Roland Reed Co.; per. ad., Providence, R I.

Vaughan, Miss Effie, soubrettes and light juveniles, Mlle. Rhea Co.; dram. agts., Simmonds & Brown; per. ad., New York Dramatic News.

Verney, Samuel H., char. old men and eccentric. Harry Miner s Silver King Co. No. 2; per. ad., 725 Washington st., Boston.

Vernon, Miss Ida, old women; dram. agts., Brooks & Dickson; per. ad., 409 W. 13th st., New York.

Victor, Lester, character comedy, Mlle. Aimee English Comedy Co.; dram. agts., Simmonds & Brown; per. ad., 271 Madison st , New York.

Vincent, James, stage manager, com. and char., Harry Miner's Silver King Co. No. 2; dram. agt., J. Alex Brown; per. ad , 316 W. 40th st., New York.

Vincent, Charles T., character comedian, Mlle. Aimee English Comedy Co.; dram. agts., Simmonds & Brown; per ad , 222 E. 14th st., New York.

Von Leer, Miss Sarah, leads, Manbury &

Overton's Wages of Sin Co.; dram. agts., Brooks & Dickson; per. ad., 336 W. 59th st., New York.

— W —

Wade, Miss Gracie, soubrettes, Harry Miner's Silver King Co. No. 1; dram. agts., Brooks & Dickson; per. ad., 157 W. 20th st., New York.

Wade, Mrs. Mary, old women, Harry Miner's Silver King Co. No. 1; dram. agts., Brooks & Dickson per. ad., 528 W. 21st st., New York.

Wainratta, Walter J., wire-walker; per. ad., Koster & Bial's Concert Hall, New York.

Waite, Charles B., leading heavies and char., Bartley Campbell's Siberia Co.; dram. agts., Simmonds & Brown; per. ad., Elm Cottage, Dunnville, Ont.

Wallace, Miss Laura, leads, Mlle. Aimee English Comedy Co.; dram. agts., Simmonds & Brown; per. ad., 83 W. Ninth st., New York.

Walker, W. J., heavies, dram. agts., Brooks & Dickson; per. ad., 559 W. 23d st., New York.

Wallace, J. J., comedian, Stranglers of Paris Co.; dram. agts., Brooks & Dickson; per. ad., Chesterfield, N. H.

Wallace, Bart W., comedian; dram. agts., Brooks & Dickson; per. ad., 55 W. 12th st., New York.

Wallace, Miss F. L., singing and soubrettes; dram. agts., Brooks & Dickson; per. ad., 302 E. 105th st., New York.

Wallace, Gus T., banjoist and comedian; per. ad., New York Clipper.

Wallis, Jas., juveniles; dram. agts., Brooks & Dickson; per ad., Hotel Lafayette, Philadelphia.

Walters, Willis W., juvenile; Harry Miner's Silver King Co. No. 1; per. ad., 9 Mangin st., New York.

Walters, Sidney (specialty), comic vocalist; dram. agt., R. Fitzgerald; per. ad., 103 Clinton Place, New York.

Walton, E. L., comedian, Shook & Collier's Storm Beaten Co.; dram. agts., Brooks & Dickson; per ad., 113 E. 24th st., New York.

Warde, Fred., tragedy star, starring in the legitimate drama; Harry F. Weed, manager; per. ad., Brooklyn Theatre, Brooklyn.

Wardell, Miss Telka, leads, Bartley Campbell's White Slave Co.; dram. agts.,

Brooks & Dickson; per. ad., 50 W. 29th st., New York.

Ware, Clarence, juvenile, Crimes of London Co.; per ad., Jersey City, N. J.

Ware, Miss Annie D., old women; dram. agts., Brooks & Dickson; per. ad., 196 W. 33d st., New York.

Warren, Edward, juveniles; dram. agts., Brooks & Dickson; per. ad., 30 E. 22d st., New York.

Warren, Geo C., juveniles; dram. agts., Brooks & Dickson; per. ad., 412 W. 58th st., New York.

Warren, Albert, leads; dram. agts., Brooks & Dickson; per. ad., 39 Sturtevant Place, Brooklyn.

Warren, Charles R., character; dram. agts., Brooks & Dickson; per. ad., 315 E. 14th st., New York.

Warren, Miss Nellie, soubrettes; J. S. Murphy Kerry Gow Co.; dram. agt., J. J. Spies; per. ad., 12 Union Square, New York.

Warren, Miss Marion, soubrettes; Gus Williams' Co.; dram. agts., Simmonds & Brown; per. ad., Greenville, Pa.

Washburne, G A., juveniles and genteel heavies; Tavernier Dramatic Co.; dram. agt., J. J. Spies; per. ad., 14 Union Square, New York.

Walters, Miss Adele, juveniles, leads; dram. agts., Brooks & Dickson; per. ad., 45 W. 26th st., New York.

Waterman, Edgar, heavies, William Stafford Co.; dram. agts., Brooks & Dickson; per. ad., 221 E. 70th st., New York.

Watt, Robt., song, sketch and dramatic author; per. ad., 610 Arch st., Philadelphia.

Watts, Miss Amelia, juveniles and soubrettes; dram. agts., Brooks & Dickson; per. ad., 36 E. 12th st., New York.

Weaver, Miss Affie, leads; dram. agts., Brooks & Dickson; per. ad., box 19, Highlands, N. J.

Weber, Miss Lisa, soubrettes and sing.; dram. agts., Brooks & Dickson; per. ad., Commercial Hotel, Chicago.

Weber, Miss Eliza, com. old women; dram. agts., Brooks & Dickson; per. ad., 39 E. 22d st., New York.

Weidman, Miss Charline, soubrette and character, Mlle. Aimee English Comedy Co.; dram. agts., Simmonds & Brown; per. ad., 390 Clinton ave., Albany, N. Y.

Welby, Miss Bertha, starring; H. A. D'Arcy, manager; per ad., 12 Union Square, New York.

Welby, Jake (specialty), comedian and dancer, New Orleans Minstrels; per. ad., 6 Tioga st., Syracuse, N. Y.

Weldon, Chas. Jas., heavies, Bartley Campbell's White Slave Co.; per. ad., 57 Walnut st., Hartford, Conn.

Wells, Wm. (specialty), ventriloquist; per. ad., 2525 Hanover st., Chicago.

Wellesly, Miss Maria, leads, Wellesley & Sterling's Danites Co ; per. ad., New York Clipper.

Wentworth, Miss Lou (specialty), vocalist; per. ad., 109 Bowery, New York.

Wentworth, Miss Maud, juveniles and soubrettes; dram. agts., Brooks & Dickson; per. ad., 1254 Lexington ave , New York.

West, Miss Jessie, soubrette, B. McAuley Co.; dram. agts., Brooks & Dickson; per. ad., 724 E. 11th st., New York.

West, Ed. W., stage or bus. manager; per. ad., Yellow Springs, O

West, Olive. leads; dram. agts., Brooks & Dickson; per. ad., 48 E. 10th st., New York.

West, Wm. L., old men; dram. agts., Brooks & Dickson; per. ad., 147 E. 16th st , New York.

Weston, Miss Florence L., soubrettes and boys; dram. agts., Brooks & Dickson; per. ad., 15 E 10th st., New York.

Wheatcroft, Nelson, leads, Bartley Campbell's Separation Co.; dram. agts, Brooks & Dickson; per. ad., Chicago.

Whedon, W. H., juveniles, Pavements of Paris; dram. agts., Brooks & Dickson; per ad., 1026 Third ave , New York

Wheeler, F. G. sciopticon entertainments; per. ad., Orange, N. J.

Wheeler, Miss Rose, juveniles, emotional; dram. agts., Brooks & Dickson; per. ad., 122 E. 16th st., New York.

Wheeler. Miss Julia, juveniles and light comedy; dram. agts., Brooks & Dickson; per. ad , 122 E. 16th st., New York.

Whiston, Jno. W., humorist; per. ad., Niagara Falls, Ontario, Can.

White, Miss Lillian, soubrettes, Atkinson Comedy Co.; per. ad , 63 Congress st., Newark, N. J.

White, Frank H., comedian, Atkinson's Comedy Co.; per. ad , 63 Congress st., Newark, N. J.

White, Miss Maude, juveniles and soubrettes, Patti Rosa Mizpah Co.; dram. agt., J. J. Spiles; per. ad., 36 W. 35th st., New York.

White, Douglas, juvenile; dram. agts., Brooks & Dickson; per. ad., 261 W. 43d st . New York.

White, F. G., comedian; dram agts., Brooks & Dickson; per. ad. Grand Opera House, Indianapolis, Ind.

White, Chas., negro comedian, Bartley Campbell's White Slave Co ; per. ad., 230 W. 35th st , New York.

White William Athwold, heavies and char. com., Louise Sylvester Co.; per. ad , New York Mirror.

White, R. C., character and old men, Brooks & Dickson's In the Ranks Co.; dram agts., Brooks & Dickson; per. ad , 41 W. 23d st., New York.

Whitecar, W. A., leads; dram. agts., Brooks & Dickson.

Whittaker, Robert (specialty), clown and trapeze; per. ad., Middle Bush, N. J.

Wideman, Ned, comedian ; dram. agts. Brooks & Dickson; per. ad , Wilkesbarre. Pa.

Wilbur, Tony (specialty), humorist and impersonator; per. ad., New York Clipper.

Wildman, Miss Clara, singing soubrette; per. ad., 313 W. Jackson st , Chicago.

Wildman, Fred. G., comedian and character old men; per. ad., 313 W. Jackson st., Chicago.

Wildwave, Willie (specialty), topical vocalist; per. ad., New York Clipper.

Wilkie, Alfred, principal tenor; dram. agt., Geo. W. Colby, 23 E. 11th st., New York; per. ad., 74 Waltham st., Boston.

Willets, Miss Mittens, leads, Fred. Warde Co.; dram. agts., Brooks & Dickson; per. ad., 44 W. 23d st., New York.

Willett and Thorne (specialty), Maggie and Harry, comedy, protean and pantomime artists ; per. ad., New York Clipper.

Williams, Fred., heavies, Brooks & Dickson's In the Ranks Co.; dram. agts., Brooks & Dickson ; per. ad., 44 W. 23d st., New York.

Williams, Tony, character comedian, Atkinson's Peck's Bad Boy Co.; per. ad., New York Clipper.

Williams, Miss Mattie, leads, Little Duchess Co ; per. ad., Great Western Printing Co., St. Louis.

Williams, Miss Jennie, juveniles and soubrettes, Daly's Vacation Co.; per. ad., 44 E. 14th st., New York.

Williams, Charles, comedian, Wyman's Wonders Co ; per. ad., New York Clipper.

Williams, J. J., character and comedy; dram.
agts., Brooks & Dickson; per. ad., 195
D., So. Boston.

Williams, O., character; dram. agts., Brooks
& Dickson; per. ad., 21 E. 15th st., New
York.

Willis, Miss Stella juveniles and soubrettes;
dram. agt., J. J. Spies; per. ad., 520
Superior st., Cleveland.

Wills, Frank M., comedian; dram. agts.,
Brooks & Dickson; per. ad., 42 W. 154h
st., New York.

Wilmot, Miss Emie, leads, Kiralfy Brothers
Sieba Co.; dram. agts., Brooks & Dick-
son; per. ad., 200 W. 128th st., New
York.

Wilson and Parker, Tony and Frank, (specialty), eccentric novelty and specialty artists;
per. ad., 409 Broad st., Providence, R. I.

Wilson, J. E., leads, Lizzie May Ulmer Co.;
dram. agts., Simmonds & Brown; per.
ad., Clinton, N. Y.

Wilson, Robert G., old men, Mlle. Rhea Co.;
dram. agts., Simmonds & Brown; per.
ad., Mansion House, Philadelphia.

Wilson, Clint E., comedian; per. ad., New
York Clipper.

Wilson, D. H., juveniles and light comedy;
dram. agts., Simmonds & Brown; per.
ad., 185 Dodge st., Cleveland, O.

Wilson, Miss Rose, juveniles; dram. agts.,
Brooks & Dickson; per. ad., 17 W. 26th
st., New York.

Wilson, Miss Gracie, soubrettes and boys,
Shook and Collier's Lights o' London Co.;
dram. agts., Brooks & Dickson; per. ad.,
326 W. 39th st., New York.

Wilson, Mrs. Kate Denin, leading heavy and
old women; dram. agts., Brooks & Dickson; per. ad., 204 W. 24th st., New York.

Windsor, Helen, juveniles; dram. agts.,
Brooks & Dickson; per. ad., P. O. box
263, W. Haven, Conn.

Winter, J. P., leads and heavies; dram. agts.,
Brooks & Dickson; per. ad., 170 ——
Brooklyn, E. D.

Witkiff, Geo., character; dram. agts., Brooks
& Dickson; per. ad., 418 Warren st.,
Brooklyn.

Wood, Miss Annie, comedy old women, Har-
rison and Gonrlay; dram. agts., Simmonds
& Brown; per. ad., 20 E. 28th st., New-
York.

Wood, George A., character and heavies;
dram. agts., Brooks & Dickson; per. ad.,
911 Morris st., Philadelphia.

Wood, John W., comedy and character; dram.
agts., Brooks & Dickson; per. ad., 251 E
13th st., New York.

Woodthorpe, Miss Georgie, soubrette, starring in Little Butterfly; per. ad., New
York Clipper.

Woodward, George, comedy and character;
per. ad., 206 E. 15th st., New York.

Wren, Miss Martha, soubrette, starring in
Amy, The Prison Flower; James Collins,
manager; dram. agts., Brooks & Dickson; per. ad., 241 E. 14th st., New York.

Wyman (specialty), magician and ventriloquist; Wyman's Wonders Co.

—— Y ——

Yarnall, Val. J., caricaturist and vocalist;
per. ad., 264 Perry st., Philadelphia, Pa.

Yeamans Miss Lola, singing, soubrettes and
boys; dram agts., Brooks & Dickson;
per. ad., 65 Fourth ave., New York.

Yeamans, Miss Jennie, leading comedienne
Parlor Match Co.; dram. agts., Brooks &
Dickson, New York.

Young, Wm. H., eccentric comedian; dram.
agts., Brooks & Dickson; per. ad., 221
W. 25th st., New York.

Young, Edwin, comedy and old men; dram.
agts., Brooks & Dickson; per. ad., 398 E.
14th st., New York.

Young, Miss Loduski, leads; dram. agts.,
Brooks & Dickson; per. ad., 130 W. 33d
st., New York.

Young, Miss Mary, responsible; per. ad.,
Baldwin Theatre, San Francisco.

Young, Fritz (specialty), acrobat and contortionist; per. ad., Theatre Comique,
Providence, R. I.

—— Z ——

Zander, O. B., properties; per. ad., 1816 S. 2d
st., Philadelphia

MANAGERS, AGENTS, ETC.

— A —

Abraham, Edw. J., agent Kiralfy Bros. Excelsior Co.; per. ad., 284 Longworth st., Cincinnati, O.

Adams, Chas. F., agent Nellie Boyd Co.; per. ad., 609 South 15th st., Minneapolis, Minn.

Andress, Chas., proprietor and manager, Andress' Carnival of Novelties and Trained Animal Show; per. ad., Great Bend, Kan.

Andrews, Charles, manager Michael Strogoff Co.

Arthur, Robert, manager Edwin Thorne Black Flag Co.; per ad., Fourth ave, New York.

Ashton, J. L, agent Edwin F. Thorne's Black Flag Co.; per. ad., 631 12th st., Detroit, Mich.

— B —

Baker, F. W., business manager Agnes Wallace-Villa Co.; per. ad., New York Clipper.

Boaye, E. E., manager Standard Dramatic Co.; per. ad., Jno. B. Jeffrey Printing Co., Chicago.

Bateman, Sheldon, business manager, Brooks & Dickson's Romany Rye Co. A.; per ad., 44 W. 23d st., New York.

Benton, E. F., manager Helen Sedgwick Silver Spur Co.

Benton, Z. H., agent, Only a Woman's Heart Co.; per. ad., 85 John st., New York.

Beresford, Frank, business manager, Bandit King Co.; per. ad., New York Dramatic News.

Bernard, Harry, acting manager or advance agent, Elliot's American 4 Comedy Co.; per. ad., 1328 Moore st., Philadelphia.

Birch, Billy, manager and proprietor Birch's San Francisco Minstrels; per. ad., 186 W. 3d st., New York.

Bishop, Chas. J., man. C. B. Bishop; per. ad., 12 Union Square, New York.

Bixby, Frank L., manager Madison Square Hazel Kirke Co.; per. ad., Madison Square Theatre, New York.

Blumenthal, Geo. A., press agent Alvin Joslin Comedy Co.; per. ad., New York Clipper.

Bouvier, Alfred, business manager; per. ad., Madison Square Theatre, New York.

Braden, Findly, manager Holmes Grover in I O U; per. ad., 3000 North 5th st., Philadelphia.

Brennan, H. R., business manager, Bill's Theatre Co.; per. ad., 118 W. Houston st., New York.

Brooks & Dickson, proprietors and managers Romany Rye companies A and B, In the Ranks Co., La Charbonniere Co., Ristori Co.; per. ad., 44 W. 23d st., New York.

Burnett, A. B., advance agent Bella Moore Mountain Pink Co.; per. ad., Anderson, Ind.

Burns, Chas. B., manager Carrie Stanley Co., per. ad, Enquirer, Cincinnati, O.

Burnside, Will S., business manager; per. ad., New York Clipper.

Burton, James T, advance and business manager; per. ad., Norwich, N. Y.

— C —

Callahan, Charles E., manager and proprietor Lizzie Evans Co.

Cameron, A. D., business agent McNeil Family Musical Comedy Co.; per. ad., North Attleboro, Mass.

Cameron, W. T., manager Eilani Fun in a Boarding School Co.; per. ad., New York Clipper and Dramatic News.

Campbell & MacDonough, proprietors and managers Bartley Campbell's Siberia, Separation and White Slave companies; per. ad., 1193 Broadway, New York.

Canby, Albert H., agent John T. Raymond Co.; per ad., Journalists' Club, 104 Walnut st., Philadelphia.

Carleton, William, proprietor and manager Carleton's English Opera Co.

Chapman & Sellers, managers Her Atonement Co.

Chase, Arthur B., manager Mlle. Rhea Co.; per. ad., Holyoke, Mass.

Clapham, George T., manager Thatcher, Primrose & West's Minstrels.

Clapham, Harry J., manager Barlow & Wilson's Minstrels; per. ad., Flemingville, Tioga Co., New York.

Clark, Wm. S., advertising agt. People's Theatre; per. ad., People's Theatre, New York.

Clark, Harry M., manager and proprietor of

Whiteley's Original Hidden Hand Co.; per. ad., care John B. Jeffery Show Pt'g Co., Chicago, Ill.

Clayburg, Edward, propietor and manager Stranglers of Paris and Creole companies; per. ad., 12 Union Square, New York.

Collins, Chas H., business manager W. J. Scanlan Co.; per. ad., 174 Lacrosse st., Detroit, Mich.

Comstock, Alex., manager Morton & Bell's Our Strategists; per. ad., Haverly's Theatre, Philadelphia

Cone, Spencer, advance agent Williams & Tillotson's Lynwood Co.; per. ad., 10 E. 14th st., New York.

Coney, S. P., manager, Howard Athenaeum Comedy Co.; per. ad., Howard Athenaeum, Boston, Mass.

Connor, Wm., manager John McCullough Co.; per. ad., St. James's Hotel, New York.

Cook, Chas. E., manager John Murray's Man Without a Country Co.; per. ad., Bo ton Job Print, Boston.

Corbyn, Sheridan, manager Frank Mayo's Nordeck Co ; per. ad., Criterion, 2 Union Square, New York.

Craus, S. B., business manager; per. ad.; New York Clipper.

Crossen, James F., manager Crossen's Banker's Daughter Co.; per. ad., 216 E. 9th st., New York.

— D —

Daly, Augustin, manager and proprietor Daly's Theatre Co.; per. ad., Daly's Theatre, New York.

D'Arcy, H. A., manager Bertha Welby Co.; per. ad., 12 Union Square, New York.

Davis, J. R., European agent Barnum's Show and manager Chang Museum and Novelty Co.; per. ad., 2 Spruce st., New York.

Dawson, Sam M., business manager Robt. McWade Rip Van Winkle Co.

Deaver, Jno. N., agent Mr. & Mrs. W. J. Florence; per. ad., Pepper's Hotel, Baltimore, Md.

Dickson, John T., business manager Brooks & Dickson's Romany Rye Co. B; per. ad., 44 W. 23d st., New York.

Dickson, J. W., business manager or advance agent; per ad., New York Clipper.

Donaldson, J., jr., manager Two Johns Comedy Co.

Draper, S., manager S. Draper's Double Uncle Tom's Cabin Co.; per. ad., 295 Pennsylvania st , Buffalo, N. Y.

Dudley, Walter, manager Broadway Theatre Co ; per. ad. New York Clipper.

Duffy, Will J., business agent, Carrie Swain Co.; per. ad. 130 W. Houston st., New York.

Dunne, Jno. W., proprietor and manager Patti Rosa Mizpah Co.; per. ad. 12 Union Square, New York.

Dunwick, Fred A. J , business manager and treasurer, press and advance agent; per. ad. Glens Falls, N. Y.

Durban, C. L., advance agent Williams & Tillotson's Queena Co.; per. ad. 44 W. 22d st., New York.

— E —

Earle, Graham, manager Earle Dramatic Co.; per. ad., care Hasselman-Journal Co., Indianapolis, Ind.

Eddy, Jerome H., press agent; per. ad , 64 East 14th st. New York.

Edwards, Maze, general agent and business manager; per. ad., Fifth Avenue Theatre. New York.

Edwards, W. A., business manager Effie Ellsler Co.; per. ad. Baldwin Theatre, San Francisco, until December, thereafter 12 Union Square, New York.

Ennis, J. P., business manager Rice's Surprise Party, dram. agt. E. E. Rice's National Musical Agency; per. ad. 1249 Broadway, New York.

— F —

Fargo, C. E., manager Hyer's Colored Comedy Co.; per. ad. New York Clipper or John B. Jeffery Printing House, Chicago, Ill.

Field, R. M., manager Edwin Booth; per. ad , Boston Museum, Boston, Mass.

Fitch, Carl Irving, business manager or advance agent; per. ad., 231 E. 34th st., New York.

Fitchett, George H , manager Hyde & Behman's Minstrels; per. ad. 408 Gold st , Brooklyn, N. Y.

Floyd, G. W., manager N. C. Goodwin Co.

Ford, Clint G., proprietor and manager Ford's Metropolitan Dramatic Co ; per. ad , Dawson Springs, Hopkins Co. Ky.

Frank, Joseph, manager Gardiner's Only a Farmer's Daughter Co.; per. ad , 12 Union Square, New York.

Franklin, J. E , general agent Golden Troupe per ad , Hasselman-Journal Co., Indianapolis, Ind.

Fraser, Knowlan, manager Tavernier Dramatic Co.; per. ad., 161 Devonshire st., Boston.

Frese, H. C., business manager Charles A. Gardner's Karl the Peddler Co.; per. ad., 16 Calhoun Place, Chicago.

Frohman, Charles, manager Minnie Maddern Caprice Co., Pulse of New York Co., etc.; per. ad., 18 W. 23d st., New York.

Frohman, Daniel, manager Madison Square Theatre Traveling companies; per. ad., Madison Square Theatre, New York.

Frohman, Gustave, manager New Lyceum Theatre and Lyceum Theatre Traveling Companies; per. ad., Lyceum Theatre, New York.

— G —

Gardiner, C. R., manager and proprietor Only a Farmer's Daughter Co.; Only a Woman's Heart Co., Zozo the Magic Queen Co.; per. ad. 12 Union Square, New York.

Goodwin, Frank L., manager Clara Morris Co.

Goodnow & Johnson, proprietors and managers Maude Atkinson Co.; per ad., Chicago News-Letter.

Goodrich, E. F., manager The Leopold s Frivolity Co.; per ad., 10 Union Square, New York.

Gotthold, E. M., advance agent Brooks & Dickson's Romany Rye Co. B.; per ad., 41 W. 23d st., New York.

Gourlay, Robert, business manager Harrison and Gourlay; per ad., Gourlay Bros., Detroit, Mich., and New York Dramatic News.

Graham, Binford & Edwards, managers Lillian Brown's Jollities; per ad., St Louis, Mo.

Graves, C. L., business manager Brooks & Dickson's Romany Rye Co.; per ad., 112 Fourth ave., New York.

Greene, Henry, business agent Calender's Minstrels; per ad., Madison Square Theatre, New York.

Gregg, C. A., manager Bella Moore Co.; per ad., Wiggins Block, Cincinnati, O.

Griste, Chas. B., manager J. Newton Gotthold's Micaliz Co., per ad., 23 E. 14th st., New York.

Greandler, Herman F., business manager Fulton's Juvenile Creole Minstrels; per ad., Maywood, Cook County, Ill.

— H —

Hall, Frank, advance agent Gardiner s Zozo the Magic Queen Co.; per ad., 12 Union Square, New York

Hamilton, F. C., business manager Dickson's Sketch Club; per ad., Pope's Theatre, St. Louis.

Hanley, M. W., manager Hanley's Dan's Tribulations; per ad., Harrigan and Hart's Theatre, Broadway, New York.

Harrison, Sam'l, manager Harrison & Gourlay Co.; per ad., care of Gourlay Bros., Detroit, Mich.

Hayden, Wm. R., manager T. W. Keene. per. ad., National Printing Co., Chicago.

Henry, Hi, manager Hi Henry Minstrels, per ad., Gowanda, N. Y.

Herne, James A., manager Herne's Hearts of Oak; per. ad., Dorchester, Mass.

Hicks, John C., manager Skiff, Gaylord & Hicks' Minstrels; per. ad., P. O. Box 27, Towson, Md.

Hickey, John M., manager Smith, Waldron, Cronin & Martin's Grotesque Comedy Co.; per. ad., 12 Union Square, New York.

Hill, J. M., manager Margaret Mather Co.; per. ad., Clark and Madison sts., Chicago.

Hilton, Edward P., manager Olympic Theatre; P. O. Box 289, St. Paul, Minn.

Hine, Harry, advance agent Harry Miner's Silver King Co. No. 2; per. ad., People's Theatre, New York.

Howorth, John, manager Howorth's Hibernica; per. ad., Maplewood, Mass.

Hume, E. E., business manager and treasurer Harry Miner's Silver King Co. No. 2; per. ad., People's Theatre, New York.

Hyde, Richard, manager Hyde & Behman's Operatic, Spectacular Minstrels; per. ad., Hyde & Behman's Theatre, Brooklyn.

— I —

Irving, Frank, manager Patti Rosa Co.; per. ad., 12 Union Square, Square, New York.

Irving, Phil. H., manager Arne Walker Dramatic Co.; per. ad., New York Clipper.

— J —

Johnson, J. P., manager Oliver Dond Byron Co.; per. ad., 1937 Master st., Philadelphia.

June, George W., general agent Kiralfy Bros.' spectacular productions; per. ad., Washington Square, New York.

— K —

Kahn, Gustave, manager Kiralfy Bros.' Excelsior Co.; per. ad., 39 W. Washington Square, New York.

Kennedy, Harry, manager Bartley Campbell's White Slave Co.; per. ad., Morton House, New York.

Keyser, Samuel, manager Master Walker Whiteside Co.; per. ad., Palmer House, Chicago, Ill.

Kiralfy Bros., proprietors and managers Excelsior, Sieba and other spectacular productions; per. ad., Washington Square, New York.

Krause, Otto, manager Jennie Holman Combination; per. ad., Amboy, Ill.

Kusel, Wm. S., assistant manager Shelby's Academy of Music, Chicago, Ill.

— L —

Lane, Ed. H., advance agent and manager Mason & Morgan's Uncle Tom's Cabin Co.; dram. agts., Skiff & Morgan, Chicago; per. ad., 908 Rock st., Rockford, Ills.

Leese, John S., manager J. Newton Gotthold Micaliz Co.; per. ad., 23 E. 14th st., New York.

Lennox, Geo. H., advance agent; per. ad., Staunton, Va.

Lewis, W. D., advance agent and treasurer; per. ad., 1409 43d st., Chicago.

Levy, Joseph, manager Lawrence Barrett Co.

Lister, Will T., advance agent Fanny Mountcastle Sea of Ice Co.; per. ad., Newton, Ia.

Lombard, Thos. C., manager Chas. A. Gardner's Karl the Peddler Co.; per. ad., 16 Calhoun Place, Chicago, Ill.

— M —

Mack, J. H., general manager Harry Miner's Silver King companies; per. ad., People's Theatre, New York, or Wooster, O.

Madigan, E. H., advance agent Cook's Circus (summer); per. ad., 271 Hamilton st., Cleveland, O., or Beaumont, Tex.

Maeder, Frank, manager Salsbury's Troubadours; per. ad., 866 Broadway, New York.

Maeder, Fred G., manager Carrie Swain Co.; per. ad., 12 Union Square, New York.

Magie, John G., manager Hanlon's Le Voyage en Suisse; per. ad., 64 E. 14th st., New York.

Mann, Harry, manager W. J. Scanlan Co. and A Parlor Match Co.; per. ad., 1166 Broadway, New York.

Mann, T. H., business manager Wilbur Opera Co.; per. ad., P. O. Box 253, Randolph, Mass.

Maubury & Overton, proprietors and managers Hoop of Gold Co., Wages of Sin Co.

Mayer, Marcus R., general agent Henry Irving; per. ad., Grand Opera House, New York.

McCaull, John A., proprietor and manager McCaull Comic Opera Co.; per. ad., Casino, New York.

McDonald, Charles, manager Crimes of London; per. ad., New York Mirror.

McLellan, H. K., manager Original Nashville Students; per. ad., 151 Wabash ave., Chicago, Ill.

McNamara, J. M., business manager Madison Square combinations; per. ad., Madison Square Theatre, New York.

McNeil, W. B., manager and proprietor McNeil Family Musical Comedy Co.; per. ad., Meadville, Pa.

Melville, Leonard, press agent Gardiner' Only A Woman's Heart Co.; per. ad., 12 Union Square, New York.

Melville, Paul, press agent Gardiner's Only a Farmer's Daughter Co.; per. ad., 12 Union Square, New York.

Mendum, Charles A., manager Poole & Gilmore Seven Ravens Co.; per. ad., Niblo's Garden, New York.

Merrill, James A., business agent or treasurer, Stafford-Foster Co., per. ad., 1812 Jefferson st., Philadelphia.

Mestayer, William, manager We, Us & Co. Combination; per. ad., New York.

Miaco, Alfred F., manager his own New Humpty Dumpty; per. ad., Clipper office, New York.

Miner, Harry, proprietor and manager People's Theatre, Bowery Theatre and Eighth Avenue Theatre, New York; Harry Miner's Silver King companies, Nos. 1 and 2; Harry Miner's American Dramatic Directory; per. ad., People's Theatre, New York.

Morris, George O., manager The Power of Money and Little's World; per. ad., Great Western Printing Co., St. Louis.

Morrisey, James W., business manager Brooks & Dickson's La Charbonniere Co.; per. ad., 44 W. 23d st., New York.

Mortimer, Gustave, manager Roland Reed Co.; per. ad., Brooklyn Times, 26 Broadway, Brooklyn, N. Y., or Riverside, R. I.

5

Moulton and Baker, proprietors and managers Bennett and Moulton Opera Co.; per. ad., Salem, Mass.

Moulton, Gus, general agent Thatcher, Primrose and West's Minstrels.

Murray, J. Duke, business agent **Milton Nobles' Co.; per. ad., 711 Fulton st., Chicago.**

— O —

Ogden, Josh E., manager George S. Knight Comedy Co.; per. ad., dramatic papers, News and Mirror.

Oliver, Harry, business agent Athletic Base-Ball Club; per. ad., 204 N. 8th st., Philadelphia.

Osborne, Henry, manager Osborne's Oddities; per. ad., Clipper office, New York.

Owen, Garrett W., proprietor and manager Owen's Legitimate Dramatic Co.; per. ad., 145 W. 16th st., New York.

Owen, Jack, manager Gardiner's Only **A Woman's Heart Co.; per. ad., 12 Union Square, New York.**

— P —

Paddock, H. D., manager Maggie Mitchell **Co.; per. ad., Long Branch, N. J.**

Pastor, **Tony,** manager Tony Pastor's Own Co.; per. ad., Fourteenth Street Theatre, New York.

Patrick, J. C, manager Davene & Austin Allied Shows; per. ad., New York Clipper.

Paul, Frank W., manager M. B. Curtis; per. ad., New York Dramatic News.

Pearl, C. C., business manager Original New Orleans Minstrels; per. ad., New York Clipper.

Pelham, **Fred,** manager The McGibeny Family; per. ad., Everett House, New York;

Pennoyer, Gus. A., manager Lotta Co.

Phippe, Jas. H., manager lectures, concerts, etc.; per. ad., 25 Union Square, New York.

Pickett, **A. St. J., manager Great** Southern Co.; per. ad., Georgetown, **Ky.**

Pitou, Augustus, proprietor and manager Off to Egypt Co.; per. ad., 1165 Broadway, New York.

Poole & Gilmore, proprietors Seven Ravens Co.; per. ad., Niblo's Garden, New York.

Price, **Ed. H., manager Fanny Davenport;** per. ad., Canton, Pa.

Prouty, **Ed. W., manager Agnes Wallace-**

Villa Co.; per. ad., P. O. Box 289, Spencer, Mass.

Purdie, Francis B., acting manager Geo. C. Miln Co.; per. ad., 3 Windsor Block, Indianapolis, Ind.

— R —

Randall, Wm. W., bus. manager Madison Square Theatre Rajah Co.; per. ad., Madison Square Theatre, New York.

Randall, Harry, bus. manager McCollin Opera Co.

Randolphe, J. W., business manager Davene & Austin Allied Shows; per. ad., **New York Clipper.**

Reid, **T. F, manager Neil Burgess Vim Co.;** per. ad., P. O. Box 6, Highlands, Monmouth Co., N. J.

Rentfrow, J. H., **manager Rentfrow's Jolly** Pathfinders; per. ad., 257 E. Bridge st., Grand Rapids, Mich.

Rhoades, P. B., business agent J. S. Murphy Kerry Gow Co.; per. ad., 12 Remington Block, Syracuse, N. Y.

Rice, Peter, business manager Two Johns Comedy Co.

Rice, E. E., proprietor and manager Rice's Pop and Adonis companies; per. ad., 1240 Broadway, New York.

Rile, Harry F., advance agt.; per. ad., 3099 N. 5h st., Philadelphia, Pa.

Robb, John H., manager Gus Williams Co.

Roberts, N. D., manager John Stetson's Monte Cristo Co.; per. ad., 174 Pine st., Brooklyn, N. Y.

Roberts, C. W., advance agent Harry Miner's Silver King Co. No. 1; per. ad., People's Theatre, New York.

Roberts, **E. M., manager Madison Square** Theatre May Blossom; per. ad., Madison Square Theatre, New York.

Rockwood, H. A., manager Madison Square Rajah Co.; per. ad, Madison Square Theatre, New York.

Rogers, John R., manager Minnie Palmer's My Sweetheart Co.

Ross, Willis, business manager E. A Sothern Co.; per. ad., 111 East 26th st., New York.

Rust, F. C., business manager or agent, Baker & Farren Co.; per. ad., 146 So. Salina st., Syracuse.

— S —

Sanger, Frank, manager Sanger's Bunch of Keys Co.

Sargent, H. J., manager Jarisch Co.; per. ad., box 1505 Plainfield, N. J.

Sawtelle, J. Al., manager Sawtelle Comedy Co.; per. ad., 65 Delevan st., Rochester, N. Y.

Scammon, A. Q., agent Two Johns Co.; per. ad., 12 Union Square, New York.

Schroeder, Chas. N., business manager Fifth Avenue Theatre, New York.

Scott, Frank W., business manager the Hanlons; per. ad., 561 Washington st., Boston.

Schutz, Eugene, business manager Louise Sylvester Co.; per. ad., 201 E. 14th st., New York.

Senion, Harry W., manager Silbon & Elliott's Cupid Co.; per. ad., 1543 Third ave., New York.

Sheridan, Wm. H., manager Star Minstrel and Specialty Co.; per. ad., New York Clipper.

Shook & Collier, proprietors and managers Union Square Theatre Co. Lights o' London companies, Eastern and Western; Ruth's Devotion Co.; per. ad., Union Square Theatre, New York.

Shrader, P. W., agent Heywood's Mastodon Minstrels; per. ad., Rushville, Ind.

Simpson, E. F., business manager San Francisco Minstrels; per. ad., 136 West 3d st., New York.

Sisson, Oscar P., manager Six Peas in a Pod Co.; dram. agt., J. Alex. Brown; per. ad., Sisson's Lodge, P. O. Box 147, Madeira, O.

Smart, Harry C., manager Thompson's Opera Co. (Beggar Student); per. ad., 41 E. 10th st., New York.

Smith, John P., manager E. A. Sothern Crushed; or Whose are They? Co.; per. ad., 12 Union Square, New York.

Snelbaker, Col. T. E., manager Alice Oates Ideal Opera Bouffe Co.; per. ad., Washington, D. C.

Sprague, Dan J., business manager and treasurer Alvin Joslin Comedy Co.

Stetson, John, manager James O'Neill Monte Cristo Co.; per. ad., Fifth Avenue Theatre, New York.

Stern, Ben., manager Brooks and Dickson's In the Ranks Co.; per. ad., 44 W. 23d st., New York.

Sterling, Wm. E., manager Wellsley & Sterling Danites Co.; per. ad., New York Clipper.

Stevens, John A., proprietor and manager Unknown Co.; per. ad., New Park Theatre, New York.

Stevens, B. D., manager B. McAnley Co.; per. ad., 319 W. 23d st., New York.

St. Maur, J., manager Eric Bayley Comedy Co.; per. ad., Everett House, New York.

Strakosch, Edgar, acting manager Mlle. Aimee English Comedy Co.; per. ad., 247 E. 13th st., New York.

Sydney, Geo. S., manager Tony Denier's Humpty Dumpty Pantomime Co.; per. ad., 141 Cambridge Place, Brooklyn, N.Y.

Taylor, Ed., manager Janauschek Co.; per. ad., 33 E. 14th st., New York.

Taylor, H. S., business manager Joseph Jefferson Co.; per. ad., 23 E. 14th st., New York.

Tayleure, C. W., manager Mrs. F. S. Chanfrau Co.; per. ad., Boston Theatre.

Taylor, Jack, treasurer and business agent J. H. Keane's Mrs. Partington Co.; per. ad., New York Dramatic News.

Tayleure, Roland L., manager Lillian Olcott Co.; per. ad., 162 South Elliott Place, Brooklyn, N. Y.

Templeton, John, manager Fay Templeton Opera Co.; per. ad., 182 Fulton st., New York.

Thompson, Denman, proprietor and manager Joshua Whitcomb Co.; per. ad., New York Clipper.

Thompson, W. A., proprietor and manager Thompson Opera Co. (Beggar Student); per. ad., 41 E. 10th st., New York.

Thorpe, Chas. R., manager Fanny Mountcastle Sea of Ice Co.; per. ad., care C. W. Kidder, Philadelphia, Pa.

Thurnaek, Edw., general agent Laura E. Dainty Mountain Pink Co.; per. ad., Grand Opera House, Chicago, Ill.

Tompkins, Eugene, manager Rag Baby Co.; Zanita Co.; per. ad., Boston Theatre, Boston, Mass.

Trall, Edward, business agent Tony Denier's Pantomime Co.; per. ad., 141 Cambridge Place, Brooklyn.

Ulmer, Geo. T., manager Lizzie May Ulmer Dad's Girl Co.; per. ad., North Scituate, Mass.

Van Wyck & Mack, managers Annie Berlein Co.; per. ad., 138 Fifth ave., New York.

Vetter, Max J., advance agent; per. ad., Altoona, Pa.,

Villa, Sam. B., manager Agnes Wallace-Villa Co.; per. ad., New York Clipper.

Walker, Smiley, advance agent; dram. agts., Brooks & Dickson; per. ad., Bijou Opera House, New York.

Mr. and Mrs.

Henry Osborne

IN THE FARCICAL COMEDY

OF

The Osborne Oddities.

JOS. P. CONYERS'

Boss Knivett, in Romany Rye,

SEASON 1884-'85.

Address BROOKS & DICKSON, 44 West 23d Street,

New York.

Wallick, James H., manager Bandit King Co.; per. ad., Sinclair House, New York, or Tremont, Chicago, Ill.

Warner, Chas. J., advance agent or business manager, Standard Dramatic Co.; per. ad., Rome, Ga.

Warren, E. L., advance agent; per. ad., 44 Wilber st., Utica, N. Y.

Washburne, John H., business manager or treasurer, Harry Miner's Silver King Co. No. 1; per. ad., People's Theatre, New York.

Waterman, A. R., business manager Chanfran Co.; per. ad., New York Clipper.

Weed, Harry F., manager Fred. Warde Co.; per. ad., Brooklyn Theatre, Brooklyn.

Weed, L. E., business manager Baker and Farron Co.

Welty, G. M., manager, Nellie Boyd Co.; per. ad., Dixon, Lee County, Ill.

Weston, Harry, business agent and manager; per. ad., 108 5th st., Milwaukee, Wis.

Wheeler, H. E., advance agent, Gardiner's

Only a Farmer's Daughter Co.; per. ad., 12 Union Square, New York.

Wilber, A. R., manager Wilber & Ryan's Minstrels; per. ad., New York Clipper.

Williams & Tillotson, managers, Lynwood Co. and Queena Co.; per. ad., 10 E. 15th st., New York.

Williams, Harry M., manager, Williams' Co.; per. ad., 64 E. 14th st., New York.

Williams, Arth. G., manager Miss. Katherine Gray; per. ad., Grand Opera House, Richmond, Ind.

Wilson, Harry T., manager Atkinson's Peck's Bad Boy Co. No. 1; per. ad., 32 Pemberton square, Boston, Mass.

Wilton, George W., manager J. K. Emmet.

Witting, Edward, manager William Stafford; per. ad., New York Mirror.

Yale, Charles H., manager Gallagher, Gilmore & Gardner's Devil's Auction Co.; per. ad., New Central Theatre, Philadelphia.

Yearance, Frank L., business manager; per. ad., 238 William st., New York.

DRAMATIC AUTHORS, ADAPTERS, ETC.

Baker, Benjamin, ass't sec. Actors' Fund, New York; "A Glance at New York in 1848," "New York As It Is; or, Mose," "Bohea Man's Girl," burlesque of "Bohemian Girl," etc.

Baker, George M., 47 Franklin st., Boston; "Better Than Gold," "Our Folks," "The Flower of the Family," etc.

Barnard, Ed. K., Detroit, Mich.; "Fernleigh; or, a Dark Career."

Barnes, Elliot, New York; "Only a Farmer's Daughter," "Ruth's Devotion," "The Artist's Daughter," etc.

Barron, Elwyn A., Inter-Ocean, Chicago; joint author (with Morgan Bates) "A Mountain Pink." *

Barrymore, Maurice, Haymarket Theatre, London, Eng.; "Najezda."

Bates, Morgan, Inter-Ocean, Chicago; joint author (with E. A. Barron) "A Mountain Pink."

Belasco, David, Madison Square Theatre, New York; "La Belle Russe," "Hearts of Oak," "May Blossom," "Stranglers of Paris," etc.

Boker, George H., Philadelphia; "Mahomet," "Francesca da Rimini."

Boucicault, Dion, New York; "London Assurance," "Old Heads and Young Hearts," "The Shaughraun," "The Octoroon," "Robert Emmet," etc.

Bradford, Joseph, Sunday Courier Office, Boston; "Our Bachelors," "Cherubs" and "One of the Finest."

Burnett, Mrs. Frances Hodgson, Washington, D. C.; joint author (with W. H. Gillette) "Esmeralda."

Campbell, Bartley, 1193 Broadway, New York; "My Partner," "Galley Slave," "Fairfax," "Siberia," "White Slave," "My Geraldine," "Separation," "Paquita," etc.

Carleton, Wm., New York, 325, "Fritz in Ireland."

Cazauran, A. R., Union Square Theatre, New York; "Aurora Floyd," "Miss Multon," "French Flats," "Kisses," "Fatal Letter," etc.

Childs, Nathaniel, 14 Harvard st., Charlestown District, Boston; "Dreams," "Hiawatha," "Larks."

Ciprico, George M., San Francisco; "Fates and Furies," "A Daughter of Nature," "After Twenty Years."

Claflin, F. H., Faulkner, Mass.; "Princess Ider," "J. Alma," "Tramps."

Clemens, Samuel L. (Mark Twain), Hartford, Conn.; "Colonel Sellers."

Daly, Augustin, Daly's Theatre, New York; "Pique," "Divorce." "Under the Gaslight," "Frou Frou," "7-20-8," "Needles and Pins," "Wooden Spoon," etc.

Dazey, C. T., Fargo, Dak.; "An American King."

Ellis, H. Wayne, 61 E. 14th st., New York; "Rich and Poor," "Quogne P'int," "Gotham."

Fawcett, Edgar, New York; "False Friend," "Ocean View," "Americans Abroad," "Arnold and Andre."

Foster, Charles, People's Theatre, New York; "Bertha the Sewing Machine Girl," "Neck and Neck," "Swamp Angels," "Buffalo Bill's Pledge," etc.

Freund, John C., Freund's Weekly Office, New York; "True Nobility."

Fuller, George, New York; "Midget."

Fuller, W. H., New York; "Off to Egypt."

Gaylor, Charles, New York; "Fritz." "Connie Soogah," "Jacqnine; or, Paste and Diamonds," "The Young Prince," "Jalma," etc.

Gill, William, New York; joint author (with George Jessup) "In Paradise," "Hands Off," etc.

Gillette, W. H., New York; "The Professor," joint author (with Mrs. Frances Hodgson Burnett), "Esmeralda," "The Secretary."

Goodwin, J. Cheever, Bijon Theatre, Boston; "Evangeline," "Pippins."

Green, Clay, San Francisco; "M'liss." "Under a Polar Star," etc.

Grover, Leonard, New York; "Our Boarding House," "Lispet," "My Son-in-Law," "All Crazy."

Gunther, A. C., New York; "Fresh the American," "Two Nights in Rome," "D. A. M.," "Zozo the Magic Queen," etc.

Harris, Francis A., 59 Chambers st., Boston; "My Son."

Harrigan, Edward, Theatre Comique, New York; the "Mulligan" series of dramas, "Investigation," etc.

Harte, Bret, "Two Men of Sandy Bar."

Henderson, Miss Ettie, Long Branch, N. J.; "Almost a Life," "Miss Rose," "Claire and the Forge Master," etc.

Higgins, D. K., and M. O., Philadelphia; joint authors, "Burr Oaks."

Hoey, George, New York; "A Child of the State," "Under the Upas."

Howard, Bronson, New York; "Saratoga," "Banker's Daughter," "Diamonds," "Old Love Letters," "Baron Rudolph," etc.

Howells, William D., Louisburg Square, Boston; "A Counterfeit Presentment," "Yorick's Love."

Hoyt, Charles H., Hotel Derby, Boston; "Bunch of Keys," "Rag Baby," "Gifford's Luck," "A Parlor Match."

Jessup, George, Everett House, New York; "Dollars and Sense," "The Gentleman from Nevada." Joint author (with William Gill) "In Paradise," etc.

Johnson, Mrs. Annie Lewis, Philadelphia; "Plasar, Queen of the Miners," etc.

Kidder, E. E., New York; "Three of a Kind," etc.

Lancaster, E. W., New York; "Estelle."

Lloyd, David D., New York; "For Congress."

Locke, E. A., 24 Dwight st., Boston; author of "A Messenger from Jarvis Section," "Meda," "Nobody's Claim."

Maeder, Fred. G., "Cad the Tom Boy," "Help," "Vacation," "Stranglers of Paris," etc.

Magnus, Julian, New York; "Conscience," "Marcel."

Marble, Scott, National Printing Company, Chicago; "Furnished Rooms," "State's Attorney," "Muggs' Landing," "Over the Garden Wall," "Wonderful Book," etc.

Marble, Earl, 31 Alexander ave., Boston; "Gyp, Junior," "Lee-li-nau."

Marsden, Fred., New York; "Musette," "Zara," "Nemesis," "Called to Account," "Cheek," "Humbug," etc.

Mathews, J. Brandon, New York; "Marjory's Lovers," "Edged Tools."

Mayo, Frank, Canton, Pa.; "Nordeck."

McClosky, J. J., Brooklyn; "Across the Continent," "Pomp," "On Hand," "Fatal Glass," "Kentuck," etc.

McKaye, Steele, Lyceum Theatre, New York; "Hazel Kirke," "Won at Last," "Rose Michel," "Through the Dark."

Meredith, Harry, Philadelphia; "Ranche 10," "My Life."

Miller, Joaquin, Washington, D. C.; "The Danites," "'49," "Silent Man," "Tally Ho!" etc.

Moore, J. Owen, Washingtonville, Orange Co., N. Y.; "Tempted," "Strife," "Allatoons."

*Morris, Robert Griffin, Telegram Office, New York; "Old Shipmates," "Pulse of New York."

* Murphy, Con. T., Chicago; "Karl the Peddler," "Mizpah," "Little Butterfly."

Neafie, J. A. J., New York; "Harolde, the Envoy of Artois," "Beatrice, the Self-Doomed."

Nobles, Milton; "Phœnix," "Interviews," "Love and Law," etc.

Pidgin, Chas. F., 11 Mt. Vernon st., Boston; "The Electric Spark" (music by Chas. D. Blake), "Wanted—A Partner" (music by Henry Walden), "Peck's Bad Boy and His Pa," "Cambyses; or, The Pearl of Persia" (music by W. J. D. Leavitt), "Tactics" (music by W. J. Bert-Hall).

Poole, John F., Niblo's Theatre, New York; "The Duke's Jester," "Faust" (burlesque), "The Gaelic Chief; or, The Gathering of the Clans," "Wealth and Worth," "Shin Fane," "War Eagle," etc.

* Pond, Anson, New York; "Her Atonement."

Robertson, Ian ("Karl Forster"), Boston Museum, Boston; "Nunky."

Rosenfeld, Sidney, New York; "Dr. Clyde," "The Private Secretary," "Rosemi Shell," "Well-Fed Dora," etc.

* Rowe, Geo. Fawcett, New York; "Brass," "Pop," "The Geneva Cross," "New York and London," "Fifth Avenue," "Wolfert's Roost," etc.

Schwab, Emil, 282 Washington st., Boston; "A Trip to Africa."

Smith, Dexter, Boston Theatre, Boston;" Boc-caccio, '"Musketeers," "Countess Adele," "Favart," "Cobwebs" ("Wanted, A Partner"), and joint author (with Eugene Tompkins) of "Zanita," etc.

Spencer, Edward, Baltimore; "Kit."

Stephens, John A., New Park Theatre, New York; "Passion's Slave," "Unknown"

Sullivan, T. R., Boston Museum, Boston; "A Midsummer Madness," "Papa Perichon," "Little Duke," "Hearts Are Trumps."

Swartz, E. J., Telegram office, Philadelphia; "Dad's Girl."

Taylenre, Clifton W., "East Lynne," "Banker's Wife," "Parted," etc.

Taylor, Howard P., New Park Theatre, New York; "Caprice."

Tillotson, J. K., New York; "Planter's Wife," "Queena," "Lynwood."

Tompkins, Eugene, Boston Theatre; joint author (with Dexter Smith) "Zanita."

Vider, Louis, Union Square Theatre, New York;" Immolation," "Mary of Scotland," "Tabaret," "The Roses."

Wallack, Lester, Wallack's Theatre, New York; "Rosedale," "The Veteran," "Americans in Paris,""Central Park."

Woolf, B. E., 2 Bromfield st., Boston; "Hobbies," "Mighty Dollar," "Pounce & Co.," "Fantine," "Doctor of Alcantara," etc.

Wolf, Mark, 221 Tremont st., Boston; "Bijou," "Our Queen," "Who Is It?"

Young, W. A., Chicago; "Pendragon," "The Rajah."

MUSICAL DIRECTORS, COMPOSERS, ETC.

Binns, Jack, band leader and cornet soloist; per. ad., 136 E. 19th st., New York.

Borgman, Chas. E., musical director, Detroit Opera House; per. ad., 141 Griswold st., Detroit, Mich.

Bowron, W. L., musical director; dram. agts., Brooks & Dickson; per. ad., 102 W. 17th st., New York.

Braham, John J., musical director, Bijou Theatre, Boston.

Bronson, J. O., leader of orchestra and E or B cornet; per. ad., New York Clipper.

Brown, W. Eaton, musical director; per. ad., Providence, R. I.

Catlin, Edward N., musical director, Park Theatre, Boston.

Clark, Wm. F., leader of orchestra and band, solo cornetist, pianist and violinist; per. ad., Atlanta, Ga.

Connelly, M., musical director; dram. agts., Brooks & Dickson; per. ad., Medford, Mass.

Conrad, Frank, musical director, Tony Denier's Pantomime Co.; per. ad., 183 Washington st., Brooklyn, N. Y.

Cook, Fred E., orchestra leader and violinist; per. ad., Hartford, Conn.

De Bang, Johan G., musical director and organist, J. H. Keane's Mrs. Partington Co.; per. ad., New York Mirror.

Dittmar, Charles F., musical director, Zozo the Magic Queen ; per. ad., 960 Summit ave., Jersey City Heights, N. J.

Dorer, L. A., musical director, Patti Rosa Co.: per ad., 112 E. 8th st., New York.

Drescher, Valentine, musical director, Bunch of Keys Co. No. 2; dram. agts., Simmonds & Brown; per. ad., Syracuse, N. Y.

Englander, L, musical director, Thalia Theatre, New York; dram. agts., Brooks & Dickson; per. ad., 257 E. 72d st., New York.

Farmer, Harry, musical **director; per. ad.,** New York Mirror.

Florance, William, musical director, dramatic arranger; per. ad., Irving Park, Cook Co., Ill.

Gardner, S. H., Kiralfy Bros. Sieba co ; dram. agts., Brooks & Dickson; per. ad., 20 E. 3d st , New York.

Gaylord, A. E, musical **director Murphy** Kerry Gow Co.; per ad. **Weiting Opera** House, Syracuse, N. Y.

Haslam, W. Elliot, musical director, **dram.** agts., Brooks & Dickson; per. ad., 305 W. 25th st., New York.

Hassler, Simon, musical director Chestnut Street Opera House, Philadelphia, and composer of dramatic music; per. **ad.,** 214 S. Eighth st., Philadelphia.

Iotropidi, Frederic, musical director and composer, Carleton's English Opera Co.; **per.** ad., Manhattan Chess Club, 104 E. **14th st., New York.**

Kenny, James C., musical director, **Roland** Reed Co., New York.

Kerker, Gustave, musical conductor, Bijou Opera House, New York

Kreissing, Hans, musical director, 866 Broadway, New York.

Level, musical director; dram. agts., Brooks & Dickson ; per. ad., 207 W. 23d st., New York.

Loesch, George, musical director, **Howard** Atheneum, Boston.

Lothian, Napier, musical director, **Boston** Theatre, Boston.

Mullaly, John, musical director, Globe Theatre, Boston.

Nellsen, Wilhelm, musical director and composer; dram. agt., J. Alexander Brown; per. ad., 234 E. 34th street, New York.

Oslander, John, musical director; per. ad., New York Mirror.

Perlet, Hermann H., **musical** director, Fay Templeton Opera Co.; dram. agt., H. L. Slayton, Chicago; per. ad., care of Sohmer & Co.'s warerooms, E. 14th st., New York.

Pfaff, Paul, musical director; dram. agts., **Brooks & Dickson; per.** ad., 156 E. 98th **st., New York.**

Pnerner, Charles, musical director, **Fifth Avenue Theatre, New York.**

Pnerner, Henry, musical director, **Fourteenth** Street Theatre, New York.

Purdy, George, musical director, Boston Museum, Boston.

Reiter, Ernest, musical director; dram. agts., Brooks & Dickson; per. ad., 277 W. 22d st., New York.

Ruttenber, C. B., musical director; dram. agts., Brooks & Dickson; per. ad., 31 W. 125th st., New York.

Simpson, Alfred L , musical director; per. ad., 12 Union Square, New York.

Spencer Alexander, musical director and composer, Wilbur Comic Opera Co.; dram. agt., J J Spies; per. ad , 43 E. Washington Place, New York.

Stahl, Richard, musical director; per. ad., New York Mirror.

Taylor, W. **E., musical** director; dram. agts., Brooks **& Dickson;** per. ad , 128 E. 23d st., New **York.**

Warner, Charles W., cornetist and musical director, Harry Lacy's Planter's Wife Co.; per. ad., Hastings, Mich.

Widmer, Henry, musical director; dram agts., Brooks & Dickson; per. ad., 243 W. 46th st , New York.

Vollman, Isidor, musical director, Harrison and Gourlay Co.; dram. agts., Simmonds & Brown; per ad , 81 Avenue C, New York.

Von Gericke, William, musical director, Boston Music Hall, Boston.

DRAMATIC AGENTS.

BROOKS & DICKSON (dramatic), 44 W. 23d st., New York.

Brown, J. Alex. (dramatic and variety), 64 E. 14th st., New York.

Cambridge, Arthur G. (dramatic and variety), 77 S. Clark st., Chicago, Ill.

Castle, George (variety and dramatic), 46 and 48 Clark st., Chicago, Ill.

Cuddy, J. Phelan (dramatic, variety and minstrels, 511 Clinton st., Brooklyn.

Fitzgerald, Dick (variety), 10 Union Square, New York.

Hilton, Edw. P. (variety and dramatic), St. Paul, Minn.

Ligon & Baker (variety), 101 E. 14th st., New York.

Rice, E. E., National Musical Agency (musical only), 1249 Broadway, New York.

Skiff & Morgan (dramatic and variety), 101 Clark st., Chicago, Ill.

Simmonds & Brown (dramatic), 1166 Broadway. New York.

Spies, J. J. (dramatic), 12 Union Square. New York.

SCENIC ARTISTS.

Bechtel, Ralph M., scenic artist; per. ad., Shelby's Academy of Music. Chicago, Ill.

Blum, Mose, scenic artist; per. ad., Cleveland, O.

Close. L. R. & Co., scenic artists, 525 and 527 Main st., Kansas City, Mo.

Collins, John A., scenic artist, Park Theatre, Brooklyn, N. Y.

Dudocq. Louis, scenic artist; per. ad., 303 W. 17th st., New York.

Fox & Schaefler, scenic artists, New Park Theatre, New York.

Goatcher, Phil., scenic artist, Wallack's Theatre, New York.

Marston Richard, scenic artist, New York.

Mazzanovich, John, scenic artist, 1227 Broadway, New York.

Merry Harley, scenic artist. Swiss Cottage, Flatbush, L. I

Mills, Charles E., scenic artist, 1603 Broadway, New York.

Noxon, Albert & Toomey, scenic artists. St. Louis, Mo.

Reinold, A. J., scenic artist, 57 University Place.

Sosman & Landis, scenic artists, 277 and 279 S. Clark st., Chicago.

Opera House, Cleveland.

GUS HARTZ,

Lessee and Manager.

The most complete and best appointed Theatre in the United States.

Manager HARTZ has just improved the house, and now it is complete in every detail. A NEW GRAND ENTRANCE. NEW AND BEAUTIFUL TOILET ROOMS FOR LADIES AND GENTLEMEN.

For open dates and terms address the Manager, Cleveland, O.

Lannon's Opera House,

Corner King and Pitt Streets,

ALEXANDRIA, VA.

Season of 1884-85.

Just completed. Seating capacity, 1300. Open for all first-class troupes. Will rent or share.

J. M. HILL & Co.,

Steam Printers,

Managers.

Rockville Opera House,

ROCKVILLE, IND.

TATE & STROUSE, Managers.

Seating capacity, 726 ; 14 charges of scenery, 8 dressing rooms. Lighted with gas and heated by steam throughout. Seated with Andrews' opera chairs.
On the Logansport Division of the Vandalia R.R., about midway between Terre Haute and Crawfordsville. Population 2,500. Population to draw from, including contributing towns, 10,000.
Private outside entrance to stage. Proscenium, 28x31 feet. Stage back of Proscenium, 10x53 feet in the clear.

I. Robbins' Opera House,

SHENANDOAH,

Schuylkill County, Pa.

Population, 20,000. Occupation is coal mining. The miners get paid monthly in cash and spend it freely for amusement.

Gem Opera House,

WASHINGTON, N. C.

Population of town, 3,000.

Seating capacity of house, 800 to 1,000.

First-class attractions only wanted

Walker's Hall,

GEORGETOWN, S. C.

Seating capacity 500; well lighted and heated.

The above hall has just been completed, and the Drama will be presented to the people of Georgetown from its stage for the first time in the history of the town. A new field is open to the Dramatic Fraternity in a population of 2,600 hungry for this new source of pleasure. Georgetown is a seaport 60 miles north of Charleston, S. C. For description see " Theatre Directory—South Carolina."

Alf. Dorian,

The Great, The Wonderful,

Champion Serpent Man of the World (barring no one).

With C. R. Gardiner's Zozo, the Magic Queen – Spectacular.

Permanent address:
Care *Clipper*, New York.

Chas. E. Mills,

1603 BROADWAY, NEW YORK

Manager for amateurs, churches, clubs, etc.; stage and scenery to let—so built as to fit any space, complete with drop curtain and lights. Everything furnished for entertainments, and company or any special talent for benefits.

A Page Solely to the Profession.

Members of the profession and managers have felt the need of some systematization of the dramatic profession in America, which would enable them more readily to negotiate engagements and to find the peculiar talent which their various productions demand. Such a systematization is the design of that portion of the Directory devoted to the profession. Every intelligent person interested in the actor's art has deplored its irregular and unstable character, and its annually recurring period of anxious negotiations between the close of one season's engagement and the opening of the next, has always been an unusually trying feature of the business to the actor himself. It is intended to make "The Professional Directory" a guide for managers and the profession, so that they may negotiate with and secure the talent they desire for the following season previous to the close of the current one. This, we feel assured, will go far in contributing a comfortable feeling of security in the actor's employment, and will remove he necessity of his spending the usual (and notoriously uncomfortable) Summer upon "The Rialto," enabling him to give his vacation to recuperation, rest and the mental improvement which success in his exacting art absolutely demands.

The Professional Directory this season is very far from complete and perfect; indeed, in the short period within which the whole Directory was compiled (less than eight weeks) it was impossible to perfect it, and hardly more was contemplated than to prepare for the next annual edition by exhibiting how useful such a Directory might be. From necessity it is this season a subordinate feature; but in following editions this Professional Directory will be made the leading feature. With the cordial co-operation of the profession it can be made all and more than has been contemplated.

The Directory will hereafter be issued each year between the 1st of August and the 1st of September, due notice being given through the dramatic papers of the exact date. Each member of the profession is requested as soon as he or she has made an engagement for the season of 1885-'86, to forward to this office the following facts: *Name; line of business; company engaged with (season 1885-'86); home or permanent address.* If no engagement has been made up to August 1st, send all the above facts, with the exception of "comp ny engaged with." Members of the profession are particularly requested to make it a point to forward their information at the earliest possible date, as they can thereby insure its insertion and also lessen the vast burden of work which the compilation of the Directory entails, all of of which is very largely increased when returns are not received until the last few days previous to publication. For the reception of this information, and for the purpose of extending information which cannot be obtained from other sources, the office of the Directory will be open throughout the year; and the publisher desires to assure each member of the profession that whatever information can be given will be most cheerfully extended.

Annoyance and inconvenience from mistakes in names and addresses can only be avoided by each person taking extreme care that letters of proper names and figures of addresses be plain and unmistakable. This will be recognized as an important point when it is recollected that there are no data for te revision but the information given. In giving addresses, that one should be given through which mail will reach you with the least possible delay during your season upon the road.

An important feature of the Theatre Directory to the profession is the guide it contains to the hotels of the whole country. Their names and rates will be found at the end of, and separated from, the data given about each town. This is deemed a feature of peculiar value, and with the ample time which a year affords the profession can be promised that it will be as nearly perfect as possible in the next annual edition.

The rates given as "special rates" have been furnished by those hotels as their special reduction to the profession; and we specially request that any charges above the rates given should be promptly reported to this office

It is already apparent that the demands for advertising space in the next edition will be very large, hence members of the profession who contemplate advertising will secure more desirable positions by early applications for space.

Finally, the Directory exists solely to advance the interests of the profession; its aim is to aid you and advance the actor's art. Its design can be accomplished only with your hearty co-operation. No charge will be made for the insertion of the information requested, and the price of the book will be kept within the reach of every member of the profession.

To Managers of Combinations and Theatres.

The "Theatre Directory" has been prepared with the view of serving the interests of both combination and theatre manager. Its design is to give to the manager of a combination every fact about a town or theatre which he must know, or which it is desirable he should know before booking his attraction. To be useful to him, the Directory must be absolutely reliable, unexaggerated, complete and correct. When it ceases to be relied upon by combination managers, it ceases to be useful to theatre managers. To make it absolutely reliable the same system *must* be observed with each and every theatre. It is obvious to managers of theatres who receive the annual information blanks that our system should be rigidly observed in making returns.

Every inquiry has been based upon the experience of twenty-six years upon the road, and each one is in reference to some detail which a shrewd and intelligent manager will demand. *Specific answers* must hereafter be made to each inquiry. To such inquiries as "size of stage" "number sets of scenery," "number of sheets bill poster can accommodate," etc., such answers as the following were frequently made: "Large enough for any play," "full stock," "complete stock," "abundant," "any amount," etc., etc. When managers of theatres reflect that the basis upon which such a reply is made varies as widely as do the theatres themselves, it will be apparent that such answers are next to worthless to combination managers. As far as possible they have been excluded in the present edition, and in subsequent editions will be excluded entirely.

To make the Directory subserve the interest of the combination, manager is to make it subserve the sole and only interest of the theatre manager; hence the necessity of adhering rigidly to the above plan; and, by doing so, the manager of a theatre will most advance his own interests.

The Directory will hereafter be issued annually at some date between the 1st of **August** and 1st of September. We should be promptly advised of any changes in your houses. The office of the Directory will be open throughout the year for the receipt of such information, and to extend to patrons any information that may be requested. The returns for the edition of 1885-'86 cannot be in too early.

The Directory has already firmly established a footing, and is destined to be a permanent institution of the amusement business in America. Therefore, managers of theatres should make it a regular part of the preparations for a subsequent season to properly prepare and revise for the Directory the details of their theatres. Each year managers will find it renewed, revised and enlarged, with new features that will not only make it desirable to possess, but will make it necessary that a careful revision and addition of details be made.

Managers of combinations will confer a special favor upon the publisher by reporting all cases in which details of theatres or towns have been incorrectly given, misrepresented or exaggerated. It is the aim to make the Directory a *reliable guide*, and co-operation is quite as much to your interests as to that of the publisher. The cost of the work is such that little profit can be realized at the low price at which it is sold. Nevertheless, it has been determined to retain the original price, so that the work may extend its benefits to even the humblest member of the profession.

From present indications, the edition of 1885-'86 will reach fully 10,000, and advance applications for advertising space are already numerous. Therefore, managers of theatres and managers of combinations who contemplate advertising, will find it to their interest to make early application so that they may secure desirable space.

THEATRE DIRECTORY.

ALABAMA.

BIRMINGHAM, 15,000. R. R., Ala. Great Southern; Georgia Pacific; Louisville & Nashville. Opera House, John P. O'Brien, manager; seating capacity, 1,200; rental, share only; license yearly. Size of stage, 40x49; number sets scenery, 24; bill poster, Opera House. Newspapers: daily, Iron Age; weekly, Advocate, Observer (Sun.)... Hotels: Relay, regular rates, $2.50 (special also), Gault, Richards, Kentucky, Nixon's, St. Charles.

Sublett Hall; seating capacity, 230.

DEMOPOLIS, 1,500. R. R., East Tenn., Va. & Ga. Opera House, Wm. H. Welch, manager; seating capacity, 400; rental, one night $15, three $30, license included; share also. Size of stage, 18x34; number sets scenery, 6; bill poster, Wm. Manning. Newspaper: News-Journal (Sat.)..... Hotels: City (special rates), Lister.

EUFAULA, 4,000. R. R., Montgomery & Eufaula; South Western. Eufaula Opera House, A. A. Cowne, manager; seating capacity, 800; rental, one night $30, three $65, license included; share also. Size of stage, 30x40; number sets scenery, 14; bill poster, J. Daniels. Newspaper: News and Times, tri-weekly,..... Hotels: National, regular rates, $2 (special also), Commercial, Finnerty, Central.

Shorter Opera House, P. H. Morris, manager.

Hart's Opera House; seating capacity, 500.

FLORENCE, 3,000. R. R., Memphis & Charleston. Morrison's Hall, seating capacity, 300; rental, one night $15; State, county and city license, $23. Size of stage, 18x15; number sets scenery, 3; bill poster, H. B. Harrison. Newspapers: Times (W.), Republican (Tu.).... ..Hotels: Harrison, regular rates, $1.50 (special also), National, Florence.

Town Hall, seating capacity, 800.

Masonic Hall; seating capacity, 500.

GADSDEN, 4,000. R. R., East Ala.; and Coosa River steamers. Kyle's Opera House, R. B. Scott, manager; seating capacity, 780; rental, one night $50; share also; license yearly. Size of stage, 38x40; size of proscenium opening, 18x20; height from stage to grooves, 13; height from stage to rigging loft, 18; depth under stage, 8; 5 dressing rooms under stage; number sets scenery, 14; stage carpenter, James W. Carlin; bill poster, Ed Caldwell; number of sheets can accommodate, 400. Newspapers: Times (Th.), advertising rates special; News (W.), advertising rates special......Hotels, Exchange, special rates, $1.25; Kittrell, special rates, $1.25.

GREENSBORO, 2,000. R. R., Cin., Selma & Mobile. Dorman's Hall. A. M. Dorman, manager; seating capacity, 400; rental, one night $10; three $25; license, $5. Size of stage, 15x30; number sets scenery, 4; bill poster, John Evans. Newspapers: Beacon (Tu.), Southern Watchman (Th.)......Hotels: Cowin, Johnson.

GREENVILLE, 2,500. R. R., Louisville & Nashville. New Greenville Theatre, Frank Kohn, manager; seating capacity, 450; rental or share. Size of stage, 20x14; full set scenery; bill poster, R. O. Walter. Newspaper: Advocate (W.)......Hotels: Ehebert, Perry, Mallett, Marion.

City Hall, McMullan, manager; seating capacity, 500.

HUNTSVILLE, 8,000. R. R., Memphis & Charleston. Opera House, Oscar R. Hundley, manager; seating capacity, 1,000, rental, one night $35, three $75, license included; share also. Size of stage, 20x24; number sets scenery, 8; bill poster, Winslow Dyer. Newspapers: Democrat (W.), Advocate (Th.), Independent (Th.).   Hotels: Huntsville (special), McGee, Commercial.

MOBILE, 40,000. R. R., L. & N.; M. & O. Mobile Theatre, J. Tannenbaum, manager; seating capacity, 900; share only; license, yearly. Size of stage, 65x22; size of proscenium opening. 35x30, height from stage to grooves, 18; height from stage to rigging loft, 35; depth under stage, 9; traps, 3; number sets scenery, 35; leader of orchestra, S. Schlesinger; stage carpenter, John G. Hines; bill poster, City Bill Posting Co; theatrical teamster, F. T. Penny. Newspapers: daily, Register; adv. rates, yearly contract; Gossip, yearly contract; weekly, Gazette (Sun.), advertising rates, special contract.. ....Hotels: Battle House; special rates, $2; St. James, special rates, $1.50 to $2.

Temperance Hall; seating capacity, 700. Size of stage, 33x33; fair stock scenery.

Odd Fellows' Hall; seating capacity, 1,000

MONTGOMERY, 25,000. R. R., L. & N.; Mobile & M.: M. & Western. Montgomery Theatre, J. Tannenbaum, manager; seating capacity, 1,100; rents, share only; license, by the year. Size of stage, 56x76; size of proscenium opening, 32x28; height from stage to grooves, 18; height from stage to rigging loft, 32; depth under stage, 6½; traps, star, vampire, centre trap and bridge; number sets scenery, 22; musical director, E. Hille; scenic artist, Gus Hines; stage carpenter, F. Feeley; bill poster, Theatre; number of sheets can accommodate, 1,000. Newspapers: daily, Advertiser, adv. rates, yearly contract ; Gossip (theatrical paper), yearly contract; weekly, Advertiser (Sunday), 20c. a line.......Hotels: Exchange, special rates, $1.50 to $3 ; Windsor, $1.50 to $3 ; Merchants', $1.25 to $2; Madison House and Capitol City, $1.25 to $2.

McDonald's Opera House, G. F. McDonald, manager; seating capacity, 1,000; rental, $30 share also; license yearly. Size of stage, 40x50; size of proscenium opening, 28x 6 ; height from stage to grooves, 18 ; height from stage to rigging loft, 60; depth under stage, 11 ; working bridges, 3 traps; number sets scenery, 30; musical director, Louis Hanson; stage carpenter, Mr. Willson; bill poster, Opera House; number of sheets can accommodate, 800; rates per sheet, 3c.; theatrical teamster, W. E. Haygood.

Three halls ; seating capacity, 500 each.

OPELIKA, 4,000. R. R., Western R'y of Ala.; Columbus & Western: Eastern Ala.; Goodwater & Va. R'y. Renfro Opera House, Isaac Hayman, manager; seating capacity, 850; rental, one night, $4), share also; license yearly. Size of stage, 25x47; size of proscenium opening, 11x20; height from stage to grooves, 12; height from stage to rigging loft, 19; depth under stage, 5; traps, 1 centre; number sets scenery, 16; stage carpenter, Robert Taylor; bill poster, Opera House. Newspaper: Times (Th.)......
Hotel : Opelika House, special rates, $1.50.

Rink Hall; seating capacity, 800.

SELMA, 10,000. R. R., Eastern Tenn.; Va. & Ga.; Louisville & Nash.; Cin., Selma & Mobile. Harmony Hall, Louis Gerstman, manager; seating capacity, 550; rental, one night, $40, share also, license included. Leader of orchestra, Leonce Joseph; bill poster, J. S. Jacob; rates, 3c.; theatrical teamsters, M. G. Meyer, P. H. Norris. Newspapers : daily, Times, advertising rates per inch, 50c.; Mail, advertising rates per inch, 50c......Hotels: St. James, special rates, $1.75; Commercial, special rates, $1.50.

Opera House destroyed by fire, January, 1883. Rebuilding for season of 1885-86.

Gilman's Hall, seats 450.

TALLADEGA, 4,000. R. R., Tenn., Va. & Ga. City Hall, B. Frank Coker, manager; seating capacity, 400; rental, one night $25, three $60, license included. Size of stage, 15x 35; number sets scenery, 6; bill poster, Frank Coker. Newspapers : Mountain Home (W.), Reporter, (W.)..... Hotels : Commercial, regular rates, $2 (special also), Exchange, Talladega.

TROY, 3,000. R. R., Mobile & Girard (terminus.) Minchener's Hall, F. Minchener, manager ; seating capacity, 450 ; rental, one night $15, three $35; license $10 to $15. Size of stage, 20x38; number sets scenery, 5 ; bill poster, Ben Minchener. Newspapers :

Messenger (Th.), Enquirer (Sat.)......Hotels: Parker, City, regular rates $2 (special also).

TUSCALOOSA, 5,000. R. R., Ala. Gt. Southern. Centennial Hall, Fitts Brothers, managers; seating capacity, 500; rental, one night $15, three $40; share also. Size of stage, 25x30; number sets scenery, 5; bill poster, Lyman Nunuler. Newspapers: Gazette (Th.), Times (Wed.).... ..Hotels: Washington, Druid City, Broadway.

UNION TOWN, 1,800. R. R., Alabama Central. Kittrell's Hall, W. P. Kittrell, manager.

ARKANSAS

ARKADELPHIA, 2,000. R. R., St. L., I. M. & So. City Hall, seating capacity, 500; rental one night $1, three $3; license, $5. Size of stage, 16x30; bill poster, G. B. Blish. Newspaper: Southern Standard.......Hotel: Reames, regular, $2.

EUREKA SPRINGS, 6,400; R. R., Eureka Springs. Academy of Music, Geo. Bodell, manager; seating capacity, 450; size of stage, 13x20. Newspapers: Herald, Echo (W.). Republican........Hotels: Perry, Southern, Metropolitan, Hancock.

FAYETTEVILLE, 3,000. R. R., St. L. & San Francisco. Van Winkle Hall, J. S. Hurlbut, manager; seating capacity, 500; rental, one night $10; license, $5. Newspapers: Democrat (Th.), Sentinel (W.), Blade...... Hotels: Mountain, Petty, Van Winkle, McElroy.

Bright's Hall; seating capacity, 500.

FORT SMITH, 7,000. R. R., Little Rock & Fort Smith; St. Louis & Frisco. Academy of Music, J. H. Clendening, manager; seating capacity, 700; rental, one night $35; three $100, share also; license included. Size of stage, 27x24; size of proscenium opening, 21x24; height from stage to grooves, 16; height from stage to rigging loft, 34; depth under stage, 8; number sets scenery, 8; bill poster, Geo. H. Williams, number sheets can accommodate, 200; rates per sheet, 3½ cts.; theatrical teamsters, McLoud & Moore. Newspapers: daily, Tribune; advertising rates, special contract; Evening News, special contract; weekly, Elevator (F.); Independent (W.), News (Sat.). Hotels: McKibben, special rates, $2; Le Grande, special rates, $1.50 to $1.75; Grand Central, special rates, $1.25 to $1.50.

HELENA, 5,000. R. R., Ark. Midland; St. L., Iron Mt. & Southern. Opera House, Crebs & Fitzpatrick, managers; seating capacity, 800; rental—; license yearly; share also. Size of stage, 20x47; height from stage to grooves, 16; height from stage to rigging loft, 25; depth under stage, 8; number sets scenery, 14; bill posters Geo. Foster, Joe Shepard; theatrical teamsters, J. T. Ramsey, S. C. Pipper. Newspapers: daily, World; weekly, Golden Echo (Sat.), Patriot (Sat.)........Hotels: Delmonico, Shelby.

Coolridge Hall; seating capacity, 600.

Turner Hall; seating capacity, 250.

HOPE, 2,000. R. R., St. L., I. M. & Southern. Whaley Hall, W. Shirer, manager; seating capacity, 500; rental, one night $15; license, $10; share also. Size of stage 20x21; bill poster, W. Shirer. Newspapers: Radical (W.), News (W.), Pine Torch (Sat.)........Hotel: McGee, regular, $2.

HOT SPRINGS, 8,000. R. R., Hot Springs & Malvern. Hot Springs Opera House, J. L. Butterfield, manager; seating capacity, 800; rental, share only, license included. Size of stage, 30x33; height to rigging loft, 47; number sets scenery, 10; stage carpenter, Thomas Alvin; bill poster, L. A. Thomas. Newspapers: daily, Sentinel, News......Hotels: Sumpter, reg., $2.50 to $3.50 (special also); Arlington, special, $1.75 to $3, Avenue, special, $1.75 to $3; Waverly, special, $1.75 to $3; French, special, $1.75 to $3; Clifton, special, $1.75 to $3.

City Hall; Andrew Brnon, manager; seating capacity, 500; rental, one night $10; three $25; license, $10.50. Size of stage, 15x30; number sets scenery, 6.

LITTLE ROCK, 30,000. R. R., St. Louis, Iron Mountain & So.; Memphis & Little Rock; Fort Smith. New Capital Theatre, Geo. H. Hyde, manager; seating capacity, 1,000; rental, share only. Size of stage, 36x50; size of proscenium opening, 22x27; height from stage to grooves, 14; height from stage to rigging loft, 30; depth under stage, 10; **traps**, 3; number sets scenery. 15; musical director, Cohen; scenic artist, G. W. Wolf; **stage** carpenter, D. E. Edwards; **bill poster**, C. M. Rome; theatrical teamster, W. S. **Davis** & Son. Newspapers: daily, Gazette, advertising rates, special contract; Democrat...... Hotels: Capital, special rates, $1.50—$2.00; Deming, special rates, $1.25—$1.75; Grand Central, special rates, $1.25—$1.75; City, Adams.

Grand Opera House, **R. A.** Little, manager; seating capacity, **1,000**; rental, one night **$100**, three $250, license included; share also. Size of stage, 32x48; size of proscenium opening, 26x26; height from stage to grooves, 14½; height from stage to rigging loft, 28; depth under stage, 8; traps, **3**; number sets scenery, full stock; leader of orchestra, Adolph Cohen; **scenic** artist, Wolf; stage carpenter, D. C. Edwards; **bill** poster, Opera House; **number of sheets can accommodate**, 1,000; rates, 3 to 4c.; theatrical teamsters, **W. O. Davis & Co.**

Academy of Music. Size of stage, 22x16.

Alexander Hall; seating capacity, 500.

Concordia Hall; seating capacity, 300.

PINE BLUFF, 3,500. R. R., Little Rock M. R. & Texas. Opera House, J. B. Trulack, manager; seating capacity, 800; size of stage, 31x48. Newspapers: Press, Eagle (Th.).. Hotel: Ritchies'; regular rates, $2—$2.50.

PRESCOTT, 2,000. R. R. St. Louis, Iron Mountain & South. Opera House, Isaac Moore, manager; seating capacity, 300; rental, one night, $20; license, $6; share also. Size of stage, 13x24; number sets scenery, 4; bill poster, Isaac Moore. Newspapers: Despatch, Nevada Picayune (W.)... ..Hotel: Johnson, regular rates, $2.

RUSSELLVILLE, 1,500. R. R., Little Rock & Fort Smith. Masonic Hall; seating capacity, 300; rental, one night, $6. Size of stage, 22x26; bill poster, Robert Irvin. Newspapers: Democrat (Th.)......Hotel: White's.

TEXARKANA, 5,000. R. R., St. Louis, Iron **Mountain & So.; Texas &** Pacific; Texas & St. Louis. Opera House, Thos. Orr, manager; seating capacity, **500**; rental, one night $25 three $60; license $12; share also. Size of stage, 25x60; number sets scenery, 12; bill poster, Jas. Doyle. Newspapers: daily, Inter-State; weekly, Democrat.... .Hotels: Draughon, regular rates, $2.50, (special also); Cosmopolitan, Redler, Benefield.
Shea Hall.

CALIFORNIA.

CLOVERDALE, 3,000. R. R., San **Francisco** & Northern Pacific. Eureka Hall; seating capacity 400. Newspapers: Pacific **Sentinel** (Th.), Reveille (S).. ...Hotels: United States, regular rates, $2 (special also).

Masonic Hall, seating capacity, 200.

COLUSA, 2,800. Colusa Theatre, J. **Furth** and J. Grover, managers; seating capacity, 500; rental, one night $15; three $35; license, $11. Size of stage, 20x40; number sets scenery, 10; bill poster, F. B. Hatch. Newspapers: Sun (S)   Hotels, Colusa, regular rates, $2 (special also), Eureka and National.

GILROY, 2,500. R. R., South Pacific. Music Hall, seating capacity, 800; rental, one night, $15; license, $8. Size of stage, 19x21; number sets scenery, 8; bill poster, L. Cleveland. Newspapers: Advocate (Sat.), Valley Record (Sat.)....Hotels: Williams, Southern Pacific. Gilroy Theatre.

GRASS **VALLEY, 5,000.** Hamilton **Hall.** Newspapers: Daily Tidings, Union .....Hotel: Holbrook, regular rates, $1.50—$8 (special also).

HEALDSBURG, 2,500. R. R., San Francisco & North Pacific. Truitt's Theatre, R. K. Truitt, manager; seating capacity, 700; rental, one night $22, three $45; license, $2.50. Size of stage, 22x18; size of proscenium opening, 20x22; depth under stage, 6; number sets scenery, 3; leader of orchestra, E. Learch; scenic artist, George Modaria; stage carpenter, Mr. J. Jones Shafer; bill poster, Frank; number of sheets can accommodate, 200; rates per sheet, 4c.; theatrical teamster, Harry Trultt. Newspapers; Enterprise (Th), Flag (Sat.). ....Hotels: Sotome, special rates, $1.50.

LOS ANGELES, 18.000. R. R., So. Pacific. Turn Verein Hall, J. Kuhrt, manager; seating capacity, (500); rental, one night, $25; license, $11. Size of stage, 21x17; number sets scenery, 11; bill poster, John Osbourn. Newspapers: daily, Express Republican, Free Lance, Herald, Times; weekly, News (Mon.), Porcupine (Sat.), South West (Sat)...... Hotels: Cosmopolitan, regular rates, $2 to $3; Pico, regular rates, $2 to $3; Grand Central, United States, White.

Child's Opera House, Col. A M. Gray, manager; seating capacity, 1,500

Hearn's Hall, seating capacity, 400.

Union Hall, seating capacity, 400.

Horticultural Pavilion, seating capacity, 2,000.

Merced Theatre, seating capacity, 600.

Club Theatre.

MARYSVILLE, 7,000. R. R., Cal. Northern; Central Pacific. Marysville Theatre, G. W. Harris, manager; seating capacity, 900; rental one night $25, three $65; license, State and county, $6. Size of stage, 21x40 ; fair stock scenery ; bill poster, J. A. McCormack. Newspapers : daily, Appeal; weekly, Advocate (S)...... Hotels : Western regular rates, $1.50—$2, United States, Golden Eagle.

Turner's Hall, seating capacity, 500.

Waterworks Hall, seating capacity, 300.

City Hall, seating capacity, 300.

MERCED, 3,000. R. R., Central Pacific. Washington Hall, Reidy and Quigley, managers; seating capacity, 350; rental one night, $15; license, $6. Size of stage, 2 x32; number sets scenery, 10; bill poster, J. P. Stanton. Newspapers :, Express (Sat.), Argus (Sat.), Star (Th.) .....Hotels: El Capitan, Fooley.

National Hall; B. Grogan, manager; rental one night, $8. Size of stage, 11x21.

MODESTO, 2,000. R. R., Central Pacific. Rogers' Hall, S. P. Rogers, manager; rental one night, $20; no license. Size of stage, 20x18; fair stock scenery. Newspapers: daily, Strawbach; tri-weekly, Farmers' Journal; weekly, Herald (Th.), News (F.)......Hotels: Ross, regular rates, $2 (special also), Prentiss.

NEVADA CITY, 3,250. Nevada Theatre, Geo. F. Jacot, manager; rental one night, $40, license included. Newspapers: daily, Transcript; tri-weekly, Herald......Hotels: National Exchange, special rates; Union, special rates, $1—$2.50.

NORTH SAN JUAN, 1,000. San Juan Theatre, O. P. Stedger, manager; rental one night $10, three $24; no license. Size stage, 18x25; number sets scenery, 5; bill poster, Peter Hildebrand. Newspapers: Times (Sat.)......Hotels, National. Revere.

OAKLAND. 50,000. R. R., Central Pacific. Dietz Opera House, A. C. Dietz, manager; seating capacity, 900; rental one night $50, three $125, license included. Size of stage, 27x45; full stock scenery; bill poster, Stilwell Bros. Newspapers: daily, Tribune, Times; semi-weekly,7 Independent; weekly, Press (Sat.), Sentinel (W.)......Hotels; Galindo, regular rates, $2 to $2.50 (special also); Tubbs, regular rates $2.50 (special also); Windsor, special rates; Grand Central, Newland, Centennial, Chase, Roberts, Kohler.

PETALUMA, 6,500. R. R., San Francisco & Northern Pacific. Petaluma Theatre, G. M. Brush, manager; seating capacity, 1,000; rental, one night, $25; license, $6, share also; Size of stage, 20x30; fair stock scenery; bill poster, G. M. Brush. Newspapers: Argus (Sat.), Courier (W.)......Hotels: American, Washington City.

Turner Hall, G. M. Brush, manager; seating capacity, 800. Size of stage, 14x20.

RIVERSIDE, 3,000. R. R., Southern Pacific; California Southern. Pavilion Theatre, J. E. Langley, manager; seating capacity, 1,000; rental, one night $25, three $60; license, $5. Size of stage, 24x56; size of proscenium opening, 18x27; height from stage to grooves, 14; depth under stage, 8; traps, one; number sets scenery, 7; bill poster, T. E. Langley; rates per sheet, 4c. Newspapers: Press and Horticulturist (Sat.), Independent ....Hotels: Glenwood, St. George.

1884.   1885.

FRANCIS B. PURDIE,

ACTING MANAGER

George C. Miln Dramatic Company.

Permanent Address:

3 WINDSOR BLOCK, INDIANAPOLIS, IND.

MAURICE F. DREW,

JUVENILE LEADS.

Philip Roystern, in Romany Rye

SEASON 1884-'85.

Address BROOKS & DICKSON, 44 West 23d Street,

New York.

SACRAMENTO, 25,000. R. R. Central Pacific. Metropolitan Theatre, Jos. Baily, manager; seating capacity, 1,500; rental, one night, $50; license, city and county, $11. Size of stage, 30x60; full set scenery; bill poster, Wm. Coswell. Newspapers: daily, Bee, Union; semi-weekly, Journal; weekly, Leader (Sat.), Capital (Sat.) ....Hotels: Arcade, regular rates, $2.50 (special also); Orleans, Union, Golden Eagle, Capitol, Western, State Pacific, Langham.

Odd Fellows Hall; seating capacity, 500.

Pavilion Hall; seating capacity, 500.

SAN BERNARDINO, 1,800. R. R., Cal. Southern. Opera House, Walters & Brinkmeyer managers.

SAN DIEGO, 2,150. R. R., Mexican National. Opera House. Newspapers: daily, Union, semi-weekly, Sun...... Hotel: Horton, regular rates, $2 (special also).

SAN FRANCISCO, 250,000. R. R., Central Pac.; South. Pac.; San. F. and Nor. Pac.; Sonoma Valley Baldwin's Theatre, Al. Hayman, manager; seating capacity, 1,690; rental, share only, license included. Size of stage, 42x66; size of proscenium opening, 35x31½; height from stage to grooves, 20; height from stage to rigging loft, 65; depth under stage, 9; traps, 3; number sets scenery, 75; musical director, Louis Homier; scenic artist, Forrest Seabury; stage carpenter, Robert Abrams; bill posters, Keyt & Co.; T. N. Dunphy & Co.; rates, &c.; theatrical teamsters, California Transfer Co. Newspapers: daily, Chronicle, Call, Examiner, Alta, Post, Bulletin; advertising rates per inch, $2.50; morning papers, $10 per inch per week; evening, $7.50 per inch per week... ...Hotels: Baldwin, special rates, $2.50; Palace, special rates, $3.00; Occidental, $2.50; Russ. $10 per week.

Tivoli Opera House, Joseph Kreling, manager; seating capacity, 1,600; play only stock comic and grand opera companies; size of stage, 31x60; proscenium opening, 31x32; height from stage to grooves, 18; height from stage to rigging loft, 60; depth under stage, 10; traps, 2 centre traps, 4 quarter traps, 4 strip traps, 1 bridge, sinks from front to back of stage provided with slots; number sets scenery, 100; musical director, Gustave Hinrichs; scenic artist, George Bell; stage carpenter, Henry Burkes.

Grand Opera House, Frederick W. Bert, manager.

California Theatre, Frederick W. Bert, manager; seating capacity, 2,500; share only; full stock scenery.

Oakland Theatre, Frederick W. Bert, manager; seating capacity, 2,000; size of stage, 30x 60; full set scenery.

Emerson's Theatre, Wm. Emerson, manager.

Bella Union Theatre, Harry Montague, manager; seating capacity, 1,300; size of stage, 40x45; full stock scenery.

Platt's Hall.

Adelphi Theatre.

Metropolitan Temple.

Standard Theatre.

Woodward's Gardens.

Buckley's Hall.

Union Hall.

Bush Street Theatre, M. B. Leavitt, manager.

SAN JOSE, 16,000. R. R., South Pacific Coast; Central Pacific. California Theatre, Chas. F. Macy, manager; seating capacity, 1,100; rental, one night $65, two $125; license, $8. Size of stage, 38x50; size of proscenium opening, 28x32; height from stage to grooves, 14; height from stage to rigging loft, 28; depth under stage, 3; traps, 1; number sets scenery, 14. Leader of orchestra. Geo. Parkman, Jr.; bill poster, Charles W. Williams; number of sheets can accommodate, 800, rates per sheet, &c.; theatrical teamster, L. M. Jewett. Newspapers: daily, Mercury, advertising rates per inch, $2; Times, per line 15 cents; Herald, City Item. .... Hotels: Auzerais, special rates, $2.50; Lick House, Russ House, special rates, $1.25; St. James, special rates, $1.50.

San Jose City Market Hall; seating capacity 1,200.

Music Hall, seating capacity 1,000.

Opera House, seating capacity, 1,100.

SANTA BARBARA, 5,000. Opera House. Bill poster, T. Rosenberg. Newspaper: daily, Independent Press......Hotel: Arlington.

SANTA CLARA, 2,700. R. R., P. C. & S. P. C. Widney's Hall, Widney, manager; seating capacity, 40J; rental, one night $20; three $55; license, $1.50. Size of stage, 15x22; height from stage to grooves, 12; depth under stage, 2; number sets scenery, 3 ; bill poster, H. T. Wright; number of sheets can accommodate, 200; rates per sheet, 4 cents. Theatrical teamster, town drayman. Newspaper: Journal, (Sat)., rates per inch, 50 cents ......Hotel: Santa Clara, special rates, $2 to $2.50, Vallego.

SANTA CRUZ, 6,000. R. R., So. Pacific Coast; Santa Cruz. Bernheim's Music Hall, J. Bernheim, manager; seating capacity, 800; rental, one night, $10, two $15; license $8. Size of stage, 18x25; number sets scenery, 5 ; bill posters, Hussey & Walker. Newspapers : Courier-Item (Th.), Sentinel (Sat.)......Hotels: Pacific, regular rates, $2.50 to $3 (special also); Wilkins, $1.50 to $2 (special also), Ocean, St. Charles.

Opera House, Richard Thompson, manager; seating capacity, 550; rental, one night $30; three $75; license $9. Size of stage, 40x50; number sets scenery, 5.

SANTA ROSA, 5,000. R. R., San Francisco & Nor. Pacific. Opera House, Oscar Morrison, manager. Size of stage, 16x36; fair stock scenery; bill poster, A. S. Harrington. Newspapers: daily, Republican; weekly, Democrat (Sat.)......Hotels : Occidental, regular rate $2 (special also), Grand, Santa Rosa, American.

STOCKTON, 12,000. R. R., Central Pacific. Mozart Hall, Eugene Lehe, manager; seating capacity, 900; rental, one night, $10; license, city and county, $11. Size of stage, 12x30; number sets scenery, 9; bill poster. P. H. Clifford. Newspapers : daily, Herald, Independent, Mail; weekly, Banner (Sat.), Once a Week (Sun.)......Hotels : Yosemite, regular rate, $2 and $3; Grand Central, Mansion, Eagle, Commercial.

Hickman's Hall, seating capacity, 450.

Turn Verin Hall, seating capacity, 1,000.

Stockton Theatre, seating capacity, 1,500.

National Hall, seating capacity, 2,000.

Pioneer Hall, seating capacity, 600.

VALLEJO, 8,000. R. R., Cal. Pacific & Northern. Farragut Theatre, R. B. Loyall, manager; rental, one night $25, three $65; license, $10. Size of stage, 28x50; number sets scenery, 8; bill poster, George A. Bakston. Newspapers : daily, Chronicle, Times. Hotels : Bernard, Howard.

VISALIA, 1,400. R. R., Central Pacific. Centennial Hall, J. McCarthy, manager; seating capacity, 300; rental, one night; $12.50; share also. Size of stage, 20x16. Newspapers : Delta (Th.), Journal (Th.), Times (Th)......Hotel : Palace.

YREKA, 1,500. Kessler's Theatre, J. P. Kessler, manager; seating capacity, 500; rental, one night, $10; license, $5. Size of stage, 15x20; number sets scenery, 4; bill poster, James Irwin. Newspapers : semi-weekly, Journal; weekly, Union (Th.)......Hotel : Franco-American.

CONNECTICUT.

ANSONIA, 5,000. R R., Naugatuck: New Haven & Derby. Ansonia Opera House, Dana Bartholomew, manager; seating capacity, 1,000; rental one night, $35; three, $90; license, $5; share also. Size of stage, 25x25; fair stock scenery; bill poster, Thomas Ruth. Newspapers: Sentinel (W.)......Hotel: Railroad, regular, $2 (special also).

BETHEL, 3,500. RR., Danbury & Norwalk; Shapang. Fisher's Hall, John F. Nichols, manager; seating capacity, 400; rental one night, $10; share also; license, $1. Size of stage, 14x36; size of proscenium opening, 8x16; height from stage to grooves, 8; height from stage to rigging loft, 10; depth under stage, 3½; traps, 1, center; number sets scenery, 8; leader of orchestra, Elgin Andrews; scenic artist, Christ Zarmedier; stage carpenter, G. H. Nichols; bill poster, Chas. Taylor; number of sheets can accommodate, 25; rates, 4c.; theatrical teamster, David Taylor. Newspapers: daily, Danbury News; weekly, Danbury News (Wed.)......Hotel Fox, special rates, $1.25.

BIRMINGHAM, 5,000. R.R., New Haven & Derby. Nathan's Hall, David Nathan, manager; seating capacity, 500; rental one night, $18; license, $5. Size of stage, 20x40; bill poster, G. C. Allis. Newspaper: Transcript (W.). ....Hotels: Bassett, regular, $2 (special also): Birmingham.

BRIDGEPORT, 35,000. R.R., Housatonic; Naugatuck; N. Y., N. H. & H. Hawe's Opera House, H. V. Hawes, manager; seating capacity, 1,300; rental one night. $85; share also. license included. Size of stage, 45x65; height from stage to grooves, 20; height from stage to rigging loft, 55; depth under stage, or cellar, 10; scenery, full stock; bill poster, H. H. Jennings; theatrical teamster, H. H. Jennings. Newspapers: daily, Post; News ...., Hotels: Atlantic, special rates, $2; Sterling, special rates, $2.

St. John's Hall, George Keeler, manager, seating capacity, 800; rental one night. $20; three, $50. Size of stage, 11x20.

Lyceum, seating capacity, 600.

G. A. R. Hall, seating capacity, 150.

St. Georges' Hall, seating capacity, 300.

Franklyn Hall, seating capacity, 675.

BRISTOL, 5,000. R.R., New York & New England. Town Hall, S. A. Olcott, manager; seating capacity, 600; rental, one night, $15; bill poster, Edward Brose. Newspapers: Press (Th.), Times (Sat.)......Hotels : Gridley, regular rates, $2 (special also); Bristol.

CHESTER, 1,000. R.R., Hartford & Connecticut Valley. Town Hall, C. E. Lord, manager; seating capacity, 470; bill poster, C. E. Lord. Newspapers: News, New Era, Advertiser......Hotel: Chester, regular rates, $2 (special also).

COLLINSVILLE, 3,000. R.R., Hartford & Connecticut: New Haven & Northampton. Union Hall, C. S. Osborn, manager; seating capacity, 500; rental, one night, $12; three, $28. Size of stage, 18x20; number sets scenery, 5; bill poster, A. F. Osborne. Newspaper: Herald (Th.) .....Hotel: Valley, regular rates, $2 (special also).

DANBURY, 15,000. R.R., Danbury & Norwalk; Housatonic; New York & New England: N. Y. City & Norwich. Opera House, C. L. Taylor, manager; seating capacity, 1,500; share only. Size of stage, 30x60; size of proscenium opening, 20x30; height from stage to grooves, 18; height from stage to rigging loft, 36; depth under stage, 3; number sets scenery, 8; leader of orchestra, Harry Biddiscome; stage carpenter, W. J. Taylor; bill poster, Opera House; number of sheets can accommodate, 1,500; theatrical teamster, Wm. Hitchcock. Newspapers : daily, Danbury News; weekly, Danbury News (Wed.), Democrat (Sat.), Republican (Tu.)......Hotels : Turner House, Wooster House, regular rates, $2 (special also), New England.

Benedict's Opera House.

Wildman's Opera House.

DANIELSONVILLE, 3,500. R.R., Norwich & Worcester: New York & New England. Music Hall, H. N. Clemens, manager; seating capacity, 800; rental, one night, $20; three, $50; license included. Size of stage, 26x22; size of proscenium opening, 20x22; height from stage to grooves, 20; height from stage to rigging loft, 30; number sets scenery, 5; stage carpenter, E. S. Carpenter; bill poster, E. S. Carpenter; number of sheets can accomodate, 500; rates, &c ; theatrical teamster, W. Withereld. Newspaper : Transcript (Wed.). ...Hotels: Attawagan, special rates, $1 to $1.50; Olive Branch, special rates, $1.

GOODSPEED'S LANDING, 3,200. R.R., Connecticut Valley. Goodspeed's Opera House, W. H. Goodspeed, manager; seating capacity, 850; rental, one night, $40, license included; share also; bill poster, W. H. Goodspeed. Newspaper: Advertiser......Hotel : Golsten.

GRANBY, 3,000. R.R., Canal; N. H. & Northampton. Holcomb's Hall, C. P. Loomis, manager; seating capacity, 300; rental, one night, $5. Size of stage, 7x14; depth under stage, 2; number sets scenery, 5; leader of orchestra, W. C. Griffin; stage carpenter, Henry Cooley; bill poster, Arthur Emerson; theatrical teamster, M. N. Clark. .....Hotel: Pearson's, special rates, $1.50.

GREENWICH, 10,000. R. R., New York & New Haven. Ray's Hall (new), John H. Ray, manager; seating capacity, 1,200; rental, one night, $30, three, $60; share also; license,

—— THE ——

Worcester Excursion Car Company,

WORCESTER, MASS.   115 Broadway, New York.

CAPITAL, $250,000.

JEROME MARBLE, President.   W. H. SHUEY, Superintendent.
CHAS. B. PRATT, Treasurer.   A. B. F. KINNEY, Secretary

—— PATRONIZED BY ——

Mr. HENRY E. ABBEY, Mr. EDWIN BOOTH, Mr. DION BOUCICAULT,
Mr. HENRY IRVING, Mr. JOSEPH JEFFERSON, Mr. CHARLES E. LOCKE,
Mr. JOHN STETSON, Mr. THEODORE THOMAS, Miss MARY ANDERSON,
Mme. SARAH BERNHARDT, Miss LILLIE LANGTRY, FRAU FRIEDRICH
MATERNA, Mme. HELENA MODJESKA, Mme. CHRISTINE NILSSON,
Mme. ADELINA PATTI, Miss ELLEN TERRY, Miss EMILY WINANT,
and many others well known to the theatrical world.

This Company is prepared to supply Managers or Stars with private Hotel and Sleeping
Cars at a reasonable daily rental.

These elegant coaches are expressly designed for parties requiring the use of private or
"special" cars which may be run on any railway, and are thoroughly equipped with everything necessary for safety, comfort and convenience. They are equipped with combination
couplers, automatic air brakes, improved heaters, electric bells, parlor and dining room
furniture, bedding, bed and table linen, silver, china, kitchen utensils, etc.

Commodious coal and baggage lockers are located under each car as shown in the above cut
of the "Yellowstone."

Three competent men—Porter, Cook and Waiter—accompany each car.

DIAGRAM OF PLAN E, SCALE 16 ft. to 1 inch.

A—Grand Saloon, with sixteen   F—Butler's Pantry.   N—Stationary Sofa Seats.
    double Berths.   G—Kitchen.   O—Refrigerator.
B—Stateroom, with double parlor   H—Luggage Locker.   R—Bath Tub.
    Bed.   I—Car Heater.   S—Pantry Table, making
C—Stateroom, with upper and lower   J—Range.   double bed at night.
    Berths.   K—Fire-Proof Safe.   T—Passage.
D—Ladies' Toilet   L—Silver Locker.   U—Coal Storage.
E—Gentlemen's Toilet.   M—Linen Locker.   W—Private Refrigerator.

For terms, diagrams or other information, apply to

W. H. SHUEY, SUPERINTENDENT, 115 Broadway, New York.

$2. Size of stage, 30x22; size of proscenium opening, 15x22; height from stage to grooves, 15; height from stage to rigging loft, 16; depth under stage, 8, number sets scenery, 3; bill poster, John Reynolds   Newspaper: Graphic (Sat.)......Hotels: Lenox special rates, $1.25; Morton, regular rates, $2 (special also).

HARTFORD, 42,000.   R. R., Hart. & Conn. Val.; Hart. & Conn. West., N. Y. & N. E.: N. Y., N. H. & H.   Robert's Opera House. Wm. H. Roberts. manager; seating capacity, 1,700; share only; license, $5.   Size of stage, 40x80; size of proscenium opening, 42x36; height from stage to grooves, 20; height from stage to rigging loft, 43½; depth under stage, 11. traps, 5; scenery, full set; musical director, J. Blasius; scenic artist, Geo. W. Doylon. stage carpenter, Youman Stebbins; bill poster, David Engle; number of sheets can accommodate, 3,500; rates, 5 cents; theatrical teamster, Edson Sessions. Newspapers: daily, Courant, Post, Times, Telegram; weekly, Journal (Sun.), Globe (Sun.)..... Hotels: Allyn, regular rates, $3 (special also); United States, regular rates, $2.50 to $3 (special also); Park Central, regular rates, $2.50 (special also); City, regular rates $2.50 (special also).

America Theatre (variety), Le Clair & Ferguson, managers; seating capacity, 1,100; rental, one night $30, three $45; license $4; share also.   Size of stage, 22x20; leader of orchestra, Prof. Pearson; scenic artist, Jas. Wylie.

American Theatre, W. S. Ross, manager; seating capacity, 850; license, $1 per week; share also.   Size of stage, 46x23; scenery, full set.

Union Hall, Henry Cornell, manager; seating capacity, 625.

Allyn Hall, Robt Allyn, manager; seating capacity, 1.400.

New National Theatre.

MERIDEN, 25,000.   R. R., New York, New Haven & Hart.   Delavan Opera House, T. H. Delavan, manager; seating capacity, 1,200; rental, one night, $75, three, $200; share also, license included.   Size of stage, 44x70; size of proscenium opening, 31x35; height from stage to grooves, 18; height from stage to rigging loft, 65; depth under stage, 14; traps, 6; number sets scenery, 15; leader of orchestra, H. A. Foster; stage carpenter, John Bags; bill poster, Meriden Opera House Bill Posting Co.; number of sheets can accommodate, 1,000, rate, 4c.; theatrical teamster, Opera Teaming Co.   Newspapers: daily Republican; Press-Recorder..... Hotels: Winthrop, regular rates, $3; Meriden, special rates, $1.50 to $2; Harrison, special rates, $1.50 to $2; City, special rates, $1 50 to $2; Circle, special rates, $1.50 to $2.

City Hall; seating capacity, 1,000; rental, one night. $35.

Circle Hall; seating capacity, 300.

Grand Army Hall ; seating capacity, 400.

MIDDLETOWN, 12,000.   R. R., Hartford & Conn. Valley; N. Y., N. H & H.   McDonough Hall, A. M. Colgrove, manager; seating capacity, 750; rental, one night, $50, license included, share also.   Size of stage, 18x30. number sets scenery, 15; bill poster, A. B. Colgrove.   Newspapers :   daily, Herald; weekly, Constitution (Tu.)......Hotels : McDonough, regular rates, $2 to $2.50 (special also); Kilbourne, regular rates, $2 (special also); Clarendon.

MILFORD, 3,000.   R. R., N. Y., N. H. & H.   Town Hall; bill poster, F. C. Tuthill...... Hotel: Milford, regular rates, $2 (special also.)

MYSTIC, 6,000.   R R., New York, Providence & Boston.   Central Hall; Ira W. Jackson, manager; seating capacity, 700; rental, one night, $16, share also, license, $2; size of stage, 25x30; size of proscenium opening, 18x20; height from stage to grooves, 20; height from stage to rigging loft, 21; depth under stage, 6; trap, 1; number sets scenery, 5; leader of orchestra, F. S. Bidwell; stage carpenter, Oliver Batty, jr.; bill poster, Oliver Batty,ljr.; number of sheets can accommodate, 125; rates, 4c.; theatrical teamster, Henry W. Morgan.   Newspapers: weekly, Press (Th.); advertising rates, 50c. Inch; Journal, (Fr) 50c. inch......Hotel : Hoxey House, special rates, $1.50.

NAUGATUCK, 6,000.   R.R., Naugatuck: N. Y., N. H. & Hart.   Gem Opera House, Jacques & Beardsley, managers; seating capacity, 850; rental one night, $35; share also, license included.   Size of stage, 25x55; size of proscenium opening, 20x28; height from stage to grooves, 14; height from stage to rigging loft, 22; depth under stage, 5; number sets scenery, 10; leader of orchestra, C. Reed; stage carpenter, H. Squires; bill posters, Jacques & Beardsley; number of sheets can accommodate, 500; rates, 4c ; theatrical teamster, W. N. Osborn. Newspapers; Review (Fri.), advertising rates, 75c. an inch; Enter, rise (Fri.). .Hotels : American, special rates, $1.50; Naugatuck, regular rates, $2 (special also).

NEW BRITAIN, 20,000. R. R., N. Y., N. H. & Hart.: N. Y. & N. Eng. New Britain Opera House, John Hanna, manager; seating capacity, 1,000; rental, one night, $50, three , $150; share also; license included. Size of stage, 33x60; size of proscenium opening, 22x29; height from stage to grooves, 18; height from stage to rigging loft, 40 ; depth under stage, 8; traps, 3; **full set** scenery; leader **of orchestra**, Charles Miller; stage carpenter, T. J. Lynch; **bill poster, J. J. Spears; number of** sheets can accommodate, **800; rates, 5c.; theatrical teamster, J. J. Spears. Newspapers: daily,** Herald, **advertising rates, yearly contract; semi-weekly, Herald (Tu. & Th.); weekly, Observer (Tu.), advertising rates, $1 an inch; Record (Fri.), advertising rates, $1 an inch** .....Hotels: **Strickland, special rates, $1.50; Bassett, special rates, $2; Humphrey, special rates, $1.50.**

Turner Hall, William Siering, manager; seating capacity, 800; rental, one night, $25; **license, $3; share also.** Size of stage, 16x47; number sets scenery, 10.

NEW HAVEN, 70,000. R.R., N. Y., N. H. & Hart.; Shore **Line; Air** Line; N. H. & Northampton. Carll's Opera House, P. R. Carll, manager; **seating** capacity, 2,500; rental, one night, $150; share also. Size of stage, 70x75; size of proscenium opening, 42x36; height from stage to grooves, 25 (adjustable); height from stage to rigging loft, 80; depth under stage, 25; stage all traps, sinks and bridges; scenery, complete stock; musical director, S.A.Wass; bill poster, Jas. Blakeslee; theatrical teamsters, Smedley Bros. & Co., Beck & Bishop. Newspapers; daily, Register, advertising rates, $1.50 per inch; Journal and Courier, rates, same; News, rates, same; Palladium, rates, same; Union, rates, same ...... Hotels: Elliott, special rates, $1.25 to $4; **Tremont,** special rates, $1.25 to $4; Austin, special rates, $1.25 to $2.

New Haven Opera House, Horace Wall, manager; seating capacity, 1,200; rental, share **only,** license included. Size of stage, 70x74; size of proscenium opening, 23x34; height from stage to grooves, 21; height from stage to rigging loft, 42; depth under stage, 16; traps, all necessary; number sets scenery, 20; musical director, A. P. Mallon; stage carpenter, H. Nicholson.

Grand Opera House, Clark Peck; manager; seating capacity, 1,000; rental, one night, $70, three, $180, license included. Size of stage, 42x80; full set scenery.

Athenæum, seating capacity, 600.

American Theatre.

Loomis's Temple of Music, seating capacity, 400.

NEW LONDON, 12,000. R. R., New London, Norwich; New York, Providence & Boston. New York, New Haven & Hartford. Laurence Hall, Laurence & Co., managers; seating capacity, 1,100; rental, one night, $35, share also. Size of stage, 23x33½; height from stage to rigging loft, 16; number sets scenery, 5; bill poster, Wm. J. Adams; number of sheets can accommodate, 300; rate, 5c. Newspapers: daily, Day; advertising rates per inch, 75c.; Telegram, advertising rates per inch, 75c.; weekly, Week **(Th.),** advertising rates per inch, 50c.,......Hotels : Crocker, regular rates, $2.50 to $3 (special rates also); Metropolitan (adjoining Hall), regular rates, $2; Central, Bacon, regular rates, $2 (special also).

Arion Hall, seating capacity, 500.

Allyn Hall, seating capacity, 600.

Music Hall, James A. Wilkinson, manager; seating capacity, 1,000.

NEW MILFORD, 3,900. R. R., Housatonic. Town Hall, **seating capacity,** 800; rental, one **night, $20; number sets scenery, 4; bill poster, C. M. Booth. Newspaper:** Gazette (F.) ......Hotels New England, regular rates, $2 (special also); **New Milford.**

NEWTOWN, 4,000. R. R., Housatonic; New York **& New England.** Sanford's Hall, Henry **Sanford, manager;** rental, one night, $8; seating capacity, 300. Newspaper : Bee (Fri.) ......Hotels : Grand Central, regular rates, $2 (special also).

NORFOLK, 1,500. R. R., Hartford & Connecticut Western. Village Hall, J. N. Cowles and R. I. Cossey, managers; seating capacity, 500; rental, one night, $10, share also, no license. Size of stage, 12x35; number sets scenery, 4..... Hotel : Stevens House.

NORWALK, 14,000. R. R., Danbury & Norwalk. Opera House, S. K. Stanley, manager; seating capacity, 900; rental, one night, $25, three, $55, license included. Size of stage, 24 x 36; number sets scenery, 12; bill poster, J. F. Buxton. Newspapers : Gazette (Tu.); Advertiser (Sat.)

NORWICH, 22,000. R. R., New London Northern; Norwich & Worcester. Breed Hall, Wm. M. Williams, manager; seating capacity, 1,000; rental, one night $20; three $75; license, $5; share also. Size of stage, 35x36; height from stage to grooves, adjustable; height from stage to rigging loft, 25; depth under stage, 4; traps, 2; number sets scenery, 4. Musical director, Chas. A. Yeager. Bill posters, Andrews & Roath; number of sheets can accommodate, 400; rates, 5c. Theatrical teamster, Henry Kelley. Newspapers: daily, Bulletin, advertising rates per inch, $1; weekly, Courier (Wed.), $1; Cooley's Weekly (Fri.), People's Gazette (Fri.).... Hotels: Wauregan, special rates, $1.50 to $2; American, special rates, $1; Union Square, $1.50 to $2.

Franklyn Hall, seating capacity, 500.

Town Hall, seating capacity, 800.

Treadway Hall, seating capacity, 600.

PLAINVILLE, 1,930. R. R., N. H. & Northampton; N. Y. & New England. Morgan's Hall, W. P. Morgan, manager; seating capacity, 450; rental, one night, $10. Bill poster. F. C. White. Newspaper: News (Th.)...... Hotels: Allderige, regular rates, $2 (special also); Eagle.

Newton's Hall.

PORTLAND, 5,000. R. R., N. Y., N. H. & Hartford. Waverly Hall, W. W. Coe, manager; seating capacity, 350; rental, one night, $8, no license. Size of stage, 20x25; number sets scenery, 3. Bill poster, Lewis Haling..... Hotel : Edwards, regular rates, $2 (special also).

PUTNAM, 5,827. R. R., N. Y. & N. Eng. Union Hall, A. F. Leach, manager; seating capacity, 800; rental, one night, $25, license included. Size of stage, 27x50; number sets scenery, 7. Bill poster, A. F. Leach. Theatrical teamster, Albert A. Mason. Newspapers: Patriot (Fri.), Sunbeam (Wed.).. Hotels: Bigbee, regular rates, $2 (special also); Elm Street and Commercial.

ROCKVILLE, 7,000. R. R., New York & New England. Henry Hall, E. S. Henry, manager; seating capacity, 700; rental, one night $40, license included; share also; local and sharing agents, Bolton & Foote, box 447; musical director, D. E. Barnard; scenic artist, Charles Wood, theatrical teamsters Rodgers & Doolan; bill poster, James Burton. Newspapers: Leader (Th.), advertising rates, 75c. per inch: Journal (Fri.), $1..... Hotels: Rockville, regular rates, $2 (special also), Brooklyn.

Opera House, C. White, manager; rental, one night $15; seating capacity, 780; number sets scenery, 5; theatrical teamsters, Rodgers & Doolan.

SOUTHINGTON, 5,411. R. R., New Haven & Northampton. Town Hall, C. D. Barnes, manager; seating capacity, 700; rental, one night, $20, no license; size of stage, 18x22; bill poster, George Bristoll; theatrical teamsters, Deney & Lewis. Newspapers: Phoenix (Fri.) ....Hotels : Bradley, regular rates, $2 (special also), Ocean.

SOUTH MANCHESTER, 3,500. R. R., New York & New England. Cheney's Hall, R. O. Cheney, manager ; seating capacity, 800 ; fair stock scenery. Newspaper : Herald.

SOUTH NORWALK, 1,800. R. R., Danbury & Norwalk; N. Y., N. H. & Hartford. Music Hall, F. M. Knapp, manager; seating capacity, 1,100; rental, one night, $40, three, $100, share also; size of stage, 25x60; full set of scenery; bill poster, John Buxton. .... Newspapers : Republican (Sat.), Sentinel (Th.)...... Hotels : Mahackemo, regular rates, $2 (special also), City, Warwick.

SPRAGUE, 3,500. R. R., New York & New England (Baltic station). Sprague Hall, H. L. Aldrich, manager; seating capacity, 600; rental, one night, $30, three, $80; size of stage, 30x40; size of proscenium opening, 10x10. ....Hotel : Baltic, special rates, $1.50.

STAFFORD, 6,000. R. R., New London, Northern. Central Hall. F. H. Bate, manager; seating capacity, 400; rental, one night $12.50, three $30, share also; license included. Size of stage, 18x30 ; size of proscenium opening, 9x24; height from stage to grooves, 10; height from stage to rigging loft, 12; depth under stage, 3; number sets scenery, 5; leader of orchestra, J. W. Dimock; stage carpenter, H. M. Day; bill poster, Gary Brothers; theatrical teamster, Gary Brothers. Newspaper: Press (Th.) .....Hotels : Stafford Springs, regular rates, $2 (special also), Central.

STAMFORD, 1,300. R. R., New Canaan, New York, New Haven & Hartford. Town Hall, S. C. Waterbury, manager; seating capacity, 1,500; rental, one night $40, three $80; license, $3. Size of stage, 35x60; height from stage to grooves, 16; number sets scenery, 6; bill poster, A. Brown; number of sheets can accommodate, 300. Newspapers: Advocate (Fri.), Comet (Sat.). Herald (Wed.).....Hotels : Stamford, regular rates, $2. Union.

STONINGTON, 4,000. R. R., New York, Providence & Boston; Stonington line of steamers. Borough Hall, James Penderton, manager; seating capacity, 600; share only ; license included. Size of stage, 12x60 ; size of proscenium opening, 18x30; number sets scenery, 5; bill poster, D. D. Burtch; number of sheets can accommodate, 240 ; theatrical teamster, A. A. Dewey. Newspaper : Mirror (Sat.)......Hotels : Wadawanuck, regular rates, $2 (special also), Ocean, special rates, $1.25.

Music Hall, O. F. Pendleton, manager; seating capacity, 100; rental, one night $7; license, $3. Size of stage, 21x14.

THOMPSONVILLE, 4,300. R. R., New York, New Haven & Hartford. Franklyn Hall, B. F. Lord, manager; seating capacity, 600; rental, one night, $15; share also. Size of stage, 18x18; number sets of scenery, 4; bill poster, B. F. Lord. Theatrical teamster, S. Hood. Newspaper: Press (Th.).......Hotel: Thompsonville.

TORRINGTON, 4,000. R.R., Naugatuck. Granite Hall, Chas. McNeil, manager; seating capacity, 400; rental, one night, $13; three, $33, license included; share also. Size of stage, 14x24; number sets of scenery, 4; bill poster, F. R. Matthews; number of sheets can accommodate, 125. Theatrical teamster, T. G. Alldis. Newspaper: Register (Sat.)......Hotels: Allen, American.

WALLINGFORD, 6,000. R. R., New York, New Haven and Hartford. Town Hall; seating capacity, 400; rental, one night, $10; three, $24; no license. Size of stage, 15x30. Bill poster, Edward Allen. Newspaper. Forum (Sat.) .....Hotels: Hoff: regular rates, $2 (special also); Wooster, Ingraham. ,

WATERBURY, 21,000. R. R., Naugatuck; New York & New England. City Hall, Jean Jacques, manager; seating capacity, 1,300; rental, one night $60, three $175; license, $5; share also. Size of stage, 35x30; height from stage to grooves, 15; height from stage to rigging loft, 20; number sets scenery, 12; bill posters, Partree & Barker; theatrical teamsters, Partree & Barker. Newspapers: daily, American, Republican; weekly, Democrat (Sat.)..... Hotels : Scoville; regular rates, $2.50 (special also); Park, Francklyn, regular rates. $2 (special also).

Irving Hall, H. P. Corry, manager; seating capacity, 600; rental, one night $20, no license; size of stage, 15x30.

WEST MERIDEN, 20,000. R. R., New York, New Haven & Hartford. Opera House, C. S. Perkins, manager, seating capacity: 1,000 ; rental, one night $60; share also; license included. Size of stage, 70x45; number sets scenery, 12; bill posters, Delevan & Spears. Newspapers; daily, Republican, Recorder......Hotels: Meriden, Bixbee.

WESTPORT, 3,477. R. R., New York. New Haven & Hartford. National Hall; seating capacity, 600; rental one night, $8. Newspaper: Westporter (Sat.)..... Hotel: Westport.

WILLIMANTIC, 11,000. R. R., New York & New England; New London & Northern; N. Y., N. H. & Hartford. Loomer Opera House, S. F. Loomer, manager; seating capacity, 1,100; bill poster, J. H. Gray; number sheets can accommodate, 1,500; theatrical teamster, J. H. Gray. Newspapers: Journal (Fri.), advertising rates, 75c. per inch; Chronicle (Wed.), advertising rates, 75c. per inch .. ...Hotels: Brainard, special rates, $1.50

to $2; Commercial, $1.50 to $2; Revere, $1.50 to $1.25; **Enropean, $1.** Pay days, 15th to to 20th of each month at mills and shops.

Franklin Hall, J. H. Gray, manager; seating capacity, 700.

Franklyn Hall, Alpaugh and Hooper, managers; seating capacity, **600.**

WINSTED, 7,000. R. R., Hartford & Conn.; West Naugatuck. Winsted Opera House, **J.** E. Spaulding, manager; seating capacity, 1,200; rental, one night $25; license, $3. Size of stage, 26x50; number sets scenery, 8; bill poster, D. C. Andrews; number sheets can accommodate, 100; theatrical teamster, W. P. Jones. Newspapers: Argus (Sat.), Press (Th.).... Hotels: Clarke, regular, $2 (special also); Winsted, Beardley

COLORADO.

BOULDER, 5,000. R. R., Union Pacific; Den. & Rio Grande. Berlin's Hall, Berlin & Co., managers; seating capacity, 500; rental, one night $20, three $30; license, $5. Size of stage, 20x50; size of proscenium opening, 12x25; height from stage to grooves, 14 ; number sets scenery, 6; bill poster, Joe Campbell; name of theatrical teamster, Harris & Wilson. Newspapers: daily, Herald; weekly, Banner (Tu.), Sentinel (Fr.)......Hotels: American, special rates, $1; Brainard's, regular, $2 to $2.50 (special also).

Union Hall, A. J. Mackey, manager; seating capacity, 400; rental, one night, $10; three, $25; license, $20 per week; share also.

BUENA VISTA, 3,000. R.R., Denver & Rio Grande; Union Pacific. Opera House, E. H. Hiller, manager; seating capacity, 300; rental, one night $20, three $45; license, $3 to $5. **Size of** stage, 20x30; number sets scenery, 8; bill poster, McWilson. Newspapers: **Times (F.), Herald** (Th.)......Hotels: **Lake,** regular rates, $3; Grand Park.

CANON CITY, 2,500. R. R., Denver & Rio Grande. **Blake's Hall, H.** T. Blake, manager; seating capacity, 275; rental, one night, **$25; three, $60; license,** $5. Size of stage, 16x30; fair stock scenery. Newspapers: Gazette **(Sat.), Record** (Sat.), Reporter (Th.) ....Hotels : McClure, regular, $2.50; Victoria, Turner

CENTRAL CITY, 3,000 (suburbs **3,000 more).** R. R., Colorado **Central, branch of U. P. R.** R. Central Opera House, H. M. Hale, manager; seating capacity, 800; rental one night, $40, three $100, share also; license included. Size of stage 40x50 ; size of proscenium opening, 25x25; height from stage to grooves, 20; height from stage to rigging loft, 40; depth **under** stage, 10; number sets scenery, 8 ; leader of orchestra, Albert Lintz ; bill poster, Opera House; number of sheets can accommodate, 400; rates per sheet, 5c. News **paper:** daily, Register Call, advertising rates per inch, $2, line 30c. Hotels : Teller, special rates, $2 to $2.50; Granite.

City Hall, seating capacity, 300.

Belvidere, rental, $15.

COLORADO SPRINGS, 7,000. R. R., Denver & New Orleans; Denver & Rio Grande. Opera House, A. S. Welch, manager; full stock scenery; bill poster, J. W. Sullivan. Newspapers: daily, Gazette, Republic.. ...Hotels: Springs, National.

DENVER, 70,000. R. R., Union Pac.; Den. & Rio Grande; Bur. & Mo.; Den., Mo. & Or ; Union Pac. Tabor Grand Opera House, Peter McComb, manager; seating capacity, 1,500; rental, share only. Size of stage, 45x75; size of proscenium opening, 31x33; height from stage to grooves, 20; height from stage to rigging **loft,** 60; depth under stage, 12; traps, 6, and 2 bridges; number sets scenery, 50. Musical director, E. O. Wolff; stage carpenter, J. C. Alexander; **bill poster,** J. A. Reed; number of sheets can accommodate, 1000. Theatrical teamsters, Denver Transfer Co. Newspapers: **daily, News,** advertising rates, 50c. square; Republican, advertising rates, 50c. square ; **Times 4cc. square;** weekly, Opinion (Sat.), Inter-Ocean, (Sat.)...... Hotels Windsor, **rates to profession,** $2.50 to $5.00; St. James, $2 to $4; Charpiots, $1.50 to $2.50

Academy of Music, McFadden Bros., managers; seating capacity, 1,150 ; **share** only. Size of stage, 40x69; size of proscenium opening, 30x33; height from stage to grooves, 20; height from stage to rigging loft, 52; depth under stage, 8; traps, 1 vampire; full stock scenery; musical director, Koenigsburg; scenic artist, Berky ; stage carpenter, Chas.

McGuire; bill posting done by house; number of sheets can accommodate 1,500; rates per sheet, 4c.; theatrical teamster, Denver Transfer Co.

Grand Opera House, W. S. Morse, manager; seating capacity, 1,500; share only; size of stage, 45x70; number sets scenery, 40. Bill poster, Opera House.

Turner Hall, seating capacity, 900; small stage.

Palace Theatre, Chase & Co., managers.

Armory Hall.

Standard Hall.

FORT COLLINS, 3,000. R. R., Colorado Div. U. P. S. G. S. L. & P. Ft. Collins Opera House, Jay H. Boughton, Manager; seating capacity, 1,000; rental, one night $35, three $75, license, included share also. Size of stage, 30x40; size of proscenium opening, 19x20; height from stage to grooves, 14; height from stage to rigging loft, 20; depth under stage, 6; number sets scenery, 12; bill poster, Opera House; number of sheets can accommodate, 300; rates per sheet, 4c; theatrical teamster, John Douglas. Newspapers: weekly, Courier (Wed.), Express, (Th.).... Hotels: Commercial, regular rates, $2 (special also), Windsor.

GEORGETOWN, 5,000. R. R., Union Pacific. McClellan Opera House, Mrs. Catherine McClellan, manager; seating capacity, 1,000; rental one night, $20, three $50. Size of stage, 30x50. Newspapers: Miner (Sat.), Courier (Th.)..... Hotels: De Paris, regular rates, $3; Barton, American, Phelps, Yates.

GOLDEN CITY, 3,000. R. R., Union Pacific. Opera House, —. Ackert, manager; seating capacity, 400; rental, one night, $20, license included; fair stock scenery. Newspapers: Transcript (Wed.), Globe (Sat.) ....Hotels: Garhorew, regular rates, $3 (special also); Babcock, Golden, Astor.

GREELEY, 3,000. R. R., Union Pacific; G. S. L. & P. Jackson's Opera House, H. B. Jackson, manager; seating capacity, 400; rental one night, $20; three nights, $45, share also; license, $5. Size of stage, 18x30; size of proscenium opening, 13x18; height from stage to grooves, 12; height from stage to rigging loft, 14; number sets scenery, 3; leader of orchestra, George W Fisk; bill poster, R. S. Ferguson; theatrical teamster, James Beetham. Newspapers: Sabine (Wed.), Sun (Tues.), Howitzer (Th.)...... Hotels: Oasis, special rates, $2; Exchange, special rates, $1.25 to $2; Colorado House, special rates, $1.25 to $2.

GUNNISON, 5,000. R. R., Denver & Rio Grande. Opera House, Smart & Mullen, managers; seating capacity, 650; rental, one night, $50; three, $135, share also. Size of stage 16x35; number sets scenery, 8. Newspapers: daily, News-Democrat; Review, Press; weekly, Sun (Sat.)..... Hotels: Mullen, Tabor, Dawson.

LEADVILLE, 20,000. R. R., Denver & Rio Grande; South Park Branch of U. P. Tabor Opera House, J. H. Cragg, manager; seating capacity, 800; share only. Size of stage, 34x60; size of proscenium opening, 17x22; height from stage to grooves, 16; height from stage to rigging loft, 19; depth under stage, 4½; traps, 3; number sets scenery, 12; musical director, John Parker; scenic artist, Burkey, of Tabor Grand, Denver; stage carpenter, H. C. Sprague; bill posters, John Coleman & Co.; number of sheets can accommodate, 500; rates per sheet, 4c.; theatrical teamsters, Scott & Allen Transfer Co. Newspapers: daily, Herald, advertising rates, per inch, $1; Chronicle, Democrat; weekly, News (M.)..... Hotels: Clarendon, special rates, $1.50 to $3.00; Grand, special rates, $1.25 to $1.50; Windsor, regular rates, $2.50 (special also); St. James, Fremont, American, Charipiet's, Lindell, Alvord and Metropolitan.

National (variety), Mike Goldsmith, manager.

Bella Union (variety), James Duffy, manager.

PUEBLO, 4,000. R. R., Atch., Top. & S. Fe; Den. & New Or.; Den. & Rio Grande. Opera House, C. D. Montgomery, manager; seating capacity, 700; fair stock scenery; bill poster, G. C. Budd. Newspapers: daily, Chieftan; weekly, Commercial Standard (Sat.) ... Hotels: Numa, regular rates, $3 (special also), Lindell, Grand Central, Victoria, Pacific, Commercial, National.

Chillicothe Hall, G. W. Perkins & Co., managers; seating capacity, 400; rental, one night, $20. Size of stage, 13x28.

New Opera House.

James O. Barrows,

LEADING COMEDY,

Aimee English Comedy Company.

Permanent Address:

SIMMONDS & BROWN,

1166 Broadway, New York.

Mr. H. M. PITT.

THE RAJAH.

TRIUMPHANT SUCCESS

FROM MASSACHUSETTS TO CALIFORNIA.

"The best actor of his kind the Madison Square Theatre Management has sent us."—*San Francisco Daily Examiner.*

Disengaged Season 1885 and 1886.

Address: MADISON SQUARE THEATRE.

SILVER CLIFF, 5,000. R. R., Den. & Rio Grande. Roberts Hall, seating capacity, 400. Newspapers: Tribune (Sat.), Herald.

TRINIDAD, 3,000. R. R., Atch., Top. & S. Fe; Den., Rio Grande. Jaffa's Opera House, Jaffa Bros., managers; seating capacity, 800; rent only. Size of stage, 24x30; size of proscenium opening, 24x30; number sets scenery, 8; bill poster, J. S. Lawson. Newspapers: daily, News, Advertiser......Hotels: Grand Union, regular rates, $4 to $4 (special also), United States, Trinidad, Baker.

Mitchell's Hall, E. F. Mitchell, manager; seating capacity, 250; rental, one night, $20; three $50; license, $5, share also. Size of stage, 18x30; number sets scenery, 2.

DELAWARE.

DELAWARE CITY, 1,500. R. R., Phil., Wil. & Balt. (via Porters); Newark & Delaware City. Eagle Hall, H. F. Mullin, manager; seating capacity, 250; rental, one night $5; two, $8; license, none. Size of stage, 10x18; height from stage to grooves, 16; height from stage to rigging loft, 20; depth under stage, or cellar, 4; theatrical teamster, Jester. ......Hotels: Kidd's, special rates, $1; Bradway's, special rates, $1, Delaware City.

DOVER, 3,600. R. R., Phila., Wil. & Balt. Culbarth's Hall; seating capacity, 200. Newspapers: Delawarean (Sat.), Sentinel (Sat.)......Hotels: Capital, regular rates, $1.50 (special also); Delaware.

MIDDLETOWN, 2,000. R. R., Phil., Wil. & Balt. Middletown Hall, J. R. Hall, manager; seating capacity, 500; rental, one night, $15. Size of stage, 15x60; number sets scenery, 3; bill poster, J. W. Makens; theatrical teamster, J. W. Hayes. Newspapers: Transcript (Fri.)......Hotels: National, Middletown.

WILMINGTON, 50,000. R. R., Phil., Wil. & Balt.; Wil. & North; Balt. & Phil. Grand Opera House, Jesse K. Bayles, Manager; seating capacity, 1,404; rental one night, $75; three $225, license yearly; share also. Size of stage, 45x75; size of proscenium opening, 33x40; height from stage to grooves, 20; height from stage to rigging loft, 38; depth under stage, 10; traps, 4; well stocked with scenery; musical director, Tule Reybold; scenic artist, Chas. J. Hawthorne; stage carpenter, I. A. Righter; bill poster, George W. Jackson; rates per sheet, 4c. theatrical teamster, Jos. H. Seal; Newspapers: daily, Republican, advertising rates per line, 6c.; Every Evening, advertising rates per line, 6c.; News, advertising rates per line, 6c.; Commercial, advertising rates per line, 6c. .....Hotels: Clayton, Grand Opera, Lafayette, Delaware, United States, European.

Institute Hall, seating capacity, 800.

Masonic Hall, seating capacity, 1400.

Odd Fellows Hall, seating capacity, 600.

DISTRICT OF COLUMBIA.

WASHINGTON, 200,000. R R., B. & O.; B. & Pot.; Pennsylvania; Virginia Midland; Richmond & Fredericksburg. National Theatre, Rapley & Kinsley, managers; seating capacity, 1,600; share only; license included; size of stage, 48x80; size of proscenium opening, 45x45; height from stage to grooves, 20; height from stage to rigging loft, 56; depth under stage, 5½; traps, all necessary; full complement of scenery; musical director, Chris Arth; scenic artist. E. W. Carpenter; stage carpenter, W. A. T. Phillips; bill poster, Lloyd Moxley; rates per sheet, 3c.; theatrical teamster, George Knox. Newspapers: daily, Post, advertising rates, special contract; Republican, rates, same; Star and Critic, rates same; weekly, Herald, Post, Republic, Capital, Gazette, Chronicle.......Hotels: National, special rates, $1.50, to $2; Riggs, Ebbitt, Arlington, Metropolitan

Lincoln Hall; A. S. Pratt & Sons, manager; seating capacity, 1,000; rental one night $75; three, $200, license included. Size of stage, 25x35; no scenery.

Willard's Hall; seating capacity, 800; rental one night $35, three $75; license, $5. Size of stage, 25x40; number sets scenery, 3.

Theatre Comique, Thomas E. Snellbaker, manager: **seating** capacity, 2,200; share only. Size of stage, 32x40; full sets scenery.

New Washington Theatre, Jake Budd, manager.

Arlington Theatre, Thomas Hickey, manager.

Ford's Opera House, John T. Ford, manager: **share only: full stock scenery.**

Driver's Summer Garden, George W. Driver, manager.

Grand Opera House, J. W. Albaugh, manager.

Odd Fellows Hall, seating capacity, 1,000.

Marine's Hall.

Tallmadge Hall.

FLORIDA.

FERNANDINA, 2,800. R. R., Florida Transit. Lyceum Hall, **G. Stark, manager; seating capacity, 400; rental, one night $15,** three $30. **Size of stage, 22x39; number sets scenery, 4.** Newspaper: **Mirror (Sat)....** Hotels: Egmont, Mansion, Strathmore, **Florida Dell.**

GAINESVILLE, 5,000 (in Winter, 8,000). R. R., Savannah, Florida & Western; Florida Southern; Florida Transit. Simonson's Opera House, John J. Liesuer, manager; seating capacity, 1,000; rental, share only, license included. Size of stage, 27x20; depth under stage, 4; number sets scenery, 6. Newspapers : daily, Advocate, advertising rates per inch, $1; weekly, Plaindealer (W), advertising rates per **inch,** $1. Hotels : Arlington, special **rates,** $1.50; Magnolia, special rates, $1.

Opera House. **Size of stage,** 20x18; **number** sets scenery, 2.

JACKSONVILLE, 18,000 **(in Winter, 35,000).** R. R., Savannah, Florida & Western; South Florida; Florida R'y **& Navigation Co.** Park Theatre, J. C. Carlisle, manager; seating capacity, 1,300; share only. Size **of** stage, 28x60; size of proscenium opening, 22x22; height from stage to grooves, **16;** height from stage **to** rigging loft, 19; depth under stage, 7½; traps, 4; number **sets** scenery, 10; scenic artist, Henry Bennett; stage carpenter, L Dingy; bill poster, **P.** McMurray; number of sheets can accomodate, 150; rates per sheet, 4c.; theatrical teamster, M. L. Bartridge. Newspapers : daily, Times-Union, advertising rates per inch, $1; Herald, advertising rates per inch. $1; weekly, Times-Union (Sun.) Hotels : St. James, special rates, $1 to $3; Everett, $1 to $3; Windsor, $1 to $3.

Grand Opera House, **Lowden &** Donnard, managers; **seating capacity, 1,200. Size of stage, 45x60; full set scenery.**

Polk's Hall, J. F. Gilbert, manager; seating capacity, 600; **rental, one night $25, three** $50. **Size of stage,** 25x35; number sets scenery, 5.

Metropolitan Hall, J. B. Tongui, manager; seating capacity, 650; license, $20; number **sets** scenery, 5.

National Hall, seating capacity, 600.

LAKE CITY, 1,800. R. R., Florida R'y & Navigation Co.; Florida & Western. Cleveland's Hall, S. Boteler Thompson, manager; seating capacity, 200; rental, one night $15, two $25; license, 15. Size of stage, 14x19; size of proscenium opening, 8x17; number sets scenery, 5; leader of orchestra, Ferd. Waltz; bill poster at Hall; theatrical teamsters, Baya & Moodie, Cone & Hardon. Newspapers : Reporter (Fri), advertising rates per inch, $1; Star (Th), advertising rates per inch, $1...... Hotels: Thrasher, special rates, $1.50; Borum, special rates, $1.50; Chicago, special rates, $1.50.

MONTICELLO, 1,300. R. R., Florida Central & Western. Lyon's Hall, G. W. Lyons, manager; seating capacity, 300; rental one night, $10. Newspaper: Constitution...... Hotels: Monticello; Porter; Madden.

PALATKA, 1,600. R. R., Florida Southern; Jack., Tam. **& Key West. New** Opera House, **J. E.** Rider, manager.

PENSACOLA, 7,000. R. R., Pensacola & Atlantic; Pensacola & Perdido. Opera House, E. **A. Hamilton, manager;** bill poster, L. A. Andrews. Newspapers: semi-weekly, Advance-Gazette, Commercial ...... Hotels: Continental, regular rates, $3 (special also) ; European, regular rates, $2, (special also); Merchants; Santa Rosa. Powell. City.

Odd Fellows Hall; seating capacity, 750.

Germania Hall; seating capacity, 1 000.

Sullivan's Opera House.

Bay View Varieties.

ST. AUGUSTINE, 2,400. R. R., Jack. St. A. & H. R.; St. John's. Long's Hall, Jno. G. Long, manager; seating capacity, 350; rental one night, $15; license, $10; no scenery. Newspapers: Press (Sat.); St. Johns Weekly (F.)... .... Hotels: St. Augustine; Florida.

TALLAHASSE, 2,500. R. R., Florida Central & Western. Galile's Hall, A. Galile, manager; seating capacity, 400; rental one night, $10; license, city and county, $10; number sets scenery, 4. Newspapers: Economist (Sat); [Floridian (Tu.) .... Hotels: Leon, regular $3 (special also); City.

GEORGIA.

ALBANY, 3,500. R. R., Bruns. & Western; Sav., Fla. & West.; South Western. Willingham's Hall, T. H. Willingham, manager; seating capacity, 500; rental one night, $25; three, $55; license, $2.50. Size of stage, 20x47; number sets scenery, 7; bill poster, Wm. Lewis. Newspaper: daily, Advertiser ...... Hotels: Bogen, regular, $2, (special also); Commercial; Barnes.

AMERICUS, 3,700. RR., South Western. Opera House, Glover & Perry, managers; seating capacity, 850; rental one night, $40; three $100, license included, share also. Size of stage, 30x15; number sets scenery, 10; bill poster, Opera House. Newspapers: tri-weekly, Recorder; semi-weekly, Republican ...... Hotels: Barlow, regular, $2 (special also); Perry. Commercial.

City Hall, J. E. Hall, manager; seating capacity, 400; rental one night, $20; license, $5 to $10. Size of stage, 15x30.

ATHENS, 7,000. R. R., Georgia. Deupree Opera House, W. C. Jones, manager; seating capacity, 900; rental one night, $40, three $100, license included, share also. Size of stage 30x30; fair stock scenery; bill poster. W. H. Jones. Newspapers: daily, Banner Watchman; weekly, Chronicle (Fri.), Record (Tu.) .... Hotels: Commercial, regular rates $2.50 (special also); Clinard, regular rates, $2 (special also), Clifford, Newton.

Derby's Hall, A. Evans, manager ; seating capacity, 300; rental one night $45, license included; fair stock scenery.

ATLANTA, 50,000. Eight railroads' termini, Atl. & W. Pt.: Cen. of Ga.. E Tenn., Va., G.: Ga. R. R.; Ga. Pac.; Rich. & Dan.; Western & Atlantic. Opera House, L. de Give, manager; seating capacity, 2,000; share only, license included. Size of stage, 40x67; size of proscenium opening, 32x34; height from stage to grooves, 19; height from stage to rigging loft; 42: depth under stage, 6; traps, 3; number sets scenery, full set; leader of orchestra, Alfred Wurm ; Stage carpenter, Arthur Swoope ; bill posters, Kress & Dooley; number of sheets can accommodate, 7,500, rates, 4 c ; theatrical teamster, Captain Ballard's Baggage Transfer Co.. Newspapers: daily, Constitution, adv. rates $1 per inch; Journal, rates, $1 per inch; weekly, Record (Sun.), rates, $1 per inch; Mail (Mon). rates. $1 per inch; Georgia Cracker (Sun.), rates, $1 per inch.. ...Hotels: Kimbal, special rates, $1.50; Markham, special rates, $1.50; National, special rates, $1.50; Weinmeister, special rates, $1.50.

Concordia Hall; seating capacity, 500; small stage; number sets scenery, 3.

AUGUSTA, 35,000. R. R., Georgia; Cent. of Ga.; Port Royal; Aug., South Carolina & Charlotte; A. & K. Masonic Theatre, S. H. Cohen, manager; seating capacity, 1,500; rental, one night $80, three, $200; share also; no license. Size of stage, 50x40; size of proscenium opening, 30x30; height from stage to grooves, 18; height from stage to rigging loft, 40: depth under stage, 10; traps, 3; number sets scenery, 25; leader of orchestra, Wiegand; Scenic artist. Phil. Green; stage carpenter, Wm. Hughes; bill poster, Theatre; teamster, Transfer Co. Newspapers: daily, Chronicle, adv. rates, per inch $1; News. rates.

Hotel Palace,

SPRINGFIELD, ILL.

D. J. BLOCK, Proprietor.
Cor. 4th and Washington Streets.

Headquarters for first-class theatrical troupes. Most convenient to Opera House. Special rates to the profession.

International Hotel,

European plan.

Rates, . . $1 per day.

Next door to Park and opposite Globe Theatres,

BOSTON,   MASS.

City Hotel,

PROVIDENCE, R. I.

This hotel, under its new management, has been newly furnished and refitted, and we make a special rate to the profession from $1.25 to $1.50 per day; located near the theatres and depot.

J. S. DOYLE, Lessee.

James Phelan Cuddy,

THEATRICAL AGENT,

(Variety, Dramatic and Musical Departments.)

Editor and Publisher
THE AMERICAN ACTOR,
A Monthly Publication.

Residence,
511 Clinton St., BROOKLYN, N. Y.

Jos. E. Nicol,

MUSICAL DIRECTOR,

Aimee English Comedy Co.

Address:
SIMMONDS & BROWN,
or 22 Vanauden St.,
Auburn, N. Y.

Fred. A. Dunwick.

BUSINESS MANAGER AND TREASURER.

Press and Advance Agent.

GLENS FALLS,
Warren County,
New York.

Al. K. Feeley,

STAGE MANAGER

Aimee English Comedy Co.

Permanent address:
SIMMONDS & BROWN,
1166 Broadway,
New York.

Harry Oliver,

BUSINESS AGENT
with
ATHLETIC BASE BALL CLUB,
Season 1884, re-engaged for season 1885.

Permanent address:
204 North 8th St.,
Philadelphia, Pa.

75c. per inch...... ...Hotels : Planters', special rates, $1.50 to $2 ; Augusta, special rates, $1.50 to $2; Globe, special rates $1.50 to $2.

Augusta Opera House, N. K. Butler, manager; seating capacity, 800, rental —— share also.

BAINBRIDGE, 15,000. R. R., Sav., Fla. & Western Court House. S. F. Burkett, manager; seating capacity, 400; rental, one night, $5; license, $5; bill poster, Jack Cold, Newspaper: Democrat (Th.), ...Hotels : Sharon, Innes.

BARNESVILLE, 2,000. R. R., Central of Georgia. Granite Hall, Stafford Blalock & Co. managers; seating capacity, 600; rental, one night $16, three $40; license included; share also. Size of stage, 24x10; bill poster, Scott Fletcher. Newspapers : Gazette (Th.), News (Sat.) .... Hotels : Lyon, Logan.

BRUNSWICK, 3,000. R. R. Brunswick & Western; East Tennessee; Virginia & Georgia. L'Ariosa Hall, E. J. Coney, manager; seating capacity, 600; rental one night, $20 ; two, $35 ; license, $2.50; share also. Size of stage, 20x10; number sets scenery, 12; bill poster, Robert Bailey. Newspapers : Advertiser (Sat.) .....Hotels: Nelson, regular rates, $2 to $2.50; (special also): Mansion.

Finny's Hall, J. E. DuBeqna, manager ; seating capacity, 300 ; rental one night, $15; license, $10. Size of Stage, 15x18; number sets scenery, 3.

McCromn's Hall; seating capacity, 200.

Dillon's Hall; seating capacity, 200.

CARTERSVILLE, 3,000. R. R., East & W. R. R. of Ala ; Western & Atlantic. City Opera House; seating capacity, 600; rental, one night, $15; license included. Size of stage, 25x28; number sets scenery, 4. Newspapers: American (Tri.), Free Press (Th). ......Hotel : St. James.

COLUMBUS, 12,000. R. R., Col. & Rome; Col. & West.; Mobile & Ga.; So. Western. Springer Opera House; seating capacity, 1,300; rental, one night $70, three $140; license included; share also. Size of stage, 33x32; height from stage to grooves, 18; height from stage to rigging loft, 25; depth under stage, 5; bill poster, Nelson Green theatrical teamsters; Mundy & Robinson. Newspapers: daily, Enquirer (Sun.), Times. ....Hotels : Rankin, regular rates, $2.50 (special also); Central.

CUTHBERT, 2,200. R. R., South Western R'y. Powell's Hall, T. S. Powell, manager; seating capacity, 400; rental, one night, $15; three, $30; share also; license, $3.50. Size of stage, 20x30; size of proscenium opening, 12x22; height from stage to grooves, 12; height from stage to rigging loft, 16; depth under stage, 4; number sets scenery, 4; bill poster, janitor of hall; number of sheets can accommodate, 300; rates, 3c; theatrical teamsters, Pearce & Ridgeway. Newspapers: Enterprise, advertising rates per inch, 75c.; The Appeal, advertising rates per inch, 75c......Hotels : Cobb, special rates, $1.50 to $2; Carver, regular rates, $2 (special also).

DALTON, 3,000. R. R., East Tenn. Va. & Ga.; Western & Atlantic. Previtt Hall, B. F Previtt, manager; seating capacity, 300; rental one night, $12.50; three, $27; license, ten tickets. Size of stage, 18x25; number sets of scenery, 5; bill poster, Mr. Ganz. Newspapers: Argus (Sat.), Citizen (Th.)....Hotels; National, regular rates, $2; (special also); Rudd, Exchange.

GAINSVILLE, 3,000. R. R., Ga.; Rich. & Danville. Chandler's Hall, T. S. Campbell, manager; seating capacity, 400; rental one night, $10; three, $18; license, $10. Size of stage, 16x24. Newspapers; Eagle (Th.); Press (W.); Southron (Tri.)......Hotels: Arlington, regular rates, $2 (special also).

GRIFFIN, 4,000. R. R., Central of Ga.; Sav Ga. & N. Ala. Schenermann's Opera House A. Schenermann, manager; seating capacity, 600; rental one night, $25; three, $50, license included, share also. Size of stage, 19x24; number sets of scenery, 6; bill poster, Hiram Goddard. Newspapers; daily, News, weekly, Sun (Sun.)......Hotels: National, regular rates, $2 (special also), Nelm, Georgia, Goddard.

LA GRANGE, 3,000. R. R., Atlanta & West Point. Truett's Opera House, J. C. Truett, manager; seating capacity, 400; rental one night, $35; no license. Size of stage, 20x12; number sets of scenery, 6; bill poster, Todd Chelver. Newspaper: Reporter (Th.). .... Hotel: La Grange, regular rates, $2 (special also).

7

MACON, GA., 23,000. R. R., **Central** of Georgia; East **Tennessee**, Virginia & Georgia; **South** Western. Academy of Music, H. Horne, manager; **seating** capacity, 1,150; rental one night, $90; three, $160, share also; license, $10. Size of stage, 40x60; size of proscenium opening, 40x30; height from stage to grooves, 30; height from stage to rigging loft, 56; depth under stage, 15; traps, 4; number sets scenery, full sets; leader of orchestra, F. A. Guttenberger; stage carpenter, J. H. Deming; bill poster, Burr Brown; rates per sheet, 4c; theatrical teamster, Burr Brown. Newspapers: daily, Telegraph and Messenger; advertising rates per inch, $1.50......**Hotels:** Brown, special rates, $2 to $2.50; Lanier, $1.50 to $2; National, $1.50 to $2.

Ralston Opera House, A. Block, manager; **Brooks & Dickson, New York** agents; seating **capacity, 900; rental one night, $50;** three, $125; license, city and county, $10, share also. **Size of stage, 30x50.**

Masonic Hall, James Wells, manager; seating capacity, 700; rental one night, $27.50; three, **$70, share also. Size of stage, 20x35; number sets scenery,** 5.

New **Opera House.**

Huff's Hall; seating capacity, 250.

MADISON, 2,000. R. R., Georgia. Foster's Hall, T. C. Foster, manager; seating capacity, 300; rental one night, $10; three, $25; license, $2.50 to $3. Size of stage, 15x30; no scenery. Newspaper: Madisonian (Sat.)......Hotel: Hough, regular rates, $2 (special also).

MARIETTA, 2,227. R. R., Mari. & North Georgia; Western & Atlantic. Nichold's Hall, A. C. Heggie, manager; seating capacity, 500; rental one night, $10; three, $30; license, city and county, $10. Size of stage, 12x30; number sets scenery, 4; bill poster, Wm. Cox. Newspaper: Journal **(Th)**......Hotels: Kenesaw, regular rates, $1.50 (special also) Cooper.

MILLEDGEVILLE, 3,800. **R. R.**, **Central of Georgia**; Georgia & Kentucky. Brake's Opera House, Brake & Grieve, managers; **seating** capacity, 600; rental one night, $25; three, $65, license included, share also. Size **of stage**, 30x50; full stock scenery; bill poster, Opera House. Newspapers, Chronicle **(Sat)**; Vidette (Sat.); Recorder (Tu.)......Hotels: Oconee, regular rates, $2 (special also); Stembridge.

NEWMAN, 3,000. R. R., Atlanta & West Point; Savannah, Griffin & Northern Alabama. Reese's Opera House, G. R. Bradley, manager; seating capacity, 600; rental one night, $25; three, $50, share also; license yearly. **Size** of stage, 24x33; number sets scenery, 6; bill poster, G. R. Bradley. Newspapers: Herald (Tu.); Advertiser (Fri.). Hotels: Yancy, regular rates, $2 (special also), $1 to $1.25; Virginia, $1 to $1.25; Commercial, $1 to $1.25.

ROME, 10,000. R. R., East Tenn., Va. **& Ga.;** Rome. Nevin Opera House, M. A. Nevin, manager; seating capacity, 900; rental **one** night, $75; three, $150; license included; share also. Size of stage, 30x45; number sets scenery, 15; bill poster, Walter Langston. Newspaper: daily, Bulletin, Courier......Hotels: Central, regular rates, $2 (special also); Sargent, regular rates, $2 (special also).

SAVANNAH, 40,000. R. R., Savannah; Florida & Western; Central of Georgia; Charleston & Savannah. Savannah Theatre, T. F. Johnson, manager; seating capacity, 1,512; rental one night, $100; three, $240; license, $3; share also. Size of stage, 40x30; size of proscenium opening, 30x32; height from stage to grooves, 16; height from stage to rigging loft, 35; depth under stage, 8; traps, 6; number sets scenery, 30; leader of orchestra, Henry E. Ghecks; stage carpenter, Frank Hamilton; bill poster, E. W. Fisher; theatrical teamster, John Feely. Newspapers: daily, News, advertising rates per inch, $1.50; Times, 75c. inch......Hotels: Pulaski, special rates, $2.50; Screven, special rates, $2.50; Marshall, special rates, $1.50 to $2.

Mozart Hall; seating capacity, 800; rental one night, $35. Size of stage, 24x35; no scenery.

Masonic Temple; seating capacity, 600.

St. Andrews; seating capacity, 700.

Centennial; seating capacity, 400.

Metropolitan Hall; seating capacity, 300.

Armory; seating capacity, 500.

THOMASVILLE, 2,500. R. R., Savannah, Florida & Western. City Hall, seating capacity, 350; fair stock scenery; bill poster, Albert Stogoll. Newspapers: Enterprise (W.); Times (Sat.)..... Hotels: Mitchell, Gulf.

Court House; seating capacity, 300.

WASHINGTON, 2,400. R. R., Georgia. Floyd's Opera House, John D. Floyd, manager, seating capacity, 550. Newspaper: Gazette (Fri.), ...Hotel: Washington.

WEST POINT, 2,000. R. R., Atlanta & West Point; Western Ala. Library Hall, W. B. Higginbotham, manager; seating capacity, 300; rental one night, $15; three, $20; license included; share also. Size of stage, 18x20; number sets scenery, 4; bill poster, manager Hall. Newspaper: Enterprise (Fri.)......Hotels: Chattahoochee, regular $2.50 (special also), Higganbothem, Shamrock.

Wright's Hall.

Lyceum.

ILLINOIS.

ABINGDON, 2,500. R. R., Chicago, Burlington & Quincy; Ill. Central. Foltz Opera House, F. P. Foltz, manager; seating capacity, 400; rental, one night $10, three $25; license, $1.50 to $2. Full sets scenery; bill poster, S. Willis. Newspaper: Argus (Fri.) .... Hotel: Foltz House, special rates, $1.25; Skinner's, special rates, $1.25.

ALEDO, 2,000. R. R., Chicago, Burlington & Quincy. Union Hall, Marker & Dunlap, managers; seating capacity, 500; rental, one night $10, three, $25; license, $2.50. Size of stage, 16x30; size of proscenium opening, 10x16; height from stage to rigging loft, 12; depth under stage, 2½; traps, 1; number sets scenery, 5; leader of orchestra, P. Woods; theatrical teamster, N. Jenner. Newspapers: Democrat (Th.); Record (Tu.) ......Hotels: Crosier; Button, regular $2 (special also); Aledo.

ALTON, 10,000. R. R. Chic. & Alton; C., B. & Q. City Hall Opera House, Mather & Co., managers; seating capacity, 900; rental, one night $20, three, $60; share also; license, $3. Size of stage, 40x50; size of proscenium opening, 15x25; height from stage to grooves, 18½; height from stage to rigging loft, 20; depth under stage 4; traps, 1; number sets scenery, 10; leader of orchestra, John Hoffman; scenic artist, Clark Cox; stage carpenter, Barus Coogan; bill poster Mather & Co.; number of sheets can accommodate, 1,500; rates, &c., theatrical teamster, John Collins. Newspapers: daily, Democrat, advertising rates per line, 10c.; Telegraph, rates 10c. line; weekly, Banner (Th.), rates 10c. line.......Hotels: Madison, special rates, $1.50; Brent, special rates, $1 to $1.25.

Root's Opera House, Danvers & Co., managers; seating capacity, 600; rental, one night $35; three, $80; share also; license included. Size of stage, 26x40; size of proscenium opening, 13x20; height from stage to grooves, 11; height from stage to rigging loft, 19; depth under stage, 15; mechanical traps; number sets scenery, 20; bill posters, Danvers & Co.; number sheets can accommodate, 580.

Mercantile Hall, Lewis & Detrich, managers; seating capacity, 650; rental, one night $25, three, $60; license, $5.50. Size of stage, 24x40; fair stock scenery.

Turner Hall; seating capacity, 300.

AMBOY, 3,000. R. R., Chicago, Burlington & Quincy; Illinois Central. Opera House, J. B. Graves, manager; seating capacity, 500; rental, one night, $15, license included. Size of stage, 14x22; bill poster, J. B. Graves. Newspapers: Journal (W.), News (Sat.)...... Hotels: Bristol, regular rates, $2 (special also); Smith.

Fasoldt Hall, W. H. Fasoldt, manager; seating capacity, 500; rental, one night, $15; three, $30; license, $3; number sets scenery, 10.

ANNA, 2,500. R. R., Illinois Central. Ussery's Opera House, Will. O. Ussery, manager; seating capacity, 600; rental, one night, $10, no license, share also. Size of stage, 13x40; fair stock scenery; bill poster, George Boon; number of sheets can accommodate, 250; theatrical teamster, Theo. Mullins. Newspaper: Talk (Fri.)......Hotels: European, regular rates, $2 (special also); Winstead, Otrich.

Concert Hall, A. G. Button, manager; seating capacity, 400; rental, one night, $5; license $2.50; no scenery.

OPERA HOUSE, St. Catharines, Ontario.

Seats 1,200; situated on the ground floor. | | 26 miles from Buffalo, 32 from Hamilton, 72 from Toronto

ARCOLA, 2,000. R. R., Illinois Central, Illinois Midland. Armory Hall, J. M. Sylvester manager; seating capacity, 670; rental, one night, $10; license, $2.50. Size of stage, 24x24 number sets scenery, 6; bill poster, Spelman Bros.; theatrical teamster, Ed. Hood; Newspapers: Herald (Sat.), Record (Sat.)..... Hotels: Belvedere, regular rates, $2 (special also): Terre Haute, Franklin, De Armond.

ARLINGTON, 650. R. R., Chicago, Burlington & Quincy. Young's Hall, Michael Young, manager, seating capacity, 300; rental, one night, $6 three, $15; license, $1.50. Size of stage, 15x21; number sets scenery, 5; bill poster, M. Young. Newspaper: Herald (Sat.) ..... Hotel: Arlington.

ASTORIA, 2,000. R. R., Chicago, Burlington & Quincy. Carter's Hall, Dilworth Carter, manager; seating capacity, 450; rental, one night, $10, three $25; license, $1.50. Size of stage, 27x25, size of proscenium opening, 16x19; height from stage to rigging loft, 16; depth under stage, 4; traps, 1; number sets of scenery, 9; theatrical teamster, J. D. Fenton. Newspaper: Argus (Wed.)..... Hotels: Commercial, special rates, 75c., Cottage, special rates, 75c., Hoffman, special rates, 75c.

ATLANTA, 1,600. R. R., Chicago & Alton; Ill. Midland. Murphy Hall. C. H. Turner, manager; seating capacity, 750; rental, one night, $19, three, $24, license, $2. Size of stage, 20x50; size of proscenium opening, 12x18; height from stage to grooves, 14; depth under stage, 8; traps, 1; number sets scenery, 7; bill poster. Frank Johnson. Newspaper; Argus (Fri.)..... Hotels: Coleman, Atlanta, regular rates, $2 (special also).

AURORA, 15,000. R. R., Chicago, Burlington & Quincy; Chicago & Iowa. Opera House, R. W. Corbett, manager; seating capacity, 900; rental, one night, $40, three, $100; license included; share also. Size of stage, 24x28; height from stage to grooves, 16; height from stage to rigging loft, 30; depth under stage, 5; number sets scenery, 13; bill poster, Aurora Amusement Association; theatrical teamster, E. P. Cleveland. Newspapers: daily, Post, Express, News..... Hotels: Fitch, special rates, $1.50: Tremont, (special.)

BATAVIA, 4,000. R. R., Chicago, Burlington & Quincy; Chicago & Northwestern. Music Hall. C. A. Lewis, manager; seating capacity, 660; rental, one night, $15; three, $36. Size of stage, 22x40; size of proscenium opening, 20x20; height from stage to rigging loft, 16; traps, 1; number sets scenery, 10; stage carpenter, 8. Hampton: bill poster, G. A. Lewis. Newspaper: News (Th.)..... Hotel: Review, special rates, $1.

BEARDSTOWN, 4,000. **R. R.,** Chi., Bur. & Quincy: Ohio & Miss. Opera House, J. E. Pulnam, manager; seating capacity, 800; rental, one night $25, license $4; share also. Size of stage, 25x50; number sets scenery, 7; bill poster, manager Opera House; number sheets can accommodate, 200; theatrical teamster. Park House baggage man. Newspapers: Enterprise (Tu.), Illinoian (Sat.)..... Hotel: Park, regular rates, $2 (special also).

BELLEVILLE, 15,000. R. R., Illinois & St. Louis; Louisville & Nashville. City Park Theatre, L. E. Tieman, manager; seating capacity, 800; rental, --, license $2.50, share also. Size of stage, 30x40; number sets scenery, 12; bill poster, Peter Kelly; theatrical teamster, L. E. Tieman. Newspapers: daily, News-Democrat; weekly, Advocate (F.), Republican (F.)..... Hotels: Thomas, regular rates, $2 (special also); Hinckley, regular rates $2 (special also); National, Belleville.

BELVIDERE, 3,000. R. R., Chicago & Northwestern. Union Hall, C. B. Loop, manager; seating capacity, 800; rental, one night $15, license, $3 to $5. Size of stage, 20x30; number sets scenery, 4; bill poster, Robert Smiley; theatrical teamster, T. O. Simpson. Newspapers: North Western (Sat.), Standard (Tu.) .....Hotels: Julien, regular rates, $2 (special also); American.

BLOOMINGTON, 20,000. R. R., Chic. & Alton; Ill. Cent.; Indiana, Bloom. & W.; Lake Erie & West. Grand Opera House, Tillotson & Fell, managers; seating capacity, 1,000; rental, one night, $70, three, $175, license $5, share also. Size of stage, 30x18; number sets scenery, 16; bill posters, Tillotson & Fell; theatrical teamsters, McBean & Foster. Newspapers: daily, Bulletin, Independent, Leader, Pantagraph. Hotels: Ashley, regular rates, $2 (special also); Phoenix, regular rates, $2 (special also); Watt's.

Durley Hall, Tillotson & Fell, managers; seating capacity, 1,500; rental, one night, $70, three, $175, license, $5; share also. Number sets scenery, 15.

Phoenix Hall; seating capacity, 800.

New Turner Hall.

BRAIDWOOD, 7,000. R. R., Chic. & Alton. Music Hall, John Bradbent, manager; seating capacity, 750; rental, one night, $25, three, $60, license included; share also. Size of stage, 18x43; number sets scenery, 8; bill poster, manager of Hall. Newspapers: **daily,** Independent; weekly, Gazette (F.), Reporter (Sat.)...... Hotel: Broadbent, regular rates, $2 (special also).

BUSHNELL, 3,000. R. R., Chic. Burl. & Quincy; Wabash, St. L. & Pac. Opera House, **H.** L. Randall, manager; seating capacity, 700; rental, share only, **license** included. Size **of** stage, 25x65; size of prosenium opening, 16x30; height from stage to grooves, 14; height from stage to rigging loft, 30; **depth** under stage, 4½; traps, 1, number sets scenery, **10; leader of** orchestra, Ed. Pierce; **bill** poster, Opera House; number **sheets can** accommodate, 300; theatrical **teamster, John** Cole. Newspapers: **Record** (Fri.), Democrat (Th.)....... Hotels: Hendec, **special rates,** $1.50 to $2; **Bushnell, special rates,** $1 to $1.25

Union Hall, Clark & Son, managers; seating capacity, 350; rental, one night, $10, license $1.50 to $2. Size of stage, 14x18.

CAIRO, 9,000. R. R., Ill. Cen.; Mobile & Ohio; Cairo & Vincennes; St. L. & Cairo; St. L. & Iron Mt., South Tex. & St. L. Opera House, Thomas M. Shields, manager; seating capacity, 1,300; rental, share only, license included. Size of stage, 40x60; height from stage to grooves, 18; hight from stage **to** rigging loft, 55; depth under stage, 10; number sets scenery, 20; bill poster, **C.** Hardy; theatrical teamster, Steve Bradley. Newspapers daily, Argus, Bulletin...... Hotels: Halliday, regular rates, $2.50 (special also), Arlington, Waverly.

Atheneum, Dan Hartman, manager; full set scenery.

Theatre Comique.

CAMBRIDGE, 2,000. R. R., Rock Island & Peoria. Armory Hall, Elliott Hinman, manager; seating capacity, 550; rental, one night, $15, two, 20; license, $2; share also. Size of stage, 22x45; bill poster, Oscar Etter. Newspapers: Chronicle (Th.), Local Reporter (F.), Prairie Chief (Sat.) Hotels: Central, regular rates, $2, (special also); Cambridge, Thatcher.

CAMP POINT, 1,130. R. R., Chic., Bur. & Quincy. Wabash Armory Hall, H. Follhemer, manager; seating capacity, 500. Size of stage, 23x20. Newspaper: Journal (Th.) ....Hotel: Adams.

CANTON, 5,000. R. R., Chic., Burlington & Quincy; Wabash. Canton Opera House, Abbott and Hemple, managers; seating capacity, 800; rental, one night, $20; three, $50; license, $3; share also. Size of stage, 23x40; number sets scenery, 7; bill poster, Charles T. Wilson; theatrical teamster, Adams Express. Newspapers: Ledger (Th.), Republican (Th.), Register (Th.)........ Hotels: Churchill, regular rates, $2 (special also); Canton.

CARBONDALE, 3,000. R. R., Grand, **Tower & Carbondale;** Ill. Cen.; St. Louis Coal. Moody's Opera House, J. M. Richart, manager; **seating** capacity, 500; share only. Size of stage, 20x38; number sets scenery, 3; bill poster, Thomas Brown; theatrical teamster, George Rogers. Newspapers: Free Press (Sat.), Criterion Democrat (Sat.)........ Hotels: Gager, regular rates, $2 (special also), Newell.

CARLINVILLE, 4,000. R. R., Chicago & Alton. City Opera House, W. E. Belliner, manager; seating capacity, 600; rental, one night $15, three $35; license, $3; share also; size of stage, 19x30; size of prosenium opening, 18x24; height from stage to grooves, 11; height from stage to rigging loft, 30; depth under stage, 6; trap, 1; number sets scenery, 4; scenic artist, Dr. Betteworth; bill poster, Opera House; number of sheets **can accommodate,** 300; rates 4c. Newspapers: Democrat (Wed.), **advertising rates—special con-** tract; Enquirer (Wed.), special contract......**Hotel:** St George, special rates, $1 to $1.50

CARLYSLE, 3,000. R. R., Ohio & Mississippi. Schlafly's Hall, Schlafly Brothers, managers; seating capacity, 510; rental, **one night $10, three $24;** license, $1; share also. Size of stage, 18x27; number sets scenery, 4; theatrical teamster, D. H. Colwell. Newspapers: Constitution and Union (Th.), Banner (Th.).....Hotels: Truesdale, Norris City.

CARMI, 3,000. R. R., Louisville & Nashville, Wabash. Opera House, George Guex, manager; seating capacity, 400; rental, one night $12; license, $5; width of stage, 30; fair stock scenery; bill poster, Walter Thompson. Newspapers: Times (Tu.), Courier Democrat (Wed.)..... Hotels: Damron, regular rates, $2 (special also).

Berry's Hall; seating capacity, 500.

Viskniskki Hall; seating capacity, 300.

CARPENTERSVILLE, 500. R. R., Chicago & North Western. Library Hall, G. F. Arvedson, manager; seating capacity, 300; rental, one night $3 to $7; no license. Size of stage, 16x22; small stock scenery.....Hotel : Harvey.

CARROLLTON, 2,500. R. R., Chicago & Alton ; Litchfield, Carrolton & Western. Pierson's Opera House, Robert Pierson, manager; seating capacity, 600; rental, one night $8 to $10; license, $1 to $3; number sets scenery, 3; bill poster, Opera House. Newspapers: Gazette (Sat.), Patriot (Fri.).....Hotels: Hinton, regular rates, $2 (special also). Occidental, St. James.

CARTHAGE, 2,000. R. R., Chicago, Burlington & Quincy; Wabash. Spitter's Opera House, J. E. Helfrich, manager; seating capacity, 400; rental, one night, $15, three, $37.50, share also, license included. Size of stage, 18x28; size of proscenium opening, 10x17½; height from stage to grooves, 11; height from stage to rigging loft, 12; depth under stage, 4; trap, 1; number sets scenery, 5; leader of orchestra, Lew Moore; scenic artist, Robert Hansford; stage carpenter, W. W. Bower; bill poster, W. W. Bower, rates, 3c ; theatre teamster, L. P. Hobbe. Newspapers: Republican (Wed.), 10c. line; Gaze line..... Hotels: Patterson, special rates, $1; Stevens, special rates, $1.

CENTRALIA, 5,000. R. R., Ills. Central ; Jacksonville South Eastern. Sadler's Opera House, M. B. Sadler, manager; seating capacity, 600; rental, one night, $25; license, $2.50, $10, share also. Size of stage, 25x42, full set scenery; bill poster, M. Wright; theatrical teamster, Adams' Express. Newspapers: daily, Times: weekly, Democrat (Sat.), Sentinel (Th.)......Hotels: Centralia, regular rates $2 (special also). European, Park, Occidental.

CHAMPAIGN, 5,500. R. R., Ills. Central; Wabash; Indiana, Bloomington & Western. Eichberg's Opera House, Max Eichberg, manager; seating capacity, 650; rental, one night, $15, three, $35, license, $3. Size of stage, 20x40; full set scenery; bill poster, Selden Nye; number sheets can accommodate 600; theatrical teamster, Wm. Hoffman. Newspapers: daily, Gazette; weekly, Signal (Th.), Times (Sat.)......Hotels: Carter, regular, $2 (special also), Doane (special also), Moore, Scott.

Champaign Opera House, H. Swanell, manager; seating capacity, 800; rental, one night, $15, three, $35, license, $3, share also. Size of stage, 22x20; full set scenery.

CHARLESTON, 3,000. R. R., Indianapolis & St. Louis; Toledo, Cin. & St. Louis. City Hall; M. E. M. Crory, manager; seating capacity. 500; rental, one night, $10, license, $3, $5, share also. Size of stage, 16x18; number sets scenery, 7; bill poster, John Hart. Newspapers: Courier (Th.), Plaindealer (Th.), Herald (Sat.)......Hotels: Charleston, regular rates, $2 (special also), Maple.

CHATSWORTH, 1,200. R. R., Ills. Central; Wabash. Town Hall, J. G. True, manager; seating capacity, 300; rental, one night $5, three, $15, share also. Size of stage, 14x26; number sets scenery, 5. Newspaper: Plaindealer (Sat.)......Hotels: Cottage, special; Commercial.

CHENOA. 1,200. R. R., Chicago & Alton; Wabash, St. L. & Pacific. Opera House, G. T. Cornley, manager; seating capacity 300; rental, one night $10, three $20; license, $1; share also. Size of stage, 12x28; size of proscenium opening, 10x16; height from stage to grooves, 12; height from stage to rigging loft, 13; Depth under the stage, 4; traps, 2; number sets scenery, 8; leader of orchestra, L. Luce; theatre teamster, L. Arnold. Newspaper: Gazette (Th.)......Hotels: Exchange, special rates, $2; Harris, special rates, $1.

CHILLICOTHE, 2,000. R. R., Chicago, R. I. & Pacific. Hunter's Opera Hall, H. A. Hunter, manager; seating capacity, 700; rental, one night $10, three $25; license, $1 and $2; share also. Size of stage, 17x22; no scenery. Newspapers: Independent (Sat.), Reporter (Wed.)......Hotel: Wood.

JOHN W. JENNINGS,

(COMEDIAN,)

SPECIALLY ENGAGED for SEASON OF '83 & 84

TO PLAY

HIS SUCCESSFUL CREATION OF

JAIKES

IN

Miner's Silver King Company, No. 1.

Permament Address :

Care of W. H. MINNICK, Fourth Avenue, New York.

JOSEPH FRANK,

GENERAL MANAGER

C. R. Gardiner's Attractions:

ONLY A FARMER'S DAUGHTER COMPANY;

ZOZO THE MAGIC QUEEN COMPANY;

ONLY A WOMAN'S HEART COMPANY

Permanent Address :

12 Union Square, - - - - - - - New York.

DRAMATIC AGENT, J. J. SPIES.

CHICAGO, 650,000. R. R., Baltimore & Ohio; Chicago & Alton; Chicago & Eastern Illinois; Chicago & Grand Trunk; Chicago & Northwestern; Chicago, Burlington & Quincy; Chicago, Rock Island & Pacific; Chicago, Milwaukee & St. Paul; Chicago, St. Louis & Pacific; Chicago, St. Louis & Western; Illinois Central, Lake Shore & Michigan Southern; Michigan Central; Pittsburg, Ft. Wayne & Chicago; New York, Chicago & St. Louis; Wabash. Grand Opera House, John A Hamlin, manager; seating capacity, 1,500; rental, share only; license yearly. Size of stage, 42x80; size of pro-cenium opening, 31x35; height from stage to grooves, 20; height from stage to rigging loft, 90; fly beams, 17; depth under stage, 8; traps, full set; scenery, full set; musical director, Armand Butterot; scenic artist, Walter Burridge; stage carpenter, John Faust; bill posters,'Broad way & Felsner's B. P. Co.; number of sheets can accommodate, unlimited; rates per sheet, 3c to 4c; theatrical teamsters, Caryl Young Co., Garden City Express, News papers: daily, Tribune, Times, Inter-Ocean, Herald, News, Mail, Staats Zeitung, Journal; weekly, News Letter (Sat.) Indicator, Music and Drama......Hotels: Tremont, special rates, $2 to $3.50; Sherman, same; Palmer, same; Grand Pacific, same; Briggs, $1.50 to $2; Merchants, $1 to $1.50; St Cloud, same; Commercial, same.

New Chicago Opera House, John W. Norton, manager; seating capacity, 2,200. (See advertisement).

Haverly Theatre, C. H. McConnell, manager; seating capacity, 2,500; rental, share only; license yearly Size of stage, 45x70; size of proscenium opening, 34x34; first-class equipment; musical director, George Bowron; scenic artist, Charles E. Petford; stage carpenter, A. Mackenzie.

Hooley's Theatre, R. M. Hooley, manager; seating capacity, 1,500; share only. Size of stage, 45x55; size of proscenium opening, 34x36; height from stage to grooves, 20; height from stage to rigging loft, 65; depth under stage, 10; traps, Star, Vampire, Hamlet, Macbeth, 3 sinks, 2 bridges; number sets scenery, 40; musical director, Francis Timhone; scenic artist, Charles H. Ritter; stage carpenter, A. H. Bond.

McVicker's Theatre, J. H. McVicker, manager; seating capacity, 1,800; rental, share only. Size of stage, 54x77; size of proscenium opening, 30x32; height from stage to grooves, 20; height from stage to rigging loft, 59; depth under stage, 11; all usual traps; musical director, Henry Doehne; scenic artist, J. H. Rogers; stage carpenter,John Bairstow.

Academy of Music, Daniel Shelby, manager; seating capacity, 2,000; share only. Size of stage, 38x75; size of proscenium opening, 36x34; height from stage to grooves, 20; height from stage to rigging loft, 63; depth under stage, 10; traps, 6; scenery complete in every detail; musical director, Charles Nitschke; scenic artist, Ralph Betchel; stage carpenter, Frank Bishop.

Standard Theatre, Whitney and Dyer, managers; seating capacity, 2,000; share only; license included. Size of stage, 60x60, size of proscenium opening, 35x32; height from stage to grooves, 20; height from stage to rigging loft, 65; depth under stage, 12; traps, 3; number sets scenery, 45; musical director, Frank L. Cook; scenic artist, Lem L. Graham; stage carpenter, Charles Brownell.

Criterion Theatre, Charles Engle, manager; seating capacity, 1,000, share only. Size of stage, 60x72; size of proscenium opening, 45x36; height from stage to grooves, 20; height from stage to rigging loft, 65; traps, all kinds; full set scenery; musical director, James Morrison; scenic artist, W. J. Drake.

National Theatre, C. K. Mortimer, manager; seating capacity, 1,200 (play a stock company). Size of stage, 50x50; size of proscenium opening, 28x30; height from stage to grooves, 18; height from stage to rigging loft, 34; depth under stage, 12; traps, all kinds; scenery complete; musical director, Jacob Schmidt; scenic artist, Thomas J. Curran; stage carpenter, Oliver Hugg.

Lyceum Theatre (variety), Thomas L. Grenier, manager; John Morrissey, business manager; seating capacity, 2,200. Size of stage, 35x28; size of proscenium opening, 48x28; height from stage to grooves, 18; height from stage to rigging loft, 60; depth under stage, 8; number sets scenery, 15; musical director, Charles Fischer; scenic artist, Thomas Mowes; stage carpenter, Benjamin P. Lee.

Olympic Theatre (variety), Wm. Emmett, manager; seating capacity, 1,100.

Halsted Street Opera House.

Chicago Museum, Shelby and Goodwin, managers.

Kohl & Middleton's Museums, C. E. Cole and George Middleton, managers.

Central Music Hall, Milward Adams, manager; seating capacity, 1,800; rental, one night, $125; no license. Size of stage, 25x45; no scenery.

Hershey Music Hall, Clarence Eddy, manager; seating capacity, 800; rental one night $40, two $75; no license. Size of stage, 18x35.

Weber Music Hall, Curtis & Mayer, managers; seating capacity, 400; rental one night $25, three $60; license $10. Size of stage, 9x30.

Farwell Hall; seating capacity, 1,760.

CHRISMAN, 540. R. R., Ind., Bloom. & Western; Wabash. Scott's Hall, Isaac Scott, manager; seating capacity, 250. Size of stage, 16x23: number sets scenery, 5. Newspaper: Advance (Sat)......Hotel: Hammond.

CLINTON, 3,500. R. R., Ill. Central; Springfield & Gil.; Wabash. Razey's Opera House, A. W. Razey, manager; seating capacity, 500; rental, one night, $15; three, $35; license, $3.50, share also. Size of stage, 20x45; size of proscenium opening, 9x19; height from stage to grooves, 10; height from stage to rigging loft, 11; depth under stage, or cellar, 3; traps, 1; number sets scenery, 5; leader of orchestra, W. Z. Dewey; bill poster. Opera House; number of sheets can accommodate, 100; rates, 3c ; theatrical teamster, H. B. Taylor. Newspapers: Public (Fri), Register (Fri.). Tribune (Fri), advertising rates, 5c. per line.....Hotels; Magin, special rates, $1 25 to $1.50; City, special.

COBDEN, 1,000. R. R., Ill. Central. Miller's Opera House, A. J. Miller, manager; seating capacity, 400; rental, one night $10, three $20; license, $2 50. Size of stage, 15x40; number sets scenery, 6. Newspaper: Sentinel (Th)......Hotel: Phillips', regular rates, $1.50 (special also), Rolff.

CORDOVA, 430. R. R., Chicago, Milwaukee & St. Paul. Johnson's Hall, rental one night. $4, license $1.

DANVILLE, 13,000. R. R., Wabash, Chicago, & Eastern Illinois; Indiana, Bloomington & Western; Danville, Olney & Ohio River. Grand Opera House, Leslie Davis, manager; seating capacity, 1,000; rental, share only. Size of stage, 42x60; size of proscenium opening, 30x30; height from stage to grooves, 18; height from stage to rigging loft, 50; depth under stage, 9; traps, 2; number sets scenery, 15; leader of orchestra, Prof. Semon; stage carpenter, George Kice ; bill poster, Davis & Co.; number of sheets can accommodate, 2,000; rates, 4c; theatrical teamsters, Danville Transfer Co. Newspapers : daily, News, Commercial; weekly, Ledger, (Sun.); advertising rates, yearly contract, ...Hotels : Arlington, special rates, $1.50 to $2: Aetna, special rates, $1.50 to $2; Tremont, $1 to $1.50.

Lincoln Opera House, Leslie Davis, manager; seating capacity, 700; rental, one night $40, three $100; license, yearly. Size of stage, 25x40; size of proscenium opening, 18x25; height from stage to grooves, 13; height from stage to rigging loft, 20; depth under stage, 5; number sets scenery, 12; leader of orchestra, Chas. Wyeth; stage carpenter, Geo. A. Kice.

Armory Hall; seating capacity, 200.

Gaiety Theater; seating capacity, 300.

DECATUR, 14,000. R. R., Ill. Cen.; Ill. Midland; Wabash; Ind., Bloom. & West.; Pek., Lin. & Dec. Opera House, F. W. Haines, manager; seating capacity, 1,000; rental, one night $50, three $125; share also, license included. Size of stage, 30x60; size of proscenium opening, 28x30; height from stage to grooves, 18; height from stage to rigging loft, 45; depth under stage, 10; number sets scenery, 12 ; leader of orchestra, Olof Bull; stage carpenter, F. W. Haines; bill poster, F. W. Haines; number of sheets can accommodate, 300 to 1,000; rates, 4c ; theatrical teamster, Street Railway Co. Newspapers : daily, Republican, Herald, Review......Hotels : St Nicholas, special rates, $1.50 to $2; New Dening, special rates, $1.50 to $2; Palace, special rates, $1.25 to $1.50.

DE KALB, 2,700. R. R., Chicago & North Western. Haish's Opera House, Paul Hoam, manager; seating capacity, 550; rental, one night $15, three $40; license included. Size of proscenium opening, 10x17; height from stage to grooves, 15; height from stage to rigging loft, 23; depth under stage, 4; traps, 1; number sets scenery, 5 ; leader of orchestra, Wall Cheney; bill poster, R. Trimball; theatrical teamster, C. Whitmore. Newspapers : Chronicle (Sat.), Review (Th.). Hotel Glidden, regular rates, $2 (special also).

DELAVAN, 2,000. R. R., Chic. & Alton; Peo., Dec. & Evans. Phillips' Opera House, H. Phillips, manager; seating capacity, 600; rental, one night $10, three $20; license, $3; share also. Size of stage, 18x60; full set scenery; bill poster, Opera House; theatrical teamsters, Horton Bros. Newspapers: Advertiser (Tb.), Times (Th.). ....Hotels: Central, regular rates, $2 (special also); Delavan, Rosse.

DIXON, 4,000. R. R., Chic. & N. W.; Ill. Cent. Dixon Opera House, John V. Thomas, manager; seating capacity, 800; rental, one night $30, three $65; license, $2.50; share also. Size of stage, 18x42; number sets scenery, 5; bill poster, C. M. Cropsey; theatrical teamster, C. M. Cropsey. Newspapers: Sun (W.); Telegraph (Th)......Hotels: Nachusa, regular rates, $2 (special also); Washington, Waverly, Keystone.

Union Hall, S. E. Ellis, manager; seating capacity, 475; rental, one night, $15; license, $3. Size of stage, 14x50; no scenery.'

DUNDEE, 1,500. R. R., Chic. & N. W. Hunt's Hall, H. E. Hunt, manager; seating capacity, 400; license, $2.50. Size of stage, 22x40; number sets scenery, 7..... Hotels: Commercial, regular rates, $2 (special also); Dundee.

DU QUOIN, 3,000. R. R., Ill. Cent.; St. L., Alt. & T. H. Elston's Hall, William L. Elston, manager; seating capacity, 600; rental, one night, $15; license, $2; share also. Size of stage, 19x38; number sets scenery, 6; bill poster, J. W. Hurd. Newspapers: Press (Fri.), Tribune (Th.)..... Hotels: St. Nicholas, regular rates, $2 (special also); City, Planter's.

Schnaidy's Hall; seating capacity, 800.

City Hall; seating capacity, 500.

DWIGHT, 1,600. R. R., Chic. & Alton; Ind., Ill. & Iowa. Kepplinger Hall, George G. Kepplinger, manager; seating capacity, 600; rental, one night $8, three $18; license, $3. Size of stage, 16x24; number sets scenery, 3; bill posters, Kemin & Culkins. Newspaper: Star (Fri)......Hotels: McPherson, regular rates, $2 (special also); Schmaus, Amos.

EARLVILLE, 2,000. R. R., Chic., Bur. & Quincy; Rockford & Northern. Robinson Hall, J. W. Turner, manager; seating capacity, 500; rental, one night $10, three $25; license, $1.50, share also. Size of stage, 22x30; fair stock of scenery. Newspaper: Leader (F.) .Hotels: Wallace, regular rates, $2 (special also); Earl.

EDINBURG, 600. R. R., Ohio & Miss. Harrington's Hall, Geo. P. Harrington, manager; seating capacity, 400; fair stock scenery. Newspaper: Herald (W.).

EDWARDSVILLE, 3,000. R. R., Wabash, St. Louis & Pacific; Tol., Cin. & St. Louis. St. James' Opera House, H. Kirkpatrick, manager; seating capacity, 600; rental, one night $15, three $35; license, $3. Size of stage, 21x36; size of proscenium opening, 14x26; height from stage to grooves, 12; height from stage to rigging loft, 16½; depth under stage, 3; number sets of scenery, 7; bill poster, Frank Kirkpatrick; number of sheets can accommodate, 250; rates, &c.; theatrical teamster, Tom McCune. Newspapers: Republican (W.) advertising rates per line, 15c.; Intelligence (W.); advertising rates per line, 15c.; Democrat (Sat.), advertising rates per line, 15c.......Hotel: St. James, special rates, $1 to $1.50. Opera House connected with hotel by bridge.

Armory Hall, E. Phillips, manager; seating capacity, 400; rental one night, $8; license, $3.50. Size of stage, 20x20; fair stock scenery.

EFFINGHAM, 3,400. R. R., Ind. & Ill. Southern; Ill. Central; Vandalia Line; Wabash. Register Opera House, A. Gravenhorst, manager; seating capacity, 500; rental, one night $15, three $33; license, $2; share also. Size of stage, 16x22; number sets of scenery, 4; bill poster, Bradford Whitney; theatrical teamster, John Fink. Newspapers: Democrat (Fri.); Republican (W.).. ...Hotels: Effingham, regular rates, $2 (special also): St. Louis, Pacific, Fleming, Western, Ohio, Cincinnati.

ELGIN, 12,000. R. R., Chic. & N. Western; Chic., Mil. & St. Paul. Du Bois Opera House, M. W. Du Bois, manager; seating capacity, 1,200; rental, one night $30, three $65; license, $5, share also. Size of stage, 30x30; number sets scenery, 17; bill posters, Barker & Gates; theatrical teamster, Joe Hendricks. Newspapers: daily, Frank, News...... Hotels: Jennings, regular rates, $2 (special also); Nolting, special rates; Kimball, Western, Central, New Windsor, Commercial.

ELMWOOD, 2,000. R. R., Chic., Bur. & Quincy. Liberty Hall, J. H. Clarke, manager; rental, one night $10, share also; fair stock scenery. Newspapers: Gazette (Th.), Messenger (Fri.)......Hotels: Elmwood, Leota, special rates.

EL PASO, 2,000. R. R., Illinois Central, Wabash. City Hall. Newspaper: Journal (Sat.) ......Hotel: Campbell; regular rates, $2 (special also).

EUREKA, 2,000. R. R., Chic., St. Louis & Western; Wabash. Davis Hall, Arthur Etkin, manager; seating capacity, 500; rental, one night $6, three $15; license, $4. Size of stage, 12x40; number sets scenery, 3. Newspapers: Journal (Th.). Hotels: Francks, regular rates, $2 (special also); Little.

EVANSTON, 5,000. R. R., Chicago & N. Western. Union Hall; seating capacity, 400. Newspapers: Index (Sat.), semi-weekly, North Western.....Hotels: Avenue, regular rates, $2 (special also); French, Lakeside.

FAIRBURG, 3,000. R. R., Wabash. Du Bois Opera House, T. A. Du Bois, manager; seating capacity, 1,600; rental, one night $10, three $24; license, $1 to $2. Size of stage, 20x50; number sets scenery, 5; bill posters, Du Bois & Murdoch. Newspaper: Independent Blade (Sat.)..... Hotel: Fairburg, regular rates, $2 (special also).

FARMER CITY, 2,000. R. R., Illinois Central; Ind., Bloom & Western. Bean's Opera House, Bean Bros., managers; seating capacity, 500; rental, one night $8, three $20, license, $2; share also. Size of stage, 18x29; number sets scenery, 10; bill poster. Jos. Ball. Newspapers: Journal (Fri.); Reaper (Sat.)......Hotels: regular rates, $2 (special also); Central.

Germania Hall, R. Hefti, manager; seating capacity, 700; rent, share also.

FARMINGTON, 2,000. R. R., Central Iowa; Chicago, Burlington & Quincy. Opera House, Heaton & Yates, managers; seating capacity, 400; rental, one night $10, three $25, license included; share also. Size of stage, 16x0; number sets scenery, 12. Newspapers: Bugle (F.), Home Visitor (F.)..... Hotels: Farmington, regular rates, $2 (special also), Excelsior, Mason.

FREEBURY, 1,100. R. R., Cairo Short Line. Freeburg Saengerhall, officers of the Freeburg Saengerband; seating capacity, 300; rental, one night $10; license, $3. Size of stage, 14x22; height from stage to grooves, 14......Hotels: Freeburg, St. Clair.

FREEPORT, 12,000. R. R., Chicago & Northwestern; Chicago, Milwaukee & St. Paul; Illinois Central. Wilcoxon Opera House, M. H. Wilcoxon, manager; seating capacity, 800; rental, share only; license, $4 to $6. Size of stage, 24x23; size of proscenium opening, 17x32; height from stage to grooves, 14½; height from stage to rigging loft, 22; depth under stage, 8; number sets scenery, 10; leader of orchestra, Henry Schroeder; bill poster, Opera House; theatrical teamsters, Crane & Estabrook. Newspapers: daily, Journal, Bulletin; weekly, Journal (Wed.), Bulletin (Th.), Democrat (Sat.), Banner (Sat.), advertising rates, special contract......Hotels: Brewster, Clifton, Pennsylvania, regular rates, $2 (special also).

Germania Hall, R Hefti, manager; seating capacity, 800; rental, one night $25, three $65; license, $3 to $6. Size of stage, 24x26; number sets scenery, 10.

Armory Hall, John Waltz, manager.

FULTON, 2,000. R. R., Chicago & North Western; Chic., Mil. & St. Paul. Music Hall, A. B. Hansen, manager; seating capacity, 300; rental, one night $7, three $15. Size of stage, 25x15; number sets scenery, 1. Newspapers: semi-weekly, Journal; weekly, Star (Th.) ....Hotels: Robinson, regular $2, (special also); Union, Junction, Central.

College Hall, A. A. Griffith, manager; seating capacity, 500; rental, one night $5, to $10, three $15 to $25; license, $2 to $3; number sets scenery, 4.

GALENA, 7,000. R. R., Chic. & N. Western; Ill. Central. Turner Hall, Chas. Schroeder, manager; seating capacity, 1,000; rental, one night $20, three $55, license included; share also. Size of stage, 25x40; number sets scenery, 10; bill poster. care Gazette office; theatrical teamster, Joe Brown. Newspapers: daily, Gazette; weekly, Industrial Press (Th.)...... Hotels: European, regular $2, (special also); De Soto, regular $2 (special also).

Galena Atheneum, Wm. L. Metzger, manager.

Davis Hall; seating capacity, 600.

GALESBURG, 12,000. R. R., Chicago, Burlington & Quincy. Opera House, Nick Brelchwald, manager; seating capacity, 1,200; rental, one night, $35; share also, license included. Size of stage, 28x30; bill poster, Frank B. Kirch; theatrical teamster, John Johnson. Newspapers; daily, Republican, Register; weekly, Plaindealer, (Fri.), Press and People (Fri.)........Hotels: Union, regular rates $2 (special also); Brown's, regular rates $2 (special also).

GALVA, 3,000. R. R., Chic., Burl. & Quincy; Rock Island & Peoria. Liberal Hall, C. E. Davis, manager; seating capacity, 300; rental, one night $10, three $20; license, $1 to $2. Size of stage, 11x21; number sets scenery, 5; bill poster, T. W. Patterson; theatrical teamster, Wm. Douge. Newspapers: News (Th.), Standard (Fri.)......Hotels: Albro, City, Baker, Galva.

Temperance Hall, G. W. Hought, manager; seating capacity, 700; rental one night, $10: license, $2, share also. Size of stage, 18x24; number sets scenery, 4.

GENESEO, 3,500. R R., Chicago, Rock Island & Pacific. Freeman's Hall, Pliny Freeman, manager; seating capacity, 600; rental, one night, $20, license included. Size of stage. 20x24; number sets scenery, 9; bill poster, Jas. Bracken. Newspapers: News (Th. Republic (Fri.)......Hotels: Geneseo, regular $2 (special also), City.

GENEVA, 1,500. R R., Chicago & North Western, Chicago, Burl. & Quincy. School Hall, John H. Green, manager; rental, one night $6; three, $18. Size of stage, 17x39; size of proscenium opening, 10x16; height from stage to grooves, 10½; number sets scenery, 9; theatrical teamster, Archie Scott. Newspapers: Republican (Fri.); advertising rates, 5c; per line, 50c. per inch. Hotels: Union; special rates, $1.

GIBSON CITY, 1,400. R. R., Illinois Central; Lake Erie & Western; Wabash. Union Hall, J. B. Lott, manager; seating capacity, 350; rental, one night $5; three, $12; license, $2. Size of stage, 16x16; number sets scenery, 3; bill poster, Wm. Bartell. Newspapers: Enterprise (Th.); Courier (F.) .. ..Hotels: Gault, regular $2 (special also).

GOLCONDA, 1,400. Pierce's Hall, D. G. Thompson, manager; seating capacity, 600; fair stock scenery. Newspapers: Herald (Fri.)......Hotels: Field, regular $2.

GRAYVILLE, 2,000. R. R., Peoria, Decatur & Evansville; Wabash. Band Hall, W. W. Coulter, manager; seating capacity, 350; rental, one night, $5; three, $14; license, $1 to $3. Size of stage, 12x15; no scenery; bill poster, W. W. Coulter; theatrical teamster, Coles Bros. Newspapers: Independent (Th.)... ..Hotels: Mitchell, regular $2 (special also); Grayville, Rigall, Butler.

Cooke's Opera House, Ben S. Marsh, manager; seating capacity, 400; rental, one night, $15; license, $3; share also. Size of stage, 21x28; number sets scenery, 15.

GREENVILLE, 2,500. R. R., Vandalia Line. Armory Hall, Ward Reid, manager; seating capacity, 500; rental, one night $10, three $22; license, $3; share also. Size of stage, 25x50; number sets scenery, 4; bill poster, Will. J. Fonks. Newspapers: Advocate, (Th.), Sun (F.)......Hotels: Thomas, regular rates, $2 (special also); Franklin.

GRIGGSVILLE, 2,000. R. R., Wabash, St. Louis & Pacific. Simmon's Hall, L. W. McMahan, manager; seating capacity, 325; rental, one night $10, three $20; license, $1. Size of stage, 13x34; size of proscenium opening, 9x17; depth under stage, 3½ feet; traps, 2; number sets scenery, 3; theatrical teamster, J. M. Cree. Newspaper: Independent Press (Th.) ....,Hotel : Cree House; regular rates, $2 (special also).

HARVARD JUNCTION, 1,800. R. R., Chicago & N. Western; Kenosha and Rockford. Ayer's Hall, G. Ayer, manager; seating capacity, 600; rental, one night $10; license, $3 to $5; number sets scenery, 8. Newspaper: Independent (Fri.) .....Hotels : Harvard, regular rates, $2 (special also); Ayers.

HAVANA, 3,000. R. R., Wabash. Andrus Hall, Ransdell Bros., managers; seating capacity, 300; rental, one night, $10; license, $3. Size of stage, 22x40; fair stock scenery : bill poster, Peter Lindberg. Newspapers : Republican (F.), Democrat (F.)......Hotels : Taylor, regular rates, $2 (special also), Mason.

HENRY, 2,000. R. R., Chicago, Rock Island & Pacific. Bickerman's Opera House, J. Watercoit & Co., managers; seating capacity, 700; share only. Size of stage, 22x40; size of proscenium opening, 12x20; height from stage to rigging loft, 20; depth under stage, 4½; traps, 2; number sets scenery, 5; orchestra, Henry Cornet Band; scenic artist, Ruggles; stage carpenter, Sam Sperry; bill poster, Sam Sperry; theatrical teamster, Paskell House. Newspapers: Republican (Th.)......Hote's: Paskell, special rates, $1.25; Camp, special rates, $1.

HOOPESTON, 2,000. R.R., Chicago & E. Illinois; Lake Erie & Western. McFerren's Opera House, J. S. McFerren, manager; seating capacity, 600; rental, one night $15; three $30; license, $1 to $2. Size of stage, 20x24; number sets scenery, 6; bill poster, T. B. Tennery. Newspapers: daily, Chronicle; weekly, Journal (Tu.) ..... Hotels: Dickover, regular rates, $2 (special also); Central, Arlington, Phœnix.

Clark's Hall, W. H. Clark, manager; seating capacity, 500; rental, one night $8, three $14, license, $2. Size of stage, 18x24; number sets scenery, 7.

HYDE PARK, 35,000. R.R., Ill. Central. Flood Hall, Dr. J. R. Flood, manager; seating capacity, 600; rental, one night, $20 to $25, three $60; no license. Size of stage, 16x30; no scenery. Newspaper: Herald.

JACKSONVILLE, 1,200. R.R., Wabash, St. L. & Pac.; P.,P. & J.; Chicago & Alton.; Jacksonville, South East & North West. Strawn's Opera House, Frank C. Taylor, manager; seating capacity, 850; rental, share only; license, $5. Size of stage, 15x70; size of proscenium opening, 16x28; height from stage to grooves, 12; depth under stage, 3; number sets scenery, 10; leader of orchestra, Reuben Clarke; stage carpenter, James Hayden; bill poster, Geo. W. Starks; number of sheets can accommodate, 1,500; rates per sheet, 4c.; theatrical teamster, D. C. McCoy. Newspapers: daily, Journal, Courier......Hotels: Dunlap, special rates, $1.50 to $2.50; Rataschak, special rates, $1.50 to $2; Southern, special rates, $1.25 to $2.

The Odeon, L. W. Chambers, manager; seating capacity, 330; rental one night, $10 to $15; small stock scenery.

JERSEYVILLE, 3,500. R.R., Chicago & Alton; Wabash, St. L. & Pac. Willinger Opera House, Shephard & Cory, managers; seating capacity, 500; rental, one night, $15; license, $2.50. Size of stage, 17x25, traps, 1; number sets scenery, 5; bill poster, Shephard & Cory; theatrical teamster, James Finck. Newspapers: Democrat (Th.), advertising rates yearly contract; Republican Express (Fri.), advertising rates, yearly contract; Independent (Wed.), advertising rates, yearly contract......Hotels: Commercial, special rates, $1.85; National, special rates, $1; Jersey, special rates, $1.

JOLIET, 20,000. R.R., Chicago & Alton. C. R. I. & P.; M. C.; Cb. & S.W. Opera House E. S. Barney, manager; seating capacity, 950; rental, one night $40, three $100, license included. Size of stage, 36x60; size of proscenium opening, 28x30; height from stage to grooves, 18; height from stage to rigging loft, 38; depth under stage, 9; traps, 3; number sets scenery, 20; musical director, Jos. Bayne; stage carpenter, T. Hasey; bill poster, Opera House: number of sheets can accommodate, 1,000; rates per sheet, 4c.; theatrical teamster, E. F. Palmer. Newspapers: daily, Press, advertising rates per inch, 50c.; Republic (Sun.), advertising rates per inch, 50c.....Hotels: St. Nicholas, special rates, $1.25 to $1.50; Short's, special rates, $1.25 to $1.50; Robertson's, special rates, $1.25 to $1.50.

Robesson Hall; seating capacity, 600.

KANKAKEE, 6,500. R.R., Cin. Ind. St. Louis & Chic.; Ill. Central; Ind. Ill. & Iowa. Kankakee Opera House, F. Swannell, manager; seating capacity, 500; rental, one night $15, three $37; license, $3; share also. Size of stage, 20x22; number sets scenery, 8; bill poster, Geo. Keady. Newspapers: Gazette (Th.), Times (W.). ...Hotels: Commercial, regular rates, $2 (special also); Central, special rates.

KEITHSBURGH, 1,500. R.R., Central of Iowa; Chicago, Burlington, & Quincy. Opera House, Tom. A. Marshall, manager; seating capacity, 500; rental, one night $20, three $45; share also; license included. Size of stage, 15x25; height from stage to grooves, 17; depth under stage, 8; traps, 2; number sets scenery, 6; leader of orchestra, Wm. Kolkenbeck, Jr.; stage carpenter, Wm. Green; bill poster, Jno. C. Pursal; theatrical teamster, Wm. Trick. Newspapers: Times (Wed.), advertising rates per inch, $1; News (Th.), advertising rates per inch, $1 ....Hotel Central, special rates, $1.25.

Mr. J. W. PIGOTT

Character and Comedy.

Address :   WALLACK'S THEATRE.

KEWANEE, 4,500. R. R., Chicago Burlington & Quincy. Liberty Hall; seating capacity, 500; rental, one night $10. Size of stage, 18x38. Newspapers; Courier (Wed.), Independent (Th.)...... Hotel: Kewanee, regular rates, $2 (special also).

KNOXVILLE, 2,000. R. R., Chicago, Burlington & Quincy. City Hall; seating capacity, 500; rental one night, $10. Size of stage, 20x30; no scenery. Newspaper; Republican (Wed.)........ Hotels : Hebard, regular rates, $2 to $2.50 (special also); Knoxville, Virginia.

LACON, 2,400. R. R., Chicago & Alton. Rose's Opera House, T. H. Rose, manager; seating capacity, 500; rental, one night $15; license, $2; share also. Size of stage, 16x40; number sets scenery, 6; bill poster, Arno Anskie; theatrical teamster, Wm. Itell. Newspapers ; Journal (Wed)., Democrat (Fri.)......Hotels: Taggart, regular rates, $2 (special also; Rose.

Stire Hall, Stire & Gell, managers; seating capacity, 300; rental, one night $10, three $24; license, $2. Size of stage, 16x20; number sets scenery, 3.

LANARK, 2,000. R. R., Chicago, Milwaukee & St. Paul. Hess Opera House, W. H. Hess, manager; seating capacity,(600; rental, one night $25, three $60; share also, license included. Size of stage, 20x30; size of proscenium opening. 12x18; height from stage to grooves, 10; height from stage to rigging loft, 12; depth under stage, 4; number sets scenery, 4; bill poster, W. G. Staley; number of sheets can accommodate, 150; rates per sheet, 4c. Newspapers: Gazette (Wed.), advertising rates, 5c per line; News (Fri.), 5c per line......Hotels: Lanark, special rates, $1; Germania, special rates, $1.

Sherwood's Hall, Geo. W. Sherwood, manager; seating capacity, 300.

LA SALLE, 10,000. R. R., Chicago, Rock Island & Pac'fic; Illinois Central. Turner Hall. W. E. Birkenbuell, manager; seating capacity, 700; rental, one night $20, three $50; license, $5; share also. Size of stage, 20x40; number sets scenery, 6; bill poster, Chas. McFredon; theatrical teamster, M. Corcoran. Newspapers: Express (Fri.); Times (Sat.); Democrat Press (Th.)......Hotels: Harrison, regular rates, $2 (special also); City, La Salle.

Oriental Hall, H. H. Meadows, manager; seating capacity, 600; rental, one night $10, three $25; license, $5; share also. Size of stage, 25x29; fair stock scenery.

Opera House; seating capacity, 1000.

LENA, 1,520. R. R., Ills. Central. Beine's Opera House, F. E. Beine, manager ; seating capacity, 450 ; rental, one night $9 ; license, $1. Size of stage, 14x22 ; fair stock scenery. Newspaper : Star (Fri.)......Hotels : White, regular rates, $2 (special also); Lena.

LeROY, 1,600. R. R., Ind. Bloom, & Western ; Wabash. Smith & Murray's Hall, Smith & Murray, managers ; seating capacity, 600. Size of stage, 20x44 ; fair stock scenery. Newspaper : Enterprise (Fri.). Hotels : Keenan, regular rates, $2 (special also); LeRoy.

Young's Hall, D. Young, manager ; seating capacity, 400 ; rental, one night $5, three $10 ; license, $2. Number sets scenery, 5.

LEWISTON, 2,000. R. R., Chicago, Burlington & Quincy. Beadle's Opera House, W. T. Davidson, manager; seating capacity, 850 ; rental, one night $10 ; license, $3 ; share also. Size of stage, 20x40 ; fair stock scenery ; bill poster, Barrett & Weaver. Newspapers : News (Th.); Democrat (Wed.)......Hotels : Standard, regular rates, $2 (special also).

LINCOLN, 6,000. R. R., Chicago & Alton ; Peoria, Decatur & Evansville ; Wabash. Gillett's Hall, Jas. H. Hill, manager ; seating capacity, 600 ; rental, one night $18, three $40 ; license, $4 ; share also. Size of stage, 25x30 ; full set scenery ; bill poster, Chas. Hummell. Newspapers : daily, Journal ; weekly, Herald (Th.), Tribune (Fri.), Times (Th.) .....Hotels : Lincoln, regular rates, $2 (special also) ; Commercial (special also); Spitly.

Opera House, W. W. Stokes, manager ; seating capacity, 800 ; rental ——license, $4 ; share also. Size of stage, 18x30.

8

LITCHFIELD, 5,000. R. R., Ind. & St. Louis; Jacksonville South Eastern; Wabash. City Hall, City Marshall, manager; seating capacity, 400; rental, one night $8, license included. Size of stage, 14x24; fair stock scenery; bill poster, Jno. W. Burns. Newspapers: Advocate, (Sat.), Courier (Th.), Monitor (Sat)......Hotels: Phœnix, regular rates, $2 (special also); Bowlby, special, Central, Planter's.

German Hall; seating capacity, 400.

Ferguson's Hall: **seating capacity, 500.**

LOCKPORT, 3,000. R. R., Chicago & Alton. Norton's Opera House, George B. Norton, **manager; seating capacity, 700; rental, one night** $20, three $45, license included; share also. **Size of stage, 18x42; full set scenery; bill** poster, Opera House; theatrical teamster, **G. B. Norton.** Newspapers: **Phœnix** (Th.), **Commercial** Advertiser **(Th.)**......Hotel: City.

Lull & Lynde's Hall, Lull & Lynde, managers; seating capacity, 300. Size of stage, 12x20; no scenery.

MACOMB, 400. R. R., Chicago, Burlington & Quincy. Chandler's Opera House, **Charles** T. Chandler, manager; seating capacity, 900; rental, one night $15, three $20, license, $3.50. Size of stage, 22x50; number sets scenery, 6; bill poster, J. H. Smith. Newspapers: Eagle (Sat.), By-stander (W.)......Hotels: Miller, regular rates, $2 to $3 (special also); St. Elmo, Randolph.

MARSEILLES, 3,000. R. R., Chicago, Rock Island & Pacific. Occidental Hall, J. Gage, manager; seating capacity, 300; rental, one night $7.15, three $15; no license. Size of **stage, 18x20; no scenery; bill poster,** William Knickerbocker; theatrical teamster, P. Dittmann. Newspaper: **Register (Sat.)**..... Hotels: Beckwith, **regular** rates, $2 (special also); Marseilles.

MARENGO, 2,000. R. R., Chicago & **Northwestern.** Marengo Opera House, R. M. Patrick, manager; seating capacity, 800; rental, **one** night $30, three $75, share also, license included. Size of stage, 25x50; size of proscenium opening, 20x24; height from stage to grooves, 16; height from stage to rigging loft, 26; depth under stage, 5; number sets scenery, 12; scenic artist. Moses; stage carpenter, Dnar; bill poster, Opera House; number of sheets can accommodate, 50; theatrical teamster, H. B. South. Newspaper: Republican, (Fri.), advertising rates, 5c. per line......Hotel: Ryder, special rates, $1 25.

Lansing Hall.

MARSHALL, 1,900. R. R., **Vandalia Line;** Wabash. Armory Hall. Newspapers: **Herald (Tu.), Illinoian** (Sat.), **Messenger (W.)**......Hotel: Sherman, regular rates $1.50 (special also).

MASON CITY, 2,000. R. R., Chicago & Alton; Wabash. **La** Forge **Hall, Welles** Corey, manager; seating capacity, 400; rental one night, $8; license, $3; **share also.** Size of stage, 15x30; number sets scenery, 4; bill poster, Henry Kile; **theatrical** teamster, A. A. Broker. Newspapers: Independent (Fri.), Journal (Fri.)......**Hotels:** Sherman, regular **rates,** $2 to $3 (special also); St. Nicholas.

MATTOON, 8,000. R. R., Illinois Central; Indianapolis & St. Louis (Bee Line); Peoria, Decatur & Evansville. Dole's Opera House, John W. Hanna, manager; seating capacity, 800; rental, one night $25, three, $60; license, $5.50; share also. Size of stage, 25x40; size of proscenium opening, 16x25; height from stage to grooves, 13; height from stage to rigging loft, 24; depth under stage, 6; traps, 1; number sets scenery, 7; leader of orchestra, George Gibler; bill poster, J. W. Hanna; number sheets can accommodate, 350; rate per sheet, 4c; theatrical teamster, Harry Sinsobaugh. Newspapers: daily, Journal; **advertising** rates, yearly contract; weekly, Gazette (F.), Commercial (Th.), Sun (Sun)......Hotels: Dole's House, special rates, $1.50 to $2; Essex House, special rates, $1.50 to $2; **Decker,** special rates, $1.

Union Hall; seating capacity, 500.

McHENRY, 2,318. R. R., Chicago & Northwestern. Riverside Hall, H. E. Wightman, manager; seating capacity, 1,000; rental, one night $5, three $8; **no** license. No stage. Newspaper: Plaindealer (Wed.)　.Hotel: Riverside.

McLEANSBORO, 2,000. R. R., Louisville & Nashville. Shoemaker's Opera House, J. M. Shoemaker, manager; seating capacity, 450; rental one night, $10; license, $1.50; share also. Size of stage, 16x38; number sets scenery, 4; bill poster, S. L. Braden. News-paper : Times (Wed.)......Hotels : Sharp, regular rates, $1.50 (special also), Grand Central.

MENDOTA, 4,500. R. R., Chicago, Bur. & Quincy; Ill. Central. Washington Hall, Wormley & Burkhards, managers; seating capacity, 800; rental, one night $10, three $30; license $5. Size of stage, 26x50; bill poster, H. Bunker. Newspapers: Bulletin (Fri.), Post (Sat.), Reporter (Sat.)......Hotels; Passenger, regular rates; $2 (special also); St. James.

METAMORA, 1,700. R. R., Chicago & Alton. Phœnix Hall, L. Portman, manager; seating capacity, 200; rental, one night $8; license, $2. Size of stage, 20x25; no scenery. News-papers: Sentinel (Th.)...... Hotels: Spiers, Metamora, Bosworth.

MINONK, 2,500. R. R., Chicago, St. L. & Western; Ill. Central. Opera House, Louis Lichtenstein, manager; seating capacity, 750; rental, one night $20, three $45; license, $2; share also. Size of stage, 16x22; number sets scenery, 6; bill poster, Henry Hinkle, theatrical teamster, T. P. Clark. Newspapers: Blade (Th.), Journal (Sat), News (Fri.)....Hotels: Webber, regular rates, $2.00 (special also); Lee, Commercial.

MOLINE, 9,000. R. R., Chicago, Rock Island & Pacific; Chicago, Bur. & Quincy; Chicago, Mil. & St. Paul. Wagner's Opera House, Wm. F. Cram, manager; seating capacity, 900; rental, one night $40, three $100, share also, license included. Size of stage, 32x76; size of proscenium opening, 22x26; height from stage to grooves, 18; height from stage to rigging loft, 30; depth under stage, 8; traps, 2; number sets scenery, 9; leader of orchestra, M. Schillinger; stage carpenter, George Ritter; bill poster, D. M. Mabie; number of sheets can accommodate, 1,500; rates per sheet, 3½c.; theatrical teamster, L. P. Nelson. News-papers: daily, Dispatch, Republican, advertising rate per inch, $1......Hotels: Kentor, Peal's, special rates, $1.50 to $2.

Timm's Hall, Ed. Kittilsen, manager; seating capacity, 400.

Christy's Hall; seating capacity, 300.

MOMENCE, 2,000. R. R., Chicago & Eastern Illinois; Indiana, Illinois & Iowa. Worcester & Lane's Hall, B. F. Holly, manager; seating capacity, 400; rental, one night $10, three $15; license, $1.50. Size of stage, 20x25; number sets scenery, 10. Newspaper: Reporter (Th.). .. ..Hotels: Duval, National.

MONMOUTH, 6,000. R. R., Central Iowa; Chicago, Burlington & Quincy. Opera House. C. Schultz, manager; seating capacity, 1,500; share only. Size of stage, 26x36; number sets scenery, 13; bill poster, Opera House; theatrical teamster, Richard O'Connell. Newspapers: daily, Gazette; weekly, Atlas (Fri.); Review (Fri.)......Hotels: Commercial, regular rates, $2 (special also); Baldwin, Windsor.

Claycomb's Hall, Scott Bros. & Co., managers; seating capacity, 800; rental, one night $10 to $25, three $30; license, $5. Size of stage, 20x50.

MONTICELLO, 2,000. R. R., Wabash. Rhoads Opera Hall, N. E. Rhoads, manager; seating capacity, 500; rental, one night $10, three $25; license, $1 to $3; share also. Size of stage, 16x40; number sets scenery, 5; bill poster, Wes. Trego. Newspapers: Bulletin (Th.), Herald (Wed.) .....Hotels: Sayre, regular rates, $2 (special also); Monticello, National.

MORRIS, 5,000. R. R., Chicago, Rock Island & Pacific. Hall's Opera House, B. B. Hull, manager, seating capacity, 700; rental, one night $15, three $30; license, $3.50. Size of stage, 17x34; number sets scenery, 5; bill poster, William Floyd; theatrical teamster, Wm. Allen. Newspapers: daily, News; weekly, Herald (Fri.), Independent (Wed.)...... Hotels: Hopkins, regular rates, $2 (special also); Carson, Wagner.

MORRISON, 2,600. R. R., Chic. & Nor. West. Library Hall, J. M. Cobleigh, manager; seating capacity, 660; rental, one night $10, three $25; license, $1 to $3. Size of stage, 18x40; number sets scenery, 7; bill poster, E. H. Graves. Newspapers: Herald (Fri), Sentinel (Th.)......Hotels: Revere, regular rates, $2 (special also); Morrison.

Milne's Opera House, C. Quackenbush, manager; seating capacity, 550; rental, one night $10; share also. Size of stage, 22x36; fair stock scenery.

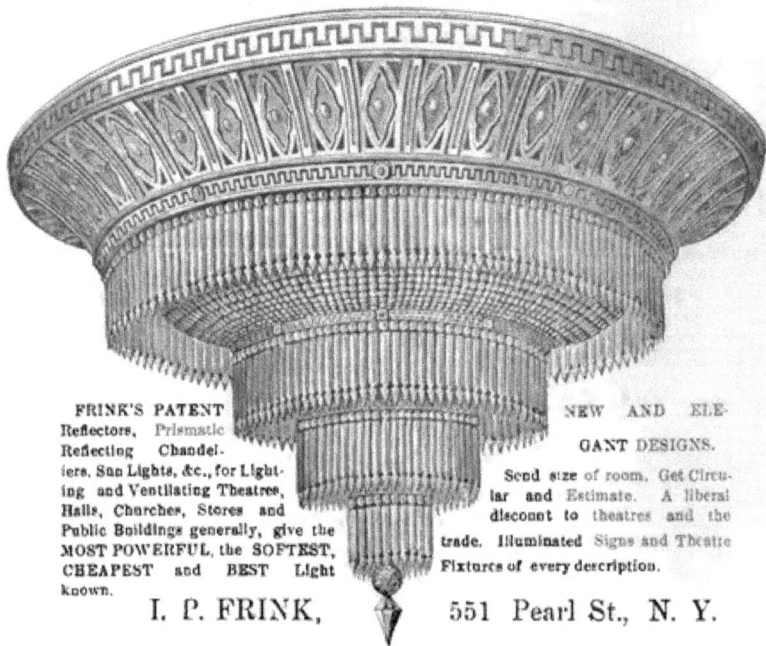

MOUNT CARMEL, 2,500. R. R., Wab., Louis., Evans. & St. L. Seiler s Hall, Sebastian Seiler, manager; seating capacity, 500; rental, one night $10, three $25; license, $1.50 to $2.50. Size of stage, 15x30; no scenery. Newspapers: Register (Th.), Republican (Fri.).... Hotels: Grand Central, regular rates, $2 (special also); Mansion.

MOUNT CARROLL, 2,000. R. R., Chic., Mil. & St. Paul. Union Hall. A. H. Lichty, manager; seating capacity, 400; rental, one night $7, three $18; license, $1; share also. Size of stage, 11x22; number sets scenery, 3. Newspapers: Herald (Fri.), Mirror (Fri.)...... Hotels: Lake, regular rates, $2 (special also); Jones.

MOUNT MORRIS, 1,500. R. R., Chic. & Iowa. Seibert Hall, Peter Knodles, manager; seating capacity, 600; rental, one night $5 to $10 license, $1 to $1.50; share also. Size of stage, 12x40; bill poster, F. F. Skinner. Newspaper: Democrat (Th.) ... Hotels: Webb, Blair.

MOUNT STERLING, 1,500. R. R., Wabash. Opera House. E. C. Brockman, manager. Newspapers: Message (Sat.). Gazette (Th.), Democrat (Sat.) . ..Hotel : Tinnen, regular rates, $2 (special also).

MOUNT VERNON, 3,000. R. R., Louisville & Nashville; Evansville & St. Louis. Shattaus Hall. A. C. Johnson & Co., managers; seating capacity, 350; rental, one night $8, three $15; license, $1 to $2. Size of stage, 18x24; number sets scenery, 3; bill poster, H. Taylor. Newspapers: Exponent (Wed.), News (Th.)......Hotel : Continental, regular rates, $2 (special also).

MURPHYSBORO, 3,000. R. R., St. Louis & Cairo; St. Louis Coal; Grand Tower & Carbondale. Deeberger's Hall, L. Hammer, manager; seating capacity, 500; rental, one night $10, three $20; license, $2. Size of stage, 18x43; number sets scenery, 4. Newspapers: Independent (Fri.), Era (Fri.)..... Hotels: Commercial, regular rates, $2 (special also); Logan.

NAPERVILLE, 2,100. R. R., Chicago, Burlington & Quincy. Scott's Hall. Willard Scott & Co., managers; seating capacity, 400; rental, one night $10; fair stock scenery; bill poster, Fred. Orcott. Newspapapers: Clarion (Wed.).. ..Hotel: American, special rates.

NASHVILLE, 2,000. R. R., Nashville, Chattanooga & St. Louis. Music Hall; seating capacity, 450; fair stock scenery. Newspapers: Democrat (Fri.), Journal (Fri.)......Hotel: Buckeye, special rates.

NAUVOO, 2,500. R. R., C. B. & Q. City Hall; John Haas, manager; seating capacity, 500; rental, one night $5, three $10; license, $1 to $10. Size of stage, 14x16; no scenery; bill poster, John Haas. Newspaper : Independent (Fri.)........Hotels: Temple, Winslow, Nauvoo.

NEWTON, 2,000. R. R., Peoria, Decatur & Evansville; Indiana & Illinois Southern. Johnson's Opera House, S. Johnson, manager; seating capacity, 700; rental (share only); no license. Size of stage, 23x40; size of proscenium opening, 14x18; height from stage to grooves, 14; height from stage to rigging loft, 18; depth under stage, 4; traps, 1; number sets scenery, 8; bill poster, Opera House. Newspapers: Press (Wed.) Times Mentor (Wed.) ... .Hotels: American, special rates, $1; Gilmore.

ODELL, 1,400. R. R., Chic. & Alton. Howard Hall, J. K. Howard, manager; seating capacity, 400; rental, one night $5, three $12; license, $2. Size of stage, 16x30; fair stock scenery. Newspaper: Centennial (Th.)......Hotel: Strawn.

OHIO, 400. R. R., Chic., Bur. & Quincy. Township Hall, Peter J. Conrad, manager; rental, one night $5; license, $2.

OLNEY, 3,558. R. R., Danville, Olney & Ohio River; Ohio & Miss.; Peoria, Decatur & Evansville. Opera House, Powers & Shultz, managers; seating capacity, 500; rental, one night $25; license, $3.50; share also. Size of stage, 22x42; number sets scenery, 14; bill poster, Newson. Newspapers: Republican (Wed.), Times (Wed.)......Hotels: Commercial, regular $2 (special also); Hathaway, National, Olney.

OREGON, 2,500. R. R., Chicago & Iowa. Union Hall, Chas. J. Nohe, manager; seating capacity, 500; rental, one night $15, three $30; license, $1 to $2.50. Size of stage, 20x40; size of proscenium opening, 10x18; depth under stage, 5; traps, 1; number sets scenery,

5; bill poster, Frank Emerson. **Newspapers: Reporter (Wed.)**, Independent (Wed.) ....Hotels: Sinnissippi, special **rates, $1 to $1.50; American,** special rates, $1.

OTTAWA, 18,000. R. R., Chi., Bur. & Quincy; Chi., Rock Island & Pac. Opera House, F. A. Sherwood, manager; seating capacity 900; rental, share **only.** Size of stage, 32x58; height from stage to grooves, 17; height from stage to rigging **loft,** 38; depth under stage, 8; number **sets** scenery, 20; bill poster, Opera House; theatrical teamster. J. **E. Caren.** Newspapers: **daily, Journal, Times;** weekly, Globe, **(Sat)** ....Hotels; Clifton, **special rates, $1.50; White's, special rates, $1.25.**

Turners' Hall, **seating capacity,** 600.

PANA, 3,200. R. R., Ill. Central; O. & Miss.; Indianapolis & St. Louis. **Hayward** Opera **House;** seating capacity, 500; rental, one night $10, three $25, license, $5. **Size of** stage, 14x27; number sets scenery, 3; bill poster, Moses Bray. Newspapers: Gazette (Sat.), **Palladium (Sat.)**... ..Hotels: St. James, regular rates, $2 to $2.50, (special also): **City, Central.**

PARIS, 6,000. R. R., Ill. Midland; Indianapolis & St. Louis; Wabash. Opera Hall, L. **A. G.** Shoaff, manager; seating capacity, 700; rental, one night $30, three $70, license, $5; share **also.** Size of stage, 22x24; number sets scenery, 7; bill poster, L. A. G. Shoaff. Newspapers: semi-weekly, Times, Beacon (Fri.), Gazette (W.)......Hotels: Paris, regular rates, $2 (special also); Commercial, regular rates, $2 (special also); Grand Central.

PAXTON, 2,000. R. R., Ills. Central; Lake Erie & Western. Clark's Hall, T. M. King, **manager; seating capacity, 500;** rental, one night $10; license, $2. Size of stage, 16x30; fair stock scenery; bill poster, G. M. Hawley. **Newspapers: Register (Wed.), Record** (Th.) ......Hotels: Blackstone, regular rates, $2 (special also); Occidental.

PEKIN, 6,500. R. R., Chicago, **St. Louis & Western;** Ind., Bloom. & Western; Peoria, Decatur & Evansville; Wabash. Empire Hall, C. B. Cummings, **manager; seating capacity,** 500; rental, one night $25; **license, $3.25.** Size of stage, 30x66; **number sets scenery.** 7; **bill poster,** A. S. Massey; theatrical teamster, F. S. Young. **Newspapers: daily. Times;** weekly, Republican (Th)......Hotels: Woodward, regular **rates, $2 (special also);** Bemis, regular rates, $2 (special **also);** White, Planters'.

PEORIA, 30,000. R. R., Chicago, **Rock** Island & Pacific; Chicago, Burl. & Quincy: **Central** Iowa,; Wabash; Ill. Mid.; Bloom. & Western; Peoria, Dec. & Evans.; **Rock Island** & Peoria. Grand Opera House, J. B. Barnes, manager; seating capacity, **2,000; rental,** share only. Size of stage, 42x72; height from stage to grooves, 20; height **from stage to** rigging loft, 60; depth under stage, 10; complete set scenery; bill poster. Opera House; theatrical teamster, E. Clarkson, Newspapers: daily, Democrat, Review. Freeman, Journal......Hotels: Peoria, regular rates, $2 (special also); Merchants', National, regular rates, $2 to 2.50 (special also).

Rouse's Opera House, R. Rouse, manager; seating capacity, 1,100; rental, one night $25, three $70; license, $5 to $10. Size of stage, 30x45; height from stage to grooves, 11½; height from stage to rigging loft, 15; depth under **stage,** 6; complete set scenery; bill poster, **M.** Kaufman.

Academy of Music, E. M. Jackman, manager; seating capacity, 1,500 Size of stage, 32x64.

Turner's Hall; seating capacity, 400.

Gable's Adelphi Theatre (variety).

PERU, 6,000. R. R., Chicago, **Rock** Island & Pacific. Turner's Hall, **Hiram** Denning, manager; seating capacity, 800; rental, one night $15, three $37.50; license $3, share also. Size of stage, 30x30; number sets scenery, 4; bill poster, John Baugert. Newspapers: Express, Herald **(W.)**......Hotels: Chambers, regular rates, **$2** (special also): Twin City.

City Hall, seating capacity, 300; rental, one night $12. **No scenery.**

PETERSBURGH, 3,000. R. R., Chicago & Alton; Wabash. **Harris** Guards Opera House, C. E. McDougall, manager; seating capacity, 500; rental, **one night** $15, three $35; license, $3; share also. Size of stage, 22x46; number sets scenery, 5; bill **poster,**

J. C. Bishop. Newspapers: Democrat (Sat.), Herald (Fri.), Observer (Sat.)..... Hotels: St. Charles, regular rates, $2 (special also); Menard.

PITTSFIELD, 3,000, R. R., Wabash. Fishell's Opera House, Albert Fishell, manager; seating capacity, 500; rental, one night $25, three $60, license included; share also. Size of stage, 23x40; number sets scenery, 11; bill poster, A. Kohn; theatrical teamster, L. Leonard. Newspapers: Herald (Wed.), Old Flag (Fri.), Democrat (Th.)......Hotels: Pittsfield, regular rates, $2 (special also); Mansion.

POLO, 2,000. R. R., Ills. Central. City Hall, Funk & Petrie, managers ; seating capacity, 500; rental, one night $10, three $20 ; license, $2. Size of stage. 14x23; number sets scenery, 7. Newspapers: semi-weekly, Clipper, Press (Sat.)......Hotels: Exchange, regular rates, $2 (special also).

PONTIAC, 4,000. R. R., Chicago & St. Louis ; Illinois Central ; Wabash. Lord's Opera House, Wallace Lord, manager ; seating capacity, 500 ; rental, one night $15, three $30 ; license, $1. Size of stage. 18x40 ; height from stage to grooves, 10 ; depth under stage, 5 ; traps, 1 ; number sets scenery, 6 ; bill posters, Scatterday & Blackmore ; number of sheets can accommodate, 500 ; rates per sheet, 3½c.; theatrical teamster, H. Blackmore. Newspapers: Sentinel (Fri.), Free Trader and Observer (Fri.), Gazette (Th.)......Hotel : Phœnix, regular rates, $2 (special also).

PRINCETON, 4,000. R. R., Chicago, Burlington & Quincy. Opera Hall, C. L. Patterson, manager; seating capacity, 600; rental, one night $12, three $30; license, $1 to $3 ; share also. Size of stage, 20x18; number sets scenery, 8 ; bill poster, J. Schlieman. Newspapers : News (Tu.), Republican (Th.), Tribune (Fri.)......Hotels : American, regular rates, $2 (special also); National.

PROPHETSTOWN. 1,200. R. R., Chicago, Burlington & Quincy. Shole's Hall, J. Sholes, manager ; seating capacity, 400 ; rental, one night $5. Newspaper: Spike (Sat.)...... Hotel: Seeley, regular rates, $2 (special also).

PULLMAN, 8,000. R. R., Chicago & Atlantic ; Ills. Central ; Mich. Central. Arcade Theatre, G. W. Hackney, manager; seating capacity, 900; rental—share only. Size of stage, 23x63 ; size of proscenium opening, 28x28 ; height from stage to grooves, 19 ; height from stage to rigging loft, 33¾ ; depth under stage, 7 ; full set scenery ; bill poster, Opera House. Newspapers: Suburban Enterprise......Hotel : Florence.

QUINCY, 42,000. R. R., Chic., Burl. & Quincy; Wabash; St. L., K. & N. W.; Hannibal & St. Joseph. Opera House, P. A. Marks, manager; seating capacity, 200; rental, share only; license, $5.50. Size of stage, 40x60; size of proscenium opening, 28x34; height from stage to grooves, 18; height from stage to rigging loft, 28; depth under stage, 8; traps, 3; number sets scenery, 18; musical director, A. H. Hackett; bill poster, W. H. Alexander; number sheets can accommodate, 2,500; rates per sheet, 4 cents; theatrical teamster, City Transfer Co. Newspapers: daily, Whig, advertising rates per inch, 50c., Herald, 50c. per inch, Journal, 50c. per inch; weekly, Review (Sat.) 50c. per inch...... Hotels: Quincy, special rates, $1.25 to $2; European, special rates, $1.50 to $2; Tremont. Theatre Comique, L. Herndon, manager.

RIVERTON, 1,500. R. R., Wabash. Opera House, R. W. Jess, manager; seating capacity, 600; number sets scenery, 7. Newspaper: Gazette.

ROBINSON, 1,800. R. R., Wabash; Ind. & Ill. Southern. Armory Hall; seating capacity, 300; rental, one night $5; license, $1.50. Size of stage, 12x12; number sets scenery, 2. Newspapers: Argus (Wed.), Constitution (Wed.)......Hotels: Robinson, regular rates, $2 (special also); St. Charles.

ROCHELLE, 2,500. R. R., Chic. & Iowa; Chic. & N. Western. Bain's Opera House, A. Bain, manager; seating capacity, 800; rental, one night $25; license, $3; share also. Size of stage, 20x50; number sets scenery, 5; bill poster, B. Marvin. Newspaper: Register (Sat.)......Hotel: Brockett, regular rates, $2 (special also).

ROCK FALLS, 1,500. R. R., Chic., Burl. & Quincy. Academy of Music, Galt & Tracy, managers; seating capacity, 950; rental, one night $25. Size of stage, 25x60, fair stock scenery. Hotel: Brevoort.

ROCKFORD, 20,000.   R. R., Chicago, Milwaukee & St. Paul; Chicago & North Western;
Chicago, Burlington & Quincy. Opera House, C. C. Jones, manager; seating capacity,
1,000; rental, share only. Size of stage, 43x60; height from stage to grooves, 18; height
from stage to rigging loft, 35; traps, 3; number sets scenery, 20; leader of orchestra, A.
Dedrickson; bill poster, Opera House. Newspapers: daily, Register, Gazette......Ho-
tels: Holland, regular rates, $2 (special also); American, regular rates, $2 (special also);
Edwards, special rates, $1.50.

Metropolitan Hall, seating capacity, 800.

Armory, Lansey & Norman, managers; seating capacity, 800.

ROCK ISLAND, 12,000.   R. R., Chicago, Rock Island & Pacific; Chicago, Burlington &
Quincy; Chicago, Milwaukee & St. Paul: Rock Island & Peoria. Harper's Theatre,
Ben Harper, manager; seating capacity, 1,000; rental, one night, $65; share also. Size of
stage, 42x60; height from stage to grooves, 18; height from stage to rigging loft, 30; depth
under stage, 7½; bill poster, A. C. Miller. Newspapers: daily, Argus, Union; weekly,
Rock Islander (Sat.)......Hotels: Harper, regular rates, $2 to $2.50 (special also): Commercial, Rock Island.

Dart's Hall, Henry Dart's Sons, managers; seating capacity, 600; rental, one night, $30; li-
cense, $5. Size of stage, 30x40; number sets scenery, 7.

ROODHOUSE, 2,500.   R. R., Chicago & Alton; Chicago, Burlington & Quincy. Armstrong's Opera House, B. P. Armstrong, manager; seating capacity, 450; rental, one
night, $10, three $25, license included; share also. Size of stage, 15x48; number sets
scenery, 7. Newspapers: Daily Eye, Journal......Hotels: Metropolitan, regular rates,
$2 (special also): St. James, Globe, Phoenix.

RUSHVILLE, 3,000.   R. R., Chic., Bur. & Quincy. New Opera House, John S. Bagby, manager; seating capacity, 600; rental, ——, share also. Size of stage, 25x43; number
sets scenery, 9; bill poster, Opera House. Newspapers: Citizen (Th.), Times (Th.)......
Hotel: Fey, regular rates, $2 (special also).

Roach Hall, J. M. Roach, manager; seating capacity, 300; rental, one night $10, three
$25; license, $2. Size of stage, 22x28; number sets scenery, 4.

SANDWICH, 2,500.   R. R., Chic., Bur. & Quincy. Union Hall, seating capacity, 300; rental,
one night $8; license, $2.50. Size of stage, 10x25; no scenery; bill poster, John McGinnis. Newspapers: Argus (Sat.) Free Press (Wed.), Gazette (Fri.)......Hotel: Commercial,
regular rates, $2 (special also).

New Opera House, J. A. Tolman, manager; seating capacity, 800. Size of stage, 15x18;
full set scenery.

SAVANNA, 2,000.   R. R., Chic., Milwaukee & St. Paul. Pulford's Hall, B. Pulford, manager; seating capacity, 600. Newspapers: Sentry (Th.), Times (Fri.). ....Hotel: Chambers, regular rates $2 (special also).

SENECA, 900.   R. R., Chic., Rock Island & Pacific; Cin., Ind., St. Louis & Chicago. Underhill's Hall, D. H. Underhill, manager; seating capacity, 300; rental, one night $10, three
$20; license, $1 to $3. Size of stage, 18x24; number sets scenery, 3; bill poster, Thomas
Woods. Newspaper: Record (Fri.)......Hotels: Clarendon, regular rates, $2 (special
also); National.

SHAWNEETOWN, 2,500.   R. R. Louisville & Nashville; Ohio & Miss. Armstrong Hall,
seating capacity, 600; rental, one night, $10; license, $5. Size of stage, 14x22; number
sets scenery, 1. Newspaper: News (Th.)......Hotel: Riverside, regular rates, $2 (special
also).

SHELBYVILLE, 4,000.   R. R., Indianapolis & St. Louis. Opera House, Philip Parker,
manager; seating capacity, 500; rental, one night $15; license, $2; share also. Size of
stage, 16x40; number sets scenery, 6; bill poster, G. Goudy. Newspapers: Democrat
(Th.), Herald (Th.), Union (Th.)... ..Hotel: Sherman, regular rates, $2 (special also).

SHELDON, 1,000.   R. R., Wabash; Cincinnati, Ind., St. Louis & Chicago. Flager's
Hall, W. B. Flager, manager; seating capacity, 350; rental one, night $10, three $20;
license, $2; share also. Size of stage, 14x40; number sets scenery, 3; bill poster, W.
Dehart. Newspapers: Journal (Th.), Reveille (F.)......Hotels: Merchants, regular
rates, $2 (special also); Railroad.

SOMONAUK, 1,000. R. R., Chicago, Burlington & Quincy. Union Hall, C. E. Wright, manager; seating capacity, 300; rental, one night $6, three, $15; license, $1; share also; Size of stage, 11x22; no scenery. Newspaper: Reville (F.)..... Hotel: Exchange, regular rates, $1.50 to $2 (special also).

SPRINGFIELD, 20,000. R. R., Chicago & Alton; Wabash, St. Louis & Pacific; Illinois Central; Springfield & Northwestern. Chatterton's Opera House J. H. Freeman, manager; seating capacity, 1,300; rental, share only; license yearly. Size of stage, 40x55; size of proscenium opening, 30x32; height from stage to grooves, 29; height from stage to rigging loft 38; depth under stage, 9; traps, 4; unmber sets scenery, 28; leader orchestra, Goldsmith; stage carpenter, Harry Snow; bill poster, Opera House; theatrical teamsters, Little & Son. Newspapers: daily, Journal, Monitor, Register; weekly, Mirror (Sat.), Journal (Wed.), Monitor, (Wed.) Register (Wed.)......Hotels: Palace (special rates); St. Nicholas, regular rates, $2 (special also); Leland, regular rates, $2.50 (special also); Revere, special rates, $1.50.

ST. CHARLES, 2,500. R. R., Chicago & North Western. Irwin's Hall, Wm. C Irwin, manager; seating capacity, 600; rental, one night $10, three $30; license, $2; no scenery. Newspapers: Chronicle (Fri.). ....Hotel: Mallory, regular rates, $2 (special also).

STERLING, 8,000. R. R., Chicago & North Western; Chicago, Burlington & Quincy. Academy of Music, Chamberlin Bros., managers; seating capacity, 840; rental, one night $25, three $60; license, $2.50; share also. Size of stage, 28x58; number sets scenery, 10; bill poster, Henry Vanderbeck; theatrical teamsters, Chamberlin Bros. Newspapers: daily, Blade, Gazette; weekly, Standard (Th.)......Hotels: Galt, regular rates, $2 (special also); Wallace, Leavitt, Waverly.

Wallace Opera House, Hamilton S Wallace, manager: seating capacity, 1,000: rental, one night $25. Size of stage, 21x23; fair stock scenery.

STILLMAN VALLEY. R. R., Chicago, Mil. & St. Paul. Opera Hall, L. Dickerman, manager; seating capacity, 575; rental, one night $10, three $25; no license; share also. Size of stage, 20x40; number sets scenery, 18; bill poster, L. Dickerman......Hotel: Stillman Valley.

STREATOR, 11,000. R. R., Chicago & Alton; Chicago, Burlington & Quincy; Chicago, St. Louis & Western; Ind., Ills. & Iowa; Wabash. Plumb's Opera House, Watson & Swan, managers; seating capacity, 1,290; rental, one night $40, three $90; share also. Size of stage, 32x60; full set scenery; bill posters, Eades & Anderson; theatrical teamster, J. Williams. Newspapers: daily, Free Press, Monitor; weekly, Times (Fri.) ... .Hotels: Plumb, regular rates, $2.50 (special also); American, Streator, Gerger. City.

Oriental Hall, J.J. Gerathy, manager; seating capacity, 800; rental, one night $30, three $75; license. $3; share also. Size of stage, 24x50; number sets scenery, 12.

Armory, seating capacity, 500.

SULLIVAN, 3,000. R. R., Decatur, Peoria & Evansville; Wabash. Titus Opera House, J. B. Titus, manager; seating capacity, 700; rental, one night $15, three $30; no license; share also Size of stage, depth, 25; fair stock scenery; bill poster, Charles R. Thomasson Newspapers: Journal (Th.) Progress (Th.)......Hotels: Maple, regular rates, $2 (special also); Eden City.

SYCAMORE, 3,500. R. R., Chicago & North Western; Cortland & Chicago. Wilkin Hall, John L. Pratt, manager; seating capacity, 400; rental, one night $10, three $21; license, $3; share also. Size of stage, 20x40; number sets scenery, 7; bill poster, M. Culihan. Newspapers: semi-weekly, Republican; weekly, City Weekly (Tu.)......Hotels: Winn, regular rates, $2 (special also); Ward.

TAMPICO, 1,000. R. R., Chicago, Burlington & Quincy. Aldrich Hall, J. C. Aldrich, manager; rental, one night $4; license, $1. Newspaper: Tornado (Sat.).. ...Hotel: City.

TAYLORSVILLE, 3,000. R. R., Ohio & Miss.; Wabash. Vandeveer's Opera House, H. M. Vandeveer, manager; seating capacity. 800; rental, one night $25; license, $3; share

also. Size of stage, 25x30; full set scenery; bill poster, O. Young. Newspapers: Democrat (Th.), Republican (W.), Journal (Th.)......Hotels : Globe, regular rates, $2 (special also); City.

Steinway Hall, D. D. Shumway, manager, seating capacity, 700; rental, one night, $5; license, $3. Size of stage, 12x20; fair stock scenery.

TOLONO, 1,500. R. R., Ill. Cent.; Wabash. City Hall, J. M. Armstrong, manager; seating capacity, 300 ; rental, one night $10, three $21 ; license, $2 to $3. Size of stage. 14x26. Newspaper : Herald (Fri.) Hotel : Leonard, regular rates, $2 (special also).

TUSCOLA, 2,000. R. R., Ill. Cent.; Ind., Bloom. & West. Tuscola Opera House, Carraway, Henderson & Co., managers ; seating capacity, 900 ; rental, one night, $15 three $30; license, $3; share also. Size of stage, 25x40 ▶ number sets scenery, 4 ; bill poster, O. M. Metchman; theatrical teamster, Chas. Carners. Newspapers: Review (Fri.), Journal (Sat.) Hotels : Beach, regular rates, $2 (special also); Central.

URBANA, 3,300. R. R., Ind., Bloom. & West.; Wabash. Busey's Hall, M. W. Busey, manager; seating capacity, 500; rental, one night $12, three $24; license, $2 to $3; share also. Size of stage, 16x24; number sets scenery, 6; bill poster, S. L. Nye, (Champaign, Ill.); theatrical teamsters, Heller & Foy. Newspaper: Herald (Wed.)......Hotels : Griggs, regular rates, $2 (special also); St. Nicholas.

Tieman's Opera House, seating capacity, 800; rental, one night $15, three $30; license, $2 to $3. Size of stage, 18x24; number sets scenery, 12.

VANDALIA, 3,000. R. R., Ill. Cent.; Vandalia Line. Fehren Hall, W. A. Riddell, manager; seating capacity, 600; rental, one night $10, three $25. Size of stage, 20x24; number sets scenery, 5; bill poster, W. A. Riddell; theatrical teamster, Jas. Chandler. Newspapers: Democrat (Wed.), Union (Wed.)......Hotels: Dieckman, regular rates, $2 (special also); Ohmer.

VERMONT, 2,000. R. R., Chic., Bur. & Quin. Mershon Hall, J. & H. Mershon, managers; seating capacity, 500; rental, one night $8, three $20. license $3; share also. Size of stage, 18x30; number sets scenery, 4; bill poster E. R. Thomas. Newspaper: Chronicle (Fri.)......Hotels : American. Standard.

VIRGINIA, 2,000. R. R., Ohio & Miss.; Wabash. Trotter's Opera House, Geo. W. Martin. manager; seating capacity, 300; rental, one night $8, two $15: license $2.50. Size of stage, 12x14; number sets scenery, 3; bill poster. H. Coll. Newspapers: Enquirer (Sat.), Gazette (Fri.).... Hotels : regular rates, $2 (special also).

WARREN, 2,000. R. R., Chic., Mil. & St. Paul; Ill. Central. Barton Opera House. Major, Barton, manager; seating capacity, 350; rental, one night $10; license $3. Size of stage 15x17; fair stock scenery. Newspaper : Sentinel (Th.) .....Hotels: Burnett, regular rates, $2 (special also); Barton.

WARSAW. 5,000. R. R., Wabash. Saenger Hall; seating capacity, 400; rental, one night $10, three $25; license. $3.50. Size of stage, 15x40; number sets scenery, 2; bill poster Chas. McKee. Newspaper: Bulletin (Sat.)......Hotels : Adams, regular rates $2 (special also); Warsaw.

WASHINGTON, 2,000. R. R., Chicago & Alton: Chicago, St. Louis & Western; Wabash. Thompson's Opera House, W. H. Long, manager. Newspapers: Herald (Th.), Republican (Wed.). Hotel: Sherman, regular rates, $2 (special also).

WAUKEGAN, 7,000. R. R., Chicago & North Western. Opera House, Ponsonby & Jemison, managers; seating capacity, 600; rental, one night $20, three $50; license $3. Size of stage, 29x90; size of proscenium opening, 12x25; height from stage to grooves, 12; height from stage to rigging loft, 18; depth under stage, 5; traps, 3; number sets scenery, 6; stage carpenter, Joseph Ludlam; bill posters, Ponsonby & Jemison; number of sheets can accommodate, 300; rate per sheet, 4 cents; theatrical teamster, P. Shea; Newspapers: Patriot (Sat.), Gazette (Sat.)......Hotels: Sherman, special rates, $1.50; Waukegan, special rates, $1.50.

WENONA, 1,500. R. R., Chicago & Alton; Ill. Central. McCall's Hall, O. M. Southwell, manager; seating capacity, 450; rental, one night $10, three $25. Size of stage, 12x32; no scenery. Newspaper: Index (Th.)......Hotel: Whittaker's, regular rates, $2 (special also).

WILMINGTON, 2,500. R. R., Chic. & Alton. Empire Hall. H. H. Wise, manager; seating capacity, 400; rental, one night $8, three $15; license, $2. Size of stage, 18x32; bill poster, Wm. H. Noble; theatrical teamster, D. Smith. Newspapers: Advocate (Fri.), Review (Wed.)......Hotel: Stewart, regular rates, $2 (special also).

WINCHESTER, 1,800. R. R., Chicago, Burlington & Quincy. Chapman Hall, W. W. Chapman, manager; seating capacity, 500; rental, one night $7. Size of stage, 18x20. Newspapers: Standard (Fri.), Times (Fri.)..... Hotel: Cheseldine, regular rates $2 (special also).

WOODSTOCK, 2,000. R. R., Chicago & Northwestern. Murphy's Hall, Edward A. Murphy, manager; seating capacity, 600; rental, one night $10 to $12, three $25; license, tickets; share also. Size of stage, 20x43; number sets scenery, 6; bill poster, Theodore Beardsley. Newspapers: Advocate (Sat.), Democrat (Sat.), Sentinel (Th.)......Hotels: Waverly, regular rates $2 (special also); Richmond.

WYOMING, 2,000. R. R., Chicago, Burlington & Quincy; Rock Island & Peoria. Central Hall, G. N. Scott, manager; seating capacity, 400; rental, one night $6, three $15. Size of stage, 14x30; number sets of scenery, 3; theatrical teamster, C. Green. Newspapers, semi-weekly: Herald (Tu., Fri.), Post (Th.)......Hotel: Clifton, regular rates $2 (special also).

INDIANA.

ANDERSON, 6,000. R. R., Cleve., Col., Cin. & Ind.; Pgh., Chic., St. Louis; Cleve., Wabash & Mich.; Cleve., Ind. & St. L. Doxey Theatre, C. T. Doxey, manager; seating capacity, 750; rental——share only; Size of stage, 42x70; size of proscenium opening, 32x27; height from stage to grooves, 14; height from stage to rigging loft, 49; depth under stage, 16; traps, star, vampire, double traps and stage bridge; number sets scenery, 16; stage carpenter, G. A. Williams; bill poster, Frank Spear; number of sheets can accommodate, 1,000; rates per sheet, 4c; theatrical teamster, Harry Brelsford. Newspapers: Review, Democrat (Fri.), advertising rates, yearly contract; Herald (Fri.), advertising rates, yearly contract........Hotels: Doxey, special rates, $1.50; Lee, special rates, $1.25.

ANGOLA, 1,280. R. R., Lake Shore & Michigan Southern. Concert Hall. Newspapers: Herald (Wed.), Journal (Wed.), Republican (Wed.).......Hotel: Russell, regular rates, $2 (special also).

ATTICA, 1,280. R. R., Chicago & Great Southern; Wabash. Banta's Hall, seating capacity, 450; rental, one night $15, three $30; license, $2. Size of stage, 18x30; fair stock scenery; bill poster, Perry Toms. Newspaper: Ledger (Th.)......Hotel: Revere, regular rates, $2 (special also).

AUBURN, 1,600. R. R., Lake Shore & Michigan Southern; Wabash. Ensley's Hall, seating capacity, 500. Newspapers: Courier (Th.), Republican (Th.)......Hotel: Swineford, regular rates, $2 (special also).

AURORA, 7,000. R. R., Ohio & Miss. Grand Opera House, Henry Leive, manager, seating capacity, 800; rental, one night $25, three $55; license, $2; share also. Size of stage, 30x40; number sets scenery, 15; bill poster, Chas. McIntrye. Newspapers: Independent (Th.), Spectator (Th.),. ....Hotels: Eagle, regular rates, $2 (special also); St. Charles..

Schulzes' Hall, H. Schulzes, manager; seating capacity, 500; rental, one night $15, three $30; license, $1 to $5. Size of stage, 12x16; number sets scenery, 2.

BLOOMINGTON, 3,000. R. R., Louis; New Albany & Chicago. Mendelssohn Hall, A. R. Howe, manager; seating capacity, 400; rental, one night $10; license, tickets. Size of stage, 14x24; no scenery; bill poster, J. G. McPheeters. Newspapers : Courier (Sat.), Progress (Wed.), Telephone (Sat.)......Hotels: National, regular rates, $2 (special also) ; Orchard, Falkner.

BLUFFTON, 3,000. R. R., Fort Wayne, Cinn. & St. Louis; Toledo, Cinn. & St. Louis. Curry's Opera House, A. Curry, manager; seating capacity, 500; rental, ——; share also; license, $2. Size of stage, 25x42; number sets scenery, 5; bill poster, Wash. Acton. Newspapers: daily, Herald; weekly, Banner (Th.), Chronicle (Th.)......Hotels: Central, regular rates, $2 (special also); Oliver, Exchange.

BOURBON, 1,000. R. R., Pittsburg, Fort Wayne & Chic. Sears Opera House. Newspaper: Mirror (Th.)... ...Hotel: Rise.

BRAZIL, 5,000. R. R., Vandalia Line. Turners Hall, A. C. Campbell, manager; seating capacity, 400; rental, one night $15. Size of stage, 25x60; size of proscenium opening, 12x22; height from stage to grooves, 10; traps, 1; number sets scenery, 5; bill poster, John Dixon. Newspapers: Mirror (Fri.), Enterprise (Wed.), Register (Th.).... Hotels: Hendrix, regular rates, $2 (special also); Rigby, regular rates, $1.50 (special also).

BREMEN, 1,200. R. R., Balt. & Ohio. Wright's Opera House, J. J. Wright, manager; seating capacity, 225; rental, one night, $10, three $20; license, $1 to $3. Size of stage, 25 x30; size of proscenium opening, 11x14; height from stage to grooves, 12; number sets scenery, 3; leader of orchestra, Peter Fagely; bill poster, Opera House. Newspaper: Banner (Th.)......Hotel : Garver, special rates, $1.

BROOKVILLE, 2,500. R. R., Whitender Valley. Town Hall, Town Marshal, manager; seating capacity, 500; rental, one night $10; no license. Size of stage, 24x40; number sets scenery, 4; bill poster, City Marshal. Newspapers: American (Th.), Democrat (Th.)......Hotels : Valley, regular rates, $2 (special also); Central, Union.

CAMBRIDGE CITY, 3,000. R. R., Pittsburg, Cinn. & St. Louis; Madison & Indianapolis; Fort Wayne, Cin. & Louisville. Opera House, James McGaffrey, manager; seating capacity, 600; rental, one night $15, three $30, license included; share also. Size of stage, 25x40; full sets scenery; bill poster, R. H. Cokefair; theatrical teamster, Charles Knox. Newspapers: Tribune (Th.), Citizen (Fri.)......Hotel: Central, regular rates, $2 (special also).

Carpenter's Hall, James McGaffrey, manager; seating capacity, 800; rental, one night $12; license, $2.25. Size of stage, 25x40; full set scenery.

City Hall, James McGaffrey, manager; seating capacity, 400; full set scenery.

CLINTON, 2,500. R. R., Chic. & Eastern Ill. Opera House, J. H. Bogart, manager; seating capacity, 800; rental, ——— ; share also. Size of stage, 15x25; number sets scenery, 4; bill poster, Henry Bogardue. Newspapers: Herald (Sat.), Argus (Sat.)......Hotel: Central, regular rates, $2 (special also).

COLUMBIA CITY, 3,000. R. R., Pittsburg, Fort Wayne & Chic.; Wabash. Opera Hall, A. P. Mitten, manager; seating capacity, 1,000; rental, one night $30, three $50; license, $2; share also. Size of stage, 22x25; number sets scenery, 8. Newspapers: Commercial (Th.), Herald (Sat.), Post (Wed.)......Hotels: McDonald, regular rates, $2 (special also); Main, Commercial.

COLUMBUS, 7,000. R. R., Cin., Ind., St. Louis & Chic.; Jefferson, Madison & Indianapolis. Germania Hall, C. J. Fowler, manager; seating capacity, 500; rental, one night $12.50, three $25; license, $3 to $5. Size of stage, 20x50; number sets scenery, 11; bill poster, John Doup. Newspapers: daily, Democrat, Republican, Herald. Hotels: Bissell, regular rates, $2 (special also); St. Denis, special.

Palace Theatre; seating capacity, 2,000. Size of stage, 30x60; full sets scenery.

Opera House, John Doup, manager.

CONNERSVILLE, 6,000. R. R., Cin., Hamilton & Dayton; Fort Wayne, Cinn. & Louisville, Whitewater. Andre's Opera Hall, D. W. Andre, manager; seating capacity, 600; rental, one night $20, three $50; license included; share also. Size of stage, 21x46; number sets scenery, 10; bill poster, Robert Gringer; theatrical teamster, A. Ford. Newspapers: Examiner (Wed.), Times (Wed.)......Hotels: Grand, regular rates, $2 (special also); Huston.

COVINGTON, 2,800. R. R., Chic. & East. Ill.; Ind., Bloom. & Western; Wabash. Opera House, A. Lemp, manager; seating capacity; 600, rental, one night $12, three $30, license included; share also. Size of stage, 20x24; number sets scenery, 10; bill poster, James Huston; theatrical teamsters, Huston & Stevenson. Newspapers: People's Friend (Th.), People's Paper (Th.).... .**Hotels:** Craig's, regular rates, $2 (special also); Brown's Eagle, Brunswick.

CRAWFORDSVILLE, 9,000. R. R., Ind., **Bloom. & West.; Vandalia Line;** Louisville, New Al. & C. Music Hall, Voris & Miller, **managers; seating capacity,** 1,000; rental, **one** night $50; share also; **license yearly.** Size of **stage, 40x70; size of** proscenium opening. **32x32;** height from **stage to grooves, 18; height from stage to rigging loft,** 40; depth under **stage, 12; traps, 6; number sets scenery,** 10, **25 set pieces; leader of orchestra,** Harry **Ramsbrook; stage** carpenter, Scott Harris; **bill posters,** Voris & Miller; **number of sheets can accommodate,** 3,000; rates **per sheet, 4c.; theatrical teamster,** Skiff & Freeman's **Transfer Co.** Newspapers: daily, **Argus, News, advertising rates, per line,** 2½c; **weekly, Journal** (Sat.), Review (Sat.), **Star (Thur.), advertising rates, per line,** 2c......**Hotels:** Nutt, Robbins, regular rates, $2 (special **also);** Sherman, **$1.50 (special also;** Holou, regular rates, $1.50 (special also).

Opera House, Dr. W. D. McClelland, manager; seating capacity, 650; rental, one night $25, three $60; license, $3.50. Size of stage, 32x42; size of proscenium opening, 25x22, height from stage to grooves, 14; height from stage to rigging loft, 55; depth under stage, 6; traps, 1; number sets scenery, 10; leader of orchestra, Chas. Rutledge; bill poster, **C.** H. Voris; number of sheets can accommodate, 1,000; rates per sheet, 4c.

CROWN POINT, 2,500. **R R.,** Pgb., **Chic. & St.** Louis. Hoffman's Opera House, John G. **Hoffman** manager; seating capacity, 750; rental, one night **$20,** three **$5**; share also; **license, $2.** Size of stage, 22x37; size of proscenium opening, centre 14½, arched down to **12 feet side: width, 18; height from stage to grooves,** 12; sliding screens; height from **stage to rigging loft, 16;** depth **under stage, 11; traps, 1; number** sets scenery, 7; bill **poster, Opera House; theatrical teamsters, Muzzas & Gregg. Newspapers:** Register **(Th.), Chronicle (Tu.), Star (Fri.), advertising rates per inch, 75c.......Hotels:** Hack, **Rockwell, Mueller's, special rates, $1.**

DANVILLE, 1,600. R. R., Indianapolis & St. Louis. Lincoln Opera House, George A. Dickson, manager; seating capacity, 700. Size of stage, 25x35. Newspapers: Gazette (Tu.), Republican (Th.)......Hotel: Mansion, regular rates, $2 (special also).

DELPHI, 3,500. R. R., Louisville, New Albany & Chicago; Wabash. Lathrop & Ruffing's Opera House, John Lathrop, manager; seating capacity, 500; rental, one night $25, three $50; license, $3; share also. **Size of** stage, 18x20; number sets scenery, 6; bill poster. Charles Taylor. Journal (Wed.), **Times** (Fri.) ....Hotels: Occidental, regular rates, $2. Knight, Frisbee.

  Rinehart's Hall, Charles A. **Holt,** manager; seating capacity, 500; **rental, one night. $10, three $24;** license, **$3; size of stage,** 20x20; number **sets scenery, 12.**

EDINBURGH, 2,000. R. R., Jeffersonville, Madison **& Ind.** Washington Hall, A. W. Winterberg, manager; seating capacity, 400; rental, one night $8, three $30; license, $2. Size of stage, 20x35; number sets scenery, 6; bill poster, Jos. A. Watson; theatrical teamster, J M. Roth......Hotels: Commercial, regular rates, $2 (special also). Galt.

ELKHART, 11,000. R. R., Lake Shore & Mich. So.; Cin., Wabash & M. Bucklen Opera House, W. **B.** Vanderlip, manager; seating capacity, 1,000; rental, one night $50; also share. Size of stage, 40x57½; size of proscenium opening, 30x31; height from stage to grooves, 18; height from stage to rigging loft, 50; depth under stage, 9; traps, **two quarter, one Hamlet, and bridge;** number sets scenery, 19; bill poster, David Carpenter; **number of sheets can accommodate, any amount; rates per sheet, 3 cents; theatrical teamster, D.** Carpenter. Newspapers: daily, Review, Journal......Hotels: Clifton, **regular rates, $2 (special** also), Elkhart, **regular rates, $2** (special **also).**

  Broderick's Opera House, Thorp & Bibbins, managers; seating **capacity, 800;** rental, one **night $20,** three **$50;** license, **$2.50.** Size of stage, 26x40; number sets scenery, 8.

EVANSVILLE, 30,000. Evansville & Terre Haute; Indiana & Evansville; Louisville & Nashville; Louisville, Evansville & St. Louis; Peoria, Decataur & Evansville. **Opera** House, Thomas J. Groves, manager; Brooks & Dickson, New York **rep-**

resentatives; seating capacity, 1,225; rental, one night $60, license included; share also. Size of stage, 40x65; height from stage to grooves, 18; height from stage to rigging loft, 34; depth under stage, 8½; full set scenery; bill poster, F. M. Groves; theatrical teamster, T. W. Vensmann. Newspapers: daily, Courier, Journal; weekly, Argus (Sat.)......Hotels; St. George, regular rates, $2 (special also); Sherwood, regular rates, $2 (special also).

Appollo Theatre, John Albecker, **manager**; seating capacity, 700. Size of stage, 20x24; size of proscenium opening, 15x24; **height from stage to grooves, 14**; depth under stage, 6; traps, 1; leader of orchestra, Val Schriber.

Webber's Theatre, Geo. L. Webber, manager.

FORT WAYNE, 25,000. R. R., Wabash; Pitts., Ft. Wayne & Chicago; New York, Chicago & St. Louis; Lake Shore & Michigan Southern; Grand Rapids & Indianapolis, Ft. Wayne, Cincinnati & Louisville. Academy of Music, C. B. Woodworth, manager; Brooks & Dickson, New York representatives; seating capacity, 1,000; rental, share only, license included; size of stage, 26x31; size of proscenium opening, 14½x25; height from stage to grooves, 12½; height from stage to rigging loft, 19½; depth under stage, 3; traps, 5; number sets scenery, 13; leader of orchestra, F. J. Heinke; scenic artist, Frank King; stage carpenter, Geo. Richards; bill poster, John Ascott; number of sheets can accommodate, 2,000; rates per sheet, 4c; theatrical teamsters, Powers & Barnett. Newspapers: daily, Gazette, advertising rates per inch, 50c.; News, 50c., Sentinel, 50c., Journal, 50c.; weekly, World (Sat.) 50c......Hotels: Aveline, special rates, $2.50; Robinson, $1.50; Main, $1.35; Fleming, $1.

Grand Opera House; seating capacity 1,100.

Masonic Temple, John A. Scott, manager.

New Catholic Library Hall.

Ewing's; seating capacity, 500.

Atlantic Garden (variety).

FRANKFORT, 6,000. R. R., Toledo, Cincinnati & St. Louis; Chicago Air Line; Terre Haute & Logansport; Lake Erie & Western. Opera House, T. J. Smith, manager; seating capacity, 1,000; rental, one night $50 share also; license yearly. Size of stage, 36x64; size of proscenium opening, 20x33; height from stage to grooves, 18; height from stage to rigging loft, 40; depth under stage, 6; traps, 1; number sets scenery, 16; bill poster, Opera House; number of sheets can accommodate, 400; rates per sheet, 3c; theatrical teamster, James Lawson. Newspapers: Crescent (Wed.), advertising rates per inch, 50c.......Hotels: Coulter, special rates, $1; Frankfort, $1.

City Hall, A. J. Dawson, manager; seating capacity, 800; rental, one night $5 to $10, three $12 to $15; license, $1 to $5. Size of stage, 15x40; number sets scenery, 3.

FRANKLIN, 4,000. Jeff., Mad. & Ind.; F. F. & M. Tracy's Opera House, I. S. Tracy, manager; seating capacity, 500; rental, one night $20, three $45; share also; license, $4. Size of stage, 20x35; size of proscenium opening, 10x22; height from stage, to grooves, 10; height from stage to rigging loft, 15; depth under stage, 17; number sets scenery, 6; leader of orchestra, Samuel Vetter; bill poster, Geo. C. Whitlock; theatrical teamster, James Ward. Newspapers: weekly, Herald, Democrat, (Fri.), Jeffersonian (Th.)...... Hotel: Rickell's, special rates, $1.

GOSHEN, 8,000. R. R., Lake Shore & Mich. So.; Cin. Wabash & M. Goshen Opera House, Rogers & Krutz, managers; seating capacity, 1,000; rental, one night $25, or share; license included. Size of stage 32x65; size of proscenium opening, 18x32; height from stage to grooves, 20; depth under stage, 4; traps, 1; number sets scenery, 16; leader of orchestra, Chas. E. Rogers; stage carpenter, W. Self; bill posters, Rogers & Krutz; number of sheets can accommodate, 500; rates per sheet, 4c.; theatrical teamster, Jacob Bloom. Newspapers: daily, News; weekly, Times, (Th.), Democrat, (Wed.).........Hotels: Hascall, special rates, $1.50; Julian, special rates, $1 to $1.50; Western Union, special rates, $1 to $1.25.

Triumph Hall, D. H. Hawks, manager; seating capacity, 465; rental, one night $6, three $15, license, $1 to $8; share also. Size of stage, 24x42; number sets scenery, 6.

H. WAYNE ELLIS,

DRAMATIST,

Author of the following plays:

RICH AND POOR;

an Irish-American Comedy Drama, written expressly for Denman Thompson.

LOVE AND LAW,

a Domestic American Melodrama, written expressly for Milton Nobles (an instantaneous success at the Fourteenth Street Theatre).

QUOGUE P'INT;

an American Comedy Drama of Connecticut life in the early part of this century, abounding in "rich humor, stirring incidents, a strong and interesting story and deftly constructed." See criticism in New York *Mirror*.

GOTHAM.

The career of two sisters, traced from affluence to poverty, and a sequel; being a powerful play of American life in a great city—a play of to-day.

TOM CRASH,

an eccentric American comedy for star. Full of typical American humor—a strong story.

WHO'S THE MAJOR?

a satire upon American Club life—for star.

Several other plays in stock suitable for stars or stock companies. Plays, Opera Librettos and Burlesques written to order.

In preparation: LITTLE JACK SHEPPARD, ROBIN HOOD and DON PEDRO the BOHEMIAN.

REFERENCES: Mr. Denman Thompson, Mr. McVicker, Chicago; Mr. Harry Edwards, Mr. W. J. Florence.

J. ALEXANDER BROWN, Agent for Mr. Ellis, to whom all business letters may be addressed.

GREENCASTLE, 6,000. R. R., Ind. & St. Louis; Louisville, New Albany & Chic.; Vandalia line. Hanneman Opera House, Brattin & Blake, managers; seating capacity, 850; rental, one night $20, license included; share also. Size of stage, 25x25; full set scenery; bill poster, T. V. Alsop; theatrical teamster, City Street Car Line. Newspapers: daily, Star, Press; weekly, Banner, (Th.), Times, To.......Hotels: Grand Central, $2, (special also); Walnut Street, $2, Jones.

HARTFORD CITY, 2,500. R. R., Fort Wayne, Cin. & St. Louis; Chic., St. Louis & Pittsburg. Van Cleve Opera House, W. L. Van Cleve, manager; seating capacity, 700; rental, one night $10, three $25; license, $2; share also. Size of stage, 30x30; number sets scenery, 5; bill poster, C. W. Abbott. Newspapers: News (Th.), Telegram (Th.).....Hotels: Huffman, regular rates, $2 (special also); City.

Dick's Hall, J. H. Dick, manager; seating capacity, 300.

HUNTINGTON, 7,500. R. R., Chic. & Atlantic; Wabash. Huntington Opera House, S. M. Sayler, manager; seating capacity, 955; rental ———; share also. Size of stage, 27x50, full sets scenery; bill poster, Ellis Scarles. Newspapers: daily, News, Democrat (Th.), Herald (Wed.).....Hotels: Commercial, regular rates $2 (special also); American Exchange, National.

City School Hall, William McGrew, manager; seating capacity, 600; rental, one night $15. Size of stage, 24x36; no scenery.

Temperance Hall, A. S. Shoff, manager; seating capacity, 400; rental, one night $15. Size of stage, 16x34.

INDIANAPOLIS, 105,000. R. R., Cin., Hamilton & Dayton; Cin., Ind'l & St. Louis; Chic., St. L. & P.; Clev., Col., Cin. & I.; Ind. & St. L.; Ind. & Vin.; Ind., Bloom. & West.; Ind., Dec. & Springfield; Jeff., Mad. & Ind.; Vandalia Line; Wabash. Dickson's Grand Opera House, George A. Dickson, manager; Brooks & Dickson, New York representatives; seating capacity, 2,000; rental one night $100. Size of stage, 48x76; size of proscenium opening, 51x34; height from stage to grooves, 24; height from stage to rigging loft, 64; depth under stage, 11; all kinds traps; number sets scenery, complete stock; leader of orchestra, R. A. Miller, scenic artist, Peter Wilson; stage carpenter, Harry Grace; bill poster, John Edwards; number of sheets can accommodate, 10,000; rates per sheet, 3c.; theatrical teamster, Frank Bird's Transfer Co. Newspapers: daily, Journal, Sentinel, Times, News; weekly, People (Sat.), Herald (Sat.), Review (Sat.).....Hotels: Dennison, Bate, special rates $2; Grand, Brunswick, special rates $1 to $1.25. English, Occidental.

English Opera House, William E. English, manager; seating capacity, 2,025; rental, one night $100, three $250; share also, license included. Size of stage, 47x80; size of proscenium opening; width, 36; height from stage to grooves, 18; height from stage to rigging loft, 61; depth under stage, 12; traps, 3; number sets scenery, 50; leader of orchestra, H. D. Beissenberg; scenic artist, J. L. Williams; stage carpenter, L. C. Parker; bill posters, Harbison & Abrams; number of sheets can accommodate, 5,000; rates per sheet, 3c.

Dickson's Park Theatre E. E. Ellis, manager; seating capacity, 1,800; share only. Size of stage, 48x76; full set scenery.

Academy of Music, Jacob Crone, manager; seating capacity, 1,600; full set scenery.

Metropolitan Hall, George A. Dickson, manager; seating capacity, 800.

Gilmore's "Zoo" and Elevated Gardens (variety), Charles S. Gilmore, manager; seating capacity, 1,500. Size of stage, 35x48; full set scenery.

Masonic Hall; seating capacity, 500.

JASPER, 1,500. R. R., Louisv., Evansv. & St. L. Grand Opera House, F. Fink & Son, managers; seating capacity, 500; rental, one night $3, three $6; license, $1; leader of orchestra, Prof. Zellen; bill poster, C. Doane. Newspapers: Courier (Fri.), advertising rates, 5c. a line......Hotels: United States, special rates, $2.50 a week; Indiana, special rates, $2.50 a week.

JEFFERSONVILLE, 10,500. R. R., Jeff., Mad. & Indianapolis; Ohio & Miss. Mozart Hall, Chas. Nagle, manager; seating capacity, 850; rental, one night $15, three, $35. Size of stage, 25x50; number sets scenery, 3; bill poster, Harry Kime. Newspapers:

9

daily, News, Times ; weekly, Herald......Hotels   Falls, City, regular rates, $2 (special also); National, regular rates, $1.50 (special also); Falls View, Sherman.

KENDALLVILLE, 3,000.   R. R., **Grand** Rapids & Ind.; Lake **Shore** & Mich. Southern. Mitchell's Hall, Jno. Mitchell, **manager** ; seating capacity, 700 ; rental, one night $10. three $18 ; license, $3. Size **of stage, 20x25** ; number sets scenery, 6 ; bill poster. J. W. Birloulter ; theatrical teamster, **J. W.** Birloulter. **Newspapers :** News. (Wed.), Standard (Fri.)......Hotels: Kelley, regular rates, $2 (special also); Brock.

KNIGHTSTON, 3,000.   R. R., Chic., St. L., **& Pgh.**   Bell's **Hall, L. H.** Bell, manager; **seating capacity, 600** ; **rental, share only, including** license.   **Size of** stage, 21x40 ; size of proscenium opening, 14x20; number **sets scenery, 4.**   Newspaper : Banner (Fri.). ......**Hotels : Shipman, regular rates, $2 (special also); Valley,** Carlen.

KOKOMO, 6,500.   R. R., Chic , St. L. & Pittsburg; Toledo, Cin, & St. L.; **Wabash. Opera House, H. E.** Henderson, manager; seating capacity, 800 ; rental, **one night $40, three** $80; **license included.**   Size of stage, 25x45; size of proscenium opening, 23x20; **height from** stage to grooves, 12; height from stage to rigging loft, 24; depth under **stage, 9;** traps, 2; number sets scenery, 10; leader of orchestra, Jas. McDonald; stage carpenter, Chas. Hovens; bill poster, J. Dashnaw; number of sheets can accommodate, 300; **rates per sheet, 4c.** Newspapers: daily, Gazette-Tribune; advertising rates, yearly contract; weekly, Gazette-Tribune (Tu.), Dispatch (Th.)......Hotels: Clinton, special rates, $1.25 to $1.50; Central, $1.

LAFAYETTE, 25,000.   **R. R ,** Lake Erie & **West.; Cinn., Ind., St. L.** & C.; Wabash; Louisville, New Al. & **C.**   Grand Opera House, F. **B. Caldwell,** manager; seating capacity, **1,350; rental,** one night $75; share also; license yearly.   Size of stage, 40x48; height from stage to grooves, 22; depth under stage, 10; traps, 6; number sets scenery, 16 ; leader of orchestra, Fred. Veole; scenic artists, Noxon, Albert & Toomey; stage carpenter, Thos. Megans; bill poster, Opera House; theatrical teamster, Opera House. Newspapers: daily, Journal, Courier, Call; advertising rates per inch, 50c.; weekly, Herald (Sun.),Times (Sun.) ..   Hotels: Lahr, special rates, $1.50 to $2; St. Nicholas, special rates, $1.50 to $2; Brambel, special rates, $1 to $1.50.

Opera House Geo. A. Dickson (Indianapolis), manager; seating capacity, 1,400; rental, one night $50, license included.   Size of stage, 30x40; full set scenery.

Pythian Hall, **C. H. Crain, manager;** seating capacity, 600.   Size of stage, 20x30; no scenery.

Blue Ribbon Hall.

Armory Hall.

LA PORTE, 9,000.   R. R., Lake Shore **& Mich.** Southern; Wabash, **St. L. & P.; Chic. &** W. **Mich.**   Hall's Opera House, A. **S. Hall,** manager; seating capacity, 900; rental, one night $30, three $75, share also; license, $4.   Size of stage, 36x54; size of proscenium opening, 17x30; height from stage to grooves, 13; height from stage to rigging loft, 35; depth under stage, 9; traps, 4; full stock scenery; bill poster, James Mackey.   Newspapers: **Argus** (Th.), Herald-Chronicle (Th.), Journal (Fri.)......Hotels: Teegarden, special rates. $1.25 to $1.50; Hannah, special **rates,** $1.25 to $1.50.

La Porte Opera House, S. Lay, manager; seating capacity, 900; rental, one night $15, three $35; license, $4; share also.   Size of stage, 25x40; number sets scenery, 12.

LAWRENCEBURG, 4,000.   R. R., Cin., Ind., St. Louis & Chic.; Ohio & Miss.   Odd Fellows Hall, seating capacity, 375; rental, one night $15, three $40; license $2 to $5. Size of stage, 12x42; no scenery; bill poster, Jesse Harper.   Newspapers: Press (Th.), Register **(Th.)** ......Hotels: Hitzfield, regular rates, $2 (special also); Anderson.

LEBANON, 4,000.   R. R., Cin., Ind., St. Louis & Chic.   Cason's Opera **House**, S. L. Cason, manager; seating capacity, 600; rental, one night $25, three $65; share also.   Size of stage, 20x30; size of proscenium **opening,** 15x24; height **from** stage to **grooves,** 15; height from stage to rigging loft, 35; depth **under** stage,4; trap, 1; number **sets** scenery, 7; leader of orchestra, Charles Fullen; scenic artist, Lee O. Garrison; bill posters, Stephenson & Wesner; rates per sheet, 3½c.; theatrical teamster, T. Stephenson.   Newspapers: Pioneer (Th.), Patriot (Th.), Mercury (Th.).......Hotels: Rose, Pleasant Grove, special rates, $1.25.

LIGONIER, 2,500. R. R., Lake Shore & Mich. Southern. Union Hall. J. H. Hoffman, manager; seating capacity, 500; rental, one night $12, three $30, license included; sh re also. Size of stage, 16x18; number sets scenery, 6; bill poster. A. M. Helts; theatrical teamster, W. L. Jackson. Newspapers: Banner (Th.), Leader (Th.).... Hotels: Ligonier, regular rates, $2 (special also): Central.

MADISON, 9,500. R. R., Jeffersonville, Madison & Indianapolis. Odd Fellows' Hall, Thomas M. Calloway, manager; seating capacity, 800; rental, one night $20, three $54, license included; share also. Size of stage 20x24; number sets scenery, 10; bill poster; A. Lockard. Newspapers, daily: Courier, Star, Herald.....Hotels: Western, regular rates, $2 (special also): Central, Continental, Centennial, Broadway.

Musical Academy; seating capacity, 400.

Anger's Hall; seating capacity, 250.

Apollo Garden Theatre (variety), E. Gebest, manager.

LOGANSPORT, 18,000. R. R., Wabash, Chicago, St. Louis & Pacific; Vandalia Line. Dolan's Opera House, William Dolan, manager; seating capacity, 1,300; rental, one night $50, three $125; no license; share also. Size of stage, 31x80; size of proscenium opening, 30x33; height from stage to grooves, 20; height from stage to rigging loft, 30; depth under stage, 6½; traps, 3; number sets scenery, 16; leader of orchestra, Joe Culp; scenic artist, J. Burky; stage carpenter, Joe Louis; bill poster, James L. West; number of sheets can accommodate, 1,000; rates per sheet, 4c. Newspapers, daily: Journal, advertising rates, 50c. per inch ; Pharos, Advertiser; weekly, Chronicle (Sat.)......Hotels New Barnett, special rates, $1.75; Murdock, special rates, $1.25; New Johnson, special rates, $1.

MARION, 4,370. R. R., Chicago, St. Louis & Pittsburgh; Cincinnati, Wabash & Michigan; Toledo, Cincinnati & St. Louis, White's Hall, George White, manager; seating capacity, 500; rental, one night $15, three $40; share also. Size of stage, 24x40; full set scenery; bill poster, E. L. Kinneman; theatrical teamster, Bus Line Spencer House. Newspapers: Chronicle (Fri.), Democrat (Fri.), Republican (Fri.)......Hotels: Spencer regular rates, $2 (special also); Riverside, Tremont, Grand View.

MARTINSVILLE, 2,500. R. R., Cincinnati, Indiana, St. Louis & Chicago; Indianapolis & Vincennes. Hite & Park's Hall, P. M. Parks, manager; seating capacity, 500; rental, one night $12, license included. Size of stage, 20x30; number sets scenery, 3; bill poster, Frank Reed; theatrical teamsters, Davis & Gilpin. Newspapers: Gazette (Sat.), Republican (Th.)......Hotels : Mason, regular rates, $2 (special also); Faulkner.

MICHIGAN CITY, 10,000. R. R., Louisville, New Albany & Chicago; Michigan Central; Wabash. Mozart Hall, Louis J. Welles, manager; seating capacity, 800; rental, one night $15, three $35; license, $2; share also. Size of stage, 20x40; fair stock scenery; bill poster, Henry Miller. Newspapers : daily, Dispatch, Enterprise......Hotels : Jewell, regular rates, $2 (special also); Schulz's European Lake.

Union Hall, Ames & Halliday, managers; seating capacity, 600; rental, one night $10, three $24; license, $3 to $5. Size of stage, 15x20; number sets scenery, 5.

Conden's Hall; seating capacity, 500.

Leed's Hall; seating capacity, 500.

Lynch Hall; seating capacity, 500.

MISHAWAKA, 4,000. R. R., Chicago & Grand Trunk; Lake Shore & Michigan Southern. Hurt's Opera House, Smith & Jernegan, managers; seating capacity, 600 ; rental, one night $10, three $25; license, $2 to $4; share also. Size of stage, 26x42; number sets scenery, 7; bill poster, Frank Avery. Newspaper : Enterprise. (F.)......Hotel : Milburn, regular rates, $2 (special also).

MOORESVILLE, 1,200. R. R., Indiana & Vincennes. City Hall, J. R. Rusle, manager; seating capacity, 500. Newspaper : Monitor (Fri.)......Hotels : McCracin, Mooresville.

MOUNT VERNON, 5,000. R. R., Evansville & Terre Haute; Louisville & Nashville. Masonic Hall, Jacob Harlem, manager; seating capacity, 600 ; rental, one night $10.50 ; license, $3.50. Size of stage, 20x21; fair stock scenery ; bill poster, Theo. Tolliver. Newspapers : Democrat (Th.), Sun (Fri.), Star (Th.).. .....Hotels : Damron, regular rates, $2 (special also); European, regular rates, $2 (special also); City, Brettuns.

"FOR HE DOTH GIVE US BOLD ADVERTISEMENT."—Shakespeare

F. McLEWEE,
Patent Illuminated Signs,

CRYSTAL PRISMATIC WORK,

Scientific Gas Fitting,

GAS FIXTURES, FINE LANTERNS, RE-
FLECTORS, ETC.

Attractive Novelties in Light.

7 W. 4th STREET,

Near Broadway,　　　　　　　NEW YORK.

ESTIMATES AND DESIGNS FURNISHED.

STOCK LITHOGRAPHS.

A LARGE ASSORTMENT CONSTANTLY ON HAND.

SAMPLES FURNISHED ON APPLICATION.

—— ALSO ——

Scenes from Plays, Portraits, Etc.

EXECUTED IN THE BEST STYLE,

AT REASONABLE PRICES.

Address:　　**HENRY SIEBERT & BRO.,**

12 and 14 Warren Street, New York.

P. S.—Our stock lithographs can also be had from Ligon &
Baker, Dramatic Agents, 101 East 14th Street; also, from Marble
& Harrington, Dramatic Agency, 125 South Clark Street, Chicago.

MUNCIE. 5,000. R. R., Fort Wayne, Cincinnati & Louisville; Lake Erie & Western; Cleveland, Columbus, Cincinnati & Indianapolis. Wysor's Opera House, J. H. Wysor, manager; seating capacity, 800; rental, one night $35, three $90; license, $6. Size of stage, 27x42; number sets scenery, 9; bill poster, Opera House. Newspapers: daily, News; weekly, News (Th.); Advertiser (Sat.), Democrat (Fri.), Times (Th.)........Hotels: Kirby, regular rates, $2 (special also); Haines, regular rates, $2 (special also).

NEW ALBANY. 17,500. R. R. Jeffersonville, Madison & Indianapolis; Louisville, Evansville & St. Louis; Louisville, New Albany & Chicago. Opera House, Opera House Co., managers; seating capacity, 1,500; rental, one night $25, three $60, license included. Size of stage, 29x40; full set scenery, bill poster, Fred. G. Corbett. Newspapers: daily, Ledger; weekly, Republican (Fri.); Press, (Wed.)........Hotels: Central, regular rates, $2 (special also), Farmers' (special), Commercial (special). Phoenix, Riverside.

NEW HARMONY. 1,700. R. R. Peoria, Decatur and Evansville. Union Hall Opera House, Eugene S. Thrall, manager; seating capacity, 600; rental, one night $12, three $30; license, $1. Size of stage, 26x22; size of proscenium opening, 18x22; height from stage to grooves, 14; height from stage to rigging loft, 25; depth under stage, 5; traps, 1 centre; number sets scenery, 15; leader of orchestra, William M. Bennett; scenic artist, W. Crisp; stage carpenter, Louis Hamilton; bill poster, J. D. Jones; number of shoe scan accommodate, 60; rates per sheet, &c.; theatrical teamster, Charles Boyer. Newspaper: Register (Fri.).....Hotels: Viet's, special rates, $1; Randolph, special rates, $1.

NEW CASTLE. 4,000. R. R. Pan Handle: Ind., Bloom. & West.; Ft. Wayne, Cin. & Louisv.; New Castle. Palace Theatre, J. W. Fontz, manager; seating capacity, 500; rental, one night $12, three $30; license $2; share also. Size of stage, 28x40; size of proscenium opening, 15x20; height from stage to grooves, 12; depth under stage, 3½; traps, 1; number sets scenery, 12; leader of orchestra, Ernest Moore; scenic artist, Alonzo McCarben, stage carpenter, Henry Kinsey; bill posters, A. W. Alexander, James Bruce, jr.; number of sheets can accommodate, 350; rates per sheet, 3c.; theatrical teamster, Samuel Wooster. Newspapers: Courier (Th.), advertising rates, 10c. per line; Mercury (Fri.), 10c. per line; Democrat (Th.), 10c. per line......Hotels: Bundy, special rates, $1.25; Junction, special rates, $1.25.

Jennings' Hall, L. A. Jennings, manager; seating capacity, 475; rental, one night $12, three $30; license, $2; share also. Size of stage, 24x34; size of proscenium opening, 12x16; height from stage to grooves, 10; depth under stage 3; number sets scenery, 5.

NOBLESVILLE. 3,500. R. R., Wabash, St. Louis & Pac.; Anderson, Lebanon & St. Louis. New Opera House, J. F. Wild, manager; seating capacity, 600; rental, share only, license included. Size of stage, 28x50; size of proscenium opening, 18x24; height from stage to grooves, 14; height from stage to rigging loft, 25; depth under stage, or cellar, 8; number sets scenery, 7; leader of orchestra, Geo. Shirts; scenic artist, T. B. Tont; stage carpenter, John Atkins; bill poster, C. R. Underwood; number sheets can accommodate, 500; theatrical teamster, Mark Daly. Newspapers: Ledger (Fri.), advertising rates, 5c. per line; Independent (Fri.), advertising rates, 5c. per line. Hotels: Wainwright, special rates, $1.25 to $1.50; Ross, special rates $1.

NORTH MANCHESTER. 2,500. R. R., Cin. Wabash & M.; Wabash. Hamilton Opera House, S. C. Hamilton, manager; seating capacity, 500; rental, one night $12, three $30; license, $1. Size of stage, 25x36; size of proscenium opening, 16x20; height from stage to grooves, 12; height from stage to rigging loft, 16; depth under stage, 4; traps, 1, center; number sets scenery, 8; leader of orchestra, W. E. Thomas; bill poster, Kide Hamilton; number of sheets can accommodate, 200; rates per sheet, 4c; theatrical teamster, C. D. Johnson. Newspaper: Journal (Th.), advertising rates, 5c. per line......Hotels: Grimes, special rates, $1.25; Sexton, special rates, $1; Bolin Boarding House, special rates, $1.

PERU. 8,000. R. R., Wabash. Emerik's Opera House, C. M. Emerick, manager; seating capacity, 1,300; rental, one night $65, three $125; license, $3; share also. Size of stage, 31½x22; number sets scenery, 6; bill poster, L. M. Clark. Newspapers: Sentinel (Th.), Republican (Fri.)......Hotels: Bares, regular rates, $2 (special also); National (special), Broadway, Keller, Mansion, Tremont, American, Peru, St. James.

Concord Hall, E. T. Andres, manager; seating capacity, 800; rental, one night $40, three $25. Size of stage, 15x22; number sets scenery, 6.

Bradley's Opera House; seating capacity, 800.

Union Hall.

PLYMOUTH, 3,500. R. R., Pitts., **Ft. Wayne & Chic.**; Vandalia Line; Wabash, Centennial Opera House, Jno. Hohan, manager; seating capacity, 500; rental, one night $15, three $30; license, $2. Size of stage, 33x42; number sets scenery, 10; bill poster, Frank Lawson. Newspapers: **Democrat** (Th.), Republican (Th.), **Restitution** (Th.)......Hotels: Ross, regular rates, $2 (special also); Vinedge, Parker.

PORTLAND, 1,700. R. R., Grand Rapids & Indiana; Lake Erie & **West.** Kirkendall Hall, **E. B Kirkendall, manager**; **seating** capacity, 700. Newspapers: Herald (Th.), Commercial (Th.), **Sun** (F.)......Hotel: Hawkins, regular rates, $2 (special also).

PRINCETON, 3,500. R. R., **Evansville & Terre Haute**; Louisville, Evansville & St. Louis. Euterpe Hall, Lewis **& Dimick, managers**; **seating capacity, 600**; rental, one night, $18; license, $2; share also. Size of stage, 24x46; fair stock scenery; bill posters, Lewis & Dimick. Newspapers: **Clarion** (Th.), **Democrat** (Sat.)......Hotels: Lagow; regular rates, $2; Offenfield's, Donald.

RENSSELAER, 1,500. R. R., **Louisville, New Albany &** Chicago. Rensselaer Opera House, Willey & Sigler, managers; seating capacity, 600; rental, one night, $15; three $35, license included; share also. Size of stage, 18x36; bill poster, Geo. Spitler. Newspapers: Sentinel (Th.), Republican (Th.)......Hotels: Nowel's, regular rates, $2 (special also); Makuver.

RICHMOND, 16,000. R. R., Chicago, St. Louis & **Pacific**; Cin., Ham. & Dayton: **Grand Rapids & Ind.** Grand Opera House, Wm. H. Bradbury & Son, managers; seating capacity, 800; rental, one night $25, three $60; license, one night $3; share also. Size of stage, 30x60; size of proscenium opening, 27x27; **height from stage to** grooves, 18; depth under stage, 10; traps, 2; **number sets scenery**, 10; leader of orchestra, Prof. Otto Schmidt; stage carpenter, **John Fleming**; bill poster, Opera House; number of sheets can accommodate, 50; rates per sheet, 4c.; **theatrical teamsters**, street car stables, or Jas. A. Mahan. Newspapers: daily Palladium, **advertising rates, special contract**; Item, advertising rates, special contract; Independent, **advertising rates, special contract**; weekly, Register (Sun.), advertising rates, special contract; Telegram (Th.), advertising rates, special contract... ..Hotels: Huntington Grand, **special rates, $1.50 to $2.50**; Arlington, special rates, $1.50 to $2.50.

Phillips Opera House, **Dobbins Bros.**, managers; seating capacity, 1,400; rental, one night $30, three $75; share also. Size of stage, 40x50; number sets scenery, 12.

New Park Theatre, Sim. Dobbins, manager; seating capacity, 2,000.

ROCHESTER, 4,000. R. R., Chic. & Atlantic; Wabash. Davidson's Academy of Music, **W. H.** Davidson, manager; seating capacity, 1,000; rental, one night $30, three $50, license included; share also. Size of stage, 28x10; number sets scenery, 12; bill poster, C. A. Haskins. Newspapers: Republican (Th.), Sentinel (Sat.), Tribune (Fri.)......Hotel: Central, regular, $2 (special also).

ROCKVILLE, 2,500. R. R., Terre Haute & Logansport Division of the Vandalia. Rockville Opera House, Tate & Stronse, managers; seating capacity, 800; share only; license, yearly. Size of stage, 25x53; size of proscenium opening, 21x28; height from stage to grooves, 16; height from stage to rigging loft, 30; depth under stage, 5; traps, 3; number sets scenery, 14; scenic artists, Matthew & Sons; bill poster, James Akers; theatrical teamster, W. N. Carlisle. Newspapers: Republican (Wed.), Tribune (Th.), Eagle (Sat.), advertising rates, 2½ c. **per line**......Hotels: Parke, Rockville; special, $1.25.

SEYMOUR, 4,000. R. R., Jeffersonville, Madison & **Indianapolis, Ohio & Miss.** Rooney's Opera House, W. P. Rooney, manager; seating capacity, **600; fair stock** scenery; bill poster, **Jesse** Bartup; theatrical teamster, Ed. Corthrum. Newspapers: daily, Business, **Democrat**......Hotels: Jonas, regular, $2 (special also); Faulkner, Harvey.

Union Hall, W. P. Rooney, manager; seating capacity, 400; **rental**, one night $10; license, **$3**. Size of stage, 12x30; number sets scenery, 2.

SHELBYVILLE, 4,000. R. R., Cin., Ind., St. Louis & Chicago; Jeffersonville, Madison & Indianapolis. Blessing's Opera House, John **Blessing**, manager; seating capacity, 600;

rental, one night $15, three $35; license, $3. Size of stage, 16x40; number sets scenery, 12; bill poster, Frank P. Mather. Newspapers : daily, Democrat; weekly, Republican (Th.), Volunteer (Th.)......Hotels : Ray, regular rates, $2 (special also); Keck, Jackson, Indiana.

SOUTH BEND, 22,000. R. R., Lake Shore & Michigan Southern; Chicago & Grand Trunk; Michigan Central, Logansport & Vandalia. Good's Opera House, John J. McElrain, manager; seating capacity, 1,000; rental, one night $25, three $60; share also; license included. Size of stage, 30x50; size of proscenium opening, 18x26; height from stage to rigging loft, 25; depth under stage, 3½; traps, 1; number sets scenery, 20; leader of orchestra, Prof. Lorenz Eibel; bill poster, Jasper B. Toms; number sheets can accommodate, 2,000; theatrical teamster, Ireland. Newspapers : daily, Times, Register, Tribune ; weekly, Times, Register, Tribune......Hotels : Oliver House, Sheridan, Grand Central, St. James.

Price's Theatre; seating capacity, 500.

SPENCER, 2,500. R. R., Indianapolis & Vincennes. Opera House, J. W. Davis, manager; seating capacity, 800; rental, one night $15, three $35; share also. Size of stage, 22x28; number sets scenery, 17; bill poster, Opera House. Newspapers : Democrat (Fri.), Journal (Th.), Republican (Wed)......Hotels : National, regular rates, $1.50 (special also); Lucas, Moore.

SULLIVAN, 3,000. R. R., Evansville, Terre Haute & Chicago. Sullivan Opera House, R. M. Dear, manager; seating capacity, 800; rental, one night $25, three $60; share also; license included. Size of stage, 22x56; size of proscenium opening, 20x27; height from stage to grooves, 14; height from stage to rigging loft, 20; depth under stage, 6; traps, 1 centre; number sets scenery, 15; bill poster, H. J. Smith; number of sheets can accommodate, 150; rates per sheet, 3c.; theatrical teamsters, Russell & Giles. Newspapers : Times (Wed.), advertising rates, special contract; Democrat (Wed.), advertising rates, special contract; Union (Wed.), advertising rates, special contract......Hotels : McCammon, special rates, $1.50; Grigsby, special rates.

TERRE HAUTE, 30,000. R. R., Chic. & East Ill.; Evansv. & Terre Haute ; Ill. Midland ; Ind. & St. L. ; Vandalia Line. Opera House, J. Naylor, manager; Brooks & Dickson, New York representatives ; seating capacity, 1,600 ; rental, one night $60 ; license included; share also. Size of stage, 38x28 ; height from stage to grooves, 19 ; height from stage to rigging loft, 41½ ; depth under stage, 7 ; full set scenery ; bill poster, J. M. Dishon ; theatrical teamster, C. P. Slaub. Newspapers : daily, Courier, Gazette. . ....Hotels : National, regular rates, $2 (special also) ; Terre Haute, regular rates. $2.50 (special also).

Dowling Hall ; seating capacity, 1,200.

Adelphi Theatre, Thomas Shawnessy, manager.

Atlantic Theatre ; variety.

Turner Hall.

TIPTON, 3,000. R. R., Wabash, St. Louis & Pac.. Lake Erie & West. Kleyla Theatre. Johr. S. Jolly, manager; seating capacity, 800; rental, share only; license included. Size of stage, 30x60 ; size of proscenium opening, 15x24 ; height from stage to grooves, 12 ; height from stage to rigging loft, 18 ; depth under stage, 3 ; traps, 1 ; number sets scenery, 12 ; leader of orchestra. G. M. Lebo ; scenic artist, Jno. S. Jolly ; stage carpenter, W. Motes ; bill poster, Jno. S. Jolly ; number of sheets can accommodate. 500 ; rates per sheet, 3c.; theatrical teamster, Marion Axtell. Newspapers : Advocate (Th.), Times (Fri.)......Hotels : Commercial, special rates. $1.25; National, special rates. $1 ; Indiana, special rates, $1.

Tipton Opera House. More & Newcomers, managers ; seating capacity, 550; rental, one night $15, three $30 ; license included ; share also. Size of stage, 22x44 ; number sets scenery, 9.

UNION CITY, 5,000. R. R., Chicago, St. Louis & Pittsburgh ; Cleveland, Columbus, Cin. & Indianapolis; Dayton & Union. Opera House, A. B. Shuyler, manager; seating capacity, 800 ; rental, one night $15, three $30 ; license, $3 to $8. Size of stage, 20x22 ; number sets scenery, 12 ; bill poster, E. M. Stone ; theatrical teamster, Trissell.

Newspapers : Eagle (Th.), **Times (Sat.)**...... .Hotels : **Branham**, regular rates, $2 ; Doty, **Winslow.**

VALPARAISO, 6,500. R. R., Chic. & Grand Trunk; Pittsburgh, Ft. Wayne & Chicago; N. Y., Chic. & St. Louis. Academy of Music, J. M. McGill, manager; seating capacity, 800; rental, one night $30, three $50; license, $3; share also; bill poster, **J. M.** McGill; theatrical teamster, J. M. McGill. Newspapers: daily, Vidette, weekly, Herald (Th.), Messenger **(Wed.),** Republican (Wed.)......**Hotels:** Merchants, regular rates $2 (special also); Gould (special); Commercial, **Tremont; Central.**

VINCENNES, **13,000. R. R., Evansville &** Terre Haute; Ohio & **Miss.; C. & V.;** Ind. & **Vin.; Wabash & P. C. Green's Opera House,** Frank Green, manager; seating capacity, **1,00); rental, share only; license yearly. Size of stage,** 24x30; size of proscenium opening, **20x24; height from stage to grooves, 16; height from stage to** rigging loft, 20; depth under stage, **5; traps, one centre; number sets** scenery, 11; **leader** of orchestra, Frank Blume; stage carpenter, Ellis Sparrow; **bill poster, J. J.** Cunningham; number **of sheets** can accommodate, 300; rates per sheet, 3 cents; theatrical teamster, Wm. Green. **Newspapers :** daily, Sun, Commercial......Hotels: La Plante, special rates, $1 to $2; American, regular rates, $2 (special also).

WABASH, 4,500. R. R., Cin., Wabash & Mich.; Wabash. Harter's Opera House, Harter Bros., managers; seating capacity, 800; rental, one night $30, three $60; no license, share **also.** Size **of stage,** 40x30; number sets scenery, 12; bill posters, Harter Bros.; the-**atrical teamster, Pat.** Ivory. Newspaper: Courier (Fri.), Plaindealer (Fri.)..... Hotels: **Lutz, regular** rates, $2 (special also); Tremont, regular rates, $2 (special also); National.

WARSAW, 4,000. R. R., Pgh., Fort Wayne & Chic.; Cin., Wabash & Mich. Opera House, Al. F. Ruch, manager; seating capacity, 800 to 1,000; rental, one night $20, three $45; **share also;** license included. Size of stage, 42x60; size of proscenium opening, 25x25; **height from** stage to grooves, 12; height from stage to rigging loft, 18 to 20; depth under stage, 8; traps, **1;** number sets scenery, 10; scenic artist, Alex. F. Ruch; stage carpenter, Louis Ruch; **bill** poster, Louis Ruch. Number of sheets can accommodate, 250 ; **rates** per sheet, 4c.; theatrical teamster, under Opera House management. |Newspapers: daily, Times, adv. rates, per line, 10c.; weekly, Republican (Th.), Union (Fri.), Wasp (Sat.)......Hotels: Kirtley, special rates, $1 to $1.25; American, regular rates, $2 (special also).

WASHINGTON, **5,000. R. R.,** Ohio & Miss., Indianapolis & Evansville. Tannton Opera **House; seating capacity, 650;** rental, one night $20. Size of stage, 17x24; fair stock **scenery; bill poster. Will Vansion.** Newspapers: daily, Gazette; weekly, Democrat **(Sat.)......Hotels: Hyatt, regular rates,** $2 (special also); **Meredith, regular** rates, **$2 (special also); Germantown.**

WESTVILLE, 1,000. R. R., Louisville, New Albany & Chic. **Opera Hall,** W. W. Webster, manager; seating capacity, 400; rental, one night $15; license, **$1.** Size of stage, 17x22; fair stock scenery; bill poster, **C.** Freeman. Newspapers: Indicator (Th.), Times (Th.) ...Hotels: Cole, Flood.

WILLIAMSPORT, 1,500. R. R., Wabash. Court House Hall; seating capacity, 450. Newspapers: Commercial, (Th.), Republican (Th.)......Hotel: Home.

WINAMAC, 2,500. R. R., Chic., St. Louis & Pittsburgh. Varpillath's Opera House, J. D. Varpillath, manager; seating capacity, 600; rental, one night $30, three $50; license, $5; share also. Size of stage, 20x44; number sets scenery, 8; bill poster, Opera House. Newspapers: Journal (Sat.), Republican (Th.)......Hotels: Gilkey, regular rates, $2 (special also); Frain.

WINCHESTER, 3,000. R. **R., Clev. Columbus, Cincinnati & Ind.;** Grand Rapids & Indiana. City Hall, C. E. Magee, manager; seating capacity, 400; rental, one night $10, three $25; license, $1; share also. Size of stage, 16x40; number **sets** scenery, 3; bill poster, **H. Hobbick.** Newspapers: Democrat (Tu.), Herald **(Wed.), Journal** (Wed.)...... **Hotels:** Irvin, regular rates, $2 (special also); Franklin, **City.**

ZIONSVILLE, 1,500. R. R., Cin., Indianapolis, St. Louis & Chicago. Clark's Opera Hall, B. F. Clark, manager; seating capacity, 500; rental, one night $8; license, $1.50; share also. Size of stage, 18x20; number sets scenery, 7; **bill** poster, manager hall. Newspaper: Times (Th.) Hotel: Alford.

IOWA.

ACKLEY, 2,500. R. R., Central Iowa, Ill. Central. City Hall, F. Perkiewicz, manager; seating capacity, 300; rental, one night $7; license, $2 to $5. Size of stage, 14x30; no scenery; bill poster, R. Bush. Newspapers: Enterprise. (Fri.): Tribune (Wed.)........ Hotels: Revere, regular rates. $2 (special also): Ackley.

ADEL, 2,000. R. R., Wabash. McLaughlin's Opera House, D. B. McLaughlin, manager; seating capacity, 600; rental, ———; share also. Size of stage, 17x42; fair stock scenery. Newspapers: Democrat (Th.); News (Wed.); New Era (Th.)......Hotel: Forrester, regular rates. $2 (special also).

AFTON, 2,000. R. R., Chicago, Burlington & Quincy. Johnson Hall, Syp & Emmons, managers; rental, one night $5; license, $2; seating capacity, 300. Size of stage, 16x23; number sets scenery, 4; theatrical teamster, Geo. Simonds, Newspapers: Enterprise (Th.), Tribune News (Wed.)......Hotels: Madison, regular rates, $2 (special also); Occidental.

AGENCY CITY, 1,200. R. R., Chicago, Burlington & Quincy. Chamberlain's Hall; seating capacity, 250; rental, one night $5: license, $1......Hotel: Harden.

ALBIA, 3,300. R. R., Central Iowa; Chicago, Burlington & Quincy; Wabash. Townsend's Opera House, J. E. Townsend, manager; seating capacity, 600; rental, one night; license, $3 to $7. Size of stage, 22x50; number sets scenery, 7; bill poster, Geo. Farrar; theatrical teamsters, Cramer & Noble. Newspapers: Democrat (Fri.), Era (Sat.), Union (Tu.). ..... Hotels: Creamer, regular rates, $2 (special also); Delmonico, C. B. & Q. House.
Seifert's Hall, Chas. E. Griffin, manager.

AMES, 1,500. R. R., Chicago & Northwestern. Opera Hall, Bradley & Reed, managers; seating capacity, 500; rental, one night $12. Size of stage, 25x85; fair stock scenery; bill poster, Chas. Kilman. Newspaper: Intelliger (Sat.)......Hotels: West. regular rates, $2 (special also): Cottage.

ANAMOSA, 2,500. R. R., Chic. & N. Western; Chic., Mil. & St. Paul. Holt's Opera Hall; seating capacity, 400; rental, one night $15; license included. Size of stage, 18x22; fair stock scenery; bill poster, Wm. Leach. Newspapers: Eureka, (Th.), Journal, (Th.) ... Hotels: Gillen, regular $2, (special also), Central.
Lehmkuhns Hall, seating capacity, 300 ; rental, one night $15; license, $2. Size of stage, 12x16; no scenery.

ANGUS, 3,500. R. R., Des Moines & F. Dodge; Minn. & St. Louis. Thomas Opera House, L. S. Thomas, manager; seating capacity, 450; shares also; rental, one night $20; three $50 ; share also ; license, $3. Size of stage, 16x40; size of proscenium opening, 10x10; height from stage to grooves, 10; depth under stage, 3½; traps, 1 ; number sets scenery, 6 ; billposter, N. L. Graham ; theatrical teamster, Jno. D. Williams. Newspapers: Black Diamond, (Sat.), Tenderfoot, (Thur.).. ...Hotel: Orono.

ATLANTIC, 6,000. R. R., Chic., R. Isl. & P.; C. B. & Q ; C. & Nor. W. Bacon's Opera House, H. E. Bacon, manager; seating capacity, 600; rental, one night $35; share also; three $100; license included. Size of stage 32x44; size of proscenium opening, 20x24 ; height from stage to grooves,13; height from stage to rigging loft, 30; depth under stage, 8; traps, 1; number sets scenery, 11; bill poster, H. E. Bacon: number of, sheets can accommodate, 200; rates per sheet, 4c.; theatrical teamsters, Walker Bros. Newspapers: daily, Telegraph, advertising rates per inch, 50c.; weekly, Messenger, (Fri.), Democrat, (Fri.) ....Hotels: Reynolds, special rates, $1 to $1.25; Park, special rates, $1.25; Commercial, special rates, $1.
Whitney's Hall, F. H. Whitney, manager. seating capacity, 400 ; rental, one night $8; license, $2; share also. Size of stage, 20x23; number sets scenery, 7.

AVOCA, 1,500. R. R., Chic. Rock Island & Pacific. Opera House, Coffman & Harlow, managers; seating capacity, 450; rental, one night $15; share also. Size of stage, 18x38; fair stock scenery;. Newspapers: Delta, (Th.), Herald, (Wed.)......Hotel: Railroad, regular, $2 (special also).

C. B. BISHOP,

COMEDIAN,

—— SUPPORTED BY ——

The Bishop Comedy Company.

———

MANAGER AND PROPRIETOR,

CHAS. J. BISHOP

———

12 UNION SQUARE, NEW YORK.

BEDFORD, 2,500. R. R., Chic. Bur. & Quincy. Steele Opera House, Chas. Steele, manager; seating capacity, 600; rental, one night $15; license, $2.50. Size of stage, 26x30; fair stock scenery; bill poster, Wm. Hankins. Newspapers: Southwest, (Fri.), Democrat, (Sat.), Republican, (Th.) .....Hotel: Bedford, regular, $2 (special also).

BELLE PLAINE, 2,000. R. R., Chicago & Northwestern. Phœnix Hall, Wm. A. Hunter, manager; seating capacity, 400; rental, one night $15, three $35; share also. Size of stage, 19x20; number sets scenery, 9. Newspapers: Independent (Wed.), Union (Wed.) .....Hotels: Burley, regular rates, $2 (special also); Sherman.

BELLEVUE, 1,500. R. R., Chicago, Milwaukee & St. Paul. Kochenian Hall; seating capacity, 350. Newspaper: Leader (Th.)......Hotel: Bower.

BLOOMFIELD, 2,500. R. R., Chicago, Burlington & Kansas City; Wabash. Taylor's Opera House, J. A. Taylor, manager; seating capacity, 300; rental, one night $7, three $30; license, $3.50; fair stock scenery. Newspapers: Republican (Th.), Democrat (Th.) ......Hotel: Wilson, regular rates, $2 (special also).

BOONE, 3,400. R. R., Chicago & Northwestern. Metropolitan Hall, A. K. Wells, manager; seating capacity, 400; rental, one night $15, three $30; license, $2. Size of stage, 16x30; bill poster, W. H. Wright. Newspaper: Democrat (Wed.), Republican (Wed.), Standard (Sat.)......Hotels: Lincoln, regular rates, $2 (special also); Eagle, St. James.

City Hall, R. Sutton, manager; fair stock scenery.

Opera House; seating capacity, 500.

BROOKLYN, 1,500. R. R., Chicago, Rock Island & Pacific. Opera House; seating capacity, 400; rental, one night, $8; license, $2; fair stock scenery. Newspaper: Chronicle (Fri.)......Hotel: Skinner, regular rates, $2 (special also).

BURLINGTON, 20,000. R. R., Chicago, Burlington & Quincy; C. B. & K. C.; B. & N. W.; B. C. R. & N.; Wabash. Opera House, Geo. A. Duncan, manager; seating capacity, 1,200; share only. Size of stage, 40x50; height from stage to grooves, 20; height from stage to rigging loft, 50; bill poster, Geo. A. Duncan; theatrical teamster, Burlington Express Co. Newspapers: daily, Gazette, Hawkeye; weekly, Reporter (Th.), Post (Sat.).....Hotels: Gorham, regular rates, $2.50 (special also); Barrett, regular rates, $2 (special also); Union, regular rates, $2.

Grimes Opera House, R. M. Washburne, manager; seating capacity, 1 000; rental, ——; share also; license included. Size of stage, 30x60; number sets scenery, 10.

Turner Hall, John A; Dalldorf, manager; seating capacity, 700.

Academy of Music, R. S. Lyle, manager.

Mozart Hall, seating capacity, 1,000.

CALMAR, 1,000. R. R., Chicago, Milwaukee & St. Paul. Landin's Hall, C. W. Geisen, manager; seating capacity, 200. Newspaper: Clarion (Sat.)......Hotel: George, special rates.

CARROLL, 2,500. R. R., Chicago & N. Western. Music Hall, B. H. Dolls, manager; seating capacity, 550; rental, one night, $15; license, $2. Size of stage, 16x20; fair stock scenery; bill poster, Geo. Marette. Newspapers: Herald (Wed.), Sentinel (Sat.) ......Hotels: Burke, regular rates, $2 (special also); Commercial.

CASCADE, 1,200. R. R., Chicago, Milwaukee & St. Paul. Crawford's Hall, Crawford Bros., managers; seating capacity, 500. Newspaper: Pioneer (Fri.).. ...Hotel: Key City regular rates, $2 (special also).

CEDAR FALLS, 5,000. R. R., Burl., Cedar Rapids & Northern; Ill. Central; W. I. & Neb. Pfeiffer's Opera House, C. H. Brown, manager; seating capacity, 1,000; rental, one night $75, share also; license included. Size of stage, 26x46; size of proscenium opening, 15x22; height from stage to grooves, 13; height from stage to rigging loft, 19; depth under stage, 10; number sets scenery, 10; bill poster, Opera House; number of sheets can accommodate, 225, rates per sheet, 4c.; theatrical teamster, M. Davis. Newspapers: Gazette (Fri.), Journal (Th.) Hotel: Burr's, special rates, $1.50; Commercial, special rates, $1.50; Monitor, special rates, $1.

CEDAR RAPIDS. 18,000. **R. R.**, **Chicago** & Northwestern; Chic., **Mil.** & St. Paul; Burl., Cedar Rapids & Northern. **Greene's** Opera House, C. G. **Greene**, manager; Brooks & Dickson, New York representatives; seating capacity, 1,200; rental, share only; license, yearly. Size of stage, 40x60; size of proscenium opening, 30x33; **height** from stage to grooves, 18; height from stage to rigging **loft**, 36; depth **under stage, 9**; traps, 4; number sets scenery, 21; leader of orchestra, **Len.** H. Salisbury; stage carpenter, George H. Nelson; bill poster, Opera **House**; number of sheets can accommodate, 400; theatrical teamsters, Lynch & Noble. **Newspapers: daily**, Gazette, advertising rates, yearly contract; Republican, **yearly contract;** Herald, yearly contract; weekly, Times (Th.), yearly contract; Chat **(Sat.), yearly contract......Hotels:** Northwestern, special rates, $1.50 to **$2: Grand, $1.50 to $2.50;** Southern, $1.50 to $2.

CENTREVILLE, 2,500. **R. R.**, **Chic.**, **Rock Island &** Pacific; Wabash. Russell's Opera **House; seating capacity, 450;** rental, one **night**, $8; license, $3; fair stock scenery; bill poster, **M. E. Lowther; theatrical teamsters,** W. T. Ogle & Co. Newspapers: Citizen (Wed.), **Industrial Iowegian (Fri.), Journal (Wed.)......**Hotels: Keystone, special: **Continental.**

CHARITON, 3,500. R.R., Chicago, Burlington & Quincy. Mallory's Opera Hall, William Reed, manager; seating capacity, 400; rental, one night $15, three $35; share also; license included. Size of stage, 20x40; size of proscenium opening, 14x24; height from stage to grooves, 12; height from stage to rigging loft, 17; depth under stage, 6; traps, 2; number sets scenery, 14; leader of orchestra, Wm. Reed; stage carpenter, John Reed; bill poster, John Callahan; **theatrical teamster, Samuel** St. John. Newspapers: Patriot (Tu.), **advertising rates 10c. per line;** Democrat **(Tu.),** 10c. per line......Hotels: Bates, special rates, **$1, $5 per week.**

CHARLES CITY, 2,500. **R. R.**, **Chic.**, **Mil. & St. Paul; Ill.** Central. Raymond's Hall, H. C. Raymond, **manager; seating capacity, 300;** rental, one night $10, three $25; license, $2. Size of **stage, 19x24; no scenery.** Newspapers: Advocate (Tu.), Standard (Fri.), Intelligencer (Th.)......**Hotels: Union, regular rates, $2** (special also); Lenard.

Mahara's Opera Hall.

CHEROKEE, 2,000. **R. R.**, **Ill.** Central. Maple Hall, Robert Buchanan, manager; seating capacity, 230; rental, one night $12; license, $2; share also. Size of stage, 16x20. Newspapers: Courier (Fri.), Free Press (Tu.)......Hotels: Washington, regular rates, $2 (special also); Fountain.

CLARINDA, 3,800. R. R., **Chic.**, **Bur. &** Quincy; Hnmeston & Shenandoah. Hawley Opera House, F. W. Parrish, manager; seating capacity, 500; rental, one night $15; license, 3; share also. Size of stage, 40x40; fair stock scenery. Newspapers: Herald (Wed.), Journal **(Sat.), Democrat (Th.)** .. Hotel: Linderman, regular rates, $2 (special also).

CLINTON, **12,000. R. R.**, Chic. & Northwestern; Chic., Mil. & St. Paul; Bur., Cedar Rapids & Northern. Doris' Opera House, Chas. E. Fenlon, manager; seating capacity, 1,200; rental, one night $55; share also; license, $3. Size of stage, 30x60; size of proscenium opening, 30x35; height from stage to grooves, 15; height from stage to rigging loft, 24; depth under stage, 16; traps, 2; number sets scenery, 12; leaders of orchestra, Bulen & Calnan; scenic artists, Andrews & Son; stage carpenter, Harry Tate; bill posters, Opera House; number of sheets can accommodate, 600; rates per sheet, 4 cents; theatrical teamsters, Pronk & McKinley. Newspapers: daily, News; advertising rates, yearly contract; Herald, yearly contract; weekly, Age (Fri.), yearly contract; Herald (Tu.), yearly contract......Hotels: Revere, special rates, $1.50 to $2; Central, special rates, $1.50 to $2; Gerhard, special rates, $1 to $1.50.

Music Hall, Chas. E. Fenlon, manager; seating capacity, 800; rental, one night $40; share also; license, $3. Size of stage, 30x60; size of proscenium opening, 18x30; height from stage to grooves, 12; height from stage to rigging loft, 20; depth under stage, 4; traps, 2; number sets scenery, 10; leader of orchestra, Bulen & Calnan; scenic artists, Andrews & Son; stage carpenter, Will Russell; bill poster, Chas. E. Fenlon.

CORYDON, 1,300. R. R., Wabash. Opera Hall, Wm. Hughes, manager; seating capacity, 400; rental, one night $15 ; license, $1. Size of stage, 16x20 ; number sets scenery, 7; bill poster, D. W. C. Gallup. Newspapers : Democrat (Th.), Times (Th.)......Hotels : Palace, regular rates, $2 (special also); Union, Cottage.

COUNCIL BLUFFS, 27,000. R. R., Union Pacific; Sioux City & Pacific; C. & N. Western ; Chicago, R. I. & Pacific ; Milwaukee & St. Paul ; Wabash ; St. Louis & Pacific ; Chicago, Burlington & Quincy ; K. C. and St. Jo.; all terminate at this point. Dohany's New Opera House, John Dohany, manager ; seating capacity, 1,060 ; rental, one night $65, two $130 ; share also; license included. Size of stage, 38x60 ; size of proscenium opening, 30x30 ; height from stage to grooves, 18 ; height from stage to rigging loft, 44 ; traps, 2 ; depth under stage, 9 ; number sets scenery, 14 ; leader of orchestra, John Adolf ; bill poster, W. C. Niethank. Newspapers : daily, Nonpareil, Globe, Herald ..... Hotels : Ogden, special rates, $1.50 to $2 ; Pacific, special rates, $1.50 to $2 ; Bechtell's, special rates, $1.50 to $2.

Bloom & Nixon's Opera House, Jno. W. Kilgore, manager ; seating capacity, 1,000 ; rental, one night $20 ; license included ; share also. Size of stage, 40x60 ; number sets scenery, 15.

CRESCO, 2,500. R. R., Chic., Mil. & St. Paul. Lyric Hall, Lomas Bros., managers; seating capacity, 800 ; rental, one night $10, three $25 ; share also ; license, $2 to $3. Size of stage, 16x18; size of proscenium opening, 12x18; height from stage to grooves, 12; number sets scenery, 6; bill poster, Syman Eastman. Newspapers : Times (Th.), Plain Dealer (Th.) ..... Hotels : Tremont, Strother.

CRESTON, 8,000. R. R., Chicago, Burlington & Quincy. Creston Opera House, Beach & Syberkrop, managers ; seating capacity, 1,000 ; share only ; license, $5. Size of stage, 35x60; number sets scenery, 30 ; bill poster, Opera House. Newspapers: daily, Gazette; weekly, Commonwealth (Fri.) ..... Hotels : Summitt, regular rates, $2 (special also); Commercial, Central.

DAVENPORT, 25,000. R. R., Chicago, Rock Island & Pacific; Chicago, M. & St. Paul. Burtis' Opera House, A. L. Skeels, manager; seating capacity, 1,400; rental, share only, license included. Size of stage, 61x32; height from stage to rigging loft, 36; depth under stage, 9; traps, 3; full set scenery; musical director, Prof. Otto; scenic artist, Mr. Moses; stage carpenter, Mat Lamb; bill posters, Albert Kackles; theatrical teamster, Alex. Roberts. Newspapers : daily, Gazette, advertising rates, yearly contract; Democrat, yearly contract; Du Demokrat, yearly contract ..... Hotels: Kimball, special rates, $1.50 to $3, St. James, special rates, $1.50 to $2; Newcomb, special rates, $1.50 to $2.
Library Hall; seating capacity, 500; fair stock scenery.

DECORAH, 3,500. R. R., Chic., Mil. & St. Paul. Steyer's Opera House, J. Steyer, manager; seating capacity, 500; rental, one night $20, three $50. Size of stage, 15x22; full set scenery; bill poster, H. L. Cross. Newspapers: Journal and Press (Wed.), Posten (Wed.), Republican (Th.) ..... Hotels: Winneshiek, regular rates, $2 (special also); St. Cloud.

DELAWARE, 500. R. R., Ill. Central: Chic., Mil. & St. Paul. Stone Hall, R. Boone, manager; seating capacity, 400.

DELHI, 700. R. R., Chic., Mil. & St. Paul. Heath's Hall, M. T. Heath, manager; seating capacity, 350; rental, one night $3, three $8, license included; share also. Size of stage, 14x30; bill poster, W. F. Neal. Newspaper: Monitor (Th.) ..... Hotels: Harding, Iowa.

DENNISON, 2,000. R. R., Chic. & Northwestern. Germania Hall, R. Huard, manager: seating capacity, 600; rental, one night $15; license, $2; share also. Size of stage, 25x30; fair stock scenery; bill poster, Tom Broadhurst. Newspapers: Bulletin (Tu.), Review (Fri.) ..... Hotels: Commercial, regular rates, $2 (special also); Jaeggar, Fargo.

DES MOINES, 40,000. R. R., Chic., Rock Island & Pacific; Chic. & North Western; Chic. Burl. & Quincy; Chic., Mil. & St. Paul; Wabash; Wis., Iowa & Neb.; Des M. & Ft. Dodge; Des M. & Osceola. New Grand Opera House, W. W. Moore, manager; seating capacity, 1,500; rental, share only. Size of stage, 50x54, size of proscenium opening, 30x32; height from stage to grooves, 18; height from stage to rigging loft, 60; depth under stage, 8; traps, 3; number sets scenery, 33; stage carpenter, E. Stoll; bill poster, W. W. Moore; number of sheets can accommodate, 3,500; rates per sheet, 4c.; theatrical teamsters, A. T. Johnson & Son. Newspapers: daily, Register, adv. rates per line, 10c.;

Leader, **adv. rates** per line, 25c.; weekly, News, adv. rates per line, 25c.: Times (Sat), adv. rates per line, 25c.; Mail (Sat.)...... Hotels: Kirkwood, special rates, $1.50 to $2: Alern, special rates, 1.50 to $2; Morgan, $1.25 to $2.

Foster's Opera House, Wm. Foster, manager; seating capacity, 1,160; rental, one night $50, license included, share also. Size of stage, 35x50; size of proscenium opening, 30x28; height from stage to grooves, 18; height from stage to rigging loft, 40: **depth** under stage, **9;** traps, 3; full sets scenery; leader **of** orchestra, R. Robinson; **scenic** artist, Clarence Bennett, stage carpenter, Oscar **Crocket;** bill poster, Wm. Foster; **number** of sheets **can accommodate,** 3,000; rates **per sheet, 4c.**

Lewis' Opera House, Brandt & Willcox, **managers; seating capacity, 1,600; rental,** ——, share also; full set scenery.

DE WITT, 3,000. R. R., Chic. & N. Western; Chic., Mil. & St. Paul. De Witt Opera **House, George K. Ryder, manager;** seating capacity, 700; **rental, one night $15, three $35, license included; share also.** Size of stage, 30x42; **number sets scenery, 8; bill poster, Opera House. Newspaper:** Observer (Wed.)...... **Hotel: Gates, regular rates, $2 (special also).**

DEXTER, 1,400. R. R., Chic., Rock Island & Pacific. Swihart's Hall, Simon Swihart. manager; seating capacity, 250; rental, one night $5; license, $1. Size of stage, 14x22. Newspaper: Herald (Fri.)...... Hotels: Kilpatrick, Johnson.

DUBUQUE, 20,000. **R. R.,** Ill. Central; Chic., Mil. & St. Paul. Opera House, Duncan & Waller, **managers; seating capacity, 900; rental, one night $50, three $125, license in-cluded; share also.** Size of stage, 35x64; size **of** proscenium opening, 23x32; height from **stage to grooves, 17; height** from stage to rigging loft, 28; depth under stage, 8; traps, 2: **number sets scenery,** 20; leader of orchestra, Henry Wunderleich; stage carpenter, James **Seward; bill poster,** Jim Brooks; number of sheets can accommodate, 1,000; rates per **sheet,** 4c.; **theatrical teamster, Dubuque Omnibus Co**. Newspapers: daily, Hera'd, Times, Telegraph...... Hotels: **Key City, special rates, $1.50;** Julien, special rates, $2; Lorimier, special rates, $1.50.

City Hall, seating capacity, 600.

Turner's Hall, seating capacity, 800.

DUNLAP, 1,500. **R. R., Chic. & N. Western.** Dunlap Opera House, S. J. Patterson, man-ager; seating capacity, 400. **Newspaper: Reporter (Th.), adv. rates per line, 1c..** ... Hotel: Railway.

EDDYVILLE, 1,100. R. R., Chicago, Rock Island & Pacific; **Central of Iowa. Leggett's Opera House, E.** Leggett, manager ; seating capacity, 250. **Size of stage, 24x14; fair stock scenery; bill poster, Ed.** Leggett. Newspaper: **Advertiser (Sat.)......** Hotels: **Plough, regular** rates, $2 (special also); McKenna.

ELDORA, 2,000. R. R., Central of **Iowa.** Porter & Moir's Opera House, Porter & Moir, managers; seating capacity, 700; rental, one night $15, three $30; share also. Size of stage, 16x44; number sets scenery, 6; bill poster, C. H. Hollister. Newspaper: Herald (Wed.), Ledger (Fri.), Telephone (Th.)..... Hotel: Edgington, regular rates $2 (special also).

ELKADER, 1,200. R. R., Chicago, Milwaukee & **St. Paul.** Boller's Hall. V. Boller, man-ager; seating capacity, 400. Newspapers: **Journal** (Wed.), Register (Fri.)...... Hotel Bordman, regular rates, $2 (special also).

EMMETSBURG, 2,000. R. R., Chicago, Milwaukee & St. Paul; Burlington, **Cedar Rapids & Northern.** Ormsby's Music Hall, Ormsby Bros. & Co., managers; seating capacity, 500; rental, one night $15, three $35; share also; license, $1 to $2. Size of **stage,** 20x42; size of proscenium opening, 14x20; height from stage to grooves, 12; height **from** stage to rig-ging loft, 14; depth under stage, 3½; number sets scenery, 6; theatrical teamster, J. E. Scott. Newspapers: Reporter (Th.), Pilot (Th.), Democrat (Th.) ..Hotels; Wa-verly, special rates, $1.25; St. James, special rates, $1.

FAIRFIELD, 3,500. R. R., Chicago, Rock Island & Pacific. Seaman's Opera House, H. Seaman, manager; seating capacity, 500; rental, **one night** $16; license, $3; share also.

Size of stage, 20x44; bill poster, Harry F. Wertz. Newspapers: daily, Journal; weekly, Ledger (Wed.), Tribune (Th.)... ...Hotels: Leggett, regular rates. $2 (special also); Davis.

FARLEY, 800. R. R., Chicago, Mil. & St. Paul; Illinois Central. Public Hall, O'Connell Bros., managers; seating capacity, 400. Hotel: American.

FAYETTE, 1,500. R. R., Chicago, Mil. & St. Paul. Duncan Hall, H. G. Pest, manager; seating capacity, 500; Newspaper: Postal Card (Tu.) Hotel: Fayette, regular rates. $2 (special also).

FORT DODGE, 5,000. R. R., Illinois Central; Des Moines & Ft. Dodge; Ft. Dodge & Ft. Ridg.; Minn. & St. Louis. Fessler's Opera House, D. Fessler, manager; seating capacity, 1,000; rental, one night $35, three nights $90; license, $2; share also. Size of stage, 20x30; full set scenery; bill poster, W. Dermer. Newspapers: daily, Times; weekly, Messenger (Th.), Gazette (Wed.)......Hotels: Duncombe, regular rates, $2 (special also), Arlington, Fort Dodge.

FORT MADISON, 6,000. R. R., Chicago, Burlington & Quincy; Chicago, Burlington & Kansas City; Fort Madison & North Western. Concordia Opera House, Charles Doerr, manager; seating capacity, 400; rental, one night $15, three $40; license, $3. Size of stage, 22x35; size of proscenium opening, 13x18; height from stage to grooves, 11; height from stage to rigging loft, 14½; depth under stage, 3½; traps, 2; number sets scenery, 8; leader of orchestra, Emil Dassau; scenic artist, E. Dassau; stage carpenter, Gus. Thomas; bill posters, Kistner & McClellan; rates per sheet, 4c.; theatrical teamster, Amzi Morrison. Newspapers: daily, Potonowok, Plain Dealer; weekly, Democrat (Wed.), Plain Dealer (Fri.)......Hotels: Anthes, special rates, $2; Metropolitan, special rates, $1 to $1.50; Kasten, special rates, $1.

GORDON GROVE, 1,200. R. R., Chicago, Burlington & Quincy. Opera House, A. B. Sterns, manager; seating capacity, 500; rental, one night $10; license $1. Size of stage, 21x24; fair stock scenery. Newspaper: Express (Th.)......Hotel: Ohio.

GLENWOOD, 1,800. R. R., Chicago, Burlington & Quincy. Glenwood Opera House, I. G. Cullen, manager; seating capacity, 400; rental, one night $15, license included. Size of stage, 23x38; number sets scenery, 6; bill poster, C. B. Claiborne. Newspapers: Gazette (Sat.), Journal (Sat.), Opinion (Sat.)... ...Hotel: Glenwood, regular rates, $2 (special also).

GREENFIELD, 1,500. R. R., Creston & Northern. Opera House, John J. Hetherington, manager; seating capacity, 400; rental, one night $15, three $35; share also; license, $2. Size of stage, 16x40; size of proscenium opening, 11x20; depth under stage, 3; traps, 1; number sets scenery, 4. Newspapers: Transcript (Th.), advertising rates per line, 5c.; Reporter (Th.), 15c. per inch; Review (Th.), 5c. per line......Hotels: Kirkwood, special rates, $1.25; Wilson.

GRINNELL, 2,500. R. R., Chicago, Rock Island & Pacific; Central of Iowa. Preston's Opera House, Preston & Proctor, managers; seating capacity, 700; rental, one night $20; license, $4; share also. Size of stage, 25x35; fair stock scenery; bill poster, Opera House. Newspapers: semi-weekly, Herald, Independent; weekly, Signal (Sat.)......Hotel: Chapin, regular rates, $2 (special also).

Stewart's Hall; seating capacity, 350; rental, one night $10, three $25; no license. Size of stage, 12x16; no scenery.

GRUNDY CENTRE, 1,000. R. R., Burlington, Cedar Rapids & Northern. Orchestra Hall, Orchestra Hall Co., managers; seating capacity, 500. Size of stage, 16x30; number sets scenery, 6. Newspapers: Argus (Th.), Republican (Wed.), Courier (Fri.)......Hotel: Citizens', regular rates, $2 (special also).

GUTTENBERG, 1,500. R. R., Chicago, Mil. & St. Paul. Turner Hall, Robt. Horsh, manager; seating capacity, 800......Hotel: Central, regular rates, $2 (special also).

HAMBURG, 3,000. R. R., Chicago, Bur. & Quincy; Kan. City, St. Jo. & Council Bluffs. Opera House, C. W. Benton, manager; seating capacity, 500; rental, one night $15; license, $4.50. Size of stage, 20x44. Newspapers: News (Wed.), Times (Fri.)......Hotel: Commercial, regular rates, $2.50 (special also).

McKunch Hall, W. Bostern, manager; seating capacity, 600. Size of stage, 24x44.

THEATRICAL TRUNKS

——AND——

BASKETS.

After thirty years experience in manufacturing, we are
enabled to offer the

Theatrical Profession

an article which, for strength, lightness and dura-
bility, is unsurpassed.

*ALL SIZES AND STYLES CONSTANTLY ON HAND
OR MADE TO ORDER.*

J. C. GILLMORE & CO.,

FACTORY AND SALESROOM:

18 and 20 Fourth Ave., New York.

HAMPTON, 1,700. R. R., Central of Iowa; Dubuque & Dakota. Harriman's Opera House, O. B. Harriman, manager; seating capacity, 800; rental, one night $12, three $30; license, $2; share also. Size of stage, 15x40; number sets scenery, 4; bill poster, E. J. Stonebreaker. Newspapers: Chronicle (Sat.), Recorder (Wed.)......Hotels: Beede, regular rates, $2 (special also); Phœnix, Cannon.

HARLAN, 3,000. R. R., Chic., Rock Island & Pac.; Cin., C. & N. W. Long's Opera House, P. B. Hunt, manager; seating capacity, 750; rental, one night $45, three $100; license included. Size of stage, 26x44; size of proscenium opening, 12x20; height from stage to grooves, 14; height from stage to rigging loft, 12; depth under stage, 4; traps, 2; number sets scenery, 10; leader of orchestra, T. B. Rail; bill poster, Jas. Durham; theatrical teamster, Bus. Line. Newspapers : Tribune (Wed.), Republican (Th.).......Hotel, City, special rates, 1 to $1.50.

INDEPENDENCE, 4,000. R. R., Ill. Central; Burl. Cedar Rapids & Northern. King's Opera House, Chas. King, manager; seating capacity, 800; rental, one night $15; license, $3. Size of stage, 24x52; number sets of scenery, 5; bill poster, Josh. Young. Newspapers: Bulletin (Tu.), Journal (Fri.), Conservative, (Wed.), Advocate (Th.)......Hotels, Empire, regular, $2, (special also); Wheeler, Turner.

Leytze Hall, A. Leytze, manager; seating capacity, 350; rental, one night $12; license, $3 to $10. Size of stage, 6x16; no scenery.

INDIANOLA, 2,500. R. R., Chicago, Rock Island & Pacific; Chic., Burl. & Quin. Opera Hall, J. W. Campbell, manager; seating capacity, 500; share also ; rental, one night $15, three $35; license, $2.50 per night. Size of stage, 20x42; size of proscenium opening, 13x19½; height from stage to grooves, 15; depth under stage, 3½; traps, 2; number sets scenery 6; leader of orchestra. William Richy; bill poster, McNabb; number of sheets can accommodate, 50; rates per sheet, 4c.; theatrical teamster, David Parker. Newspapers: Herald (Th.), Advocate (Th.), Tribune (Th.)........Hotels: Central, special rates, $1, Madison, special rates, $1.

IOWA CITY, 10,000. R. R., Chic., Rock Island & Pac.; Burl., Cedar Rapids & Northern. Clark & Hill's Opera House, J. N. Coldren, manager ; seating capacity. 1,000 ; rental, one night $40, three $100; share also; license included. Size of stage, 32x60 ; height from stage to grooves, 15; height from stage to rigging loft, 21 ; depth under stage, 6 ; number sets scenery, 10; bill poster, Opera House; theatrical teamster, Frank F. Luse. Newspapers: daily, Republican, weekly, Press (Wed.), Vidette-Reporter (Fri.)...... Hotels : St. James, regular rates, $2 (special also) ; Palace, regular rates, $2 (special also.)

IOWA FALLS. 1,000. R. R., Ill. Central. Opera House, R. A. Casleton, manager; seating capacity, 500; rental, one night $8; license, $2. Size of stage, 16x40; fair stock scenery. Newspapers: Citizen (Sat.), Sentinel (Wed.) .....Hotels: Jones, Western, Woods, special rates.

Leonard & Chesboro Opera Hall; seating capacity, 500; rental, one night $10, three $25; license, $2. Size of stage, 18x24; no scenery.

JEFFERSON, 2,000. R. R., Chicago and N. Western; Wabash, St. Louis and Pacific. Opera House, Gallagher & Thompson, managers; seating capacity, 400; rental, one night $15, three $35; license, $1 to $3; share also; license included. Size of stage, 15x21; size of proscenium opening, 10x20; height from stage to grooves, 9½; depth under stage, 3; traps, 1; number sets scenery, 5; bill poster, Sim De Witt; number of sheets can accommodate, 100; theatrical teamsters. W. D. Chandler, A. Gibson. Newspapers : Bee (Th.), advertising rates, 10c. per line; Argus (Wed.), 10c. per line......Hotels : Revere, special rates, $1 to $1.25; Head, special rates, $1 to $1.25.

JESUP, 1,000. R. R., Ill. Central. Bank Opera House; seating capacity, 400; license, $1. Size of stage, 15x25; number sets scenery, 4; bill poster, S. L. Clark. Newspaper : Times (Tu.)......Hotels : Evergreen, Julian.

KEOKUK, 16,000. R. R., Chic., Rock Island & Pac.; Chic., Burl. & Quin.; Wabash & So. Pac. Keokuk Opera House, Harrison Tucker, manager; seating capacity, 1,300; rental, one night $75, three $150; share also. Size of stage, 34x58; size of proscenium opening, 30x30; height from stage to grooves, 18; height from stage to rigging loft 54; depth under

10

stage, 14; traps, 5; number sets **scenery**, 10; leader of orchestra, Chas. Miller; **scenic** artist, Peter Vandersberg; stage carpenter, Grant Springer; bill poster, Austin Bland; number sheets can accommodate, 1,750; rates per sheet, 4c; theatrical teamsters, W. S. Ivine, H. C. Sloten. Newspapers: daily, Gate City, advertising rates, 20c. per line; Constitution, advertising rates, 20c. per line; Democrat, advertising rates, 15c. per line; weekly, Post (Th.), News, (Sat.)......Hotels: Patterson, **special** rates, $1.25 to $1.50; Stanleigh, special rates, $1.25 to $1.50.

Gibbons' Opera House, seating capacity, 1,000; share only. **Size of** stage, 40x50; fair stock scenery.

Baker's Hall, seating capacity, **600.**

KEOSAUQUA, 1,200. R. R., Chic., **Rock Island & Pacific.** Opera House, J. B. Bleakmore; manager; seating capacity, **250; rental, one night** $8, three $18; license, $2. Size **of** stage, 15x18; number sets scenery, **5; bill poster,** Opera House. Newspapers: Republican (Th.), **Democrat (Th.)......Hotels:** Russell, regular rates, $2 (special also): Shepperd.

KNOXVILLE, 3,000. R. R., Chic., Bur. & Quincy; Chic., R. I. & Pacific. Knoxville Opera House, R. H. Law, manager; seating capacity, 500; rental, one night $10, three $25; license, $3.50; share also. Size of stage, 20x30; number sets scenery, 7; **bill** poster, Opera House. Newspapers: Journal (Wed.), Express (Tu.), Reporter (Fri.)...... Hotels: Amos, regular rates, $2 (special also); Tremont.

LANSING, **2,000. R. R., Chic., Mil. &** St. Paul. Germania Hall, M. Kernat, manager; seating capacity 500; **fair stock scenery. Newspapers :** Journal (Wed.), Mirror (Fri). ......Hotel : Unfschmidt, regular rates, **$2 (special also).**

LA PORTE CITY, 1,800. **R. R.,** Burl., Cedar Rapids & Northern. Opera Hall, or G. A. R. **Hall, A.** U. Evarts **and** J. C. Adams, managers; seating capacity, 500; rental, one night $12, three $30; share also; license, $2. Size of stage, 16x38; size of proscenium opening, 14x20; height from stage to grooves, 12½; height from stage to rigging loft, 14; depth under stage, 3; traps, 1; number sets scenery, 11; no orchestra; stage carpenter **J. C.** Adams; bill poster, Dell Mitchell. Newspapers : Progress (Wed.), Review (Th). ......Hotels: National, special rates, $1.

LE MARS, 5,500. R. R., Chi., St. Paul, Minn. & Omaha; Ill. Central. Hoyt's Opera House, H. L. Hoyt, manager; seating capacity, 900; rental, one night $40, three $75; share also; license $2. Size of stage, 65x28; number sets scenery, 10; bill poster, Isaac Lankford. Newspapers: daily, Sentinel; weekly, Democrat (Fri.); Dispatch (Tu.)......Hotels: Richard's, regular rates, $2 (special also), Revere.

Apollo Hall, Geo. E. Pew, manager; seating capacity, 450; rental, one night $15, three $40; **share** also; license $1 to $15. Size of stage, 18x48; number sets scenery, 5.

LEON, **2,000.** R. R., **Chi., Bur. &** Quincy; Des Moines, Osceola & So. Hildreth's Opera House, J. F. Hildreth, manager; seating capacity, 600; rental, one night $10, three $25, license included; share also. Size of stage, 22x44; size of proscenium opening, 18x16; height from stage to grooves, 10; height from stage to rigging loft, 18; depth under stage, 4½; traps, 1; number sets scenery, 6; leader of orchestra, W. T. Kelly; stage carpenter, S, Peniwell; bill poster, Milton Simmons; number sheets can accommodate, 500; rates per sheet, 2c.; theatrical teamster, Wm. Glaze. Newspapers: Journal (Th.); Democrat-Reporter (Wed.) .....Hotels: Ward's, special rates, $1; Sales, special rates, $1; Beck, special rates, 75c.

LYONS, 4,000. R. R., Chi. & N. Western; Chi., Mil. & St. Paul. Odeon Hall, Justus Lund, manager; seating capacity, 500; rental, one night $15; license $2 to $3. Size of stage, 25x50; number sets scenery, 12; bill poster, Jacob Thomson. Newspapers: Advertiser (Th.); Mirror (Sat.)......Hotels: American, regular rates, $2 (special also); Union, Transit, City.

Masonic Temple; seating capacity, 400.

Murphy's Hall; seating **capacity, 350.**

MALCOLM, 800. R. R., Chic., Rock Island & Pacific. Opera House; seating capacity, 350; rental, one night $5; license, $1.50; fair stock scenery. Newspaper: Gazette (Tu.)...... Hotel: Central.

Chickering Hall.

STAGE

CHICKERING HALL,
151 and 153 Tremont St., Boston.

FLOOR

BALCONY

This beautiful hall, just opened to the public, and so long needed in Boston, is fitted up regardless of expense, and has all modern conveniences.

It is lighted by the Edison Isolated Light, and its acoustic properties and ventilation are perfect. It has a seating capacity of four hundred and sixty-two (462), all numbered seats.

For Pianoforte Recitals, Readings and Chamber Concerts, this hall has no equal in Boston

151 and 153 TREMONT STREET,
BOSTON, MASS.

MALVERN, 7,100. R. R., Chic., Bur. & Quincy; Wabash. Opera House. Newspaper: Leader (Th.) .... Hotel: Judkins, regular rates $2 (special also).

MANCHESTER, 3,000. R. R., Illinois Central. City Hall, Charles H. Day, manager; seating capacity, 600; rental, one night $15, three $45; share also; no license. Size of stage, 18x66; size of proscenium opening, 14x27 height from stage to grooves, 13½; depth under stage, 3; number sets scenery, 10; bill poster, J. B. Andrews; number sheets can accommodate, 300; rates per sheet, 4c.; theatrical teamster, F. E. Evans. Newspapers: Democrat (Wed.), Press (Fri.) ..... Hotels: Clarence, special rates, $1.25; Globe, special rates, $1.25.

MAQUOKETA, 3,500. R. R., Chicago & Northwestern; Chicago, Mil. & St. Paul. Opera House, Wm. Current, manager; seating capacity, 700; rental, one night $20, three $50; share also; license, $2. Size of stage, 20x36; size of proscenium opening, 12x20; height from stage to grooves, 15; height from stage to rigging loft, 15; depth under stage, 3; traps, 1; number sets scenery, 5; leader of orchestra, Prof. F. Kreger; scenic artists, Slauter & Stanley; stage carpenter, Wm. Current. Newspapers: Record (Wed.), advertising rates, 5c. per line; Sentinel (Th.), 15c. per line; Excelsior (Sat.), 10c. per line...... Hotels: Emery, special rates, $1 to $1.25; Decker, $1.25 to $1.50.

MARENGO, 2,500. R. R., Chic., R. I. & Pacific. Stover's Opera House, M. W. Stover, manager; seating capacity, 600; rental, one night $15, three $40; license, $1; share also. Size of stage, 20x41; number sets scenery, 5; bill poster, J. B Lion; theatrical teamster, John Lindsay. Newspapers: Democrat (Th.), Republican (Wed.)...... Hotels: Clifton, regular rates, $2 (special also); Park, Lafayette, Central, Parnell, Union.

MARION, 4,000. R. R. Chic., Mil. & St. Paul. Marion Opera Hall, J. I. Berryhill, manager; seating capacity, 600; rental, one night $15, three $35; license, $1 to $3. Size of stage, 20x30; number sets scenery, 7; bill poster, Robert Magee. Newspapers: Pilot (Th.), Register (Wed.) ..... Hotel: Park, regular rates, $2 (special also).

MARSHALLTOWN, 9,000. R. R., Chicago & North Western; Central of Iowa. Woodbury Hall, L. C. Goodwin, manager; seating capacity, 800; rental, one night $25, three $60; license, $5; share also. Size of stage, 22x30; number sets scenery, 8; bill poster, L. C. Goodwin. Newspapers: daily, Times-Republican; weekly, Statesman (Sat.)........ Hotels: Tremont, regular rates, $2 (special also); Boardman, Bowler.

MASON CITY, 4,500. R. R., Chic., Mil. & St. Paul; Central of Iowa. Parker's Opera House, H. T. Parker, manager; seating capacity, 800; rental—share only; license, $3. Size of stage, 28x44; size of proscenium opening, 16x22; height from stage to grooves, 14; height from stage to rigging loft, 24; depth under stage, 4; traps, 1; number sets scenery, 14; bill posters, H. G. & A. T. Parker; number of sheets can accommodate, 400; rates per sheet, 3c. Newspapers: Republican (Wed.), advertising rates, 10c. per line; Express (Sat.), advertising rates, 10c. per line; Times (Wed.), advertising rates, 10c. per line......Hotels: St. Charles, special rates, $1.50 to $2; Dyer House, special rates, $1.25 to $2; Albion, special rates, $1 to $1.50; Zoller, special rates, $1; Slocum, $1 to $1.50.

Lloyd & Tuttle's Hall, Lloyd & Tuttle, managers; seating capacity, 400; rental, one night $10, three $25; license, $2 to $2.50. Size of stage, 16x28; number sets scenery, 3.

McGREGOR, 3,500. R. R., Chic., Mil. & St. Paul. Atheneum, Thos. Arnold, manager; seating capacity, 700; rental, one night $15. Size of stage, 25x50; full set scenery; bill poster, E. D. Ryan; theatrical teamster, John Mann. Newspapers: News (Wed.), Times (Th.)........Hotels: Hofschmidt, Evans.

MECHANICSVILLE, 1,000. R. R., Chic. & North Western. Opera House, W. H. Sturges, manager; seating capacity, 300; rental, one night $8; license, $1. Size of stage, 18x18; fair stock scenery. Newspaper: Press (Fri.)......Hotel: City.

MITCHELL, 2,500. R. R., Illinois Central. Court House; seating capacity, 300; rental, one night $5. Size of stage, 12x40; bill poster, Geo. Botham. Hotel: Lewis.

MISSOURI VALLEY JUNCTION, 1,150. R. R., Chic. & North Western; Sonix City & Pacific. Town Hall, A. L. Tamislede, manager; seating capacity, 220; rental, one night $7; license, $5; share also. Size of stage, 12x18; number sets scenery, 3; bill poster, W.

— THE —

ERIE RAILWAY,

"The Landscape Route of America,"

— IS THE —

SHORT AND DIRECT ROUTE from NEW YORK

— TO —

BINGHAMTON, OWEGO, CLEVELAND, DETROIT,

ELMIRA,

BUFFALO,

NIAGARA

FALLS,

CINCINNATI,

ST. LOUIS,

CHICAGO.

A

DOUBLE
TRACK

of

STEEL RAILS
with

ROCK BALLAST

And FAST TRAINS.

A

SPLENDID

EQUIP-

MENT
of

PULLMAN'S
PALACE,

DAY, BUFFET
and

Sleeping Coaches.

WESTINGHOUSE AIR BRAKES and
MILLER PLATFORM AND COUPLER.

For further and more particular Information as to Rates, Routes, Pullman Coach Accommodation, etc., etc., etc, apply to any Erie Ticket Agent, or to

JNO. N. ABBOTT,
Gen'l Passenger Agent.
New York.

J. BUCKLEY,
Gen'l Eastern Passenger Agent.
401 Broadway, New York.

H. Donohue. Newspapers: People's Defender (Th.), Times (Fri.)......Hotels: Commercial, regular rates, $2 (special also); Union.

MONTICELLO, 2,800. R. R., two branches Chic., Mil. & St. Paul. Monticello Opera House, Ross & Foster, managers: seating capacity, 800; rental, one night $18, three $15; share also; license, $2. Size of stage, 20x60; size of proscenium opening, 18x25; height from stage to grooves, 14; depth under stage, 10; traps, 2; number sets scenery, 10; leader of orchestra, W. H. Monroe; bill poster, Levi Fuller; number of sheets can accommodate, 200; rates per sheet, 3c.; theatrical teamster, Pat Conners. Newspapers: Express (Th.), Times (Wed.)......Hotels: Lovell, special rates, $1.50; Clifton, special rates, $1.

MOUNT AYR, 2,000. R. R., Chic., Bur. & Quincy. Cole & Pratt's Opera House. Cole & Pratt, managers: seating capacity, 350; rental, one night $7, three $14; license, $1 to $3; share also. Size of stage, 30x10; number sets scenery, 5; bill poster, Johnny Morrison: Newspapers: Journal (Th.). Onward (Th.), Record (Th.)......Hotels: Ellis, regular rates, $2, (special also); Crawford, Currie.

MOUNT PLEASANT, 5,000. R. R., Chic., Bur. & Quincy; St. Louis, Keokuk & Nor. Western. Union Hall, W. E. Bass, manager; seating capacity, 1,000; rental, one night $10, three $25; license, $5; share also. Size of stage, 23x40; number sets scenery, 7; bill poster, C. S. Moore; theatrical teamster, W. P. Saunders. Newspapers: Free Press, (Th.), Herald (Th.), Journal (Th.)......Hotels: Hazelton, regular rates, $2 (special also); Harlan, regular rates, $2, (special also).

Saunders Opera House, W. E. Bass, manager; seating capacity, 1,100; rental, one night $10, three $25. Size of stage, 24x30; number sets scenery, 2.

MUSCATINE, 12,000. R. R., Chic., Rock Island & Pac.; Burl., Cedar Rapids & Northern. Odds' Opera House, L. W. Olds, manager: seating capacity, 900; rental, one night $25, three $60; license, $3 to $5.50; do not share. Size of stage, 18x30; size of proscenium opening, 24x26; height from stage to grooves, 14; height from stage to rigging loft, 28; depth under stage, 4; traps, 2; number sets scenery,13; leader of orchestra, Icoff & Beaty; bill poster, Wm. Amlong; number of sheets can accommodate, 400; rates per sheet, 2c.; theatrical teamster, Johns. Newspapers: daily, Journal, advertising rates per line, 10c.; Tribune, advertising rates per line, 10c........Hotels: Commercial, special rates, $1.25, Webster, special rates, $2.

Stein's Music Hall, S. G. Stein, manager; seating capacity, 700; rental, one night $15, three $40; share also. Size of stage, 17x38; number sets scenery, 12.

Tremont Hall, S. G. Stein, manager; seating capacity, 650; rental, one night $15, three $40; license, $5 to $9.50. Size of stage, 16x32; number sets scenery, 8.

Hare's Hall; seating capacity, 500.

NEVADA, 2,000. R. R., Chic., & Nor. Western. Opera Hall, McCord & Briggs, managers; seating capacity, 600; rental one night $17, license included. Size of stage, 23x26; number sets scenery, 8; bill posters. Bishop Bros. Newspapers: Highway (Sat.), Representative (Wed.), Watchman (Fri.)........Hotel: Vincent, regular rates, $2 (special also).

NEW SHARON, 1,000. R. R., Central of Iowa. Concert Hall, D. Stanton, manager; seating capacity, 400; rental, one night $8; license, $1. Size of stage, 16x40; number sets scenery, 7. Newspaper: Star (Wed.)......Hotels: Pacific, Sharon.

NEWTON, 3,500. R. R., Chic., Rock Island & Pacific; N. & M.; Central of Iowa. Union Hall, Arthur J. Wright, manager; seating capacity, 550; rental, share only; license yearly. Size of stage, 14x22; size of proscenium opening, 14x22; height from stage to grooves, 9; height from stage to rigging loft, 14 front, 9 back; depth under stage, 4; traps, 1; number sets scenery, 5; no orchestra; scenic artist, W. W. De Long; bill poster, Chas. E. Mitchell; number of sheets can accommodate, 400; rates per sheet, 3c.; theatrical teamster, Bewyer Bros. Newspapers: Journal (Wed.), advertising rates per line, 5c. to 10c.; Democrat (Th.), 5c. to 10c.; Herald (Fri.), 5c. to 10c. .....Hotel: Johnson's, special rates, $1.50; Delmonico, regular rates, $2 (special also).

NORTHWOOD, 1,300. R. R., Central of Iowa. Bur., Cedar Rapids & Northern. Music Hall, R. C. Pike, manager; seating capacity, 300; rental, one night $6, three $15; license,

$2 to $3; share also. Size of stage, 16x16; no scenery. **Newspapers:** Eagle (Th.), Index (Th.)..... Hotels: Dwelle, regular rates, $2 (special also); **Miller,** Northwood.

OGDEN, 800. R. R.. Chic. & North Western; Minn. & St. **Lonis.** Opera House. Newspaper: Reporter (Th.)...... Hotel: King, regular rates, $2.

OSAGE, 3,000. **R. R.,** Ill. Central. Sprague's Academy of Music; seating capacity, 1,000. Size of stage, **25x50;** bill poster, Manager Academy of Music. Newspapers: Press (Th.), News (Th.)..... Hotels: Merchants', regular rates, $2 (special also): Lawn.

OSCEOLA, 2,000. R. R., Chic., Bur. & Quincy; **Des Moines,** Osceola & Southern. Opera **House, B.** Prichett, **manager;** seating capacity, 700. Size of stage, 22x16; fair stock **scenery. Newspapers:** Democrat (Th.), Sentinel (Th.)......Hotels: Kohler, regular rates, $2 (special also); Merchants.

OSKALOOSA, 8,000. R R , Central of Iowa; Chic., Bur. & Quincy: Chic., Rock Island & **Pacific;** Keokuk & Des Moines; B. & W. Masonic Opera House, G. N. Beechler, manager; seating capacity, 1,000; rental, share only; license yearly. Size of stage, 35x58; size of proscenium opening, 18x20; height from stage to grooves, adjustable; height from stage to rigging loft, 20; depth under stage, 9; traps, 1; number sets scenery, 16; leader of orchestra, Horace Shadell; bill poster, Fred Beckman, jr.; number of sheets can accommodate, 400; theatrical teamster, Oskaloosa Livery & Transfer Co. Newspapers: semi-weekly, Herald (Th. and **Sat.),** advertising rates, yearly contract; Globe (Sat.) yearly contract; Standard (Fri.), yearly contract...... Hotels: Downing, special rates, $1.50 to $2; Burnett, special rates, $1.25 to $1.50.

OTTUMWA, 13,000. R. R, Chic., Bur. & Quincy: Chic., Rock Island & Pacific; Chic., Mil. & St. Paul; Wabash. Lewis Opera House, Conn Lewis, manager; seating capacity, 1,500; rental, one night $45, three $90; share also; license yearly. Size of stage, 32x65; size of proscenium opening, 26x32; height from stage to grooves, 16; height from stage to rigging loft, 26; depth under stage, 4; traps, 4; number sets scenery, 12; leader of orchestra, Carl Swabkey; scenic artist, Hugh Lansing; stage carpenter, Harry Howser; bill poster, Opera House; number sheets can accommodate, 500; rates per sheet, 4c.; theatrical teamster, Opera House. Newspapers: daily, Courier, advertising rates, yearly contract; Democrat, yearly contract; weekly, Press (Sat.), yearly contract......Hotels: Ballingall, special rates, $1.50 to $2; Baker, $1 to $2; Revere, $1.

Market Street Opera House; seating capacity, 650; rental, one night $15, three $35; license $6; share also. Size of stage, 20x27; number sets scenery, 6.

OXFORD JUNCTION, 1,000. R. R., Chic., R I. & Pacific. **National Hall,** F. Nowacheek, manager; seating capacity, 300; bill poster, Manager Hall. **Newspaper: Mirror** (Th.) ......Hotel: **Central.**

PANORA, 1,100. R R., Wabash. Opera House, L. J. Pentacost, manager; seating capacity, 300; rental, one night $10, three $25; license, $1. Size of stage, 18x40; no scenery; bill poster, Opera House. Newspaper: Vedette (Fh.)......Hotel : Panora, regular rates, $2 (special also).

PELLA, 3,000. **R.R ,** Chic., R. I. & Pac. Pella Opera House, L. Bach, manager; seating capacity, 400; rental, one night $10, three $25; license, $3. Size of stage, 19x40; number sets scenery, 4; bill poster, Orange D. Post; theatrical teamster, D. Wells. Newspaper: Blade (Th.)..... Hotels American, regular rates, $2 (special also); Sterling, Gardiner.

PERRY, 1,500. Chic., Mil. & St. Paul; Des Moines & Fort Dodge. Union Hall, Lunt & Leaton, managers; seating capacity, 500; rental, one night $10, three $20; license, $2; share also. Size of stage, 12x25; no scenery; bill poster, R. S. Lunt. Newspapers: Chief (Fri); Pilot (Wed.)......Hotels: City; regular rates, $2 (special also); Perry.

POSTVILLE, 1,000. R.R., Bur., Cedar Rapids & Northern; Chic., Mil. & St. Paul. Turner Hall, John Thoma, manager; seating capacity, 500. **Newspapers: Post** (Fri.), Review **(Sat.).** ...Hotel: Commercial, regular rates, $2 (special also).

PRAIRIE CITY, 1,900 R. R., Chic., R. I. & Pac. (K. & D. Div.) Union Hall. W. G. Clements, manager; seating capacity, 500; rental, one night $10, three $20; license, $1; share also. Size of stage, 22x18; number sets scenery, 4. Newspaper: News (Fri.) ..... Hotels: Atkins, regular rates, $2; Feather's.

RED OAK. 5,000. R. R. Chic., Bur. & Quincy. Bryson's Hall, Bryson & Son, managers; seating capacity, 500; rental, one night $15, three $35; license, $3 to $5. Size of stage, 25x40; fair stock scenery; bill poster, W. A. Fisher. Newspapers: Express (Fri.), Telephone, (Wed.), Record (Tu.)...... Hotels : Central, regular rates, $2 (special also). Judkins, Depot.

Roache's Hall; seating capacity, 350; rental, one night $15; license, $1 to $3. Size of stage, 14x32; no scenery.

Bishop's Opera House; seating capacity, 1,000.

SABULA, 1,500. R. R., Chic., Mil. & St. Paul. Blenner Hall. Jerry Blenner, manager ; seating capacity, 500. Newspapers : Gazette (Sat.)...... Hotel : Eldredge, regular rates, $2 (special also).

SAC CITY. 2,500. R. R., Chic. & North Western. Opera House, Jas. N. Miller, manager ; seating capacity, 700; rental, one night $10; license included; share also. Size of stage, 24x50 ; number sets scenery, 5 ; bill poster, Jas. N. Miller. Newspapers : Democrat (Th.), Sun (Fri.)...... Hotels: Hendricksen, special rates; Stanley.

SANBORN, 1,000. R. R., Chic., Mil. & St. Paul. Roden Hall, A. H. Roden, manager; seating capacity, 800. Newspaper : Pioneer (Fri.)........ Hotel : Clark, regular rates, $2 (special also).

SHELDON, 1,200. R. R., Chic., Mil. & St. Paul; Chic., St. Paul, Minneapolis & Omaha. White's Hall, D. S. White, jr., manager; seating capacity, 350; rental, one night $10; license, $5. Size of stage, 14x48; no scenery. Newspapers: Mail (Th.), News (Th.) ......Hotel; Sheldon, regular rates, $2 (special also).

SHENANDOAH, 2,000. R. R., Chic., Bur. & Quincy; Humeston & Shenandoah; Wabash. Norton & West's Opera House, Norton & West, managers; seating capacity, 600; rental, one night $20. Size of stage, 24x50; fair stock scenery; bill poster, J. C. Brookfeet. Newspapers: Post (Sat.), Reporter (Fri.), Republican (Th.)..... Hotels: Lytle, regular rates, $2 (special also); Grand Central. Park.

Williams' Hall; seating capacity, 300; rental, one night $4; license, $3. Size of stage, 12x30; no scenery.

SIBLEY, 800. R. R., Chic., St. Paul, Minn. & Omaha. Academy of Music, Close Bros. & Co., managers; rental, ——, share also. Newspaper: Gazette (Fri.)...... Hotel; Sibley, regular rates, $2 (special also).

SIGOURNEY, 2,500. R. R. Chic , R. I. & Pacific; Chic., Mil. & St. Paul. Yerger's Opera House, Frank S. Yerger, manager; seating capacity, 600; rental, one night $10, three $27; license, $3. Size of stage, 14x22; number sets scenery, 5; bill poster, J. W. Burke; theatrical teamster, James Adams. Newspapers: Courier (T.), News (T.), Review (Wed.)...... Hotels: Page, regular rates, $2.50 (special also); Commercial, Beatty.

SIOUX CITY, 10,000. R. R., Chic., Mil. & St. Paul; Chic., St. Paul, Minn. & Omaha; Ill. Central; Sioux City & Pacific. Academy of Music, William Grady, manager; seating capacity, 650; rental, one night $25; license, $5. Size of stage, 22x50; number sets scenery, 5; bill poster, Wm. Grady. Newspaper: daily, Journal, Times; weekly, Courier (Fri.) ..... Hotel: Hubbard, regular rates, 2 (special also): Merchants (special); St. Elmo, Madison.

SPIRIT LAKE, 1,500. R. R , Bur.. Cedar Rapids & Northern. Rice Opera House, John A. Moak, manager; seating capacity, 400; rental, one night $15, three $30; license, $2; share also. Size of stage, 17x12; number sets scenery, 4. Newspapers: Beacon (Fri.), Journal (Wed.)...... Hotels: Crandall, Baxter, Commercial, Lake, Park.

STUART, 3,000. R. R., Chic., Rock Island & Pacific. Opera House, Savage & Ryan, managers; seating capacity, 600; rental, one night $15; license, $2 to $3; share also. Size of stage, 18x45; number sets scenery, 5; bill poster, J. W. Rose; theatrical teamster, Wm. Warren. Newspaper: Locomotive (Fri.)...... Hotels: Dean, regular rates $2 (special also); Iowa.

STORM LAKE, 2,500. R. R., Ill. Central. Rawson Opera House, —— Rawson Manager; seating capacity, 1,000; rental, one night $20, three $50; share also; license, $2. Size of stage, 20x48; size of proscenium opening, 12x22; height from stage to grooves, 12; height from stage to rigging loft,18; depth under stage, 8; traps, 1; number sets scenery, 8; leader of orchestra, Geo. Robinson; stage carpenter, Samuel Ellis; bill poster, Opera House; number of sheets can accommodate, 500; rates per sheet, 4c.; theatrical teamster, Joy Clemonds. Newspapers: Tribune (Sat.), Pilot (Th)......Hotel: City, regular rates, $2 (special also); Park, regular rates, $1.

Brown Brothers' Hall; Brown Brothers, managers; seating capacity, 225; rental, one night $10, three $20; license, $1 to $2; share also. Size of stage, 20x21; no scenery.

TAMA CITY, 1,500. R. R., Chicago & North Western ; Chi., Mil. & St. Paul. Soleman's Opera House, H. Soleman, manager; seating capacity, 500; fair stock scenery. Newspapers: semi-weekly, Free Press; weekly, Herald (Fri.)
Merchants' Hall; rental, one night $7; license, $2.50; no scenery.

TIPTON, 2,000. R. R., Chicago & North Western. City Hall, J. C. Reichert, manager; seating capacity, 500; rental, one night $10, three $25; license, $3; share also. Size of stage, 12x44; number sets scenery, 6. Newspapers : Advertiser (Th.), Conservative (Wed.)......Hotels: Fleming, regular rates $2 (special also); Palmer, Hartson.

VILLISCA, 1,500. R. R., Chicago, Burlington & Quincy. Opera House, H. D. Dolson, manager; seating capacity, 400; rental, one night $10, license included. Size of stage, 16x30. Newspaper: Review (Th.)......Hotels: Commercial, regular rates, $2 (special also); Western.

VINTON, 3,500. R. R., Burlington, Cedar Rapids & Northern. Watson's Opera House, Sam. H. Watson, manager; rental, one night $20, three $50; license, $2; share also; fair stock scenery; bill poster, W. T. Phelps. Newspapers : semi-weekly, Eagle; weekly, Herald (Tu.), Observer (Fri.)......Hotels: Ralyea, regular rates, $2 (special also); Central, City.

WASHINGTON, 3,000. R. R.. Chicago, R. Island & Pacific; Burlington & North Western, Everson's Opera House, N. Everson, manager; seating capacity, 800; rental, one night $15, three $40; license, $3. Size of stage, 19x22; number sets scenery, 7; bill posters, Amusement Circle. Newspapers: Press (Wed.), Gazette (Fri.), Democrat (Wed.)..
Hotel: Bryson, regular rates, $2 (special also).

WATERLOO, 8,000. R. R.. Illinois Central; Burlington, Cedar Rapids & Northern; W. I. & Neb. Burnham's Opera House, E. W. Burnham, manager; seating capacity, 1,000; rent or share. Size of stage, 34x60; size of proscenium opening, 28x30; height from stage to grooves, 18; height from stage to rigging loft, 45; depth under stage, 9; number sets scenery, 20; bill poster, Opera House. Newspapers : semi-weekly, Tribune: weekly, Courier (Wed.), Reporter (Th.) ...Hotels : Logan, regular rates, $2 (special also); Central, regular rates, $2 (special also); Irving.

WAUKON, 2,000. R. R., Chicago, Mil. & St. Paul. Boomer's Opera House, Boomer Bros., managers; seating capacity, 500; rental, one night $10, three $22; license, $2.50; share also. Size of stage, 40x18; bill poster, Theodore Manch. Newspapers: Democrat (Wed.), Standard (Th.)......Hotels: Mason, regular rates, $2 (special also); Central.

WAVERLY, 2,500. R. R., Ill. Central. Opera House, C. H. Burrows, manager; seating capacity, 700; rental, one night $25, three $65; license, $3; share also. Size of stage, 22x44; number sets scenery, 10; bill poster, Opera House. Newspapers : Independent (Th.), Democrat (Fri.), Republican (Th.) ...Hotels : Bremer, regular rates, $2 (special also); Waverly.

WEBSTER CITY, 4,000. R. R., Chicago & N. Western ; Ill. Central. Wilson's Opera House, Frank E. Wilson, manager; seating capacity, 700; rental, one night $25; share also. Size of stage, 23x66; full set scenery; bill poster. Opera House; theatrical teamster, H. Witte. Newspapers : Advertiser (Tu.), Argus (Fri.), Freeman (Wed.)......
Hotels : Grand Central, regular rates, $2 (special also); Wilson, Brown, Hamilton, Potter.

WEST LIBERTY, 1,900. R. R., Chic.. Rock Island & Pacific; Bur., C. Rapids & Northern, Liberty Hall. Newspaper: Enterprise (Th.)......Hotels: Illee.

WEST UNION, 2,000. R. R., Bur., **Cedar Rapids & Northern**; Chic., Mil. & St. Paul. Zeigler Hall, Joe. Hobson, manager; seating capacity, 300; rental, one night $12, three $28; license, $2 to $5; share also. Size of stage, 15x40; number sets scenery, 7. Newspapers: semi-weekly, Gazette; weekly, Argo, (Wed.), Union (Tu.)......Hotels: Descent, Delmonico.

WHAT-CHEER, 2,200. R. R., Bur., **Cedar Rapids & Northern**. Opera House. Lortcher Bros., managers; seating capacity, 640; rental, one night $25; license, $2.50; number sets scenery, 4; bill poster, R. **M. Law.** Newspapers; Patriot (Wed.), Reporter (Wed.)...... Hotels: Commercial, Clifton.

WINTERSET, 4,800. R. R., Chic., **Rock Island & Pacific**. Opera Hall, M. Tiduck, manager; seating capacity, 400; rental, one night $15, three $40; license, $2. Size of stage, 18x24; number sets scenery, 6. Newspapers: Madisonian and Chronicle (Th.), News (Wed.).   Hotels: St. Nicholas, regular rates, $2, (special also); Tremont.

KANSAS.

ABILENE, 4,500. R. R., Union Pacific. Bonebrake Opera House, W. H. H. Bonebrake, manager; seating capacity, 800; rental——share only; license included. Size of stage, 24x48; size of proscenium opening, 14x24; height from stage to grooves, 12; height from stage to rigging loft, 16; depth under stage, 4; traps, 1; number sets scenery, 10, stage carpenter, W. B. Smith; bill poster, Opera House; number of sheets can accommodate, 140; rates per sheet, 4c. Newspapers: Gazette (Fri.), Chronicle (Fri.), Reflector......Hotels: Henry, special rates, $1.50; Continental, special rates, $1; Cottage, special rates, $1.

ARKANSAS CITY, 3,000. R. R., Atch. **Topeka & Santa Fe**. Highland Opera House, H. P. Farrar, manager; seating capacity, 700; rental, —— share also; no license. Size of stage, 30x40; number sets scenery, 15. Newspapers: Democrat (Tu.), Traveller (Wed.) .....Hotels: Perry, regular rates, $2 (special also); Leland, Central, Avenue.

ATCHISON, 17,000. R. R., Mo., Pac., Atch., **Topeka & Santa Fe**; Han. & St. Joe. New Opera House, L. M. Crawford manager; Brooks & Dickson, New York representatives; seating capacity, 1,000; rental, one night $65 three $175; license, $5; share also. Size of stage, 35x56; height from stage to grooves, 16; height from stage to rigging loft, 34; number sets scenery, 20; bill poster, Opera House; theatrical teamster, Omnibus Co. Newspapers daily, Champion, Patriot, Globe; weekly, Call (Sun.)......Hotels: Otis, regular rates, $2; Lindell, regular rates, $2.

BELOIT, 2,500. R. R., C. B. of Union Pac.; Soloman Branch of Kansas Pac. Beloit Opera House, Ben. Shaw, manager; seating capacity, 600; rental, one night $15; share also, license included. Size of stage, 25x28; size of proscenium opening, 20x27; height from stage to grooves, 14; height from stage to rigging loft, 19; depth under stage, 8; traps, 1; number sets scenery, 5; leader of orchestra, A. Manifold; bill poster, Chas. Burt. Newspapers, Gazette, (Fri.), Courier, (Th.), Democrat, (Fri.)......Hotels: Brunswick, special rates, $1; **Avenue**, special rates, $1.50.

BURLINGAME, 1,800. R. R., Atchison, **Topeka & Santa Fe**, Manhattan, Alma & Burlingame. Union Hall, L. R. Spaulding, manager; seating capacity, 500; rental, one night $20, license included. Size of stage, 30x50; number sets of scenery, 5; bill poster, H. A. Barker. **Newspapers**: Herald (Sat.), Chronicle (Th.), Democrat (Wed.)......Hotels: Shepard, regular rates $2, (special also); Barker.

BURLINGTON, 3,000. R. R., Missouri Pacific; Southern Kansas. Opera house, W. J. Kent, manager; seating capacity, 400; rental, one night $12; license, $5. Size of stage, 22x18; full set scenery; bill poster, Ham. Hinsley. Newspapers: Independent, (Fri.), Patriot, (Fri.), Republican, (Th.)......Hotels; Morris, regular rates, $2 (special also); Patton.

CALDWELL, 1,300. R. R., Atchison, **Topeka & Santa Fe**. Opera House, Frank Jones, manager, seating capacity, 800; rental——; share also; fair stock scenery. Newspaper: Journal (Th.).   Hotel: Leland, regular rate, $2 (special also).

— THE —

Crimes of London,

UNDER THE MANAGEMENT OF

CHARLES McDONALD.

The GREATEST MELODRAMA OF MODERN TIMES.

We Carry Our Own Scenery
(SPECIAL).

OUR OWN MAGNIFICENT MILITARY BAND

— AND —

ORCHESTRA,

UNDER THE LEADERSHIP OF THE FAMOUS NATHAN CARL.

*THE MOST VARIED ASSORTMENT OF STAND WORK
AND LITHOGRAPHS EXTANT.*

Managers are requested to send addresses for newspaper notices.
Direct as per route in dramatic papers.   Address:

CHARLES McDONALD, Manager.

CAWKER CITY, 1,200. R. R., Missouri Pacific. Grand Army Hall, Geo. A. Latham, manager; seating capacity, 300; rental, one night $6; license, $3. Size of stage, 24x20; fair stock scenery. Newspapers: Journal (Wed.), Public Record (Th.)..... Hotel: Whitney. regular rates, $2 (special also).

CHANUTE, 1,500. R. R., Missouri Pacific; Southern Kansas. Williams' Hall, Geo. W. Williams, manager; seating capacity, 500; rental, one night $12; license, $2.50. Size of stage, 14x30; fair stock scenery; bill poster, Jesse Martin. Newspapers: Blade (Th.), Times (Th.).... Hotels: Sherman, Lindell, Occidental.

CHERRYVALE, 3,000. R.R., Kansas City, Ft. Scott & Gulf; St. Louis & San Fran.; South'n Kansas. Cherryvale Opera House, O. F. Carson, manager; seating capacity, 400; rental, one night $7.50; share also. Size of stage, 16x30; number sets scenery, 2. Newspapers: Torch (Wed.); Globe News (Fri.).... Hotels: Leland, regular rates, $2 (special also; Commercial.

CHETOPA, 3,000. R. R., M. K. & T. Branch of Mo. Pac. Chetopa Opera House, E. W. Clark, manager; seating capacity, 500; rental, one night $14, three $50; share also; license, $3. Size of stage, 22x37; size of proscenium opening, 13x20; height from stage to grooves, 12; height from stage to rigging loft, 14; depth under stage, 8; traps, 1; number sets scenery, 5; leader of orchestra, George Spangler; bill poster W. M. Roberts; theatrical teamster, J. W. Columbia. Newspaper: Advance (Wed.); advertising rates, yearly contract.... Hotel: National, special rates, $1.50 to $2.

CLAY CENTRE, 5,000. R. R., Union Pacific; Kansas Central. Opera House, C. E. Gifford, manager; seating capacity, 500; rental, one night $25, three $60; share also; license included. Size of stage, 24x40; height from stage to grooves, 12; depth under stage, 4; traps, 1, number sets scenery, 5; bill poster, Opera House; number of sheets can accommodate, 300; rates per sheet, 3c. Newspapers: Dispatch (Th.), advertising rates, special contract: Times (Th.), special contract; Firebrand (Th.), special contract. Hotels: Dispatch, special rates, $1.50; Henry, special rates, $1.50; Resort, special rates, $1.

COFFEYVILLE, 2,500. R. R., Southern Kansas. Opera House, Well Bros., managers; seating capacity, 700; rental, one night $15, three $40; license, $5. Size of stage, 20x48; size of proscenium opening, 14x20; height from stage to grooves, 14; height from stage to rigging loft, 19; depth under stage, 5; number sets scenery, 6; leader of orchestra, Chas. Merriman; scenic artist, J. M. Sherbury; stage carpenter, James Scoville; bill poster, W. Currier; theatrical teamster, A. H. Boothby. Newspapers: Journal (Sat.), advertising rates, 5c. per line; Enterprise (Fri.), 5c. per line...... Hotels: Eldridge, special rates, $1.25, Southern, special rates, $1; Forest, special rates, $1.

COLUMBUS, 2,000. R. R., Kansas City, Ft. Scott & Gulf; St. Louis & San Fran. Opera House, Harlan Bros., managers; seating capacity, 700; bill poster, N. M. Parker. Newspapers Border Star (Sat.), Courier (Th.), News (Th.) Advocate (Fri.)..... Hotel: Gulf, regular rates, $2.

DODGE CITY, 2,000. R. R., Atch., Topeka & Santa Fe. Dodge City Opera House, Walter Streator, manager; seating capacity, 350; rental, one night $25; three $45; license, $5. Size of stage, 21x24; no scenery. Newspapers: Democrat (Sat.), Globe (Tu.), Times (Th.)......Hotels: Dodge, regular rates, $2 (special also); Wright, Great Western.

EMPORIA, 9,000. R. R., Atch., Topeka & Santa Fe, Missouri Pac.; South. Kan. Whitley's Opera House, H. C. Whitley, manager; seating capacity, 900; rental, one night $40; three $100, license included; share also. Size of stage, 34x60; number sets scenery, 16; bill poster, Austin Hathaway. Newspapers: daily, News, Republican; weekly, Democrat (Wed.)......Hotels: Coolidge, regular rates, $2 (special also); Windsor, Merchants' Fifth Avenue, Park Place.

Jay's Opera House, William Jay, manager; seating capacity, 600. Size of stage, 18x24; number sets scenery, 4

Bancroft Hall; seating capacity, 600.

Eskridge Hall; seating capacity, 200.

EUREKA, 3,000. R. R. Atch., Top. & Santa Fe, St. Louis, Fort Scott & Wichita. Eureka Opera House, Morris & Pierce, managers; seating capacity, 600; rental, one night $30, three $45, license included. Size of stage, 19x42; size of proscenium opening, 12x24;

depth under, stage, 3½; traps, 1; number sets scenery, 5; leader of orchestra, Thos. Lewis; bill poster, Joseph Dixon; theatrical teamster, J. A. McCoy. Newspapers: Republican (Fri.), Herald (Th.). Messenger (Fri.)......Hotels: Greenwood, special rates. $1.75; Forrest City, special rates, $1.25; Union, Jackson, special rates, $1.

FLORENCE, 2,000. R. R., Atch., Top. & Santa Fe. Florence Opera House, A. Z. Hamilton, manager; seating capacity, 650; rental, one night $25, three $50; no license; share also. Size of stage, 50x25; number sets scenery, 5; bill poster, Harry Hinkle. Newspaper: Herald (Sat.)......Hotels: Clifton, regular rates, $2 (special also); Florence, American.

FORT SCOTT, 12,000. R. R., Missouri, Pacific; Fort Scott & Wichita; Kansas City, Fort Scott & Gulf; Kansas City, Fort Scott & Springfield. Fort Scott Opera House, W. P. Patterson, manager; seating capacity, 800; rental, share only; license included. Size of stage, 28x50; size of proscenium opening, 13x26; height from stage to grooves, 12; height from stage to rigging loft, 18; depth under stage, 5; traps, 3; number sets scenery: 14; leader of orchestra, Jay Brothers; scenic artist, W. O. Thomas; stage carpenter, Richard Fowler; bill poster, Oscar Slater; number of sheets can accomodate, 400; rates per sheet, 4 cents; theatrical teamster, Southwestern Bus Co. Newspapers: daily, Monitor Herald; weekly, Banner (Th.)......Hotels: Huntington, special rates, $1.50; Wilder, special rates, $1.50; Tremont, special rates, $1.25.

GALENA, 2,500. R. R., Kansas City, Fort Scott & Gulf; St. Louis & San Francisco. Opera House, Gove & Stone, managers; seating capacity, 600. Newspaper: Republican (Fri.) ......Hotel: Willard, regular rates, $2 (special also).

GARNETT, 2,000. R. R., Missouri, Pacific, Southern Kansas. Stouch Opera House, W. R. Stouch, manager; seating capacity, 400; rental one night $10; three $25, license $2.50. Size of stage, 14x22; number sets scenery, 4. Newspapers: Republican (Fri.); Journal (Sat.)......Hotels: Commercial, regular rates $2 (special also); St. James.

GIRARD, 3,500. R. R., Kansas City, Fort Scott & Gulf; Kansas Southern; St. Louis & San Francisco. Pamton's Hall, manager, James S. James; seating capacity, 500; rental, share only; license included. Size of stage, 35x50; size of proscenium opening, 12x19; height from stage to grooves, 14; depth under stage, 4; traps, 1; number sets scenery, 6; theatrical teamster, Mansfield. Newspapers: Press (Th.), Herald (Th.) .....Hotels: St. James, special rates, $1.50; Commercial, special rates, $1.50; St. Paul, special rates, $1.00.

HIAWATHA, 3,000. R. R., Missouri Pacific; Union Pacific. Hiawatha Opera House, A. N. Ruley, manager; seating capacity, 400; rental, one night $25, license included; share also. Size of stage, 18x50; full set scenery; bill poster, Opera House. Newspapers: Messenger (Sat.), World (Th.)......Hotels: Hiawatha, regular rates, $2 (special also); Commercial.

HUTCHINSON, 3,500. R. R., Atchison, Topeka & Santa Fe. Hutchinson Opera House, W. T. Atkinson, manager; seating capacity, 800; rental, ——; share also. Size of stage, 25x50; number sets scenery, 11; bill poster, Thomas Harman. Newspapers: Herald (Sat.), News (Th.), Democrat (Sun.)... ..Hotels: Reno, regular rates, $2 (special also); Windsor, Occidental, Howard.

INDEPENDENCE, 3,000. R. R., Southern Kansas. Opera House, A. Brinckman, manager; seating capacity, 600; rental, one night $30; license, $3.25. Size of stage, 16x32; number sets scenery, 3; bill poster, Milt. Gregory. Newspapers: daily, Reporter; weekly, Kansan (Wed.), Tribune (Wed.), Kansas Star (Fri.)......Hotels: Caldwell, regular rates, $2 (special also); Main Street, Hoober. Commercial.

Payne's Opera House, H. L. Payne, manager; seating capacity, 700; rental, one night $30, three $60; share also; license, $3. Size of stage, 24x24; number sets scenery, 9.

IOLA, 1,800. R. R., St. Louis, Fort Scott & Wichita; Southern Kansas. Iola Opera House, C. H. Declude, manager; seating capacity, 350; rental, one night $10; license, $3. Size of stage, 20x40; number sets scenery, 5. Newspapers: Courant (Th.), Register (Fri.)...... Hotels: Central, regular rates, $2; Penn, Leland.

JUNCTION CITY, 3,500. R. R., Missouri Pacific; Union Pacific. Opera House, A. L. Barnes, manager; seating capacity, 625; rental, one night $30, three $50; license, $5;

share also. Size of stage, 31x65; number sets scenery, 10; bill poster, H. Gibbon. Newspapers: Republican (Fri.), Tribune (Th.), Union (Sat.)......Hotels: Bartell, regular rates, $2 (special also); Pershall, Pacific.

City Hall; seating capacity, 1,000.

Turner Hall; seating capacity, 200.

KINGMAN, 2,500. R. R., Wichita & Western. Tull's Hall, F. M. Tull, manager; seating capacity, 800; rental——. share also. Size of stage, 20x30; number sets scenery, 6. Newspapers: Citizen (Th.), Republican (Th.)......Hotel: Laclede, regular rates, $2 (special also).

LA CYGNE, 1,500. R. R., Kansas City, Ft. Scott & Gulf. La Cygne Opera Hall, Geo. C. Wyndcoop, manager; seating capacity, 600; rental, one night, $15, three $35; license included. Size of stage, 21x43; number sets scenery, 9; bill poster, Henry Lockwood. Newspaper: Journal (Sat.)......Hotels: La Cygne, regular rates, $2 (special also); Sinclair, Commercial.

LAWRENCE, 14,000. R. R., Union Pacific; Atch., Top. & Santa Fe; Southern Kansas. Bowersock's Opera House, W. F. March, manager; seating capacity, 1,000; rental, share only; license included. Size of stage, 24x60; size of proscenium opening, 30x30; height from stage to grooves, 16; height from stage to rigging loft, 30; depth under stage, 18; traps, 2; number sets scenery, 12; leader of orchestra, John Buch; stage carpenter, Wm. Begge; bill poster, W. Begge; number of sheets can accommodate 1,000; theatrical teamster, Geo. Fricker, omnibus line. Newspapers: daily, Journal; Herald; weekly, Germania (Th.)......Hotels: Eldridge, special rates, $1.50; Windsor, special rates, $1.25; Lawrence, special rates, $1.25.

Liberty Hall, Andrew Terry, manager; seating capacity, 1,100; rental, one night $20 to $35; license, $3 to $5. Size of stage, 20x21; number sets scenery, 3.

LEAVENWORTH, 25,000. R. R. Atch., Top. & Santa Fe; Chicago Rock Island & Pacific; K. C., St. J. & C. B., Missouri Pacific; Union Pacific. Opera House, Lester M. Crawford, manager; seating capacity, 800; rental, one night $60, three $150; share also, license included. Size of stage, 40x65; number sets scenery, 20; bill posters, Crawford & Brooks. Newspapers: daily, Standard, Times; weekly, Chronicle (Sat.)...... Hotels: Planters', regular rates, $2 (special also); Continental, regular rates $2 (special also); Mansion, Delmonico.

Laing's Hall, Jno. M. Laing, manager; seating capacity, 800; rental, one night $18, three $45; share also. Size of stage, 20x48; no scenery.

Unmethun Opera House; seating capacity, 800.

Odd Fellows' Hall; seating capacity, 800.

LYONS, 1,200. R. R., Atch., Topeka & Santa Fe. Butler's Opera House, T. A. Butler, manager; H. C. Taylor, assistant manager; seating capacity, 500; rental, one night $25, three $60; share also; license included. Size of stage, 20x22; size of proscenium opening, 14x18. Newspapers: Republican (Th.), Democrat (Th.), Prohibitionist, (Th.) ......Hotel: Commercial, special rates, $1.50.

MANHATTAN, 3,000. R. R., Union Pacific; Man. Alma & Burlingame. Moore's Opera House, H. S. Moore, manager; seating capacity, 600; rental, one night $25, three $65; share also; license yearly. Size of stage, 30x17; full set scenery; bill poster, Opera House. Newspapers: National (Fri.), Republic (Fri.)......Hotels: Adams, regular rates, $2 (special also); Commercial, Cottage.

Colisseum Theatre, Moore & Elliott, managers; seating capacity, 600; rental, one night $15, three $35; license, $3; share also. Size of stage, 16x40; fair stock scenery.

Peak's Hall, Aug. Peak, manager; seating capacity, 300; rental, one night $7, three $18; license, $1; share also. Size of stage, 12x27; number sets scenery, 2.

MARION, 3,000. R. R., Atch., Top. & Santa Fe. Compton Opera House, Geo. F. Roberts, manager; seating capacity, 800; fair stock scenery. Newspapers: Democrat (Th.), Record, (Fri.)... .Hotel: Bailey, regular rates, $2 (special also).

MARYSVILLE, 2,200. R. R., Union Pacific. Turner Hall, Aug. Holm, manager; seating capacity, 400; rental, one night $10; license, $5. Size of stage, 20x23; fair stock scenery ; bill poster, **Joe. Cottrell.** Newspapers : Democrat (Fri.), News (Fri.), Post (Th.) .....Hotels : Sherman, regular rates, $2 (special also); Tremont.

McPHERSON, 2,800. **R. R., Union Pacific ; Kans.** Pacific. McPherson Opera House, Howard & Bartholomew, **managers ; seating** capacity, 600 ; rental, one night $25, three $60; share also; license **included.** Size of stage, 25x40 ; size of proscenium opening, 12x15; height from stage to grooves, 15; height from stage to rigging loft, 18; depth under stage, 4 ; traps, 1 ; **number sets** scenery, 8 ; leader of orchestra J. S. Howard ; scenic artists, D. K. Node **& B. McFadden** ; stage carpenter, **Joe.** Haith ; bill poster, **Opera House ; number of sheets** can accommodate, 250 ; rates per **sheet,** &c.; theatrical teamster, A. B. Smith. **Newspapers :** Freeman (Th.), advertising rates, special contract; **Republican (Th.), advertising rates, special** contract ; **Press (Th.),** advertising rates, special contract........Hotels: Union, Merchants', McPherson.

NEWTON, 4,300. **R. R., Atchison, Topeka & Santa Fe. Opera House, George W. Seaton,** manager; seating capacity, **500; rental, one night $15; license, $5. Size of stage,** 18x20; number sets scenery, 2. Newspapers: Democrat (Fri.), Kansan (Th.), Republican **(Fri.)** ....Hotel: Howard, regular rates, $2 (special also); New Grand Opera House.

NORTH TOPEKA, 15,000. R. R., Union Pacific; Atchison, Topeka & Santa Fe. Luken's Opera House, J. A. Luken, manager; seating capacity, 800; rental, one night $20, three $50; license, $2; share also. Size of stage, 29x50; number sets scenery, 12; bill poster, Opera House. Newspapers: Good Tidings, Mail, Times.........Hotels: Palace, Adams.

OLATHE, 3,000. **R. R., Kansas City,** Fort Scott & Gulf; Kansas Southern, Hayes' Opera House, George B., **Lord, manager;** seating capacity, 700; rental, one night $25, three **$65; share also; license included.** Size of stage, 18x40; traps, 1; number sets scenery, 3; **bill poster, John K. King. Newspapers:** Democrat (Th.), Patron (Th.), Star (Th.)... Hotels: American, Hackett.

OSAGE CITY, 3,000. R. R., Atchison, Topeka **& Santa Fe.** City Opera House, Howe & Co., managers; seating capacity, 600; rental, ——; share also. Size of stage, 29x50; number sets scenery, 7; bill poster, Henry Anderson. Newspaper: Free Press (Th.)......
Hotels: Osage City, regular rates, $2 (special also); Palace.

Union Hall; seating capacity, 800; rental, one night $20, three $50; license included. **Size of stage, 24x50;** number sets scenery, 12.

OSWEGO, 3,500. R. R., Missouri Pacific; St. Louis & San Francisco. **Oswego Opera House. L. S.** Crum, manager; seating capacity, **350;** rental, one night $12, **three $30; license.** $5; **share also.** Size of stage, 20x30; number sets scenery, 6; bill posters, **Brandas & Mitchell.** Newspapers: Independent (Fri.), Democrat (Fri.), Republican (Th.)......**Hotels: Oswego, regular** rates, $2 (special also); Star, Condon, American.

OTTAWA, 7,000. R. R., Kansas City, Burlington & Santa Fe; Missouri Pacific; Southern Kansas. Ottawa Opera House, **A.** W. Barker, manager; seating capacity, 500; rental, one night $30; license, $3.50; share also. Size of stage, 30x50; number sets scenery, 20; bill poster, Opera House. Newspapers, daily: Republican; weekly: Journal and Triumph (Th.), Herald (Th.)......Hotels: **Johnson,** regular rates, $2 (special also); Hamblin, Centennial, Shannon, Occidental.

Hamblin **Opera House;** E. L. **Clark, manager.**

PAOLA, 4,000. R. R., **Kansas** City, **Fort Scott & Gulf; Mo.** Pac. Paola Opera House, L. D. White, manager; seating capacity, **600; rental, one** night $30; three $50; license, $5; **share also.** Size of stage, 22x40; number sets scenery, 10; bill poster, J. **D.** Sloane. Newspapers: Republican (Fri.), Times (Th.), Spirit (Fri.)... ...Hotels: Grimshaw, regular rates, $2; Reed, Paola, Commercial.

Globe Hall, L. D. White, **manager; seating capacity, 600; license, $5.** Size of stage, 18x22; **full set scenery.**

PARSONS, 7,000. R. R., Kansas City, Fort Scott & Gulf; Missouri **Pacific.** Edwards' Opera House, E. H. Edwards, manager; seating capacity, 800; rental, one night $35; share also; license included. Size of stage, 28x50; number sets scenery, 7; bill poster. Walter Decker. Newspapers: daily, Eclipse, Sun......Hotel: Abbott, regular **rates,** $2 (special also).

SABETHA, 1,700. R. R., Union Pacific. **G. A. R. Hall, D. D. Wickins,** manager; seating capacity, 1,000; rental, one night $25; **share also**; license included. Size of stage, 30x14; **fair stock scenery**; bill poster, **manager Hall.** Newspaper: Republican (Th.)...... Hotels : Hooks', regular rates, $2 (**special also**); World, Haxton's.

SALINA, 1,100. R. R., Union Pacific. **Opera House, T. Bond,** manager; seating capacity, 800 ; **rental,** one night $25. **Size of stage,** 25x40; fair stock scenery. Newspapers : Herald **(Th.),** Independent **(Sat.),** Journal (Th.)......Hotels : Pacific, regular rates, $2 (special also); Metropolitan.

SENECA, 2,000. R. R., St. Joseph & Western. **Seneca Opera House, Strafford & Ford,** managers; seating capacity, 600; rental, share only; license included. Size of stage, 30x35; size of proscenium opening, 14x20; **number sets scenery,** 6; leader of orchestra, Chas. Scraaf; bill poster, Joseph Guffy. **Newspapers : Tribune** (Wed.), Courier (Th.)...... Hotels: Commercial, **special rates, $1.25;** Cameron, special rates, $1.

SOLOMON **CITY,** 1,300. R. R., **Union Pacific.** Wall's Hall, Wall Bros., managers; seating capacity, 350; rental, one **night $15**; **share also**; no license. Size of stage, 14x20; **full set scenery.** Newspaper: **Sentinel (Wed.)**......Hotels: Hall, regular rates, $2 (special also); Roach's.

STERLING, 1,500. R. R., Atchison, **Topeka & Santa Fe. Goodson's Opera House.** B. H. Beattie, manager; seating capacity, 500; rental, one night $10; license, $4. Size of stage, 16x40; fair stock scenery; bill poster, **Wm. Porter.** Newspapers: Bulletin (Th.), Gazette (Th.).....Hotels: Green Mountain, regular **rates, $2 (special also); Morris.**

STRONG CITY, 850. **R. R.,** Atchison, Topeka & Santa Fe. Opera House, E. A. Hildebrand, manager; **seating capacity,** 400; rental, one night $15; **share also**; license included. Size **of stage, 16x20**; fair stock scenery; bill poster, T. Brandt. Newspaper: Independent (Fri.)......**Hotel: Clay's.**

TOPEKA, 30,000. R. R., Atchison, **Top.** & Santa Fe; **Union Pacific.** Grand Opera House, Wood & Updegraff, managers; Brooks & Dickson, **New York representatives;** Corydon F. Craig, business manager; seating capacity, 1,600; rental, **share only, license included.** Size of stage, 60x67; size of proscenium opening, 35x28; height **from stage to grooves,** 18; height from stage to rigging loft, 50; depth under stage, 15; **traps, 3; number sets** scenery, 30; stage carpenter, John Albaugh; bill poster, John Albaugh; number of sheets can accommodate, 1,500; rates per sheet, 3 cents; theatrical **teamster, Transfer** Co. Newspapers: daily, Capital, advertising rates, yearly contract; Commonwealth, advertising rates, yearly contract; Journal, advertising rates, yearly contract......Hotels: Windsor, special rates, $1.50 to $2; Fifth Avenue, special rates, $1.50 to $2; **Copeland,** special rates, $1.50 to $2; Gordon, special rates, $1.50 to $2.

Topeka Opera House, Lester M. Crawford, manager; seating capacity, **1,100;** rental, one night $65; share also; license included. **Size of** stage, 38x48; size of proscenium opening, 28x27; height from stage to grooves, **16;** height from stage to rigging loft, 28; depth under stage, or cellar, 10; traps, 2; number **sets** scenery, 30; leader **of orchestra,** Louis Heck, Jr.; bill poster, L. M Crawford.

Globe Theatre, George Fredericks, manager; (add. Theatre Comique, Kansas City.)

TROY, 1,000. R. R., Union Pacific; Burlington & **Missouri River.** Court House Hall; seating capacity, 300; rental, one night $3; license **$5 to $10 per week. Size of stage, 10x15.** Newspaper: Chief (Th.)......Hotels: Higby, **regular rates, $2 (special also).**

WAMEGO, 2,300. R. R., Union Pacific. Leach's Opera House, Lew. **B. Leach, manager;** seating capacity, 500; rental, ——, **share also**; license yearly. **Size of stage, 26x46;** number sets scenery, 16; bill poster, Opera House. Newspaper: **Reporter (Fri.)......Hotels:** Ames, regular rates, $2 (special also); Merritt.

WASHINGTON, 1,500. R. R., Missouri Pacific. Knowles Opera House, O. L. Taylor, manager; seating capacity, 700; rental, one night $30; share also; license included. Size of stage, 30x40; fair stock scenery; bill poster, Charles Pitcher. Newspapers: Republican (Fri.); Register (Sat.)..... Hotels: Central, regular rates, $2 (special also); Commercial, American.

WELLINGTON, 4,000. R. R., Atchison. Topeka & Santa Fe; Southern Kansas. Wood's Opera House, H. L. Woods, manager; seating capacity, 800; rental, one night $35; share also; license included. Size of stage, 22x25; fair stock scenery; bill poster, Opera House. Newspapers : Press (Th.), Wellingtonian. (Th.)......Hotels : Phillips, regular rates, $2 (special also); Larned, Barnard.

WICHITA, 7,000. R. R., Atchison, Topeka & Santa Fe; St. Louis & San Francisco; St. Louis, Fort Scott & Wichita. Turner's Opera House, J. A. Ask, manager ; seating capacity, 1,000; rental, one night $30, three $80; license $5.50; share also. Size of stage, 20x35; number sets scenery, 12; bill posters, Craddock & Davis. Newspapers ; daily, Times; weekly, Beacon (Wed.), Eagle (Th.), New Republic (Th.)......Hotels ; Occidental, regular rates, $2 (special also); Douglass Avenue, Tremont.

Eagle Hall; seating capacity, 600.

Russell Hall; seating capacity, 350.

WINFIELD, 5,000. R. R., Atchison, Topeka & Santa Fe; Kansas City, Lawrence & So. Manning's Opera House, T. B. Myers, manager; seating capacity, 800; rental, one night $15, three $40; share also; license, $5. Size of stage, 20x50; size of proscenium opening, 16x20; height from stage to grooves, 10; height from stage to rigging loft, 25; depth under stage, 8; traps, 1; number sets scenery, 6; leader of orchestra, George Crippen; bill poster, J. M. Read ; rates per sheet, 4 cents; theatrical teamster. Arthur Bangs. Newspapers; Telegram (Th.), Courier (Th.).. ..Hotels : Central, special rates, $1 to $2; Boettine, special rates, $1 to $2; Old's, $1.

WYANDOTTE, 12,000 (closely surrounding 6,000 more). R. R., Missouri Pacific; all roads entering Kansas City. Dunning's Opera House, Robert G. Dunning, manager; seating capacity, 800; rental, one night $25, three $65; share also; license included. Size of stage, 25x43; size of proscenium opening, 18x21; height from stage to grooves, 18; height from stage to rigging loft, 22; depth under stage, 4; traps, 1; number sets scenery, 8; bill poster, R. G. Dunning; rates per sheet 3c; theatrical teamsters, Wm. Richards, John Mount. Newspapers: daily, Kansas City (Mo.), Times, Journal, Star. Wyandotte Column; advertising rates per line, 15c.; weekly, Herald (Th.), Gazette (Fri.), Chief (Th.), advertising rates, 10c......Hotel: Ryus, special rates, $1 to $1.50; Garno, special rates, $1.

YATES CENTRE. 1,000. R. R., St. Louis, Fort Scott & Wichita. Ray & Yates' Opera House, D. M. Ray, manager; seating capacity, 500; rental, one night $15; no license. Size of stage, 16x30; fair stock scenery. Newspapers; Argus (Th.), News (Fri.), ... Hotels; Bailey, regular rates, $2 (special also).

KENTUCKY.

BOWLING GREEN, 8,000. R. R., Louisville & Nashville. Oden Hall, James F. Hackney, manager; seating capacity, 1,000. Size of stage, 30x40; number sets scenery, 12; bill poster, J. Winslow. Newspapers: daily, Times; semi-weekly, Gazette-Democrat (Fri.), Watchman (Sat.)......Hotels: Morehead, Potter, regular rates, $2 (special also); Merchants', Commercial, Kentucky.

COVINGTON, 35,000. R. R., all roads entering Cincinnati. Odd Fellows' Hall, F. E. O. Brooks, manager; seating capacity, 600; rental, one night $15, three $35; license, ten times price of one admission. Size of stage, 18x21; height from stage to grooves, 16; height from stage to rigging loft, 25; depth under stage, 5; traps, 2; number sets scenery, 5; bill poster, O. P. Fairchild. Newspapers: daily, Commonwealth; Cincinnati daily papers......Hotel: Arlington.

CYNTHIANA, 3,500. R. R., Kentucky Central. Æolian Hall, Keller & Tucker, managers; seating capacity, 800; rental, one night $20; full set scenery; bill posters, Keller & Tucker. Newspapers: Democrat (Fri.), News (Th.), Times (Wed.)......Hotels: Smith's, regular rates, $2 (special also).

DANVILLE, 4,000. R. R., Cinn., N. Orleans & Tex. Pacific. James' Hall; seating capacity, 400; rental, ——; share also; full set scenery; bill poster, T. B. Williams. Newspapers:

11

Advocate (Fri.), Tribune(Fri.)   Hotels: Gilcher's, **regular** rates, $2; Clemens', regular rates, $2 (special also); Central.

ELIZABETHTOWN, 3,000.   R. R., Chesapeake, Ohio & **South Western**; Louisville & Nashville. Bryan Hall, Bryan, **Warren** & Co., managers; seating **capacity**, 500; rental, **one** night $10, three $25; no license. **Size** of stage, 20x40; number **sets** scenery, 2; bill poster, Lewis Helm. Newspaper : News (**Fri.**). ....Hotels : Showers', regular rates, $2 (special, also); Hill.

FRANKFORT, 10,000. R, R., Louisville & Nashville; Chesapeake & Ohio. Opera House, A. C. Wood, manager; **seating capacit**y, 800; rental, **share only**, license included. **Size of stage, 35x54; size of proscenium opening, 28x40; height from** stage to grooves, 18; **height from stage to rigging loft, 30; depth under stage, 7; traps, 2;** number sets scenery, **13; stage** carpenter, **Heffner; bill poster,** Wood; **number of sheets can** accommodate, 500; **rates per** sheet, 4c.; **theatrical** teamster, Heffner. **Newspapers : daily,** Yeoman, yearly contract; weekly, Roundabout (Sat.).... Hotels : **Capital, special rates $1.25 to $1.50;** Buhr's, $1.25 to $1.50; Merryweather's, $1 to 1.50.

Major Hall, H. G. Banta, manager; seating capacity, 1,000; **rental, one** night $25; **three** $67.50; share also; license included. Size of stage, 30x35; number sets scenery, 8.

FRANKLIN, 3,100. R. R., Louisville & Nashville. Wade's Hall, H. K. Wade, manager; seating capacity, 500; rental, one night $12.50; three $30, license included. Size of stage, 18x40; number sets scenery, **6;** bill poster, Tom Travis. Newspaper : Favorite (Th.) .Hotels : Harris, regular rates, $2 (special also); Hern, Boissesu.

GEORGETOWN, 4,000. **R. R., Cin., N. O. & Tex. Pac.** Barlow's Opera House, E. C. Barlow & Son, managers; seating capacity, 700; rental, ——; share also; full set scenery Newspaper : Times (Wed.)   .Hotel : Welles, regular rates, $2 (special also).

GLASGOW, 2,600. R. R., Louis. & Nash. Bowler Hall, James Murrell, manager; seating capacity, 500; rental, one night $12.50; fair stock scenery; **bill poster,** J. Murrell. Newspaper: Times (Wed.) .....Hotel: Murrell's, **regular** rates, $2 (special also).
Morris Hall, **J. F.** Hackney, manager, **seating capacity, 320.**

HARRODSBURG, 3,000. R. R., Cin. South.; Cin., N. O. & Tex. Pac ; Southw'n of Ky **Cardmell's** Opera House, L. D. Cardmell, manager; seating capacity, 750; rental, one **night $2),** three $60, license included. Size of stage, 52x50; size of proscenium opening, **16x24;** height from stage to grooves, 14; height from stage to rigging loft, 24; depth under **stage, 16;** traps, 1; number sets scenery, 12; scenic artist, Will Clark; stage carpenter, **C. E. Clark; bill** poster, Opera House; number of sheets **can accommodate, 500; rates per sheet, 3c.;** theatrical **teamster,** R. E. Coleman. Newspaper: **Citizen (Sat.), advertising rates, 10c.** per line .....**Hotel:** National, special rates, $1.25.

HENDERSON, 10,000. R. R., **Louisville &** Nashville; **Ohio River.** New Opera House, R. E. Cook, manager; seating capacity, 800; rental, **one** night $50, three $125; share also; license included. Size of stage, 30x40; size of proscenium opening, 18x22; height from stage to grooves, 12; height from stage to rigging loft, 20; depth under stage, 9; traps, 2; number sets scenery, 7; dressing rooms, 5; leader of orchestra, A. Tonini; stage carpenter, P B. Trible; bill poster, Spaulding Trible; rates per sheet, 4c.; theatrical teamster, Ad. Carlisle. Newspapers: Journal (Sat.), advertising rates, yearly contract: News (Sat.), special contract; Reporter, semi-weekly (Tu. & Fri.), special contract......Hotels : **Hord,** special rates; Central, special rates; Commercial, regular rates, $2 (special also).

HOPKINSVILLE, 7,300. R. R., Louisville & **Nashville. Holland's Opera** House, A. D. Rodgers, manager; seating capacity, 650; share only; license yearly. **Size** of stage, 36x30; number sets scenery, **16;** bill poster, Opera House. Newspapers: semi-weekly, Kentuckian; weekly, New Era (Fri.)......Hotels: **Phoenix, regular** rates, $2 (special **also); Cooper,** Burbridge. European.

Mozart Hall, T. E. Lawson, manager; seating capacity, 500; rental, one night $30, three **$75.** Size of stage, 21x24; number sets scenery, 7.

City Hall; seating capacity, 600.

Holloway Hall; seating capacity, **$1,200.**

LANCASTER, 2,500. R. R., Kentucky Central. Lancaster Opera House, Sandifer & Miller, managers; seating capacity, 600; rental, one night $18, three $50, share also; license yearly. Size of stage, 30x33; size of proscenium opening, 16x38; height from stage to grooves, 14; height from stage to rigging loft, 33; number sets scenery, 5; bill poster, Alex. Miller; number sheets can accommodate, 300; theatrical teamster, J. W. Griffin. Newspaper: News (Thu.) .....Hotels: Miller House, special rates, $1.50; Lancaster, regular rates, $? (special also).

LEXINGTON, 20,000. R. R., Ches. & Ohio; Louisville & Nashville; Kentucky Central; Cin. Southern. Opera House, R. B. Marsh, manager; seating capacity, 1,000; rental, one night $50, three $125, license included; share also. Size of stage, 37x45; size of proscenium opening, 35x24; height from stage to grooves, 18; height from stage to rigging loft, 30; depth under stage, 6; traps, 8; number sets scenery, 15; leader of orchestra, Frank J. Wolf; stage carpenter, Geo. Lightner; bill poster, Opera House; rates per sheet, 3c. and 4c.; theatrical teamster, Lex. Transfer Co. Newspapers: daily, Press, Transcript, News; weekly, Observer (Sun.), Republican (Sat.) .....Hotels: Phœnix, special rates, $2; Ashland, $1.50; Florentene, $1.25 to $1.50.

Melodeon Hall; seating capacity, 450.

LITCHFIELD, 1,000. R. R., Ches., Ohio & Southwestern. Heyser Opera House; seating capacity, 450; rental, one night $10 to $12; license, $1.50 to $5. Size of stage, 33x11; height from stage to grooves, 11; fair stock scenery. Newspaper: Sunbeam (Fri.), advertising rates per line, 2½c. .....Hotels: Heyser, special rates, $1.50 to $2; Thomas, $1.50 to $2; Sisk, $1.50 to $2.

LOUISVILLE, 110,000. R. R., Louis. & Nashv.; Ohio & Mis.; Jeff. Mad & Ind.; L., N.A. & Cory.; L., N.A. & Chic.; Chic. & Ohio. Masonic Temple Theatre, Meffert & Friedlander; seating capacity, 1,300; rental, share only. Size of stage, 50x50; size of proscenium opening, 20x36; height from stage to grooves, 18; height from stage to rigging loft, 60; depth under stage, 6; number sets scenery, 30; musical director, Henry Burck; scenic artist, D. T. Elly; stage carpenter, E. A. Martin; bill poster, Heverin Bros.; number of sheets can accommodate, 1,000; rates per sheet, 3c.; theatrical teamster, S. T. Moore. Newspapers, daily, Courier-Journal, advertising rates per inch $1.20; Commercial, advertising rates per inch, $1.25; weekly, Argus, (Sun.), advertising rates per inch, $1. Hotels: Galt House, special rates, $2; Louisville, special rates, $2 to $3; Standiford, special rates, $1.50 to $2.50.

New Grand Theatre, J. H. Whallen, manager; seating capacity, 2,200; share only. Size of stage, 45x80; size of proscenium opening, 31x42; height from stage to grooves, 18; height from stage to rigging loft, 48; depth under stage, 14; traps, 4; full stock scenery; musical director, Ed. Morback; scenic artist, James Ettoy.

McCauley's Theatre, T. D. McCauley, manager; seating capacity, 1,555; rental, share only. Size of stage, 40x80; full set scenery.

Opera House, T. D. McCauley, manager; seating capacity, 1,100. Size of stage, 45x65; full set scenery.

Grand Central Theatre and Garden, T. J. Nolen, manager.

Liederkranz Hall; seating capacity, 1,800.

Tivoli Theatre, J. H. Whallen, manager.

Harris Museum, Jas. Revell, manager; seating capacity, 1,200; number sets scenery, 16.

MADISONVILLE, 3,000. R. R., Louisville & Nashville. Mile's Opera House, S. T. Miles, manager; seating capacity, 750; rental, one night, share only; license yearly. Size of stage, 26x35; size of proscenium opening, 14x25; height from stage to grooves, 10; height from stage to rigging loft, 14; number sets scenery, 10; leader of orchestra, C. Speed; bill poster, Chas. Schnumel; number sheets can accommodate, 100. Newspapers: Times (Wed.), Gleaner (Fri.) ....Hotels: Belmont, special rates, $1 to $1.50; Barnes, $1 to $1.25.

MAYFIELD, 3,000. R. R., Chic., Ohio & South Western. Opera House, T. A. Slaughter, manager; seating capacity, 400; rental, share only; license included. Size of stage, 14x44; size of proscenium opening, 10x25; depth under stage, 4; traps, 1; number sets scenery, 2. Newspapers: Democrat (Th.), Monitor (Fri.) ... Hotel: Southern, regular rates, $1.50 (special also).

Freund's Weekly.

A Review of Music and the Drama.

PUBLISHED EVERY SATURDAY
At 835 BROADWAY, NEW YORK.

JOHN C. FREUND,   -   -   -   Editor.

ITS PRINCIPAL AIM.

While it is read by the most intelligent and refined members of the dramatic profession, FREUND'S WEEKLY reaches a very large class of musical people who do not read any other dramatic paper. While it aims to be, above all, a NEWSpaper, it rejects the scandals of the profession, which can only be enjoyed by those who wish to degrade the stage or see it brought into disgrace. It deals fearlessly and without favor with all subjects relating to the kindred professions. By excluding from its columns coarse abuse, vulgar praise and the prurient sensationalism of the daily press, it aims by example to elevate the standard of public taste by dealing with artists solely in their relation to art. It is only necessary to compare it with other papers of its class to convince intelligent and refined readers—the only class it caters for—that it contains the best features of all without those which disgrace dramatic and musical journalism.

ITS PRINCIPAL FEATURES.

COULISSES CHAT—FREUND'S WEEKLY makes a special feature of musical and dramatic NEWS, both original and selected, covering every important city in the United States, Canada and Europe, carefully classified under the following departments

  I. MANAGERS AND AUTHORS, identified with the profession who do not appear upon the stage.
  II. MUSICAL NEWS, concerning all combinations, except those identified with the dramatic stage.
  III. DRAMATIC NEWS, including minstrel troupes and specialty combinations of the best class.
  IV. THE FOREIGN STAGE, including both the lyric and spoken drama.

CORRESPONDENCE—Covering every city and town in the United States and Canada possessing a theatre or opera house, giving a weekly chronicle of musical and dramatic events on the American Continent.

LONDON AND PARIS LETTERS—From able correspondents, giving a weekly review of the principal events of the English and Continental stages.

LATEST NEWS—Including news by telegraph and cable despatches up to the time of going to press on Thursday of each week.

TRAVELING COMPANIES—FREUND'S WEEKLY list of advance dates is the most complete list of the kind published, because it is edited with the most care. It is only necessary to know the character of the entertainment to find it in its proper department. FREUND'S WEEKLY list is the only one published and (copyrighted) in which the attractions are classified according to the character of the entertainments given, indexed alphabetically, according to the initial letter of the last name of the star being always used, or the initial letter of the attractions "featured," as follows :

  I. Italian, German and French opera and concert companies of the first class.
  II. English opera companies.
  III. Minstrel troupes and other musical entertainments.
  IV. Musical, Comedy and Burlesque companies.
  V. Specialty combinations, booked only in first-class theatres.
  VI. Melodrama, Spectacular and Pantomime companies, in which mechanical scenery, etc., form a principal feature.
  VII. Dramatic companies, of which the principal feature is the star.
  VIII. Dramatic companies, in which the play is featured, or, if playing more than one, indexed according to the name under which the company is advertised.

This list is invaluable for local managers and representatives of hotels and transportation companies, who will find it the most complete and correct list published.

TERMS.—Single Copies, ten cents; Subscription, One Year, in advance, three dollars.

HARRY E. FREUND, Publisher and Proprietor.

MAYSVILLE, 6.500. R. R., Kentucky Central. Washington Opera House, Chas. H.
Frank, manager; seating capacity, 600; rental, one night $20, license included. Size
of stage, 36x47; full set scenery; bill posters, Taylor & Dillon. Newspapers: Bulletin
(Th.), Republican (Sat.), Eagle (Wed.)......Hotels: Central, regular rates, $2 (special
also); Hill, European, Bancroft.

Court House; seating capacity, 500.

Neptune Hall; seating capacity, 300.

MT. STERLING, 5,000. R. R., Ches. & Ohio; E. L. & B. S. Bristow's House, J. M.
Kelly, manager; seating capacity, 500; rental, one night $20, three $50, license
included. Size of stage, 25x18, size of proscenium opening, 12x14; height from stage to
grooves, 11½; height from stage to rigging loft, 12; height under stage, 4; number sets
scenery, 5; leader of orchestra, E. S. Fogg; bill posters, Hall & Shore; number of sheets
can accommodate, 365; rates per sheet, 4c.; theatrical teamster, G. E. Coleman. Newspapers: Sentinel (Th.), advertising rates, 10c. per line; Gazette (Tu.), advertising rates,
10c. per line ......Hotels: National, special rates, $1.50; Turner, special rates, $1.25.

Masonic Hall, John J. Cornelison, manager; seating capacity, 350; rental, one night $20;
license, $5; share also.

NEWPORT, 21,570. R. R., Louisville & Nashville. Odd Fellows' Hall; seating capacity 400.
Newspapers: tri-weekly, Journal.

Turner's Hall, seating capacity, 500.

NICHOLASVILL, 2,500. R. R., Cincinnati Southern. Sparks' Opera House, J. H. Dorman,
manager; seating capacity, 750; rental, one night $25, three $40; share also; license included. Size of stage, 20x25; size of proscenium opening, 18x22; height from stage to
grooves, 14; height from stage to rigging loft, 18 and 28; depth under stage, 4; number
sets of scenery, 8; bill poster, J. H. Dorman; number of sheets can accommodate, 200;
rates per sheet, 3c.; theatrical teamster, J. D. Carlisle. Newspaper: Courier (Fri.), advertising rates, 5c. per line......Hotels: Verandah, special rates, $1 to $1.25; Jessa-
mine, special rates, $1 to $1.25.

OWENSBORO, 10,000. R. R., Owensboro & Nashville. Grand Opera House, A. Hill & Co.,
managers; seating capacity, 900; rental, one night, $50, three $125; share also; license included. Size of stage, 40x50; full set of scenery; bill poster, John Blanford. Newspaper: semi-weekly, Messenger......Hotels: Planters', regular rates, $2 to $2.50 (special
also); McCullough's, Palmer's, Brooks'.

Hall's Opera House, Frank L. Hall, manager; seating capacity, 900; rental, one night $35,
three $75; share also. Size of stage, 22x24; number sets scenery, 7.

Griffith's Hall; seating capacity, 500.

City Hall; seating capacity, 500.

PADUCAH, 12,000. R. R., Chicago, Ohio & South Western; Ohio River Boats. Morton's
New Opera House, Morton, Kirkland & Quigley, managers; seating capacity, 1,000;
rental, share only; license, $10. Size of stage, 40x55; size of proscenium opening,
23x30; height from stage to grooves, 16; height from stage to rigging loft, 33; depth
under stage, 4; number sets scenery, 10; leader of orchestra, Chas. W. Gilbert; stage
carpenter, John Artz; bill poster, Opera House; theatrical teamster, Richmond House
Baggage Wagon. Newspapers: daily, News, Standard......Hotels: Richmond, Marshall.

St. Clair Hall, Lambkin & Clark, managers; seating capacity, 1,000; rental, one night
$35, three $95; share also; license included. Size of stage, 36x60; fair stock scenery.

PARIS, 5,000. R. R., Kentucky Central. Odd Fellows' Hall; seating capacity, 300; bill
poster, T. O. Bashford. Newspapers: semi-weekly, Bourbon News; weekly, Advertiser
(Fri.), Kentuckian (Wed.) Citizen (Fri.)......Hotels: Bourbon, regular rates, $2 (special
also); Bradford, Gore, Gleeson, Terrapin, Southwestern.

PRINCETON, 2,500. R. R., Chesapeake, Ohio & South Western, Opera House, W. S.
Powell, manager; seating capacity, 500; rental, one night $10, three $25; license, $2.50;
share also. Size of stage, 20x22; number sets of scenery, 4; bill poster, T. J. Hoodenfile.
Newspaper: Banner (Th.)......Hotels: Commercial, regular rates, $2 (special also);
Bank.

RICHMOND, 3,500. R. R., Kentucky Central. Opera House, A. C. Green, manager; seating capacity, 800; rent or share; license yearly. Size of stage, 25x23; number sets scenery, 7; bill poster, John Christopher. Newspapers. Herald (Wed.), Register (Fri.) ..... Hotels: Garnet, Roberts.

Park Theatre, Wherrin & Stockton, managers; seating **capacity,** 600; rent or **share**; license yearly. Size of stage, 24x40; number sets scenery, 8.

Arnold's Theatre, James H. Arnold, manager.

RUSSELLVILLE, 2,500. R. R., Louisville & Nashville, Owensboro & Nashville. Ryan's **Hall, C. H.** Ryan, manager; seating capacity, 400; rental, **one** night $15, three $30; **share also**; license included. Size of stage, 18x30; number sets scenery, 3; bill **poster,** Richard Mosby. Newspapers: Herald, Enterprise (Wed.)... ..Hotel: Armstrong, regular rates, $2 (special also).

SHELBYVILLE, 3,000. R. R., Louisville & Nashville. Layton Hall, Geo. **Petney, man**ager; seating capacity, 600; rental, one night $25; full set scenery; bill poster, **T. S.** Baxter. Newspaper: Sentinel (Th.) .....Hotel: Armstrong, regular rates, **$2 (special also).**

STANFORD, 2,000. R. R., Louisville & Nashville; Kentucky Central. Stanford Opera House, W. P. Walton, manager; seating capacity, 600; rental, one night, $25, three $50, share also; license included. Size of stage, 20x50; number sets scenery, 8; bill poster, E. C. Walton. Newspaper: semi-weekly, Journal.. .Hotels: Meyers, regular rates, $2 (special also); St. Asaph.

LOUISIANA.

ALEXANDRIA, 3,000, R. R., Texas Pacific: Morgan's, Louisiana & Texas. Exchange Hall, John De Lacy, manager; seating capacity, 800; rental, one night $10; license, $10. Size of stage, 28x35; number sets scenery, 8. Newspapers: tri-weekly, Democrat ; weekly, Express (Sat.)......Hotels : Exchange, regular rates, $2 (special also); **Samo.**

City Hall; seating capacity, 450. Size of stage, 18x25.

BATON ROUGE, 8,000. R. R., Miss. Valley; Morgan's, La. & Texas. Pike's Theatre, A. H. **Hoguet,** manager ; seating capacity, 500; rental, one night, $35; license included. Size of **stage,** 24x45; full set scenery; bill poster, manager Hall. Newspapers: daily, Advocate; weekly, Truth (Fri.)..... Hotels: Capital, regular rates, $2 (special also); Bank, special.

BAYOU SARA, 2,000. Freyhan Hall, **J.** Freyhan, manager; seating capacity, 300; **rental, one** night $25; share also; **license** included. Size of stage, 20x30. Newspaper : **Sentinel** ......Hotels Witcher's, Alexandre.

DONALDSONVILLE, 4,000. R. R., Texas & Pacific. Silver Cornet Band Hall; seating capacity, 200; rental, one night $25; no license. Size of stage, 30x40; number sets scenery, 12. Newspapers : Democrat (Sat.), Chief (Sat.)......Hotel : Lee, regular rates, $2 (special also).

LAKE CHARLES, 5,000. R. R., Texas & New Orleans. Fricke's Opera House, Wm. **C.** Fricke, manager; seating capacity, 600; share only. Size of stage, 30x30; number **sets** scenery, 10; bill poster, Opera House. Newspapers : Commercial (Sat.), Echo **(Sat**) ..... Hotels : Haskell's, **Lake,** Cosmopolitan, Hawkins', Commercial.

MONROE, 3,500. R. R., Vicksburg, Shreveport & Pacific. Gerspach Opera House, **John** Gerspach, manager; seating **capacity,** 600; rental, one night $30, three $70, license included. Size of stage, 18x24; **full** set scenery Newspapers : Bulletin (Wed.); Telegraph (Fri.) ....Hotels: Enmenger's, regular rates, $2 (special **also)**; Ouachita, Monroe.

MORGAN CITY, 3,000. R. R., Morgan, La. & Tex. Whitney Opera House, Geo. Drews, manager; seating capacity, 500; rental, one night $30, **three $17.** Size of stage, 20x30; number sets scenery, 5; bill poster, D. Grammond. Newspapers : Free Press (Th.); Review (Sat.)......Hotels : **City,** regular rates, $2 (special also); Commercial.

NATCHITOCHES, 1,500. Freeman Hall, seating **capacity, 250**; rental, one night, **$7.50. Size** of stage, 15x30; number sets scenery, 2. Newspaper: **Vindicator (Sat.)......Hotel: Harris,** regular rates, $2 (special also).

NEW IBERIA, 3,000. R. R., Morgan's, La. & Texas. Serrett's Hall, F. Serrett, manager. Newspapers: Journal (Sat.); Star (Sat.)......Hotels: Serrett, regular rates, $2 (special also).

NEW ORLEANS, 300 000. R. R., Illinois Central, Louisville & Nashville; Morgan's Louisiana & Texas; N. Or. & Miss, Valley; N. Or. & Northeastern; Texas & Pacific. St. Charles Theatre, D. Bidwell, manager; seating capacity, 3 000; rental, share only; license yearly. Size of stage, 63x72; size of proscenium opening, 32x38; height from stage to grooves, 21; height from stage to rigging loft, 56; depth under stage, 9; traps, 3; complete stock scenery; bill poster, manager; number of sheets can accommodate, 6,000. Newspapers: daily, Chronicle, Item; Picayune, States, Times-Democrat............ Hotels: St. Charles, regular rates, $3 (special also); City, regular rates, $2 (special also); St. Louis, Cosmopolitan, Cassidy's.

Grand Opera House, D. Bidwell, manager; seating capacity, 1,800; rental, share only. Size of stage, 70x80; size of proscenium opening, 33x36; height from stage to grooves, 27; height from stage to rigging loft, 65; depth under stage, 28; traps 6 and 4 sets complete stock scenery.

Bidwell's Academy of Music. D. Bidwell, manager; seating capacity, 2,000; share only. Size of stage, 45x50; size of proscenium opening, 30x32; height from stage to grooves, 29; height from stage to rigging loft, 45 (will be raised); depth under stage, 7; traps, 3; complete stock scenery.

Grunewald Opera House, Eugene Robinson, manager; seating capacity, 1,200; rental, share only; license yearly. Size of stage, 35x60; size of proscenium opening, 30x28; height from stage to grooves, 17; number sets scenery, 18; musical director, Henry Grolling; name of scenic artist, Dresser; bill poster, A. Webber.

Park Theatre (Variety), Samuel S. McLean, manager. Size of stage 25x35; number sets scenery, 7.

Hamilton's New Varieties, A. E. Hamilton, manager; seating capacity, 1,000.

Werlein Hall, P. Werlein, manager; seating capacity, 700.

West End Pavilion, J. Alexander Brown, manager.

Spanish Fort Opera House.

National Theatre.

Faranta's Pavilion.

OPELOUSAS, 3,000. R. R., Morgan's La. & Texas. Varieties Hall, C. Deitlein, manager; seating capacity, 700; rental, one night $10; license, $10; no scenery; bill poster, Wm Smith. Newspapers: Courier (Sat.), Democrat (Sat)......Hotels: Eureka, regular rates, $2.50 (special also); Bailey

Latour's Hall; seating capacity, 300.

SHREVEPORT, 10,000. R. R., N. O. Pacific; Texas Pacific; Vicksburg & Shreveport; East & West Texas. Tally's Opera House, Hyams, Leonard & Carter, managers; seating capacity, 600; rental, one night $60, three $125; license; share, 30 per cent. 2 nights, 35 per cent. 1 night. Size of stage, 30x35; number sets scenery, 6; stage carpenter, T. J. Seaton; theatrical teamster, T. J. Seaton. Newspapers: daily, Times, Democrat...... Hotels: City, special rates, $1.50; Compton, regular rates, $2.50 (special also).

Brewers' Hall; seating capacity, 1,000.

Anderson's Hall; seating capacity, 750.

THIBODAUX, 2,000. R. R., Morgan's La. & Texas. Waverly Hall, Brand & Legrande, managers. Newspaper: Sentinel (Sat.)......Hotel: Stranger's, regular rates, $2 (special also).

VERMILLIONVILLE, 22,000. R. R., Morgan's La. & Texas; Galveston, Harrisburg & San Antonio. St. John's Hall; seating capacity, 400; rent or share; license, $5. Size of stage, 18x25; fair stock scenery. Newspaper: Advertiser (Sat.)... ..Hotels: Crescent, regular rates, $2 to $2.50 (special also); Lafayette, Sallar.

MAINE.

AUGUSTA, 8,700. R. R., **Maine Central.** Granite Hall, C. B. Morton, manager; seating capacity, 1,200; rental, one night $25; license, $5; full set scenery. Size of stage, 25x25; bill poster, W. H. Walker; theatrical teamster, J. W. Harlow. Newspapers: daily, Journal; weekly, New Age (Fri.)......Hotels: Augusta, regular rates $2 (special also); Cony, Mansion.

Meonian Hall; seating capacity, 1,000.

BANGOR, 20,000. R. R., Maine Central. Bangor Opera House, **Frank A.** Owen, manager; seating capacity, 1,100; rental, share only; license, yearly. **Size of** stage, 35x65; size of proscenium opening, 31x31; height from stage to grooves, 18; height from stage to rigging loft, **40**; depth under stage, 10; traps, 2; number sets scenery, 15; leader of orchestra, **M.** H. Andrews; scenic artist, O. Ackerman; stage carpenter, E. H. Stockman; bill **poster,** Thos. W. Burr; number of sheets can accommodate, 1,500; rates per sheet, 4c.; **the**atrical teamster, N. B. Williams. Newspapers: daily, Whig, Commercial......**Hotels:** Bangor, special rates, $1.50 to $2.50; Penobscot Exchange, Windon, $1.25 to $2; Bangor Exchange, $2.

Music Hall, M. H. Andrews, manager; seating capacity, 650; rental, one night $15; share also. Size of stage, 8x24; no scenery.

Norombega Hall, C. E. Lovell, manager; seating capacity, 1,100; rental, one night **$50,** three $40; license, $5. Size of stage, 30x50; number sets scenery, 9.

City Hall; seating capacity, 800.

BATH, 8,000. R. R., Knox & Lincoln, Maine Central. Columbian Hall, Jos. M. Sorell, manager; seating capacity, 800; rental, one night $20; three $50; license, $5; share also; number sets scenery, 4; bill poster, manager of hall. Newspapers: daily, Times; weekly, Independent (Sat.)......Hotels: Sagadahoc, regular rates $2 (special also); Bath, Columbian, Shannon.

City Hall; seating capacity, 500.

Music Hall; seating capacity, 500.

BELFAST, 6,000. R. R., Maine Central. Hayford Opera House, Charles **J.** Burgess, manager; seating capacity, 900; rental, one night $30, license, $5; share also. Size of stage, 25x40; fair stock scenery; bill poster, Opera House; theatrical teamster, Belfast Livery Co. Newspapers: Age (Th), Journal (Th.)......Hotels: American, regular **rates, $2** (special) also; New England.

BIDDEFORD, (with Saco), 22,500. R. R., Boston & **Maine** Eastern. City Opera House, Brooks Brothers, managers; seating capacity, 1,000. Size of stage, 50x30; size of proscenium opening, 20x25; height from stage to grooves, 12½; height from stage to rigging loft, 22; depth under stage, 4½; traps, 3; number sets scenery, 10; leader of orchestra, E. Sampson; bill poster, Sam. Parsons; number of sheets can accommodate, 700; rates per sheet, 3c.; theatrical teamster, Charles Millkin. Newspapers, daily: Journal, advertising rates per inch, **50c.**......Hotels: Biddeford, rates to profession, $1.50 to $2; Commercial, rates to profession, **$1 25.**

BREWER, 3,200. R. R., **Maine Central.** Town Hall; seating capacity, 300; **rental, one** night $3 to $4; no license. **Size of** stage, 5x30.

BRUNSWICK, 5,500. R. R., Maine Central. Town Hall, Emery A. Crawford, manager; seating capacity, 1,500; rental, one night $30, three $60; license, $2. **Size of** stage, 25x49; size of proscenium opening, 23x29; traps, 2; number sets scenery, **6**; bill poster, John Dunning; theatrical teamster, Crawford's Express. Newspapers: Herald (Sat.), Telegraph (Th.)......Hotel: Tontine, regular rates $2 (special also).

BUCKSPORT, 3,500. R. R., Maine Central. Emery Hall, Emery & Sons, managers; seating capacity, 700 ; rental, one night $10; license, six tickets; share also. Size of stage, 25x20; full set scenery; bill poster, Alva B. Ames... ...Hotels: Robinson, regular rates, $2 (special also); Eldredge.

CALAIS, 10,000. R. R., N. B. & C ; St. Croix & Penob, St. Croix Hall, H. C. Grant, manager; seating capacity, 900; rental, one night $15, three $25; share also; license, $2. Size of stage, 24x56; size of proscenium opening, 18x23; height from stage to grooves, 16; height from stage to rigging loft, 25; depth under stage, 4; traps, 3; number sets scenery, only drop curtain and wings; leader of orchestra, M. Silverston; stage carpenter, J. Sanders; bill poster, H. Clenant; number of sheets can accommodate, 300; rates per sheet, 4c.; theatrical teamster, D. M. Gardner. Newspapers: Times (Tn.), Advertiser (Th.), Courier (Th.)......Hotels: American, Exchange, special rates, $1.25.

DAMARISCOTTA, 1.000. R. R., Knox & Lincoln. Lincoln Hall; rental, one night $12. Newspapers: Herald and Record (Th.)......Hotel: Maine, regular rates, $2 (special also).

DEXTER, 3,700. R. R. Maine Central. Town Hall, W. B. Goff, manager; seating capacity, 700; rental, one night $15, three $30; no license. Size of stage, 20x22; number sets scenery, 12; bill poster, Henry Fitzgerald. Newspapers : Eastern State (Th.), Gazette (Fri.)......Hotel : Merchant, regular rates, $2 (special also), Dexter.

DOVER, 1,700. R R., Bangor & Piscataquis. Central Hall, W. C. Woodbury, manager; seating capacity, 600; rental, one night $12, license included. Size of stage, 19x14; full set scenery; bill poster, manager of Hall. Newspaper ; Observer (Tb.) ....Hotels: Blethen, Exchange.

EASTPORT, 4,000. R. R., nearest at St. Stephens, N. B., 30 miles. Steamboat communication every day east and west. Memorial Hall, selectmen, managers; (Hall engaged Mondays and Fridays); seating capacity, 600; rental, one night $10, three $30, license included. Size of stage, 16x30; height from stage to ceiling, 16; depth under stage, 7; leader of orchestra, T. Mabee; scenic artist, Harry Harrington; stage carpenter, Everett Newcomb; bill poster, Albert Gilligan; theatrical teamster, H. C. Harrington. Newspaper: Sentinel (Wed.) advertising rates, $1 per inch......Hotels : Passamaquoddy, special rates $1.50; Island, special rates, $1 25.

ELLSWORTH, 5,300. R. R., Maine Central. Hancock Hall, C. S. Stover, manager; seating capacity, 700; rental, one night $30. Size of stage, 16x34; fair stock scenery; bill poster, James McLane. Newspaper: American (Th.)......Hotels: American, Franklin.

FARMINGTON, 4,000. R. R., Maine Central ; Sandy River. Drummond Hall, S. B. Pillsbury, manager; seating capacity, 400; rental, one night $6, three $15 ; no license. Size of stage, 12x18 ; no scenery. Newspapers : Chronicle (Th.), Journal (Sat.)......Hotels: Stoddard, Forrest.

GARDINER, 5,000. R. R., Maine Central. Coliseum, A. W. McCausland, manager; seating capacity, 2,000 ; rental, share only ; license included. Size of stage, 38x55 ; size of proscenium opening, 25x32 ; height from stage to grooves, 18 ; height from stage to rigging loft, 40 ; depth under stage, 8 ; number sets scenery, 7 ; leader of orchestra, A. R. Protheroe; scenic artist, J. W. Berry; stage carpenter, Harrison Potter; bill poster, J. W. Kimball ; number of sheets can accommodate, 500 ; rates per sheet, 4c. Newspapers : daily, Journal, Advocate, advertising rates, yearly contract ; weekly, Journal (Wed.), advertising rates, yearly contract ; Reporter (Sat), advertising rates, yearly contract ; Register (Fri.), advertising rates, yearly contract ; Bee (Wed.), advertising rates, yearly contract........Hotels : Evans, special rates, $1.50 ; Johnson, special rates, $1.50.

Johnson Hall, B. Johnson, managers ; seating capacity, 800 ; rental, one night $20, license included. Size of stage, 32x19 ; number sets scenery, 6 ; bill posters, S. W. Kimball ; theatrical teamsters, Harridian & Nevel. Newspapers : Journal (Wed.), Reporter (Sat.).... .Hotels : Evans, regular rates, $2 (special also) ; Johnson.

HALLOWELL, 4,000. R. R., Maine Central. Wilson Hall, Chas. Wilson, manager; seating capacity, 900 ; rental, one night $20 ; share also ; no license. Size of stage, 27x42; number sets scenery, 8 ; bill poster, Jno. C. McCluer ; theatrical teamster, Jno C. McCluer. Newspaper : Register (Sat.)........Hotels : Hallowell, regular rates, $2 (special also).

HOULTON, 4,000. R. R., New Brunswick & Maine Central. Opera House, Albion P. Haywood, manager; seating capacity, 800; rental, one night $10, three $25; license, $2 to $4. Size of stage, 22x50; size of proscenium opening, 18x23; height from stage to

THE NEWS LETTER.

EDITED BY D. DALZIEL.

PUBLISHED IN

NEW YORK AND CHICAGO.

Subscription, $4.00 per annum.

Advertising rates, 12 1-2 cents per line (agate.)

Address all communications to

D. DALZIEL,

44 W. 23d St., New York, N. Y.   87 Clark St., Chicago, Ill.

grooves, 13; traps 1; number sets scenery, 7; leader of orchestra, Van Robinson; stage carpenter, H. K Whitcomb; bill poster, Wm. Gallagher; number of sheets can accommodate, 150; rates per sheet, 3½; theatrical teamster, Thomas Flowers. Newspapers: Pioneer (Mon.), Times (Wed.), advertising rates, $1 per inch......Hotels : Exchange, special rates, $1.25; Snell, special rates, $1.50; Clark's, special rates, $1.25.

Music Hall, H. T. Frisbie, manager; seating capacity, 800; rental, one night $10, three $25; license, $2 to $3; share also. Size of stage, 50x17; number sets scenery, 6.

Crarey's Hall; seating capacity, 400.

KENNEBUNK, 3,500. R. R., Boston & Maine; Eastern. Mousams Hall, J. E. Lord, manager; seating capacity, 500; rental, one night $12; no scenery; bill poster, J. F. Noyes. Newspaper : Star (Fri.).. .. ..Hotels : Mousam, Lowell's.

LEWISTON, 20,000. R. R., Maine Central & Grand Trunk Music Hall, Charles Horbury, manager; seating capacity, 1,274; rental or share; license, yearly. Size of stage, 38x60; size of proscenium opening, 30x30; height from stage to grooves, 17; height from stage to rigging loft, 34; depth under stage, 8; traps, 5; number sets scenery. 20; bill poster, Charles Horbury; number sheets can accommodate, 2,000; theatrical teamster. Joseph Woodbury. Newspapers : daily, Journal; weekly, Gazette (Fri) .... Hotels : Marston, regular rates, $2 (special also), Exchange, regular rates, $2 (special also); De Witt, regular rates (special also).

Lyceum Hall, Horace C. Little, manager; seating capacity. 1,000; rental, one night $25, three $60; license included. Size of stage, 23x30; number sets scenery, 6.

City Hall; seating capacity. 2,000.

MACHIAS, 2,500. Libby Hall; seating capacity, 500; rental, one night $5; three nights $15; no license; share also. Size of stage, 40x20; no scenery. Newspapers : Republican (Sat.), Union (Tu.).. ...Hotels : Eastern, Clare's, Machias.

NEWPORT, 1,750. R. R., Maine Central. Meriden Hall, J. S. Sargent, manager; seating capacity, 450; rental, one night $5, three, $9, no license. Size of stage, 22x40; number sets scenery, 6; bill poster, H. Smith; theatrical teamster, Frank Pushar......Hotel: Shaw.

OLDTOWN, 3,400. R. R., Maine Central; Bangor & Piscataquis. Town Hall, J. M. Jellison manager; seating capacity, 800; rental, one night $10. Size of stage, 15x45; fair stock scenery; bill poster. J. M. Jellison....Hotels: Colman; Cousins.

PORTLAND, 24,000. R. R., Bos. & Me ; East.; Gd Trunk; Intern'l S. S. Co. ; Me. Cent., Port. & Og.; Port & Roch.; Port. Steam Pkt. Co. Portland Theatre, Frank Curtis; manager; seating capacity, 1,150; rental, one night $75, three $200; license included; share also. Size of stage, 34x59; height from stage to grooves, 18; height from stage to rigging loft, 32; depth under stage, 5; bill poster, Portland Theatre ; theatrical teamster, A. Baker. Newspapers: daily, Advertiser, Argus, Press, Express .. ..Hotels: Falmouth, regular rates, $2.50 to $3; Preble, regular rates, $2.50 to $3; United States, regular rates, $2 (special also); City, regular rates, $2 (special also).

Portland Museum. J. T. Wyer, manager; seating capacity, 800; rental. one night $60, license included; full set scenery.

City Hall, George H. Libby, manager; seating capacity, 1,200; rental, one night $84, three $226; license included. Size of stage, 26x60; full set scenery.

Lyceum Theatre, Mortimer & Sterling, managers.

Music Hall; seating capacity, 800.

ROCKLAND, 8,000. R. R., Knox & Lincoln; Boston & Bangor steamers. Farwell Hall J. B. Porter, manager; seating capacity, 900; rental, one night $20, three $30; share also; license, $5. Size of stage, 22x20; size of proscenium opening, 13x24; height from stage to rigging loft, 18; number sets scenery, 8; bill poster, G. L. Black; number of sheets can accommodate, 250; rates per sheet, 5c.; theatrical teamster, G. L Black. Newspapers: Courier-Gazette (Tu), Opinion (Fri.), Free Press (Tu.)......Hotels: Thorndyke, special rates, $2; St. Nicholas; special rates, $1.75; Lindsey, special rates. $1.50.

SACCARAPPA, 4,000. R. R., Portland & Rochester. Odd Fellows' Hall, C. B. Woodman, agent; seating capacity, 600; rental one, night $15, three $30; license included. Size of stage, 12x24. Newspapers: Chronicle (Fri.) .....Hotels: Presumpscot, Highland, special rates; $1.

Weston's Hall, Geo. H. Raymond, manager; seating capacity, 310; rental, one night, $6, three $12; no scenery.

SACO, 6,000. R. R., Boston & Maine, Eastern. City Hall, Geo. F. Owen, manager; seating capacity, 750; rental, one night $25, license, six tickets. Size of stage, 25x44; no scenery; bill poster, S. Parsons (Biddeford). Newspapers: daily, Times; weekly, Journal (Fri.), Sentinel (Sat.)......Hotel: Saco, regular rates, $2 (special also.)

Patten's Hall; seating capacity, 400.

SKOWHEGAN, 5,000. R. R., Maine Central (terminus). Coburn Hall, Chas. F. Jones, manager; seating capacity, 1,200; rental, one night $15, three $30 to $35; no license. Size of stage, 23x24; size of proscenium opening, 15x22½; height from stage to grooves, 16½; height from stage to rigging loft, 18½; depth under stage, 3¼; traps, 1; number sets scenery, 6; scenic artists, P. & A. L. Weston; stage carpenter, C. C. Grover; bill poster, A. J. Ordway; number of sheets can accommodate, 200; rates per sheet, 4c; theatrical teamster, G. E. Goodwin, H. P. Thing. Newspaper: Reporter (Wed.), advertising rates, $1 per inch .Hotels: Heselton, Coburn, special rates, $1.50; Skowhegan, $1.

SOUTH BERWICK, 4,000. R. R., Boston & Maine; Eastern. Newichawanick's Hall, J. V. Nealy, manager; seating capacity, 500; rental, one night $10, l cense included. Size of stage, 26x15; no scenery; bill poster, J. P. Noys. Hotels: Paul's, South Berwick, Jones, Salmon Falls.

WALDOBORO, 4,000. R. R., Maine Central. Clark's Hall, E. O. Clark, manager; seating capacity, 500; rental, one night $8; fair stock scenery; bill poster. Thomas P. Shay. Newspaper: News (Fri.)......Hotel: Medomak.

WATERVILLE, 6,000. R. R., Maine Central. Town Hall, Geo. H. Esty, manager; seating capacity, 800; rental, one night $15, license included; share also. Size of stage, 19x19; number sets scenery, 5; bill poster, F. J. Hill; theatrical teamster, J. M. Wall. Newspapers: Mail (Fri.); Sentinel (Fri.)......Hotels: Elmwood, Williams', Smith.

WINTHORP, 3,000. R. R., Maine Central. Packard Hall, H. W Packard, manager; seating capacity, 700; rental, one night $10, three, 25; no license. Size of stage, 23x44; number sets scenery, 3; bill poster, Thomas Dealy. Newspaper: Budget (Sat.) .... Hotel: Winthorp.

MARYLAND.

ANNAPOLIS, 6,500. R. R., Annapolis & Elk Ridge. Masonic Hall, G. A. Culver, manager; seating capacity, 500; rental, one night, $20, three $40; share also; license included Size of stage, 19x38; number sets scenery, 8; bill poster, Jack Adams. Newspapers: daily, Herald; weekly, Gazette (Tues.), Republican (Sat.), Record (Sat.)......Hotels: Maryland, regular rates, $3; City , Carroll.

Assembly Room; seating capacity, 300.

BALTIMORE, 400,000. R. R., Balt. & Ohio; Balt. & Phila.; Nor. Cen.; Phila., Wil. & Balt.; West Md.; Md. Cen. Academy of Music, S. W. Fort, manager; seating capacity, 1,800; rental, one night $150; share also; license, yearly. Size of stage, 75x82; size of proscenium opening, 53x55; height from stage to grooves, 21; height from stage to rigging loft, 85; depth under stage, 40; traps of every description, and sinks for flat; number sets scenery, 50; musical director, Adam Itzel, Jr.; scenic artist, Carpenter; stage carpenter, Ben Morrison; bill poster, A. P. Houck; number of sheets can accommodate, 10,000; rates per sheet, 3c.; theatrical teamsters, Baltimore Transfer Company, Geagan. Newspapers: daily, American (Sun. also); News (Sun. also); Herald (Sun. also); Day (Sun. also)......Hotels: Carrollton, special rates, $1 to $3.50; Barnum's, special rates, $1 to $3.50; Pepper's, special rates, $1 to $1.50; Adler's, special rates, $1.

Ford's Grand Opera House, John T. Ford, manager (also of Ford's Opera House, Washington, D. C.); seating capacity, 2,000; rental, one night $100, three $250; license, yearly; share also. Size of stage, 65x80; size of proscenium opening, 40x45; height from stage to grooves, 18; height from stage to rigging loft, 35; depth under stage, 24; traps, complete set; full set scenery; musical director, Prof. Weber; scenic artist, Geo. W. Hyland; stage carpenter, Geo. W. Vanderwerken; bill posters, Wachtel & Co.; number of sheets can accommodate, 4,000; rates per sheet, 2½c.

Front Street Theatre, Dan. A. Kelly, manager; seating capacity, 2,500; rental, share only; license, yearly. Size of stage, 72x65; size of proscenium opening, 30x36; height from stage to grooves, 22; height from stage to rigging loft, 70; depth under stage, 18; traps — star, vampire, and traps of all description; number sets scenery, 40; musical director, Prof. Richard Wagner; scenic artist, James Thomas; stage carpenter, A. P. Martin.

Kernan's Monumental Theatre, James L. Kernan, manager; seating capacity, 2,300; share only. Size of stage, 60x62; size of proscenium opening, 37x35; height from stage to grooves, 20; height from stage to rigging loft, 50; depth under stage, 10; traps, 2; number sets scenery, 30; musical director, Prof. Ludeke; scenic artist, Milton Slemmer; stage carpenter, Wm. H. R. Foster; bill posters, Wachtel & Co.; number of sheets can accommodate, 5,000; rates per sheet, 3c.

Albaugh's Holliday Street Theatre, John W. Albaugh, manager; seating capacity, 1,700. Size of stage, 45x72; size of proscenium opening, 38x38; height from stage to grooves, 20; height from stage to rigging loft, 65; depth under stage, 16; complete stock scenery; musical director, Adam Rosenberger; scenic artist, Milton Slemmer; stage carpenter, James Walsh.

Odeon Theatre (Variety), E. M. Castine, manager; seating capacity, 600. Size of stage, 25x33; size of proscenium opening, 15x22.

Harris Museum, Col. G. O. Starr, manager; seating capacity, 2,100. Size of stage, 43x60; size of proscenium opening, 55x39; height from stage to grooves, 17; height from stage to rigging loft, 50; depth under stage, 8; trap, centre; number sets scenery, 15; musical director, F. H. Roble; scenic artist, Will Bayard; stage carpenter, Phil Taylor.

Masonic Temple, J. Likes, manager; seating capacity, 1,300.

Maryland Institute; seating capacity, 1,400.

Eagle Palace Theatre (Variety), Frederick Loeber, manager.

New Museum, Dan Herzog & Co., managers.

CUMBERLAND, 15,000. R. R., Cumb. & Penn.; Balt. & Ohio; Penn. Academy of Music, Chas. J. Saunders, manager; seating capacity, 1,200; rental, one night $50, three $100; share also; leader of orchestra, Michal Weisel; scenic artist, Frank Davis; stage carpenter, David Walter; bill poster, Charley Inix; theatrical teamster, Thomas Robison. Newspapers: daily, News, Times; weekly, Civilian (Sun.), Courier (Th.), Independent (Sat.)..... Hotels: Queen City, special rates, $2; Windsor, special rates, $1.25; St. Nicholas, special rates, $1.

Belvidere Hall; seating capacity, 500.

EASTON, 3,500. R. R., Branch of Penn. R. R. (Del. & Chesapeake). Music Hall, M. M. Higgins, manager; seating capacity, 480; rental, one night $15 to $30; license, $4.25. Size of stage, 15x44; size of proscenium opening, 30x22; depth under stage, 6½; traps, 3; number sets scenery, 5. Newspapers: Star (Tu.), Ledger (Th.), Gazette (Sat.) .... .Hotels: Brick, American.

FREDERICK, 9,000. R. R., Baltimore & Ohio; Pennsylvania. Opera House; seating capacity, 800; rental, one night $25; license, $3. Full set scenery; bill poster, Ed. Butler. Newspapers: daily, Call; weekly, Examiner (Wed.), Union (Th.)......Hotels: City, regular rates, $2 (special also); Carlin, Groff, Dill, Central.

City Hall, Jacob Dadsminaw, manager; seating capacity, 800; rental, one night $25; license, $3. Size of stage, 26x26; fair stock scenery.

Junier Hall; seating capacity, 600.

FROSTBURG, 5,000. R. R., Cumb. & Penn. Odd Fellows' Opera House, T. G. Dillion, manager; seating capacity, 600; rental, one night $15, share also. Size of stage, 60x40; full set scenery; bill poster, R. Bean. Newspaper: Mining Journal (Sat.)......Hotels: Grand Central, special rates $1; St. Cloud, special rates, $1.25.

Opera House, O. J. Moat, manager; seating capacity, 450; rental one night $12; three $25; license, $3. Size of stage, 25x28; size of proscenium opening, 14x20½; height from stage to grooves, 16; height from stage to rigging loft, 18; depth under stage, 4; number sets scenery, 12; leaders of orchestra, George Hocking & Son; bill poster, Thomas Payne; theatrical teamster, Wm. Parker.

HAGERSTOWN, 8,500. R. R., Balt. & Ohio; Cumberland Valley; Shenandoah Valley Western Maryland. Academy of Music, E. W. Mealey, manager; seating capacity, 750; **rental, one night $30; three $75;** license $2.50. share also. Size of stage, 40x30; number **sets scenery, 16; bill poster, Samuel B.** Oliver. Newspapers: daily, Globe, News; weekly, **Herald and Torchlight (Th.), Mail (Fri.)** ..... Hotels: Baldwin, regular rates, $2 (special **also); Franklin, special rates; City, Central,** Antietam

Lyceum Hall, F. Dorsey Herbert, manager; seating capacity, 600; rental, one night $15; three $35; number sets scenery, 6.

HAVRE DE GRACE, 3,000. R. R., **Phila., Wilmington & Balt.** City Hall, seating capacity, **400;** rental, one night $15; license, $3 to $5. Size of stage, 25x45; number sets scenery, **3;** bill poster, M. Vandiver. Newspapers: bi-weekly, Electric Light, Republican (Fri.) ..... Hotels: City, Harford, Adams.

Spencer Hall; seating capacity, 175.

MT. SAVAGE, **1,500.** R. R., Cumberland & Penn. Odd Fellows Hall, John Klein, manager; seating capacity, 250; rental, one night $6, three $15. Size of stage, 10x20; height from stage to grooves, **8; theatrical** teamster, McMullen **Bros** ..... Hotel; Varnum, special rates, $1.25.

WESTMINSTER, 3,000. **R. R.,** Western Maryland. Odd Fellows Hall; seating capacity, **500;** bill poster, T. K. Webster. Newspapers: Sentinel (Sat.), Advocate (Sat.) ..... Hotels: City, regular rates, $1.50 (special also); **Wilson, Wheeler's, Marsh, Central,** Anchor, Westminster, Benford.

Sons of Temperance Hall; seating capacity, 200.

MASSACHUSETTS.

ADAMS, 8,500. R. R., Pitts. & North Adams (branch of B. & A.). Town Hall, Dr. C.W. Burton, manager; **seating capacity, 1,000; rental, one night $25, three $60;** license, $3; share also. Size of stage, 16x46; size of proscenium opening, 20x22; height from stage to grooves, **16;** height from stage to rigging loft, 23; number sets scenery, 5; bill poster, David Crosier; number of sheets can accommodate, 135; rates per sheet, 4c.; theatrical teamster, David Crosier. Newspaper: Freeman (Fri.), advertising rates, $1 **per inch** ..... **Hotel:** Greylock, special rates, $1.50 to $1.75.

ALLSTON, 1,500. R. R., Boston & Albany. Union Hall, **J. W.** Hollis, manager; seating capacity, 500; fair stock scenery; bill posters, Harrison & McLane.

AMESBURY, 10,000. R. R., Eastern (branch at Newburyport). Merrimac Opera House. M. Kelly, manager; seating capacity, 1,000; rental, one night $35, three $75; license, $2.50; share also Size of stage, 30x50; size of proscenium opening, **15x28;** height **from** stage to grooves, 13; depth **under** stage, 8; number sets scenery, 15; bill poster, Opera House Bill Posting Co.; number of sheets can accommodate, 250; rates per sheet, 4c.; theatrical teamster, Thomas Brown. Newspapers: Villager (Wed.), News (Sat.) ..... Hotel: American, special rates, $1 50 to $1.75.

AMHERST, 4,292. R. R., New London Northern. Palmer's Hall, D. W. **Palmer,** manager; seating capacity, 550; rental, one night $10 to $15; license, $2. **Size of** stage, 16x50; no scenery; bill poster. David Warren; theatrical teamster, Henry Jackson. Newspaper: Record (Wed.). ..Hotels: Amherst, regular rates, $2 (special also); Woods.

ASHLAND, 2,318. R. R., Boston & Albany; Hopkinton. Town Hall, Town Clerk, manager; seating capacity, 400; rental, one night $7; no scenery. Newspaper: Advertiser (Fri.) ..... Hotels: Central, Ashland.

ATHOL, 5,000. R. R., Fitchburg, Boston & Albany (branch from Springfield). Skating Rink, Albert Ellsworth, manager; seating capacity, 800. Size of stage, 20x64; size of proscenium opening, 26x26; leader of orchestra, H. A. Preston; bill poster, H. M. Slate. Newspaper: Transcript (Th.).....Hotels: Bangor, Slater, Pequoig.

Starr Hall; Talbot & Drake, managers; seating capacity, 600; rental, one night $15 to $25. Size of stage, 40x18; full set scenery.

ATTLEBORO, 12,000. R. R., Boston & Providence; Old Colony. Union Hall, L. W. Dean, manager; seating capacity, 640; rental, one night $16; license, $3. Size of stage, 30x40; number sets scenery, 4; bill poster, L ,T. Starkey; theatrical teamster, L. T. Starkey. Newspapers: Advocate (Sat.), **Chronicle** (Sat.). .... Hotels: Park Street, regular rates, $2 (special also); Ryder.

BEVERLY, 9,000. R. R., Eastern. Lefavour Opera House, Israel Lefavour manager; seating capacity, 814; rental, one night $35, three $85; share also; license, $1. Size of stage, 28x50; size of proscenium opening, 22x30; height from stage to grooves, 22; height from stage to rigging loft, 28; depth under stage, 4; number sets scenery 2; leader of orchestra, C. Holden; bill poster, Luther Cahoon; number of sheets can accommodate, 150; theatrical teamster, P. Hogerzieel. Newspapers: Citizen (Sat.), Times (Wed.)..... Hotels: Avenue, special rates, $1; Bantoul, special rates, $1.

Town Hall, Wm. H. Lovett, manager; seating capacity, 800; rental, one night $20, license included; no scenery.

BOSTON, 400,000. R. R., Boston & Albany; Boston & Maine; Boston & Lowell; Boston & Providence; Boston, R. B. & Lynn; **Eastern;** Boston, Wm. & Shore; Fitchburg; International Steamship Co.; Mass. **Central;** New York & New England; Old Colony; Port. Steam Packet Co. Boston Theatre, Eugene Tompkins, manager; seating capacity, 3,017; share only. Size of stage, 90x90; size of proscenium opening, 40x48; height from stage to grooves, 20; height from stage to rigging loft, 70; depth under stage, 32; traps, 4 centre, 6 working, 4 quarter, 6 sinks; musical **director, Napier Lothian; scenic artist, Charles S.** Getz; stage carpenter, Wm. P. Prescott; bill posters, J. T. Donnelly, Kelley & Wogan; rates per sheet, 3c. Newspapers: daily, **Advertiser, Star, Transcript, Herald, Globe,** Traveller, Journal, Post......Hotels: **International, special rates, $1; Adams, special** rates, $2; Tremont, special rates, $3; **New Marlboro, special rates, $1.50);** Metropolitan, special rates, $1.25 to $1.50; Creighton, **$1.50.**

Bijou Theatre, Bijou Theatre Co., **H. B. Lonsdale,** managers; seating capacity, 900; rental, share only; license, yearly. Size of stage, 32x60; size of proscenium opening, 25x30; height from stage to rigging loft, 65; musical **director, John J. Braham;** scenic artist, Ed. Le Moss; stage carpenter, P. Henderson.

Park Theatre, Abbey & Schoeffel, **managers;** seating capacity, 1,200; share only. Size of stage, 43x63; size of proscenium opening, 38x33; height from stage to grooves, 38; height from stage to rigging loft, 62; depth under stage, 7; traps of all kinds; full stock scenery; leader of orchestra, E. N. Catlin; scenic artist, J. S. Schnell; stage carpenter, J. D. Lundy.

Dudley Street Opera House (Roxborough), **W. C. Blodgett, manager;** seating capacity, 700; rental, one night $40, three $100; license, $4; share also. Size of stage, 60x60; size of proscenium opening, 30x25; height from stage to grooves, 25; height from stage to rigging loft, 34; depth under stage, 4; traps, 1; number sets scenery, 25; leader of orchestra, S. C. Nason; stage carpenter, G. H. Keefe.

Globe Theatre, John Stetson, manager; seating capacity, 2,000.

Parker Memorial Hall; seating capacity, 850.

Boston Museum, R. M. Field, manager; seating **capacity, 1,500.**

Howard Athenaeum, Isaac B. Rich and William Harris, managers; seating capacity, 1,800; share only. Size of stage, 42x32; size of proscenium opening, 34x33; height from stage to grooves, 18; height from stage to rigging loft, 27; depth under stage, 13; traps, 6; leader of orchestra, George Quesh; scenic artist and stage manager, George B. Radcliffe; stage carpenter, B. B. Harris.

Windsor Theatre, G. E. Lothrop, manager; seating capacity, 1,000; rental, one night $100, three $250; license included; share also. Size of stage, 45x50; size of proscenium open-

ing, 30x28; height from stage to grooves, 36; height from stage to rigging loft, 45; full set scenery; leader of orchestra, J. Daurin; scenic artist, W. C. Turner; stage carpenter, Geo. W. Palmer.

Boston Music Hall, A. P. Peck, manager; seating capacity, 2,400; rental, one night $150, three $125; license, $1.

Horticultural Hall, Fredk. Kyle, manager.

Boylston's Museum, G. E. Lothrop, manager; seating capacity, 600.

Tremont Temple; seating capacity, 2,523.

Union Hall; seating capacity, 1,000.

Association Hall; seating capacity, 700.

Gaiety Theatre; seating capacity, 800.

Oakland Garden.

BRIDGEWATER, 3,500. R. R., Old Colony. Town Hall, H. O. Lawrence, manager; seating capacity, 400; rental, one night $10; no scenery. Newspaper: Independent (Fri.).... . Hotel: Heyland, regular rates, $2 (special also).

BROCKTON, 20,000. R. R., Old Colony. City Theatre, W. W. Cross, manager; seating capacity, 1,500. Size of stage, 43x72; size of proscenium opening, 31; height from stage to grooves, 18; height from stage to rigging loft, 52; depth under stage, 8; traps, 1; number sets scenery, 13; leader of orchestra, Mace Gay, Jr.; scenic artist, Jacob A. Johnson; stage carpenter, Frederick W. Mozart; billposter, Wm. Faunce; number of sheets can accommodate, 1,000; rates per sheet, 4c.; theatrical teamster, Merritt's Express. Newspapers: daily, Enterprise; Gazette (Sat.), Enterprise (Sat.)......Hotels: Belmont, Holbrook, regular rates, $2; (special also).

Brockton Opera House, Henry L. Bryant, manager; seating capacity, 1,300; rental, ——; share also. Size of stage, 35x15; full set scenery.

Murray Hall, Ellis Packard, manager; seating capacity, 650; rental, one night $15, three $35. Size of stage, 15x20; number sets scenery, 4.

Music Hall, Henry L. Bryant, manager; seating capacity, 1,000; rental, one night $40, license included; full set scenery.

Cunningham Hall; seating capacity, 400.

BROOKFIELD, 2,800. R. R., Boston & Albany. Town Hall, G. W. Oakes, manager; seating capacity, 775; rental, one night $8. No scenery; bill poster, J. W. Oakes. Newspaper: Times (Th.)......Hotels: Brookfield, regular rates, $2 (special also); Central.

BROOKLINE, 8,100. R. R., Boston & Albany; New York & New England. Opera Hall; seating capacity, 1,500. Newspaper: Chronicle (Sat.)......Hotel: De West.

Lower Hall; seating capacity, 500.

Goddard Hall; seating capacity, 300.

CAMBRIDGE, 52,740. R. R., Fitchburg. Union Hall, W. A. Bullard, manager; seating capacity, 1,500; rental, one night, $50, three $120. No scenery; bill poster, J. M. McLane. Newspapers: daily, Herald, Crimson, weekly, Chronicle (Sat.); News (Sat.), Press (Sat.) .... Hotels: Prospect, regular rates, $2 (special also); Porter's.

Lyceum Hall; seating capacity, 500; rental, one night $15; no scenery.

Sander's Theatre; seating capacity, 1,200.

Gothic Hall.

CAMPELLO, 5,500. R. R., Old Colony. Opera House, Ira A. Leach, manager; seating capacity, 600. Newspaper: Herald (Sat.)

CANTON, 5,000. R. R., Boston & Providence. Brook's Music Hall, Wm. W. Brooks, manager; seating capacity, 700; rental, one night $20, three $50; no license. Size of stage, 22x40; number sets scenery, 10; bill poster, John W. Tirrell; theatrical teamsters, Byam Bros. Newspaper: Journal (Fri.) Hotels: Brown's, regular rates, $2 (special also); Massaposgo, Cobb.

Memorial Hall, Wm. O. Chapman, manager; seating capacity, 900; rental, one night $25; no scenery.

CHESHIRE, 1,800. R. R., Boston & Albany (Branch). Dean's Hall, George Z. Dean, manager; seating capacity, 250; rental, one night $5. Stage, movable platform; no scenery. ......Hotel: Hoosic Valley.

12

CHELSEA, 25,000. R. R., Eastern. Academy of Music, J. B. Field, manager; seating capacity, 1,350; rental, one night $80; license yearly; share also. Size of stage, 38x68; size of proscenium opening, 30; height from stage to grooves, 17; height from stage to rigging loft, 20; depth under stage, 8; traps, 7; stage carpenter, John Robertson; bill poster, Wm. Carroll; rates per sheet, &c.; theatrical teamsters, Wilson, Cheney & Son. Newspapers: Pioneer and Telegraph (Sat.); Advocate (Sat.); Record (Sat.).. ....Hotels City, special rates $1.25; Broadway, Highland.

CHICOPEE, 11,300. R. R., Connecticut River. Well's Opera House, William E. Wheeler, manager; rental, ——; share also; license, $2. Size of stage, 26x26; full set scenery; bill poster, William E. Wheeler; theatrical teamster, William E. Wheeler......Hotels Cabot, regular rates, $2 (special also); Chicopee.

Town Hall; seating capacity, 1,000.

Cabot Hall; seating capacity, 400.

CHICOPEE FALLS, 12,000. R. R., Connecticut River. Union Temperance Hall, T. C. Page, manager; seating capacity, 250; rental, one night $7.50; three $15; license, $2. Size of stage, 20x22; number sets scenery, 4......Hotel: Wildes'.

Wildes' Hall; A. T. Wildes, manager; seating capacity, 450; rental, one night $12, three nights, $25; share also. Size of stage, 16x32; full set scenery; bill poster, A. T. Wildes.

CLINTON, 10,000. R. R., Old Colony. Worcester & Nashua. Town Hall, William Newhall, manager; seating capacity, 1,300; rental, one night $35. Size of stage, 20x45; number sets scenery, 14; bill poster, J T. Coulter; theatrical teamster, George S. Gibson. Newspapers: semi-weekly, Times; weekly, Courant (Sat.)......Hotels: Clinton, regular rates, $2 (special also); Oriental.

Below Hall: seating capacity, 600; rental, one night $15; number sets scenery, 3.

DANVERS, 6,000. R. R., Boston & Maine ; Eastern. Gothic Hall, Sam. C. Putnam, manager ; seating capacity, 400; rental, one night $12, three $30. Size of stage, 12x25 ; no scenery ; bill posters, Warren & Goodall ; theatrical teamster, A. B. Woods. Newspapers : Mirror (Sat.), Times (Wed.)..... .Hotels Danvers, regular rates, '$1.50 (special also); Central.

Peabody Institute; seating capacity, 1,000.

Porter's Hall; seating capacity, 400.

Town Hall; seating capacity, 300.

DEDHAM, 5,000. R. R., Boston & Providence. Memorial Hall, Jas. Griggs, manager; seating capacity, 700 ; rental, one night $15 ; no scenery; bill poster, C. R. Griggs. Newspapers: Standard (Sat.), Transcript (Sat.)......Hotel: Phœnix

Temperance Hall ; seating capacity, 300.

Tapeley's Hall ; seating capacity, 200.

EAST DOUGLAS, 3,000. R. R., New York & New England. Thayer's Hall, Asa Thayer, manager ; seating capacity, 400 ; rental, one night $10, three $25. Size of stage, 18x22 ; size of proscenium opening, 11x20 ; number sets scenery, 4 ; bill poster, Frank Marsh. .Hotels: East Douglas, special rates, $1 to $1.50.

EAST HAMPTON, 4,400. R. R., Conn. River, New Haven & Northampton. Town Hall, E. R. Bosworth, manager; seating capacity, 800; rental, one night, $15 to $20; number sets scenery 9; bill poster, R. A. Frizzell. Newspaper: News and Enterprise (Fri.).. Hotel: Mansion.

FALL RIVER, 49,500. R. R., Fall River, Old Colony. Academy of Music, Geo. Hackett, manager; seating capacity, 2,050; rental, one night $75. Size of stage, 50x70; full set of scenery; bill posters, Fall River Bill Posting Co. Newspapers: daily, News; Herald; weekly, Advance (Sat.)......Hotels: Narragansett. regular rates, $2.50 (special also); Wilbur, regular, $2 to $2.50 (special also); Le Grange, Thurston.

Opera House, Durfee, Russell & Co., managers; seating capacity, 950.

Music Hall; seating capacity, 600.

Temple Hall; seating capacity, 800.

People's Museum (variety), John Daly, manager.

FITCHBURG, 15,000. R. R., Old Colony (Nor. Div.). Whitney's Opera House, Fred. A. Currier, business manager; seating capacity, 1,014; rental, one night $60; share also; Size of stage, 28x40; size of proscenium opening, 26x29; height from stage to groove, 10; height from stage to rigging loft, 28 ; depth under stage, 4½; traps, 3; number sets scenery, 9, stage carpenter, John Burke; bill poster, Eugene Sanderson; number of sheets can accommodate, 300; rates per sheet, &c.; theatrical teamsters, L. M. Wheeler & Son, F. W. Bennett. Newspapers: daily, Sentinel, Tribune; weekly, Sentinel, Tribune (Th.) Hotels: American, special rates, $1.25 to $1.55; Fitchburg, special rates, $1.25 to $1.55.

City Hall, Chas. T. Cushing, manager; seating capacity, 1,100 ; rental, one night $38, three $100; no license. Size of stage, 25x30; number sets scenery, 6.

Crocker's Hall; seating capacity, 600.

Board of Trade; seating capacity, 600.

FLORENCE, 3,000. R. R., New Haven & Northampton; Cosmian Hall, A. G. Hill, manager; seating capacity, 650; rental, one night $20; share also; license, $1. Size of stage, 24x40; height from stage to groove, 5; depth under stage, 5; traps, 2; number sets scenery, 10; leader of orchestra, Fred. T. Atkins; stage carpenter, C. R. Flood; number of sheets can accommodate, 96; theatrical teamster, E. B. Howes. Newspapers: daily, Herald; weekly, Gazette (Th.), Journal (Fri.)......Hotels : Florence, Mansion, Cottage.

FOXBORO, 2,950. R. R., Old Colony. Town Hall, Town Clerk, manager; seating capacity, 600; rental, one night, $10; no license. Size of stage, 15x22; no scenery. Newspaper; Times (Fri.)......Hotel : Cocasset.

FRANKLIN, 5,000. R. R., New York & New England. Daniels' Hall, J. H. Daniels, manager; seating capacity, 400; rental, one night $10. Size of stage, 15x22; height from stage to groove, 14; bill poster, R. H. Davidson; theatrical teamster, J. H. Daniels. Newspaper : Sentinel (Sat.)......Hotel : Central, special rates, $1.25.

GARDNER, 8,000. R. R., Fitchburg; Boston, Barre & Gardner Town Hall, Albert Lovejoy, manager; seating capacity, 1,100; rental, share only, license included. Size of stage, 17x22; size of proscenium opening, 15x24; height from stage to groove, 11; height from stage to rigging loft, 14; number sets scenery, 6; bill poster, T. C. Moore; number of sheets can accommodate, 500; rates per sheet, &c.; theatrical teamster, T. C. Moore. Newspapers: Democrat (Wed.), News (Sat.), advertising rates, 75c. per inch......Hotels : Windsor, special rates $1.50; Richards, Gardner, special rates $1.25.

GLOUCESTER, 20,000. R. R., Eastern. City Hall, City Clerk, manager ; J. O. Bradstreet, local manager; seating capacity, 1,000; rental, one night $35, three $95; license, $3; share also. Size of stage, 25x35; size of proscenium opening, 13x27; height from stage to grooves, 13; number sets scenery, 6; bill poster, George H. Bradstreet; theatrical teamster, Albert Lane. Newspapers: daily, News, Breeze; weekly, Advertiser (Th.)...... Hotels : Webster, regular rates, $2 (special also); Gloucester, Atlantic.

Rogers' Hall; seating capacity, 500.

Scientific Hall; seating capacity, 250.

GREAT BARRINGTON, 5,000. R. R., Housatonic. Town Hall, H. G. Winegar, manager; seating capacity, 800; rental, one night $15; fair stock scenery; bill poster, John Kerr. Newspaper: Courier (Wed.)..... Hotels : Berkshire, Miller.

GREENFIELD, 5,000. R. R., Fitchburg; Hoosac Tunnel Line; Conn. River. Greenfield Opera House, E. M. Slocomb, manager; seating capacity, 1,000; rental, one night $25, three $55; share also; license, $5. Size of stage, 30x70; Size of proscenium opening, 28x28; height from stage to grooves, 14; height from stage to rigging loft, 30 ; depth under stage, 4 ; number sets scenery, 12 ; leader of orchestra, C. F. Eddy; scenic artists, Ronet and Richmond; stage carpenter, F. A. Bickford ; bill poster, E. M. Slocomb; number of sheets can accommodate, 700; rates per sheet, &c.; theatrical teamster, Sainford Kent. Newspapers : Gazette (Mon.), advertising rates, $1 per inch; Reform (Fri.), advertising rates, $1 per inch.... Hotels: Morrison, special rates, $1.50 to $2; American, special rates, $1.50 to $2.

HAVERHILL, 24,000. R. R., Boston & Maine. Academy of Music; James F West, manager; seating capacity, 1,500. Size of stage, 40x67; size of proscenium opening, 21x33; height

THE
BEST AND CHEAPEST
NUMBERED
COUPON
TICKETS
IN THE WORLD

GLOBE
PRINTING
HOUSE,
112 & 114 NORTH 12TH ST.
PHILADELPHIA.

ROYAL ALBYCRUM THEATRE
GRAND TIER.
6
Thursday, January 1.
BOX G Grand Tier, 4 Guineas

BOX G
GRAND TIER.
6

THE CASINO.
Wednesday Evening, Oct. 8.
McCAULL
Opera Comique Co.
8
$12.00

OPERA HOUSE
Wednesday Evening, Oct. 15.
45
PARQUET
ADMIT ONE

QUET
Oct. 15.
15

CHESTNUT ST THEATRE
Wednesday Evening, Sept. 19.
22 BALCONY
ADMIT ONE

1 P 60
BALCONY
Sept. 19.
23

ACADEMY
Friday E
30 ORC
ADMIT ONE.

METROPOLITAN OPERA HOUSE
Friday Evening, Mar. 11.
DRESS CIRCLE

PEOPLES THEATRE
Wednesday Evening, Oct. 22.
10 Orchestra Circle
ADMIT

O 10
Orch

I 202
PARQUET
Oct. 15.
45

ACADEMY OF MUSIC.
Friday Matinee, Oct. 3.
BARTHOLOMEW'S
EQUINE PARADOX
Orchestra Chair, 50c.
F

BROOKLYN THEATRE.
Friday Evening, Oct. 24.
11 BOX G
ADM

HAVERLYS THEATRE
Wednesday Evening, Oct. 15.
PARQUET
ADMIT ONE.

WALLACK'S
Thursday Evening, Oct. 1.
4 BOX

COOPER & HOUSE
BANDIT KING
ARQUET

PITTSBURGH
A HOUSE
day Evening, Oct. 8.
ORCHESTRA.
ADMIT ONE.

O 5
ORCHEST
38

STREET THEATRE
Matinee, Oct. 18.
BALCONY

N 24
BALCONY
53

NOVELTY THEATRE
Friday Evening, Sept. 26.
30 Orchestra Chair.
ADMIT ONE

GS STREET OPERA HOUSE
Evening, Sept. 18.
BOX B
ADMIT ONE

B
BOX
Sept. 18.
11

THIRD AV. THEATRE
Monday Evening, Oct. 6.
BOX D
42

NEW CENTRAL THE
Saturday Evening, Oc.
43 PARLOR CH
ADMIT

S THEATRE
Wedne
57

GRAND OPERA HOUSE
Tuesday Evening, Nov. 4.
90 BOX A
ADMIT ONE.
GOOD FOR THIS DATE ONLY

90
Nov. 4.
BOX
A

THEATRE
Oct. 1.
43 CHAIR

L 46
43

ACADEMY OF MUSIC
Friday Evening, Sept. 26.
30 ORCHESTRA. 50c.
ADMIT ONE.
for this Date Only.

HARRIS
NEW MAMMOTH
ORCHEST

LIBRARY HALL
Wednesday Evening, Sept. 10.
BALCONY
ONE.

6 D 398
BALCONY
Sept. 10.
12

WALNUT STREET THEATRE
Evening, Sept. 17.
ORCHESTRA.
ADMIT ONE.
FOR THIS DATE ONLY

2
ORCHESTRA
Sept. 17.
72
28

HARRIS DIME MUSEUM
Wednesday, Oct. 15, MATINEE.
53 DRESS CIRCLE
ADMIT ONE.
GOOD FOR THIS DATE ONLY

BALCONY
WEDNESDAY MATINEE,
Mar. 25th, '85

3 B
BALCONY
Mar. 25.
2

of stage to rigging loft, 55; number sets scenery, 13; bill poster, Geo. J. Dean; theatrical teamster, Charles M. Cox. Newspapers: daily, Bulletin, Gazette and Laborer...... Hotels Webster, regular rates, $2 (special also); Eagle, Clinton, Hotel Opera.

HOLLISTON, 3,180. R. R., Boston & Albany. Town Hall, John Baker, manager; seating capacity, 600; rental, one night $10; no license; number sets scenery, 3; theatrical teamster, John Shippee. Newspaper: Transcript (Fri.)........Hotels: Hollis, regular rates, $2 (special also); Shippee.

HOLYOKE, 30,000. R. R., Conn. River; N. H. & Northampton. Holyoke Opera House, Chase Brothers, managers; seating capacity, 1,000; rental, one night $75, license included. Size of stage, 50x91; size of proscenium opening, 30x33; height from stage to grooves, 30; height from stage to rigging loft, 50; depth under stage, 12; traps, 4; number sets scenery, full set; leader of orchestra, James Coakley; bill poster, James Coakley; number of sheets can accommodate, 500; rates per sheet, 5c.; theatrical teamster, H. Smith. Newspaper: daily, Transcript, weekly, Herald.........Hotels: Windsor, special rates, $1.75; Holyoke, Palatine, special rates, $1.75; Belmont, special rates, $1 to $1.25.

City Hall; seating capacity, 1,300.

Parson's Hall; seating capacity, 800.

HUDSON, 3,600. R. R., Fitchburg; Mass. Central. Town Hall, Geo. De Sawyer, manager; seating capacity, 800; rental, one night $20; number sets scenery, 3; bill poster, J. G. Bugbee; theatrical teamster, Chas. Houghton. Newspaper: Pioneer (Sat.)...... Hotels: Mansion, Hudson.

IPSWICH, 4,000. R. R. Eastern. Town Hall, J. H. Lakeman, manager; seating capacity, 700; rental, one night $17; no license. Size of stage, 28x30; no scenery: bill poster, J. H. Lakeman; theatrical teamster, Jennings. Newspaper: Chronicle (Sat.)......Hotels: Ogawam, regular rates, $1.50 (special also); International.

LAWRENCE, 50,000. R. R., Boston & Lowell; Boston & Maine. Manchester & Lawrence; Eastern. Lawrence Opera House, T. A. Sweeny, manager; seating capacity, 1,550; rental, one night $75 to $80; share also; license, ten tickets Size of stage, depth, 50; width, 67; size of proscenium opening, 36x37; height from stage to grooves, 16; depth under stage, 7; traps, 3; number sets scenery, 10; leader of orchestra, E. T. Collins; stage carpenter, A. L. Grant; bill poster, Lawrence Bill Posting Co.; number of sheets can accommodate, 5,000; rates per sheet, 5c.; theatrical teamster, H. W. Foster. Newspapers: daily, American, Eagle; weekly, Journal (Fri.), Sentinel (Fri.), advertising rates, yearly contract.....Hotels: Essex, special rates, $1.25 to $1.50; Franklin, special rates, 1.50 to $2; Brunswick, special rates, $1.25 to $1.50.

City Hall, W. H. Merrow, manager; seating capacity, 1,250; rental, one night $40; license, ten tickets; share also. Size of stage, 21x25; number sets scenery, 13.

Saunder's Hall, Caleb Saunders, manager; seating capacity, 600; rental, one night $18, three $40; license, tickets. Size of stage, 10x40; no scenery.

Music Hall; seating capacity, 350.

LEE, 4,000. R. R., Housatonic. Memorial Hall, J. C. Schaffner, manager; seating capacity, 450; rental, one night $10; no scenery; bill poster, H. A. Peck; theatrical teamster, E. L. Cogswell. Newspapers: Gleaner (Wed.)......Hotels: Morgan, Norton.

Northrop's Hall; seating capacity, 300.

LEOMINSTER, 5,000. R. R. Fitchburg; Old Colony. Town Hall, James M. Bronson, manager; seating capacity, 800; rental, one night $13, three $36. Size of stage, 18x50; no scenery; bill poster, Porter Whitney; theatrical teamster, Josiah Pierce. Newspapers: Enterprise (Wed.). Telephone (Fri.)......Hotels: Leominster, regular rates, $2 (special also); Linden.

LOWELL, 75,000. R. R., Boston & Lowell; Boston & Maine; Old Colony. Huntington Hall, John F. Cosgrove, manager; seating capacity, 1,500; rental, one night $60; share also. Size of stage, 45x33; size of proscenium opening, 30x30; height from stage to grooves, 16; height from stage to rigging loft, 17; number sets scenery, 20; bill poster, Huntington Hall; number of sheets can accommodate, 3,000; rates per sheet, 5c.; theatrical teamster, Huntington Hall. Newspapers, daily: Citizen, advertising rates, yearly contract; Courier, advertising rates, yearly contract; T.mes, advertising rates, yearly contract; Mail, advertising rates, yearly contract......Hotels: St. Charles, special rates, $1.25 to $1.50; American, special rates, $1.50 to $2; Dresser, regular rates, $2 (special also); Merrimack, regular rates, $2 (special also).

Music Hall: William H Emery, **manager**; seating capacity, 900; **share** only. Size of stage, 40x65; full set scenery.

Mechanics' Hall; seating capacity, 500.

LYNN, 50,000. R. R., Eastern; Boston, Revere, Beach & Lynn. Music Hall, J. F. Rock, manager; seating capacity, 1,200; rental, one night $80, three $200, license $5; share also; Size of stage, 41x31; height from stage to grooves, 16; leader of orchestra, C. Ward; **stage** carpenter, Chas. Wells; bill posters, Young & Thomas; theatrical teamsters, **Young & Thomas**. Newspapers: daily, Item, Bee, advertising rates per inch, $1; weekly, **Transcript (Fri.).**......Hotels: **Sagamore**, special rates, $1.25; Kirtland, special **rates, $1.25.**

Odd Fellow's Hall, E. E. Davis & Co., managers; seating capacity, **1,000; rental, ——; license, $2.** Size of stage, 24x30; number sets scenery, 7.

G. A. R. Colliseum; seating capacity, 3,500.

MALDEN, 13,000. R. R., Boston & Maine. City Hall, City Treasurer, manager; seating capacity, 600; rental, one night $15; no license. No scenery; bill poster, H. A. Morse. Newspapers: Mirror (Sat.); Press (Sat.). ..Hotels: Evelyn, regular rates, $2 (special also); Howard, Pratts.

Bailey's Hall; seating capacity, 500.

Marten's Hall; seating capacity, **400.**

Ballou's Hall; seating capacity, 400.

MANSFIELD, 2,800. R. R., Old Colony; Boston & Providence. Mansfield Town Hall, William B. Rogerson, manager; seating capacity, 700; rental, one night $15, three .$26. Number sets scenery, 2; theatrical teamsters, L. R. King. Newspaper: News. Hotel: Mansfield House.

MARBLEHEAD, 8,000. R. R., Eastern. Abbot Hall, Frank Dodge, manager; seating capacity, 1,081; rental, one night $50, three $150; share also; license, 12 tickets. Size of stage, 25x35; size of proscenium opening, 12x30; height from stage to grooves, 13; height from stage to rigging loft, 24; number sets scenery, 8; scenic artist, Eben Colley, **bill poster**, Frank Dodge; number sheets can accommodate 350; rates per sheet, 4c.; theatrical teamster, P. P. Eustis. Newspapers: daily, Item; advertising rates **per line,** 10c.: **Bee;** advertising rates per line, 10c.; weekly, Statesman (Sat.), **advertising rates, $4 per inch; Messenger (Fri.), advertising rates, $4.25 per inch......Hotels: American:** rates to profession, $1.25.

MAYNARD, 3,000. R. R., Fitchburg (Marlboro Branch). Co-operative Hall, Dennis Casey, manager; seating capacity, 600; rental, one night $12, **three** $30; bill poster, F. F. Robertson. Newspapers: Journal (Fri.), Enterprise (Wed.)... ..Hotels: Maynard, Maple.

MARLBORORO, 11,000. R. R., Fitchburg; Old Colony. Riley's Opera House, F. W. Riley, manager; seating capacity, 800; rental, one night $25, three $60; license, $1; share **also**. Size of stage, 19x26; number sets scenery, 8; bill poster: George Mawson; theatrical teamster, F. E. Cummings; Newspapers: Advertiser (Wed.), Mirror-Journal (Sat.), Times (Thu.)......Hotels: Central, regular rates, $2 (special also); Gates, Temple, Marlboro.

Fairmont Hall, F. W. Riley, manager; seating capacity, 800; rental, one **night** $12.50.

Town Hall, Town Clerk, manager.

Berry's Hall; seating capacity, **500.**

MEDFORD, 7,500. R. R., Boston & Maine. Town Hall; seating capacity, 350; bill **poster,** S. Derby. Newspaper: Mercury (Fri.)......Hotels: Medford, Mystic, Simpson.

Brook's Hall; seating capacity, 300.

Mystic Hall; seating capacity, **200.**

Music **Hall: seating capacity, 400.**

MIDDLEBORO, 6,500. R. R., Old Colony. Town Hall, Wm. R. Wood, manager; seating capacity, 1,200; rental, one night $25; do not share. Size of stage, 16x35; size of proscenium opening, 20; number sets scenery, 1; bill poster, Capt. A. Baker; theatrical teamster, B. Folger. Newspapers: Gazette (Fri.), News (Th.).... . Hotel: Nemasket.

MILFORD, 10,000. R. R., Boston & Albany; New York & New England. Music Hall, Music Hall Co., manager; **seating capacity, 920.** Size of stage, 40x36; number sets scenery, 10; leader of orchestra, A. C. Johnson; bill poster, W. E. Cheney; number of sheets can accommodate, 1,000; theatrical teamster, J. C. Symonds. Newspaper: Journal (Wed.)..... Hotels: Mansion, special rates, $1.50; Lincoln, $1.50; Milford, $1.25.

Town Hall, R. H. Montague, manager; seating capacity. 800; rental, one night $15; no scenery.

Lyceum Hall, S. P. Carpenter, manager; seating capacity, 400; rental, one night $1.50; number sets scenery, 3.

Washington Hall; seating capacity, 450.

Irving Hall; seating capacity, 350.

MILLBURY, 5,200. R. R., Boston & Albany; Providence & Worcester. Town Hall, H. B. Lovell, manager; seating capacity, 800; rental, one night $20, no license. Size of stage, 25x22; no scenery; bill poster, H. S. Gerry; theatrical teamster, Benj. Boyd...... Hotels: **Central, St. Charles, Tourtelotte.**

MONSON, 4,000. R. R., New London; Northern. Central Hall, Norcross & Reynolds, managers; seating capacity, 850; rental, one night $15, three $40. Size of stage, 15x20; **height** from stage to grooves, 11; **number sets scenery,** 6; bill poster, Norcross & Reynolds; number sheets can accommodate, 2; theatrical teamster, Monson House...... **Hotel: Monson**

NATICK, 8,500. R. R., Boston & Albany. Concert Hall, Edward Clark, manager; seating capacity, 1,300; rental, one night $35, license included. Size of stage, 21x35; size of proscenium opening, 12x21; number sets scenery, 5; bill poster, Edgar Hayes. Newspapers: Citizen (Fri.), Bulletin (Fri.).... . Hotel: Wilson, regular rates, $2, (special also).

Washington Hall, C. W. Childs, manager.

NEW BEDFORD, 32,000. R. R., Old Colony; Fall River. Grand Opera House, J. C. Omey, manager; seating capacity, 1,300. Size of stage, 48x60; size of proscenium opening, width, 30; height from stage to grooves, 18; height from stage to rigging loft, 40; depth under stage, 8; traps, 5; number sets scenery, 17; leader of orchestra, C. S. Berry; stage carpenter, M. P. Whitfield; bill poster, Opera House; number of sheets can accommodate, 2,000; rates per sheet, &c.; theatrical teamsters, Driscol & Tript. Newspapers: daily, Standard, Mercury; weekly, Star (Sat.)...... Hotels: Parker, special rates, $2.50; Bancroft, special rates, $1.50 to $1.75; Mansion, special rates, $1.50 to $1.75.

Waite's Music Hall, Benjamin H. Waite, manager; seating capacity, 800; rental, one night, $30; license, $2; full set scenery.

Liberty Hall, A. S. Anthony, manager; seating capacity, 1,400; rental, one night $50, three $140; share also; license included. Size of stage, 40x60; full set scenery.

City Hall; seating capacity, 400.

Pierian Hall; seating capacity, 750.

NEWBURYPORT, 14,000. R. R., Boston & Maine; Eastern. City Hall, George H. Stevens, manager; seating capacity, 1,040; rental, one night $50, license included. Size of stage, 29½x35; size of proscenium opening, width, 28½; number sets scenery, 6; leader of orchestra, L. W. Piper; stage carpenter, George W. Mansen; bill posters, Noyes, Dodge & Noyes; number sheets can accommodate, —; rates per sheet, &c.; theatrical teamsters, S. M. Noyes & Co. Newspapers: daily, Herald, Germ; weekly, Visitor (Sat.)...... Hotels: Merrimac, regular rates, $2 (special also).

Washington Hall; seating capacity, 800.

Central Hall; seating capacity, 900.

NEWTON, 17,500. R. R., Boston & Albany. Elliott Hall, H. Van Buskirk, manager; seating capacity, 900; **rental, one night $40; no** scenery; bill posters, Harrison & McLane; the

atrical teamster, Kilbourne Express. Newspapers: Graphic (Sat.), Journal (Sat.)......
Hotels: Hunnewell, Newton.

City Hall, J. B. Wellington, manager; **seating capacity, 800**; rental, one night, $25; **no scenery.**

NORTH ABINGTON, 4,000. **R. R.,** Old Colony, Hanover Branch. Standish Hall, E. P. Boynton, manager; **seating capacity,** 800; rental, one night $15, three $50. Size of stage, 15x24; bill poster, Herbert Tanner; theatrical teamster, Tanner Express. Newspapers Public, Herald, Journal......Hotel: Cullen House.

NORTH ADAMS, 16,000. R. R., Boston & Albany; Fitchburg; Boston Hoosac Tunnel & W. Wilson's Hall, F. E. Swift, manager; seating capacity, 800; rental, one night $20, three $45; license, $5; share also. Size of stage, 24x48; fair stock scenery; bill poster, **Thomas Ryan;** theatrical teamster, J. B. Flagg. Newspapers: News (Sat.), Transcript (Th)......Hotels: Richmond, regular rates, $2 (special also); Wilson, regular rates, $2 (special also); Commercial.

Armory Hall, C. T. Sykes, manager; seating capacity, 800; rental, one night $15; no scenery.

NORTHAMPTON, 13,000. R. R., Conn. River; N. H. & Northampton. Opera House, Geo. S. Whittick, manager; seating capacity, 700; rental, one night $35; share also; license, $1. Size of stage, 24x40; size of proscenium opening, 16x22; height from stage to grooves, 13; **height from stage to rigging loft,** 20; depth under stage, 3½; traps, 3; number sets scenery, 13; leader of orchestra, A. N. Baldwin; stage carpenter, J. J. Raleigh; bill poster, Geo. S. Whittick; number sheets can accommodate, 300; rate per sheet, &c.; theatrical teamster, H. S. Backnam. Newspapers: daily, Herald; weekly, Gazette (Tu.), advertising rates, $1 per inch; Journal (Fri.), $1 per inch......Hotels: Mansion, special rates, $2; Hampshire, special rates, $1.75; City, special rates, $1.50.

Town Hall, H. E. Hillman, manager; seating capacity, 600. Size of stage, 15x20; no scenery.

NORTH ATTLEBORO, 13,000. **R. R., Boston & Providence.** Wamsutta Opera House, H. B. Davenport, manager; **seating capacity, 800; rental, one** night $30; license, $3; share also. Size of stage, 38x40; number sets scenery, 12; bill poster, Opera House; theatrical teamster, C. E. Ward. **Newspaper:** Chronicle (Sat.)......Hotel: Wamsutta, regular rates, $2 (special also).

NORTH BROOKFIELD, 4,700. **R. R.,** Boston & Albany. Town Hall, P. J. Downey, manager; seating capacity, 600; rental, one night $12; no scenery; theatrical teamster, **H. A. Knight.** Newspaper : Journal (Sat.) .....Hotel: Batcheller.

ORANGE, 4,500. R. R., Fitchburg. Putnam Opera House, J. Putnam, manager; seating **capacity, 1,000;** rental, one night $35, three $65. Size of stage, 21x54; number sets scenery, 8; bill poster, W. H. Lang; theatrical teamster, W. H. Conner. Newspaper : Journal (Fri.) .....Hotels: Mansion, Putnam.

PALMER, 5,000. R. R., Boston & Albany; New London & Northern. Wales Hall, Palmer Dramatic Club, managers; seating capacity, 550; rental, one night, $15; fair stock scenery. Newspaper: Journal (Fri.)......Hotels: Week's, regular rates, $2 (special also); Nassowanno, Tockwatton.

PEABODY, 10,000. R. R., Eastern; Salem & Lowell; Horse Cars to Salem, Beverley & Lynn. Town Hall, N. C. Patterson, manager; seating capacity, 1,550; rental, one night $40; license, $5. Size of stage, 31x46; size of proscenium opening, 17x37 ; height from stage to grooves, 17; height from stage to rigging loft, 42; number sets scenery, 4; leader of orchestra, Ripton; stage carpenter, Orin Goodwin; bill poster, Andrews; theatrical teamster, Henry Wilson. Newspapers: daily, Item, News; weekly, Press (Wed.), Reporter (Sat.)......Hotel: Baldwin, regular rates, $1.50 (special also).

Peabody Institute, John McKean, manager; seating capacity, 800; rental, one night $25; no scenery.

Temperance Hall; seating capacity, 300.

PITTSFIELD, 15,000. R. R., Boston & Albany; Housatonic. Academy of Music, C. Quackenbush, manager; seating capacity, 1,100; rental, ——; license, $3; share also. Size of stage, 40x80; full sets scenery; bill poster, Frank Durkee; theatrical teamster,

Samuel Bridges. Newspaper: daily, Journal; weekly, Eagle (Th.), Sun (Th.).... Hotels: American, regular rates, $2 (special also); Burbank, regular rates, $2 (special also); Berkshire.

Burbank's Opera House; seating capacity, 1,200.

Music Hall; seating capacity, 400.

PLYMOUTH, 7,100. R. R., Old Colony. Davis Hall, James E. Thompson, manager; seating capacity, 850; rental, one night $20; license, $2 to $5. Size of stage, 25x25; number sets scenery, 7; bill posters, Harlowe, Pickard & Thompson; theatrical teamster, George Bagnall. Newspapers: Free Press (Sat.), Memorial (Th.). .... Hotels: Samoset, regular rates, $2 (special also); Central, Brastow, Franklin, Manomet, Plymouth Rock.

Odd Fellows' Hall, W. W. Avery, manager; seating capacity, 850; rental, one night $15, three $37; share also. Size of stage, 18x24; number sets scenery, 6.

Leyden Hall; seating capacity, 400.

Lyceum Hall; seating capacity, 450.

Standish Hall; seating capacity, 400.

PROVINCETOWN, 4,500. R. R., Old Colony. Masonic Hall, A. P. Hannum, manager; seating capacity, 550; rental, one night $15, three $35; no license. Size of stage, 16x22; no scenery; bill poster, manager of hall. Newspaper: Advocate (Th.)...... Hotels: Pilgrim, regular rates $2 (special also), Central, Gifford, Atlantic.

QUINCY, 12,000. R. R., Old Colony. Robertson Hall, W. P. Meseroe, manager; seating capacity, 500; rental, one night $7, three $15; share also. Size of stage, 15x20; no scenery; bill poster, C. T. Stancomb. Newspaper: Patriot (Th.)...... Hotels: Robertson, regular rates, $2 (special also); Atlantic, Great Hill, Albion, Linden, Willow, Beach, Wollaston.

Town Hall, James E. Maxim, manager; seating capacity, 700; rental, one night $15, three $35; no license. Size of stage, 18x24; no scenery.

Revere Hall; seating capacity, 200.

Faxon's Hall; seating capacity, 350.

RANDOPH, 4,000. R. R., Old Colony. Stetson Hall, Calvin Boyd, manager; seating capacity, 800; rental, one night $15; no license. Size of stage, 14x21; no scenery; bill poster, E. A. Perry; theatrical teamster, Gove's Express. Newspaper: Register (Sat.) .....Hotels: Howard, Sumner.

ROCKLAND, 6,000. R. R., Old Colony; Hanover's Branch. Phœnix Hall, J. A. Macdonald, manager; seating capacity, 650; rental, one night, $15, three $35; share also; no license. Size of stage, 28½x36; height from stage to grooves, 12; height from stage to rigging loft, 10; depth under stage, 4; traps, 1; number sets scenery, 6; leaders of orchestra, Beals & Wheeler; bill posters, McCarthy & Mansfield; number of sheets can accommodate, 40; theatrical teamsters, Randall & Burrell Express. Newspaper : Standard, Journal (Fri.) ......Hotel: Sherman House.

ROCKPORT, 5,000. R. R., Eastern, Gloucester Branch. Town Hall; seating capacity, 800; rental, one night $15 to $25. Size of stage, 15x30; no scenery; bill poster, Wm. Parsons ; theatrical teamsters, Harvey, Tarr & Co. Newspaper : Review (Sat.)........ Hotels: Smith's, Clark, Sheriden, Rockport.

SALEM, 30,000. R R., Boston & Lowell; Eastern. Mechanic Hall, Jos. S. Foster, manager; seating capacity, 1,110; license, $5; Size of stage, 33x34 ; full set scenery ; bill poster, N. W. Andrews; theatrical teamsters, Edson & Harry Lewis. Newspapers: daily; News, Post; semi-weekly, Gazette, Register ....Hotels : Essex, regular rates, $2 to $2.50; Lafayette, Central, Farragut.

Lyceum Hall, G. L. Streeter, manager; seating capacity, 600; rental, one night $12; license, $1. Size of stage, 15x30; no scenery.

Central Hall; seating capacity, 500.

SHELBURNE FALLS, 2,500. R. R., Fitchburg. Union Hall, H. W. Swan, manager; rental, one night $10; no license. Size of stage, 16x24; number sets scenery, 4; bill poster, L. Gordon; theatrical teamster, A. E. Kemp .... Hotel: Shelburne.

SOMERVILLE, 27,000. R. R., Boston & Albany ; Boston & Lowell ; Boston & Maine; Eastern ; Fitchburg; Mass. Central. Bacon Hall, B. F. Johnson, manager: : seating capacity, 800; rent or share. Size of stage, 20x30; number sets scenery, 12; bill poster, Jas. McLane; theatrical teamster, A. L. Prescott. Newspapers: Journal (Sat.), Truth (Sat.)..... Hotels: Warren, regular rates, $2 (special also); Oasis.

SOUTH ABINGTON, 3,000. R. R., Old Colony. Village Hall, A. Davis, manager; seating capacity, 700; rental, one night $15; no license. Size of stage, 13x62; no scenery; bill poster, C. B. Dobson, theatrical teamster, J. M. Penniman. Newspaper: Times (Fri.). ..... Hotels: Standish, Pratt.

SOUTH ADAMS. R. R., Pittsfield & No. Adams. Collins' Hall, Isaac Collins, manager; seating capacity, 600; rental, one night $18, three $39. Size of stage, 15x32; number sets scenery, 5; bill poster, Isaac Collins. Newspaper: Freeman (Sat.)..... Hotel: Graylock.

SOUTHBRIDGE, 7,000. R. R., New York & New England. Opera House, Dresser & Page, managers; seating capacity, 800; rental, one night $25, three $35; number sets scenery, 11; bill poster, Opera House; theatrical teamster, J F. Parker. Newspapers: Herald (Th.), Journal (Fri.).. ...Hotel: Dresser.

SPENCER, 9,000. R. R., Boston & Albany. Town Hall, H. P. Draper, manager; seating capacity, 800; rental, one night $30, three $40, license included. Size of stage, 24x18; size of proscenium opening, 16x20; height from stage to grooves, 16; depth under stage, 3; leader of orchestra, A. R. Hallett; bill poster, H. P. Draper; number sheets can accommodate, 80; rates per sheet, 4c.; theatrical teamster, Fred Linermore. Newspaper: Sun (Fri.)......Hotels: Massasoit, special rates, $1.50; Spencer, special, $1.

SPRINGFIELD, 35,000. R. R., Boston & Albany; N. Y. & N. H.: Conn. River. Gilmore's Opera House, W. C. Le Noir, manager; seating capacity, 1,300; rental, one night $75; license, $2; share also. Size of stage, 31½x56; size of proscenium opening, 27; height from stage to grooves, 20; height from stage to rigging loft, 34; depth under stage, 6; traps, 4; full set scenery; leader of orchestra, C. H. Southland; stage carpenter. Richard Kelley; bill posters, Le Noir & Perkins; number of sheets can accommodate, 300 to 500; rates per sheet, 4c.; theatrical teamster, Wm. Sheban. Newspapers: daily, Republican, advertising rates, 10c. per line; Union, advertising rates, 10c. per line......Hotels: Haynes, special rates, $1.75 to $2; Gilmore, special rates, $1.25 to $1.50; Warwick, special rates, $1.50; Converse, special rates, $1.25.

Haynes' Music Hall; seating capacity, 1,000; rental, one night $65, license included. Size of stage, 35x50; full set scenery.

City Hall, City Clerk, manager; rental, one night $30 to $50; no license; no scenery.

Lincoln Hall; seating capacity, 500.

Winkler's Winter Garden, B. Winkler, manager.

STOUGHTON, 5,000. R. R., Boston & Prov., Old Colony. Town Hall; seating capacity, 900; rental, one night $30, license included. Size of stage, 20x25; fair stock scenery; bill poster, F. A. Shepherd; theatrical teamster, Fisher's Express........Hotels : Stoughton, Drake's, Chemung, Keith's.

Atwood's Hall; seating capacity, 550.

TAUNTON, 23,000. R. R., Old Colony. Music Hall, A. B. White, manager; seating capacity, 1,020; rental, one night $30; license, $3; share also. Size of stage, 33½x55; size of proscenium opening, 17x28; height from stage to grooves, 15; height from stage to rigging loft, 23; depth under stage, 12; traps, 2; number sets scenery, full set; leader of orchestra, James Boardman; stage carpenter, J. Mitchell; bill poster, J. H. Mitchell; number of sheets can accommodate, 1,000; rates per sheet, 4c. ; theatrical teamster, Chas. A. Field. Newspapers: daily, Gazette, Republican (Fri.)......Hotels: City, regular rates, $2.50 (special also); Windsor, special rates, $1.50; Central, special rates, $1.50; Wilde, special rates, $1.50.

TURNERS FALLS, 6,000. R. R., Fitchburg; Northampton & New Haven. Colle Opera House, Fred. Colle, manager; seating capacity, 900; rental, one night $25; share also; license, 6 tickets. Size of stage, 20x50; size of proscenium opening, 23x23; height from stage to grooves, 14; height from stage to rigging loft, 16½; depth under stage, 4;

traps, 2; number sets scenery, 10; leader of orchestra, Fred. Colle; bill poster, **Edward Slocum Greenfield.** Newspapers; Reporter (Wed.)........Hotel: Farren, special rates, $1.25.

WAKEFIELD, 5,700. R. R., **Boston & Maine. Town Hall, seating capacity, 1,200; rental, one night $25, three $60. Size of stage, 20x24; no scenery; bill poster, F. J. Coker.** Newspapers: **Bulletin** (Sat.), **Banner** (Sat.).... ...Hotels; McMillan, special rates: **Albion,** Leggett.

Cates' Hall; seating capacity, 700.

Walton's Hall; seating capacity, 500.

WALTHAM, 15,000. R. R., Fitchburg; Mass. Central. **Music Hall, Wm. D. Bradstreet, manager; seating capacity, 1,037; share only. Size of stage, 28x60; size of proscenium opening, 26x30; height from stage to grooves, 16; height from stage to rigging loft, 30; depth under stage, 15; number sets scenery, 10; leader of orchestra, T. H. Rollinson; stage carpenter, Thomas Nunney; bill poster, Frank McGuInness; number of sheets can accommodate, 500; rates per sheet, 4c** Newspapers: daily, Tribune, advertising **rates** per line, 15c.; weekly, Record (Fri.), advertising rates 40c. per inch; Free Press **(Fri.),** advertising rates, 25c. per inch........Hotels · Central, special rates, $1.25 to $1.50; Prospect, special rates, $1.50.

Rumford Hall, Frank McGuinness, manager; seating capacity, 700; rental, one night, $40 to $60, license included; share also. Size of stage, 12x15; full set scenery.

WARE, 5,000. R. R., **Boston & Albany. Music Hall, D. A. Jennison, manager; seating capacity, 600; rental, one night $15. Size of stage, 40x60. Newspapers:** Enterprise (Sat.), Gazette (Fri.), Standard (Sat)......Hotel: Hampshire, regular rates, **$2** (special also).

WAREHAM, 3,500. R. R., Old Colony. **Webster Hall, M. C. Moroney, manager; seating capacity, 400; rental, one night $8, three $20. Size of stage, 15x32; no scenery; bill poster, Fred. Hinkley. Newspapers: News** (Sat.), **Times** (Sat.)......Hotels: Thompson, Wankinco, Kendrick.

WARREN, 4,000. R. R., Boston & Albany. **Town Hall, M. B. Ramsdell, manager; seating capacity, 700; rental, one night $15; no license. Size of stage, 18x24; full set scenery; bill poster, Wm. Carey; theatrical teamster, Jno. Daily. Newspaper:** Herald (Fri.) ......Hotels: Warren, regular rates, $2 (special also); Coles, Fessenden.

Armory Hall, J. E. Dana, manager; seating capacity, 400; rental, one night $12, license included. Size of stage, 15x18; number sets scenery, 6.

WEBSTER, 7,000. R. R., N. Y. & N. Eng.; Nor. & Wor. Branch; B. & A., branch. **Music Hall, E. S. Hill, manager; seating capacity, 1,000; rental, one night $25, three $48; license, $2. Size of stage, 28x40; size of proscenium opening, 17x28; height from stage to grooves, 17; height from stage to rigging loft, 28; depth under stage, 5; traps, 1; number sets scenery, 12; bill poster, E. S. Hill; number of sheets can accommodate, 275; rates per sheet, 4c.; theatrical teamster, C. Whitford. Newspapers: Times** (Fri.); Eagle (Fri.)......Hotel : Joslin, special rates, $1.25 to $1.50.

WESTBORO, 5,000. R. R., Boston & Albany. Town Hall, manager; seating capacity, 546; rental, one night $12 to $15; license, **eight** tickets. Size of stage, 16x30; no scenery; bill poster, **Frank Sandra.** Newspaper: **Chronotype** (Sat.)......Hotels: Westboro, Whitney

WESTFIELD, 8,500. R. R., New Haven & Northampton; Boston & Albany. **Music Hall P. W. Howe,** manager ; seating **capacity, 750; rental,** one night **$25, three nights $60.** license included. Size of stage, 25x50; size of proscenium opening, 14x20; height from stage to grooves, 10; height from **stage to rigging loft, 15; depth under** stage, 8; traps, 1; number set scenery, 8; leader **of orchestra, Cland Alstrom;** stage carpenter, P. W. Howe; **bill poster, W. R. Loomis; number of sheets can accommodate, 500;** rates per sheet, 4c.; theatrical teamster, J. F. Freeman. Newspaper: **Times** (Wed.), advertising rates **per inch, $1**.......Hotels: Central, **special rates, $1.50 to $2;** Wilmarth, special rates, **$1.50** to $2.

WINCHENDON, 3,200. R. R., Boston & Albany; Boston, Barre & Gardner; Cheshire. **Town Hall, A. S. Parkes, manager; seating** capacity, 600; rental, one night $30; no scenery. Newspaper: **Courier** (Fri.)......Hotels : American, Tremont.

WOBURN, 12,000. R. R., Boston & Lowell; **Woburn Branch. Lyceum Hall.** W. Hammond, manager; seating capacity, 650; **rental, one night $25; license, $1.** Size of stage, 18x25; **size of** proscenium opening, 13x20; **number sets** scenery, 8; leader of orchestra, J. C. **Hearne; bill poster, S. H. Cutter; number of sheets can accommodate, 300; rates per sheet, 4c.; theatrical teamster, R. S. Spaulding.** Newspapers : Courier (Sat.), Journal (Fri.), **Advertiser (Th.), Union (Sat.)......Hotel : Central, special rates, $1.50.**

WORCESTER, 70,000. R. R., Boston & Albany, Boston, Barre & Gard.; New York & New England; Providence & Worcester; **Worcester & Shrewsbury;** Worcester, Nash. & Roch. Worcester Theatre, **Chas. Wilkinson, manager; seating capacity, 1,438; rental, share only;** license included. Size of stage, 37x75; size of proscenium opening, 28x33; height from stage to grooves, 18; height from stage to rigging loft, 34; depth under stage, 9; traps, 8; number sets scenery, 30; leader of orchestra, **E. D.** Ingraham; scenic artist, none employed; stage carpenter, **Thomas Doran; bill poster, L. B. Fiske; number of** sheets can accommodate, 5,000; **rates per sheet, 4c.; theatrical teamsters, L. R. Spooner,** John Hickey. Newspapers: daily, Spy, Gazette; weekly, Journal (Fri.), advertising rates, yearly **contract..... Hotels : Bay State, special rates, $2;** Lincoln, special rates, $1.50; **Waldo, special rates, $1.25; Waverly, special rates, $1.25;** United States, special rates, **$1.25.**

Mechanics' Hall, C. W. Wentworth, manager; seating capacity, 2,000; rental, one night $60, three $150; share also. Size of stage, 24x45; size of proscenium opening, 18x30; **height from** stage to grooves, 15; **number sets scenery, 10.**

Washburn Hall, C. W. Wentworth, **manager; seating capacity, 600; rental, one night $10 to** $35; license, $3; share also. Size of stage, 12x30; number sets scenery, 5.

Horticultural Hall, Charles Brooks, **manager; seating capacity, 650; rental, one night $15,** three $40; license, $5. Size of stage, 23x24; full set scenery.

Music Hall; **seating capacity, 1,500; rental, one night $60; license, $5.** Size of stage, 32x35, full set scenery.

YARMOUTH PORT, 2,465. R. R., **Old Colony. Lyceum Hall,** R. H. Harris, manager; seating capacity, 325 ; rental, one **night $8, three $20.** Size of stage, 13x20. Newspapers: Register (Sat.), Item (Fri.)

MICHIGAN.

ADRIAN, 10,000 R. R., L. S. & Mich. Southern; **Wabash. Opera House, C. M. Croswell,** manager; seating capacity, 1,100; **rental, one night $40, three $110; share also; license** included. Size of stage, 30x60; height **from stage to rigging loft, 22; depth under stage** 9; number sets scenery, 10; bill poster, **Chas. Van Ostrand.** Newspapers: daily, Record, Times; weekly, Press (Fri.)......**Hotels: Lawrence, Central, regular rates $2 (special** also); Commercial, Gibson.

ALBION, 5,500. R. R., Lake Shore **& Mich. So.;** Michigan Central. Albion Opera House, M. C. Moore, manager; seating **capacity, 800; rental, one night $35; share also; license** included. Size of stage, 28x30; **number sets scenery, 8; bill poster, Opera House.** Newspapers: Mirror (Fri.), Republican **(Fri.)......Hotels: Albion, regular rates, $2 (special** also).

ALLEGAN, 3,400. R. R., Chicago **& West Michigan; Grand Rapids & Indiana; Lake** Shore & Michigan Southern; **Michigan & Ohio. Empire Hall, C. H. Adams, manager;** seating capacity, 500; **rental, one night $10, three $26; license, $3; share also.** Size of stage, 18x18; number sets **scenery, 7; bill poster, C. H. Adams.** Newspapers: Democrat (Wed.), Gazette (Sat.), **Journal and Tribune (Fri.)... ..Hotels : Sherman, regular** rates, **$2** (special also); Allegan, **Chaffee City.**

ALPENA, 8,000. Connected by daily steamer **with** Detroit. Opera House, G. L. **Maltz.** manager; **seating capacity, 600; rental, one night $25, three $50; share** also; license included. **Size of** stage, 25x60; number sets scenery, 10. Newspapers: Argus (Wed.), Pioneer (Fri.),. . Hotels: Fletcher, regular rates, $2 (special also); Alpena, Galling.

Theatre Comique (variety).

ANN ARBOR, 12,000. R. R., Michigan Central; Toledo, Ann Arbor & Northern Michigan. Grand Opera House, A. J. Sawyer, manager; seating capacity, 1,200; rental, one night $75, three $150. Size of stage, 30x60; size of proscenium opening, 27; height from stage to grooves, 16; height from stage to rigging loft, 50; depth under stage, 20; traps, 2; number sets scenery, full set; hill poster, C. A. Edwards; theatrical teamster, J. A. Polhemus. Newspapers: Argus (Fri.), Courier (Fri.), Democrat (Th.)......Hotels: St. James, special rates, $1.50; Cook, special rates, $1.50

Hill's Opera House; seating capacity, 1,200; rental, one night $40, three $75; share also; license included. Size of stage, 26x30; full set scenery.

ASHLAND, 1,700. R. R., Chic. & W. Mich. Opera House ; seating capacity, 600 ; rental, one night $15. Newspapers : Times, Press........Hotels : Miller, McNulty.

AU SABLE, 2,500. O'Toole Hall, J. T. Perry, manager ; seating capacity, 350 ; rental, one night $10, three $25 ; license, $2. Size of stage, 25x25 ; number sets scenery, 3. Newspaper : Saturday Night........Hotels : National, regular rates, $2 (special also), Lee, Eagle.

BANGOR, 2,200. R. R., Chicago & W. Mich. Miller's Opera House, J. G. Miller, manager; seating capacity, 400 ; rental one night $10. Size of stage, 18x22 ; fair stock scenery ; hill poster, Will. Doris. Newspapers : Reflector (Fri.), Advance (Th.) .....Hotels : Schrlug, Russell.

BATTLE CREEK, 10,000. R. R., Mich. Central ; Chicago & Grand Trunk ; Mich. & Ohio. Hamblin's Opera House, C. J. Whitney, manager ; seating capacity, 1,000 ; rental, one night $50, three $120 ; share also ; license, $5. Size of stage, 32x32 ; size of proscenium opening, 13x25; height from stage to grooves, 14 ; height from stage to rigging loft, 24; depth under stage, 4 ; traps, 1 ; number sets scenery, 14 ; leader of orchestra, Prof. Theo. Martin ; stage carpenter, C. E. Ireland ; hill poster, W. H. Eldred ; number of sheets can accommodate, 2,000 running feet ; rates per sheet, &c.; theatrical teamsters, Beaver & Williams. Newspapers : daily, Journal, Republican ; weekly, Sunday Call. ....Hotels : Williams, special rates, $1.50 to $2 ; Lewis, special rates, $1.50 to $2 ; Grand Central, 75c. to $1.50.

Centennial Hall, N. P. Simons, manager ; seating capacity, 450 ; rental one night, $10, three $24 ; share also; license included. Size of stage, 16x36 ; number sets scenery, 4 hill poster. N. P. Simons.

BAY CITY, 30,000. R. R., Michigan Central; Flint & Pere Marquette. Weston Opera House, J. Buckley, manager; seating capacity, 1,200; rental, one night $50, three $120; share also. Size of stage, 35x75; size of proscenium opening, 24x32; height from stage to grooves, 16; height from stage to rigging loft, 40; depth under stage, 8; traps, 2; number sets scenery, full set; leader of orchestra, Prof. Hudson; scenic artists, Walthen & Sons; stage carpenter, Wallin; hill poster, Chas. Bloomfield; rates per sheet, 3c.; theatrical teamsters, Birney Bros. Newspaper: daily, Tribune, Press, Call, adv. rates, special contract........Hotels: Foster, special rates, $2.50 to $3; Campbell, special rates, $1.50 to $2; Brunswick, special rates, $1 to $1.25.

Nonpareil Theatre, Wm. Fuller, manager.

BIG RAPIDS, 5,000. R. R., Chic. & W. Mich.; Detroit, Lansing & Northern; Grand Rapids & Ind. Opera House, T. W. Adams, manager; seating capacity, 800; rental, one night $8; license, $5; share also. Size of stage, 28x40; full set scenery; hill poster, Opera House. Newspaper: daily, Pioneer; weekly, Current (Wed.); Herald (Fri.)......Hotels: Northern, regular rates, $2 (special also); Bracket.

BLISSFIELD, 1,500. R. R., Lake Shore & Mich. So. Clinton Hall, A. B. Williams, manager; seating capacity, 500; number sets scenery, 2. Newspaper: Advance (Fri.) ..Hotel: Wheeler.

BUCHANAN, 3,200. R. R., Mich. Central; St. Joseph's Valley. Kinyon's Hall, H. H. Kinyon, manager; rental, one night $5, three $12; license, $1; share also. Size of stage, 13x34; number sets scenery, 1; hill poster, Seth Strau. Newspapers: Independent and Reporter (Tb.), Record (Th.)......Hotels: Tremont, Major.

Opera House, Rough Bros., managers; seating capacity, 700.

CADILLAC, 3,300. R. R., Grand Rapids & Ind. Forrester's Opera House, J. H. Hixson, manager; seating capacity, 600; rental, one night $30, three $45; license $3; share also. Size of stage, 26x38; number sets scenery 8; bill poster, Tompson Kent. Newspapers: News (Sat.), Times (Fri.)......Hotels: Snow's, regular rates, $2 (special also); McKinnon, Balfour.

Holbrook & May's Hall, Holbrook & May, managers; seating capacity, 2 0; rental, one night $5. Size of stage, 14x25; no scenery.

CALUMET, 8,500. R. R., Mineral Range. St. Patrick's Hall, John Cuddihy, manager; seating capacity, 500; rental, one night $15, three $40; no license. Size of stage 26x35; number sets scenery, 2; bill poster, H. P. Larson. Newspaper: News (Sat.)......Hotels: Calumet, Commercial, Pacific.

CARO, 2,100. R. R., Michigan Central. Opera House, George R. Rolston, manager; seating capacity, 700; bill poster, George W. Smith. Newspapers: Advertiser and Citizen (Th.), Jeffersonian (Fri.) .....Hotel: Caro, regular rates, $2 (special also).

CASNOVIA, 2,600. R. R., Chic. & W. Mich. Toppin's Hall, R. H. Toppin, manager; seating capacity, 200; rental, one night $3; license, $1; share also. Size of stage, 10x22; bill poster, Postmaster. Newspaper: Herald (Sat.)......Hotels: Edie, Hylers, Hicks.

Hyler's Hall, Wm. Hyler, manager; seating capacity, 500,

CASSOPOLIS, 1,200; R. R., Chic. & Grand Trunk ; Mich. Central. Goodwin's Hall, F. Goodwin, manager; seating capacity, 350 ; rental, one night $5; license, $1. Size of stage, 16x18 ; fair stock scenery. Newspapers : Democrat (Th.), Vigilant (Th)...... Hotels: Exchange, regular rates, $2 (special also); Cass.

CHARLEVOIX, 1,100. Lewis Hall, Dl. Lewis, manager; seating capacity, 600; no scenery. Newspapers: Journal (Th.), Sentinel (Wed.)......Hotel : Bridge Street.

Bartholomew's Opera House.

CHARLOTTE, 3,700. R. R., Chic. & Grand Trunk; Mich. Central. Sampson Hall, A. H. Sleater, manager; seating capacity, 900; rental, one night $15, three, $30; license, $2; share also. Size of stage, 22x24; number sets scenery, 8; bill poster, A. H. Sleater. Newspapers: Caller (Sat.), Leader (Th.), Republican (Fri.)......Hotels: Sherwood, Phoenix.

CHEBOYGAN, 3,300. R. R., Mich. Central. Town Hall; seating capacity, 550; no license. Number sets scenery, 2. Newspapers ; Democrat (Th.), Tribune (Sat.) .....Hotel: Grand Central, regular rates, $2 (special also).

New Opera House.

CHELSEA, 1,600. R. R., Michigan Central. Town Hall, J. L. Gilbert; seating capacity, 600 ; rental, one night $25, three $40; license, $3; share also. Size of stage, 20x40; number sets scenery, 6; bill poster, Samuel Hasalschwardt. Newspaper: Herald (Th.)...... Hotels: Chelsea, McKone.

COLDWATER, 7,000. R. R., Lake Shore & Mich. So. Tibbitts' Opera House, B. S. Tibbits, manager; seating capacity, 1,000; rental, one night $50, three $100; share also; license included. Size of stage, 34x53; full set scenery; bill poster, Opera House. Newspapers: semi-weekly, Republican, Courier (Sat.), Sun (Th)......Hotels : Southern Michigan, regular rates. $2 (special also); Bolster, St. James.

CONSTANTINE, 3,000. R. R., Lake Shore & Mich. Southern. Union Hall Theatre, Chas. M. Hazlitt, manager; seating capacity, 600; rental, one night $15, three $30; share also; license included. Size of stage, 48x30; number sets scenery, 5; bill poster, Silas Kline. Newspaper: Mercury (Th.)......Hotels: Wells, regular rates, $2 (special also); Constantine.

CRYSTAL FALLS, 5,300. R. R., Chic. & North Western. Doucet Opera House, J. M. Essinger, manager; seating capacity, 400; rental, one night $15, three $30; share also. Size of stage, 28x30; number sets scenery, 7; bill poster, Opera House .. ...Hotels: Adams, Davis, Lockwood.

DECATUR, 1,500. R. R., Mich. Central. Town Hall, J. G. Haynes, manager; seating capacity, 300. Newspaper: Republican (Wed.)......Hotel: Duncombe.

WEST SHORE ROUTE.

New York, West Shore & Buffalo Railway.

THE HANDSOMEST PASSENGER COACHES

AND

Pullman Buffet, Parlor and Sleeping Cars

Ever placed in service on any line.

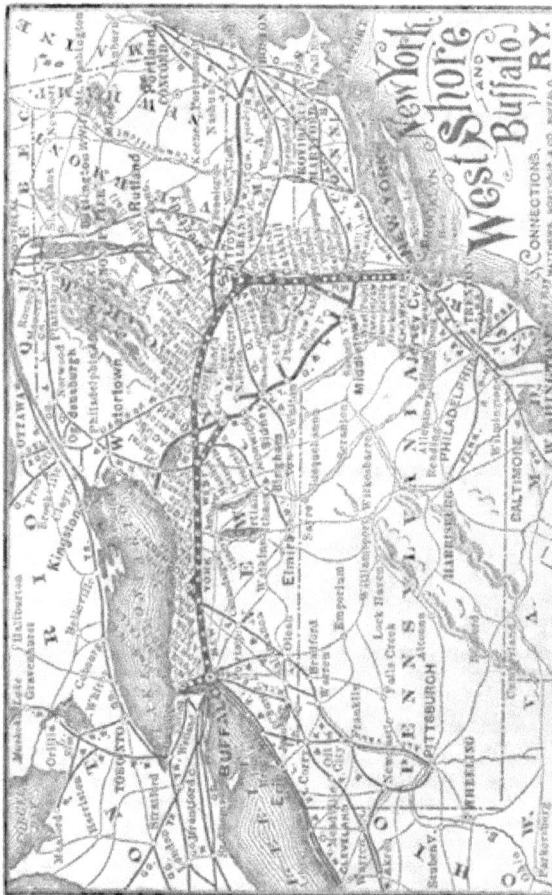

HENRY MONETT, General Passenger Agent.

E. V. SKINNER, Gen'l Eastern Passenger Agent.

363 Broadway, N. Y.

DEERFIELD, 1,000. R. R., Lake Shore & Mich. So.; Mich. Central. Burnham's Hall, E. E. Bornham, manager; seating capacity, 600; number sets scenery, 2. Newspaper: Record (Fri.)

DETROIT, 165,000. R. R., Detroit, Gd. Hav. & Milwaukee; Detroit, Lansing & Northern; Grand Trunk; Wabash; Michigan Central; Lake Shore & Michigan So. White's Grand Theatre, Charles O. White, manager; seating capacity, 2,700; rental, share only. Size of stage, 55x100; size of proscenium opening, 35x40; height from stage to grooves, 20; height from stage to rigging loft, 54; depth under stage, 4; traps, 5; number sets scenery, 20; leader of orchestra, Mark Kelntz; scenic artists, Walthen & Sons; stage carpenter, Joseph Jamison; bill posters, Goodwin & Henry; number sheets can accommodate, 4,000; rates per sheet, 3 cents; theatrical teamster, Detroit Transfer Co. Newspapers: daily, Free Press, News, Post, Times, Journal; weekly, Chaff (Sat.)..... Hotels: Russell, special rates, $1 to $2; Griswold, special rates, $1 to $2; Brunswick, special rates, $1 to $2; Standish, special rates, $1 to $2.

Whitney's Grand Opera House, C. B. Blanchett, manager; Brooks & Dickson. New York representatives; seating capacity, 2,000. Size of stage, 44x74; height from stage to grooves, 20; height from stage to rigging loft, 65; depth under stage, 12, leader of orchestra, Prof. Heintz; scenic artist, A. Chevalier; stage carpenter, John Hanna; bill posters, Goodwin & Henry, city bill posters; rates per sheet, 3 cents; theatrical teamster, Hartford & Co.

Detroit Opera House, C. A. Shaw, manager; seating capacity, 1,909; rental, one night $100, three $250; share also; license included; number sets scenery, full set; leader of orchestra, C. E. Borgman, scenic artist, Robert Hopkins; stage carpenter, M. W. Leslie; bill poster, H. W. Walker; number of sheets can accommodate, 3,000; rates per sheet, 3 cents.

Detroit Museum (late Park Theatre), Prof. George W. Ryder, manager.

Detroit Music Hall, Charles White, manager; seating capacity, 3,500. Size of stage, 40x70.

Academy of Music, John P. Long, manager.

Merrill Hall; T. P. Palmer, manager.

Harmonic Hall, Julius Milchers, manager.

Theatre Comique, Charles N. Welch, manager; seating capacity, 1,200; rental, ——; share also. Size of stage, 30x35; full set scenery.

DEXTER, 1,100. R. R., Mich. Cent. Red Ribbon Hall, R. P. Copeland, manager; seating capacity, 300; bill poster, James Wilsey. Newspaper: Leader (Sun.)..... Hotels: Blanchard, regular rates, $2 (special also); Exchange, Eureka, Franklin.

Sills' Hall, G. S. Sills, manager; seating capacity, 450.

DOWAGIAC, 2,500. R. R., Mich. Cent. Public Hall, D. Lyle, manager; seating capacity, 600. Newspapers: Republican (Th.), Times (Wed.)......Hotels: Continental, regular rates, $2 (special also); Commercial.

DUNDEE, 1,100. R. R., Lake Shore & Mich. South.; Mich. & Ohio. Munger's Hall, A. D. Gilmore, manager; seating capacity, 700; number sets scenery, 2. Newspaper: Reporter (Fri.).....Hotel: Bingham.

EAST SAGINAW, 30,000. R. R., Flint & Pere Marquette; Mich. Central; Port Huron & N. W.; Detroit & Bay City. Academy of Music, S. G. Clay, manager; seating capacity, 1,500; share only. Size of stage, 39x56; size of proscenium opening, 32x30; height from stage to grooves, 20; from stage to rigging loft, 67½; depth under stage 8; traps, 3; number sets scenery, 25; leader of orchestra, Prof. Julius Reiss; scenic artist, J. B. Gray; stage carpenter, Fred. McWithy; bill poster, S. G. Clay; number of sheets can accommodate, 3,000; rates per sheet, 3c.; theatrical teamsters, Bartow & Enwright. Newspapers: daily, Courier, advertising rates, 10c. per line; Herald, advertising rates, 10c. per line; News, advertising rates, 12c. per line; weekly, Courier (Th.), Herald (Th.) ......Hotels: Bancroft, regular rates, $2.50 to $3.50; Everett, special rates, $1.50 to $1.75; Sherman, special rates, $1 to $1.15; Marshall, $1 to $1.25.

Germania Theatre, Clay & Burkley, managers; seating capacity, 1,200; rental, ——; share only; license, none. Size of stage, 39x60; size of proscenium opening, 20x85; height from stage to grooves, 18; height from stage to rigging loft, 24; depth under stage.

8; traps, 1; number sets scenery, full set; leader of orchestra, Prof. Price; scenic artist, Walthen; stage carpenter, Fred. McWithy; bill poster, S. G. Clay; number of sheets can accommodate, 5,000; rates per sheet, 3 to 4c.; theatrical **teamster**, Omnibus Line.

Bordwell's Opera House (Variety).

Varieties Theatre; seating capacity, 630.

Brewer Hall, A. P. Brewer, manager.

EATON RAPIDS, 2,700. **R. R.,** Lake Shore & Mich. So.; **Mich.** Central, Red Ribbon Hall, J. M. **Reynolds, manager;** seating capacity, 500. Newspapers: Journal (Fri.), **Times (Th.).** . . . . .Hotels: **Anderson,** regular rates, $2 **(special** also); Frost, regular **rates,** $2 (special also); **Morgan.**

ESCANABA, 3,700. R. R., Chic. & N. W. **Music Hall;** rent or **share;** fair stock scenery. Newspaper: Iron Point **(Sat.)** . . . . . .Hotel: **Ludington, regular rates,** $2 (special also.)

FENTON, 2,900. R. R., Detroit. Grand Haven & Milwaukee. **Colwell Hall,** J. W. **Topping, manager;** seating capacity, 800 ; rental, one night $10, three $25; share **also; license,** $1 **to** $1.50. Size of stage, 22x24 ; size of proscenium opening, 28x22; height from stage **to grooves,** 15; height from stage to rigging loft, 28; depth under stage, 5; traps, 1; **number sets** scenery, 4; leader of orchestra, J. F. Hepler; scenic artist, J. C. Perry; stage car-**penter, J.** Carmer; bill poster, Joe M. Abbott; theatrical teamster, J. R. Rogers. News-papers ; Courier (Sat.), Gazette (Fri.), Independent (Sat.) . . . . . .Hotels: Denis, special rates, $1.25; Lansing, special rates, 75c. to $1.

FLINT, 10,000. R. R., Chicago & Grand Trunk; Flint & Pere Marquette. Music Hall, H. A. Thayer, manager; seating capacity, 1,100; share only. Size of stage, 37x60; number sets **scenery, 12; bill poster,** H. A. Thayer. **Newspapers:** daily, Journal; weekly, Globe **(Th.), Democrat (Sat.)** . . . . .Hotels: Bryant, regular rates, $2 (special also); Sherman, **Thayer, Brotherton, Dayton, Mason.**

Fenton Hall; **seating capacity, 800; rental, one night** $30, **three** $60; license, tickets; share **also. Size of stage,** 20x21; **number sets scenery,** 13.

FRANKFORT, 1,300. Temperance Hall; no scenery. **Newspaper: Express (Wed.).** . . . . . . **Hotel:** Forrest Avenue, regular rates, $2 (special also).

May's Hall; no scenery.

GRAND HAVEN, 5,500. R. R., Chicago & W. Mich.; Detroit, Grand Haven & Milwaukee. Music Hall, J. A. Stevenson, manager; seating capacity, 600; rental, **one** night $20, three $50, license included. Size of stage, 20x40; number sets scenery, 4; bill poster, **J. A.** Stevenson. Newspapers: Courier-Journal (Sat.), Herald (Fri.), News-Journal **(Th.)** . . . . . .**Hotels:** Cutler, regular rates, $2 (special also); Kirby, **Andres, City.**

Cutler House Hall; seating capacity, 400.

GRAND RAPIDS, 45,000. **R. R., Mich.** Central, G. R. **&** Indiana; Detroit, G. H. & Mil-waukee; Michigan Southern; Chicago & West Mich. Powers Opera House, Wm. H. Powers, manager; seating capacity, 1,500; rental, one night $75, three $200; share also; license included. Size of stage, 33x60; size of proscenium opening, 36x29; height from stage to grooves, 18; height from stage to rigging loft, 60; depth under stage, 9; traps, 5; number sets scenery, full set ; leader of orchestra, Walter Miles; stage carpenter, Ed. Warrington; bill poster, Geo. N. Leonard; rates per sheet, 4c.; theatrical teamsters, Ball & Waters. Newspapers: daily, Eagle, Leader, Times, Democrat. . . . .**Hotels:** Mor-ton, regular rates, $2.50 to $3 (special also); Sweet s, regular rates, $2.50 to $3 (special also); Eagle, regular rates; Rathbun, regular rates; Bridge Street **House,** regular rates.

Redmond's Grand Opera House, F. P. Thayer, manager; **seating** capacity, 1,600; rental, one night $75, three $175; share also. Size of stage, 32x50; height from stage to grooves, 18; height from stage to rigging **loft,** 32; full set scenery

Smith's Opera House (variety), **W. H.** Smith, manager.

Luce's Hall; seating capacity, 900.

Adelphi Hall; seating capacity, 500.

GRASS LAKE, 2,000. R. R., **Mich. Central. Town Hall,** D. W. Clark, manager. News-paper: News (Th.)

Union Hall, B. B. Lamon, manager.

HANCOCK, 7,000. R. R. Marquette, Houghton & Ontonagon; M. R. St. Patrick Hall, Rich Rourke, manager; seating capacity, 800; rental, one night $15, three $40. Size of stage, 24x19½; size of proscenium opening, 15x19½; height from stage to grooves, 12; number sets scenery, 5; bill poster, John Verhoven. New-paper: Mining Journal (Tues.). ......Hotels: Northwestern, special rates, $1.50; Lakeview, regular rates. $2 (special also).

Germania Hall; seating capacity, 300. Size of stage, 15x20; fair stock scenery.

HARTFORD, 2,000. R. R., Lake Shore connected with Central. Reynolds' Opera House. Mrs. Julia Reynolds, manager; seating capacity, 600. Size of stage, 14x20; size of pro scenium opening, 11x20; height from stage to rigging loft, 14; depth under stage, 4; traps, 1; number sets scenery, 5. Newspaper: Dayspring (Fri.)......Hotels: Barrett, special rates, $1; Olds, regular rates. $3 (special also).

HASTINGS, 3,200. R. R., Mich. Central. Union Hall, W. S. Goodyear & Co., managers; seating capacity, 500. Newspapers: Banner (Fri.), Democrat (Th.), Journal (Th.)...... Hotels: Hastings, regular rates. $2 (special also); Newton, Central.

HILLSDALE, 4,800. R. R., Lake Shore & Mich. So. Underwood's Opera House, Geo. M. Underwood, manager; seating capacity, 1,200; rental, one night $25, three $60; share also. Size of stage, 24x24; full set scenery; bill poster, A. H. Dolles. Newspapers: Business (Sat.), Democrat (Fri.), Herald (Th.), Leader (Fri.), Standard (Th.).....Hotels: Smith's, regular rates, $2 (special also); Randell, Mosher.

Sutton's Opera House, S. Golloway, manager; seating capacity, 600; rental, one night $15, three $30; license, $5. Size of stage, 45x16; number sets scenery, 10.

HOLLAND, 3,000. R. R., Chicago & West, Mich. Lyceum Opera House, C. L. Waring, manager; seating capacity, 500; rental, one night $10, three $20; license included. Size of stage, 20x33; size of proscenium opening, 14x18; height of stage to grooves, 16; height from stage to rigging loft, 26; depth under stage, 12; number sets scenery, 5; leader of orchestra, Dr. D. McGee; stage carpenter, J. R. Kleyn; bill poster, J. Van Den Berg; number of sheets can accommodate, 150; rates per sheet, 4c; theatrical teamster, John Serier. Newspaper: News (Sat.)......Hotels: City, special rates, $1.25; Phoenix, special rates, $1.

HOUGHTON, 2,600. R. R., Mineral Range; Marquette, Houghton & Ontonagon. Miller's Hall, Mr. H. Miller, manager; seating capacity, 800; rental, one night $15, three $32; license, $10. Size of stage, 35x40; full set scenery; bill poster, T. Daniels. Newspaper: Gazette (Th.)......Hotels: Douglass, regular rates, $2 (special also); Butterfield, Miller's.

HOWELL, 3,000. R. R., Det., Lans. & Nor. Howell Opera House, T. M. Hunter, manager; seating capacity, 825; share also; rental, one night $15, three $50; license, $2; share also. Size of stage, 26x44; size of proscenium opening, 19x20; height from stage to grooves, 13; height from stage to rigging loft, 22; depth under stage, 5½; traps, 1; number sets scenery, 8; scenic artist, S. E. Landis (Chicago); stage carpenter, R. T. Holmes; bill poster, proprietors; number of sheets can accommodate, 250; rates per sheet, 4c.; theatrical teamster, T. J. Winegar. Newspapers: Republican (Th.), advertising rates, $3 per column; Democrat (Wed.), advertising rates, $3 per column......Hotels: National, special rates, $1.25; Commercial, special rates, $2.

Weimeister Hall, John Weimeister, manager; seating capacity, 400; rental, one night $7. Size of stage, 16x20.

HUDSON, 3,150. R. R., Lake Shore & Mich. So. Fowle's Opera House, G. Fowle, manager; seating capacity, 600; license, $2. Size of stage, 20x20; number sets scenery, 7; bill posters, Schemerhorn Bros. Newspapers: Gazette (Fri.), Post (Fri.)......Hotels: Comstock, regular rates, $2 (special also); Hudson.

Union Hall, M. M. Maxon & Co., managers; seating capacity, 500; rental, one night $10; license, $2.50.

IONIA, 5,300. R. R., Det., Lans. & Nor.; Det., Grand Haven & Mil. Armory Hall. Kim R. Smith, manager; seating capacity, 800; rental, one night, $30; share also; license included. Size of stage, 22x40; number sets scenery, 8; bill poster, Thos. Keys.

– THE –

NEW YORK MIRROR

ORGAN OF THE THEATRICAL MANAGERS AND DRAMATIC PROFESSION OF AMERICA.

PUBLISHED EVERY THURSDAY,

At No. 12 UNION SQUARE, NEW YORK

HARRISON GREY FISKE, EDITOR.

THE MIRROR has the largest dramatic circulation in America. It is the leader of opinion in the special field it covers. Abroad it is quoted as the authority on dramatic affairs in this country. Its able editorial corps is supplemented by a staff of over four hundred correspondents. The latest news by telegraph is a special feature. The whereabouts of all traveling companies are found in its "Dates Ahead," a special department, carefully revised each week.

*THE MIRROR UPHOLDS THE **LOFTIEST** AIMS OF THE PROFESSION.*

IT IS NEWSY, GOSSIPY AND BRIGHT, WITHOUT **OPENING** ITS COLUMNS TO SCANDAL AND SENSATION.

As an Advertising Medium it is Invaluable to Manager and Actor.

SUBSCRIPTION PRICE, - - - - - - -	FOUR DOLLARS A YEAR
ADVERTISEMENTS, - - - - - - -	TWENTY CENTS A LINE
(Subject to discounts for continuance.)	
READING NOTICES, - - - - - - -	THIRTY CENTS A LINE

FOR SALE BY ALL NEWSDEALERS.

Newspapers: daily, Mail, Sentinel; weekly, National (Fri.), Standard (Fri.).....
Hotels — Bailey, regular rates, $1 (special also); Clarendon, regular rates, $2 (special also); Washington, Union, Sherman, Revere.

Smith's Hall; seating capacity, 400.

Bayard's Hall; seating capacity, 400.

IRON MOUNTAIN, 3,700. R. R., Chic. & N. Western. Marchand Opera House, seating capacity, 350; number sets scenery, 5. Newspaper: Range (Sat.). .....Hotel: Jenkens.

ISHPEMING, 8,000. R. R., Chic. & N. Western; Marquette, Houghton & Outonagon. Opera House, F. M. Norton, manager; rent or share; license $5. Size of stage, 20x36; fair stock scenery; bill poster, Opera House. Newspaper: Iron Agitator (Sat.).......
Hotels: Nelson, Barnum, Commercial.

Austin's Hall, Chas. Ham, manager; seating capacity, 500; rental, one night $10, three $25, license, $3 to $5. Size of stage, 25x32; number sets scenery, 5.

McKay's Hall; seating capacity, 1,200.

Nora Hall; seating capacity, 600.

JACKSON, 23,000. R. R., M. C.: Ft. Wayne; G. R. V.; Gr. Trunk; L. S. & M. S.; Jackson, Lansing & Saginaw. Hibbard Opera House, C. J. Whitney, manager; Brooks & Dickson, New York representatives; seating capacity, 1,135; rental, one night $75, three $200, license included. Size of stage, 32x64; size of proscenium opening, 32x29; height from stage to grooves, 17; height from stage to rigging loft, 34; depth under stage, 10; traps, 2; number sets scenery, 25; leaders of orchestra, Ninnis Bros.; scenic artist. E. D. Smith; stage carpenter, W. D. Greg; bill poster, G. W. Stevenson; rates per sheet, 4c.; theatrical teamsters, Knapp & Sutton. Newspapers: daily, Patriot, advertising rates per inch, 50c.; Citizen, advertising rates per inch, 50c.; Courier, advertising rates per inch, 50c.; weekly, Star (Sat.), advertising rates, 50c. per inch; Advertiser (Sat.), advertising rates, 50c. per inch......Hotels: Hibbard, special rates, $2; Hurd, special rates, $1.50); Commercial, special rates, $1.

Union Hall; seating capacity, 1,500; rental, one night $40, three $90; license, $5; share also. Size of stage, 40x50; number sets scenery, 12.

KALAMAZOO, 16,000. R. R., Michigan Central; Grand Rapids & Indiana; Lake Shore & Mich. Southern. Opera House, Jeffrey & Powelson, managers; seating capacity, 1,200; rental, one night $25, three $60, license included; share also. Size of stage, 32x60; size of proscenium opening, 20x22; height from stage to grooves, 19; depth under stage, 5; trape, 1; number sets scenery, 14; leader of orchestra, John Baker; scenic artist, Wm. H. Powelson; stage carpenter, F. W. Downey; bill poster, W. R. Solomon; number of sheets can accommodate, 2,000; rates per sheet, 3c.; theatrical teamster, Boardman. Newspapers: daily, Gazette, Telegraph; weekly, Telegraph (Tu.), Gazette (Fri.), Herald (Sun.) ......Hotels: Burdick, special rates, $2.50; Kalamazoo, $2.; American, $1.50; Burk's, $1.

Academy of Music, B. A. Bush, manager; seating capacity, 1,350; rental, one night $75, license, $3. Size of stage, 33x32; size of proscenium opening, 32x32; height from stage to grooves, 20; height from stage to rigging loft, 43; depth under stage, 9; traps, 3; number sets scenery, 31; leader of orchestra, G. B. Balum; stage carpenter, Joseph Bidwell; bill poster, G. A. Bush; number of sheets can accommodate, 1,000; rates per sheet, 3c.; theatrical teamster, Boardman Ruse.

Union Hall; seating capacity, 600.

KALKASKA, 1,100. R. R., Grand Rapids & Ind. Irving Hall, A. H. Bleazby, manager; seating capacity, 200; rental, one night $7, three $15; share also. Size of stage, 14x23. Newspapers: Kalkaskian (Fri.), Leader (Th.)......Hotels: Exchange, Manning, Kiddle.

Town Hall; no scenery.

LANSING, 10,000. R. R., Chic. & Grand Trunk; Jackson, Lansing & Saginaw; Detroit, Lansing & Northern; Lake Shore & Michigan Southern. Buck's Opera House, Mayton, manager; seating capacity, 1,000; rental, one night $50, three $130, license included. Size of stage, 30x48; size of proscenium opening, 27x27½; height from stage to grooves, 16; height from stage to rigging loft, 20½; depth under stage, 8; traps, 1; number sets scenery, 21; leader of orchestra, Jas. Richmond; stage carpenter, Jas. Emerson; bill poster, V. W. Tooker; number of sheets can accommodate, 275; rates per sheet, 3c.; theatrical teamsters, Porter & Goodrich. Newspapers: daily, Telegram, advertising rates, yearly contract; News, yearly contract; tri-weekly. Republican (Tu., Th. and Sat), yearly contract; Journal (Fri.), yearly contract; Sunday Siftings (Sat.), yearly contract......Hotels: Lansing, special rates, $1.50 to $2; Hudson, $1.50; Commercial, $1.

Mead's Hall, J. I. Mead, manager; seating capacity, 800; rental, one night $10, three $18; license, $5. Size of stage, 17x44; number sets scenery, 9.

Hart's Hall, A. N. Hart, manager; seating capacity, 450.

LAPEER, 4,300. R. R., Chic. & Grand Trunk; Michigan Central. White's Opera Hall, J. Havener, manager; seating capacity, 600; rental, one night $15; fair stock scenery. Newspapers: Clarion, (Th.), Democrat. (Wed.)........Hotels: Abrams', regular rates, $2 (special also); Park, Marshall, American, Donaldson. Mannering Hall.

LESLIE, 2,600. R. R., Mich. Central. Union Hall, A. Young Leslie, manager ; seating capacity, 500; rental, one night $3 to $6; license, $3 to $10; number sets scenery, 7. Newspaper: Local (Fri.)......Hotel; Allen, regular rates, $2 (special also).

LOWELL, 2,000. R. R., Detroit & Grand Haven. Music Hall, Chandler Johnson, manager; seating capacity, 600; rental, one night $4 to $10, three $15 ; share also ; license, $1 size of stage, 16x43; size of proscenium opening, 13x20; depth under stage, 4 ; traps, 1; number sets scenery, 6; bill poster, Frank Eddy : rates per sheet, 4c.; theatrical teamster, Edgar Morse. Newspaper: Journal (Wed.), special contract .....Hotels : Davis, special rates, $1; Commercial, special rates, $1; Travis, special rates, $1.

Train's Hall, **J. C. Train,** manager; seating capacity, 550; **rental,** one night $6, three $12; license, $1 to $2. Size of stage, 16x22; fair stock scenery.

LUDINGTON, 3,200. R. R., Flint & Pere Marquette. Opera House, Cooper & Wells, managers; seating capacity, 600; **rental, one night, $12,** three $25; license, $5. Size of stage 22x32; number sets scenery, **5; bill** poster, **Opera** House. Newspapers: Appeal (Th.), Democrat (Sat.), Record (Th.)......Hotels: **Elliot',** regular rates, $2 (special also); Marshall, Clinton.

MACKINAC ISLAND, 800. R. R., Mich. Central; Grand Rapids & Indiana. Fenton's Hall, C. B. Fenton, manager; seating capacity, 300; rental, one night $10, three $25; license, $2. Size of stage, 16x26; size of proscenium opening 10x10; depth under stage, 3; number sets scenery, 4; leader of orchestra, A. Perault; theatrical teamster, Thomas Chambers. ......Hotels: Astor, special rates $1.50; Mackinac, special rates, $1.50.

Truscott's Opera House, George Truscott, manager; seating capacity, 300; rental, one night $12; license, $1.50. Size of stage, 14x24.

MACKINAW, 1,120. R. R., Grand Rapids & Ind.; Michigan Central. Fenton Hall; rental, **one night $15,** three $35: license, $3. Size of stage, 16x26......Hotels: Astor, St. Cloud. **Mission.**

MANCHESTER, 2,600. R. R., Lake Shore & Mich South. Goodyears' Hall, Goodrich Conklin, manager; seating capacity, 800; rental, one night $10, three $22; license, $1 to $2. Size of stage, 20x85; full stock scenery; bill poster, Joe Goodyear. Newspaper : Enterprise (Th.).....Hotel: Goodyear, regular rates, $2 (special also).

MANISTEE, 12,000. R. R., Flint & Pere Marquette. Scandinavian Hall, P. J. Miller, manager; seating capacity, 850; **rental,** one night $20, three $30; share also; license, $3. Size of stage, 24x50; size of proscenium opening, 16x22; **height from stage to** grooves, 12; height from stage to rigging roft, 24; depth under stage, 8; traps, 1; number sets scenery, 8; leader of orchestra, Charles Gerloch; bill poster, E M. Washburne; number of sheets can accommodate, 450; rates per sheet, 3c.; theatrical **teamster,** Henry Rademaker. Newspapers: Times (Th.), Democrat (Tu.), Advocate (Sat), **Standard** (Sat): advertising rates $1 per ¼ column......Hotels: Dunham, Metropolitan, Exchange, regular rates, $2 (special also).

Temperance Hall, C. D. Gardiner, manager; seating capacity, 600; rental, one night $15, three $37.50; license, $4. **Size of** stage, 20x30; number sets scenery, 12.

MARQUETTE, 7,000. R. R., Detroit, Mackinaw & Marquette; Marquette, Houghton & Ontonagon. Red Ribbon Hall, W. A. Burt, manager; seating capacity, 300; rental, one night $10 to $12, three $40; license, $5. Size of stage, 14x24; number sets scenery, 4; bill posters, West & Co. Newspaper: Morning Journal (Sat.).... Hotels: North Western, regular rates, $2 (special also); Cozzen.

Coles Hall, W. A. Burt, manager; seating capacity, 350; rental, one night $10. Size of stage, 16x20; number sets scenery, 3.

Opera House, P. M. Everett, manager.

Mather's Hall; seating capacity, 600.

MARSHALL, 5,000. R. R., Michigan Central; Michigan & Ohio. Eagle Opera House, Thomas Mearns, manager; seating capacity, 1,000; rental, one night $2, three $4, license, $3. Size of stage, 25x35; full set scenery; bill poster, John H. Beau. Newspapers: daily, Chronicle; weekly, Expounder (Th.); Statesman (Fri.).... Hotels: Tremont, regular rates, $2 (special also), Toutine, Ford's.

Academy of Music; seating capacity, 500.

Wagner Hall; seating capacity, 400.

MASON, 2,000. R. R., Mich Central; J. L & Saginaw Branch. Rayner Opera House, Chas. J. Rayner, manager; seating capacity, 850; rental, one night $25; share also; license, $1.25 to $5. Size of stage, 30x44; depth under stage, 8; number sets scenery, 18; leader of orchestra, F. Fragel; stage carpenter, E. Rob; bill poster, C. J. Rayner; theatrical teamster, S. H. Worden. Newspapers: News (Th.), Democrat (Th.)...... Hotel: Donnelly, special rates, $1.50.

MAYFIELD, 1,500. R. R., Grand Rapids & Ind. School Hall, H. Stevens, manager; seating capacity, 500.

MENOMINEE, 2,100. R. R., Chic. & N. Western; Milwaukee & Northern. Forvilly Hall, seating capacity, 1,000; rental, one night $10, three $25. Size of stage, 18x25; number sets scenery, 9; bill poster, W. J. Hall. Newspaper: Herald (Th.) ....Hotel: Kirby, regular rates, $2 (special also).

Centennial Hall, S. M. Stevenson, manager; seating capacity, 250; rental, one night $10; license, $4. Size of stage, 12x14; number sets scenery, 4.

MIDDLEVILLE, 1,100. R. R., Mich. Central. Red Ribbon Hall, E. D. Sprague, manager; seating capacity, 500. Newspaper: Republican (Th.)......Hotels: Johnson, Dibble, Millville.

Leonard's Hall, P. Leonard, manager; seating capacity, 500.

MIDLAND, 2,500. Flint & Pere Marquette. Opera House, Clay & Buckley, managers (East Saginaw). Newspapers: Republican (Th.), Sun (Th.)......Hotels: Sherwood, regular rates $2 (special also); St. James, Exchange.

MILFORD, 1,800. R. R., Flint & Pere Marquette. Ferguson's Opera House, J. J. Buford, manager; seating capacity, 500; rental, one night $7, three $18; license, $1.50. Size of stage, 20x34; height from stage to grooves, 13; height from stage to rigging loft, 10; depth under stage, 3; traps, 1; number sets scenery, 5; bill poster, W. J. Buford. Newspapers: Times (Fri.), Review (Th.)......Hotels: Central, special rates, $1.50; Milford, special rates, $1.50.

MONROE, 1,000. R. R., Michigan Central; Lake Shore & Michigan Southern. Opera Hall, J. K. Wilder, manager; seating capacity, 500; rental, one night $25, three $50, license, included. Size of stage, 45x14; number sets scenery, 4. Newspapers: Commercial (Fri.), Democrat (Th.), Index (Wed.)......Hotels: Park, regular rates, $2 (special also); Stoug's, regular rates, $2 (special also).

City Hall, George W. Bowlsly, manager; seating capacity, 450; rental, one night $15, three $35; share also; license included. Size of stage, 18x30; fair stock scenery.

Kremer's Hall; seating capacity, 600.

Beauban; seating capacity, 600.

MONTAGUE, 5,200. R. R., Chic. & West. Mich. Opera House, Burrows & Jones, managers; seating capacity, 750; rental, one night $25, three $50; share also. Size of stage, 27x30; number sets scenery, 8; bill poster, Opera House. Newspaper: Lumberman (Sat.). ....Hotels: Franklin, regular rates, $2 (special also); Montague.

MOUNT PLEASANT, 2,500. R. R., Flint & Pere Marquette; Toledo, Ann Arbor & Northern. Mount Pleasant Opera House, D. Scott Partridge, manager; seating capacity, 500; rental, one night $15, three $40, license included; share also. Size of stage, 40x40; size of proscenium opening, 28x30; height from stage to grooves, 20; height from stage to rigging loft, 40; traps, 1; number sets scenery, 12; leader of orchestra, D. Woodworth; scenic artist, A. Walthen & Son; stage carpenter, W. R. Humphrey; bill poster, Charles D. Smith; number of sheets can accommodate, 500; rates per sheet, &c.; theatrical teamster, Wm. Woodbury. Newspaper: Enterprise (Wed.), advertising rates, 10c. per line. ......Hotel: Bennett, special rates, $1 to $1.25.

MUSKEGON, 20,000. R. R., Chicago & West Michigan. Opera House, Fred. N. Reynolds, manager; Brooks & Dickson, New York representatives; seating capacity, 1,000; rental, one night $60, three $150, license included. Size of stage, 38x64; size of proscenium opening, 30x32; height from stage to grooves, 16; height from stage to rigging loft, 16; depth under stage, 5; traps, 2; number sets scenery, 14 ; leader of orchestra, E. Aubrie; stage carpenter, Gilbert Forbes; bill posters, Reynolds & Leonard; number of sheets can accommodate, 400; rates per sheet, 3c.; theatrical teamster, L. B. Morse. Newspapers: daily, Chronicle, advertising rates, $5 for ¼ col.; News, $5 for ¼ col.; Journal, $5 for ¼ col......Hotels: Occidental, special rates, $1.50 to $2; Arlington, special rates, $1.25 to $1.50; American, special rates, $1.

Rifenberg Hall, Joseph Ireland, manager; seating capacity, 450; rental, one night $15, three $30; license, $3. Size of stage, 16x20; number sets scenery, 7.

Mason Hall; seating capacity, 650; fair stock scenery.

NASHVILLE, 1,600. R. R., Mich. Central. Opera House, E. Chipman, manager; seating capacity, 500; bill poster, Opera House. Newspaper: News (Sat.)......Hotels: Wolcott, Nashville.

NEGAUNEE, 4,500. R. R., Chicago & N. W.; Marquette & Western; M. H. & O. McDonald's Opera Hall, D. McDonald, manager; seating capacity, 400; rental, one night $15, three $35; license, $5. Size of stage, 18x42; size of proscenium opening, 18x22, height from stage to rigging loft, 13; depth under stage, 3½; number sets scenery, 5; leader of orchestra, John Stecker; stage carpenter, L. Gilmet; bill poster, C. S. Barnes; theatrical teamster, Suass. Newspapers: daily, Marquette Journal, weekly, Herald (Th.) ......Hotel: Breitung, regular rates, $2 (special also).

Winter's Opera House, Wheelock & Winters, managers; seating capacity, 490; rental, one night $20, three $45. Size of stage, 18x20; number sets scenery, 5.

NILES, 6,000. R. R., Wabash & Michigan Central. Peak Hall, Brown & Marston, managers; seating capacity, 800; rental, one night $30, three $50; license, $2; share also. Size of stage, 16x20; number sets scenery, 5; bill posters, Brown & Marston. Newspapers: Democrat (Sat.), Mirror (Wed.), Republican (Th.)......Hotels: Pike's, regular rates, $2 (special also); Clifton, Reading, Bond.

Kellog's Hall; seating capacity, 700

NORWAY, 3,200. R. R. Chic. & N. Western. O'Callaghan's Opera House; seating capacity, 450; fair stock scenery. Newspaper: Chronicle (Sat.)......Hotel: Caldwell.

OTSEGO, 1,600. R. R., Lake Shore & Mich. So. Edsell's Opera House, Edsell & Travis, managers; seating capacity, 600; rental, one night $10, three $20; license, $1; share also. Size of stage, 20x50; number sets scenery, 5; bill poster, Geo. H. Woodward. Newspaper: Union (Fri.)......Hotels: Exchange, regular rates, $2 (special also); Commercial, Lutkin.

OVID, 1,550. R. R., Detroit, Grand Haven & Milwaukee. Marvin's Opera House; seating capacity, 650. Newspapers: Union (Fri.), Register (Fri.)......Hotel: Retan, regular rates, $2 (special also).

New Opera House.

OWOSSO, 3,200. R. R., Detroit, Grand Haven & Mil.; Mich. Central. Salisbury's Hall; seating capacity, 550; rental, one night $15; license, $1 and tickets. Size of stage, 12x15; fair stock scenery; bill poster, Chas. Chipman. Newspapers: News (Sat.), Press (Wed.), Times (Fri.)......Hotels: National, regular rates $2 (special also); Exchange.

Gould's Hall; seating capacity, 500; rental, one night $10; license, tickets; fair stock scenery.

OXFORD, 1,370. R. R., Mich. Central ; Pontiac, Oxford & Port Austin. Oakland Hall. John Ryman, manager ; seating capacity, 400 ; bill poster, J. W. Cannon. Newspaper : Globe (Sat.)......Hotels : Stanton, regular rates, $2 (special also) ; Commercial.

PARMA, 1,100. R R , Michigan Central. Aldrich Hal , O. Gillett; seating capacity, 500. ......Hotel : Cooley.

PAW PAW, 1,800. R R., Paw Paw. Opera House, G. W. Longwell, manager ; seating capacity, 400. Newspapers: Free Press and Courier (Wed.), Herald (Fri), True Northerner (Th.)........Hotels : Dyckman, regular rates, $2 (special also); Clifton.

Town Hall ; seating capacity. 300.

PONTIAC, 5,600. R R , Pontiac & Port Austin ; Detroit, G. H. & Milwaukee ; Michigan Air Line Div. of Grand Trunk. Clinton Hall, C. B. Pittman, manager; seating capacity, 700; rental, one night $20, three $50 ; license, $2. Size of stage, 45x40 ; size of proscenium opening, 18x32 ; height from stage to grooves, 16 ; height from stage to rigging loft, 28 ; depth under stage, 5; traps, 1; number sets scenery, 10 : scenic artist, Dell Douglas; bill poster, W. C. Ellwood ; number of sheets can accommodate, 500 ; rates per sheet, 4c.; theatrical teamster, N. E. Deunell. Newspapers: Gazette (Fri.). Bill Poster (Wed.) ......Hotels : Hodge's, special rates, $1 ; Northern, special rates, $1 ; Waverly, special rates, $1.

Washington Hall ; seating capacity, 500 ; rental, one night $8, three $15. Size of stage, 24x30 ; number sets scenery, 5.

PORT HURON, 13,000. R. R., Grand Trunk; Port Huron & Northwestern. City Opera House. Clay & Buckley, managers; seating capacity, 1,000; rental, one night $40, three $90; license, yearly; share also. Size of stage, 32x30 ; size of proscenium opening, 30x32; height from stage to grooves, 16; height from stage to rigging loft, 40; depth under stage, 8; traps, 3; number sets scenery full set; leader of orchestra, A. Wood; scenic artist, Walthen; stage carpenter, Berry; bill poster, Clay & Buckley; number of sheets can accommodate, 2,000; theatrical teamster, Geering. Newspapers: daily, Times, Telegram; weekly, Commercial (Sun.), Tribune (Sun.)........Hotel: Huron, special rates, $1.75 to $2; Whiting, special rates, $1.75 to $2.

Harder's Opera House; seating capacity, 500

Harrington's Opera House; seating capacity, 800.

PORTLAND, 2,700. R R , Detroit, Lansing & Northern. Portland Opera House, G. W. Porter, manager; seating capacity, 600; rental, one night $16, three $40; share also; license included. Size of stage, 20x22, number sets scenery, 20; bill poster, George W. Seymour; Newspapers : Courier (Fri.), Observer (Wed.)........Hotels: Welsh, regular rates, $2 (special also); National.

QUINESEC, 3,100. R R , Chic. & Northwestern. Buel Opera House; seating capacity. 500; full set scenery......Hotel : Quinesec.

REED CITY, 3,000. R. R., Flint & Pere Marquette; Grand Rapids & Indiana. Higbe's Opera House, W. A. Higbe, manager; seating capacity, 600; rental, share only; license yearly. Size of stage, 22x43; size of proscenium opening, width, 22; height from stage to grooves, 12; number sets scenery, 12; leader of orchestra, Q. C. Hoyt ; bill poster, W. A. Higbe; number of sheets can accommodate, 90; rates per sheet, 3½c ; theatrical teamster, James Welsh. Newspapers: Clarion (Th.), News (Sat.), People (Sat.)...... Hotels: Oaks, special rates, $1.25 ; National, special rates, $1 25.

ROCHESTER, 1,300. R. R., Grand Trunk; Mich. Cent. Town Hall, T. Dahlman, manager; seating capacity, 200. Newspapers: Era (Th.), Sun (Th.)......Lambertson, regular rates, $2 (special also).

Newburg Hall; James Newburg, manager; seating capacity, 200.

SAGINAW, 17,000. R. R., Mich. Cent ; Detroit & Bay City; F. & P. M.; Sag. Valley & St. Louis. Teutonic Opera House, President of the Teutonic Opera House Co., manager; seating capacity, 1,000; rental, one night $25, three $60; license included; share also. Size of stage, 31x48; size of proscenium opening, 22x24 ; height from stage to grooves, 14½; height from stage to rigging loft, 30; depth under stage, 9; traps, 1; number sets scenery, 14; leader of orchestra, Prof. Julius Reiss; scenic artist and stage carpenter, Alb. Fuchs;

bill poster, Edward Laidley; number sheets can accommodate, 5,600; rates per sheet 3c. to 4c.; theatrical teamster, Jerry Martin. Newspapers: daily, Times, advertising rates per inch, 40c.; Sentinel, advertising rates per inch, 40c.; weekly, Valley News (Tu.), advertising rates, special contract; Saginawian (Tu.)......Hotels: Bauman, special rates, $1.25; Kirby, special rates, $1; Crowley, special rates, $1.

Temperance Hall, E. St. John, manager; seating capacity, 600; rental, one night $18, three $40; share also, license included. Size of stage, 33x11; number sets scenery, 16.

Eola Hall; seating cacapacity, 800.

ST. CHARLES, 1,000. R. R., Michigan Central. Knights of Honor Hall, W. W. Eddy, manager; seating capacity, 500. Newspaper: Independent (Th.). ....Hotels: Symes, St. Charles, Union.

ST. CLAIR, 3,000. R. R., Michigan Central. Town Hall. Newspaper: Republican (Th. ......Hotels: St. James, regular rates, $2 (special also); Oakland.

ST. IGNACE, 3,500. R. R., Detroit, Mackinaw & Marquette; Michigan Central; Grand Rapids & Indiana. Music Hall, William J. Brown; seating capacity, 600; rental, one night $10, three $20; license, $3. Size of stage, 22x20. Newspapers : semi-weekly, News (Tu. and Fri.); weekly, Free Press (Sat.)......Hotels : Bay View, special rates, $1.50; Everett, special rates, $1.50; Globe, special rates, $1.

ST. JOE, 3,800. R. R., Chicago & West Mich. Martin's Academy of Music, J. F. Martin, manager; seating capacity, 700; rental, share only; license included. Size of stage, 25x 25; size of proscenium opening, 24x25 ; depth under stage, 5; traps, 2 ; number sets scenery, 10; leader of orchestra, B. Frank Green; bill poster, O. D. Jacobs ; theatrical teamster, Geo. Reily. Newspapers: Republican (Sat.), advertising rates, 5c. per line; Traveler (Sat.)...... Hotels: Lake View, special rates, $1; Park, special rates, $2; Clifton, special rates, $1.

ST. JOHNS, 2,600. R. R., Detroit, Grand Haven & Milwaukee. Brown's Opera Hall, D. R. Brown, manager ; seating capacity, 730; rental, one night $10, three $25; share also. Size of stage, 20x35; number sets scenery, 8. Newspapers: Independent (Th.), Republican (Th.)......Hotels: Perrin, regular rates, $2, special also; St. Johns, Gibbs, Walker Street.

ST. LOUIS, 3,100. R. R., Chicago, Saginaw & Canada; Saginaw Valley & St. Louis. Martin's Opera House, H. M. Martin, manager; seating capacity, 700; rental, one night $15, three $30; license, $2; share also. Size of stage, 24x40; fair stock scenery. Newspapers: Democrat, (Th.), Herald (Fri.), Leader (Wed.)......Hotels: Commercial, regular rates, $2 (special also); Harrington, Wessel.

Holcomb Opera House, F. C. Seymour, manager; seating capacity, 900; share only. Size of stage, 30x66; bill poster, Opera House.

SOUTH HAVEN, 2,700. R. R., Michigan Central. Leighton's Opera Hall, L. A. Leighton, manager; seating capacity, 500; rental, one night $8, three $20; share also; license included. Size of stage, 35x36; full set scenery; hill poster, Joseph Lynn. Newspapers: Messenger (Fri.), Sentinel (Sat.).. ....Hotels: Pacific, regular rates, $2 (special also); Dyckman.

STANTON, 2,500. R. R., Detroit, Lansing & Northern. Turner's Opera House, Albrecht & Andrews, managers; seating capacity, 450; rental, or share; license, yearly. Size of stage, 18x44; number sets scenery, 7; hill poster, John Hartman. Newspapers: Clipper (Fri.), Herald (Sat.)......Hotels: Bailey, Stanton.

STURGIS, 3,000. R. R., Grand Rapids & Indiana; Lake Shore & Michigan Southern. Union Hall, F. W. Watt, manager; seating capacity, 500; rental, one night $10, three $21; license, $2; share also. Size of stage, 15x10; number sets scenery, 4; hill poster, Geo. W. Pearsall. Newspapers : Journal (Th.), Democrat (Wed.)...... Hotel : Elliott, regular rates, $2 (special also).

TECUMSEH, 2,500. R. R., Michigan & Ohio; Lake Shore & Michigan Southern. Opera House, Will Sutton, manager; seating capacity, 900; rental, one night $20, three $50. Size of stage, 30x50; size of proscenium opening, 25x25; height from stage to rigging loft, 15; depth under stage, 8; number sets scenery, 15; scenic artist, S. Wheeler; stage

carpenter, **Wm.** Jordan; bill poster, Wm. Jordan; rates per sheet, 3c; theatrical teamster, Chapman. Newspaper: Herald (Th.)......Hotel: Lilly, regular rates, $2 (special
also).

TEKONSHA, 1,100. R. R., Michigan Central. Opera House; seating capacity, 1,000;
rental, one night $25. Size of stage, 25x30; fair stock **scenery; bill** poster, Wm. Jordan.
Newspapers: News (Sat.) ....**Hotels: Air** Line, regular **rates,** $1.50 (special also);
Merchants'.

Batt's Hall, L. D. Batt, manager; seating capacity, 300; rental, one night $3 to $5, three
$8; license, $1 to $5. Size of stage, 20x24; no scenery.

THREE RIVERS, 3,200. R. R., Mich. Central; Lake Shore & Mich. Southern. Kelsey's
Hall; seating capacity, 500; rental, one night $10; license, $1 to $3. Size of stage, 16x20;
no scenery. Newspapers: Herald (Fri.), Reporter (Sat.), Tribune (Fri.)......Hotels:
Three Rivers, regular rates, $2 (special also); Central, Hatch.

TRAVERSE CITY, 2,500. R. R., Grand Rapids & Indiana. Library **Hall, T. W. Brown,**
manager; seating capacity, 500; rental, one night $10; license, $2; **Size of**
stage, 15x30; no scenery. Newspapers: Herald (Th.), Eagle (Fri.) .....Hotels: **Park,**
regular rates, $2 (special also); Front Street, Bandman, Occidental, Bay.

UNION CITY, 2,100. R. R., Michigan Central. Union City Opera House, J. H. Guilford,
manager; seating capacity, 600; share only; license, yearly. Size of stage,
36x30; number sets scenery, 15; **bill** poster, Opera House. Newspapers: semi-weekly,
Herald; weekly, Register (Sat.)......Hotels: Paddock, special rates, $1.25; Commercial,
special rates, $1; Union City, **regular** rates, $2 (special also).

VASSAR, 2,000. **R. R., Mich. Central; Port Huron & North Western.** Miller's Opera
House. H. A. Miller, manager; seating capacity, 800; rental, one night $15, three $30;
license, $2; **share also.** Size of stage, 16x24; number sets scenery, 6; bill poster, George
H. Maxwell. **Newspapers: Times (Th.), Pioneer (Th.)......Hotels:** Jewell, regular rates
$2 (special also); **Central, American.**

WHITEHALL, 5,600. R. R., Chicago & West Michigan. **Ruggles'** Opera House, E. M.
Ruggles, manager; seating capacity, 800; rental, one night $30; three $75; share also;
size of stage, 30x52; bill poster, L. C. Brown. Newspaper: Forum (Th). . .Hotels:
Mears', regular rates, $2 (special also); European.

YPSILANTI, 6,000. R. R., Lake Shore & Mich. Southern; Michigan Central. Ypsilanti
Opera House, H. M. Curtis, manager; seating capacity, 900; rental one night $50; share
also; license included. Size of stage, 32x48; full set scenery; bill poster, Opera House.
Newspapers: Commercial (Sat.), Sentinel (Wed.), Ypsilantian (Fri.)... ...**Hotels: European,** Hawkins, Lewis, Barton.

Lightguard Hall, S. J. Vail, manager; seating capacity, 600; rental, one night $15, three $35.
Size of stage, 22x28; full set scenery

Hewitt; seating capacity, 500.

Seminary; seating capacity, 300.

MINNESOTA.

ALBERT LEA, 2,000. R. R., Bur., Cedar Rapids & Northern ; Chicago, Milwaukee & **St.
Paul ; Minneapolis** & St. Louis. Hall Opera House, Anson Peck, manager ; bill
poster, **Heman Blackman.** Newspapers: Enterprise (Fri.), **Standard** (Tu.), Poster (Fri.)
......**Hotels :** Hall, Lake, Webber.

Court House Hall, T. J. Sheehan, manager ; seating capacity, **450** ; rental, one night $10,
three $30; license, $3 to **$10.** Size of stage, 12x24; no scenery.

ALEXANDRIA, 2,000. R. R., St. Paul, Minneapolis & Manitoba. Cowing's Opera House.
T. F. Cowing, manager ; seating capacity, 500 ; rental, one night $15, three $30; license
included. Size of stage, 36x28 ; size of proscenium, 12x17 ; height from stage to rigging
loft, 16 ; depth under stage, 3½ ; traps, 2 ; number sets scenery, 3 ; bill poster, Thos.

Costillo ; theatrical teamster, Frank Kent. Newspapers: Post (Fri.), advertising rates, 5c. per line ; News (Th), advertising rates, 5c. per line.......Hotel: Letson's, special rates, $2.

ANOKA, 5,000. R. R., St. Paul, Minneapolis & Manitoba. Washburne Opera House. Newspapers: Union (Th.), Herald (Fri.)......Hotel : Merchants'.

AUSTIN, 2,400. R. R., Chic., Mil. & St. Paul. Jones & Walsh's Hall, John Walsh, manager; seating capacity, 700; rental, one night $20; license, $2 50; no scenery; bill poster, Wm. Witham. Newspapers: Transcript (Wed), Register (Th.)......Hotels: Railway, Flick, Mansfield.

BIRD ISLAND, 850. R. R , Chic., Mil & St. Paul. Exhibition Hall, M. Donohue, manager ; seating capacity, 500. Newspaper : Union (Th.)

BRAINERD, 12,000. R. R. Northern Pacific. Sleeper Opera House, C. B. Sleeper, manager; seating capacity, 750; rental, one night $50, three $120. Size of stage, 30x45; height from stage to grooves, 14; height from stage to rigging loft, 25; depth under stage, 10; traps; 2; number sets scenery, 15; leader of orchestra, Prof. W. M Dresskell; bill poster, J. A. Bixby. Newspapers: Tribune (Sat), Dispatch (Fri.) Journal (Wed.)....... Hotels : Villard, special rates, $2; Commercial, special rates, $1.50.

CALEDONIA, 1,100 R. R., Chic., Mil. & St. Paul. Court House, Walter Goergen, manager; seating capacity, 350. Newspapers: Argus (Th.), Journal (Wed)......Hotel: Barnes.

CARVER 1,250. R. R , Chic., Mil. & St. Paul; Minneapolis & St. Louis. Turn Hall, C. A. Blomquist, manager ; seating capacity, 100. Newspapers : Free Press (Th.)........ Hotel: Planters'.

CHASKA, 1,550. R. R., Chic., Mil. & St. Paul; Minneapolis & St. Louis. Concordia Hall, Peter Iltis, manager; seating capacity, 500. Newspapers: Herald (Th.). ....Hotel: Merchants'.

CHATFIELD, 1,500. Chic. & Northwestern. Lovell's Hall, R. B. Lovell, manager; seating capacity, 350; rental, one night $3, one week $12. Size of stage, 14x25; size of proscenium opening, 10x14; height from stage to grooves, 10; depth under stage, 2½; number sets scenery, 1; leader of orchestra, H. D. Jones; theatrical teamster, J. D. Jones. Newspaper: Democrat (Sat.) ....Hotel : Medary, special rates, $1; Eureka, special rates, 50c.

CROOKSTON, 5,000. R. R., St. Paul, Minn. & Manitoba. Erresson's Hall, M. Erresson, manager; seating capacity, 450; rental, one night $15; license, $5. Size of stage 16x18; number sets scenery, 2. Newspapers; Chronicle (Tu), Journal (Th.)......Hotels: Linton, regular rates, $2 (special also); Commercial.

DETROIT, 600. R. R., Northern Pacific. Opera House, Carson & Peters, managers; seating capacity, 450; no license; fair stock scenery. Newspaper: Record (Sat.)......Hotel: Lakeside.

DULUTH, 18,000. R. R , St. Paul & Duluth; Northern Pacific; C., St. P.: M. & O. Grand Opera House, Munger & Markell, managers; seating capacity, 1,600 (actual count); rental, one night $60; share also; license included. Size of stage, 35x52; size of proscenium opening, height, 32; height from stage to grooves, 16; height from stage to rigging loft, 32; depth under stage, 4; traps, 2; number sets scenery, full set; scenic artist, W. Van Wart Davids; stage carpenter, Harry G. Carter; bill poster, Opera House; number of sheets can accommodate, 4 stands; 5c. sheet; theatrical teamsters, O'Brien & Knowlton. Newspapers: daily Tribune, advertising rates, yearly contract; Herald, advertising rates, yearly contract; weekly, News (Th.) .....Hotels: St. Louis, Bay View, Merchants', Clark.

Opera House; seating capacity, 750.

Dramatic Temple; seating capacity, 850.

Turner's Hall; seating capacity, 300.

FAIRVOUNT, 1,100. R R., Chic., Mil. & St. Paul. Albion Hall, P. Wallaston, manager; seating capacity, 300. Newspaper. Sentinel (Fri.......Hotel: Occidental, regular rates, $2 (special also).

FARIBAULT, 7,100. R. R., Chic., Mil. & St. Paul. Hill's Opera House, A. L. Hill, manager; seating capacity, 600; rental, one night $15, three $49; license, $5. Size of stage, 20x30; number sets scenery, 12; bill poster, A. B. Shipley Newspapers: Democrat (Fri.); Republican (Wed.)......Hotels: Brunswick, regular rates, $2.50; Arlington, regular rates, $2; Barron.

Kyllo's Hall; seating capacity, 600.

FARMINGTON, 1,100. R. R., Chic., Mil. & St. Paul. Music Hall, C. M. Pittman, manager; seating capacity, 400; fair stock scenery. Newspaper: Journal (Th.) .....Hotel Wiskern.

FERGUS FALLS, 7,000. R. R., Northern Pacific; St. Paul, Minneapolis & Manitoba. Sundhal's Opera House, J. F. Johnson, manager; seating capacity, 600; rental, one night $15, three $35; license, $5; share also. Size of stage, 20x20; number sets of scenery, 4; bill poster, Weatherstone. Newspapers: daily, Journal, Telegram, Sunday Morning. ......Hotels: Occidental, regular rates, $2; Bell's.

Theatre Comique; seating capacity, 350.

GLENCOE, 2,100. R. R.,Chic., Mil. & St. Paul. Court House Hall, C. B. Lincoln, manager; seating capacity, 350. Newspapers: Enterprise (Wed.), Register (Th.)......Hotels: Merchants', regular rates, $2.

HASTINGS, 4,000. R. R , Chic., Mil. & St. Paul. Music Hall, J. B. Lambert, manager; seating capacity, 500; share only. Size of stage, 20x30; number sets scenery, 5; bill poster, Geo. B. Hespeth. Newspapers: daily, News; weekly, Gazette (Sat.), New Era (Tu.), Union (Fri.) .....Hotels: Foster, regular rates, $2; Tremont, St. Joe.

Teutonic Hall; seating capacity, 600.

HOKAH, 1,250. R. R., Chic., Mil. & St Paul. Town Hall, W. H. Webber, manager; seating capacity, 500. Newspaper: Chief (Th.).... ..Hotel: Union, regular rates, $2.

HOUSTON, 530. R. R., Chic. Mil. & St. Paul. Town Hall, Fields & Briggs, managers; seating capacity, 390. Newspaper: Signal (Th.)......Hotel: Cottrell.

KASSON, 2,000. R. R., Chic & North Western. Coolidge Hall, Lyman Gerould, manager; seating capacity, 500; rental, one night $10 to $12, three $15 to $20; license, $1.50 to $2.50. Size of stage, 16x42; number sets scenery, 7; bill poster, Allen Sharer. Newspapers: Republican (Th.), Vindicator (Tu.)......Hotels: Walker's, regular rates, $2.00; American, Hanley.

LAKE CITY, 3,000. R. R., Chicago, Milwaukee & St. Paul. Academy of Music, R. Hanische, manager; seating capacity, 500; rental, one night $18, license included. Size of stage, 20x48; number sets scenery, 5; bill poster, John Danelsen. Newspapers: Graphic (Th.), Sentinel (Sat.). .Hotel: Merchants', regular rates, $2.

LANESBORO, 1,400. R. R., Chicago, Milwaukee & St. Paul. Kevin's Hall, E. Kevin, manager; seating capacity, 250; rental, one night $8; license, $2 to $5. Size of stage, 12x25; no scenery. Newspaper: Journal (Fri.)......Hotel: Lanesboro, regular rates, $2.

LITCHFIELD, 1,850. R. R., St. Paul, Minneapolis & Manitoba. Town Hall. Newspapers: Independent (Tu), News-Ledger (Th.)......Hotel: Howard, regular rates, $2.

MANKATO, 7,000. R. R., Chicago & North Western; Chicago, Milwaukee & St. Paul; Chicago, St. Paul, Minn.; Omaha. Union Hall, H. Himmelman, manager; seating capacity, 525; rental, one night $20, three $40. Size of stage, 20x42; number sets scenery, 3; bill poster, George Zenipolski. Newspapers: Free Press (Fri.), Public Spirit (Th.), Review (Tu.)......Hotels: Clifton, regular rates, $2.50; Merchants', regular rates, $2; Mankato, City.

MINNEAPOLIS, 100,000. R. R., Chicago, Milwaukee & St. Paul; Minn. & St. Louis; Minn., L'y & Mian.; St. Paul, Minn. & Man. Grand Opera House, J. Conklin, manager; seating capacity, 1,400; share only. Size of stage, 50x34; height from stage to grooves, 20; height from stage to rigging loft, 63; depth under stage, 12; full stock scenery; bill poster, M. Breslauer; number sheets can accommodate, 5,000; rates per sheet, 3c.; theatrical teamster, Matterson. Newspapers: daily, Gazette, advertising rates, per inch.

$1; Journal, advertising rates per inch, $1.50; weekly, Gazette (Sun.), advertising rates per inch, $1.25......Hotels: Nicolett, special rates, $4; St. James, special rates, $1.25 to $1.50; Clark, special rates, $1.50 to **$1.75**.

Brown's Theatre Comique, W. W. Brown, manager; seating capacity, 800; rental, one night 40 per cent., three 35 per cent., license included. Size of stage, 18x20; size of proscenium opening, 22x20; height from stage to grooves, 15; height from stage to rigging loft, 22; depth under stage, 4; number sets scenery, 10; leader of orchestra, Prof. Frank Powel; scenic artist, Pete Clansen; stage carpenter, James Smith; bill poster. M. Breslauer; number sheets can accommodate, 5,000; rates per sheet, 3c.; theatrical teamster, Theatre Comique.

Peace Opera House, George Wood, manager; seating capacity, 1,000; full set scenery.

Academy of Music; seating capacity, 1,400.

MONTEVIDEO, 1,800. R. R., Hastings Div. of C. M. & St. Paul. Court House Hall, Jas. M. Severens, manager; seating capacity, 300; rental, one night $6, three $18; license, $2. Size of stage, 18x40. Newspaper, Leader (Fri.)......Hotels: Excelsior, Dunn, Montevideo, special rates, $1.50.

Anderson Hall, Henry Anderson, manager; seating capacity, 500.

MOORHEAD, 4,000. R. R., Northern Pacific; St. Paul, M. & M. Bunn's Opera House, Walsh Partridge, manager; seating capacity, 500; rental, one night $25, three $60; share also; license, yearly. Size of stage, 21x19; size of proscenium opening, 10x21½; height from stage to grooves, 12; depth under stage, 8; traps, 3; number sets scenery, 8; leader of orchestra, Carl Fetzer; scenic artist, Chas. D. Fox; stage carpenter, R. R. Bixby; bill poster, Moorhead Bill-Posting Company; number of sheets can accommodate, 318; rates per sheet, 4c.; theatrical teamster, J. H. Barnard. Newspaper: daily, News; advertising rates, yearly contract......Hotels: Grand Pacific, special rates, $2; Jay Cooke, special rates, $1.50; Key City, special rates, $1.

NEW ULM, 3,250. R. R., Chic. & Northwestern. Union Hall, J. Bobleter, managers; seating capacity, 500; rental, one night $6, three $13. Size of stage, 24x40; bill poster, J. Bobleter. Newspapers: Post (Fri.), Review (Wed.)......Hotels: Dakota, regular rates, $2; Union, Merchants.

NORTHFIELD, 2,500. R. R., Chic., Mil. & St. Paul. Lockwood's Opera House. Newspapers: News (Sat.), Journal (Th.)......Hotels: Archer's, regular rates, $2.

ORTONVILLE, 1,400. R. R., Chic., Mil. & St. Paul. Orton Opera House, C. K. Orton, manager; seating capacity, 500. Newspapers: Herald (Th.), North Star (Tu.)

OWATONNA, 4,000. R. R., Mil. & St. Paul; Chic. & N. W. Morehouse Opera House, E. M. Morehouse, manager; seating capacity, 1,000; rental, one night $15, three $36; license, city, $3. Size of stage, 25x44; size of proscenium opening, 18x18; height from stage to grooves, 13; depth under stage, 4; traps, 3; number sets scenery, 4; leader of orchestra, Emil Thimer; bill poster, Mart E. Morehouse; number sheets can accommodate, 100; rates per sheet, 4c.; theatrical teamster, W. Nickerson. Newspapers: Herald (Tu.), People Press (Fri.), Journal (Tu.)......Hotel: Arnold, regular rates, $2; Commercial, special rates; Nickerson, special rates.

Mitchell Hall; seating capacity, 500; license, $5. Size of stage, 15x42; fair stock scenery.

PRESTON, 1,500. R. R., Chic., Mil. & St. Paul. Court House Hall, George W. Harde, manager; seating capacity, 500. Newspapers: Republican (Th.)......Hotel: Gibbett's, regular rates, $2.

RED WING, 8,000. R. R., C. M. & S. P.; Rock Island & Pacific. Casino, F. S. Webster, manager; seating capacity, 1,000; rental, one night $35, three $90; share also; license included. Size of stage, 27x53; size of proscenium opening, 11x21; height from stage to grooves, 11; number sets scenery, 8; leader of orchestra, C. E. Wilcox; bill posters, Bixby & Webster; rates per sheet, 4c.; theatrical teamsters, W. L. Webster & Co. Newspapers: Sun (Th.), Advance (Sun.), Republican (Sat.)......Hotel: St. James, special rates, $1.50 to $2; Newton, special rates, $1 to $1.25.

Music Hall; seating capacity, 600.

Opera House; seating capacity, 800.

ATLANTIC COAST LINE.

Fast Mail Route to New Orleans Exposition.

Also to CHARLESTON, AIKEN, SAVANNAH, JACKSONVILLE.

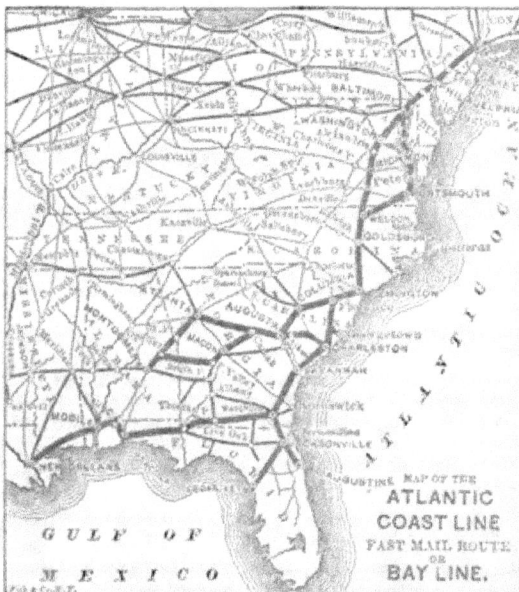

VIA
Washington,

Richmond

and

Wilmington,

TO

FLORIDA,

NEW
ORLEANS,

TEXAS.

42 Hours BOSTON
to
JACKSONVILLE.

44½ Hours
WASHINGTON
to
NEW ORLEANS.

ATLANTIC
COAST LINE
FAST MAIL ROUTE
OR
BAY LINE.

In connection also with THE BAY LINE,

The Old Established Route via BALTIMORE, OLD POINT COMFORT AND NORFOLK
AND PORTSMOUTH, VA.

Leaving New York at 3.40 P. M., via Pennsylvania R. R., with comfortable night's rest on
Chesapeake Bay.

*Pullman Sleeping Cars Boston to Washington, in connection with
Sleeper Washington to New Orleans, Pullman Buffet Cars
New York to Jacksonville, and Pullman Sleeper
Savannah to New Orleans via Pensacola.*

Tickets, Time Tables and Sleeper Car Reservations at

228 Washington St., Boston.	9 German St., Baltimore.
229 Broadway, New York.	511 Penn. Ave., Washington, D. C.
6 North Fourth St., Philadelphia.	All Eastern Offices Penn. R. R.

SOL. HAAS, **Traffic Manager,** Richmond, Va.

T. M. EMERSON, Gen. Pass. Agent, Wilmington, N. C.

H. P. CLARK, G. E. P. A., J. H. WHITE, East. P. A., 229 Broadway, N. Y

REED'S LANDING, 1,000. R. R., Chic., Mil. & St. Paul. Wilson's Hall. Knapp, Stout & Co., managers; seating capacity, 200; rental, one night $5; license, $1 to $4. Size of stage, 12x20; number sets scenery, 9; bill poster, George K. Cassidy.....Hotel: Funk.

ROCHESTER, 5,400. R. R., Chic. & Northwestern. Henny's Opera House, Charles S. Cook, manager; seating capacity, 1,000; rental, one night $20; license, $5. Size of stage, 30x48; number sets scenery, 4; bill poster, R. Taukhauser. Newspapers: Herald (Th.), Post (Fri.), Record & Union (Fri.)......Hotels: Cook, regular rates, $2; Bradley, Merchants.

Horton's Hall, C. L. Cook, manager; seating capacity, 500; rental, one night $12. Size of stage, 8x20; no scenery.

Rommel's Hall; seating capacity, 500.

Upman's Hall; seating capacity, 300.

RUSHFORD, 1,800. R. R., Chicago, Mil. & St. Paul. Edwards' Hall, C. G. Edwards, manager; seating capacity, 300; rental, one night, $8, three $18; license, $3. Size of stage, 10x20; no scenery. Newspaper: Star (Th.)......Hotels: Northwestern, regular rates, $2; Windsor, Clarendon.

SAUK CENTRE, 1,600. R. R., North. Pacific; Min. & Manitoba. Pendergart Hall, S. Pendergart, manager; seating capacity, 250; rental, one night $5 to $7; no scenery; bill poster, J. M. Johnson. Newspapers: Record (Th.), Tribune (Fri.)......Hotels: Coe, Sauk Centre, Occidental, Eastern.

SHAKOPEE, 3,000. R. R., Chic., Mil. & St. Paul; Chic., St. Paul, Minn. & Omaha. Reis Hall, Geo. Reis, manager; seating capacity, 400. Newspapers: Argus (Th.), Courier (Th.) ......Hotel: Occidental, regular rates, $2.

ST. CLOUD, 4,500. R. R., St. Paul, Minn. & Manitoba. Opera House, C. F. MacDonald, manager; seating capacity, 550; rental, one night $20, three $50; share also. Size of stage, 25x42; number sets scenery, 12; bill poster, Oscar Becker. Newspapers: Journal-Press (Th.), World (Th.), Times (Wed.)......Hotels: West, regular rates, $2; Grand, Central.

ST. PAUL, 100,000. R. R., Chic., Mil. & St. P.; Chic., St. P., M. & O.; Northern Pacific; St. P. & Duluth; St. P., Minn. & Man. Grand Opera House, L. M. Scott, manager; seating capacity, 2,300; share only. Size of stage, 50x80; size of proscenium opening, 39x38; height from stage to grooves, 20; height from stage to rigging loft, 52; depth under stage, 12; traps, 6; number sets scenery, 25; bill poster, M. Breslauer; number of sheets can accommodate, 2,500; rates per sheet, 4c; theatrical teamsters, J. B. Cook & Son. Newspaper: daily, Pioneer Press, advertising rates, per inch, $1.25 to $1.50; Globe, per inch, $1; Dispatch, per inch, 75c; weekly, Herald (Sat.), per inch, 50c......Hotels: International, special rates, $1 to $1.25; Western, special rates, $5 to $7 per week; Metropolitan, regular rates, $2.50 to $3; Windsor, regular rates, $2.50 to $3; Sherman, $2.50 to $3; St. James, $2.50 to $4.

Olympic Theatre, Edwin P. Hilton, manager; seating capacity, 900; rental, share only; license included. Size of stage, 32x45; size of proscenium opening, 15x26; height from stage to grooves, 14; height from stage to rigging loft, 30; traps, 1; number sets scenery, 10; leader of orchestra, Fred Hoppe; scenic artist, Arthur Hurtt; stage carpenter, A. L. Lauphear; bill poster, Grand Opera House; rates per sheet, 3 to 4c.; theatrical teamster, Joe St. Germain.

Market Hall.

Sherman Hall.

Music Hall; seating capacity, 500; no scenery.

Conley's Variety Theatre.

ST. PETER, 3,500. R. R., Chicago & North Western; Chic., St. Paul, Minn. & Omaha. Goethe Verein Hall, rental, one night $6; license, $5. Size of stage, 18x20; full set scenery; bill poster, Thos. M. Perry. Newspapers: Journal, (Sat.); Tribune (Wed.)......Hotels: Nicolett, regular rates, $2; Northwestern, American, Washington.

STILLWATER, 10,000. R. R., Chic., Mil. & St. Paul; Chic., St. Paul, M. & O.; St. Paul & Duluth. Grand Opera House, E. W. Durant, manager; seating capacity, 1,275; rental,

14

share only. Size of stage, 40x69; height from stage to grooves, 18; height from stage to rigging loft, 24; depth under stage, 7; bill poster, V. C. Seward; theatrical teamster, H. C. Farmer. Newspapers: daily, Sun; weekly, Gazette (Wed.), Lumberman (Fri.), Messenger (Sat.), Post (Wed.). ...Hotels: Sawyer, special rates, $2; Central, special rates, $2; Key Stone, **Union**, Northwestern.

Music Hall, Julius Duel, manager; seating capacity, 600; **rental**, one night $15, three $40, license, $5. Size of stage, 25x27; number sets scenery, **6**.

Opera Hall, E. Frederick, **manager; seating** capacity, 600; **rent or** share; license, $5. Size **of** stage, 23x25; **number sets scenery, 6**.

Hersey & Staples' Hall; **seating capacity, 800**.

WABASHA, 3,500. R. R., Chic., Mil. & St. Paul. Hirschey's Hall, O. F. Collier, manager; **seating capacity, 200; rental, one night $15; share also; licensee included**. Size of stage, 25x30; **number sets scenery, 7; bill poster**, Ben Shaw. **Newspaper:** Herald (Wed.).... Hotels: **Commercial, regular rates**, $2; **Hurde**, Smith.

WADENA, 1,350. R. R., Northern Pacific. Peak's Opera House, Spaulding **& Graham**, managers; seating capacity, 400; rental, one night $15, three $30; license yearly; **share** also. Size of stage, 18x30; number sets scenery, 2; bill posters, Opera House. **Newspaper :** Farmer (Th.)..... Hotel : Pelkey.

WELLS, 1,500. R. R., Chicago, Milwaukee & St. Paul. Wells' Public Hall, W. F. Myers, manager; seating capacity, 600; rental, one night $15, three $20; license, $1. Size of **stage**, 20x32; number sets **scenery, 3**; bill poster, W. F. Myers. Newspaper : Advocate (Th.)..... Hotels : **Wells, regular** rates, $2 (special also); American, Western, Globe.

Village Hall, F. E. Watson, manager; **seating capacity, 200.**

WILLMAR, 1,200. R. R., St. Paul, Minn. & Manitoba. Town Hall. Newspaper : Gazette **(Th.)......Hotel : Spottswood, regular rates, $2.**

WINNEBAGO CITY, 1,600. R. R., Chicago, Milwaukee & St. Paul; Chicago, St. Paul, Minn. & Omaha. Opera House, Holley & Walch, managers; seating capacity, 400; rental, one night $30, three $40; share also. Size of stage, 18x32; number sets scenery, **1**. Newspapers : News (Wed.), Press and Times (Sat.)......Hotels Kimball, regular **rates**, $2; Dond.

Moulton's **Hall**, S. Richardson, **manager; seating capacity**, 225; rental, one night **$5;** license, $3. Size of stage, 15x24; **no scenery.**

WINONA, 12,000. R.R., Chic. & Northwestern; Chic., Mil. **& St. Paul**; Green Bay, **Winona** & St. Paul. Philharmonic Hall; seating capacity, 700; rental, one night $15, three **$30;** license, $5.25. Size of stage, 30x54; full sets scenery; bill posters, Gray & Russell. Newspapers: daily, Republican; weekly, Adler (Th.), Herald (Fri.). Hotels: Jewell, regular rates, $2.50; Huff, regular rates, $2.

Normal Hall; seating capacity, 900.

Ely Hall; seating capacity, 800.

ZUMBROTA, 853. R. R., Chicago & Northwestern; Chic., Mil. & St. Paul. Parker Hall, T. D. Rowell, manager; seating capacity, 350. Newspaper: Independent (Th.)......Hotel: **Zumbrota.**

MISSISSIPPI.

ABERDEEN, 3,650. R. R., Mobile **& Ohio.** Military Institute Hall, C. M. Jordan, manager; seating capacity, 200; rental, **one** night $18.50; license, $8.50; no scenery. Newspapers: tri-weekly, Examiner; weekly, News (Sat.)......Hotels. Gordon's, regular rates, $2 (special also); Commercial, European, City.

New Opera House.

BROOKHAVEN, 3,700. R. R., Illinois Central. Varieties Theatre, E. B. Perkins, manager; seating capacity, 500; rental, one night $10, three $25; license, $7.50. Size of stage, 30x40; number sets scenery, 10; bill poster, Joseph Brown. Newspapers : Democrat **(Sat.),** Leader (Th.)......Hotels : Boswell, regular rates, **$2.**

CANTON, 3,000. R. R., Ill. Central. Odd Fellows' Hall, William Priestley, manager; seating capacity, 600; rental, one light $25, three $60; license, $7.50. Size of stage, 30x32; size of proscenium opening, 12; height from stage to grooves, 12; height from stage to rigging loft, 15; depth under stage, 3; traps, 1; number sets scenery, 4; bill poster, Green Coleman; theatrical teamster, R. W. Durfey. Newspapers: Picket (Sat.), advertising rates, special contract; Citizen (Sat.), advertising rates, special contract.....Hotels: Walker, special rates, $1; European, special rates, $1.50 to $2.

COLUMBUS, 6,500. R. R., Mobile & Ohio. Concert Hall, E. C. Lanier, manager; seating capacity, 400; rental, one night $15, three $25; license, $7.50; share also. Size of stage, 30x25; number sets scenery, 2; bill poster, Thos. B. Munroe. Newspapers: tri-weekly, Despatch; weekly, Index......Hotels: Gilmer, regular rates, $2 (special also); Dowsing.

Court House Hall; seating capacity, 600.

Concordia Hall; seating capacity, 600.

CORINTH, 2,500. R. R., Memphis & Charleston; Mobile & Ohio. Opera Hall, H. Mitchell, manager; seating capacity, 600; rental, one night $10, three $20; license, $7.50. Size of stage, 25x50; number sets scenery, 4; bill poster, T. J. Walch. Newspapers: Herald (Fri.), Democrat (Fri.)... Hotels: Corinth, regular rates, $2 (special also); Young's, Callahan, Hill.

GREENVILLE, 3,000. R. R., Georgia Pacific. Greenville Opera House, W. E. Everman, manager; seating capacity, 400; rental, one night $25, three $75; share also; license included. Size of stage, 30x30; fair stock scenery; bill poster, Caleb Dean. Newspapers: Review (Th.), Times (Sat.)......Hotels: Greenville, regular rates, $1.50 to $2.50; Dawson, Commercial.

GRENADA, 3,100. R. R., Illinois Central; Mississippi & Tennessee. Mozart Hall, W. N. Pass, manager; seating capacity, 500; rental, one night $25, three $60; license, $5 to $10. Size of stage, 12x25; number sets scenery, 3. Newspaper: Sentinel (Sat.)......Hotel: Chamberlain, regular rates, $2.

Phœnix Hall; seating capacity, 300. Size of stage 18x22.

HOLLY SPRINGS, 3,000. R. R., Illinois Central. Masonic Hall, Mosby & McCaroll, managers, seating capacity, 450; rental, one night $25, three $50; share also; license included. Size of stage, 18x40; full set scenery; bill poster, manager Hall. Newspapers: Register (Sat.), Reporter (Th.), South (Wed.)......Hotels: Holly Springs, regular rates, $2 (special also); Nuttell.

JACKSON, 7,000. R. R., Ill. Cent.; V. & M.; N., J. & C.; Y. & M. V. Robinson Opera House, W. E. Gage, manager; seating capacity, 900; rental, one night $75, three $200; license included. Size of stage, 22x40; size of proscenium opening, 13x20; height from stage to grooves, 12; height from stage to rigging loft, 30; depth under stage, 4; traps, 1; number sets scenery, 7; stage carpenter, John Elsessen; bill poster, E. T. Evans; number of sheets can accommodate 1,000; rates per sheet, 4c.; theatrical teamster, Crescent City Warehouse. Newspapers: tri-weekly, Ledger (Tu., Th. & Sat.); Clarion (Wed.), advertising rates, $1.50 per inch; Mississippian (Tu.), advertising rates, $1.50 per inch. ......Hotels: Edwards, special rates, $1.75; Spengler, special rates, $1.50; Lawrence, special rates, $1

Angelo's Hall; seating capacity, 400.

McCOMB CITY, 2,300. R. R., Illinois Central. Tegarden Hall, W. T. Tegarden, manager; seating capacity, 600; rental, one night $10, three $18; license, $4; share also. Size of stage, 17x17; number sets scenery, 5; bill poster, P. C. Wilson......Hotel: De Soto, regular rates, $2.

MERIDIAN, 8,000. R. R., Mobile & Ohio; Ala. & Gt. Southern; Vicksburg & Meridian; N. O. & N. E.; E. Tenn., Va. & Ga. Opera House, Marks, Lichtenstein & Co., managers; seating capacity, 800; rental, share only. Size of stage, 30x40; size of proscenium opening, 18x25; height from stage to grooves, 11; height from stage to rigging loft, 20; depth under stage, 4½; traps, 1; number sets scenery, 25; bill poster, Opera House. Newspapers: daily, Mercury; tri-weekly, Observer (Tu., Th. & Sat.)......Hotels: International, special rates, $1.50; St. Charles, regular rates, $2.

Bennett's Hall; seating capacity, 500.

"BEHNING"

PIANOS

Have universally received Highest Awards and Honors wherever exhibited for greatest

Purity and Evenness of Tone,

Elasticity of Touch,

Simplicity of Action,

Solidity of Construction,

Excellence of Workmanship,

And Elegance of Finish,

AND ARE PRONOUNCED BY LEADING PIANISTS AND MUSICAL AUTHORITIES

The Best Now Made.

WAREROOMS

3 W. 14TH STREET, NEW YORK.

OKOLONA, 3,000. R. R., Mobile & Ohio. McIver Hall; seating capacity, 900; rental, one night $5, three $15; license, $5. Size of stage, 15x25; number sets scenery, 4. Newspaper: Messenger (Th.)... Hotel: St. Elmo, regular rates, $2 (special also).

PORT GIBSON, 2,000. R. R., New Or., Baton R., Vicks. & Mem. Odd Fellows' Hall, John C. Watkins, manager; seating capacity, 400; rental, one night $12; license, $6.25. Size of stage, 15x25; number sets scenery, 3. Newspapers: News (Fri.), Reveille (Sat.)...... Hotels: Weekes', regular rates, $2; Banks', Gibson.

SARDIS, 1,600. R. R., Miss. & Tenn. Wall's Opera House, W. H. Wall, manager; seating capacity, 800; rental, one night $12, three $25; license, $7.50; share also. Size of stage, 18x30; number sets scenery, 3; bill poster, Joe Simmons. New-papers: News (Th.), Star (Sat.)...... Hotels: Veranda, regular rates, $2; Sardis.

SUMMIT, 2,300. R. R., Illinois Central. Lyceum Hall, G. T. Gracie, manager; seating capacity, 700; rental, one night $10, three $15; license, $2.50; share also. Size of stage, 30x40; fair stock scenery. Newspapers: Sentinel (Fri.), Intelligencer (Fri.)......Hotels: St. Peter, regular rates, 2; Foltz, Morgan.

VICKSBURG, 16,000. R. R., New Or., Baton R., Vicks. & Mem.; Vicks. & Meridian; Vicks., Shrev. & Texas. Opera House, N. Piazza, manager; seating capacity, 500; rental, one night $50, license included. Size of stage, 35x40; fair stock scenery; bill poster, Geo. De Fontaine. Newspaper: daily, Post, Herald..... Hotel: Pacific, regular rates, $2.50; Washington.

Southern Concert Hall, Wach, Enheim & Herman, managers; seating capacity, 500; rental or share; license yearly. Size of stage, 15x22; fair stock scenery.

WATER VALLEY, 4,500. R. R., Illinois Central. City Hall, F. N. Meerin, manager; seating capacity, 800; rental, one night $25, three $52.50; license included. Size of stage, 22x45; number sets scenery, 3. Newspapers: Central (Sat.), Progress (Sat.)...... Hotel: Oak Hall, regular rates, $2.

McCormack's Hall, Fly & Fly, managers; seating capacity, 300; rental, one night $10; license, $7.50; full set scenery.

YAZOO CITY, 3,270. R. R., Illinois Central. Lyceum Hall, Saul Wallerstein, manager; seating capacity, 500; rental, one night $25, three $70, license included. Size of stage, 30x50; number sets scenery, 4. Newspapers: Herald (Fri.), Sentinel (Th.)......Hotel: Richards'

MISSOURI.

APPLETON CITY. R. R., Missouri Pacific. Durley Hall; seating capacity, 580; rental, one night $15; share also; no license. Size of stage, 30x52; number sets scenery, 12. Newspaper: Journal (Th.)..... Hotel: Prier, regular rates, $2; Appleton.

BETHANY, 2,100. R. R., Chic., Bur. & Quincy. Atheneum, E. J. Fuller, manager; seating capacity, 700; rental, one night $10; license, $3; share also. Size of stage, 22x44; number sets scenery, 6. Newspapers : Broadaxe (Th.), Clipper (Th.), Republican (Th.) ......Hotels : Ramer, regular rates, $2; Poynter, Anderson, Park, Beny.

BOONEVILLE, 5,300. R. R., Missouri Pacific. Thespian Hall, J. F. Guerlich, manager; seating capacity, 500; rental, one night $15; license, $5.50. Size of stage, 25x50; number sets scenery, 6; bill poster, C. W. Tuchs. Newspapers : Advertiser (Fri.), News (Fri.), Topic (Fri.)......Hotel: City.

BOWLING GREEN, 2,000. R. R., Chic. & Alton, St. Louis, Hannibal & Keokuk. Thalia Hall, J. C. Mosely, manager; seating capacity, 650; rental, one night $10; license, $2.50; share also. Size of stage, 18x40; number sets scenery, 2; bill poster, Edward Powell. Newspapers : Post-Observer (Fri.); Times (Th.)... ..Hotel : Ingram.

BROOKFIELD, 3,000. R. R., Hannibal & St. Jo. Strawbridge Hall, E. Turner, manager; seating capacity, 400; rental, one night $15 ; share also. Size of stage, 20x40 ; number sets scenery, 2. Newspapers : Argus, (Sat.), Chronicle (Th.), Gazette (Th.)... ...Hotels: Clarke, regular rates, $2 ; Central.

BROWNSVILLE, 2,500. **R. R.**, Missouri Pacific. Olympic Hall, B. T. Bellamy, manager ; seating capacity, 500 ; rental, one night $20, three $50 ; share also ; license included. Size of stage, 26x44 ; size of proscenium opening, 17x21 ; height from stage to grooves, 13 ; depth under stage, 4½ ; **traps,** 1; bill poster, B. N. Tate ; theatrical teamster, Frank Bright. Newspaper: **Herald** (Fri.).......Hotels : **City,** special rates, $1.25 ; Central, special rates, $1.25.

BRUNSWICK, 2,500. R. R., Wabash. **City** Hall; seating capacity, 500 ; rental, one **night** $5; license, $3; no scenery. **Newspapers : Brunswicker** (Fri.), News (Sat.)......Hotels: Brown, regular **rates, $2** ; Andes.

BUTLER, 5,000 R. R., Missouri Pacific. Walton's Opera House, **Wm. E.** Walton, **manager;** seating capacity, 800; **rent or share. Size** of stage, 35x50; number sets scenery, 15; **bill poster,** Vau Nix. Newspapers: Democrat (Th.), Record **(Sat.),** Republican (Fri.), **Times** (Wed.).......Hotels : Palace, regular rates, $2; **Olive, Lindell,** Leclede.

CAMERON, 3,500. R. R , Chicago, Rock Island & Pacific ; Hannibal & St. Jo   Musser's **Opera** House, S. Musser, manager; seating capacity, 600; rental, one night, $10 **to $15;** license, $3.50. Size of stage, 20x30; number sets scenery, 5; bill posters, Gage & Gib-**bons.** Newspapers : daily, Vindicator; weekly, Observer (Th.)......Hotels : Combe, regular rates, $2; Cameron, Tremont, Western.

CANTON, 3,100. R. R., St. Louis, Keokuk & Northwestern. Town Hall, Perry Nichols, manager; seating capacity, 300; **rental, one** night $5; license, $5. Size of stage, 12x40; number sets scenery, 3; **bill poster, L. W.** Ingram. Newspapers   News (Fri.), Press **(Fri.)......**Hotel : Canton.

CARROLLTON, 3,500. R. R., Wabash. Centennial Hall, Charles S. Hill, manager; seating capacity, 500; rental, one night $15, three $35; share also; license included. Size of stage, 18x35; number sets scenery, 7; bill poster, Geo. Williams. Newspapers: daily, Democrat; weekly, Record (Sat.), Journal (Fri.)......Hotels: Florence, regular rates, $2; West Side, Getting's.

CARTHAGE, 6,000. R. R., St. Louis & San F.; Mo. Pacific. Opera House, Cassil & Hurley, managers ; seating capacity, 600; rental, one night, $25, three $60; license included. Size of stage, 20x27; size of proscenium opening, 19x20; height from stage to grooves, 11; depth under stage, 4; **traps, 2;** number sets scenery, 6 ; **bill** poster, Jos. Barrett ; rates per sheet, 4c. Newspapers : daily, Banner, advertising rates, yearly contract; Patriot, advertising rates, yearly contract......Hotels: Harrington, special rates, $1.50; **Karr, special** rates, $1.50.

Reagan's **Hall; seating capacity, 1,000.**

CENTRALIA, 1,500. R. R., Chic. & Alton ; Wabash.   People's Theatre. McMahon & Hockin, managers; seating capacity, 800; rental, one night $20; license, $2; share also. Size of stage, 35x48; fair stock scenery. Newspaper : Fireside Guard (Sat.)........Hotels: Globe, Central.

CHILLICOTHE, 6,000. R. R., Hannibal & St. Jo; Wabash. City Hall, J. C. Barkley, manager; seating capacity, 700; rental, one night $15; license, $10. Size of stage, 20x21; number sets scenery, 4; bill poster, G. W. Dorsey. Newspapers : daily, News, Tribune ......Hotels: Browning, regular rates, $2 (special also); Saunders, American.

CLINTON, 4,500. R. R., Kansas City & Southern; Missouri Pacific. Opera House, Brannum Bros., managers; seating capacity, 600; rental, one night $18; license, $3. Size of stage 30x41 ; number sets scenery, 12; bill posters, Wright & LeMar. Newspapers ; daily, advocate, Bee ; weekly, Democrat (Th.), Messenger (Th.)... ....Hotels : Allen, regular rates, $2; Heckler.

COLUMBIA, 4,500. R. R., Wabash. Haden Opera House, J. R. Campbell manager; seating capacity, 1,250; rental, one night $50, three $150; license, $5. Size of stage, 20x60; size of proscenium opening, 15x20; height from stage to grooves, 21; height from stage to rigging loft, 27; depth under stage, 10; number sets scenery, 10; stage carpenter, Frank Hays; bill poster, Frank Hays; number of sheets can accommodate, 300; rates per sheet, 3 cents. Newspapers: Statesman (Th), advertising rates, 5 cents per line; Herald

(Wed), advertising rates, 5 cents per line; Sentinel (Fr.), advertising rates, 5 cents per line.. ..Hotels: Powers, special rates, $1.50; Planters', special rates, $1.00, Central, special rates, $1.00.

DE SOTO, 2,500. R. R., St. Louis, Iron Mountain & Southern. Masonic Opera House, Gus Hamel, manager. Newspaper: Watchman (Fr.)......Hotel: De Soto, regular rates, $2 (special also).

EDINA, 2,000. R. R., A. M. & P. Div. of Wabash. Burk's Concert Hall, M. G. Biggerstaff, manager, seating capacity, 400; rental, one night $15, three $40; share also. Size of stage, 30x40; height from stage to grooves, 8; height from stage to top of rigging loft, 10, depth under stage, 3; traps, 1; number sets scenery, 4; leader of orchestra, Jacob Bishoff; stage carpenter, Jacob Bishoff, Jr.; bill poster, W. D. Pugh; number of sheets can accommodate, 30; theatrical teamster, John Jarvies. Newspapers: Sentinel (Th.), advertising rates, $1.00 per inch, Democrat (Th.), advertising rates, $1.00 per inch......Hotels: Kelley, special rates, $1.50; Victor, special rates, $1.00.

FAYETTE, 2,000. R. R., Missouri Pacific. Fayette Opera House. G. D. Tolson, manager; seating capacity, 400. Size of stage, 17½x32; size of proscenium opening, 15x15; fair stock scenery. Newspapers: Advertiser (Th.), Independent (Fri.)......Hotels : Howard, regular rates, $2 (special also): Commercial, Butler.

FULTON, 4,600. R. R., Chicago & Alton. City Hall. Charles Gebhardt, manager; seating capacity, 800; rental, one night $2, three $30; license included; share also. Size of stage, 26x42; number sets scenery, 8; bill poster, John Evans. Newspapers : Gazette (Fri.), Telegraph (Fri.)......Hotels : Palace, regular rates, $2 (special also); Powell.

Lawther's Opera House, Samuel D. Lawther, manager; seating capacity, 800: license yearly. Size of stage, 17x20; number sets scenery, 7.

GALLATIN, 1,750. R. R., Chicago, Rock Island & Pacific; Wabash. Alexander Opera House, J. W. Alexander, manager; seating capacity, 600; rental, one night $10, three $25; share also. Size of stage, 16x30; number sets scenery, 1; bill poster, Charles Shaw. Newspapers : Democrat (Sat.), Missourian (Th.)......Hotels : Palace, regular rates, $2 (special also); Commercial.

City Hall, J. M. Cravens & Co., managers; seating capacity, 600; license, $5. Size of stage, 15x40; no scenery.

GLASGOW, 2,500. R. R., Chicago & Alton; Wabash. Library Hall, J. H. Wayland, manager; seating capacity, 250; rental, one night $8; license, $2.50 to $5. Size of stage, 12x18; number sets scenery, 3. Newspapers : Central Missourian (Th.), Journal (Th.) ......Hotels : Thixton, regular rates, $2 (special also); Palmer.

HANNIBAL, 12,000. R. R., Chic., Bur. & Quincy; Hannibal & St. Joseph; Missouri Pacific; Wabash ; St. L., Hannibal & Keokuk ; St. L., Keokuk & N. W. Opera House, C. W. Winslow; seating capacity, 900; share only. Size of stage, 38x60; height from stage to grooves, 28; height from stage to rigging loft, 58; depth under stage, 9; full stock scenery; bill poster, R. M. Gill. Newspapers: daily, Courier, weekly, Independent (Sat.) ...... Hotels: Park, special rates, $3; Kettering's, Ohmer's, $2.

Academy of Music, A. H. Pierce, manager; seating capacity, 1,300; rental, one night $12.50 to $35; share also; license included. Size of stage, 42x40; number sets of scenery, 6.

Mozart Hall, W. D. Waller, manager; seating capacity, 700 ; rental, one night $35; share also; license included. Size of stage, 20x24; fair stock scenery.

Stillwell Hall; seating capacity, 800.

HARRISONVILLE, 2,600. R. R., Missouri Pacific. Barrett's Hall, M. H. Barrett, manager; seating capacity, 300; rental one night, $10; license, $3.50; share also. Size of stage, 16x25 ; bill poster, Thos. Mosley. Newspapers: Democrat (Th.), News (Fri.), Journal (Fri.)......Hotel: City, regular rates, $2 (special also).

HIGGINSVILLE, 2,000. R. R., Chic. & Alton; Missouri Pacific. Opera House, M. Wilmuth, manager; seating capacity, 400; rental, one night $18; license, $5.50. Size of stage, 12x38; fair stock scenery. Newspapers : Advance (Fri.), Post (Wed.). ....Hotel: Occidental, regular rates, $2 (special also).

HOLDEN, 2,600.   R. R., Missouri Pacific.   Englosslan Hall, G. E. Clarke, manager; seating capacity, 500; rental, one night $10; license, $4.50.   Size of stage, 8x18; fair stock scenery   Newspapers: Enterprise (Th.), Herald (Th.).   .Hotels: Bell, regular rates, $2 (special also) ; Herman.

HOPKINS, 960.   R. R., Chic., Burlington & Qnincy; Kansas City, St. Jo. & Council Bluffs. Frayne & Jeffers' Opera House, W. S. Frayne, manager; seating capacity, 450; rental, one night $10.   Size of stage, 15x20; fair stock scenery.   Newspaper: Journal, (Sat.) ....Hotel : Hopkins.

INDEPENDENCE, 6,000.   R. R., Chic. & Alton; Missouri Pacific.   Wilson's Opera House, Charles E. Wilson, manager; seating capacity, 600; rental, one night $25, three $65; share also; licenee included; bill poster, James O'Reilly.   Newspapers: Progress (Sat.) ......Hotels: Merchants', Laclede.

JEFFERSON CITY, 7,000.   R. R., Chicago & Alton; Missouri Pacific.   Bragg Hall, J. M. Clarke, manager; seating capacity, 500; rental, one night $20, three $50; license, $7. Size of stage, 18x45; fair stock scenery; bill poster, Henry Barnes.   Newspapers: daily, Journal, Tribune .....Hotels: Madison, regular rates, $2 (special also); City, McCarty, Central.

JOPLIN, 10,000.   R. R., Kansas City, Fort Scott & Gulf; Missouri Pacific; St. Louis & San Fran. Joplin Opera House, H. H. Haven, manager; seating capacity, 600; rental, one night $35, three $80; share also. Size of stage, 22x28; number sets scenery, 7; bill poster, H. H. Haven. Newspapers : daily, Herald, News... .Hotels : Joplin, regular rates $2 (special also); St. James, Pacific.

Perkins Hall.

KANSAS CITY, 100,000.   R. R., Atchison, Top. & S. Fe; Wabash; Chicago & Alton; Hannibal & St. Joseph; K. C., Ft. S. & Gulf; K. C., St. J. & C. B ; Missouri Pacific; Southern Kansas; Union Pacific.   Gillis' Opera House, Corydon F. Craig, manager; seating capacity, 1,600; share only. Size of stage, 46x124; size of proscenium opening, 37x46; height from stage to grooves, 28; height from stage to rigging loft, 58; depth under stage, 20; traps, 5; number sets scenery, 20; leader of orchestra, M. Lenge; stage carpenter, Claude L. Hagen; bill poster, K. C. Adv. Co.; number of sheets can accommodate, 3,000; rates per sheet, 3c.; theatrical teamster, K. C. Transfer Co. Newspapers: daily, Times, Journal, Star.   Hotels: Delmonico, special rates, $1.25 to $1.50; St. James, special rates, $2; Centropolis, special rates, $3; Coates, special rates, $2.25 to 2.50.

Coates Opera House, M. H. Hudson, manager; seating capacity, 1,600; share only. Size of stage, 48x68; size of proscenium opening, 35; height from stage to grooves, 20; height from stage to rigging loft, 48; depth under stage, 10; traps, 3; number sets scenery, 20; leader of orchestra, Prof. Hullett; stage carpenter, L. H. De Puy; bill poster, M. H. Hudson; number of sheets can accommodate, 10,000; rates per sheet, 3c. to 4c.

Coliseum Theatre (variety), H. D. Clark, manager; seating capacity, 1,200; do not rent; license, $5. Size of stage, 25x25; size of proscenium opening, 23x25; height from stage to grooves, 14; height from stage to rigging loft, 35; depth under stage, 15; traps, 2; number sets scenery, 20; leader of orchestra, L. F. Johns; scenic artist, W. D. Sterry; stage carpenter, Geo. Baker; bill poster, C. P. Tucker; number of sheets can accommodate, 125-3 sheets; rates per sheet, 5c.; theatrical teamster, Geo. E. Brown.

Theatre Comiqne (variety); seating capacity, 1,500. Size of stage, 25x33.

Merchants' Exchange Hall; seating capacity, 1,000.

Long's Hall; seating capacity, 600.

Walnut Street Theatre.

Kansas City Museum.

KIRKSVILLE, 3,100.   R. R., Wabash.   Masonic Hall, J. L. Porter, manager; seating capacity, 400; rental, one night $10; license, $5. Size of stage, 12x41; no scenery; bill poster, Olen Johnson. Newspapers: Democrat (Th.), Graphic (Fri.), Journal (Th.)......Hotels : Parcell, regular rates, $2 (special also); Pool's.

KNOBNOSTER, 1,500.   R. R., Missouri Pacific. Fields Hall, J. T. Baker, manager; seating capacity, 400; rental, one night $7.50; license, $4.75. Size of stage, 15x15; no scenery. Newspaper: Gem (Fri.).   Hotel: Central, regular rates, $2 (special also).

LAMAR, 3,500. R. R., Kansas City & Gulf; Missouri Pacific. Lamar Opera House, Brown & Avery; seating capacity, 800; rental, one night $30, three $60; share also; license yearly; size of proscenium opening, 16x25; height from stage to grooves, 12; height from stage to rigging loft, 21; depth under stage or cellar, 4; traps, 1; number sets scenery, 11; bill poster, Brown & Avery; number sheets can accommodate, 200; rates per sheet, 3½c.; theatrical teamster, S. E. McBride. Newspapers: Missourian (Th.), Advocate (Th.) Hotels: Lamar, special rates, $1.50; Commercial, Grayson, St. Nicholas, special rates, $1.

LEBANON, 3,500. R. R., St. Louis & San Francisco. Lebanon Opera House, Sam Farrar, manager; seating capacity, 600; rental, one night $30. Size of stage, 24x48; size of proscenium opening, 32x24; height from stage to grooves, 14; depth under stage, 4½; traps, 1; number sets scenery, 12; stage carpenter, J. W. Kendwig; theatrical teamster, Wm. Crow. Newspapers: Graphic (Fri.), advertising rates, 5c. per line; Sentinel (Fri.), advertising rates, 5c. per line; Rustic (Wed.), advertising rates, 5c. per line. Hotel: Laclede, special rates, $1.50.

LEE'S SUMMIT, 1,500. R. R., Missouri Pacific. Irvine's Opera House, Matt. Irvine, manager; seating capacity, 400; rental, one night $15, three $40, share also. Size of stage, 18x30; size of proscenium opening, 13x18; height from stage to grooves, 12; traps, 1; number sets scenery, 8; bill poster, Opera House; theatrical teamster, Sam Folk. Newspaper: Journal (Th.)......Hotel: Snow.

LEXINGTON, 5,000. R. R., Missouri Pacific; Wabash. Hagen's Opera House, Henry Hagen, manager; seating capacity, 700; rental, one night $25, two $45, three $60; license included. Size of stage, 25x40; size of proscenium opening, 14x22; height from stage to grooves, 12; height from stage to rigging loft, 18; depth under stage, 5; number sets scenery, 8; bill poster, Bob Sandefort; number of sheets can accommodate, 120; rates per sheet, 4c.; theatrical teamster, John Fogg. Newspapers: Register (Th.), Intelligencer (Sat.)......Hotels: Laclede, special rates, $1.25; Commercial, special rates, $1.25; Long's, special rates, $1.25.

Turner's Hall; seating capacity, 300.

Baehr's Hall; seating capacity, 400.

Leiderkranz Hall; seating capacity, 400.

LIBERTY, 2,000. R. R., Hannibal & St. Joe. Bank Hall, D. Gittings, manager; seating capacity, 600; rental, one night, $20; license included. Size of stage, 14x30; number sets scenery, 4. Newspapers: Advance (Fri.), Tribune (Fri.)......Hotel: Arthur, regular rates, $2.

LOUISIANA, 6,500. R. R., Chicago & Alton; Chicago, Burlington & Quincy; St. Louis, Kansas & Northwestern. Burnett Opera House (new), O. C. Beyson, manager; seating capacity, 1,000; rental, share only; license yearly. Size of stage, 40x56; size of proscenium opening, 22x36; height from stage to grooves, 16; height from stage to rigging loft, 35; depth under stage, 15; leader of orchestra, E. A. Parks; stage carpenter, Thomas McGinnis; bill poster, Wm. Shaffner; number of sheets can accommodate, 5 large boards; theatrical teamster, Ed. A. Glenn. Newspapers: Press (Wed.), Journal (Wed.), Republican (Sat.)......Hotel: Globe, special rates, $1.75.

National Hall, J. H. Rhea, manager; seating capacity, 500; rental, one night $14; license, $7. Size of stage, 18x24; number sets scenery, 5.

Parks' Music Hall, E. A. Parks, manager; seating capacity, 400; rental, one night $15, three $35; share also; license included; number sets scenery, 6.

MACON, 4,000. R. R., Wabash; H. & St. Jo. Wright's Opera House, Patton & Jackson, managers; seating capacity, 900; rental, one night $25, three $50 ; share also ; license $3 to $6.50. Size of stage, 22x21 ; size of proscenium opening, 10½x20 ; height from stage to grooves, 10½ ; height from stage to rigging loft, 16 ; depth under stage, 3½ ; traps, 1 ; number sets scenery, 6 ; leader of orchestra, Prof. Jackel ; bill poster, J. W. Patton ; number of sheets can accommodate, 400 ; rates per sheet, 4c.; theatrical teamster, Alex. Roberts. Newspapers: Free Democrat (Fri.), advertising rates, 10c. per line ; Republican (Th.), advertising rates, 10c. per line; Times (Fri.), advertising rates, 5c. per line..... Hotels: Wabash, special rates, $1.50 ; Palace, special rates, $1.25.

LIZZIE MAY ULMER,

IN THE GREAT NEW ENGLAND SOCIETY PLAY,

"DAD'S GIRL,"

Written Expressly for her by Mr. E. J. SWARTZ.

"She holds the keys to the Gates of Laughter and the Portals of Pathos."—*St. Louis Republican.*

There are few, if, indeed, there are any actresses on the American stage who have struggled for supremacy with more patience and determination than has LIZZIE MAY ULMER, and there are few, if, indeed, there are any who have entrenched themselves so firmly in public esteem. A career begun with modesty, but with a high resolve to advance—characterized throughout by the absence of ostentation; steadily strengthening itself in popularity by the force of unquestioned talent and the magnetism of a sympathetic nature—has at length reached the harvest of success. Miss Ulmer has triumphed, and to-day holds a place among the leaders of her profession.

MARSHALL, 5,000. R. R., Chicago & Alton; Kansas City Branch. Marshall Opera House, Silas Marshall, manager; seating capacity, 800; rental, share only. Size of stage, 26x44 ; size of proscenium opening, 20x22 ; height from stage to grooves, 17½ ; height from stage to rigging loft, 30; depth under stage, 8 ; traps, 1 ; number sets scenery, 12 ; leader of orchestra, Prof. Storant ; scenic artist, C. L. McFarland ; stage carpenter, C. L. McFarland ; bill poster, J. McCratne ; number of sheets can accommodate, 200 ; theatrical teamsters, Robinson & Barnhill. Newspapers: daily, News, advertising rates, 5c. per line ; weekly, Democrat (Fri.), advertising rates, 5c. per line ; Progress, (Th.), advertising rates, 5c. per line ; Republican (Th.) advertising rates, 5c. per line. .....Hotels: Ming's, special rates, $1.75; Commercial, special rates, $1.50.

MARYVILLE, 5,700. R. R., Kansas City, St. Jo. & Council Bluffs. Union Hall, F. C. McCluskey, manager; seating capacity, 500; rental, one night $10, three $30; license $2. Size of stage, 16x24; number sets scenery, 5; bill poster, Charles Philo...... Newspapers: Democrat (Th.), Republican (Th.), Times (Wed.) .....Hotels: Arlington, Luona, American, Valley, Maryville, Wills.

MEMPHIS, 2,500. R. R., Wabash. Mason's Opera House, Donnell & Bennett, managers; seating capacity, 450; rental, one night $15 Size of stage, 12x18; number sets scenery, 3; bill poster, James Whallen. Newspapers: Democrat (Wed.), National (Th.), Reveille (Th.).....,Hotels: Wabash, Central, Reddish, Star.

MEXICO, 8,300. R. R., Chicago & Alton; Wabash. Opera House, E. G. Armstrong, manager; seating capacity, 1,000; rental, one night $25, three $60; license, $5. Size of stage, 22x36; number sets scenery, 7; bill posters, Sprucing & Stacey. Newspapers: daily, Intelligencer; weekly, Ledger (Th.). Press (Wed.)......Hotels: Ring's, regular rates $2 (special also); Erver, Central, Commercial, Farris, Windsor, Jones.

MOBERLY, 8,700. R. R., Missouri Pacific; Wabash. Apgar's Opera House, G. R. Apgar, manager; seating capacity, 1,000; rent or share; full set scenery. Newspapers: daily, Headlight, Monitor, Times......Hotels: Grand Central, regular rates, $2 (special also), Merchants', regular rates $2 (special also).

Hegarty Bros.' Opera House; Hegarty Bros., managers; rent or share; full set scenery.

MONTGOMERY CITY, 2,000. Wabash, St. Louis & Pacific. Library Hall, J. D. Barnett, manager; seating capacity, 300; rental, one night $15, three $35, license included. Size of stage, 12x40; size of proscenium opening, 14x18; bill poster. Library Hall. Newspapers : Standard (Fri.), Ray (Fri.)......Hotel: Worley's.

MOUND CITY, 2,500. R. R., Kansas City, St. Jo. & Council Bluffs. Corsant & Meyer's Opera House, C. K. Corsant, manager; seating capacity, 600; rental, one night $12.50, three $30; license, $2.50; share also. Size of stage, 20x22; number sets scenery, 11; bill poster, Walter Williams. Newspaper: News (Fri.),......Hotels: Dunham, Central, Hoett, Gill's.

NEOSHA, 2,500. R. R., St. Louis & San Francisco. Opera House, W. H. Stein, manager; seating capacity, 400; rental, one night $15, license included. Size of stage, 16x40. Newspapers: Miner & Mechanic (Sat.), Republican (Fri.), Times (Th.)......Hotel: McElheny, regular rates, $2 (special also).

NEVADA, 6,000. R. R., Mo. Pacific; L. & S. Moore's Opera House, Henry C. Moore, manager; seating capacity, 900; rental, share only; license included. Size of stage, 36x58; size of proscenium opening, 24x20; depth under stage, 5; traps, 2 ; number sets scenery, 20; scenic artist, T. B. Harrison ; stage carpenter, W. D. Clark; bill poster, W. D. Clark. Newspapers : daily, Mail, Democrat; weekly, Ledger (Fri.)......Hotels: Mitchell, special rates, $1.50; Shaft's, special rates, $1.50; Richmond, special rates, $1.50.

NORTH SPRINGFIELD, 9,000. R. R., St. Louis & San Francisco; Springfield & Kansas City; Kansas City, S. & M. Frisco Opera House, J. A. Irwin, manager; seating capacity, 600; rental, share only. Size of stage, 30x44; size of proscenium opening, 18x24; height from stage to grooves, 15; height from stage to rigging loft, 22; depth under stage, 4; traps, 1; number sets scenery, 8; leader of orchestra, H M. Gier; bill poster, Jas. Ried; number sheets can accommodate, 1,000; rates per sheet, 4c. Newspapers: daily, Herald, advertising rates, yearly contract ; Southwester, advertising rates, yearly contract; Journal, advertising rates, yearly contract......Hotels: Ozark, special rates, $1.50 to $2; Metropolitan, special rates, $1.50 to $2; Central, special rates, $1.

ODESSA, 1,000. R. R., Chicago & Alton. Opera House, L. R. **Smith, manager; fair stock** scenery. Newspaper: Herald (Fri.)

PALMYRA, 3,500. R. R., Hannibal **& St.** Jo. Hanley's **Opera** House, Rice & Spencer, managers; seating capacity, 600; rent or share. Size **of** stage, 35x20; number sets scenery, 12. Newspapers: Herald (Th.), Spectator **(Fri)**.....Hotels: National, regular rate, $2 (special also); McLeod.

PRINCETON, 1.600. R. R., Chicago, Rock Island & Pacific. Buren's Hall, W. F. Buren, manager; seating capacity, 500; rental, one night, $10; license, **$4.** Size of stage, 16x24; number sets scenery, 8; **bill poster, Gus** Reeves. Newspapers: People's Press (Wed.), Telegraph (Fri.).. ...Hotels: Buckeye, regular rates, $2 (special also); Princeton.

RICH HILL, 6,000. R. R., Mo. Pacific; Kansas City, Fort Scott & Gulf. Opera House, J. Goldenberg, manager; seating capacity, 600; **rental, one night $25; three $60; share also;** license included. Size of stage, 24x50; size of proscenium **opening, 12x24; height from stage** to grooves, **10; height** from **stage** to rigging loft, **14;** depth under **stage, 5;** traps, 1; number sets scenery, 7; bill poster, J. Goldenberg; number of sheets can accommodate, 400; rates per sheet, 3½c; theatrical teamster, A. C. Cate. Newspapers: Review (Th.), Enterprise (Fri.)......Hotels: Talmage, special rates, $1.50; Merchants', special rates, $1.

RICHMOND, 3,000. R. R., Wabash. Opera House, Geo. W. Trigg, manager; seating capacity, 700; rent or share. Size of stage, 50x100; full set scenery; bill poster, John Stook. Newspapers: Conservator **(Fri.),** Democrat (Th.)......Hotels: Wasson, regular rates, $2 (special also); Hudgins.

Moshy's Opera House, C. E. **Moshy, manager; seating capacity, 600;** rental, one night $15, three $35, license **included; share also. Size of stage, 25x10; full set scenery.**

ROCKPORT, 1 100. R. R., Kansas City, St. Jo. & Council Bluffs. Academy of Music, **Dopf & Yosleyn, managers; seating capacity, 450;** rental, one night $10, three $25; **license, $5; share also. Size of stage, 25x40; number sets scenery, 4;** bill posters, **Academy of Music. Newspapers:** Journal (Sat.), Mail (Th.)......Hotels: Rockport, **Wright's.**

ROLLA, 3,000. R. R., St. Louis & San Francisco. New Era Opera House, W. J. Powell, manager; seating capacity, 400; rental, one night $25, three $50, license included. Size of stage, 20x30; fair stock scenery. Newspapers: Herald (Th.), New Era (Sat.) ... ..**Hotels:** Grant, Grandell, special rates, $1.

SAVANNAH. 2,000. R. R., Kansas City, St. Jo. & Council Bluffs. Hardy's **Hall, J. T.** Hardy, manager; seating capacity, 400; rental, one night $10; license, $2; share also; fair stock scenery; bill poster, J. T. Hardy. Newspapers: Democrat (Fri.), Reporter (Fri.), Wind Mill (Fri.)......Hotels: St. Charles, regular rates, $1 (special also); Commercial.

SEDALIA, 23,000. R. R., Missouri Pacific. Wood's Opera House, H. W. Wood, manager; seating capacity, 1,560; rental, **one** night $100, three $225; share also; license yearly. Size of stage, 40x70; number sets scenery, 30; bill poster, Charles W. Lyon. Newspapers: daily, Bazoo, Democrat; weekly, Journal (Wed)......Hotels: Sicher's, regular rates, $2 to $2.50 (special also); Garrison, regular rates, $2 to $2.50 (special also); Kaiser, Depot, Le Roy, Jay Gould.

Smyth's Hall, Charles W. Lyon, manager; seating capacity, 1,000 ; share also. Size of stage, 18x30; number sets scenery, 8.

White's Hall, seating capacity, 600.

SPRINGFIELD, 18,000. R. R., St. Paul & San Fran.; K. C., Fort S. & Gulf. Mansfield Opera House, Chas. E. Duhbs, manager; seating capacity, 600; rental, share only. Size of stage, 30x50; size of proscenium opening, 16x27; height from stage to grooves, 12; height from stage to rigging loft, 16; depth under stage, 4; traps, 1; number sets scenery, 9; leader of orchestra, T. J. Rountree; scenic artist, H. McClure; stage carpenter, Wm. Orcutt; bill poster, W. H M. Reld; number of sheets can accommodate, 300; rates per sheet, 4c.; theatrical teamster, F. S. Jones. Newspapers: daily, Herald, Journal, Leader, South West......Hotels: Metropolitan, special rates, $1.10; Southern, special rates, $1.25; Central, special rates, $1.25.

Springfield Opera House, Fricke & Newton, managers; seating capacity, 500; rental, one night $25, three $60, license included; share also. Size of stage, 30x27; full set scenery.

City Hall, McDaniel & Sheppard, managers; seating capacity, 250; license, $10. Size of stage, 72x60; no scenery.

Odd Fellow's Hall; seating capacity, 500.

Phœnix Hall; seating capacity, 400.

ST. CHARLES, 6,500. R. R., Wabash; St. Louis & Pacific. Opera House, J. N. Mittelberger & Co., managers; seating capacity, 600; rental, one night $20, three $50; share also; license, $6. Size of stage, 24x15; size of proscenium opening, 12x24; height from stage to rigging loft, 20; depth under stage, 3; traps, 1; number sets scenery, 7; bill poster, J. N. Mittelberger & Co. Newspapers: Cosmos (Wed.), News (Sat.), Democrat (Th.) . . . . . Hotels: Galt, special rates, $1 25 to $1.50; Central, special rates, $1 to $1.25; Monroe, special rates, $1.

Odd Fellows' Hall.

Opera House.

ST. JOSEPH, 50,000. R. R., Chicago, Burlington & Quincy; Wabash, Missouri Pacific; St. Joseph & Western. Tootle's Opera House, Fred F. Schrader, manager; Brooke & Dickson, New York representatives; seating capacity, 1,500; share only. Size of stage, 46x67; size of proscenium opening, 75x30; height from stage to grooves, 20; height from stage to rigging loft, 55; depth under stage, 7; traps, 4; number sets scenery, 24; leader of orchestra, E. Winkler; scenic artist, Albert C. Roberts; stage carpenter, Jacob Seippel; bill poster, John Mulvihill; theatrical teamster, St. Joseph Bus Co. Newspapers: daily, Herald, advertising rates, 15c. per line, $1 per inch; Gazette, advertising rates, 15c. per line, $1 per inch; weekly, Democrat (Sat.), advertising rates, 80c. per inch; Leader (Mon.) . . . . . . Hotels: Pacific, special rates, $2 to $2.50; St. Charles, special rates, $1.25 to $1.50; Saunder, special rates, $1.25 to $1.50.

City Hall; seating capacity, 2,000.

Turner's Hall; seating capacity, 600.

ST. LOUIS, 500,000. R. R., Chicago & Alton; Chicago, Burlington & Quincy; Illinois & St. Louis; Indianapolis & St. Louis; Louisville & Nashville; Missouri Pacific; Ohio & Missouri; St. Louis & Cairo; St. Louis & San Francisco; Wabash; Vandalia Line; Toledo, Cincinnati & St. Louis; St. Louis, Iron Mt. & So.; St. Louis, A. & T. H.; St. Louis, C. C. & St. C. Grand Opera House, John W. Norton, manager; seating capacity, 2,500; license yearly; share only. Size of stage, 38x68; height from stage to grooves, 20; height from stage to rigging loft, 55; depth under stage, 11; traps, full complement; complete stock scenery; bill poster, W. R. Cottrell; number of sheets can accommodate; 50,000; rates per sheet, 3c. and 4c.; theatrical teamster, Transfer Co. Newspapers: daily, Globe-Democrat, Tribune (Ger.), Republican, Amerika (Ger.), Post-Dispatch; weekly, Spectator (Th.), Critic (Fri) . . . . . Hotels: Southern, special rates, $1.25 to $2.50. Lindell, special rates, $1.25 to $2.50; Laclede, special rates, $1.25 to $2.50; Planters', special rates, $1.25 to $2.50; St. James', special rates, $1.25 to $2.50; Hurst's, special rates, $1.25 to $2.50.

Olympic, C. A. Spalding, manager; Brooke & Dickson, New York representatives; seating capacity, 2,400; license yearly. Size of stage, 45x80; size of proscenium opening, 38x37; height from stage to grooves, 20; height from stage to rigging loft, 62; depth under stage, 11; traps, 6; number sets scenery, any amount; leader of orchestra, B. Vogel; scenic artists, Noxon, Albert & Toomey; stage carpenter, S. J. Gates.

Pope's Theatre, Charles R. Pope, manager; seating capacity, 2,213; license paid by theatre; share also. Size of stage, 47x70; size of proscenium opening, 36x36; height from stage to grooves, 20; height from stage to rigging loft, 60; depth under stage, 10; traps, 10; number sets scenery, 100; leader of orchestra, William Withers, Jr.; scenic artist, Frank Gates; stage carpenter, James P. Bennett.

People's Theatre, William C. Mitchell, manager; seating capacity, 2,000; rental, share only; license yearly. Size of stage, 40x66½; size of proscenium opening, 25x36; height from stage to grooves, 20; height from stage to rigging loft, 58; depth under stage, 10; traps, 3; number sets scenery, 35; leader of orchestra, George Olney; scenic artist, Arthur Greenus.

Casino, George McManus & Dick Parker, managers; seating capacity, 1,100; stock theatre. Size of stage, 20x22; size of proscenium opening, 21x22; height from stage to grooves, 18; height from stage to rigging loft, 48; depth under stage, 16; traps, 2; number sets scenery, 10; leader of orchestra, J. B. Donniker; scenic artists, Noxon, Albert & Toomey; stage carpenter, William Price.

Palace Theatre, T. V. Day, manager; seating capacity, 2,000. Size of stage, 20x30; size of proscenium opening, 25; height from stage to grooves, 20; height from stage to rigging loft, 40; number sets scenery, 5; leader of orchestra, Demenic Sarli; scenic artist, John Noxon; stage carpenter, John Ross; bill poster, Charles Voris.

Edwards' Theatre, J. Edwards, manager; seating capacity, **1,500.** Size of stage, 40x28; **height from stage to grooves, 14; height** from stage to rigging loft, 20; depth under **stage, 10; traps, 3; number sets scenery, 22;** scenic artist, B. K. Hodges; stage carpenter, **H. B. Knight.**

Mercantile Library Hall, John N. Dyer, manager; **seating capacity, 1,600;** rental, $60 per night; $250 per week. **Size of stage, 38x42.**

Standard Theatre, W. H. Smyth, manager; seating capacity, 2,500.

Globe Theatre, Captain J. W. Decker, manager.

Theatre Comique, John C. Groffer, manager; seating capacity, 1,000.

Gregory's Variety Theatre, Frank Gregory & Co., managers.

Howard & Alton's Pavilion Theatre.

Broadway & Treyser's Dime Museum, James E. Barnes, manager.

St. Louis Dime Museum.

Fontaine's Theatre.

Eshler's Alhambra Theatre.

TIPTON, 1,350 R. R., Missouri Pacific. City Hall, Fitschen & Stetler, managers; seating capacity 300; rental, one night $5, three $11; license, $2.50; share also; no scenery. Newspaper: Times (Th.)......Hotel: Tipton, regular rates, $2 (special also).

WARRENSBURG, 5,000. R. R., Missouri Pacific. Empire Opera House, **McFarland &** Gear, managers; seating capacity, 600; rental, one night $15; license, $5; share also. Size of stage, 18x48; fair stock scenery; bill poster, **Capt.** Thurber. Newspapers: Journal-Democrat (Fri.), Standard (Th.), Star **(Th)... ...Hotels:** Simmons, regular rates, $2 (special also); Eads, Jacobs.

WASHINGTON, 3,700. R R., Missouri Pacific. Turner Hall, Henry J. Krog, manager; seating capacity, 400; rental, one night $10, three $25; license, $2.50. Size of stage 21x35; number sets scenery, 6; bill poster, H. J. Krog. Newspaper: Observer (Fri.)..... Hotels: Commercial, regular rates, $2 (special also); Washington, Collins, Pacific.

Liberty Hall ; seating capacity, 500.

WEBB CITY. R. R., St. Louis & San Fran. Webb City Opera House, H. H. Haven, manager; seating capacity, 600 ; rent or share; no license. Size of stage, 40x26; bill poster, Lester Aylor. Newspaper: Times (Fri.).... ...Hotels: Scott, regular rates, $2 (special also); Transit, Webb City.

WINDSOR, 1,700. R. R., Missouri Pacific. Temperance Hall, C. C. Morse, manager; seating capacity, 300; rental, one night $10, three $25; license, $2; share also. Size of stage, 18x36; fair stock scenery. Newspapers: Democrat (Wed.), Review (Fri.)....... Hotel Windsor, regular rates, $2.

NEBRASKA.

AURORA, 1,700. R. R., Burlington & Missouri River. Rogers' Opera House, H. T. Rogers **manager;** seating capacity, 400; rental, one night $25; license, $1.50; share also. Size of stage, 40x30; fair stock scenery. Newspapers: News (Fri.), Republican (Th.).. .... Hotels: Aurora, regular rates, $2 (special also); Tuttle, Commercial.

BEATRICE, 4,500. R. R., Burlington & Missouri River; Union Pacific. Beatrice Opera House, C. M. Emery, manager; seating capacity, 650; license, $2; share also. Size of stage, 21x50; number sets scenery, 5; bill poster, Opera House. Newspapers: daily, Express; weekly, Democrat (Fri.); Republican (Sat.).......Hotel: Randall, regular rates, $2 (special also): Pacific.

BLAIR, 2,400. R. R., Chic. St. Paul, Minn. & Omaha; Sioux City & Pacific. Germania Hall, Alex. Finleyson, manager; seating capacity, 350; rental, one night, $12; license, $3. Size of stage, 23x30; number sets scenery, 4. Newspapers: Pilot (Th.), Republican (Th.) ......Hotel: City, regular rates, $2 (special also).

BROWNVILLE, 1,450. R. R., Missouri Pacific. Marsh's Hall, J. H. Brody, manager; seating capacity, 500; rental, one night $12.50; license, $3. Size of stage, 18x24; number sets scenery, 3. Newspapers: Granger (Fri.), Republican (Th.)......Hotel: Marsh, regular rates $2 (special also).

COLUMBUS, 3,500. R. R., Burlington & Missouri River; Union Pacific. Columbus Opera House, John Stauffer, manager; seating capacity, 750; rental, one night $20, three $50 license included. Size of stage, 28x40; number sets scenery, 12. Newspapers: Democrat (Sat.), Journal (Wed.)... ...Hotels : Grand Pacific, regular rates, $2 (special also); Clothers, Lindell.

CRETE, 2,700. R. R., Burlington & Missouri River. Band's Opera House, E. Heley, manager; seating capacity, 1,000; share only; license yearly. Size of stage, 16x24; number sets scenery, 6; bill poster, Dan Hawkins. Newspaper: Globe (Th.)......Hotel : Cosmopolitan, regular rates, $2 (special also).

DAVID CITY, 1,800. R. R., Burlington & Missouri R.; Union Pacific. New Opera House. Newspapers: Press (Fri.), Republican (Th.)......Hotels: Commercial, regular rates $2 (special also).

DORCHESTER, 500. R. R., Burlington & Missouri River. Opera House. Newspaper: Star (Th.)

FAIRBURY, 2,000. R. R., St. Joseph & Western. Buckstaff Opera House, D. B. Cropsey, manager; seating capacity, 700; rental, one night $20, three $45 ; share also; license included. Size of stage, 29x40; size of proscenium opening, 11x18; height from stage to grooves, 14; height from stage to rigging loft, 17; depth under stage, 4½; number sets scenery, 7; theatrical teamsters, Pantier & Martin. Newspapers: Nebraskan (Th.); Gazette (Fri.)...... Hotels : Grand Central, special rates, $1.25; Pacific, special rates, $1.25.

FAIRMONT, 1,200. R. R., Burlington & Missouri River. Fairmont Opera House, John Barsley, manager; seating capacity, 500; rent or share. Size of stage, 15x40; number sets scenery, 4. Newspapers : Bulletin, (Th.), Signal (Th.)......Hotels: Pacific, regular rates, $2 (special also); City.

FALLS CITY, 4,000. R. R., Atchison & Nebraska; Missouri Pacific. Cain's Opera House, M. W. Zielle, manager; seating capacity, 600; rental, one night $20, three $50; license included. Size of stage, 25x25; size of proscenium opening, 21x22; height from stage to grooves, 18; height from stage to rigging loft, 27; depth under stage, 6; traps, 3; number sets scenery, 8; leader of orchestra, Frank Wosika; scenic artist, James Denison; bill poster, James Denison; theatrical teamster, John Honner. Newspapers: News (Th.), Journal (Th.)......Hotels: Union, Central, Commercial.

FREMONT, 6,000. R. R., Union Pacific; Sioux City & Pacific. Bullock's Opera House, George Yates, manager; seating capacity, 800; shares also; rental, one night $35, three $60; license included. Size of stage, 24x43; size of proscenium opening, 14x24; height from stage to grooves, 14; height from stage to rigging loft, 26; depth under stage, 7; traps, 2; number sets scenery, 12; leader of orchestra, C. H. Meservey; bill poster, E. F. Teal; number sheets can accommodate, 300; rate per sheet, 3c.; theatrical teamster, Chas. H. Coman. Newspapers: daily, Tribune, Herald; weekly, Journal (Sat.)...... Hotels: Enos, special rates, $1.50; New York, special rates, $1.50; European, special rates, $1.

WEBER

PIANOFORTE

COMPLETE TRIUMPH.

The wonderful OFFICIAL Report, being the basis of the U. S. Centennial award decreed to

ALBERT WEBER, New York,

—— FOR ——

GRAND, SQUARE AND UPRIGHT PIANOS.

REPORT.—"For **sympathetic, pure and rich tone, combined with greatest power** (as shown in their Grand, Square and Upright Pianos). These three styles show intelligence and solidity in their construction, a pliant and easy touch, which, at the same time, answers promptly to its requirements, together with excellence and workmanship"

A. T. GOSHORN, Director-General.   J. R. HAWLEY, President.

Attest. [Seal.] J. L. CAMPBELL, Secretary.

☞ **CAUTION.**—Beware of unscrupulous advertisers, who are trying to palm off a *certificate of private individuals*, consisting of renowned professors of Universities and Colleges, Chemists, Astronomers and Engineers, as a Centennial Award on Pianos.

The Weber Grand Piano reached the highest average over all competitors, 95 out of a possible 96; next highest on Grand Piano at 91.

Call and see the **Official** report at the Weber Rooms, and hear the Weber Pianos, which stand to-day without a **rival for "Sympathetic, pure and rich tone, combined with greatest power."**

Illustrated Catalogue, with Price List, mailed free upon application.

Warerooms, Fifth Ave., cor. Sixteenth St., New York.

Shed's Opera House, Geo. D. Marr, manager; seating capacity, 750; rental, one night $20; share also. Size of stage, 20x40; number sets scenery, 8.

Court House Hall; seating capacity, 300.

GRAND ISLAND, 1,000. R. R., Union Pacific; St. Joe & Western; B. & M. R. Bartenbach's **Opera House,** S. P. Reynard, **manager; seating capacity,** 1,000; rental, share only; Size **of stage, 26x59; size of** proscenium **opening,** 15x28; **height** from stage to grooves, 16; height **from stage to** rigging loft, 30; **depth under stage,** 6; traps, 2; **number** sets scenery, 15; **leader of orchestra,** Professor Bartling; **stage carpenter,** Thener; bill poster, Nat. Hurford; number of sheets can accommodate, 300; rates **per sheet,** 4c.; **theatrical** teamster, A. Baldwin. Newspapers: daily, Independent; weekly, Times (Th.), Herald (Wed). Democrat (Fri.).... Hotels: R. R. **House, special rates,** $1.50; Jorden, special rates, $1.50; Clarendon, special rates, $1.50.

Leiderkranz Hall, Chas. Ivers, manager; **seating capacity,** 500; rental, one night, $20; license included. Size of stage, 36x38; **fair stock scenery.**

HASTINGS. R. R., Burlington & Missouri River; Union Pacific. Liberal Hall, J. N. Lyman, manager; seating capacity—; rental, one **night** $15, three $35, license included. Size of stage, 16x40; **number sets** scenery, 6; bill poster, Harvey Williams. Newspapers: weekly, Journal, Gazette; semi-weekly, Central Nebraskian,..... Hotels: Commercial, Lepins, Denver, New England.

HEBRON. R. R., Burlington & M. R. Hebron Opera House, S. Poste, manager; **seating capacity, 500;** rental, one night $25, **three $50; share also,** Size of stage, 16x40; **no scenery;** bill **poster,** Opera House. Newspaper: Journal (Th.)........Hotels: Central, Gettis, **Sherman,** Hebron.

HUMBOLDT, 1,800. R. R., Burlington & M. R. in Neb. Samuelson Opera House, F. W. Samuelson, manager; seating **capacity,** 400; rental, one night $15, three $35; license, $2.20. Size of stage, 20x40; size of proscenium opening. 14x25. Newspaper: Advocate (Sat.), Sentinel (Fri.), Standard (Fri.)..... Hotel: Filson, regular rates, $2 (special also).

KEARNEY JUNCTION, 2,400. R. R., Burlington & Mis. River; Union Pacific. Moore's Music Hall; seating capacity, 600; **rental, one night $10;** license, $3; **fair stock scenery;** Newspapers: Journal (Wed.), New **Era** (Sat.)......Hotels: Atkins, regular rates, $2, (special also).

LINCOLN, 20,000. R. R., Burlington & Missouri River; Nebraska: Union Pacific. Frank's Grand Opera **House,** S. E. Moore, **manager; seating capacity,** 1,200; rental, share only; Size **of stage,** 40x72; size of proscenium **opening,** 22x30; **height from stage to** grooves, 22; height from stage to rigging loft, 36; depth **under stage,** 7; **traps,** 3; number sets scenery, 14; stage carpenter, W. H. Campbell; bill **poster,** S. E. Moore; rates per sheet, 4c; theatrical teamster, Grant Ensign. Newspapers: daily, Democrat, Journal, News..... Hotels: Commercial, St. Charles, Arlington, regular rates, $2 (special also).

LINCOLN, **20,000. R. R., Bur. & M. R. in** Neb.; Union Pacific. Opera House; seating capacity, **1,600;** rental, one night $75. Size of stage, 30x30; **height from stage to grooves,** 20; height **from stage to rigging loft, 25;** depth under stage, 7; **bill posters,** E. A. Church & Co.; theatrical teamsters, Bohannan Bros.

Academy of Music; seating capacity, 600.

City Hall; seating capacity, 800.

McCOOK, 1,500. R. R., Chic., Burl. **& Quincy.** Menard's Opera Hall, Wallace & Forbes, managers; seating capacity, 400; share only, license included. Size of stage, 20x40; size of proscenium, 10x20; height from **stage to grooves,** 9; number sets **scenery,** 6; bill **poster,** Opera Hall. Newspaper: Tribune **(Th.)......Hotel: B. & M. Hotel, special rates,** $1.

NEBRASKA CITY, 7,500. R. R., Burlington & Mis. River; Chic., Bur. & Quincy; Kansas City, St. Joseph & Council Bluffs. Hawke's Opera House, W. T. Canada, manager; **seating** capacity, 700; no license. Size of stage, 52x30; full set scenery. Newspapers: daily, Press, News .... Hotels: Morton, regular rates, $2 to $2.50 (special also); Grand Central, Barnum, Cincinnati.

15

NORTH PLATTE, 2,700. R. R., **Union** Pacific. Keith's Opera House, Wm. Neville, manager; seating capacity, 400; **rental,** one night $20, share also. Size of stage, 18x22; number sets scenery, 8; bill **poster, D. E.** Baker. Newspapers: Telegraph (Th.), Nebraskian (Sat.)......Hotels: **Hinman,** regular rates, $2.50 (special also); Railroad, Nebraska, California.

    Unitarian Hall, Lefille **& Tracy.** managers; seating capacity, 350; rental, one night $10; license, $5; fair stock scenery.

OMAHA, 60,000. R. R., Bur. & M. R. in Neb.; Chic., Mil. & St. Paul; Chic., St. Paul & O.; **Union Pacific;** Chic., Rock Island & Pac.; C., B. & Q.; Chic. & Northwestern; Missouri Pacific. Boyd's Opera House. Thos. **F.** Boyd, manager; E. E. Whitmore, treasurer; seating capacity, 1,700; **rental, one** night $75; share only. Size of stage, 50x75; size of proscenium opening, 35; **height from stage** to grooves, 18; height from stage to rigging loft, 70; **depth under stage,** 12; traps, 4; **number** sets scenery, 40; **leader** of orchestra, **Prof. S. Hoffman; stage carpenter, John Booth;** bill poster, Thomas Mulvihill; theatrical teamsters, Kennard **& Sharp Trans. Co.** Newspapers: daily, Herald; **advertising** rates per inch, 75c.; Bee, 75c. per inch; Republican, 75c. per inch; Dispatch, 50c **per inch**......
Hotels: Millard, special rates, $2 to $2.50; Metropolitan, special rates, $1.50 to **$2; Can**field, special rates, $1.50 to $3.

    Academy of Music, S. N. Mealls, manager; seating capacity, 700; rental, one night $50, three $100; license yearly. Size of stage, 44x27; height from stage to grooves, 15; depth under stage, 7; traps, 2; number sets scenery, 10.

    St. Elmo Theatre, John G. Nugent.

    Buckingham Theatre (variety), Nugent & Greene, managers; **seating capacity, 600. Size of stage,** 18x26.

    Creighton's Hall; seating capacity, 1,000.

    Masonic Hall; seating capacity, 600.

    Myer's Hall, seating capacity, 250.

PAWNEE CITY, 2,400. R. R., Burlington **& Missouri River.** Opera House, Spates & **Inglis,** managers; seating capacity, 1,000; rental, one night $25; share also; no license. **Size** of stage, 24x50; bill posters, Opera House. Newspapers: Banner (Fri.), Press **(Wed.),** Republican (Th.),......Hotels: Hazel, Arlington.

PLATTSMOUTH, 6,000. R. R., Chicago, Burlington & Quincy, Burlington & M. R.; Neb. **& Kansas** City; **St. Jo. & Council** Bluffs. Waterman Opera House, J. P. Young, manager; seating capacity, 1,200; rental, share only. Size of **stage,** 30x60; size of proscenium opening, 15; height from stage to grooves, 18; height **from stage** to rigging loft, 20; depth under stage, 4; traps, 5; number sets scenery, 10; **leader of** orchestra, Sam. Mathews; bill poster, J. P. Young; number of sheets **can** accommodate, 125; rates per sheet, 4c.; theatrical teamster, S. Fogleson. Newspapers; daily, Herald, Journal; week'y, Herald (Th.), Journal (Th.)......Hotels: Perkins', special rates, $1.25 to $1.50; City, special rates, $1 to $1.25; St. James, special rates, **$1** to $1.25.

    Fitzgerald's Hall, M. O'Donohue, manager; seating capacity, 600; rental, one night $15. Size of stage, 40x20; fair stock scenery.

SEWARD, 2,700. R. R. Burlington **& Missouri** River. Walker's Opera House, Thomas & Gercke, managers; seating capacity, 500; rental, one night $12; license, 2. Size of **stage,** 22x27; number sets scenery, 7. Newspapers: Blade (Wed.), Reporter **(Th.)** ......Hotels: Commercial, regular rates, $2 (special also); Windsor.

SIDNEY, 1,500. R. R., Union Pacific. White House Hall. Carl **E.** Borgquist, manager; seating capacity, 400; rental, one night $15, three $35. Size of stage, 12x24; number sets scenery, 4; bill poster, B. F. Walker. Newspaper: Plaindealer (Sat.)......Hotels: Lockwood, regular rates, $2 (special also); Metropolitan.

SYRACUSE, 1,000. R. R., Burlington & Missouri River. Erend's Opera House, E. Waite, manager. Newspaper: Journal (Fri.)......Hotel: National.

TECUMSEH, 1,500. R. R., Burlington & Missouri **River.** Opera House, W. R. Spicknall, **manager;** seating capacity, 500; rental, one night $15; license, $3.50. Size of stage, 40x23; fair stock scenery. Newspapers: Chieftain (Sat.), Journal (Th.), Torchlight **(Sat.)**......Hotels: Sherman, regular rates, $2 (special also); Caledonia, Continental.

WAHOO, 2,000. R. R., Union Pacific. Winter's Opera House. Newspapers: Independent (Th.), Tribune (Th.), Times (Fri.)......Hotel: Merchants', regular rates, $2 (special also).

WEYMORE, 2,000. R. R., Burlington & Missouri River; Union Pacific. Livsey's Opera House, Richard Livsey, manager, seating capacity, 700; rental, one night $25, three $55; share also; license included. Size of stage, 24x50; number sets scenery, 11. Newspapers: Reporter (Fri.), Eagle (Fri.)..... Hotels: Potter, regular rates, $2 (special also); Grand Central, City.

YORK, 2,500. R. R., Burlington & Missouri River. York Opera House, C. J. Nobes, manager; seating capacity, 800; share only. Size of stage, 20x40; number sets scenery, 10; bill poster, J. C. Brown. Newspapers: Republican, Democrat, Times......Hotels: Commercial, regular rates, $2 (special also); Central. .

NEVADA.

CARSON CITY, 4,600. R. R., Virginia & Truckee. Carson Opera House, John T. Preddey, manager; seating capacity, 750; rental, one night $85, license included. Size of stage, 33x50; number sets scenery, 8; bill poster, Opera House. Newspapers: daily, Index, Appeal, Tribune......Hotels: Ormsby, regular rates, $2.50 to $3 (special also); Arlington.

ELKO, 1,450. R. R., Central Pacific. Freeman's Opera House, M. P. Freeman & Co., managers; seating capacity, 350; rental, one night $30, three $45; license, $6. Size of stage, 15x22; number sets scenery, 3; bill poster, Opera House. Newspapers: daily, Independent; weekly, Free Press (Fri.)......Hotel: Depot.

Granger Hall, J. Reinhart, manager; seating capacity, 300; rental, one night $15, three $30; license, $7.50. Size of stage, 15x22; number sets scenery, 5.

EUREKA, 6,000. R. R., Eureka & Palisade. Eureka Opera House, Foley, Winzell & Sadler, managers ; seating capacity, 600 ; rental, one night, $40 ; three $120 ; license included ; share also. Size of stage, 30x38 ; number sets scenery, 10 ; bill poster, Opera House. Newspapers : daily, Leader, Sentinel........Hotels: Jackson, Parker, Turner, International.

Truckee Concert Hall, George Elston, manager.

RENO, 3,500. R. R., Central Pacific ; Nevada & Oregon ; Virginia & Truckee. Nevada Theatre, Hammond & Wilson, managers ; seating capacity, ——; rental, one night $50; share also, license included. Size of stage, 30x40 ; number sets scenery, 8 ; bill poster, Wm. H. Henderson. Newspaper: daily, Gazette, Journal........Hotels: Depot, regular rates, $2 to $2.50 (special also); International, Arcade, Pollard, Blake, Palace.

Pavilion; seating capacity, 1,500.

VIRGINIA CITY, 15,000. R. R., Virginia & Truckee. Piper's Opera House (burned 1883). Newspapers : daily, Chronicle, Enterprise........Hotels : International, regular rates, $2.50 to $3 (special also); Williams', Bixler's.

WINNEMUCCA, 1,500. R. R., Central Pacific. Centennial Hall, F. Levy & Co., managers ; rental, one night $20; license, $6. Size of stage, 12x18 ; number sets scenery 5. Newspaper: daily, Silver State..... Hotel: Winnemucca.

NEW HAMPSHIRE.

CLAREMONT, 4,300. R. R., Conn. River; Concord & Claremont. Town Hall, E. Burrell, manager; seating capacity, 700; rental, one night, $12.50; bill poster, E. Burrell. Newspapers : Advocate (Tu.), Eagle (Sat.)......Hotels : Belmont, regular rates, $2; Sullivan.

CONCORD, 1,500. R. R., Boston & Lowell; Concord. White's Opera House, B. C. White, manager; seating capacity, 1,000; rental, one night, $40; license, $5. Newspapers : daily.

Monitor; weekly, Journal; (Fri); People and Patriot (Th.)......Hotels: Eagle, special rates, $2.50; Phœnix, regular rates, $2.50 (special also); Elm, regular rates, $2.50 (special also): American.

Eagle Hall; seating capacity, 1,400.

Phœnix Hall; seating capacity, 975.

City Hall, seating capacity; 1,000.

Rumford Hall; seating capacity, 500.

DOVER, 13,000. R. R., Boston & Maine; Eastern. Coliseum, J. W. Caverly, manager; seating capacity, 1,150; share only. Size of stage, 25x70; size of proscenium opening, 30x30; height from stage to grooves, 16; height from stage to rigging loft, 24; depth under stage, 8; traps, 2; number sets scenery, 7; leader of orchestra, W. D. Taylor; bill poster, Geo. M. Gray; number of sheets can accommodate, 250; rates per sheet, 3c.; theatrical teamster, C. W. Butterfield. Newspapers: daily, Republican, advertising rates, per inch, $1.25; Democrat, advertising rates, per inch, $1.25; weekly, Enquirer (Th.), $1.25......Hotels: American, special rates, $1.50 to $2; Kimball, $1.50; Hawthorn, $1.25 to $1.50.

City Hall, Samuel Browning, manager, seating capacity, 1,000; rental one night, $39.50.

Wiggins Hall; seating capacity, 500.

Freeman Hall; seating capacity, 300.

EPPING, 1,960. R. R., Worcester, Nashua & Rochester; Concord. Pawtuckaway Hall, G. E. Smith, manager; seating capacity, 500; rental, one night $6; stage carpenter, James Riley; bill poster, James Riley; theatrical teamster, Riley. Newspaper: Leader..... Hotel: Pawtuckaway.

EXETER, 2,000. R. R., Boston & Maine. Town Hall, J. H. Taylor, manager; seating capacity, 600; rental, one night $15; fair stock scenery; bill poster, J. H. Taylor. Newspapers: Exonian (Sat.), Gazette (Fri.)......Hotels; Gorham, regular rates, $2; American, Granite.

FARMINGTON, 4,000. R. R., Boston & Maine. New Town Hall, seating capacity, 800; rental, one night $20; fair stock scenery; bill poster, J. F. Noyes. Newspaper: News (Fri.)....Hotel: Centre.

Mozart Hall; rental, one night $25. Size of stage, 15x21.

FRANKLIN FALLS, 3,700. R. R., Boston & Lowell (Northern Division). Burleigh Hall, Burleigh Bros., managers; seating capacity, 600; rental, one night $10, three $30. Size of stage, 10x16; size of proscenium opening, 10x16. Newspapers: Journal (Fri.), Transcript (Fri.)......Hotels: Young's, Winnipisogee.

GREAT FALLS, 8,000. R. R., Eastern: Boston & Maine. Tom Hall, J. F. Noyes, manager; seating capacity, 800; rental, ——; share also; license included. Size of stage, 16x44; size of proscenium opening, 12x24; number sets scenery, 22; leader of orchestra, D. P. Sweet; scenic artist, C. J. Cowell; stage carpenter, Stubb Corliss; bill poster, J. F. Noyes; number of sheets can accommodate, 200; rates per sheet, 5c.; theatrical teamster, Foos & Goodwin. Newspaper: Journal (Th.)......Hotels: Great Falls, special rates, $1.50; Grant's, special rates, $2; Granite, special rates, $1 to $1.25.

HANOVER, 3,000. R. R., Con. River & Passumsic. Kibling's Opera House, G. W. Kibling, manager; seating capacity, 600; rental, one night $15, three $32; share also; no license. Size of stage, 16x20; number sets scenery, 6; bill poster, Opera House; theatrical teamsters, Allen & Swazy. Newspapers: Journal (Sat.) .... Hotels: Dartmouth, regular rates $2 (special also).

HOOKSET, 1,500. R. R., Concord. Odd Fellows' Hall, E. Prank, manager; seating capacity, 300; rental, one night $5. Size of stage, 25x12; bill poster, E. Prank; theatrical teamster, J. O. Ingalls......Hotels: Ayer, Bonney.

KEENE, 7,000. R. R., Boston & Lowell; Cheshire; Connecticut River. City Hall, E. O. Keith, manager; seating capacity, 1,000; rental, one night $30, three $75; license included. Size of stage, 21x60; fair stock scenery; bill poster, H. C. Rice; theatrical

teamster, D. S. Willard. Newspapers: Republican (Sat.), Journal (Sat.), Observer (Th.),
Sentinel (Wed.)......Hotels: Cheshire, regular rates $2 (special also); City, Eagle.

Cheshire Hall; seating capacity, 400.

Liberty Hall; seating capacity, 400.

LACONIA, 4,500. R. R., Boston & Lowell. Folsom Opera House, F. D. Ellis, manager:
seating capacity, 500; rental, share only; license, $2 to $5. Size of stage, 18x24; size of
proscenium opening, 11x24; height from stage to grooves, 11½; depth under stage, 4;
traps, 1; number sets scenery, 6; leader of orchestra, Professor F. W. Story; scenic artist, O. L. Andrews; stage carpenter, Thomas Gay; bill posters, Truland Bros., F. D.
Ellis; number of sheets can accommodate, 200; rates per sheet, 5c.; theatrical teamsters, Truland Bros. Newspapers : daily, Democrat; advertising rates, 50c. inch; weekly. Democrat; advertising rates, 50c. inch... . .Hotels : Eagle, special rates, $1.25; Wil-
lard, special rates, $1; Laconia, special rates, $1.

LAKE VILLAGE, 2,200. R. R., Boston & Lowell. Moore's Opera House, George F. Roby,
manager; seating capacity, 600; rental, one night $12, three $30, license included. Size
of stage, 16x30; size of proscenium opening, 14x30; number sets scenery, 2; leader of orchestra, A. L. Ruble. Newspapers: daily, Laconia Democrat; weekly, Lake Village
Times (Sat.)... Hotels: Mt. Belknap, special rates, $1; Brown.

LEBANON, 3,300. R. R., Boston & Lowell. Town Hall, W. H. Richardson. manager;
seating capacity, 1,000; rental, one night $14 to $20; number sets scenery; 6, bill poster,
Carlisle; theatrical teamster, Sayers. Newspaper : Free Press (Fri.) ..Hotel : Sayers.

LITTLETON, 3,300. R. R., Boston, Concord & Montreal. Union Hall, John Ready, man-
ager; seating capacity, 800 ; rental, one night $15; number sets scenery, 4; bill poster,
John Ready; theatrical teamster, E. J. Crane. Newspapers: Journal (Fri.), Republican
(Sat.)........Hotels: Thayer, Union, Potter's.

MANCHESTER, 40,000. R. R., Concord. Manchester Opera House, E. W. Harrington, manager ; seating capacity, 1,500; size of proscenium opening, 36x36; height from stage to
grooves, 20; height from stage to rigging loft, 68; depth under stage, 14; traps, 6; number sets scenery, 20; leader of orchestra, C. F Eastman; scenic artist, Wm. Gannon;
stage carpenter, W. D. Jillson; bill poster, F. P. Colby; number of sheets can accommodate, 1,000; theatrical teamster, F. P. Colby. Newspaper: daily, Union, Mirror; weekly,
Budget......Hotels: Windsor, regular rates, $1.50 to $2; Manchester House, $1.50 to
$2; Hanover, $1 to $1.50.

Smyth's Opera House (variety), S. R. Hanford, manager ; seating capacity, 1,400 ; full set
scenery.

Music Hall (variety), Wambold & Mortimer, managers; seating capacity, 800.

NASHUA, 16,000. R. R., Boston & Lowell ; Concord ; Worcester & Nashua. Franklin
Opera House, Geo. Swain, manager; seating capacity, 925; rental, one night $40, license,
included ; share also. Size of stage, 21x35 ; size of proscenium opening, 15x22 ; height
from stage to grooves, 13 ; height from stage to rigging loft, 17 ; depth under stage,
3½ ; number sets scenery, 10 ; leader of orchestra, Cummings & Damons ; stage
carpenter, Geo. W. Brown ; bill poster, Geo. W. Davis ; number of sheets can accommodate, 600 ; rates per sheet, 5c. ; theatrical teamster, D. W. Dunckler. Newspapers :
daily, Telegraph, advertising rates, 50c. per inch ; Gazette, advertising rates, 50c. per
inch......Hotels : Indian Head, special rates, $1.50; Tremont, special rates, $1 50.

City Hall, City Clerk, manager ; seating capacity, 700 ; rental, one night $20; license, $8 ;
no scenery

NEWMARKET, 3,000. R. R., Boston & Maine. Town Hall, N. Morgan, manager; seating
capacity, 400 ; rental, one night $12, license included. Size of stage, 16x18 ; bill poster
J. F. Noyes (Great Falls); theatrical teamsters, Grant & Son. Newspaper : Advertiser
.....Hotels: Silver, Newmarket.

PENACOOK, 3,000. R. R., Northern Division of Boston & Lowell. Exchange Hall, G. W.
Abbott, manager; seating capacity, 600; rental, one night $10, three $25; license, $5.
Size of stage, 15x30; size of proscenium opening, height, full size of stage; height from

TIME ALL FILLED!

3d Annual Tour. 3d   1884—Season.—1885

"UNEQUALED SUCCESS."

THE GREATEST OF ALL MELODRAMATIC AND EQUES-
TRIAN SENSATIONS.

JAMES H. WALLICK'S

PICTURESQUE COMEDY DRAMA

In six acts and eight stirring tableaux, entitled the

"THE NEW BANDIT KING."

(OVER)

"NEW BANDIT KING,"

INTRODUCING THE FAMOUS HORSES,

Roan Charger

— AND —

Bay Raider,

*The Most Intelligent and Wonderful Animal Actors
on Earth!*

$10,000—OFFERED FOR THEIR EQUAL—$10,000.
4 Strong Original Comedy Parts.
A Specially Adapted Dramatic Company.

A Full Equipment of Scenery Runs, etc., etc., Transported in
our own Special Cars.

Below will be found a few of the

SPECIAL SENSATIONAL EFFECTS:

The Bombshell Explosion and Fire Scene.

The Dash for Liberty through a Window on Horseback, Carrying
a Woman in His Arms.

The Escape and Running Duel on Horseback (the most exciting
rally on the stage).

The Rescue of Indian Girl from the Rapids with the Lariat (a new
and original water scene).

The Spy's Ride to Death (the greatest run ever made on any stage).

The Great Bowie Knife Fight
ON HORSEBACK.

Season of 1885 and 1886 will open on or about Sept. 1.

Managers of first-class large theatres and opera houses will
please send their open dates, terms, etc., as per route of company
given in weekly dramatic papers. Address :

JAMES H. WALLICK & CO., Managers.

stage to rigging loft, 12; bill poster, W. Bonney; theatrical teamster. John Zucker. Newspapers: Rays of Light (Th.)......Hotel; Washington, special rates, $1 to $1.25

PORTSMOUTH, 10,000. R. R., Eastern; Concord & Portsmouth Music Hall, John O. Ayres, manager; seating capacity, 1,200; rental, one night $35, three $120; license included. Size of stage, 30x72; size of proscenium opening, 25x35; height from stage to grooves, 16; height from stage to rigging loft, 35; depth under stage, 8; traps, 4; number sets scenery, 7; stage carpenter, Charles Henry Kennison; bill poster, V. A. Hett; number of sheets can accommodate, 500; rates per sheet, 5c.; theatrical teamster, Hett Bros. Newspapers: daily, Chronicle, advertising rates, 10c. per inch; Times, advertising rates, 40c. per inch; weekly, Gazette (Wed.), States & Union (Fri.), Journal (Sat.) ... .Hotels: Kearsarge, special rates, $1.75 to $2; Webster, special rates, $1.50 to $1.75.

Franklin Theatre, E. Slavers, manager; seating capacity, 800; rent or share. Size of stage, 30x60; full set scenery.

Congress Hall; seating capacity, 500.

Temple; seating capacity, 1,000.

Mechanics' Hall; seating capacity, 200.

ROCHESTER, 6,000. R. R., Boston & Maine; Eastern; Portland & Rochester; Nashua & Rochester. Hayes' Hall, A. W. Hayes, manager; seating capacity, 500; rental, one night $10, three $25. Size of stage, 15x25; size of proscenium opening, 10½x15; height from stage to grooves, 13½; height from stage to rigging loft, 14½; number sets scenery, 8; leader of orchestra, L. S. Clark; scenic artist, Frank H. Orr; stage carpenter, Leander Pickering; bill poster, James T. B. Edgerly; number of sheets can accommodate, 300; rates per sheet, 4c.; theatrical teamster, E. M. Denne. Newspapers : Courier (Fri.), advertising rates, $10 per column; Anti-Monopolist (Fri.), advertising rates, $10 per column......Hotels: W. Wrisley, special rates, $1.25; Mansion, special rates, $1.25.

McDuffees' Hall, G. B. Berry, manager; seating capacity, 500; rental, one night $12; no scenery.

Heazes' Hall; seating capacity, 700.

Town Hall; seating capacity, 450.

SUNCOOK, 8,000. R. R., Concord. Suncook Opera House, J. G Bartlett, manager; seating capacity, 1,000; rental, one night $15, three $35; no license. Size of stage, 20x30; number sets scenery, 5; bill posters, Bartlett & Hayes; theatrical teamster, John Colby. Newspaper; Journal (Sat.)......Hotels: Opera Hotel, Suncook.

Hayes' Opera House, David Hayes, manager; seating capacity, 1,000; rental, one night $15; share also. Size of stage, 20x30; number sets scenery, 5.

NEW JERSEY.

ASBURY PARK, 7,600. R. R., Central New Jersey. Patterson's Opera House, Frank Patterson, manager; seating capacity, 1,226; share only. Size of stage, 25x26; number sets scenery, 8; bill poster, Opera House. Newspapers: Journal (Sat.), Republican (Sat.), Press (Sat.)......Hotels: Coleman, Grand, American, Asbury.

BLOOMFIELD, 7,000. R. R., Del., Lack. & Western; N. Y. & Greenwood Lake. Library Hall, J. Banks Reford, manager; seating capacity, 500; rental, one night $20; no license. Size of stage, 20x30; no scenery. Newspaper: Citizen (Sat.)......Hotel: Bloomfield.

BORDENTOWN, 7,000. R. R., Penn. (Amboy Division). Park Street Opera House, T. J. Murphy, manager; seating capacity, 650; rental, one night $25, three $60. Size of stage, 30x35; number sets scenery, 6; bill poster, Demmons & Murphy. Newspaper: Register (Fri.)......Hotels: Bordentown, regular rates, $2 (special also); Davis, American, City, Washington.

BRIDGETON, 1,200. R. R., Cumberland & Maurice River; New Jersey South.; West Jersey. Moore's Opera House, J. M. Moore & Sons, managers; seating capacity, 1,000; rental, one night $25 to $35; share also. Size of stage, 30x65; full set scenery; bill poster, F. D. Carll;

theatrical teamsters, **Davis** Bros. Newspapers: daily, New Chronicle; weekly, Patriot (Fri.), Pioneer (Th.)......Hotels: Davis, regular rates $2 (special also); City.

Groscup's Hall; C. C. Groscup, manager; **seating capacity, 800; rental, one night $12, three** $30; license, $8. Size of stage, 12x16; no **scenery.**

BURLINGTON, 8,500. R. R., Penn. (Amboy division). Birch's Opera House, James Birch, manager; seating capacity, 1,200; rental, one night $40, three $60; no license. Size of stage, 30x30; fair stock **scenery;** bill **poster,** Philip Galerger. Newspapers: Advertiser (Sat.), Enterprise **(Th.).. ...Hotels: Beldin,** City, Washington.

City Hall; seating capacity, **800.**

Beldin's Hall; seating capacity, 200.

CAMDEN, 10,000. R. R., Camden & Atlantic; Camden, Gloucester **& Mt. E.; Penn. (Amboy Division,); Phila. & Atlantic City;** West Jersey. Morgan Hall, Frank **J. Burr, manager;** seating capacity, 500; rental, **one** night $15, three $30. Size of stage, 17x21; **height from** stage to grooves, 18; depth under stage, 3; number sets scenery, 2; bill posters, Templeman & Dorney. Newspapers: daily, Post, Courier; weekly, Democrat (Sat.).. ...Hotels: West Jersey, regular rates, $2 (special also); Parsons, regular rates, $2 (special also).

Camden Opera House, R. Bingham, manager; seating capacity, 1,200; rental, one night $40, share also; no license. Size of stage, 30x64; full set scenery.

Lincoln Hall; seating capacity, 600.

Central Hall; seating capacity, 250.

Wildey's Hall; seating capacity, 200.

DOVER, 2,800. R. R., Delaware, Lackawanna & West. **Opera House,** Daniel Moller, manager; seating capacity, 500; rental, **one** night $10; license, $5. Size of stage, 20x40; full set scenery; bill poster, Charles Gear. Newspapers: Index (Th.), Iron Era (Sat.).....Hotels: Mansion, Jolly, Stickler, Learing.

ELIZABETH, 35,000. R. R., **Central New Jersey; Pennsylvania. Library** Hall, J. E. Marsh, manager; seating capacity, 800; rental, one night $25; **license, $3.** Size of stage, 28x56; number sets scenery, 3; **bill poster, Wm. Woodruff; theatrical** teamster, Patrick Clark. Newspapers: daily, **Herald, Journal; weekly, Leader** (Sun.)......Hotels: Sheridan, regular rates, $2 (special also); City.

Opera House; seating capacity, 800.

Arnold's Hall; **seating capacity, 400.**

ELMER. **500. R. R., West Jersey.** Reed's Hall, J. M. Reed, **manager; seating capacity,** 450..... Hotel : Hitchner.

FREEHOLD, 4,500. R. R., Freehold & New York; Pennsylvania, (Amboy Division). **Shinn's Hall,** G. W. Shinn & Son, managers; seating capacity, 1,000; rental, one night **$15,** three $35; no license. Size of stage, 24x50; number sets scenery, 1; bill poster, Frank Emmons; theatrical teamster, Wm. H. Cook. Newspapers : Democrat (Th.), Inquirer..... .Hotels : American, regular rates, $2 (special also); Washington, Union.

Seminary Hall; seating capacity, 500.

HACKENSACK, 8,000. R. R., New Jersey & N. Y.; N. Y., Ont. & W.; N. Y., Sus. & **West.; N. Y.,** W. S. & B. Irving Hall, J. C. Vanhorn, manager; seating capacity, 600; **rental, one** night $15, three $40; no license. Size of stage, 20x27; **no** scenery; bill **poster, J.** H Lanisson. Newspapers: semi-weekly, Index (Tu. and Fri.); weekly, Democrat **(Fri.),** Republican (Th.)......Hotels : Hackensack, regular rates, $2 (special also); Washington Mansion.

Anderson Hall, John J. Anderson, manager; seating capacity, **450;** rental, one night $10, three $20; no license Size of stage, 13x33; no scenery.

HACKETTSTOWN, 3,500. R. **R.,** Delaware, Lackawanna **& Western.** Shield's Hall; seating capacity, 400; rental, **one** night $15; license, $3; bill poster, manager of hall; theatrical teamster, J. McCracken. Newspapers : Gazette (Fri.), Republican (Fri.)...... **Hotels :** Warren, regular rates, $2 (special also); Clarendon, American.

HIGHTSTOWN, 3,000. R. R., Pennsylvania, (Amboy Division.) Hutchinson Hall, George D. Hutchinson, manager; seating capacity, 400; rental, one **night $8, three $18;** license.

$2. Size of stage, 12x20 ; bill poster, manager of hall. Newspapers : Gazette (Th.),
Independent......Hotels : Railroad, Washington, Luntz.

HOBOKEN, 37,000. R. R., Delaware, Lackawanna & Western. Wearing's Germania
Garden Theatre, Robert Wearing, manager; seating capacity, 1,200. Size of stage, 16x18;
number sets scenery, 8; bill poster, William Frazier. Newspapers: Advertiser (Sat.),
Journal (Sat.)......Hotels: Park, Bush, Naegli, Meyers.

Odd Fellows Hall; seating capacity, 500.

Webber's Hall; seating capacity, 500.

JERSEY CITY, 125,000. R R, Central New Jersey; Erie ; New Jersey & N. Y.; N. Y. &
Green Lake; N. Y. & Long Branch: N. Y., Sus. & West. ; N. Y., W. Sh. & B ; Penn.
Academy of Music, Wm. Henderson, manager; seating capacity, 1,400 ; share only.
Size of stage, 82x60; size of proscenium opening. 24x26; height from stage to grooves,
18; height from stage to rigging loft, 87 ; depth under stage, 4; traps, 3 ; number sets
scenery, 12; leader of orchestra, H. F. Wagner; scenic artist, T. Neville ; stage carpenter, T. S. Durkin; bill posters, Rikeman & Omelia; theatrical teamsters, Dodd & Childs.
Newspapers: daily, Journal, advertising rates per line, 10c.; Argus, advertising rates per
line, 10c.; weekly, Tattler (Sun.), rates 10c. per line......Hotels: Taylor's, Philadelphia.

Opera House, W. H. Budlong, manager ; seating capacity, 1,000 ; rental, one night $50;
three $130; share also; license included. Size of stage, 28x32; full set scenery.

Library Hall; seating capacity, 400.

KEYPORT, 2,700. R. R., Freehold & N. Y. Walling's Opera House; seating capacity, 600;
rental, one night $35; bill poster, Timothy Watts; theatrical teamster, Fred Hoffman.
Newspapers: Enterprise (Sat.), Weekly (Sat.)......Hotels: Pavilion, regular rates, $2
(special also), Mansion.

LAMBERTVILLE, 5,000. R. R., Pennsylvania, (Belvidere Division). Lyceum Hall; seating
capacity, 600; bill poster, Chas. Gallagher. Newspapers: Beacon (Fri.), Record (Wed.)
......Hotels: Lambertville, regular rates $2 (special also): Bellemonte, Union.

Halcombe Hall; seating capacity, 500.

LONG BRANCH, 7,000. R. R., N. Y. & Long Branch; N. J. South.; Pennsylvania, (Amboy
Division). Long Branch Opera House, J. V. Allstron, manager; seating capacity, 500;
rental, one night $20, three $40; share also, license included. Size of stage, 18x20; fair
stock scenery; bill poster, Opera House. Newspapers: News (Sat.), Record (Sat.)......
Hotels: West End, Ocean, Howland, Central.

Theatre Comique; seating capacity, 500.

MATAWAN, 2,000. R. R., Freehold & New York; New York & Long Branch. Washington
Hall, C. H. Wardell, manager; seating capacity, 400; rental, one night $10. Size of
stage, 12x20; no scenery; bill poster, Hal Close; theatrical teamster, Frank Bedel.
Newspaper: Journal (Sat.)......Hotel: Matawan.

MILLVILLE, 18,000. R R, West Jersey. Wilson's Opera House, James C. Wilson, manager; seating capacity, 1,000; rental, one night $35; license, $2.50 to $5; share also.
Size of stage, 25x50; number sets scenery, 12; bill poster, Lewis Murray; theatrical
teamster, Ben Davis. Newspapers: Republican (Fri.), Transcript (Fri.)......Hotels:
Doughty, regular rates, $2 (special also): Burrough, Broadstreet.

Institute Hall; H. Mulford. manager; rent or share; license, $5. Size of stage, 38x15;
number sets scenery, 13.

Morris Opera House.

MORRISTOWN, 6,500. R. R., Delaware, Lackawana & Western. Lyceum Hall, William
M King, manager; seating capacity, 750; rental, one night $30, three $50; license. —.
Size of stage, 22x34; number sets scenery. —; bill poster, Henry West; theatrical teams-
ters, Van Fleet Brothers. Newspapers: Jerseyman (Fri.), Chronicle (Sat.), Banner (Th.)
......Hotels: Mansion, regular rates, $2.50 (special also) : United States, Park.

Washington Hall ; seating capacity, 100.

MOUNT HOLLY, 6,000. R. R., Pennsylvania, (Amboy Division). Mount Holly Opera
House, J. F. Laumaster, manager; seating capacity, 600; rental, one night $25, three $60:

Miss Nellie Boyd,

SUPPORTED BY A CAREFULLY SELECTED COMPANY

IN A REPERTOIRE OF

STANDARD PLAYS.

———

A CLASSICAL ORCHESTRA.

———

G. M. WELTY,	Manager.
C. F. ADAMS,	Business Agent.
D. W. CLARK,	Musical Director.

---

no license. Size of stage, 30x50; number sets scenery, 3; bill poster, Joseph D Champman; theatrical teamster, Thos. Aitkin. Newspapers: Herald (Sat.), Mirror (Wed.), News (Tu.) .....Hotels: Arcade, regular rates, $2 (special also); Washington.

NEWARK, 146,000. R. R., Central New Jersey; Delaware, Lackawanna & Western; New York, Lake Erie & Western; Pennsylvania, (New York Division). Grand Opera House, Leonard Gray, manager; seating capacity, 1,456; rental, one night $75, three $180; license, $1; share also. Size of stage, 42x80; size of proscenium opening. 40x32; height from stage to grooves, 26; height from stage to rigging loft, 8; depth under stage, 13; traps, 5; number sets scenery, 21; leader of orchestra, Prof. Haynes; scenic artist, R Weed; stage carpenter, J Guisinger; bill posters, Evans & Hotchkiss; number sheets can accommodate, 1,600; rates per sheet, 4c.; theatrical teamster, P. Mead. Newspapers: daily, Advertiser, Journal; weekly, Call (Sun.) ....Hotels: Park, special rates, $1.50 to $2; Continental, special rates, $1 to $2.

Park Theatre, Leonard Gray, manager; seating capacity, 1,663; rental, one night $80, three $225; share only. Size of stage, 50x62; size of proscenium opening, 40x30; height from stage to grooves, 40; height from stage to rigging loft, 46; depth under stage, 13; traps, 4; number sets scenery, 22; leader of orchestra, Prof. Wagner; scenic artist, Wilder; stage carpenter, Guisinger; bill posters, Evans & Hotchkins; number sheets can accommodate, 2,000; rates per sheet, 4c.; theatrical teamster, Mead.

Atlantic Theatre, Hohweiler, manager; seating capacity, 1,100. Size of stage, 21x23; full set scenery.

Waldmann's Opera House, Fred. Waldmann, manager.

Library Hall; seating capacity   ; rental, one night $25.

Dime Museum, H. R. Jacobs, manager.

NEW BRUNSWICK, 18,000. R R., Pennsylvania, (New York Division). Opera House. Ayers D. Insler, manager; seating capacity, 1,200. Size of stage, 35x30; height from stage to grooves, 19; height from stage to rigging loft, 90; depth under stage, 12; bill poster, C. F. Shaw; theatrical teamster, James Ferguson. Newspapers : daily, Fredonian, News, Times. ......Hotels : Abbott, White Hall, McCormick's.

NEWTON, 3,400. R. R., Sussex. Library Hall, Dr. F. Smith, manager; seating capacity, 500; rental, one night $15, three $30; no license. Size of stage, 15x30; number sets scenery, 3; bill poster, James Matthews; theatrical teamsters, Brannigan & Cochran. Newspapers: Democrat (Wed.), Register (Wed.)......Hotels : Cochran, regular rates, $2 (special also); Ward.

NORWOOD, 500. R. R., Northern New Jersey. Inman Hall, James Inman, manager; seating capacity, 400; rental, one night $8; license, $2. Size of stage, 15x30; no scenery; bill poster, J. Delaney......Hotels: Whitney, American.

ORANGE, 14,000. R. R., Delaware, Lackawanna & Western; N. Y. & Greenwood Lake. Music Hall, Geo. P. Kingsler, manager; seating capacity, 950; rental, one night $40 to $60; license, $3 to $5; share also; size of stage, 28x60; height from stage to grooves, 18; height from stage to rigging loft, 24; depth under stage, 6; number sets scenery, 4; bill posters, Taylor & Co.; theatrical teamster, H. F. Ballard. Newspapers: Chronicle (Sat.), Journal (Sat.)......Hotels: Park, regular rates, $2 (special also), Morrison.

Library Hall, seating capacity, 500; rental, one night $15; license, $3 to $5.

PASSAIC, 7,500. R. R., Delaware, Lackawanna & Western; Erie. Lyceum Hall, F. Whitehead, manager; seating capacity, 700; rental, one night $15, three $30. Size of stage, 30x30; number sets scenery, 4; bill poster, M. C. Dwyre; theatrical teamster, E. Broadway. Newspapers: daily, News, Times; weekly, Herald (Sat), Item (Sat.)......Hotel: Lyceum, regular rates, $2 (special also).

Rattegue Hall.

PATERSON, 68,000. R. R., Erie; New York, Susquehanna & West.; Del., L. & W. Paterson Opera House, H. C. Stone, manager; seating capacity, 1,600; rental, one night $75; three $195, license included; share only. Size of stage, 34x36; size of proscenium opening, 32x30; height from stage to grooves, 18; height from stage to rigging loft, 56; depth under stage, 12; traps, 2 ; scenery, full set ; leader of orchestra, R. Nicholls ; scenic artist, Geo. Heinmann; stage carpenter, H. C. Stone; **bill poster,** Opera House; number sheets can accommodate, 800; rates per sheet, &c.; theatrical teamster, Edward Barlow. Newspapers: daily, Guardian, Press......Hotels: Hamilton, Franklin, United States.

Odd Fellows Hall, Robert Dalling, manager; seating capacity, 500; rental, one night $8 to $20.

Novelty Theatre, J. Van Orden, manager; seating capacity, 1,600; **rent or share;** full set scenery.

Philion's Dime Museum, E. Philion, manager.

PERTH AMBOY, 5,500. R. R. Central N. J.; Lehigh Valley; N . Y. & Long Branch; Pennsylvania (New York Division); Staten Island. City Hall; seating capacity, 400; rental, one night $10, three $20; share also; **number sets scenery,** 2; bill poster, John **Sarles;** theatrical teamster, John Sarles. Newspapers: Democrat (Sat.), Republican (Fri.)......Hotels: Central, regular rates, $2 (special also); Pennsylvania, Park.

PLAINFIELD, 12,000. R. R., Phil. & Reading; (New Jersey Central Div.) **Stillman Music Hall;** Craig A. Marsh, manager; seating capacity, 948; share only. Size of stage, 40x70; height from stage to grooves, 16; number sets scenery, 11; leader of orchestra, Voss; scenic artist, W. F. Fetters; stage carpenter, J. Furze; bill poster, Charles Cook; rates per sheet, &c. Newspapers; daily, News; weekly, Times (Wed.), Constitutionalist (Th.)......Hotel : Lang's, City, Park House, Fetherwood, Farmers, Metropolitan, special rates.

Vanderveer's Hall; seating capacity, 800.

Lang's Hall; seating capacity, 600.

Assembly Hall; seating capacity, 500.

PRINCETON, 4,000. R. R., Pennsylvania, **(N. Y. Div.) Mercer Hall,** —— Koltschmid, manager; seating capacity, 400; **rental, one night $15;** no license. Size of stage, 15x21; no scenery; bill poster, C. A. Anderson; **theatrical teamster, John G.** Skillman. Newspapers: Press (Sat.) Hotels: Nashua, **University.**

RAHWAY, 7,200. R. R., Penn., (N. Y Division). Gordon **Opera** House, Wm. E. Van Fleet, manager ; seating capacity, 800; rental, one night $40, three $100; license included. Size of stage, 33x53; fair stock scenery; bill posters, Banta & Crowell; theatrical teamster, Wm. Ruddy. Newspapers: semi-weekly, Advocate; weekly, Democrat (Fri.)... Hotels: Chamberlain, **regular rates;** $2 (special also); Melck, Park.

SALEM, 6,000. R. R., Salem; Woodstown; West Jersey. **Salem Lecture Hall.** D. Harris Smith, manager; seating capacity, 900; rental, one night **$25; share also; license included.** Size of stage, 17x46 ; size of proscenium opening. **18x25;** height from stage to grooves, 18; height from stage to rigging loft, 24; **depth** under stage, 10; number sets scenery, 8; leader of orchestra, Professor D. W. Smith; stage carpenter, G. M. Morris; bill poster, A. J. Copner ; number of sheets can accommodate, 300; rates per sheet, 3c.; theatrical teamster, W. A. Smith. Newspapers: Jerseyman (Tu.), Sunbeam (Fri.), Standard (Wed.)......Hotels: Nelson, special rates, $1.50; Garwood, special rates, $1.50 ; Schaefer, special rates, $1.25.

Rumsey Hall, J. R. Edgar, **manager;** seating capacity, 500; rental, one night $10; three $25; **no license.** Size of stage, **12x23; no** scenery.

TRENTON, 40,000. R. R., Penn.; Phila. & Reading. Taylor Opera **House,** John Taylor, **manager;** seating capacity, 1,300; share only. Size of stage, 34x65; size of proscenium **opening, 23x32;** height from stage **to** grooves, 16 to 23 (adjustable); height from stage to **rigging loft,** 47; depth under stage, 7; traps, 2; **full set of scenery;** leader of orchestra, J. H. Peterman; stage carpenter, Joseph Roff; bill poster, **John** Taylor. Newspapers; **daily, State Gazette, advertising rates per** inch, 75c.; **Times,** advertising rates per inch, 75c.; **True** American, **advertising rates** per inch, 75c.; Emporium; weekly, Advertiser (Sun.)......Hotel : Trenton, special rates, $2.50; **American,** special rates, $1.50; United States, National, Windsor.

Grand Central Theatre, Turner & Knowles, managers; seating capacity, 700 ; shares only. Size of stage, 20x38; size of proscenium opening, 15x20; height from stage to grooves, 10; height from stage to rigging loft, 18; depth under stage, **5;** traps, 1; number sets scenery,

; leader of orchestra, Mat Herrmann; stage carpenter, John Phillips; bill poster, Harry Ditmars; rates per sheet, 3c.; theatrical teamsters, Cappell Brothers.

Temperance Hall, H. B. Howell, manager, seating capacity, 600; rental, one night ——. Size of stage, 11x23. .

Washington Hall; seating capacity, 600.

Freeze's Hall; seating capacity, 400.

VINELAND, 2,000. R. R., N. J. Southern; West Jersey. Cosmopolitan Hall, S. G. Sylvester, manager; seating capacity, 700; rental, one night $10, three $24; share also. Size of stage, 22x20; number sets scenery, ——; bill poster, A. J Washburne; theatrical teamster, R. Sanderson. Newspapers: daily, Journal; News-Times; weekly, Independent (Th.) ....Hotel: Baker, regular rates, $2 (special also); Vineland.

Vineland Grand Army Hall, George A. Cheever, manager; seating capacity, 450; rental, one night $10, three $24; license, $5 to $10; share also. Size of stage, 16x23; number sets scenery, 6.

WASHINGTON, 3,300. R. R., Delaware, Lackawanna & Western. Beatty Music Hall, rental one night, $15; license, $3 to $5; bill poster, John McNally. Newspapers: Review (Fri.), Star (Th.)......Hotel: Windsor, regular rates, $2 (special also); St. Cloud.

WOODBURY, 8,000. R. R., West Jersey; Delaware River. Green's Opera House, Geo. H. Barker, manager; seating capacity, 800; rental, one night $25, three $60; license included. Size of stage, 18x22; depth under stage, 3½; traps, 7; number sets scenery, 8; bill poster, Ben Dilks; rates per sheet, 3c.; theatrical teamster, Ben Dilks. Newspapers: Constitution (Tu.), Democrat (Wed.), Liberal Press (Fri.) .... Hotels: Paul's, special rates, $2; Newton's, special rates, $2; Green Castle, special rates, $1.

Woodbury Hall, Chas. W. Starr, manager; seating capacity, 500; rental, one night $10; no license. Size of stage, 10x16; no scenery.

NEW YORK.

ADDISON, 3,300. R. R., Addison & Northern Penn.; Erie. Baldwin's Hall, seating capacity, 600; rental, one night $6 to $10; license, $1 to $2. Size of stage, 16x20. Newspapers: Advertiser (Th.), Record (Th.)......Hotels: American, regular rates, $2 (special also); Huston, Harder.

ALBANY, 100,000. R. R., N. Y. C. & H. R; Del. & Hud. C. Co.; N. Y., W. S. & B.; Del. & Lack. Leland Opera House, Mrs. Rosa M. Leland, manager; Brooks & Dickson, New York representatives; seating capacity, 1,300; rental, share only; license included. Size of stage, 38x60; size of proscenium opening, 33x37; height from stage to grooves, 19; height from stage to rigging loft, 44; depth under stage, 30; number sets of scenery, 30; musical director, W. Walters; scenic artist, Samuel Booker; stage carpenter, P. W. McDonald; bill poster, F. Keeler; number of sheets can accomodate, 1,500; rates per sheet, 4c.; theatrical teamsters, Wm. C. Perry, Wygant & Co. Newspapers: daily, Argus, advertising rates, 60c. per inch; Express, 60c. per inch; Press, 60c. per inch; Times, 60c. per inch; Journal, 60c. per inch; Post, 60c. per inch; weekly, Sunday Press, rates $1.50; Sunday Argus, $1.50..... Hotels: regular rates, $1.50 to $3; Stanwix, regular rates, $1.50 to $3; Port Orange, regular rates, $1 to $2.50; American, regular rates, $1 to $3; Belvidere, regular rates, $1.50 to $2; Brunswick, regular rates, $1.50 to $2.50.

Music Hall, George E. Oliver, manager; seating capacity 1,000; rental, one night $75, three $225; share also; license yearly. Size of stage, 36x68; number sets scenery, 36.

Stanwix Hall, Cebral Quackenbush, manager.

Novelty Theatre, Fred. Le Vantine, manager.

Tweddle Hall, seating capacity, 1,000.

ALBION, 6,500. R. R., N. Y. Cen. & Hudson River. Village Opera House, Charles D. Harris, manager; seating capacity, 650; rental, one night $20, share also; license included. Size of stage, 30x40; number sets scenery, 8; bill poster, Opera House; theatrical teamster,

S. Stockton. Newspapers: American (Th.), Republican (Wed.), Chronicle (Sat.).
........**Hotels** : Orleans, regular rates, $2 (special also); Albion, Exchange.

Bordwell Hall; seating capacity, 1,000.

Concert Hall; seating capacity, 800.

AMSTERDAM, 14,000. **R. R., N. Y. Cen. & H. R. :** N. Y., **W. S. & B.** Opera House,
A. **Z.** Neff, manager; **seating capacity, 1,750;** rental, share only; license yearly. Size
of stage, 30x58; size **of proscenium opening,** 28x32; height from stage to grooves,
17; height from stage **to rigging loft,** 33; **depth** under stage, 10; number sets scenery,
16; bill poster, **Opera House; number sheets** can accommodate, 300; theatrical teamster, Opera House. Newspapers : **daily,** Democrat; advertising rates, yearly contract;
Leader, advertising rates, yearly contract...... Hotel : Warner, special rates, $1.50;
Brunswick, special rates, ;$1.50; Commercial, special rates, $1.50; Globe, special **rates,**
$1.25.

Union Hall, Wm. H. Arnold, **manager; seating capacity, 600; rental, one night $15, three**
$35; license, $3. Size of **stage, 18x25; number sets scenery, 4.**

Newton Hall; seating capacity, 400.

Sanford Hall; seating capacity, 400.

ANTWERP, 1,500. R.R., Rome, Watertown & Ogdensburg. Ellis Hall, J. D. Ellis, manager; seating capacity, 400; rental, one night $10. Size of stage, 16x21; bill poster,
Edward Sharon. Newspaper Gazette (Wed.)......Hotels : Proctor, regular rates, $2
(special also); Foster.

ARCADE, 2,000. R. R., Buffalo, N. Y. & Philadelphia. Keystone Hall, B. F. Harty **&**
Co., managers; seating capacity, 500; rental, one night $8; license, $2. Size of stage,
14x26; no scenery. Newspaper: Leader (Wed.)......Hotels: Arcade, United States.

ATTICA, 3,700. **R. R.,** Baltimore & Ohio. **Williams' Opera House, C. F. Williams, mana-**
ger; **seating capacity, 700; rental, one night $20, three $40 ; license, 12 tickets ; share**
also. Size of stage, 30x52 ; number sets scenery, 8 ; bill poster, Opera House ; theatrical
teamster, **Charles Nichols. Newspapers : Argus (Th.), News (Th.)... ....Hotels :**
Wyoming, regular rates, $2 (special also); Western.

AUBURN, 28,000. R. R., Aub. **Branch N. Y. C. & H. R.;** Southern Central ; Ithaca,
Auburn & Western. Academy **of** Music, E. J. Matron, manager , seating capacity,
1,100 ; rental, one night $50 ; **share also** ; license included. Size of stage, 35x40 ; size **of**
proscenium opening, 30x22 ; **height from** stage to grooves, 12 ; height from **stage to**
rigging loft, 18 ; depth **under** stage, 7 ; number sets scenery, 20 ; leader of orchestra,
Ed. Nicht ; stage carpenter, John H. Roberts ; bill poster, E. J. **Watson** ; number of
sheets can accommodate, 1,000 ; rates per sheet, 4c. ; theatrical teamster, H. B. Ronnds.
Newspapers , daily, Advertiser, Dispatch, News, Anhurnian ; weekly, Dispatch (Sun.)
.Hotels: Osborne, special rates, $1.25 to $2; Gaylord, special rates, $1 to $1.50.

Shiner's Opera House, A. Shiner, manager ; seating capacity, 1,300 ; rental, one night $60.
Size of stage, 40x60; height from stage to grooves, 16; height from stage to rigging loft,
30; depth under stage, 8; full set scenery.

AVON, 2,000. R. R., Buffalo, N. Y. & Philadelphia ; Erie. Hall's Opera House, Wm. **E.**
Hall, manager ; seating capacity, 600 , rental, one night $15 ; license, $3. Size of stage,
16x18 ; full set scenery ; bill poster, M. M. Mather. Newspapers : Herald (Th.),
Avonian (Wed.)   ...Hotels : **Livingstone,** regular rates, $2 **(special also);** Newman,
Potter.

BALLSTON SPA, 5,600. **R. R.,** Delaware & Hudson Canal Co. **Gould's** Opera Hall, John
D. Wait, manager; **seating** capacity, 600; rental, one night **$20, three** $50; license, 12
tickets; share also. **Size** of stage, 24x33; number sets scenery, 7; bill poster, Mat. Lee;
theatrical teamster, **Lew** Harlow. Newspapers: Democrat (Fri.), Journal (Sat.)...
Hotels : American, regular rates, $2 (special also); Commercial, Village, Eagle, Ballston
Spa, Haner.

BALDWINSVILLE, 7,000. **R. R.,** Delaware, Lackawanna & Western. Howard Opera
House, H. Howard, manager; seating capacity, 700; rental, share only; license, $3.
Size of stage, 27x42; size of proscenium opening, 22x27; height from stage to grooves,

13; height from stage to rigging loft, 21; depth under stage, 7; traps, 1; number sets scenery, 10; leader of orchestra, George Peete; bill poster, Bob Cunningham; number of sheets can accomodate, 300; rates per sheet, 3c.; theatrical teamsters, Paul & Betts. Newspaper : daily, Syracuse, weekly, Farmer's Journal (Th.), advertising rates, yearly contract......Hotels: Seneca, $1.25 to $1.50; American, $1.25 to $1.50; Cornell, $1.25 to $1.50, special rates.

BATAVIA, 8,000. R. R., N. Y. C. & H. R.; N. Y., L. E. & W. Opera House, Harry C. Ferren, manager; seating capacity, 900; rental, one night $40, three $90, license included. Size of stage, 24x50; size of proscenium opening, 18x25; height from stage to grooves, 14; height from stage to rigging loft, 18; depth under stage, 7; number sets scenery, 12; leader of orchestra, Wm. Wood; scenic artist, Frank Cox; bill poster, Opera House; number of sheets can accommodate, 300; rates per sheet, 4c.; theatrical teamster, Opera House. Newspapers : daily, News, advertising rates, per inch, 50c.; weekly, Times (Fri.), advertising rates per inch, 50c.; Batavian (Th.), advertising rates per inch, 50c .. ..Hotels: St. James, rates, $2.50; Washburn, rates, $1.50; Hooper, rates, $1,

Ellicott Hall; seating capacity, 600.

BATH, 6,500. R. R., Rochester branch of Erie. Purdy's Opera House, M. C. Purdy, manager; seating capacity, 600; rental, one night $20, three $50; share also; license, $3. Size of stage, 20x35; size of proscenium opening, 20x24; height from stage to grooves, 18; height from stage to rigging loft, 32; cellar, 8; number sets scenery, 9; leader of orchestra, A. L. Allen; stage carpenter, W. Smith; bill poster, Wm. Miller; number sheets can accommodate, 350; theatrical teamster, Henry Collins. Newspapers : Courier (Tu.), Advocate (Fri.)......Hotels : Nichols, regular rates, $1 to $1.50; Steuben, $1.50.

French's Hall; seating capacity, 500.

New Opera House.

BINGHAMPTON, 18,000. R. R., Delaware & Hudson Canal Co. New Opera House, G. M. Furman, manager; bill poster, W. H. Vanslyk; theatrical teamster, John Mollen. Newspapers: daily, Democrat, Leader, Republican; weekly, Globe (Sun.), Tribune (Sun.). .....Hotels: Bennett, regular rates, $2 (special also); Lewis, regular rates, $2 (special also); Exchange, Spaulding.

Lester's Hall; seating capacity, 1,200.

Firemen's Hall; seating capacity, 500.

BOLIVAR, 3,400. R. R., Bradford, Eldred & Cuba; Buffalo, N. Y. & Phila.; Lackawanna & Pittsburg. Cain's Opera House, Wagner & Reis, managers; seating capacity, 900; share only. Size of stage, 28x40; full set scenery; bill posters, Opera House. Newspaper: Leader (Sat.)......Hotel: Newton, Clark.

BOONVILLE, 2,200. R. R., Utica & Black River. Opera House, A. J. Schmemsberg, manager; seating capacity, 550; rental, share only; license, 10 tickets. Size of stage, 30x30; size of proscenium opening, 10x20; leader of orchestra, R. Parsons; bill poster A. J. Schwemsberg; number of sheets can accommodate, 90; rates per sheet, 4c.; theatrical teamster, D. A. Talcott. Newspaper : Herald (Th.)......Hotels : Hulbert, special rates, $1.25; Central, special rates, $1.25.

BRIGHTON. R. R., N. Y. Central & Hudson River. Brighton Pier Theatre, Paul F. Nicholson, manager; seating capacity, 2,500......Hotel: Case.

BROCKPORT, 4,600. R. R., N. Y. Central & Hudson River. Ward Opera House, George R. Ward, manager; seating capacity, 800; rental, one night $20, three $40; license, 12 tickets; share also. Size of stage, 22x26; number sets scenery, 6; bill poster, Chas. Ruttan; theatrical teamster, James Mufford. Newspapers: Democrat (Fri.), Republican (Thur.) . ..Hotels: Getty, regular rates, $2 (special also); American.

BROOKLYN, 700,000. R. R., Long Island (connects with all railroads entering New York City). Brooklyn Theatre, W. A McConnell, manager; seating capacity, 2,000; share only. Size of stage 76x70; size of proscenium opening, 50x40; height from stage to grooves, 22; height from stage to rigging loft, 65; depth under stage, 16; traps, 5; musical director, F. W. Petcherson; scenic artist, Richard Halley; stage carpenter, T. Walker; bill posters, Kenny & Murphy. Newspapers: daily, Eagle, advertising rates, per line, 25c; Times,

– NEW –

Chicago Opera House,

COR. WASHINGTON AND CLARK STREETS,

CHICAGO, ILL.

Entirely Fire-Proof. The Finest Theatre in the West.

SEATING CAPACITY 2,200.

This magnificent temple of Drama and Opera, the largest, grandest and best located in the City of Chicago, will be completed August 1, 1885.

It will be the best arranged and most handsomely appointed place of amusement in the United States.

Address all communications to

JOHN W. NORTON,

Grand Opera House, St. Louis, Mo.

advertising rates, per line, 12c; Union, **advertising rates, per line, 15c**.......Hotels: **Clarendon, rates, $1 to $3; Mansion, $1 to $3; Pierrepont, $2 to $3.**

Grand Opera House, Knowles & **Morris,** managers; seating capacity, 2,150; share only. **Size of stage, 38x60;** size of proscenium opening, 35x32; height from stage to grooves, 25; height from stage to rigging loft, 56; depth under stage, 10; traps, 5; number sets scenery, 40; musical director, Joseph All; scenic artist, R. L. Weed; stage carpenter, George Sunder.

Park Theatre, Col. Wm. E. & Walter Z. Sinn, managers; seating capacity, 1 900; rental, share only. Size of stage, 69x71; size of proscenium opening, 42x34; height from stage to grooves, 21; height from stage to rigging loft, 68; depth under stage, 17; traps, 6; number sets scenery, 75; leader of orchestra, Prof. M. Papet; scenic artist, Henry Meyer; stage carpenter, Jas. H. Thompson.

Hyde & Behman's Theatre, Hyde & **Behman,** managers; seating capacity, 1,600; rental, share only; license yearly. **Size of stage, 37x65; size of proscenium opening, 30x36;** height from stage to grooves, 19; height from stage to rigging loft, 44; depth under stage, 10; traps, 3; full set scenery; leader of orchestra, Julius Vogler; scenic artist, Jos. De La Harpe; **stage carpenter, Louis Fernaudez.**

Lee Avenue Academy of Music **(Brooklyn, Eastern District),** Berger & Price, managers; seating **capacity, 2,000;** share only. Size of stage, 40x65; size of proscenium opening, 34x32, height from stage to grooves, 20; height from stage to rigging loft, 40; depth under stage, 12; traps, 4; number sets **scenery, 25;** leader of orchestra, Mark Isaacson; scenic artist, George Helster; stage carpenter, **John Elfers;** bill posters, Kenny & Murphy...... Hotels: Wall House, special rates, $1.50 **to $3; Bliss Hotel, special rates, $1 to $2.**

Novelty Theatre (Brooklyn, Eastern **District), Theall & Williams,** managers; Brooks & **Dickson, New York** representatives; seating capacity, 1,400; share only, license included. **Size of stage, 30x50;** size of proscenium opening, 26x27; **height from stage to grooves, 18;** height from stage to rigging loft, 33; full set scenery; leader of orchestra, Peter Frank; scenic artist, J. R. B. Ayres; **stage carpenter,** Thos. Cary; bill poster, Kenny & Murphy; theatrical teamster, F. **T. Hill.**

Standard Museum and Theatre, John W. Holmes, manager; seating capacity, 1,700; rent or share. Size of stage, 40x75; full set scenery.

Brooklyn Music Hall, Wm. R. Anderson, manager; seating capacity, 1,200; rental, one night $150. Size of stage, 25x35.

Academy of Music, E. I. Wies, manager; seating capacity, 2,000; full set scenery.

Atheneum; seating capacity, 1,200.

Gray's Broadway Theatre.

Theatre Comique.

Waverly Theatre.

BUFFALO, **250,000.** R. R., Buffalo, **N. Y. &** Phila.; Del., Lack. & Western; Erie; Grand Trunk; **L. S. &** Mich. Southern; Mich. Central; N. Y. C. & H. R.; N. Y., Chic. & St. Louis; N. Y., West Shore & Buffalo. Court Street Theatre, **J. M. Hill,** manager; seating capacity, 1,500; share only. Size of stage, 37x53; size of proscenium **opening, height,** 37, width, 31; height from stage to grooves, 18; height from stage to rigging loft, 45; depth under stage, 12; traps, 4; number sets scenery, 40; leader of orchestra, Emil Wahle; scenic artist, Leon Lempert; stage carpenter; George Thomas; bill poster, **C. M.** Whitmild; number of sheets can accommodate, 50,000; rates per sheet, 2c.; theatrical teamster, C. M. Miller. Newspapers: daily, Courier, advertising rates per inch, $1; **Express, advertising** rates per inch, $1; Times, advertising rates per inch, $1; News, **advertising** rates per inch, $1; Telegraph; weekly, **Truth** (Sun.)......Hotels: **Geneva, special rates, $2.50;** Tifft, special rates, $2.50; **Mansion, special rates,** $2 to $2.50; United States, special **rates,** $1.25 to $1.50.

Academy of Music, Maech Bros., managers; Brooks & Dickson, New York representatives; seating capacity, 1,800; rental, share only; license yearly. Size of stage, 30½x59; size of proscenium opening, 35x40; height from stage to grooves, 21; height from stage to rigging loft, 40; depth under stage, 9; full set traps; number sets scenery, 30; leader of orchestra, Joseph Kuhn; scenic artist, Horace N. Smith; stage carpenter, Thomas Duncan.

Adelphi Theatre, Joe Lang, manager; seating capacity, 1,500; rental, share only; license included. Size of stage, 30x28; size of proscenium opening, 25x28; height from stage to grooves, 16; height from stage to rigging loft, 30; depth **under** stage, 5; number sets scenery, 25; leader of orchestra, Eugene Schmidt; scenic artist, **E.** D. Skillett; stage carpenter, Wm. Dougherty,

Bunnell's Museum, H. **A. Bates, manager** ; seating capacity, 1,500. Size of stage, 30x34; leader of orchestra, W. Pastor.

St. James' Theatre, C. G. Flint, manager; seating capacity, 1,300 ; rental, one night $50; share also

Coliseum Theatre, Jerome Stensell, manager; seating capacity, 1,100.

Humphries' Alhambra Theatre (variety), J. Humphries, manager.

CANAJOHARIE, 3,400. R. R., N. Y., West Shore & Buffalo. **Nellis Opera Hall,** E. Nellis & Co., managers; seating capacity, 600; rental, one night $15, three $35. Size of stage, 14x35; **fair stock scenery;** bill poster, **D.** G. Campbell ; **theatrical teamster,** Godfrey Brown. Newspapers: Courier (Tu.), Gazette. .....Hotels : Wagner, regular **rates,** $2 (special also); Nellis Cottage.

CANANDAIGUA, 7,000. R. R., N. Y. Cen. & Hudson River; Nor. Cen. McKechnie Opera House, Stuart C. McKechnie, manager; seating capacity, 800; rental, one night $25, three $60; license, $3. Size of stage, 13x30; size of proscenium opening, 11x11; height from stage to grooves, 12; **height** from stage to rigging loft, 14; depth under stage, 5; number sets scenery, 13; leader of orchestra, Fred Remington; stage carpenter. J. Powelson; bill poster, Will Melvin; number of sheets can accommodate, 500; rates **per sheet, 3c.;** theatrical teamsters, Fletcher & Spencer. Newspapers: Journal (Wed.), advertising rates per line, 10c.; Times (Th.), 10c; Repository (Fri.), 10c....... Hotels: Canandaigua, regular rates, $1 to $1.50; Webster, $1 to $1.50; Masseth, $1 to $1.50.

Kingsbury Grand Opera House, Sherman Kingsbury, manager; seating capacity, 1,000; rental, one night $50, three $150; **license,** $4; share also. Size of stage, 37x63; **size of** proscenium opening, 24x35; **height from stage to** grooves, 16; height from stage to rigging loft, 24; depth **under stage,** 16; **number sets** scenery, 12; leader of **orchestra,** Sutton; scenic artist, D. Flevel; **stage carpenter,** F. A. Guild; bill poster, Opera House.

CANISTEO, 2,400. R. R., Erie. **Riddle** Hall; seating capacity, 400 ; rental, one night $3; **no license; fair stock scenery;** bill poster, J. **Ashley.** Newspaper: Times (Th.) .....Hotels: **Carter, regular rates,** $2 (special also); Canisteo.

CANTON, 2,600. R. R.,Rome, Watertown & Ogdensburg. **Town** Hall ; seating capacity, 1,000; rental, one night $15, **three** $40; license, $5. Size of stage, 26x45; number sets **scenery, 2;** bill poster, Tom Smith; theatrical teamster, **Oscar Brown.** Newspapers: Advertiser (Th.), **Plaindealer (Wed.)**......Hotels : Hodgkin, **regular** rates, $2 (special also); American, Commercial.

CAPE VINCENT, 2,000. R. R., Rome, Watertown & Ogden. Opera House, S. S. Block, manager; seating capacity, 1,000; rental, one night $30, three $45; share also, license included. Size of stage, 20x30; height from stage to grooves, 15; depth under stage, 3; traps, 1; number sets scenery, 4; leader of orchestra, H. N. Potter; theatrical teamster, R. Davis. Newspaper : Eagle (Th.)......Hotels: Rathbun, special rates, **$1; Railroad,** special rates, $1.

CARTHAGE, 3,500. R. R., Utica **& Black** River. Carthage Opera **House,** C. J. Clark, manager; seating capacity, 600; **rental,** one night $15, three $30; license, $2; share also; bill poster, E. Bertrand; theatrical teamster, Jacob Bartlett. Newspaper : Republican (Tu.)......Hotels : Lewis, regular **rates,** $2 (special also), Ha'ch, **Peck,** Park.

Mechanics Hall, Walsh & Myers, **managers;** seating capacity, 600 ; rental, one night, **$10, three $25;** license, $2 to $3; **share also.** Size of stage, 27x37; number sets scenery, 8.

CATSKILL, 8,700. R. R., N. Y. C. & Hudson River. Mott **& Gaylord's Opera House.** Mott & Gaylord, managers; seating capacity, 1,000; **rental,** one night $25; license, **12** tickets. Size of stage, 20x43; number sets scenery, 10; bill poster, Opera House. Newspapers; daily, Mail; weekly, Examiner (Sat.), Recorder (Fri.)......Hotels : Irving, regular rates, $2 to $2.50 (special also) ; Gunn's, **regular** rates, $2 (special also), Western, Continental

CHESTER, 2,500. R. R., N. Y., L. E. & W.; L. & Hudson. Bodler Opera House, R. P. Conklie, manager; seating capacity, 350; rental, one night $10. Size of stage, 14x17; size of proscenium opening, 10x17; height from stage to grooves, 12 ; number sets scenery, 3... ....Hotel : Howland, special rates, $1 to $1.25.

CLINTON, 1,200. R. R., Delaware & Hudson Canal Co. Opera House. Newspaper : Courier (Wed)......Hotel : Clinton, regular rates, $2 (special also).

COHOCTON, 1,000. R. R., Delaware, Lackawanna & Western ; Erie. Warner's Opera House, F. C. Cramer, manager; seating capacity, 500. Newspaper: Times (Th.)...... Hotel : Rowell, regular rates, $2 (special also).

COHOES, 25,000. R. R., N. Y. C. & H. R.; Dela. & Had Canal Co. Cohoes Opera House, P. J. Callan, manager; seating capacity, 1,000; rental, share only; license included. Size of stage, 26x67½; depth under stage, 8; number sets scenery, 12; leader of orchestra, Prof. Werner; stage carpenter, Samuel Wade; bill poster, J. Powers; number of sheets can accommodate, 1,500; rates per sheet, 3c.; theatrical teamster, Chas. Davis. Newspapers: daily, News, Dispatch; weekly, Regulator (Sun.)........ Hotel : Harmony, special rates, $1.50.

Egbert's Hall; seating capacity, 600.

Harmony Hall; seating capacity, 700.

COOPERSTOWN, 4,500. R. R., Cooperstown & Susquehanna Valley. Brown's Opera House, E. E. Jarvie, manager; seating capacity, 500; rental, one night $15 to $20; license, $3. Size of stage, 23x50; fair stock scenery; bill poster, Opera House; theatrical teamster, J. P. Mitchell. Hotels: Ballard, Central.

CORNING, 7,000. R. R., Corning, Cowanesque & Antrim; Delaware, Lackawanna & Western; Erie. Washington Hall, Kimball & Todd, managers; seating capacity, 1,000; rental, one night $20, three $50; license, $2 to $3. Size of stage, 20x30; fair stock scenery; bill poster, T. Argue. Newspapers : Democrat (Wed.), Journal (Th.)...... Hotels : Dickenson, regular rates, $2 (special also); Globe, regular rates, $2 (special also); Barry.

Barry Opera House, David Barry, manager; seating capacity, 1,100; rental, one night $25 ; fair stock scenery.

CORTLAND, 7,200. R. R., E., C. & N.; Del., Lack. & West. Taylor Opera House, E. D. Mallery, manager; seating capacity, 920 ; rental, share only, license included. Size of stage, 22x36 ; size of proscenium opening, 16x22; height from stage to grooves, 12; height from stage to rigging loft, 20; depth under stage, 5; traps, 2; number sets scenery, 7; leader of orchestra, B. R. Webster; bill poster, Claude Pelham; number of sheets can accommodate, 400; theatrical teamster, J. Gillett & Co. Newspapers: Democrat (Th.), advertising rates, 50c. per line; Standard (Th.), advertising rates, 50c. per line; News (Fri.), advertising rates, 50c. per line. ...Hotels : Cortland, special rates, $1.25 to $1.50 ; Arnold, special rates, $1.25 to $1.50.

CUBA, 3,400. R. R., Bradford, Eldred & Cuba; Buffalo, New York & Philadelphia; Erie. Palmer Hall, J. Palmer, manager; seating capacity, 1,000; rental, one night $40; license, $3. Size of stage, 20x25; number sets scenery, 5 ; bill poster, William Henderson; theatrical teamster, F. Chamberlain. Newspaper: Patriot (Fri.)......Hotels: Cuba, regular rates, $2 (special also); Western.

DANSVILLE, 6,700. R. R., Delaware, Lackawanna & Western; Erie. Opera House, Dyer Brothers, managers; seating capacity, 500; rental, one night $12; license, $3. Size of stage, 30x30; fair stock scenery; bill poster, J. M. Boughton; theatrical teamster, John Dick. Newspapers: Advertiser (Th.), Breeze (Tu.), Express (Th.) ....Hotels: Hyland, regular rates, $2 (special also); Allen, Clinton.

Union Hall; John Hyland, manager.

DEPOSIT, 2,000. R. R., Erie. Borrows Hall, E. T. Burrows, manager; seating capacity, 400; rental, one night $4, three $10; license, $4. Size of stage, 16x40; no scenery; bill poster, Darius Valentine. Newspaper: Courier (Sat.)..... Hotels: Oquaga, regular rates, $2 (special also); Western.

Oquaga Hall; H. W. Wilcox, manager; seating capacity, 400. Size of stage, 16x40.

DUNKIRK, 10,000. R. R., L. S. & M. S.; N. Y., L. E. & W.; D. A. V. & P. Opera House, Frank Gilbert, manager; **seating capacity, 1,200; rental, one night $30, three $75; license included.** Size of stage, 41x43; **size of proscenium opening, 25x25; height from stage to grooves, 14; height** from stage to rigging loft, 30; **depth under stage, 5; number sets scenery, 8; leader of** orchestra, F. W. Krafft; **stage carpenter, W. Ellis; bill poster.** William Ruediel; **number of sheets can accommodate, 350; rates per sheet, 4c.; theatrical teamster,** P. H. Murphy. Newspapers, **daily: Observer, advertising rates, 20c. per line; weekly: Journal** (Wed.), advertising **rates, $2 to $3, per inch; Advertiser, (Th.), advertising rates, $2 per** inch.......Hotels: **Hurlbert, regular rates, $1.50; Erie, regular rates, $1.50;** Eastern, regular rates, $2; St. James, **regular rates, $1 to $2.**

ELMIRA, 30,000. R. R. Lack. & **Western; El. Cort. & Northern; Erie; Tioga; North**ern Central; N. E. Bardwell, manager; **seating capacity, 1,550; share only.** Size of stage, 48x75; size of proscenium opening, 32x25; **height from stage to grooves, 16; height** from stage to rigging loft, 40; depth **under stage, 10; number sets scenery, 33; leader of** orchestra, Charles Suigerhoff; **stage carpenters, Matt Lockwood & John Brown; bill** poster, W. E. Bardwell; number of sheets can **accommodate, 5,000; theatrical teamsters,** George H. Colton, Jr., & Bro. Newspapers: **daily, Advertiser, Gazette; weekly, Tele**gram (Sun.), Tidings (Sun.).......Hotels: **Rathbun, special rates, $1.75; Wycoff, special** rates, $1.25; Delavan, Frazer.

Academy of Music, S. T. Reynolds, manager; seating capacity, 900; rental, one night $25, three $55; full set scenery.

Stancliff Hall; seating capacity, 500.

FISHKILL, 8,700. R. R., N. Y. & New **England. Fishkill Opera House, W. H. Robinson,** manager; seating capacity, 700; **rental, one night $30, three $50; license, $3; share also,** size of stage, 36x17; number sets scenery, 7; **bill poster, George Schofield.** Newspaper: **Standard (Sat.)......Hotel: Mont Julian, regular rates $2 (special also.)**

Swift's Hall; seating capacity, 600.

FLUSHING, 8,700. R. R., Long Island. Opera House; seating capacity, 600; rental, one night $10 to $22; no license; **bill poster, —— Marks.** Newspapers: daily, Journal, Times......Hotels: Flushing, Simmonds'.

FORT EDWARD, 5,000. R. R., Delaware **& Hudson Canal Co.** Bradley's Opera House C. W. Bowtell, manager; seating **capacity, 900; rental, one night $18; license, $3; share** also; bill poster, W. E. Tucker; **theatrical teamster, Charles Finn.** Newspapers: Gazette (Fri.); Advertiser (Wed.)......Hotels: **St. James, Eldridge, Milliman.**

FORT PLAIN, 3,700. R. R., N. Y. Central **& Hudson River; N. Y., West Shore & Buffalo.** Fritcher Opera House, A. P. Fritcher, **manager; seating capacity, 1,000; rental, one** night $25, three $45; license, tickets; **number sets scenery, 7; bill poster, W. D. Irwin.** Newspapers: Register (Fri.); Standard **(Wed.)......Hotels: Zoller, Montgomery Hall,** Union Hall.

FREDONIA, 4,000. R. R., Dunkirk, Alleghany Valley & **Pittsburg.** Union Hall, Frank G. Stone, manager; seating capacity, 800; rental, one night, **$15, three $35; no license;** share also. Size of stage, 21x30; number sets scenery 6; **bill poster, Lewis Henry;** theatrical teamster, George **W. Sisson.** Newspaper: Censor (Wed.).......Hotels: Park, Pemberton.

FRIENDSHIP, 2,000. R. R., N. Y., **L. E. & W.; Lackawanna & Pittsburg. Academy Hall,** J. V. Price, manager; seating capacity, 800; rental, one night $12; share also; **license** included. Size of stage, 20x35; size of proscenium opening, 14x25; height from stage to **grooves, 9;** height from stage to **rigging loft, 18; depth under stage, 5; traps, 1; number sets scenery, 8 ;** billposter, A. Worden; **number of sheets can accommodate, 300; rates per sheet, 3c.;** theatrical teamster, **J. McGann.** Newspaper: Register (Wed.), advertising rates, 10c. per line....Hotels: American, special rates, $1.50; Mansion, special rates, $1.50.

FULTON, 7,500. R. R., N. Y. & West.; Del. Lack. & West. Stephens' Opera House, John J. Stephens, manager; seating capacity, 900; rental, one night $40, three $100; share also; license included. Size of stage, 25x30; size of proscenium opening, 40x35; number sets scenery, 6; scenic artist, Suaray; bill posters, Youngs Brothers. Newspapers: Times

(Wed.), Patriot (Fri.), Observer (Sat.)......Hotels: Lewis, special rates, $1 to $1.50; Clark, special rates, $1.50; Johnson, special rates, $1.50.

Nichols' Hall, S. B. Mead, manager; seating capacity, 450; rental, one night $12, three $25; license, $2. Size of stage, 20x25; number sets scenery, 4.

GENESEO, 2,500. R. R., Erie. Concert Hall; seating capacity, 700; rental, one night. $12. Size of stage, 14x25; bill poster, George Johnson. Newspaper: Republican (Th.) Citizen (Sat.). ....Hotels: Wallace, American, Globe.

GENEVA, 7,500. R. R., Geneva & Lyons; Geneva, Ithaca & Sayre; N. Y. C. & Hud. River. Linden Hall, M. W. Hemlup, manager; seating capacity, 600; bill poster, George Stroupe. Newspapers: Advertiser (Tu.), Asteroid (Fri.), Courier (Wed.).. ...Hotels: Franklin, American.

GLEN COVE, 3,000. R. R., Long Island. Continental Hall, F. B. Palmer, manager; seating capacity, 500; rental, one night $12; three $30. Size of stage, 15x40; number sets scenery, 10; bill poster, Tuttle Dayton; theatrical teamster, Titus. Newspaper: daily, Gazette......Hotel: Snediker's, special rates, $1.50.

GLENS FALLS, 10,000. R. R., Branch, Del. & Hud. Canal Co. Glens Falls Opera House, Glens Falls Opera House Co., managers; seating capacity, 1,000; rental, share only; license included. Size of stage, 36x62; size of proscenium opening, 32x30; depth under stage, 17; bill posters, P. P. Braley & Co.; number sheets can accommodate, 150; rates per sheet, 4c.; theatrical teamsters, Goodwin & Co. Newspapers: daily, Star, Times; weekly, Messenger (Fri.), advertising rates, 50c. per line; Republican (Tu.), advertising rates, 50c. per line......Hotels Rockwell, special rates, $1.50 to $1.75; American, special rates, $1.50 to $1.75.

Little's Opera House, Colvin & Co., managers; seating capacity, 1,000; rental, one night $15; share also.

GLOVERSVILLE, 20,000, (within four mile radius.) R. R., Fonda, Johnstown & Gloversville. Memorial Hall, A. J. Kasson, manager; seating capacity, 1,200; rental, share only. Size of stage, 33x43; size of proscenium opening, 25x30; height from stage to grooves; 16; height from stage to rigging loft, 28; depth under stage, 4; traps, 1; number sets scenery, 12; leader of orchestra, Charles Hildreth; scenic artist, George Canham; stage carpenter, Theodore Foster; bill poster, Olin Sutliff; rates per sheet, 4c.; theatrical teamster, James Hanley. Newspapers: daily, Critic; weekly, Intelligencer (Th.), advertising rates, $2 per inch, Standard (Th.), advertising rates, $2 per inch......Hotels: Windsor, special rates, $1.25 to $1.50; Alvord, special rates, $1.25 to $1.50; Burlington, special rates, $1.25 to $1.50.

Mason Opera House, John Mason, manager; seating capacity, 800; rental, one night $12.50, three $30. Size of stage, 20x28; number sets scenery, 5.

Electric Choral Union Hall, C. G. Alvord, manager; seating capacity, 600; rental, one night $10, three $30. Size of stage, 21x25; number sets scenery 7.

GOUVERNEUR, 3,000. R. R., Rome, Watertown & Ogdensburg. Union Hall, C. H. Bourne, manager; seating capacity, 1,000; rental, one night $30, three $48; license, $3 share also. Size of stage, 21x36; number sets scenery, 8; bill poster, Eugene Campbell; theatrical teamster, Henry Caul. Newspapers: Free Press (Wed.), Herald & Times (Th.). ......Hotels: Fuller, Van Buren, Spencer

GOWANDA, 2,000. R. R., Erie, Buffalo & Suspension Bridge. Torrance Opera House, J. S. Torrance, manager; seating capacity, 1,400. Newspaper: Enterprise (Fri.)......Hotel: Gowanda, regular rates, $2 (special also).

HAVANA, 2,000. R. R., Northern Central. Cook's Academy, C. W. Burrows, manager Newspapers: Journal (Sat.), Republican (Th.)......Hotel: Montour.

HERKIMER, R. R., N. Y. Central & Hudson River ; N. Y., W. Sh. & B.; Herkimer, Newport & Poland. Fox Opera House, Chas. J. Fox, manager ; seating capacity, 1,000 ; rental, one night $20 to $25 ; license, 11 tickets. Size of stage, 25x25 ; number sets scenery, 13; bill poster, C. F. Dockstader. Newspaper ; Democrat (Wed.)...., .Hotel : Waverley, regular rates, $2 (special also).

HOLLEY, 1,000. R. R., N. Y. Central & Hudson River. Newton Hall, H. G. Newton, manager; seating capacity, 500 ; rental, one night $10, three $18 ; share also. Size of stage, 16x20 ; number sets scenery, 6 ; bill poster, Lloyd T. Pierce. Newspaper: Standard (Th.). . . . . Hotel: Mansion.

HOMER, 4,000. R. R., Syracuse, Bingham, & N. Y. Keator Opera House, Jacob Metzger manager ; seating capacity, 800 ; rental, one night $15, three $35 ; license, $3. Size of stage, 22x49 ; size of proscenium opening, 20x28 ; height from stage to grooves, 22 ; depth under stage, 4 ; traps, 1 ; number sets scenery, 8 ; stage carpenter, Fred. K. Wright ; bill poster, Opera House ; number of sheets can accommodate, 100 ; rates per sheet, 4c. ; theatrical teamster, G. W. Fraizer. Newspaper : Republican (Th.), advertising rates, $3.50 per quarter column........Hotels : Windsor, special rates, $1.25 ; Monsoon's, special rates, $1.25.

HORNELLSVILLE, 15,000. R. R., N. Y., L. E. & W.; Leh. Val. Shattuck Opera House, Wagner & Reis, managers (Bradford, Pa.) ; seating capacity, 1,350 ; rental, share only ; license included. Size of stage, 40x58 ; size of proscenium opening, 30x34 ; height from stage to grooves, 18 ; height from stage to rigging loft, 50 ; depth under stage, 11 ; number sets scenery, 12; leader of orchestra, J. K. Arms; stage carpenter, G. W. Hassinger ; bill poster, Opera House ; number of sheets can accommodate, 1,000 ; rates per sheet, 4c. ; theatrical teamster, A. Dugan. Newspapers : daily, Times, advertising rates, 15c. per line ; Tribune, advertising rates, 20c. per line........Hotels : Osborne, regular rates, $1.50 to $2; Nichols, regular rates, $1.50 to $2; Delaven, regular rates, $1 to $1.50.

HOOSAC FALLS, 7,000. R. R., Troy & Boston; Boston, Hoosac Tunnel & Western, Woods Hall, E. R. Westerbrook, manager; seating capacity, 500; rental, one night $25, three $60; license, $4; share also. Size of stage, 16x34; size of proscenium opening, 10½x19; height from stage to grooves, 9; height from stage to rigging loft, 14; depth under stage, 4; traps, 1; number sets scenery, 8; leader of orchestra, Mr. Moon; bill poster, Mr. Brown; theatrical teamsters, E. Leonard & Son. Newspaper: Standard (Fri.)......Hotels: Wallace, Commercial.

HUDSON, 13,000. R. R., Boston & Albany; N. Y. C. & Hud. River. Hudson Opera House, Alcott & Lisk, managers; seating capacity, 1,000; rental, one night $30, three $75; share also; license included. Size of stage, 25x50; number sets scenery, 5; bill poster, E. R. Groat; theatrical teamster, Wm. Benzle. Newspapers; daily, Register, Republican. ... ..Hotels: Worth, regular rates, $2 (special also); St. Charles, regular rates, $2 (special also); Central, Waldron.

City Hall; seating capacity, 300; rental, one night $20, three $50; license, tickets. Size of stage, 25x75; no scenery.

ILION, 5,200. R. R., N. Y. C. & Hud. Riv.; N. Y. West Sh. & Buffalo. Thomas Opera House, J. F. Thomas, manager; seating capacity, 1,000; rental, one night $30, three $75; share also; license included. Size of stage, 25x50; number sets scenery, 10; bill poster, Opera House; theatrical teamster, Frank Reese. Newspaper; Citizen (Fri.)......Hotels: Osgood, Central, National.

ITHACA, 13,000. R. R., Del., Lack. & Western ; Lehigh Valley ; Cayuga Lake ; Elmira, Cortland & Northern. Wilgus Opera House, H. L. Wilgus, manager ; seating capacity, 1,080; rental, one night $45; license yearly ; share also. Size of stage, 26x48 ; size of proscenium opening, 24x24; height from stage to grooves, 16; height from stage to rigging loft, 30; depth under stage, 4; traps, 2; number sets scenery, 14; leader of orchestra, Mr. Harris; stage carpenter, A. S. Cowles; bill poster, Opera House; number sheets can accommodate, 1,000; rates per sheet, 4c.; theatrical teamster, Chas. Ingersoll. Newspapers: daily, Journal, Democrat, Sun; weekly, Era (Fri.), Journal (Th.), Ithacan (Sat.) ......Hotels: Ithaca, special rates, $1.50 to $2; Clinton, special rates, $1 50 to $2; Tompkins, special rates, $1.25 to $1.50; Martin, special rates, $1.

Cornell Library Hall, D. F. Finch, manager ; seating capacity, 1,000 ; rental, one night $15. Size of stage, 16x26.

Academy of Music, Joseph Gobay, manager.

Journal Hall; seating capacity, 600.

JAMAICA, 4,290. R. R., Long Island. Opera House, Elijah **Nostrand**, manager; seating capacity, 600; rental, one night $16; no license; number **sets** scenery, 9; bill poster, Chas. Wood; theatrical teamster, William Hendrickson. Newspapers: Democrat (Tu.), Standard (Sat.)......Hotel: Jamaica.

Town Hall, Starr Edwards, manager.

JAMESTOWN, 11,000. R. R., N. Y., P. & O.; Dunkirk & Titusville. Allen's Opera House, **A. E. Allen, manager; seating capacity,** 1,200; share only. Size of stage, 40x90; size **of proscenium opening, 26x32; height from stage to** grooves, 18; height from stage to **rigging loft, 40; depth under stage, 12; traps, 3;** number sets scenery, 26; leader of orchestra, Prof. **Wilbur; scenic artist,** Horace N. **Smith;** stage carpenter, Gus De Laine; **bill poster, A. E. Allen; number of sheets can** accommodate, 600; rates per sheet, 4c.; theatrical teamster, J. Green. Newspapers: **daily,** Journal, Messenger; weekly, Standard (Fri.), **Democrat (Wed.)....Hotels: Opera, special rates, $1; Weeks', special rates, $1.25;** Sherman, **special rates, $1.50.**

JOHNSTOWN, 6,000. R. R., Fonda, Johnstown & Gloversville. **Kennedy's Opera House,** E. Kennedy, manager; seating capacity, 700; rental, one night $15; license, **$3; share** also. Size of stage, 20x30; number sets scenery, 6; bill poster, E. M. Brown; **theatrical** teamster, E. M. Brown. Newspapers: Democrat (Wed.), Republican (Th.)......Hotels: Johnston, regular rates, $2 (special also), Longfield, Harden.

KEESEVILLE, 2,700. Association Hall, C. M. Boynton, manager; seating capacity, 461; rental, one night $10, three $22; license, $1 to $3. Size of stage, 20x40; number sets **scenery, 4;** bill poster, T. E. Beaumont. Newspaper: Republican (Th.).. ...Hotel: Adi-**rondack,** regular rates, $2 (special also).

KINGSTON, 20,000. R. R., N. Y., W. Sh. & B.; Ulster & Delaware; **Walkill** Valley, Music **Hall, Dubois** & Nichols, managers; seating capacity, 1,200; rental, one night $35, three $75; share also; license included. Size of stage, 28x42; full set scenery; bill poster, W. H. Freer; theatrical teamsters, **Winter Bros. Newspapers: daily, Freeman, Leader;** weekly, Argus (Wed.).. ..Hotels: Eagle, **regular rates, $2 (special also); Kingston,** regular rates, $2 (special also); Mansion.

Washington Hall; seating capacity, 1,000.

Vorhees' Hall; seating capacity, 900.

Samson's Hall; seating capacity, **1,150.**

Opera House.

LANSINGBURGH, 8,000; R. R., Troy & Boston. Concert **Hall, H. S.** Dickson, manager; **seating capacity, 600; rental,** one night $35, license included. Size of stage, 28x46; leader **of** orchestra, Irvin **Hyatt; stage** carpenter, Sandholt; **bill poster, J.** Caswell; theatrical teamsters, Vanderheyden & Morse. Newspaper: Courier (Fri.)......Hotels: American, Phœnix.

LE ROY. R. R., Erie; N. Y. C. & H. R. Maloney Hall, John Maloney, manager; seating capacity, 700; rental, one night $12, three $15; license, $2 to $3; share also. Size of stage, 15x22; number sets scenery, 8; bill poster, Billy Carey; theatrical teamster, Jake King. Newspapers: Gazette (Wed.), Courier (Fri.), Times (Wed.).....Hotels: Lampson, regular rates, $2 (special also); Collins, Eagle.

LITTLE FALLS, 7,000. R. R., N. Y. C. & H. R.; N. Y., **West Shore** & Buffalo. Opera House; seating capacity, 1,100; bill poster, John Fleming; **theatrical** teamster, John Dooley. Newspapers: News (Fri.), Journal & Courier (Tu.). ....Hotel: Girvan, regular rates, $2.50 (special also); Metropolitan, regular rates, $2 **to $2.50;** Hinchman, Bradford, Cottage, Grand Central.

Skinner Opera House, S. A. Skinner, manager; seating **capacity,** 1,000; rental, **one night $30; no license. Size of** stage, 30x50; full set scenery.

LIVONIA, 2,000. R. R., Erie. Prescott Hall, E. R. Bolles, manager; seating capacity, 500; **rental,** one night $10, three $25; license, 6 tickets. Size of stage, 16x24; number sets scenery, 6; bill poster, H. H. Ray. Newspaper: Gazette (Fri.)......Hotels: Livonia, Commercial, Church.

LOCKPORT, 14,000. R. R., Erie; N. Y. Central & Hudson River. Hodge's Opera House, John Hodge, manager; Brooks & Dickson, New York representatives; seating capacity, 2,000; rental, one night $40, three $100, license included. Size of stage, 35x33; height from stage to grooves, 18; height from stage to rigging loft, 25; depth under stage, 7; number sets scenery, 15; bill poster, Jas. H. Staats; theatrical teamster, Rupert Pickles. Newspapers: daily, Journal, News, Union......Hotels: American, special rates, $1.50; Judson, $1.50.

Arcade Hall; seating capacity, 1,000.

LOWVILLE, 3,700. R. R., Utica & Black River. Roscoe Opera House, George Sherwood, manager; seating capacity, 500; rental, one night $15, three $35; no license; share also. Size of stage, 33x16; number sets scenery, 7; bill poster, George Sherwood; theatrical teamster, L. S. Andrus. Newspapers: Journal and Republican (Th.), Democrat (Wed.), Times (Th.).... Hotels: Kellogg, regular rates, $2 (special also); Central, Barr's, Campbell.

LYONS, 6,300. R. R., Geneva & Lyons; N. Y. Central & Hudson River; N. Y., West Shore & Buff. Parshall Memorial Hall, Dwight & Chamberlain, managers; seating capacity, 1,000; rental, one night $50; share also; license included. Size of stage, 35x57; number sets scenery, 24; bill poster, manager of Hall; theatrical teamster, Robert Smith. Newspapers: Grin and Bear It (Sat.), Republican (Th.), Press (Wed.)......Hotels: Congress Hall, regular rates, $2 (special also); Graham, National, Lyons.

Tower's Hall; seating capacity, 1,000.

MALONE, 8,500. R. R., Ogdensburg & Lake Champlain. Lawrence Opera House, A. H. Merritt, manager; seating capacity, 650; rental, one night $15, three $35; license, $5; share also. Size of stage, 25x30; number sets scenery, 6; bill poster, M. B. Cheesebro; theatrical teamsters, Jones & Martin. Newspapers: Gazette (Fri.), Palladium (Th.) ......Hotels : Ferguson, regular rates, $2 (special also); Hogle, Elmwood.

Concert Hall, James S. Amsden, manager; seating capacity, 600; rental, one night $15, three $33; license, $2.50; share also. Size of stage, 25x40; number sets scenery, 5.

MARYVILLE, 2,900. R. R., Lake Chautauqua. Bemus Opera House, Dr. R. F. Curtis, manager; seating capacity, 400; rental, one night $6, three $15. Size of stage, 15x30; number sets scenery, 5. Newspaper: Sentinel.. ...Hotels: Chant, Maryville.

MATTEAWAN, 3,900. R. R., N. Y. & New Eng.; Newburg, Dutchess & Conn. Music Hall, Samuel K. Philips, manager; seating capacity, 700; rental, one night, $8; no license. Bill poster, Geo. Schofield. Newspapers: Journal (Th.)......Hotel: Deddie.

MAYVILLE, 1,500. R. R., Buffalo, New York & Philadelphia. Mayville Opera House, Kibbe, Bly & Co., managers; seating capacity, 400; rental, one night $8, two $14; share also. Size of stage, 12x20; height from stage to grooves, 12; height from stage to rigging loft, 20; depth under stage, 3; traps, 1; number sets scenery, 6; bill poster, Will. Dean; theatrical teamster, J. H. Flagler. Newspapers: Era (Mon.), Sentinel, (Wed.) ......Hotels: Mayville, special rates, $1; Odell, special rates, $1; Banjean, special rates, 85c.

MECHANICVILLE, 3,000. R. R., Boston, Hoosac Tunnel & Western; Delaware & Hudson. Crosby Opera House, C. F. Crosby, manager; seating capacity, 1,000; rental, one night $40; share also; license included. Size of stage, 18x35; size of proscenium opening, 13½; height from stage to grooves, 11; height from stage to rigging loft, 15½; depth under stage, 6; traps, 1; number sets scenery, 5; leader of orchestra, A. E. Andrews; scenic artist, Charles Huest; stage carpenter, A. M. Waite; bill posters, P. H. Reeves & Co.; theatrical teamster, Charles Patrick. Newspapers: daily, Troy Times; weekly, Mercury (Fri.)......Hotels:|Smith's, special rates, $1.25 to $1.50; Burnop, special rates, $1.25 to $1.50; Hart, special rates, $1.25 to $1.50.

Town Hall; Jairus Pratt, manager; seating capacity, 400; rental, one night $8. Size of stage; 9x38; fair stock scenery.

MEDINA, 5,000. R. R., Niagara Falls Branch of N. Y. Central & H R. Bent's Opera House, Fred J. Gates, manager; seating capacity, 1,000; rental, one night $25, three $60; share also; license, $3. Size of stage, 23x26; size of proscenium opening, 13x30; height from stage to

grooves, 12½; height from stage to rigging loft, 14½; depth under stage, 4; traps, 1; number sets scenery, 12; leader of orchestra, J. Swett; stage carpenter, John Swobe; bill poster, Opera House; number sheets can accommodate, 400; rate per sheet, 4c.; theatrical teamster, Opera House. **Newspapers: daily, Times,** advertising rates, per inch, 75c.; **weekly, Tribune** (Th.), 10c. per line, $1 per inch; **Register** (Th.), 10c. per line, $1 per inch. **Hotels:** Hart, special rates, $1 to $1.50; Bancroft, special rates, $1 to $1.50.

MEXICO, 2,200. R. R., Rome, Watertown & Ogdensburg. Town Hall, D. Boyd, manager; seating capacity, 800; rental, one night $10; license, tickets. Size of stage, 20x28; no scenery; bill poster, John Dididier. Newspaper: Independent (Th.). Hotels: Boyd, Mexico.

MIDDLEPORT, 1,300. R. R., N. Y. C. & H. R. Opera House; bill poster, Opera House. Newspaper: Mail (Sat.). Hotels: Pierce, Vernon.

MIDDLETOWN, 10,500. R. R., N. Y., L. E. & West.; N. Y., Ont. & West.; N. Y., S. & W. Bull's Opera House. Albert Bull, manager; seating capacity, 800; rental, one night $35, three $95; license included. Size of stage, 28x45; size of proscenium opening, 12x15; height from stage to grooves, 12; depth under stage, 4; traps, 3; number sets scenery, 12; bill poster, Charles E. Sharpe; number of sheets can accommodate, 300; rates per sheet, 4c.; theatrical teamster, S. Redfield. Newspapers: daily, Press, Argus.........Hotels: Grand Central, regular rates, $2 (special also); Commercial, Russell.

MORAVIA, 2,000. R. R., Southern Central. Peacock's Opera House, Titus & Townsend, managers; seating capacity, 800; rent or share; license yearly. Size of stage, 20x25; number sets scenery, 6; bill posters, Arnold Bros. Newspapers: Republican (Th.), Register (Fri.)..... Hotel: Goodrich, regular rates, $2 (special also).

MOUNT MORRIS, 3,000. R. R., New York & Phila.; Del., Lack. & Western; Erie. Livingstone Hall; D. W. Bacon, manager; seating capacity, 1,000; rental, one night $10, three $24; license, $3. Size of stage, 16x24; full set scenery; bill poster, William Hading; theatrical teamsters, McAvilly & Gamble. Newspapers: Enterprise (Sat.), Union (Th.), ...Hotels: Scoville, Eagle, American, Dodge.

NEWARK, 4,500. R. R., N. Y. Cen. & Hud. Riv.; N. Y., West Shore & Buf. Washington Hall, D. L. Ford, manager; seating capacity, 450; rental, one night $10 three $30; license, ten tickets; share also. Size of stage, 20x23; number sets scenery, 9; bill poster, C. has. Harrington; theatrical teamster, F. S. Parks. Newspapers: Courier (Th.), Union (Sat.) ......Hotel: Newark, regular rates, $2 (special also).

NEWBURG, 20,000. R. R., Erie (Newburg branch); Newburg, Dut. & Ct.; N. Y. C. & H. R., by ferry from Fishkill; N. Y. & N. E., by ferry from Fishkill Landing. Newburg Opera House, Wm. D. Dickey, manager; seating capacity, 1,200; rental, one night $35, three $90; share also; license, $5. Size of stage, 37x40; size of proscenium opening, 14x18; height above grooves, 14; depth under stage, 7; traps, 1; bill poster, George Gardner; number sheets can accommodate, 400; rates per sheet, 4c.; theatrical teamster, Lewis H. O'Brien. Newspapers: daily, Journal, Register.........Hotels: United States, special rates, $1 50 to $1.75; Merchants', special rates, $1.50 to $1.75; Orange, $1.40 to $1.50.

NEWPORT, 1,200. R. R., Herkimer, Newport & Poland. Newport Opera House, Will. H. Switzer, manager; seating capacity, 600, rental, one night $15; license, $5; share also. Size of stage, 15x20; number sets scenery, 5; bill poster, J. H. Willoughby; theatrical teamster, James P. Kanon. Newspaper: Register (Sat.).........Hotels: Ingham, Hawkins.

NEW ROCHELLE, 6,000. R. R., N. Y., New Haven & Hartford. Town Hall; seating capacity, 700; rental, one night $15; no license; share also. Size of stage, 30x40; no scenery; bill poster, Edward Kelly; theatrical teamster, Miller Bownel. Newspapers: Pioneer (Sat.), Press (Sat.).........Hotels: LeRoy, regular rates $2 (special also); Huguenot.

NEW YORK, 1,300,000. R. R., Central New Jersey; Erie; Del., Lack. & Western; Long Island; N. Y. & Long Branch; N. Y. & Greenwood Lake; N. J. & N. Y.; New Jersey South.; N. Y. Central & Hudson River; N. Y. City & Northern; N. Y., N. H. & H.; N. Y., Susq. & Western; N. Y., West Shore & Buffalo; Pennsylvania; etc., etc.

Academy of Music, Academy of Music Co., managers; Aug. L. Brown, president; H. R. Le Roy, secretary and treasurer; Andrew J. Murphy, assistant secretary and treasurer and superintendent; seating capacity, 2,500; rental, one night $250. Size of stage, 70x84; size of proscenium opening, 46x48; height from stage to grooves, 24; height from stage to rigging loft, 78; depth under stage, 10; musical directors, Signor Arditi, Theodore Thomas, etc.; scenic artist, Charles Fox; stage carpenter, C. E. Lange.

Bijou Opera House, Miles & Barton, lessees and managers.

Casino, Rudolph Aronson, manager; seating capacity, 1,200. Devoted to the production of comic opera.

Comedy Theatre, H. M. Valentine, manager; James A. Hamilton, treasurer; seating capacity, 700; traps, 2; musical director, Joyce; advertising agent, A. A. McDonald : stage carpenter, John A. Martin; gas engineer, Fred. Kinzler.

Daly's Theatre, Augustin Daly, manager; seating capacity, 1,200; musical director, Henry Widmer; scenic artist, James Roberts; stage carpenter, James Tait.

Fifth Avenue Theatre, John Stetson, manager, seating capacity, 1,300. Size of stage, 45½x30; size of proscenium opening, 29x28; musical director, Charles Puerner; scenic artist, H. L. Reid; stage carpenter, Daniel Shea.

Fourteenth Street Theatre, Samuel Colville, lessee and sole manager; James T. Maguire, treasurer; Alexander Fitzgerald, stage manager; Henry E. Hoyt & Bro., scenic artists; A. D. Peck, machinist; Joseph D. Wray, master of properties ; Richard Francis, gas engineer; Mr. Henry Puerner, musical director; J. W. Rosenquest, manager's assistant.

Grand Opera House, Henry E. Abbey, lessee & manager; Wm. W. Tillotson, acting manager; John H. Bones, treasurer; Myron B. Rice, assistant treasurer; share only. Size of stage, 71x65; size of proscenium opening, 35x38; height from stage to grooves, 22; height from stage to rigging loft, 51; depth under stage,23; full set traps; complete sets scenery; musical director, Albert Anderson; stage manager, W. H. Flohr; scenic artist, Thomas Weston; master machinist, H. Weaver; property master, J. S. Ellick; gas engineer, James Stewart, Jr.; doorkeeper, S. D. Singleton; advertising agent, J. H. Geary.

Lyceum Theatre, and Lyceum Theatre School of Acting; director of theatre, Steele Mackaye; director of school, Franklin Sargent; business director, Gustave Frohman; secretary, Charles MacGeachy.

Madison Square Theatre, proprietors and managers, M. H. Mallory & Co.

Metropolitan Opera House, Metropolitan Opera House Company, managers; secretary and treasurer, Edmund C. Stanton; superintendent, A. A. Arment; musical director and conductor, Dr. Leopold Damrosch; leader of orchestra, Herr Reinhard Richter; chorus masters, Herr Lund, Herr Rechelt ; stage manager, Herr Wilhelm Hock; stage carpenter, Gifford; scenic artist, Fox; property master, Bradwell; wardrobe mistress, Miss Berg : perruquier, C. Meyer; costumers, Herr Riteroth (Brunswick), L. Stern (Berlin); armorer, Bradwell; music librarian, Russel; orchestra manager, Kayser; director of stage band, Leypold; prompter, Mrs. Buschmann.

Mt. Morris Theatre, Jno. W. Hamilton, manager.

New Park Theatre, Frank B. Murtha, manager; seating capacity, 1,800; Size of stage, 40x100; size of proscenium opening, 30x36; height from stage to grooves, 26; height from stage to rigging loft, 60; depth under stage, 8; scenic artists, Fox & Schaffer; stage carpenter, Jas. A. Curwood.

Niblo's Garden, John J. Poole & E. G. Gilmore, managers; seating capacity, 2,930; share only. Size of stage, 49x76; size of proscenium opening, 37x43; height from stage to grooves, 32; height from stage to rigging loft, 62; depth under stage, 86; musical director or leader of orchestra, A. W. Hoffman; scenic artist, J. Mazzanovitch ; stage carpenter, W. Crane.

People's Theater, Harry Miner, sole proprietor and manager; Wm. S. Moore, assistant manager; Jno. R. Topham, treasurer; seating capacity, 2,600. Size of stage, 47x100; size of proscenium opening, 28½x30 ; height from stage to grooves, 20 ; height from stage to rigging loft, 55; depth under stage, 10; scenery, unlimited quantity; musical director, J. B. Holding; scenic artist, John Quinn; master machinist, Al. Young; master of properties, John G. Williams; gas engineer, Wm. Burke.

Star Theatre, Lester Wallack, sole proprietor, manager; seating capacity, 1,700; size of stage, 50x71; size of proscenium opening, 36x26; height from stage to grooves, 20; height from stage to top of rigging loft, 42; depth under stage, or cellar, 8; scenic artist, Geo. Dayton; stage carpenter, A. Fillery.

Thalia Theatre, Gustav Amberg, manager; seating capacity, 1,800; musical director, Prof. Poelz; scenic artist, Stoekel; stage carpenter, Klaus; bill poster, Weijki.

Theatre Comique, Harrigan & Hart, managers. Size of stage, 33x24; size of proscenium opening, 32x26; height from stage to grooves, 19; height from stage to rigging loft, 42; depth under stage, 19; musical director, D. Braham; scenic artist, C. Withum; stage carpenter, M. McMurray.

Third Avenue Theatre, Mr. and Mrs. McKee Rankin, proprietors and managers; Joseph Arthur, acting manager; Otto J. Ahlstrom, treasurer; seating capacity, 1,800; musical director, Emil Habercorn; scenic artist, R. Halley; stage carpenter, Wm. Hughes; master of properties, G. Burnton; advertising agent, Isaac M. Wall.

Union Square Theatre, Shook & Collier, managers; Leigh S. Lynch, business manager; W. E. Hudson, treasurer; E. H. Gouge, secretary; seating capacity, 1,900. Size of stage, 50x38; size of proscenium opening, 48x32; height from stage to grooves, 25; height from stage to rigging loft, 55; traps, 15; number sets scenery, 239; musical director, Henry Tissington; scenic artist, Richard Marston; stage carpenter, G. B. Winne.

Wallack's Theatre, Lester Wallack, sole proprietor, manager; acting manager, J. Gilbert; stage manager, Arthur Wallack; stage director, H. Edwards; treasurer, Theodore Moss; seating capacity, 1,300. Size of stage, 38x64; size of proscenium opening, 31½x34; height from stage to rigging loft, 75; depth under stage, 20; musical director, Michael Connolly; scenic artist, Philip Goatcher; prompter, James S. Wright; master machinist, F. Dorrington; properties, E. Siedle; gas engineer, J. F. Driscoll.

Harry Miner's Bowery Theatre (variety), Harry Miner, sole proprietor and manager; A. H. Sheldon, business manager; Thos. W. Moore, treasurer; seating capacity, 3,200. Size of stage, 33x45; size of proscenium opening, 28x24; height from stage to grooves, 17½; height from stage to rigging loft, 48; depth under stage, 20; traps, 4; full set scenery; leader of orchestra, Thomas Maguire; scenic artist, R. Smith; master machinist, James Taylor; advertising agent, John Gedney; assistant treasurer, Geo. Hoppert; cashier, J. H. Casey; officer, John Kennedy.

Harry Miner's Eighth Avenue Theatre (variety), Harry Miner & Thos. Canary, proprietors; Fred. H. May, treasurer; seating capacity, 2,300. Size of stage, 30x47; size of proscenium opening, 24x23½; height from stage to grooves, 18; height from stage to rigging loft, 50; depth under stage, 10; stage manager, Louis Robie; musical conductor, Thos. Hindley; scenic artist, Richard Smith; stage carpenter, Harry R. Bradley; property master, Wm. H. Banm; advertising agent, Burt Pierson.

Koster & Bial's Concert Hall (variety), Koster & Bial, managers; musical director, Jesse Williams.

London Theatre (variety), Donaldson & Webster, proprietors; James Donaldson, jr., manager; Edwin A. Boll, treasurer; seating capacity, 2,000. Size of stage, 28x26; height from stage to grooves, 15; height from stage to rigging loft, 29; depth under stage, 8; leader of orchestra, Robert Recker; director of amusements, E. D. Gooding; advertising agent, Edward F. Denike; master of properties, Ed. Mills; mechanical engineer, Geo. N. Veritzan.

National Theatre (variety), Michael Heumann, manager; J. T. Dudley, treasurer; seating capacity, 1,200; share only. Size of stage, 24x40; size of proscenium opening, 25x20; height from stage to grooves, 15; height from stage to rigging loft, 28; depth under stage, 9; number sets scenery, 10; leader of orchestra, Prof. Ph. Loesch; director of amusements, Alf. A. Wallace; scenic artist, George Becker; stage carpenter, J. F. Post.

Tony Pastor's Theatre (variety), Tony Pastor, manager; seating capacity, 1,000; license yearly; share only. Size of stage, 43½x50; size of proscenium opening, 22x28; height from stage to grooves, 18½; depth under stage, 20; leader of orchestra, Adolph Nichols; scenic artist, Edward Simmons; stage carpenter, Henry Liphart.

NIAGARA FALLS, 4,900. **R. R.**, Erie ; Grand Trunk ; Michigan Central ; N. Y. Central & Hudson River ; N. Y., West Shore & B. Prospect Park Pavilion, Prospect Park Co., managers ; seating capacity, 600. Size of stage, 20x40 ; number sets scenery, 3. Newspapers: daily, Gazette; weekly, Courier (Sat.)......Hotels Spencer, Niagara, Cataract, International.

NORWICH, 5,000. **R R., D., L. & W.; N. Y.**, On. & W. Breeze Opera House, Breeze & Clark, managers; **seating capacity,** 1,000; rental, share only; license included. Size of stage, 36x50; size **of proscenium** opening, 18x25; height from stage to grooves, **14; height from** stage **to rigging loft, 20;** depth under stage, 5; traps, 2; number sets scenery, 10; **bill poster,** Breeze **Opera House; theatrical** teamster, M. Tanner. Newspapers: **semi-weekly,** Telegraph **(Tu. and Sat.); advertising rates, yearly** contract; weekly, Union (Th.), **yearly** contract; **Post (Fri.), yearly contract; Sentinel (Th.)...** ..Hotels: Spaulding, **special rates, $1; American, special rates, $1; Eagle, special rates,** $1 to $1.50.

Academy of Music, **C. G.** Sumler, manager; seating capacity, **800; rental, one** night **$15,** three $40; license, **$3 to $5.** Size of stage, 21x45; full set scenery.

NUNDA, 2,800. R. R., Buffalo, New York & Philadelphia; Erie; **Lackawanna & Pittsburg**. Academy of Music, C. K. Sanders, manager; seating capacity, 600; rental, **one night,** $10; license, $?. Size of stage, 24x40; full set scenery; bill poster, John Provo; theatrical teamster, J. E. Paine. Newspapers: Herald (Fri), News (Sat.).. ...Hotel: Nunda.

NYACK, 4,000. R. R., Northern N. J.; N. Y. Cen. & Hudson R ; N. Y. West Shore & Buff.; N. Y., Ont. & Western. Opera House; seating capacity, 600; rental, one night **$8;** bill poster, John E. Weeks; theatrical teamsters, Matthews Express. Newspapers: Chronicle (Wed.), City & Country (Fri.), Journal (Sat.)......Hotels: St. Nicholas, York.

Voorhis Hall, E. M. Voorhis, manager; seating capacity, 600 ; rental, one night, $25; license, $5. Size of stage, 23x40; number sets scenery, 5.

OGDENSBURG, 10,000. R. R., Rome, Watertown & Ogden.; **Utica &** Black River; Ogden. & L. C.; Grand Trunk; St. L. & O. New Opera House, Geo. **L.** Ryan, manager; seating capacity, 1,200; share only; license included. Size of stage, 40x64; size of proscenium opening, 30x36; height from stage to grooves, 20; height from stage to rigging loft, 56½; depth under stage, 10; full set scenery; leader of orchestra, Prof. Donmonchel; stage carpenter, Nelson Como; bill poster, John Ashwood; theatrical teamster, John Ashwood. Newspapers : daily, Journal, advertising rates, special contract; semi-weekly, News (Wed., Sat.), advertising rates, special contract; weekly (Th.), advertising rates, **special** contract......Hotels : Seymour, special rates, $1.50 to $2 · Windsor, special **rates $1 to $1.50; Johnson, special** rates, $1.

OLEAN, 6,000. **R. R.**, Erie; Buffalo, New York & Philadelphia; Lackawanna & Pittsburg; **Olean, Brad. &** W. Olean Opera House, Wagner & Reis, **manager,** Bradford. Pa. Seating **capacity,** 1,000; rental, share only; license, yearly. **Size of** stage, 32x57 ; size of proscenium opening, 24x28; height from stage to grooves, 16; height from stage to rigging loft, 30; depth under stage, 10; number sets scenery, 30; bill posters, Wagner & Reis, Bradford, Pa.; number of sheets can accommodate, 1,000 ; rates per sheet, 4c. Newspaper: daily, Times......Hotels: Grand Central, special rates, $1.25 to $2.00; Moore, special rates, $1.50 to $2.00; Olean, special rates, $2.

ONEIDA, 6,000. R. R., New York, Ontario & Western; New York Central & Hudson River. Oneida Opera House, Dr. M. Cavana, manager; seating capacity, 1,200; rental, one night $30, three $75; share also; license, yearly. Size of stage, 48x35; number sets scenery, 32; bill poster, L. Lounsbery; theatrical teamsters, Haslem & Wilson. Newspapers: Union (Th.), Dispatch (Fri.), Free Press (Sat.), Post (Sat.)......Hotels: Eagle, Brunswick, Allen, Bacon, Madison, Globe.

Devereaux Opera House; Dr. M. Cavana, manager; seating capacity, 1,000; rental, one **night $25, three** $60; share also; license, yearly. Size **of** stage, 30x35; number sets **scenery, 23.**

ONEONTA, 3,500. R. R., Delaware & Hudson Canal Co. Stanton Opera House, H. G. Wood, manager; seating capacity, 700; rental, one night $25 ; license, $2. Size of stage, 20x40; full set scenery; bill poster, Charles Warner ; theatrical teamster, O. N. Beach. Newspapers: Herald (Th.), Press (Th.).. ...Hotels: Central, regular rates, $2 (special also); Susquehanna, Hathaway.

OSWEGO, 25,000). R R.,'D., L. & W.; R., W. & O ; N. Y., On. & W. Academy of Music. W. B. Phelps, manager; seating capacity, 900; rental, one night $40, three $100; share also; license, yearly. Size of stage, 26x50; size of proscenium opening, 15x25; height from stage to grooves, 13; height from stage to rigging loft, 21; depth under stage, 4; traps, 2; number sets scenery, full set; leader of orchestra, Prof. E. Faveau; bill poster, Mose Arden; number sheets can accommodate, 500; rates per sheet, 4c.; theatrical teamster, C. R. Lewis. Newspapers : daily, Times, advertising rates, yearly contract ; Palladium, advertising rates, yearly contract .....Hotels : Lake Shore, special rates, $1.25 to $1.50 ; Doolittle, special rates, $1.50 to $2.

Mansard Hall; seating capacity, 700.

OWEGO, 6,000. R. R., Delaware. Lackawanna & Western ; Erie; Southern & Central. Wilson Hall, S. F. Fairchild, manager; seating capacity, 1,200; rental, one night $25, license included. Size of stage, 26x50; height from stage to grooves, 16; height from stage to rigging loft, 20; depth under stage, 6; full set scenery; bill poster, P. H. Romine ; theatrical teamster, Sweet & Wilson. Newspaper : daily, Blade ; weekly, Gazette (Th.), Times (Th), Record (Sat.)......Hotels : Central, Ah-wa-go, Exchange.

PALMYRA, 5,000. R. R., N. Y., C & Hud. Riv.; N. Y., West Shore & Buffalo. Village Hall, H. D. Sanders, manager; seating capacity, 600; rental, one night $35, three $35; no license. Size of stage, 15x25; number sets scenery, 6; bill poster, manager of Hall; theatrical teamster, W. H. Bump. Newspapers: Courier (Fri.), Journal (Th)......Hotels: Palmyra, Eagle, Exchange.

PEEKSKILL, 8,000. R. R., N. Y. Cen. & Hudson River. Dramatic Hall, Durrin Bros., managers, seating capacity, 800; rental, one night $5. Size of stage, 20x22; number sets scenery, 5; bill poster, F. S. Cunningham; theatrical teamster, Abe Blight. Newspapers: Blade (Tu.), Democrat (Sat.), Messenger (Th.)......Hotels: Eagle, Continental, Exchange.

Military Hall; seating capacity, 500.

PENN YAN, 3,400. R. R., North. Cent.; Lake Kenka Steam Navigation Co. Cornevell's Opera House, Abe V. Master, manager; seating capacity, 1,000; rental, one night $25, three $60; license, tickets; share also. Size of stage, 25x50; number sets scenery, 18; bill poster, Opera House; theatrical teamster, Nicholas Wolover. Newspapers: Democrat (Fri.), Express (Wed.), Chronicle (Wed.)......Hotels: Benham, regular rates, $2 (special also); Krapp, Shearman, Central.

PERRY, 1,800. R. R., Silver Lake R'y. Olin Opera House, Olin & Nobles, managers; seating capacity, 800; rental——; share also; no license. Size of stage, 42x20; scenic artist and stage carpenter, A. R. Chands; bill poster and press agent, J. H. Terry. Newspaper : Press (Th.)..... Hotels : Walker, special rates, $1; Hartford, $1.25.

Smith's Hall, M. A. Lovejoy, manager ; seating capacity, 800; rental, one night $5, three $12; license, six tickets; share also. Size of stage, 25x35; number sets scenery, 3.

PHELPS, 1,700. R. R., New York Central & Hudson River; Sodus Bay & Southern. Gibson Hall, D. White, manager; seating capacity, 400; rental, one night $8; number sets scenery, 3; bill poster, Frank Pettit. Newspapers : semi-weekly, Advertiser; weekly, Citizen (Th.)......Hotels : Phelps.

PHŒNIX, 2,800. R. R., Cooperstown & Susquehanna Valley. Windsor Hall, James Duffey, manager; seating capacity, 800; rent or share. Size of stage, 28x40; number sets scenery, 9; bill poster, John Butts. Newspaper : Register (Th.)......Hotels : Howard, regular rates, $2 (special also); Windsor.

PLATTSBURGH, 9,000. R. R., Del. & Hud. Canal Co.; Champlain Transportation Co.; Chateaugay. Palmer's Hall, Charles Palmer, manager; seating capacity, 600; rental, one night $10, three $21; license, $3 to $5. Size of stage, 18x42; bill posters, J. H. Barton & Co. Newspapers: daily, Telegram; weekly, Republican (Sat.), Sentinel (Fri.)...... Hotels; Cumberland, regular rates, $2 (special also); Witherill, regular rates, $2 (special also); Fouquet.

Academy Hall; seating capacity, 520.

PORT BYRON, 3,400. R. R., N. Y. Cen. & Hud. River; N. Y., West Shore & Buffalo, Masonic Hall, Richard Hoff, manager; seating capacity, 600; rental, one night $10, three $21; license, $3. Size of stage, 10x18; no scenery; bill poster, John Brodie; theatrical teamster, C. C. Rumsey. Newspaper: Chronicle (Sat.)......Hotels: Howard, National.

PORT CHESTER, 5,000. R. R., N. Y., New Haven & Hartford. Port Chester Rink, Owen P. Smith, manager; seating capacity, 1,000. Size of stage, 16x25; size of proscenium opening, 11; height from stage to grooves, 12; height from stage to rigging loft, 13; depth under stage, 7; bill poster, H. S. Townsend; number of sheets can accommodate, 80; rates per sheet, 4c.; theatrical teamster, Fred Poor. Newspaper: Journal (Th.), advertising rates per inch, $1......Hotels: Irving, special rates, $1.25; Walker, special rates, $1.25; Windsor, special rates, $1.25.

Irving Hall, Charles H. Felix, manager; seating capacity, 500; rental, one night $15, three $30; license, $3; share also. Size of stage, 16x32; number sets scenery, 2.

PORT HENRY, 5,500. R. R., Delaware & Hudson Canal Co. Opera House, J. W. Deane, manager; seating capacity, 1,000; rental, one night, $12; three, $30; license, $3. Size of stage, 25x25; fair stock scenery, bill poster, Jerry Shahan. Newspaper: Herald (Fri.) ......Hotels: Lee, Pease.

PORT JERVIS, 12,000. R. R., Erie; Port Jervis & Mon. Lea's Opera House, George Lea, manager; seating capacity, 1,200; rental, one night $25, three, $70, license included. Size of stage, 20x36; size of proscenium opening, 15x25; height from stage to grooves, 15; no rigging loft; depth under stage, 5; traps, 3; number sets scenery, 10; leader of orchestra, J. Davis; stage carpenter, Jacob Hauber; bill poster, George Lea; number of sheets can accommodate, 500; rates per sheet, 4c.; theatrical teamster, George Lea. Newspapers: daily, Union, advertising rates, yearly contract; Gazette, advertising rates, yearly contract......Hotels: Delaware, special rates, $1.50; Fowler, special rates, $1.50; Eagle, special rates, $1.

Brown's Hall; seating capacity, 800.

St. John's Hall; seating capacity, 600.

PORT RICHMOND, 4,500 (9 miles from New York City; a ferry runs every hour). Griffith Hall, Alfred Z. Ross, manager; seating capacity, 400; rental, one night $8 to $12; license, $3. Size of stage, 11x24; number sets scenery, 3; bill poster, J. Lewis. Newspapers: Sentinel, Advertiser......Hotels: Continental, Steamboat.

POTSDAM, 3,700. R. R., Rome, Watertown & Ogdensburg. Opera House; seating capacity, 1,500; rental, one night $25, license included. Size of stage, 25x30; fair stock scenery; bill posters, James Brown; theatrical teamsters, John McGilvra. Newspapers: Courier & Freeman (Wed.), Herald (Fri.) ....Hotels: Albion, Mattison.

Town Hall, S. C. Crane, manager; seating capacity, 1,500; rental, one night $16; license, $5; number sets scenery, 3.

POUGHKEEPSIE, 22,000. R R., N. Y. Central; Poughkeepsie, H. & Boston. Collingwood Opera House, E. B. Sweet, manager; seating capacity, 1,800; rental, one night $75; share also. Size of stage, 35x40; size of proscenium opening, 40x40; height from stage to grooves, 19; height from stage to rigging loft, 40; depth under stage, 10; traps, 1; number sets scenery, 20; leader of orchestra, Frank L. Schofield; scenic artist, L. Dujlocg; stage carpenter, Chas. Marshall; bill poster, E. B. Sweet; number sheets can accommodate, 1,000; rates per sheet, 4c.; theatrical teamster, Joseph Gillins. Newspapers: daily, Eagle, advertising rates per inch, $1; News, advertising rates per inch, $1; Enterprise, advertising rates per inch, $1; weekly, Courier (Sun.), advertising rates per inch, $1. ......Hotels: Nelson, special rates, $1.75; Poughkeepsie, special rates, $1.50; Morgan, special rates, $1.75.

PULASKI, 2,300. R. R., Rome, Watertown & Ogdensburg. Tucker's Hall; seating capacity, 300; rental, one night $25, three $40; license, $2. Size of stage, 24x28; number sets scenery, 5; bill poster, Helon F. Doan. Newspaper: Democrat (Th.)......Hotels: Salmon River, Palmer.

RICHBURG, 2,300. R. R., Bradford, Eldred & Cuba; Buffalo, N. Y. & Phil.; Lack. & Pittsburg. Brown's Opera House.

17

RIVERHEAD. 2,300. R. R., Long Island. Music Hall, David F. Vail, manager; seating capacity, 600; rental, one night $15, three $30; share also. Size of stage, 24x12; number sets scenery, 5; bill poster, Wm. Hicks. Newspapers: News (Tu.)......Hotels: Griffin, Long Island, Suffolk.

ROCHESTER, 105,000. R. R., Buffalo, N. Y. & Phil.; N. Y., Lake Erie & Western; N. Y. Central & Hudson River; N. Y., West Shore & Buffalo; Rochester & Charlotte; Rochester & Pittsburg. Grand Opera House, Philip H. Lehnen, manager; seating capacity, 1,400; rental, share only; license yearly. Size of stage, 40x60; size of proscenium opening, 29x39; height from stage to grooves, 16; height from stage to rigging loft, 30; depth under stage, 7; traps, 3; full set scenery; leader of orchestra, Prof. Schack; scenic artist and stage carpenter, Charles A. Holland; bill poster, George Bach; number sheets can accommodate, 5,000; rates per sheet, 3c; theatrical teamster, Rochester Transfer Co. Newspapers: daily, Union, advertising rates per inch, 75c.; Democrat, rates per inch, 75c.; Herald, rates per inch, 75c.; Post-Express, rates per inch, 75c.; weekly, Herald (Sun.) rates per inch, 75c.......Hotels: New Osborn, special rates, $1 50 to $1.75; Brackett, special rates, $1.25 to $1.50; Congress Hall, special rates, $1.25 to $1.50.

Corinthian Academy of Music, Philip H. Lehnen, manager; seating capacity, 1,400; rental, share only; license yearly. Size of stage, 40x70; size of proscenium opening, 30x 40; height from stage to grooves, 16; height from stage to rigging loft, 35; depth under stage, 9; traps, 6; full set scenery; leader of orchestra, A. H. Meyering; scenic artist, Denis Flood; stage carpenter, Henry Macarty.

Washington Hall; seating capacity, 1,200.

Falls Field Summer Theatre.

ROME, 16,000. R. R., N. Y., C. & H. R.; R. W. & O.; D. & H. C. Co. Opera House, J. H. Wheeler, manager; seating capacity, 1,200; rental, one night $35 ; license, 18 tickets. Size of stage, 35x50; size of proscenium opening, 20x24; height from stage to grooves, 14; height from stage to rigging loft, 26; depth under stage, 8; traps, 2; number sets scenery, 12; leader of orchestra, G. Schillner; stage carpenter, A. Leon; bill poster, J. N. Wheeler ; number sheets can accommodate, 500 ; rates per sheet, 3c.; theatrical teamster, C. Mack. Newspapers: daily, Sentinel; weekly, Republican (Sat.), Citizen (Fri.) ......Hotels: Stanwix, special rates, $1.25 to $1.50; Arlington, Willett.

Sink's Opera House, W. S. Sink, manager; seating capacity, 1,482; rental, one night $35, three $95; license, 17 tickets; share also. Size of stage, 24x36; full set scenery.

Wolf's Union Hall; seating capacity, 700.

RONDOUT, 22,000. R. R., N. Y. West Shore & Buffalo; N. Y. C. & H. R. Sampson Opera House, Phil. Sampson, manager ; Brooks & Dickson, New York representatives ; seating capacity, 1,200; share only. Size of stage, 28x60; size of proscenium opening, 30x32; height from stage to grooves, 16; height from stage to rigging loft, 40; depth under stage, 6; traps, 2; number sets scenery, 16; leader of orchestra, Jerome Williams ; scenic artist, Geo. Stemper; stage carpenter, John Carter; bill posting, done by house ; theatrical teamster, Winters. Newspapers: daily, Courier, Leader. Freeman......Hotel: Mansion, special rates, $1.25 to $1.50; Excelsior, special rates, $1.25 to $1.50; Eagle.

Liscomb's New Opera House, George G. Liscomb, manager; seating capacity, 1,200 ; rental, one night $35, three $75; license, $5; share also. Size of stage, 28x60; size of proscenium opening, 10x20; height from stage to grooves, 17; height from stage to rigging loft, 25; depth under stage, 5; traps, 2; number sets scenery, 15; leader of orchestra, Prof. J. Williams; scenic artist. Gilbert S. Miller; stage carpenter, F Hardwick; bill poster, W. Houghtaling; number sheets can accommodate, 500 ; rates per sheet 4c.; theatrical teamster, W. Houghtaling.

SALAMANCA, 4,300. R. R., Erie; N. Y., Pa. & Ohio; Roch. & Pitts.; Buff., N. Y. & Phila. Opera House, Hudson & Ausley, managers; seating capacity, 1,500. Newspapers: Republican (Fri.), Union (Th.).....Hotels: Dudley, regular rates, $2 (special also); Kreiger, Haymarket.

SALEM, 3,000. R. R., Del. & Hud. Canal Co. Salem Opera House, C. M. McLaurie, manager; seating capacity, 600; rental, one night $15; no license. Size of stage, 17x24; number sets scenery, 6; bill poster, William Smart; theatrical teamster, Charles Magee. Newspapers: Press (Fri.). Review (Sat.)......Hotels Ondewa, Central.

SARATOGA SPRINGS, 12,000. R. R., Adirondack; Boston, Hoos. Tun. & West.; Del. & Hud. Canal Co.; Sar. Mt. McG. & L. G. Town Hall, Hill & Connors, managers; seating capacity, 1,100; rental, one night $50, three $150; license included. Size of stage, 30x70; size of proscenium opening, 35x31; height from stage to grooves, 19; height from stage to rigging loft, 29; depth under stage, 8; traps, 2; number sets scenery, 14; leader of orchestra, H. Ensign; scenic artist, Voegtlin; stage carpenter, Harry G. Hill; bill poster, James D. Kelly; number sheets can accommodate, 300; rates per sheet, 4c.; theatrical teamster, William Granger. Newspapers: daily, Journal, advertising rates per inch, 75c. (yearly contract); Saratogian advertising rates per inch, 75c. (yearly contract); weekly, Sun (Th.), advertising rates per inch, 75c. per inch.... Hotels: Irving, special rates, $1.25 to $1.50; New York, special rates, $1.25 to $1.50.

Putnam Music Hall, Frank N. Drew, manager; seating capacity, 600; rental, one night, $40; share also. Size of stage, 26x17; number sets scenery, 6.

Lower Town Hall; seating capacity, 500.

SCHENECTADY, 15,000. R. R., Del. & Hud. Can. Co.; N. Y. C. & H. River. Union Opera House, E. W. Moore, manager; seating capacity, 1,300; rental, one night $25; license, $5. Size of stage, 30x40; full set scenery; bill poster, John Gilmon; theatrical teamster, J. Picket. Newspapers: daily, Star, Union; weekly Gazette (Fri.)..... Hotels: Given, Casley, Burns, Davis, Merchants'.

Central Garden Theatre, Chas. Camden, manager.

New Opera House.

SCHOHARIE, 1,800. R. R., Schoharie & Middleburg. Perry Hall; seating capacity, 600; rental, one night $10 to $15. Size of stage, 18x21; number sets scenery, 5. Newspapers: Republican (Th.), Union (Th.)......Hotels: Wood, Taylor.

SCHUYLERVILLE, 3,000. R. R., Boston, Hoosac Tunnel & Western. Opera House, J. H. De Ridder, manager; seating capacity, 500; rental, one night $15, three $30. Size of stage, 25x20; size of proscenium opening, width, 20; number sets scenery, 7; leader of orchestra, John McLindon; bill poster, S. R. Rice. Newspaper: Standard (Wed.)...... Hotels: Dawley, special rates, $1; Schuylerville, special rates, $1.

SENECA FALLS, 6,500. R. R., N. Y. Cen. & Hud. Riv. Daniels Hall, G. O. Daniels, manager; seating capacity, 800; rental, one night $20; license, $3. Fair stock scenery; bill poster, D. V. Hall; theatrical teamster, D. H. Burns. Newspapers: Reveille (Fri.), Call (Sat.), Courier (Th.)......Hotels: Hoeg, Globe.

Johnston's Hall; seating capacity, 500.

SKANEATELES, 3,000. R. R., N. Y. Cen. & Hud. Riv.; Skaneateles. Legg Hall, Holton & Petheram, managers; seating capacity, 500; rent or share. Newspapers: Democrat (Th.), Free Press (Sat.)......Hotel: Packwood.

SODUS, 1,500. R. R., Rome, Watertown & Ogdensburg. Sodus Opera House, Taylor & Thorne, managers; seating capacity, 650; rental, one night $7 to $10; three $15 to $20; share also; license included. Size of stage, 22x40; number sets scenery, 6; bill poster, Ed. Mills. Newspapers: Alliance (Wed.)... ..Hotels: Whitney.

SYRACUSE, 60,000. R. R., Del., Lack. & West.; N. Y. Cen. & H. Riv.; N. Y., W. Sh. & Buff.; Rome, Watertown & Ogdensburg; Syr., Ont. & N. Y. Wieting Opera House, Phil H. Lehnen, manager; seating capacity, 1,600; rental, one night $190, three $300; share also. Size of stage, 50x60; height from stage to grooves, 20; height from stage to rigging loft, 60; depth under stage, 14; complete stock scenery; bill poster, Geo. Castner; number of sheets can accommodate, 10,000; rates per sheet, 4c.; theatrical teamsters, Hunt's Baggage Co. Newspapers: daily, Journal, Herald, Standard... ..Hotels: Vanderbilt, special rates, $2 to $2.50; Empire, special rates, $1.50 to $2; Caudee, special rates, $1.25 to $1.50.

Grand Opera House, Phil H. Lehnen, manager; seating capacity, 1,300; rental, one night $190; three $300; share also. Size of stage, 40x68; height from stage to grooves, 20; height from stage to rigging loft, 40; depth under stage, 12; complete stock scenery; bill poster, Opera House.

Park Opera House, S. M. Hickey, manager.

THEATRICAL AND OPERATIC
TROUPES

who will take the trouble to examine a map of the United States will note that

— THE —

GREAT ROCK ISLAND ROUTE

reaches more good show towns than any other railway in the United States, and from its central position connects directly in Union Depots with all railways to the Pacific Coast , and in Chicago and Peoria with all the railroads leading East, Southeast or Northeast.

Every professional, man or woman, will admire the

Parlor Reclining Chair Cars,

named after the prima donna of the Operatic Stage.

We enumerate a few of the larger cities to which we run through cars :

PEORIA, DAVENPORT, ROCK ISLAND, MUSCATINE, TRENTON, Mo. ; KANSAS CITY, LEAVENWORTH, Atchison, Council Bluffs, Omaha, Des Moines, Atlantic, Ia.; Cedar Rapids, Waterloo, Ia.; St. Paul, Minneapolis and Watertown, Dak.

Special rates and accommodations for large parties.

Address :

A. B. FARNSWORTH. Gen. East'n. Pass. Agt.,
257 BROADWAY, N. Y.,

OR

R. R. CABLE,   E. ST. JOHN,
Prest. and Gen. Man'g'r.   Gen. Ticket and Pass. Agt.
CHICAGO, ILL.

Shakespeare Hall; seating capacity, 1,600.

Greely Hall; seating capacity, 1,000.

Barton Hall; seating capacity, 1,600.

TARRYTOWN, 10,000. R. R., N. Y. C. & H. R.; N. Y. C. & Northern; several steamboats. Smith's Opera House (new), Henry T. Smith, manager; seating capacity, 900; rental, one night, $25, three $55; license, $5. Size of stage, 24x40; size of proscenium opening, 18x25; height from stage to grooves, 14; height from stage to rigging loft, 31; depth under stage, 9; traps, 2; number sets scenery, 8; scenic artist, Frank Cox; stage carpenter, Opera House; bill poster, C. B. Casel, number of sheets can accommodate, 200; rates per sheet, 4c.; theatrical teamster, Opera House. Newspaper: Herald (Sat.), advertising rates, per inch, 75c...... Hotels: Perry House, special rates, $1 to $1.25; Warner, special rates.

TICONDEROGA, 4,500. R. R., Delaware & Hudson Canal Co.; Vermont Central. Weed's Opera House, F. Weed, manager; seating capacity, 600; rental, one night $30, three $45; share only; license included. Size of stage, 18x20; size of proscenium opening, 18x20; height from stage to grooves, 12; height from stage to rigging loft, 13; depth under stage, 4; traps, 1; number sets scenery, 10; leader of orchestra, E. J. Weld; bill poster, O. H. Holcomb; number of sheets can accommodate, 200; rates per sheet, 4c.; theatrical teamster, E. A. Pinchin. Newspaper : Ticonderogian (Fri.), advertising rates, 50c. per inch .....Hotels : Hall, special rates, $1.25 to $1.50; Burleigh, special rates, $1.25 to $1.50; Exchange, special rates, $1.25 to $1.50.

TONAWANDA, 8,500. R. R., Erie; N. Y. Central & Hudson River; N. Y., West Shore & Buffalo. Riesterer's Hall, Ed. Riesterer, manager; seating capacity, 700; rental, one night $10, three $25, license included. Size of stage, 18x21; number sets scenery, 4; bill poster, D. W. Rundell, theatrical teamsters, Hoeg & Rundell. Newspapers: daily, News; weekly, Enterprise (Sat.), Herald (Th.)........Hotels : American, Excelsior, Backer.

TROY, 60,000. R. R., Del. & Hudson Canal Co.; N. J. C. & H. R.; Troy & Boston. Griswold Opera House, S. M. Hickey, manager; Brooks & Dickson, New York representatives; seating capacity, 1,400; rental, one night $75, three $200; license included; share also. Size of stage, 26x60; height of stage to grooves, 18; height from stage to rigging loft, 44; depth under stage, 13; full set scenery; bill poster, Harry Wheeler; theatrical teamster, A. L. Porter. Newspapers: daily, Standard, Press, Telegram, Times......Hotels: Troy, special rates, $3; American, special rates, $1.75; Mansion.

Music Hall; seating capacity, 1,200; rental, one night $50, three $140; license included. Size of stage, 21x38; depth of stage, 9; bill poster, Dundon.

Rand's Opera House, G. Rand, manager; seating capacity, 1,500.

Grand Central Theatre, Peter Curley, manager.

TRUMANSBURG, 2,200. R. R., Geneva, Ithaca & Sayre. Opera Hall, Gregg & Buckley, managers; seating capacity, 700; rental, one night $20, three $50; license, $3 to $5; share also. Size of stage, 28x42; number sets scenery, 12; bill posters, Opera House; theatrical teamster, Opera House. Newspaper: Sentinel (Wed.)......Hotels: Central, Trembly, Cornell.

UTICA, 40,000. R. R., N. Y. C. & H. R.; D., L. & W.; U. C. & B. R.; N. Y., West Shore & B. Utica Opera House, T. L. Yates, manager ; seating capacity, 1,600 ; rental, one night $75, three $170 ; share also ; license included. Size of stage, 20½x24 ; size of proscenium opening, 29x34½ ; height from stage to grooves, 18 ; height from stage to rigging loft, 38 ; depth under stage, 7 ; traps, 5 ; number sets scenery, 24 ; leader of orchestra, James Koehl; scenic artist, Allen McKenzie ; stage carpenter, John Canfield; bill poster, T. L. Yates; number of sheets can accommodate, 1,500 ; rates per sheet, 4c.; theatrical teamsters, Dunn & Leut. Newspapers : daily, Herald, advertising rates, 75c. per inch ; Press, advertising rates, 75c. per inch ; Observer, advertising rates, 75c. per inch ; weekly, Tribune (Sun.), advertising rates, 75c. per inch......Hotel : Baggs, special rates, $2.50 to $3 ; Butterfield, special rates, $2 to $2.50 ; Grand Central, special rates, $1.25 to $1.50.

Mechanics' Hall ; seating capacity, 1,000.

City Opera House; seating capacity, 900.

UNADILLA, 3,000. R. R., Del. & Hud. Canal Co. Mulford & Siver's Hall, Robert Siver, manager ; seating capacity, 450; rental, one night $10 ; no license. Size of stage, 16x28 ; fair stock scenery ; bill poster, J. O. Burrows. Newspaper: Times (Wed.)......
Hotels: Brick, Central.

WARSAW, 3,000. R. R., Erie; Rochester & Pittsburg. Irving Opera House; seating capacity, 650; rental, one night $15; three $30; license, $2. Size of stage, 19x27; number sets scenery, 5; bill poster, Hop Salisbury; theatrical teamster, Monroe & Norton. News-papers: New Yorker (Th.), Review (Th.), Times (Th.)..... Hotels: Bingham, regular rates, $2 (special also); Cook, United States.

WARWASSING, 3,000. R. R., Midland & West Shore. Masonic, Charles B. Houston, manager ; seating capacity, 500 ; rental, one night $10, three $24; license, $3; leader of orchestra, Clayton. Newspapers: Ellenville Press (Th), Ellenville Journal (Th.).
Hotel: Constable.

WATERFORD, 4,600. R. R., Delaware & Hud. Canal Co. Town Hall, John Higgins & Co. managers; seating capacity, 500; rental, one night $15; license, 8 tickets; share also Size of stage, 15x25; fair stock scenery; bill poster, Robert Palmer. Newspaper: Adver-tiser (Fri.)......Hotels: Morgan, City, Clifton.

WATERLOO, 5,400. R. R., N. Y. Cen. & Hud. Riv. Academy of Music, Slack & Co., man-agers; seating capacity, 700; rental, one night $15, three $35; license, $3; share also. Size of stage, 18x20; number sets scenery, 9; bill poster, O. D. Terris; theatrical teamster, H. H. Kelly. Newspapers: Observer (Wed.), News (Tu.)......Hotels: Towsley, Com-mercial, Brunswick.

WATERTOWN, 12,000. R. R., Rome, Watertown & Ogdensburg. Washington Hall, E. M. Gates, manager; seating capacity, 1,200; rental, one night $40, three $60; share also; license included. Size of stage, 40x60; number sets scenery, 7; bill poster, E. G. Clark. Newspaper: daily, Times; weekly, Republican (Sun.); Post (Tu.)......Hotels: Woodruff, Globe, Crowner, Kirby.

WATERVILLE, 4,000. R. R., Delaware, Lackawanna & Western. Waterville Opera House; seating capacity, 800; rental, one night $40; no license; share also. Size of stage, 24x24; size of proscenium opening, 18x24; number sets scenery, 10; bill poster, Henry Crosby; theatrical teamster, J. F. Hamill. Newspaper: Reporter (Fri.)....
Hotel: American.

WATKINS, 3,500. R. R., Northern Central; Syracuse, Geneva & Corning; Seneca Lake Steam Navigation Co. Watkins Opera House, Watkins Opera House Co., man-agers; seating capacity, 750; rental, one night $20, three $45; share also; license, $5 or tickets. Size of stage, 30x50; size of proscenium opening, 15x18; height from stage to grooves, 12; height from stage to rigging loft, 15; depth under stage, 8; traps, 2; num-ber sets scenery, 10; bill poster, David Griffith; number sheets can accommodate, 400; rates per sheet, 4c. Newspapers: Express (Th.), Democrat (Wed.), Herald (Wed.)..... Hotels: Jefferson, Lake View, Mountain, Glen Park, Fall Brook.

Freer's Opera House; seating capacity, 800.

WAVERLY, 5,000. R. R., Delaware, Lackawanna & Western; Erie; Lehigh Valley. Waverly Opera House, C. Mullock, Jr., manager; seating capacity, 800; rental, one night $25; license, tickets; share also; number sets scenery, 12; bill poster, Opera House; theatrical teamster, J. F. Tozer. Newspapers : Advocate (Fri.), Tribune (Th.)...... Hotels : Tioga, regular rates, $2.50 (special also); American, Snyder, Courtney.

Exchange Hall; seating capacity, 600.

WEEDSPORT, 2,300. R. R., New York Central & Hudson River; New York, West Shore & Buffalo; Southern Central. Franklin Hall, Donovan, Palmer & Co , managers; seating capacity, 500; rental, one night, $10; license, 12 tickets. Size of stage, 16x22; no scenery; bill poster, Thomas Durbin. Newspapers Chief (Sat.), Sentinel (Th.)...... Hotels: Willard, Mansion, Congress.

WELLSVILLE, 4,500. R. R., Bradford, Eldred & Cuba; Erie. Opera Hall, S. F. Hanks, manager; seating capacity, 600; rental, one night $18, three $40; license, $2; share also. Size of stage, 50x70; number sets scenery, 6; bill poster, J. B. Goodliff; theatrical teamster, Wm. Steffy. Newspapers: daily, Free Press, Reporter......Hotels: Fassett, Howell.

WESTFIELD, 3,500. R. R., Lake Shore & Mich. So.; N. Y., Chic. & St. Louis. Wells' Opera House, S. V. Wells, manager; seating capacity, 600; size of stage, 22x36; fair stock scenery; bill poster, William Johnson; theatrical teamster, James Borden. Newspaper : Republican (Wed.)......Hotels : Westfield, Minton.

WHITEHALL, 5,000. R. R., Del. & Hud. Canal Co. Hall's Opera House, E. W. Hall, manager; seating capacity, 1,000; rental, one night, $25; license included; share also. Size of stage, 30x60; full set scenery; bill poster, W. D. Butts; theatrical teamster, James Farrell. Newspapers: Chronicle (Sat.) Times (Wed.)... .Hotels: Opera House Hotel, regular rates, $2 (special also); Grand Union.

WHITE PLAINS. 4,500. R. R., New York Central & Hudson River. Lafayette Hall, Wm. H. Hoatts, manager; seating capacity, 500; rental, one night $12, three $30; license, $5. Size of stage, 11x21; size of proscenium opening, 19; theatrical teamster, Augustus Bogart. Newspapers: Journal (Fri.), Westchester News (Sat.) ... Hotels: Standard, Central.

YONKERS, 20,000. R. R. New York Central & Hudson River; New York City & Northern. Music Hall, John Bright, manager; seating capacity, 1,000; rental, one night $85, three $210, license included; share also. Size of stage, 30x51; size of proscenium opening, 30x30; height from stage to grooves, 18; height from stage to rigging loft, 45; depth under stage, 8; traps, 3; number sets scenery, 13; leader of orchestra, John Bright; scenic artists, Charles Huent & F. Klug; stage carpenter, Oliver G. Parsons; bill poster, Calvin D. Gale; number sheets can accommodate, 400 to 500; rates per sheet, 4c ; theatrical teamsters, Armstrong & Whyte. Newspapers; daily, Statesman, advertising rates, per inch, $1; weekly, Gazette (Fri.), Statesman (Fri.), Times (Sat.)......Hotels: Getty's, special rates, $2; Yonkers, special rates, $1.50.

Warburton's Opera House, John Bright, manager; seating capacity, 800; rental, one night $25, three $55; license, $5. Size of stage, 16x24; number sets scenery, 14.

Radford's Hall; seating capacity, 1,000.

NORTH CAROLINA.

ASHEVILLE, 8,000. R. R., Western North Carolina. Asheville Opera House, James P. Sawyer, manager; seating capacity, 500; rental, one night $10, three $25; share also. Size of stage, 20x30; number sets scenery, 10; bill poster, E. L. Brown. Newspapers: semi-weekly, Citizen; weekly, Register (Th.), Republican (Th.)......Hotels: Swannanoa, regular rates, $2 (special also); Eagle, Bank, Barnet, Central.

BEAUFORT, 2,000. R. R., Atlantic & North Carolina. Davis' Hall, James C. Davis, manager; seating capacity, 400; rental, one night $5. Size of stage, 10x30; size of proscenium opening, 8; depth under stage, 3; bill poster, John Willis. Newspaper: weekly, Telephone (Fri.)......Hotels: Davis, Ocean View, Dunn.

CHARLOTTE, 12,000. R. R., Carolina Central, Char.; Col. & Aug.; Rich. & Danville. Opera House, L. W. Sanders & Co., managers; seating capacity, 1,200; rental, one night $60, three $150; share also; license included. Size of stage, 25x24; height from stage to grooves, 17; height from stage to rigging loft, 31; depth under stage, 4; bill poster, Nat. Gray; theatrical teamster, J. W. Wadsworth. Newspapers: daily, Journal, Observer ......Hotels: Central, special rates; $1.50 to $2; Buford, special rates, $1.50 to $2.

DURHAM, 5,000. R. R., Rich. & Danville. Stokes' Hall, Stokes & Geer, managers; seating capacity, 600; rental, one night $20, three $50; license, $15.75; share also. Size of stage, 28x22; number sets scenery, 6; bill poster, J. T. Mallory. Newspapers: daily, Reporter; weekly, Recorder (Mon.)......Hotels: Claiborne, regular rates, $2 (special also).

ELIZABETH CITY, 3,500. R. R., Norfolk Southern. Library Hall, J. E. Marsh, manager; seating capacity, 800; rental, one night $25; license, $5. Size of stage, 28x56; number

sets scenery, 3; bill posters, **Woodruff** & Smith. Newspaper: Economist (Tu.), Falcon,
(Mon.), North Carolinian (Wed.) ....**Hotels:** Albemarle, regular rates, $2 (special also);
City, Sheridan,

Harney's Theatre, **T.** Selby **Harney,** manager; seating capacity, **500.**

FAYETTEVILLE, 5,400. R. R., Cape Fear & Yadkin Valley Williams' Hall, E. B. Williams & Co., managers; seating capacity, **500;** rental, one night $30, three $80; license
included. Size of stage, 25x30; **number sets** scenery, 3; bill poster, manager of hall.
Newspaper: Observer (Th.), Sun **(Wed.)**......Hotel: Fayetteville, Clarendon.

GOLDSBORO, 5,000. R. R., Atl. & N. C.; Mid. N. C.; Rich. & Dan.; Wilmington & Weldon.
Messenger Opera House, J. E. Bonitz, manager; **seating capacity,** 900; rental, one night
$40, three $80; license $10 to $14; share also. Size of stage, 27x30; number sets
scenery, 11; bill poster, Opera House. Newspaper: semi-weekly, Messenger; weekly,
Bulletin (Sat.).......Hotel: Gregory, regular rates, $2 (special also); Bonitz, regular
rates, $2.

Town Hall, **J. A. Washington, manager; scating capacity, 400; rental, one night $5; license,**
$15. Size of stage, 20x30; no scenery.

GREENSBORO, 3,500. R. R., Rich. **& Danv.;** N. C.; N. W., N. C; Cape Fear &
Yadkin Valley. Burford Hall, D. W. C. Burford, manager; seating capacity, 600;
rental, one night $20, three $50; license, $15.75. Size of stage, 17x50; size of pro-
scenium opening, 13x17; height from stage to grooves, 17; height from stage to rigging
loft, 17; **depth** under stage, 10; traps, 1; number sets scenery, 4; bill poster, Bill Sloan;
rates per sheet, &c. Newspaper: daily, Workman; advertising rates per inch, $1.
Hotels: Burford, special rates, $1.50; Central, regular rates, $2 (special also); McAdoo,
regular rates, $2.50 (special also).

HENDERSON, 3,300. R. R., Oxford & Henderson; Raleigh & Gaston. Burwell Hall, Burwell Bros , managers; seating capacity, 700; rental, one night $20, three $50; license, $5;
share also. Size of stage, 15x23; number sets scenery, **5; bill** poster, manager of hall.
Newspaper: Gold Leaf (Th.)......**Hotels:** Henderson, **regular rates, $2** (special also);
Central, regular rates, $2 (special also).

Opera House; seating **capacity,** 1,000

KINSTON, 3,000. R. R., Atlantic & North Carolina. Loptin's Opera House, S. H. Loptin,
manager; **scating capacity, 800;** rental, share only; license included. Size of stage.
24x24; size of proscenium opening, 12x24; height from stage to grooves, 13; depth under
stage, 3½; traps, 1; number sets scenery, 4. Newspaper, Free Press (Th.)......Hotel:
Nnon's, special rates, **$1.25.**

NEW BERNE, 7,000. R. R., Atlantic & North Carolina. New Berne Theatre, John **C.**
Green, manager; seating capacity, 500; rental, one night $25; share also, license in-
cluded. Size of stage, 40x20; size of proscenium opening, 15x18; height from stage **to**
grooves, 12; height from stage to rigging loft, 16; depth under stage, 8; traps, 2; number
sets scenery, 11; bill poster, New Berne Theatre; number sheets can accommodate, 200;
rates per sheet, 4c.; theatrical teamster, Jonas Daniels. Newspaper : daily, Journal
...Hotels: Central, **special rates, $1** to **$1.50 ;** Gaston, special rates, $1 to $1.50.

RALEIGH, 13,000. R. R., Raleigh & Gaston; Raleigh & Augusta; Richmond **& Danville.**
Tucker **Hall, R.** S. Tucker, manager; seating capacity, 800; rental, **one night $40, license**
included. **Size** of stage, 27x41; size of proscenium opening, 16x22½; **height from stage to**
grooves, 18; height from stage to rigging loft, 18; depth under stage, 3; **traps, 3; number**
sets **scenery, 11;** leader of orchestra, M. Pauli; stage carpenter, **Charles Tucker;** bill
poster, **G. H.** Mullin; number of sheets can accommodate, **500; rates per sheet,** 4c.;
theatrical teamster, John O'Kelly. Newspapers: daily, **News & Observer, advertising**
rates, per inch, **$1 ;** Chronicle, advertising rates, per **inch, $1;** **Visitor, advertising**
rates, per inch, $1   .Hotels : Tucker, regular rates, **$2 (special also);** Yarbrough,
regular rates $2 (special also).

Metropolitan Hall; seating capacity, 1,200.

Holtoman Hall; seating capacity, 1,500.

REIDSVILLE, 2,200. R. R., Richmond & Danville; Philadelphia & Reading. Ellington Opera House, E. J. Ellington, manager; seating capacity, 600; rental, one night $15; license, $8; share also. Size of stage, 20x40; number sets scenery, 5; bill poster, Opera House. Newspapers: Times (Th.), Weekly (Tu.)......Hotels: Piedmont, Exchange.

SALISBURY, 4,500. R. R., Richmond & Danville; Western & North Carolina. Meroney's Opera House, seating capacity, 500; rental, one night $15, three $35; license, $15 75. Size of stage, 20x40; number sets scenery, 7; bill poster, John Morgan. Newspapers: Watchman (Th.), Examiner (Th.)......Hotels: Mount Vernon, regular rates, $2 (special also); Boyden, National.

STATESVILLE, 1,500. R. R., Charlotte. Columbia & Augusta; Western & North Carolina. Opera House, J. S. Van Pelt, manager; seating capacity, 306; rental, one night $25; license included. Size of stage, 18x21; fair stock scenery; bill poster, Charles Davis. Newspapers: American (Sat.), Landmark (Fri.)......Hotels: St. Charles, regular rates, $2 (special also); Central.

TARBORO, 3,360. R. R., Albemarle & Raleigh; Wilmington & Weldon. Opera House, D. Lichtenstein, manager; seating capacity, 500; rent or share, license yearly. Size of stage, 26x26; fair stock scenery; bill poster, Edward Dancy. Newspapers: Guide (Sat.); Sentinel (Sat.); Southerner (Th.).....Hotels: Tarboro, regular rates, $2 (special also); Bryant.

WASHINGTON, 3,000. R. R., Jamesville & Washington. Opera House; seating capacity, 1,000; rental, one night $20, three $50; share also. Size of stage, 17x29; size of proscenium opening, 13x21; height from stage to grooves, 15; depth under stage, 4; number sets scenery, 6. Newspaper: Gazette (Th.), advertising rates per line, 10c......Hotel: De Willer, regular rates $2 (special also).

WILMINGTON, 21,000. R. R., Carolina Central; Wil. & Weldon; Wil., Col. & Aug. Opera House, E. I. Pennypacker, manager; seating capacity, 1,000; rental, one night $60, three $150; share also; license included. Size of stage, 32x50; full set scenery; bill poster, B. Fuller. Newspapers: daily, Star, Review; weekly, Post (Sun.)......Hotels: Commercial, special rates, $1.25; Purcell, regular rates, $2 (special also).

City Hall; seating capacity, 1,500.

Brooklyn Hall; seating capacity, 300.

WILSON, 1,300. R. R., Wilmington & Weldon. Willis Momona Opera House, C. F. Willis, manager; seating capacity, 750. Newspapers: Advance (Fri.), Mirror (Fri.).....Hotel: Briggs, regular rates, $2 (special also).

WINSTON, 6,500. R. R., Richmond & Danville. Brown's Opera House, Samuel A. Smith, manager; seating capacity, 1,000; rental, one night $25, three $50; license, $5 to $12; share also. Size of stage, 25x50; number sets scenery, 3; bill poster, Thomas Pfhel. Newspapers: daily, Pilot; weekly, Leader (Tu.), Republican (Th.), Sentinel (Th.)......Hotels: Merchants', regular rates, $2 (special also); Central.

OHIO.

ADA, 1,800. R. R., Pitts., Ft. W. & Chic. Opera House, A. Shaw, manager. Size of stage, 30x45; number sets scenery, 15. Newspaper: Record (Wed.)......Hotel: Commercial, regular rates, $2 (special also).

AKRON, 32,463. R. R., Cleveland, Mt. V. & Del. ; N. Y., Pa. & Ohio ; Pitts., Cleveland & Toledo ; Valley. Academy of Music, W. G. Robinson, manager ; Brooks & Dickson, New York representatives ; seating capacity, 1,000 ; rental, one night $60, three $150 ; share also ; license yearly. Size of stage, 32x60 ; size of proscenium opening, 28x24; height from stage to grooves, 17½ ; height from stage to rigging loft, 39 ; depth under stage, 4 ; traps, 4 ; number sets scenery, 21 ; leader of orchestra, C. W. Lantz ; scenic artist, William Beck ; stage carpenter, George Knox ; bill poster, M. H. Hart ; number of sheets can accommodate, 3,000 ; rates per sheet, 4c.; theatrical teamster, Charles Camp. Newspapers: daily, Beacon, advertising rates, yearly contract ; weekly, Gazette

BROOKS & DICKSON,

MANAGERS.

ROMANY RYE (A),

         IN THE RANKS,

                LA CHARBONNIERE,

LILLIAN RUSSELL,

         MME. RISTORI,

                ROMANY RYE (B),

Herman and Wills' new play, HONI SOIT.

GENERAL OFFICES,

44 W. Twenty-third Street.

NEW YORK CITY.

GENERAL DRAMATIC AGENCY.

(Sun.), Times (Wed.), Labor Union (Fri.).... Hotels : Buchtel, special rates, $1 25 to $1.50 ; Empire, special rates, $1 to $1 50; Windsor, special rates, $1 to $1 50.

Phoenix Hall ; seating capacity, 400.

ALLIANCE, 7,000. R. R., Pitts., Ft. Wayne & Chic ; Cleve. & Pitts. ; Cleve., Youngs. & Pitts. ; Alliance, Niles & Ashtabula. Marchand's Opera House, F. C. Marchand, **manager** ; seating capacity, 1,000 ; share only. Size of stage, 30x60 ; number sets scenery, 16; bill poster, Opera House ; theatrical teamster, Jesse Shidler. Newspapers: semi-weekly, Review ; weekly, Leader (Sat.), Standard (Fri.).... Hotels : Sourbeck, regular rates, $2 (special also); Chase, regular rates, $2 (special also); Arlington, Central, Vincent.

ANTWERP, 1,400. R. R., Wabash. Shirley Hall; seating capacity, 400. Newspaper: Argus (Th.).... Hotel: Exchange, regular rates, $2 (special also).

ASHLAND, 4,000. R. R., N. Y., Pa. & Ohio. Opera House, W. H Reynolds, manager; seating capacity, 800; share only. Size of stage, 40x70; number sets scenery, 13; bill poster, Opera House; theatrical teamster, Isaac Laner. Newspapers: Press (Th.), Times (Th.).... Hotels: McNulty, regular rates, $2 (special also); Central.

ASHTABULA. R. R., Lake Shore & Mich. So.; Nickel Plate; Ashtabula, Pitts. & Franklin (Division of the Lake Shore). Smith's Opera House, L. W. Smith & Son, managers; seating capacity, 850; rental, share only, license included. Size of stage, 26x42; size of proscenium opening, 17x22; height from stage to grooves, 12, height from stage to rigging loft, 16; depth under stage 8; traps, 1; number sets scenery, 10, leaders of orchestra, Chas Leek and Prof. Olland; bill poster, L. W. Smith & Son. Newspapers: Telegraph (Th.), Standard (Wed.), News (Wed.)...... Hotels: Fisk, special rates, $1.25 to $1.50; Stoll, special rates, $2; Rural, special rates, $1 to $1.25; Smith, special rates, $1 to $1.25.

ATHENS, 3,200. R. R., Cin., Wash. & Balt.; Col , Hock. Val. & Tol.; Ohio Cent. City Hall, C. H Wingas, manager; seating capacity, 600; rental, one night $20, three $40; share also; license included. Size of stage, 30x22; number sets scenery, 10; bill poster, H. C. Brown; theatrical teamster, W. B. Foster. Newspapers: Herald (Wed.), Journal (Th.), Messenger (Th.)...... Hotels: Warren, regular rates, $2 (special also); Cornell.

BELLEFONTAINE, 5,000. R. R. Clev., Col., Cin. & Ind.; Ind., Bloom & West. Grand Opera House, Grand Opera House Co., managers; seating capacity, 800; bill poster, Spence Miller. Newspapers: Examiner (Fr.), Index (Wed.), Republican (Fr.)...... Hotels : Miltenberger, regular rates, $2 (special also); Bellefontaine, Logan.

Melodeon Hall, Marquis & Jordan, managers; seating capacity, 500; rental, one night, $10, three $25; license, $2 to $3. Size of stage, 15x22; number sets scenery, 6.

BELLEVUE, 5,300. R. R., Lake Sh, & Mich. So.; N. Y., Chi. & St Louis. Opera House, Benner & Kern, managers; seating capacity, 800; rental, one night $12, three $30; license, $3 to $10. Size of stage, 17x22; number sets scenery, 7; bill poster, Opera House. Newspapers: Gazette (Wed.), News (Sat.)...... Hotels: Exchange, regular rates, $2 (special also); Ridle, Mane.

BEVERLY, 1,100. R. R., Muskingum Riv. Odd Fellows' Opera Hall, S. G. Adair, manager; seating capacity, 350; rental, one night $10, three $25; license, $1; share also. Size of stage, 18x28; full set scenery; bill poster, manager of hall. Newspaper: Dispatch (Fri.) .... Hotels: American, Lewis, Central.

BOWLING GREEN, 1,700. R. R , Bowling Green, Toledo & Indianapolis. Blank's Hall, F H. Broughton & Co., managers; seating capacity, 600; rental, one night $10. Size of stage, 18x24; full set scenery; bill poster, E. J. Orvine; theatrical teamster, Wm. White. Newspapers: Democrat (Fri.), Sentinel (Th.)...... Hotels: Central, regular rates, $2 (special also); Lease.

BRYAN, 4,400. R. R , Lake Shore & Mich. Southern. Baxter Opera House, Baxter & Nelson, managers; seating capacity, 600; rental, one night $15, three $36; license, $3; share also. Size of stage, 24x36; number sets scenery, 9 ; bill poster, Wm. Raynor. Newspapers : Democrat (Th.), Press (Th.)...... Hotels : Fountain City, regular rates, $2 (special also); Bryan, Ohio.

BUCYRUS. 4,200. R. R., Ohio Cent.; Pitts., Ft. Wayne & Chic. Rowse Hall, H. & W.
Rowse, managers; seating capacity, 500; rental, one night $15; license, $3. Size of stage,
25x30; bill posters, Fulton & Kayler. Newspapers: Forum (Fri.), News (Th), Journal
(Fri.)......Hotels: Sims, regular rates, $2 (special also); Alcorn, Monnett.

CADIZ, 2,000. R. R., Pan Handle (Pitts., Cin. & St. Louis). Cadiz Opera House, J. S.
Conwell, manager; seating capacity, 700; rental, one night $25; license, $25. Size
of stage, 20x30; size of proscenium opening, height, 12; full sets scenery; leader
of orchestra, W. P. Rea; stage carpenter, J. O. Lucas; bill poster, Wm Miller;
theatrical teamster, Wm. Johnson. Newspapers: Sentinel (Th.); advertising rates 10c.
per line; Republican, advertising rates 10c. per line......Hotels: New Arcade, special
rates, $1.25; Globe, special rates, $1.25.

Music Hall, Clark & Dewey, managers; seating capacity, 600; rental, one night $12.50,
three $25; license, $1 to $3 share also. Size of stage, 15x30; number sets scenery, 13.

CAMBRIDGE, 3,200. R. R., Balt. & Ohio; Cleveland & Marietta. Town Hall, E. W.
Stottlemire, manager; seating capacity, 400; rental, one night $9, three $20, license included. Size of stage, 20x30; bill poster, T. C. Stanley. Newspapers: daily, Times;
weekly, Democrat (Sat.), Herald (Th.)........Hotels: Eagle, regular rates, $2 (special
also); Brown, regular rates, $2 (special also); Morton.

CANTON, 25,700. R. R., Pittsburgh, F. W. & C.; Connotton Valley; Cleveland & Marietta.
Schaefer's Opera House, Louis Schaefer, manager; Brooks & Dickson New York representatives; seating capacity, 1,250; rental, share only; license, yearly. Size of stage,
31x48; size of proscenium opening, 20x30; height from stage to grooves, 16; height
from stage to rigging loft, 30; depth under stage, 10; traps, 3; number sets scenery,
18; scenic artist, C. F. Papke; stage carpenter, Robert Votaw; bill poster, address manager; number of sheets can accommodate, 16 stands; rates per sheet, 3c.; theatrical
teamsters, Hurford & Miller. Newspaper: daily, Repository, Democrat... ...Hotels:
American, special rates, $1.50; St. Cloud, special rates, $1.50 to $2; Metropolitan, special
rates, $1.25 to $1.50.

CELINA, 1,600. R. R., Lake Erie & West; Tol., Cin. & St. L.; Cin, Van Wert & Mich.
Tunnell's Hall; seating capacity, 500; rent or share; license, $1.50. Size of stage, 18x75;
number sets scenery, 6; bill poster, Wm Baker. Newspapers: Observer (Th.), Standard
(Th.)......Hotels: Ellis, regular rates, $1.50 (special also); St. Charles.

CHARDON, 1,500. R. R., Painesville & Youngstown. Chardon Opera House, S. E. Bod-
man, manager; seating capacity, 550; rental, one night $15, three $30; license, $1 to $3.
Size of stage, 20x30; size of proscenium opening, 15; height from stage to grooves, 16;
height from stage to rigging loft, 22; depth under stage, 3; traps, 3; number sets scenery,
7; leader of orchestra, Prof. Rodgers; stage carpenter, T. C. Crampton. Newspaper
Republican (Tu.)......Hotels: Chardon, regular rates, $2, (special also); Burnett
House, regular rates, $2 (special also).

CHILLICOTHE, 13,000. R. R., Cincinnati, Wabash & Baltimore; Scioto Valley; Toledo,
Cincinnati & St. Louis. Masonic Opera House, Byron W. Orr, manager; seating
capacity, 800; rental, one night $50; share also; license, $1. Size of stage, 30x38; size
of proscenium opening, 20x25; height from stage to grooves, 18; number sets scenery, 19;
leader of orchestra, Eddy Fry; scenic artist, Byron W. Orr; stage carpenter, J. Drummond; bill poster, Byron W. Orr; number of sheets can accommodate, 500; rates per
sheet, 3c.; theatrical teamster, James Smith. Newspapers: daily, News; weekly,
Gazette (Wed.), Leader (Sat.), Advertiser (Sat.) ...Hotels: Warner, special rates, $2;
Emmett, special rates, $1.50.

Clongh's Opera House, E. Kauffman, manager; seating capacity, 900; rental, one night
$40; three $100, license, $1.25; share also. Size of stage, 30x52; height from stage to
grooves, 16; height from stage to rigging loft, 31; depth under stage, 7; bill poster, E.
Kauffman; theatrical teamster, E. Kauffman.

CINCINNATI, 300,000. R. R., Cin., Ham. & Day.; C, Ind., St. L & C.; C., N. O. & Tex.
Pacific; .Cin. & Portsmouth; Cleveland, C., C. & I.; Kentucky Central; Louisville &
Nashville; Marietta & Cin.; N. Y., Pa. & Ohio; Ohio & Mississippi; Pittsburg, Cin &
St. Louis; Toledo, Cin. & St Louis. Grand Opera House, Miles & Rainforth, managers;
seating capacity, 2,200; share only. Musical director, Isaac Haig; scenic artist, De Witt C.

Waugh; stage carpenter, George Fields; bill poster, Harry Lewis; number of sheets can accommodate, 30,000; rates per sheet. 3c; theatrical teamster, Omnibus Line. Newspapers: daily, Enquirer, advertising rates, per inch, $1.50; Commercial-Gazette, per inch. $1.50; Times-Star, per inch, $1.50; Post ..... Hotels: Burnett House, special rates $2.50 to $3; Grand, special rates, $2.50 to $3; Gibson, special rates, $2.50 to $3; Palace, $2 to $3; Emery, regular rates, $3 (special also).

Havlin's Theatre, J. H. Havlin, manager; Brooks & Dickson, New York, representatives; seating capacity, 1,700. Size of stage, 38x70; size of proscenium opening, 30x30; height from stage to grooves, 18; height from stage to rigging loft, 40; depth under stage, 8.

Heuck's New Opera House, Jas. E. Fennessy, manager; Brooks & Dickson, New York representatives; seating capacity, 2,500; share only. Size of stage, 60x83; size of proscenium opening, 40x35; height from stage to grooves, 21; height from stage to rigging loft, 75; depth under stage, 12; complete stock scenery; musical director, Adam Weber; scenic artist, D. B. Hughes; stage carpenter, Jos. Morris; bill poster, John Chapman; theatrical teamster, Omnibus Co.

People's Theatre, Jas. E. Fennessy, manager; seating capacity, 1,800; share only; size of stage, 37x75; size of proscenium opening, 30x35; height from stage to grooves, 18; height from stage to rigging loft, 60; depth under stage, 12; traps, all kinds; full set scenery; leader of orchestra, H. Leopold; scenic artist, Fred Jones; stage carpenter, F. Mills; bill poster, J. Chapman.

Robinson Opera House, John Robinson, manager; seating capacity, 1,600; rent only. Size of stage, 45x90.

Coliseum Opera House, James Collins, manager; seating capacity, 3,000.

Harris Museum, P. Harris, manager; seating capacity, 600; size of stage, 30x30.

Vine Street Opera House (variety), S. Gabriel, manager; seating capacity, 800. Size of stage, 30x30.

St. Charles Music Hall, E. A. Ritter, manager.

Smith & Nixon's Hall.

Greenwood Hall.

Mozart Hall.

CLEVELAND, 250,000. R. R., Cleveland, C., C. & I.; Cleveland & Pittsburg; Cleveland, Youngstown & Pittsburg; Lake Shore & Mich. Southern; N. Y., Chic. & St. Louis; N. Y. Pa. & Ohio; Connotton Valley. Opera House, Gus Hartz, manager; seating capacity, 1,400; rental, share only; license, yearly. Size of stage, 65x80; size of proscenium opening, 38x34; height from stage to grooves, 18½; height from stage to rigging loft, 60; depth under stage, 22; traps, all kinds; number sets scenery, most complete; musical director, Prof. J. U. Thorndike; scenic artist, Simon Moesta; stage carpenter, James J. King; bill posters, T. E. Bryan & Co.; number of sheets can accommodate, 6,000; rates per sheet. 3c.; theatrical teamsters, Omnibus Transfer Co. Newspapers: daily, Leader, advertising rates, yearly contract; Herald, yearly contract; Penny Press, yearly contract; Plain Dealer, yearly contract; weekly, Sun (Sun.), yearly contract; Voice (Sun.), yearly contract; Sentinel (Sat.), yearly contract ..... Hotels: Stillman, special rates, $3.50; Weddell, special rates, $2 to $2.50; Kennard, special rates, $2 to $2.50; Forest City, special rates, $2 to $3; Prospect, special rates, $1 to $1.25; American, special rates, $1.50; Hawley, special rates, $1.50.

Academy of Music, John A. Ellsler, manager; seating capacity, 900; rental, one night $100, three $300, license included; share only. Size of stage, —; size of proscenium opening, 36x31; height from stage to rigging loft, 26; depth under stage, 6; traps, 6; number sets scenery, 40; musical director, Prof. Schoenam; scenic artist, Signor Cappannini; stage carpenter, Tom Studer; bill poster, James Bryan; number of sheets can accommodate, 1,100; rate per sheet, 4c; theatrical teamster, Transfer Co.

Globe Theatre; seating capacity, 1,028; rental, one night $40, three $105, license included; full set scenery.

Case Hall; seating capacity, 1,240; license, $5. Size of stage, 22x45; no scenery.

Drew's Museum, Charles Drew, manager.

CIRCLEVILLE, 7,000. R. R., Pitts., Cinn. & St L; Scioto Valley. Peck's Hall, Evans Krimmel manager; seating capacity, 550; rental, one night $12, three $30; license, $3.25; share also Size of stage, 18x30; number **sets** scenery, 4; bill poster, James O'Neal; theatrical teamster, E. G Binny Newspapers : daily, Herald; weekly, Watchman (Fri.), Union-Herald (Th.)......Hotels: Pickaway, regular rates, $2 (special also); American.

CLYDE, 3,700. R. R., Lake Shore & Mich. South.; Wheeling & Lake Erie. Opera **House,** C. E. Perry, manager; seating capacity, 450; rent or share; license, $1 and 8 tickets. Size of stage, 20x21; full set scenery; bill poster, W. J. De Lude; theatrical teamster, N. H. Wyatt. Newspapers: Enterprise (Th.), Advocate (Sat.).....Hotel: Nichols, Junction, St. Vincent.

COLUMBIANA, 1,800. R. R., P. F. W. & Chicago. Appleton Hall, John P. Patterson, manager; seating capacity, 400; rental, one night $10, three $25; rental, $5. Size of stage, 30x25; size of proscenium opening, 14x18; depth under stage, 4; traps, 2; number sets scenery, 6; leader of orchestra, C. M. McClure; stage carpenter, B. F. Miller; theatrical teamster, Frank Bell. Newspaper: Register (Th.)......Hotel: Patterson, regular rates, $1.50 (special also).

COLUMBUS, 70,000. R. R., Baltimore & Ohio; Clev., Col., Cincinnati & Indiana; Cleveland, Mt. V, & Delaware; Col., Hock. Val. & Toledo; Chicago, St. Louis & Pitts.; Col. & Eastern; Ind., Bloom. & West; Ohio Central; Pitts., Cinn. & St. Louis; Scioto Valley. Grand Opera House, Miller & O'Key; seating capacity, 1,500; rental, share only; license yearly. Size of stage, 40x58; size of proscenium opening, 26x33; height from stage to grooves, 18; height from stage to rigging loft, 41; depth under stage, 11; traps, 3; complete stock scenery; leader of orchestra, C. L. Schneider; scenic artist, E. B Fickes; stage carpenter, Geo. Jackson; bill poster, J. B. Miller; number sheets can accommodate, 600; rates per sheet, 4c ; theatrical teamster, Col. Transfer Co. Newspapers daily, Journal, advertising rates per inch, 75c.; Dispatch, advertising rates per inch, 75c.; Times, advertising rates per inch, 75c.; weekly, Capital (Sun.), advertising rates per inch, 75c.; News, (Sun) advertising rates per inch, 75c.; Bohemian (Sat.), advertising rates per inch, 75c. ......Hotels: Neil, regular rates, **$3 to $4;** American, $1.50 to $2; Park, $2 to $2.50.

Comstock's Opera House. F. E. Comstock. manager; seating capacity, 1,400; rental, one night, **$75;** share also; license included. Size of stage, 24x32.

Eureka Theatre, James Douglass, manager.

Pavilion **Theatre,** Richards & Roltain, managers; seating capacity, 2,200.

City Hall; seating capacity, 3,000.

COLUMBUS GROVE, 3,500. R. R , Cin.. Ham. & Dayt. Day's Academy of Music, **Marion** Lace, manager, seating capacity, 600; rental, one night $25; license, $2. Size of stage, 17x24; size of proscenium opening, 18x22 ; height from stage to grooves, 12; bill poster, Marion Lace; number sheets accommodate, 250; rates per sheet, 4c. Newspaper: Democrat (Th.), advertising rate, 10c. per line......Hotel : City, special rates $1.25.

CORNING, 4,200. R. R., Ohio Central. Monahan's Opera House, John Monahan, manager; seating capacity, 800; rental, one night $15, three $40; license, $3; share also Size of stage, 13x30 ; number sets scenery, 5. Newspaper : Times (Th.).. Hotels: Central, Globe, Park.

COSHOCTON, 4,330. R. R., Connotton Valley; Pitts., Cin., **St. Louis.** Opera House ; seating capacity, 1,000; rental, one night $30; share also; license included. Size of stage, 30x40; full set scenery; bill poster, H D. Beach. Newspapers· Age (Sat.), Democrat, (Tu.), Standard (Sat.)......Hotels : McDonald, regular rates, $2 (special also); Price. City Hall; seating capacity, 500.

CRESTLINE, 4,200. R. R., Clev., **Col.**, Cin. & Ind.; Pitts., **Ft.** Wayne & Chic. Schober's Opera House, Aug Schober, manager; seating capacity, **560;** rental, one night $10, three **$24; license $2; share also.** Size of stage, 22x28; number sets scenery, 6; bill poster, **W. Carney.** Newspapers: Advocate (Fri.), Democrat (Th.)......Hotels: Continental, regular rates, $2 (special also); National, Central, Gibson.

CUYAHOGA FALLS, 3,000. R. R., Pitts., Clev. & Tol.; Clev., Mt. Ver. & Del. James **Hall,** George Sackett, manager; seating capacity, **500;** rental, one night $10, three $25;

license, $1; share also. Size of stage, 18x22; no scenery; bill poster, F. H. Duffy; theatrical seamster, J. Hatfield. Newspaper: Reporter (Fri.)....Hotel: Perry, regular rates, $2 (special also).

DAYTON, 45,000. R. R., Cin., Ham. & Day.; Cin. Nor.; Clev., Col., Cin. & Ind.; Day. & Union; N. Y., Pa. & Ohio; Pitts., Cin. & St. Louis; Tol., Cin. & St. Louis. Weidner's Opera House, J. & P. Weidner, managers; seating capacity, 1,100; rental, one night, $40, three $120; share also. Size of stage, 30x51, size of proscenium opening, 29x29; height from stage to grooves, 20; height from stage to rigging loft, 32; depth under stage, 8; traps, 3; number sets scenery, 16; leader of orchestra, C. Dennewitz; scenic artist, D. Hughes; stage carpenter, Charles Combs; bill posters, Wolf Bros.; theatrical teamster, P. A. McGowen. Newspapers: daily, Democrat, advertising rates, per inch, 75c.; Journal, advertising rates, per inch, 75c.; Herald, advertising rates, per inch, 75c....Hotels: Beckel, special rates, $2; Phillips, special rates, $1.50; Arlington, special rates, $1; Palmer, special rates, $1.

Grand Opera House (formerly Music Hall), Larry H. Reist, manager; seating capacity, 1,500; share only. Size of stage, 45x90; size of proscenium opening, 40x40; height from stage to grooves, 20; height from stage to rigging loft, 25; depth under stage, 16; traps, 2; number sets scenery, 18; leader of orchestra, G. H. Marsteller; scenic artist, Walter P. Wilson; stage carpenter, Henry Bandendistle; bill posters, Wolf Bros.; number of sheets can accommodate, 10,000; rate per sheet, 3c.; theatrical teamster, P. P. Mosler.

NATIONAL MILITARY HOME, 5,000. R. R., Home Avenue; Tol., Cin. & St. L. Memorial Hall, Amusement Committee, managers; seating capacity, 1,500; share also. Size of stage, 40x75; size of proscenium opening, 24x32; height from stage to grooves, 17; height from stage to rigging loft, 23; depth under stage, 8; traps, 4; number sets scenery, 15; stage carpenter, Sam. Harderson; theatrical teamster, Home....Hotel: Home.

Beckel Opera House; seating capacity, 800.

DEFIANCE, 8,000. R. R., Balt. & Ohio; Wabash. Meyers Hall; seating capacity, 500; full set scenery; bill poster, G. W. Eiser. Newspapers: daily, Journal; weekly, Express (Th.); Times (Sat.). Herald (Wed.)......Hotels: Russell, regular rates, $2 (special also); Crosby, regular rates, $2 (special also).

DE GRAFF, 1,400. R. R., Clev., Col., Cin. & Ind. Weller Hall, E. Weller, manager; seating capacity, 500; rental, one night $10, three $20; license, $2; share also. Size of stage, 20x40; number sets scenery, 7; bill poster, Nate Strayer; theatrical teamster, Wm. Posh. Newspaper: Buckeye (Fri.)......Hotels: Miami, regular rates, $2 (special also); Buckeye.

DELAWARE, 10,000. R. R., Clev., Col., Cin. & Ind.; Col., Hock. Valley & Tol. City Opera House, Clippinger & Rutter, managers; seating capacity, 1,012; rental, one night $40, three $100; share also; license included. Size of stage, 30x60; number sets scenery, 20; bill poster, Opera House; theatrical teamster, Bus Line. Newspaper: daily, Chronicle; weekly, Gazette (Th.), Herald (Th.), Signal (Wed.) ....Hotels: American, regular rates, $2 (special also); Powell, Nicholls, St. Charles.

Williams' Opera House, Harry N. Hills, manager; seating capacity, 1,000; rental, one night $15 to $30; license, $3 to $10. Size of stage, 23x36; number sets scenery, 5.

DRESDEN, 1,200. R. R., Pittsburg, Cincinnati & St. Louis. Lemert's Hall. Newspaper: Doings (Fri.)......Hotel: Akeroyd, regular rates, $2 (special also).

EAST LIVERPOOL, 7,000. R. R., Cleveland & Pittsburgh. Opera House, Geo. J. B. Phillips, manager; seating capacity, 900; rental, one night $30, three $75; license, yearly. Size of stage, 22x22; size of proscenium opening, 16x16; height from stage to grooves, 14; height from stage to rigging loft, 18; depth under stage, 4; traps, 2; number sets scenery, 11; bill poster, Wm. Bridge; number of sheets can accommodate, 200; rates per sheet, 3c.; theatrical teamster, Henry Benington. Newspapers, weekly: Review (Sat.), advertising rates, 50c. per inch; Gazette (Th.), advertising rates, 50c. per inch......Hotels: Thompson, special rates, $1 to $1.25; Dobbs, special rates, $1.

Deldrick's Opera House, J. L. Deidrich, manager; seating capacity, 400; rental, one night $10, three $25; share also. Size of stage, 15x17; number sets scenery, 6.

McNicoll's Opera House; H. E. McNicoll, manager; seating capacity, 800.

EATON, 3,500. R. R., Cin., Ham. & Day. **Opera House**, E. H. Allison, manager; seating capacity, 600; rental, one night $50. **three $45**; license includ.d. Size of stage, 21x41; full set scenery; bill poster, Thomas J. **Tibbals**; theatrical teamster, M. Ryan. News-paper; **Democrat** (Th.).......Hotels: Reicher, regular rates, $2 (special also).

ELMORE, 1,500. **R. R**., Lake Shore & Mich. So. Opera **Hall**, Johnson & Haskins, mana-gers; seating capacity, 400; **rental, one night $8**, three $20; share also; license, $1 Size of **stage**, 20x24; size of proscenium opening, 9x19; depth under stage, 4; traps, 1; number **sets** scenery, 5; bill poster, Johnson & Haskins; number of sheets can accommodate, 60; rates per sheet, 4c.; theatrical teamster, John **Goff**. Newspapers: Tribune (Fri), ad-vertising rates, 5c. per line. Hotels: Elmore, special rates, $1; American, special rates, $1.

ELYRIA, 5,500. R. R., Cleveland, Lorain & Wheeling; Lake Shore & Mich. Southern. Elyria Opera House, W. B. Gates, manager; seating capacity, 1,000; rental, one night $25, three $50; license included. Size of stage, 30x40; number sets scenery, 14; bill post-er, W. W. **Bruce**; theatrical teamster, B. F. Small. Newspapers: Constitution (Th.), Republican (**Th.**) ....Hotels: Beebe, regular **rates**, $2 (special also,; American, regular rates, $2 (special also); Metropolitan, National.

Town **Hall**; seating capacity, 750; rental, **one night $15**; license included. Size of stage, 18x20).

FINDLAY, 6,000. R. R., Lake Erie & **Western**; Ind., Bloomington & Western; Toledo & Ind. Davis' Opera **House**, J. C. Bushon, **manager**; seating capacity, 800; rental, one night $25, three $60; share also; license yearly. Size of stage, 33x50; size of proscenium opening, 10x30; height from **stage to** grooves, 16; height **from** stage to rigging loft, 22; depth under stage, 6; number **sets** scenery, 16; leader of orchestra, Mr. Wineland; bill **poster**, Opera House Co.; **number of sheets can accommodate, 250**; rates per sheet, 4c.; theatrical **teamster**, Stanley **Moore**. Newspapers ; daily, Jeffersonian, advertising rates per inch, $1; **Star**, advertising rates per inch, **$1**; weekly, **Republican** (Fri.). Courier (Th.). .....Hotels : Joy's, special rates. $1.50 to **$2**; **Commercial, special rates, $1.25 to $2**; Sherman, special rates, $1; Central, **special rates, $1**.

FOSTORIA, 5,300. R. R., Baltimore **& Ohio**; Col., Hocking Valley & Toledo; Lake Erie & Western; N. Y., Chic. & St. Louis; **Ohio** Central. Audes Opera **House**, W. P. Howell, manager; seating capacity, 800; **rental**, one night $20, three **$45; share also license** in-cluded. Size of stage, 30x60; number sets scenery, 15; bill **poster**, J. A. **Flickinger**. Newspapers: Democrat (Th.), Observer (Th.), Review (Fri.). ....Hotels: Hayes', regular rates, $2 (special also), Central.

Liberty **Hall**, Eschelman & Hale, managers; seating capacity, 400; **rental, one night $8**, **three $21; license**, $1.50 to $3; share also. Size of stage, 22x30; full set scenery.

FREMONT, 10,000. **R. R**., Lake Shore & Mich. So.; Lake Erie **& Western**; Wheeling & Lake Erie. Opera Hall, F. Heine, manager; seating **capacity, 800**; rental, one night $15; license, **$3; Size of** stage, 40x37; size of proscenium **opening**, 16x24; depth under **stage**, 3; traps, 4; **number** sets scenery, 5; leader of orchestra, Gus. Spicher; scenic artist, P. Phillips; stage carpenter, Jas. Steiniy; bill poster, James Thompson; **theatrical teamster**, John Steward. Newspapers: Messenger (Th.); Journal (Fri.); **Courier** (Th.)...... Hotels: Roch, regular rates, $2 (special also); Ball, regular rates, **$2** (**special also**); Croghan.

Mammoth Hall; seating capacity, 1,000.

Union Hall; seating capacity, 800.

GALION, 7,500. R. R., Clev., Col., Cin. **& Ind.**; N. Y., Pa. & Ohio. City Opera Hall, A **Brokaw**, manager, seating capacity, **900**; rental, one night $15; license, $2 Size of stage, 25x50; **number** sets scenery, 27; bill **poster**, S. F. Riblet. Newspapers: Inquirer (Fri.); **Noose (Sat.)**; Sun-Review (Fri.) .....**Hotels**: Central, regular **rates**, $2 (special also); Capitol.

Central Opera **House**, H. R. Kelley, manager; **seating capacity, 550**; rental, one **night $12**; **share also**; license included. Size of stage, 22x22; full set scenery.

GALLIPOLIS, 5,300. R. R., Col., Hock. Val. & Tol. Aleshire Hall, W. S. Kerr, manager; seating capacity, 600; rental, one night $15, three $35; license, $3. Size of stage, 16x

18

17; number sets scenery, 6; bill poster, Frank Lepert. Newspapers: daily, Tribune; weekly, Bulletin (Tu.), Herald (Sat.), Journal (Th.)......Hotels; Dufour, regular rates, $2 (special also; Wendell, St. Charles, Ecker.

GARRETTSVILLE, 2,200. R. R., N. Y., Pa. & Ohio. Buckeye Hall, G. Horton, manager; seating capacity, 700. Newspaper: Journal (Th.)....... Hotel: Cannon, regular rates, $2 (special also).

GREENVILLE, 5,500. R. R., Cin., **Van Wert & Mich.;** Chic., St. L. & Pittsburg: **Dayton & Union.** **Opera House, R. S.** Frizell, manager; seating capacity, 700; rental, one night. **$35; share also; license included.** **Size of stage, 25x40;** number sets scenery, 12; bill **poster, Daniel Murphy.** **Newspapers:** **Democrat (Wed.),** Advocate (Th.), Die Post (Sat.), **Journal (Fri.), Courier (Sat.)......Hotels: Turpen, regular rates,** $2; Wagner.

Music Hall, Frank McWheeney, manager; seating capacity, 800; rental, one night, $10 to **$20; license, tickets; share also; number sets scenery, 3.**

HAMILTON, 15,000. R. R., Cin., **Ham. & Day.; C.,** H. & I.; N. Y., Pa. & Ohio; Cin., H. & R. Globe Opera House, A. Myers, manager; seating capacity, 1,200; **rental, one night** **$35, three $85, share also;** license yearly. Size of stage, 30x30; size of proscenium opening, 18x50; height from stage to grooves, 15; height from stage to rigging loft, 19; traps, 1; number sets scenery, 10; stage carpenter, Kuhne; bill poster, Kuhne; number sheets can accommodate, 1 500 to 2,000; rates per sheet, 4c. Newspapers: daily, News, advertising rates, yearly contract; weekly, Democrat (Th.), Observer (Fri.)......Hotels: St. Charles, special rates, $1.25; Central, special rates, $1.25; Stronb, special rates, $1.25.

Beckett Hall, Jacob Lorenz, manager; seating capacity, 600; **rental,** one night $20; **license, $3.** Size of stage, 20x25.

HANOVERTON, 500. R. R., Cleveland & Pittsburg. Hanover Hall, **S. M. Borson, manager;** **seating** capacity, 300......Hotel: Mansion.

HICKSVILLE, 2,000. R. R., Baltimore & Ohio. Pettit Opera House, B. S. Pettit, manager; seating capacity, 550; size of proscenium opening, 18x20; number sets scenery, 9; leader of orchestra, G. F. Knight; bill poster, J. O. Russ. Newspaper: News (Th.)......Hotels: Union, special rates, $1; Aldine, special rates, $1.

HILLSBORO, 3,600. R. R., Cin. & Eastern; Cin., **Wash. & Balto.** Music Hall, C. S. Bell, manager; seating capacity, 800; rental, one night $15, three $30; license, $2. Size of stage, 17x43; number sets scenery, 4; bill poster, **Chas.** Clay. Newspapers: daily, Gazette; weekly, **News (Wed.),** Herald (Sat.)... ..**Hotels:** Kramer, regular rates, $2 (special also); **Ellicott, Woodrow.**

HOLGATE, 1,200. R. R., Baltimore & Ohio; Tol., Cin. & St. Louis. Holgate Opera Hall; **seating** capacity, 500. Size of stage, 16x22; fair stock scenery. Newspaper: Times **(Th.)**

HUDSON, 2,100. R. R., Clev., Mt. Ver. & Del.; Cleveland & Pittsburg. Adelphian Hall, C. W. Farrar, manager; seating capacity, 800; rent or share. Size of stage, 25x30; fair stock scenery; bill poster, A. G. Benson; theatrical teamster, Wm. Bond. Newspaper: Enterprise (Fri.) .....Hotel: Mansion, regular rates $2 (special also).

IRONTON, 11,000. R. R., Scioto Valley; Toledo, Cin. & St. L. Masonic Opera House, B. F. Ellsberry, manager; seating capacity, 950; rental, share only; license included. Size of stage, 23x32; size of proscenium opening, 19x25; height from stage to grooves, 14; height from stage to rigging loft, 24; depth under stage, 9; traps, 2; number sets scenery, 10; leader of orchestra, J. M. Stroble; scenic artist, B. V. Hicks; stage carpenter, Jos. Barnes; bill poster, Opera House; number sheets can accommodate, 800; rates, 3c; theatrical teamster, E. W. Jones. Newspapers: Register (Wed.), advertising rates yearly; Bee (Sat.), advertising rates, special contract; Irontonion (Fri.), advertising rates, contract......Hotels: Ironton, special rates, $1.50; Sheridan, special rates, $1.50; Massie, special rates, $1.

Union Hall, W. A. Murdock, manager; seating capacity, 750; rental, one night $18, three $40; license, $5.50; share also. Size of stage, 18x24; number sets scenery, 7.

JEFFERSON, 1,200. R. R., Lake Shore & Mich. So. Town Hall; seating capacity, 700; rent or share; fair stock scenery. Newspapers: semi-weekly, Sentinel; weekly, Gazette (Fri.). ..Hotels: American, regular rates, $2 (special also); Beckwith.

KENT, 4,000. R. R., Connotton Valley; N. Y., Pa. & Ohio; Pittsburg & Western. Opera House, W. S. Kent, manager; seating capacity, 500; rental, share only; license yearly. Size of stage, 21x22; size of proscenium opening, 13½x23; height from stage to grooves, 13½; height from stage to rigging loft, 16½; depth under stage, 3½; number sets scenery, 7; bill poster, B. A. Brewster; number sheets can accommodate, 300; rates per sheet, 4c. Newspapers : Bulletin (Th.), advertising rates, per inch, $2; News (Th.), advertising rates, per inch, $2......Hotel : Continental, special rates, $1 to $1.25; Collins, special rates, $1 to $1.25.

KENTON, 5,500. R. R., Chic. & Atlantic; Ind., Bloom. & Western, (Ohio Division). Dickson's Grand Opera House, Henry Dickson, manager; seating capacity, 1,295; share only; license yearly Size of stage, 42x70; number sets scenery, 25; bill posters, Dickson & Lawrence; theatrical teamster, Thos. Maple Newspapers: Democrat (Th.), Republican (Th.)..... Hotels : Reese, regular rates, $2 (special also); Southard, regular rates, $2 (special also); Scott, Dugan, Franklin.

City Hall; seating capacity, 800.

LANCASTER, 9,000. R. R., Cincinnati & Muskingum Valley ; Toledo, Columbus & Hocking Valley. Chestnut Street Opera House, Sandy G. V. Griswold, manager ; seating capacity, 900 ; rental, share only. Size of stage, 29x50 ; size of pro-scenium opening, 24x26 ; height from stage to grooves, 18 ; height from stage to rigging loft, 30 ; depth under stage, 9; traps, 3; number sets scenery, 12 ; leader of orchestra, J. E. Rudebaugh; scenic artist, M. Anubrustic ; stage carpenter, H. Eckert ; bill poster, Chas. Scoville ; theatrical teamster, John Cleery. Newspapers : semi-weekly, Gazette (Tu. and Fri.), advertising rates, yearly contract; weekly, Eagle (Th.), advertising rates, yearly contract; Republican (Th.), advertising rates, yearly contract......Hotels: Martin, special rates, $1.25 ; Ynithoff, special rates, $1.25; Talmadge, regular rates, $2 (special also).

City Hall, Geo. C. Stonebremer, manager ; seating capacity, 500; rental, one night $20, license included; share also. Size of stage, 40x50; number sets scenery, 3.

LEBANON, 3,500. R. R., Cin. Northern; Toledo, Cin. & St. Louis. Opera House, seating capacity, 900; rental, one night $20; three $48 ; license included. Size of stage, 30x60; number sets scenery, 10 ; bill poster, Jacob Egbert; theatrical teamster, J. M. Thompson. Newspapers : daily, Star ; semi-weekly, Gazette ; weekly, Patriot (Fri.) ......Hotels: Lebanon, regular rates, $2 (special also).

LEETONIA, 2,500. R. R., N. Y., Pa. & Ohio ; Pitts., Ft. Wayne & Chic. Forney's Opera House, M. T. Forney, manager ; seating capacity, 600). Newspaper : Democrat (Fri.).....Hotel : Hartzell, regular rates, $2 (special also).

LIMA, 12,500. R. R., Pittsburg, Fort Wayne & Chicago; D. & M.; Chicago & Atlantic; Lake Erie & Western. Faurot Opera House, O. E. Latham, manager; seating capacity, 1,000; rental, one night $100; three $225; share also; license included. Size of stage, 58x60; size of proscenium opening, 40x30; height from stage to grooves, 18; height from stage to rigging loft, 70; depth under stage, 12; traps, 5; number sets scenery—full sets; leader of orchestra, Mr. Johnson; stage carpenter, Harry Bell; bill poster O. E. Latham; number of sheets can accommodate, 800); rates per sheet, 4c; theatrical teamster, Wm. Pangle. Newspapers: daily, Republican, advertising rates (yearly contract), 10c. per line; semi-weekly, Democrat (Wed. and Sat.), advertising rates, 10c. per line; weekly, Times (Sat.), advertising rates, 10c. per line......Hotels: Lima, special rates, $2 to $2.50; Barnet, special rates, $1.50 to $2.50; French's, special rates, $2 to $2.50.

Faurot Music Hall, O. E. Latham, manager. Size of stage, 35x18; no scenery.

City Hall; seating capacity, 650; rental, one night $25, three $75; license, 8 tickets; share also. Size of stage, 23x30; number sets scenery, 12.

LOGAN, 3,200. R. R., Col., Hock. Val. & Tol. Rempel's Opera House, F. F. Rempel, manager; seating capacity, 1,000; rental, one night $30; three $40; share also. Size of stage, 16x36; number sets scenery, 10; bill poster, J. C. James. Newspapers : Sentinel (Th), Gazette (Th.)......Hotels: Rempel, regular rates, $2 (special also); American, Bunz.

LONDON, 3,700. R. R., Pitts., Cin. & St. Louis; Ind., Bloom. & Western. Music Hall, W. R. Park, manager; seating capacity, 450; rental, one night $45, three $95; share also; license included. Size of stage, 18x26; number sets scenery, 11; bill posters, City

Bill Posting Co ; theatrical teamster, **Morris Welsh**. Newspapers : Enterprise (Wed.), Democrat (Wed.), Times (Fri.) .... Hotels: Phifer, regular rates, $2 (special also); Madison, regular rates, $2 (special also).

MANSFIELD, 10,000. R. R., Baltimore & **Ohio**; Northwestern Ohio; N. Y., Pa. & Ohio; Pitts., Ft. W. & C.; B. & O.; P., F. W. & C., connect at Crossing. Opera House; seating capacity, 200. Size of stage, 31½x54; height from stage to grooves, 13½; height from stage to rigging loft, 16; depth **under stage, 5½**; bill poster. C. S. Longsdorf; theatrical teamster, C. S. Longsdorf. Newspapers: Courier (Fri.), Democrat (Sat.), Herald (Th.).... Hotels: St. James, special rates, $2. Wiler, special rates, $2; Sherman, special rates, $1.25.

Miller's Opera House, Joe Miller, **manager**; seating capacity, 600.

MARIETTA, 8,000. R. R., Cleveland & **Marietta**; Cin., Wash. & Balto.. City Hall, Thos. Hancock, manager; seating capacity, 1,290; rental, one night $25 ; share also. Size of stage, 53x72; size of proscenium opening, 23x33; height from stage to grooves, 15½; height from stage to rigging loft, 28; depth under stage, 15½; traps, 2; number sets scenery, 12; leader of orchestra, Dan **Baker**; bill poster, Chas. Straws ; number sheets can accommodate, 200; rates per sheet, 4c.; theatrical teamsters, Dye Bros. Newspapers: semi-weekly, Register; advertising rates 10c. per line; weekly, Leader (Tu.); advertising rates 10c. per line; Times (Th.); advertising rates 10c. per line..... Hotels : **National**, special rates, $1.50 to $2; St. Cloud, special rates, $1; Bizant's, $1.

MARION, 6,000. R. R., Chic. & **Atlantic**; Clev., Col., Cin. & Ind.; Col., Hoc. Val. & Tol; New York, Pa. & Ohio. Music Hall, **C. C. Pettit, manager**; seating capacity, 750 ; rent or share. Size of stage, 3 5x55; number sets scenery, 12; bill poster, James Joy. Newspapers: daily, Star; weekly, Mirror (Th.), Independent (Th.) .....Hotels: Marion, regular rates, $2 (special also); Kerr.

City Hall; seating capacity, 350. Size of stage, 20x31; number sets scenery, 2.

MARYSVILLE, 4,500. R. R., Cleveland, C., Cin. & **Indianapolis**. City Opera House, John F. Zwerner, manager; seating capacity, 850; rental, one night $30, three $75; share also; license included. Size of stage, 34x36; size of proscenium opening, 26x14; height from stage to rigging loft, 20; depth under stage, 8; traps, 1 ; number sets scenery, 11; leader of orchestra, Wm. Lampart; scenic artist, Geo. Zwerner ; stage carpenter, Jas. Gibson; bill poster, Sam Fry; number sheets can accommodate, 800 ; rates per sheet, 4c. theatrical teamster, John Sellers. Newspapers: weekly, Journal (Tu.), advertising rates $1 per inch; Tribune, (Fri); advertising rates $1 per inch......Hotels : Continental, special rates, $1 to $1.50.

MASSILLON, 10,000. R. R., Pitts., Ft. Wayne & Chic ; **Cleve.**, **Loraine & Wheeling**; W. & L. E ; M. & C , Cleve., Akron & Col. Bucher's Opera House, J. G. Bucher, manager; seating capacity, 900; rent or share. Size of stage, 35x55; size of proscenium opening, 20x33; **height** from stage to grooves, 14; height from stage to rigging loft, 30; depth under stage, 7; traps, 3; number sets scenery, 19; bill poster, Chas. S. Traphagen; theatrical teamster, C. S. Traphagen. Newspapers: American (Tu.), Independent (Th.)...... Hotels: Park, regular rates, $2 (special also); Waverly, regular rates, $2 (special also).

Madison Hall; seating **capacity, 500.**

McCONNELLSVILLE, 3,000. On the **Muskingum River, two steamers daily.** Music Hall, Robert L. Morris, manager; seating capacity, 550; rental, one night $10; license, $2. Size of stage, 26x38; number sets scenery, 9; bill poster, Geo. N. Scott. Newspapers: Democrat (Fri.), Herald (Fri.)...... .Hotels: Adams', regular rates, $2 (special also); Koons'.

MIAMISBURG, 3,100. R. R , Cin., Ham. & Dayton; Clev., Col., Cin. & Ind. Gwinner's **Opera Hall**, Fred. Gwinner, manager; seating capacity, 500; rental, one night $8, three $21; license, $2. Size of stage, 30x35; number sets scenery, 4; bill poster, Charles O. Miller. Newspapers: Bulletin (Fri.), News (Th.)......Hotels: Baum, regular rates, $1.50 (special also), Washington.

MIDDLEPORT, 3,500. R. R., C., H. V. & T.; Ohio & Cin.; also on Ohio River. Coe's Opera House, S. P. Coe, manager; seating capacity, 500; rental, one night $25; share also; license yearly. Size of stage, 20x40; size of proscenium opening, 10x20; height from stage to grooves, 12; number sets scenery, 5. Newspapers: Herald (Fri.). Republican (Wed.)......Hotels: Grand View, special rates, $1; Central, special rates, $1.

MIDDLETOWN, 6,400. R. R., Cin., Hamilton & Dayton; Cleve., Col., Cin. & Indianapolis. Leibee's Opera House, James E. Wooley, manager; seating capacity, 500; rental, one night $15, three $35; license, $2; share also. Size of stage, 20x22; number sets scenery, 6; **bill poster**, Opera House. Newspapers: **daily**, Argus; weekly, Journal (Fri.). Signal (Sat.) Hotel: United States.

Wooley's Bijou Theatre, James E. Wooley, manager; seating capacity, 500. Size of stage, **20x30; number sets scenery, 12.**

MILAN, 1,300. R. R., Wheeling & Lake Erie. Town Hall; seating capacity, 600; rental, one night $10. Size of stage, 20x24; number sets scenery, 3; bill poster, L. Minard. Newspaper: Advertiser (Sat.). ....Hotels: Park, Ferguson, Klein.

MINERVA, 2,000. R. R., Cleveland & Pittsburgh; Connotton Valley; Cleveland, Youngstown & Pittsburgh. Yengling's Opera House, W. J. Yengling, manager; seating capacity, 600; rental, share only; license included. Size of stage, 15x40; size **of proscenium opening, 12x18; height from stage to grooves, 12; height from stage to rigging loft, 18; number sets scenery, 8; leader of orchestra, M. M. Perdue; stage carpenter, Jerry Myres; bill poster, John Yengling; number sheets can accommodate, 40; theatrical teamster, Abia Stackhouse; Newspaper: News (Fri.)......Hotels: St. James, special rates, $1 to $1.25; Center, special rates, $1 to $1.25; Jackson, special rates, $1 to $1.25; Ungerer, special rates, $1 to $1.25; Jackson,** special rates, $1 to $1.25.

MOUNT GILEAD, 1,600. R. R., Clev., Col., Cin. & Ind.; Ohio Central. Levering Hall; **seating capacity, 800; rental, one night $10,** three $25, license included. Size of stage, **20x66; fair stock scenery; bill poster, G. G. Lidz.** Newspapers: Sentinel (Th.), Register (Wed.)...... Hotels: G'obe, **regular rates, $2** (special also); American.

MOUNT VERNON, 7,000. R. R., **Baltimore & Ohio;** Cleveland, **Mt.** Vernon & Delaware. Woodward Opera House, L. G. Hunt, manager; seating capacity, 900. Size of **stage, 25x43; bill poster, W. T. Critchfield.** Newspapers: semi-weekly, Tribune; weekly, Banner (Th.), Republican (Th.)......Hotels: **Curtis, regular rates, $2** (special also); Rowley, regular rates, $1.50 (special also); Philo.

Kirk Opera House, L. G. **Hunt,** manager; seating **capacity, 650; rental, one night $15;** license, $3; share also. **Size of stage, 25x40; number sets scenery, 9**

NAPOLEON, 4,500. R. R., **Wabash.** Beckmann's Hall, **Fred** Beckman, **manager: seating** capacity, 600; **rental, one night $8,** three $15; license, **$1 to $5.** Size **of stage, 20x40; number sets scenery, 12; bill poster,** Chas. Tyler. Newspapers: **Democrat,** Northwest **(Th.), Signal (Th.)......Hotels:** Miller, regular rates, $2 (special also); Wasus.

NELSONVILLE, 3,900. R. R., Col., Hoc. Val. & Tol. Opera Hall; rent or share. Newspapers: News (Th.), Republican (Th.)......Hotels: Dew, regular rates, $2 (special also).

NEVADA, 1,300. R. R., Pitts., Fort Wayne & Chic. Balliet Hall, Balliet & Goodbread, managers; seating capacity, 500; rental, one night $5, three $10; license, $1. Size of stage, 20x20; number sets scenery, 3; bill poster, John Price. Newspaper: Enterprise (Fri.)......Hotels: Commercial, regular rates, $2 (special also); Centra'.

NEWARK, 10,000. R. R., Baltimore & Ohio; Pittsburg, Cleveland & **St. Louis.** Wallace's Opera House; seating capacity, 900; rental, one night $20. **Size of stage, 40x50;** height from stage to grooves, 15; height from stage to rigging loft, **25**; depth under stage, 6; bill poster, J. H. Miller; theatrical teamster, Long Bros. Newspaper : daily, Advocate; weekly, American (Fri.), Banner (Wed.)........**Hotels:** American; Lansing, regular rates, $2 (special **also);** Tobb's, regular rates, **$2 (special** also).

Music Hall, Geo. Wallace, manager; seating capacity, 800.

NEWCOMERSTOWN, 1,200. R. R., Cleveland & **Marietta;** Pittsburg, Cincinnati & St. Louis. Crater's Hall, **J. G. Crater, manager; seating** capacity, 400; fair stock scenery. Newspaper : Index (Th.)

NEW LEXINGTON, 1,700. R. R., Ohio Central ; Pittsburg, Cincinnati & St. Louis. Smith's Opera House, **F. J. Smith,** manager; seating capacity, 500. Size of stage, 20x25; number sets scenery, 4. Newspapers ; Herald (Th.), Tribune (Th.).. ..Hotels : New Central, regular rates $2 (special also).

NEW LISBON, 2,700. R. R., N. Y., Pa. & Ohio. Opera House, Wm. Monaghan, manager; seating capacity, 460; rental, share only; license, $1 to $3. Size of stage, 20x45; number sets scenery, 10, bill poster, Frank Gaily; theatrical teamster, James Hill. Newspapers: Buckeye State (Th.), Tribune (Th.)......Hotels: Cowan, regular rates, $2 (special also); Central, special rates, $1.25; Hostetter.

NEW LONDON, 2,300. R. R., Clev., Col., Cin. & Ind. Town Hall, George W. Ransom, manager; seating capacity, 500; rental, one night $15, three $30; license, $1. Size of stage, 40x16; number sets scenery, 6; bill poster, Dan. Parkin. Newspaper: Record (Wed.)......Hotels: Gregory, regular rates, $2 (special also); Kellenger.

NEW PHILADELPHIA, 5,500. R. R., Clev. & Pitts; Clev., Loraine & Wheeling. Opera House, John Barry, manager; seating capacity, 500; rental, one night $15, three $30; license, $1; share also. Size of stage, 24x60; number sets scenery, 5; bill poster, Charles Barry. Newspapers: Argus (Th.), Democrat (Th.), Advocate (Th.)......Hotels : Exchange, regular rates, $2 (special also); Gerin. Schmidt.

NEW VIENNA, 1,100. R. R. Marietta & Cin. Peale's Hall, T. P. Peale, manager; seating capacity, 400; rental, one night $10, three $25; license included. Size of stage, 18x24; number sets scenery, 4; bill poster, Chas. Wine. Newspaper: Record (Fri.)......Hotels; Miller, regular rates, $2 (special also ; Union, Harrison.

NILES, 4,000. R. R., Alliance, Niles & Ash.; Ash. & Pitts.; N. Y., Pa. & Ohio; Painesv. & Youngs.; Pitts., Clev. & Tol. Union Opera House, O. W. Wilson, manager, seating capacity, 600; rent or share. Size of stage, 15x17; fair stock scenery; bill posters, Hoover & Siglman. Newspaper : Independent (Fri.)......Hotels : Sanford, regular rates, $1.50 (special also); Commercial.

NORTH AMHERST, 2,300. R. R., Lake Shore & Mich. Southern. Ploto Hall, Ploto Bros., managers; rent or share; license, $2. Number sets scenery, 4. Newspaper : Free Press (Th.)......Hotels : Henery, Sherman.

NORWALK, 7,000. R. R., Lake Shore & Mich. So.; Wheeling & Lake Erie. Whittlesey's Opera House; seating capacity, 600; full set scenery; bill poster, Henry Palmer. Newspapers, daily, Penny Sun. Reflector; weekly, Chronicle (Th.), Journal (Sat.)......Hotels: Baldwin, regular rates, $2 (special also); St. Charles, regular rates $2 (special also); City.

St. Charles Hall; seating capacity, 300.

OBERLIN, 3,500. R. R., Lake Shore & Mich. So. Town Hall; seating capacity, 300. Newspaper: News (Fri.)......Hotels: Park, Hurd, regular rates, $1.50 (special also).

OTTAWA, 3,000. R. R., Cin., Ham. & Dayton. City Hall. Marion Luce, manager; seating capacity, 500; rental, one night $30, three $50; license, $2. Size of stage, 18x25; proscenium opening, 20x22; height from stage to grooves, 12; bill poster, Marion Luce; number of sheets can accommodate, 250; rates per sheet, 4c. Newspaper: Democrat, (Wed.), rate 10c. per line......Hotel: Leopold: regular rates $1.50 (special also).

Utrop's Opera House, Wm. Utrop, manager; seating capacity 800; fair stock scenery.

PAINESVILLE, 5,000. R. R., Lake Sho.e & Mich. So.; N. Y., Chic. & St. Louis; Painsville & Youngstown. Child's Hall, C. A. Hardway, manager; seating capacity, 800; rental, one night, $30; share also; license, $2 to $5. Size of stage, 20x40; number sets scenery, 8; bill poster, Arthur Higgins; theatrical teamsters, Tabor & Ingrim. Newspapers: Graphic (Fri.), Democrat (Sat.), Journal (Sat.), Telegraph (Th.)......Hotels: Coroles, regular rates, $2 (special also); Stockwell, regular rates, $2 (special also).

PIQUA, 11,000. R. R., Chic., St. L. & Pitts.; Cin., Ham. & Dayton. Conover's Opera House, W. G. Conover, manager; seating capacity, 1,000; rental, one night $40, three $100, share also; license, $2. Size of stage, 45x60; size of proscenium opening, 63x40, width, 4; height from stage to grooves, 17; height from stage to rigging loft, 40; depth under stage, 12; traps, 5; number sets scenery, 13; leader of orchestra, B. R. Kleub; bill poster, Joe Kipson; number of sheets can accommodate, 350; rates per sheet, 4c.; theatrical teamsters, Robbins & Sutton. Newspapers: daily, Call, advertising rates, 5c. per line; weekly, Journal (Th.); Leader (Sat.), Helmet (Th.)......Hotels: City, special rates, $1.25; Barrett, special rates, $1.25; Miller s, special rates, $1.

High School Hall; seating capacity, 1,200.

POMEROY, 12,000. R. R., Columbus, Hocking Valley & Toledo. Opera House, S. Davis, manager; seating capacity, 500; rental, one night $25; share also; license yearly. Size of stage, 20x40; number sets scenery, 10; bill poster, W. E. Haner; theatrical teamster, Levi Woods. Newspaper: Telegraph (Wed.)   ...Hotels: Dilcher, regular rates, $2 (special also); Remington.

PORT CLINTON, 2,100. R. R., Lake Shore & Mich. So., Turner Hall; seating capacity, 400; rental, one night $6, three $13; license, $2. Size of stage, 13x50; number sets scenery, 3; bill poster, Oliver Fows. Newspapers: Bulletin (Wed.), News (Fri.) Hotels: Clinton, regular rates, $1.50 (special also); Ottawa, Island.

PORTSMOUTH, 15,000. R. R., Scioto Valley; Marietta & Cincinnati; Cincinnati & Eastern. Wilhelm's Opera House, John Wilhelm, manager; seating capacity, 650; rental, one night $35, three $85, license included; share also. Size of stage, 20x24; size of proscenium opening, 14x24; height from stage to grooves, 18; depth under stage, 3½; traps, 1; number sets scenery, 12; bill poster, Sol Lampman; number sheets can accommodate, rates per sheet, 3c.; theatrical teamster, Peter Schafer. Newspapers: daily, Times (Sat.), advertising rates, per inch, 50c ; Tribune (Wed.), advertising rates, per inch, 50c.; Blade (Sat.), advertising rates, per inch, 50c.

RAVENNA, 4,000. R. R., Cleveland & Pittsburg; N. Y., P. & Ohio; Pitts. & Western. Reed's Opera House, C. A. & G. P. Reed, managers; seating capacity, 700; rental, one night $25, three $55, share also; license yearly Size of stage, 35x54; size of proscenium opening, 16x25; height from stage to grooves, 15; height from stage to rigging loft, 26; depth under stage, 4; traps, 2; number sets scenery, 10; leader of orchestra, John Hamm; scenic artist, Chas. E. Russell; stage carpenter, James Bacon; bill posters, C. A. & G. P. Reed; number of sheets can accommodate, 500; rates per sheet, 4c.; theatrical teamster, L. S. Ward. Newspapers: Republican (Tu.), advertising rates, 50c per inch; Press (Wed.), advertising rates, 50c. per inch......Hotels: Etna, special rates, $1.25 to $1.50; Commercial, $1.25 to $1.50.

SALEM, 5,000. R. R., Pitts., Ft. Wayne & Chic. Concert Hall, F. W. Allison, manager; seating capacity, 1,000; share only. Size of stage, 20x35; number sets scenery, 6; bill poster, manager of hall. Newspapers: semi-weekly, Republican; weekly, Vidette (Fri.), Era (Fri.)......Hotels: American, Pickett.

SALINEVILLE, 3,000. R. R., Cleveland & Pitts. Masonic Opera House, I. B. Cameron, manager; seating capacity, 350..... Hotel: McGilvery, regular rates, $2 (special also).

SANDUSKY, 22,955. R. R., Ind., Bloomington & West.; Lake Shore & Mich. So.; Balt. & Ohio; Lake Erie & West. Opera House, Wm. J. Stoffel, manager; seating capacity, 900; rental, one night $40, three $100; share also; license included. Size of stage, 36x66; size of proscenium opening, 24x30; height from stage to grooves, 18; height from stage to rigging loft, 28; depth under stage, 8; traps, 3; number sets scenery, 17; leader of orchestra, Chas. Buetz; stage carpenter, John May; bill poster, W. J. Stoffel; number of sheets can accommodate, 1,500; rates per sheet, 4c.; theatrical teamsters, Gossman Bros. Newspapers: daily, Register, advertising rates, yearly contract; Local, yearly contract; weekly, Journal (Th.). ....Hotels: West, special rates, $1 to $1.25; Sloane, $1.25 to $1.50; Cotton, $1.

Fisher's Hall; seating capacity, 800.

Linx Hall; seating capacity, 500.

SEVILLE, 800. R. R., Cleveland, Loraine & Wheeling. Town Hall. Newspaper: Times (Th.)......Hotel: Redman.

SHAWNEE, 4,000. R. R., Baltimore & Ohio. Knights of Labor Opera House, E. W. Williams, manager; seating capacity, 700; rent or share, Size of stage, 20x40; number sets scenery, 6; bill poster, Opera House, theatrical teamster, John J. Caddy. Newspaper: Banner (Th.)......Hotels: New American, regular rates, $2 (special also); Obear.

SHILOH, 1,100. R. R., Cleveland, Columbus, Cincinnati & Indianapolis. Breneman's Hall, S. S. Hunter, manager; seating capacity, 300; rental, one night $3, three $8; license, $1. Size of stage, 16x20; number sets scenery, 5; bill poster, George Hammond. Newspaper: Review (Th.)......Hotel: American.

SIDNEY, 6,230. R. R., Cin., Hamilton & Dayton; Clev., Col., Cin. & Ind. Monumental Opera Hall, Edgar & Nutt, managers; seating capacity, 800; rental, one night $35, three $75; license, $2; share also. Size of stage, 25x40; number sets scenery, 26; bill poster, Charles Rodgers; theatrical teamster, E. C. Fry. Newspapers: daily, Sentinel; weekly, Journal (Fri.), Democrat (Fri.)......Hotels: Burnett, regular rates $2 (special also); Valley City, Wagner, Bush.

Taylor's Hall, Taylor Bros., managers; seating capacity, 800; rental, one night $40. Size of stage, 25x35.

SOUTH TOLEDO, 1,800. R. R., Toledo, Cin. & St. Louis; Wabash. Union Hall; seating capacity, 300. Newspaper: New Era (Fri.)

SPRINGFIELD, 35,000. R. R., Cleve., C. C. & I.; Ind., B. & W. (O. Div.), N. Y. Pa. & Ohio; Ohio Southern; Pitts., Cin. & St. Louis. Black's Opera House, Samuel Waldman, manager; seating capacity, 1,200; rental, one night $75; three $200. Size of stage, 40x60; number sets scenery, 18; leader of orchestra, Robert Nelson; stage carpenter, Milton Myers; bill poster, H. F. Tyner; number of sheets can accommodate, 400; rates per sheet, 4c; theatrical teamsters, Holloway & Son. Newspapers: daily; Gazette, advertising rates, per inch, $1; Republic, advertising rates, per inch, $1; Transcript, advertising rates, per inch, $1......Hotels: Lagonda, special rates, $1.50; Arcade, special rates, $1.50; St. James, special rates, $1.25.

Grand Opera House, Samuel Waldman, manager; seating capacity, 1,200; share only; no license. Size of stage, 42x60; height from stage to grooves, 18; height from stage to rigging loft, 90; depth under stage, 6½; number sets scenery, 12; bill poster, H. Tyner.

New Crystal Hall, Marsh Adams, manager; seating capacity, 600. Size of stage, 25x30; fair stock scenery.

City Hall; seating capacity, 600.

STEUBENVILLE, 16,000. R. R., Cleveland & Pittsburg; Pittsburg, Cin. & St. Louis. Jarrett's Hall, D. J. Sinclair, manager; seating capacity, 800; rental, one night $30; share also; license included. Size of stage, 25x30; number sets scenery, 7; bill poster, J. M. Russell; theatrical teamster, B. F. Markes. Newspapers: daily, Gazette, Herald; weekly, Press (Fri.)......Hotels: United States, regular rates, $2 to $2.50 (special also); Mossgrove, Lowes, Imperial, St. Nicholas.

Opera Hall, Boveman Gardiner, manager; seating capacity, 350; rental, one night $15, three, $30; license, $3; number sets scenery, 5.

ST. CLAIRSVILLE, 1,300. R. R., St. Clairsville; St. Clairsville & Northern. Welday's Hall, H. C. Welday, manager; seating capacity, 400; rental, one night $7 to $10, three $15 to $20; license, $1. Size of stage, 12x40; number sets scenery, 3. Newspapers: Chronicle (Th.), Gazette (Th.)......Hotel: National, regular rates, $2 (special also).

ST. MARY'S, 3,000. R. R., Lake Erie & West. City Hall, Marion Luce, manager; seating capacity, 500; rental, one night $20, three $50; license, $2 and tickets. Size of stage, 17x20; size of proscenium opening, 18x20; height from stage to grooves, 10; bill poster, manager of hall; number of sheets can accommodate, 200; rates per sheet, 4c. Newspaper: Argus (Wed.), rates per line, 20c. .....Hotel: Durker, special rates, $1.50.

ST. PARIS, 1,200. R. R., Chic., St. Louis & Pittsburg. Town Hall. Newspapers: Dispatch (Fri.); New Era (Fri.)......Hotel: American, regular rates, $2 (special also).

TIFFIN, 10,000. R. R., Balt. & Ohio; Ind., Bloom. & West.; North West, Ohio. National Hall, E. B. Hubbard, manager; seating capacity, 1,000; rental, one night $25, three $60; license, 2; share also. Size of stage, 45x35; height from stage to grooves, 13½; depth under stage, 4; traps, 1; number sets scenery, 8; leader of orchestra, Charles Boos; scenic artist, Edward Lepper; stage carpenter, Wm. Rogers; bill poster, J. R. Lewis; number sheets can accommodate, 600; rate per sheet, 4c; theatrical teamster, George Reeme. Newspapers: daily, Herald; weekly, Tribune (Th.), Advertiser (Th.), News (Fri.). Hotels: Empire, special rates, $1.50; Shawhan, special rates, $1.50; Lang, special rates, $1.

City Hall; seating capacity, 300.

Freund's Weekly,

A Review of Music and the Drama,

PUBLISHED EVERY SATURDAY

At 835 BROADWAY, NEW YORK.

JOHN C. FREUND,   -   -   -   Editor.

ITS PRINCIPAL AIM.

While it is read by the most intelligent and refined members of the dramatic profession, FREUND'S WEEKLY reaches a very large class of musical people who do not read any other dramatic paper. While it aims to be, above all, a NEWSpaper, it rejects the scandals of the profession, which can only be enjoyed by those who wish to degrade the stage or see it brought into disgrace. It deals fearlessly and without favor with all subjects relating to the kindred professions. By excluding from its columns coarse abuse, vulgar praise and the prurient sensationalism of the daily press, it aims by example to elevate the standard of public taste by dealing with artists solely in their relation to art. It is only necessary to compare it with other papers of its class to convince intelligent and refined readers—the only class it caters for—that it contains the best features of all without those which disgrace dramatic and musical journalism.

ITS PRINCIPAL FEATURES.

COULISSES CHAT—FREUND'S WEEKLY makes a special feature of musical and dramatic NEWS, both original and selected, covering every important city in the United States, Canada and Europe, carefully classified under the following departments:

  I. **MANAGERS AND AUTHORS**, identified with the profession who do not appear upon the stage.
  II. MUSICAL NEWS, concerning all combinations, except those identified with the dramatic stage.
  III. DRAMATIC NEWS, including minstrel troupes and specialty combinations of the best class.
  IV. THE FOREIGN STAGE, including both the lyric and spoken drama.

CORRESPONDENCE—Covering every city and town in the United States and Canada possessing a theatre or opera house, giving a weekly chronicle of musical and dramatic events on the American Continent.

LONDON AND PARIS LETTERS—From able correspondents, giving a weekly review of the principal events of the English and Continental stages.

LATEST NEWS—Including news by telegraph and cable despatches up to the time of going to press on Thursday of each week.

TRAVELING COMPANIES—FREUND'S WEEKLY list of advance dates is the most complete list of the kind published, because it is edited with the most care. It is only necessary to know the character of the entertainment to find it in its proper department. FREUND'S WEEKLY list is the only one published and (copyrighted) in which the attractions are classified according to the character of the entertainments given, indexed alphabetically, according to the initial letter of the last name of the star being always used, or the initial letter of the attractions "featured," as follows:

  I. Italian, German and French opera and concert companies of the first class.
  II. English opera companies.
  III. Minstrel troupes and other musical entertainments.
  IV. Musical, Comedy and Burlesque companies.
  V. Specialty combinations, booked only in first-class theatres.
  VI. Melodrama, Spectacular and Pantomime companies, in which mechanical scenery, etc., form a principal feature
  VII. Dramatic companies, of which the principal feature is the star.
  VIII. Dramatic companies, in which the play is featured, or, if playing more than one, indexed according to the name under which the company is advertised.

This list is invaluable for local managers and representatives of hotels and transportation companies, who will find it the most complete and correct list published.

TERMS.—Single Copies, ten cents; Subscription, One Year, in advance, three dollars.

HARRY E. FREUND, Publisher and Proprietor.

TIPPECANOE CITY, 2,200. R. R., Dayton & Michigan. Chaffee's Opera House, Sam. E. Smith, manager; seating capacity, 600; rental, one night $15; share also; license, $1 to $3. Size of stage, 19x45; size of proscenium opening, 15x20; height from stage to grooves, 12; height from stage to rigging loft, 18; depth under stage, 4, traps, 1 ; number sets scenery, 7; bill poster, manager; number of sheets can accommodate, 200; rates per sheet, 3½c ; theatrical teamster, Thomas Hartley. Newspaper: Herald (Sat.) ...... Hotels: City, regular rates, $2 (special also).

TOLEDO, 60,000. R. R., Cin., Ham. & Day.; Col., Hock. Val. & Tol.; Flint & Pere Mar.; L. S. & Mich. So.; Mich. Cen.; Mich & O.; Nor. West. O.; O. Cen.; Tol. & Ind.; Tol., Ann. A. & N. M; Tol., Cin. & St. L.; Wabash; Wheel. & L. Erie. Wheeler Opera House, George W. Bills, manager; seating capacity, 1,400; rental, one night $75; license included. Size of stage, 47x80; number sets scenery, 15; bill poster, Opera House; theatrical teamsters, Transfer Co. Newspapers: daily, Blade, Telegram, Bee, Express, Post; weekly, Record (Sat.), Democrat (Sun.)..... Hotels: Boody, regular rates, $2 50 to $3 50 (special also); Madison, regular rates, $2 to $3 (special also); Burnett, regular rates, $2 (special also); Oliver, American, Union.

White's Hall, D. Coghlin, manager; seating capacity, 1,000; rental, one night, $25. Size of stage, 25x50; no scenery.

Music Hall, Wm. Baker, manager; seating capacity, 800.

Sangerfest Hall; seating capacity, 1,800.

Adelphi Theatre; seating capacity, 1,000.

Theatre Comique; seating capacity, 1,000.

TORONTO, 2,000. R. R., Cleveland & Pittsburg. Freeman's Opera House, Freeman & Puzlis, managers. Newspaper: Tribune (Wed.)

TROY, 5,000. R. R., Cin., Ham. & Day.; Ind., Bloom. & West. City Opera House, Jesse Shilling, manager; seating capacity, 700; rental, one night $25; share also; license included. Size of stage, 30x60; number sets scenery, 10; bill poster, Robert Hollis. Newspapers: Chronicle (Fri.), Union (Sat.)......Hotels: Morris, regular rates, $2 (special also); Hatfield, Gault.

UPPER SANDUSKY, 4,700. R. R., Col., Hocking Valley & Toledo; Pittsburg, Ft. Wayne & Chic. Lime's Opera House, John W. Lime, manager; seating capacity, 800; rental, one night $20, three $35; license, $2; share also. Size of stage, 32x40; full set scenery; bill poster, Opera House; theatrical teamster, Opera House. Newspapers: Chief (Sat.), Republican (Th.), Union (Th.)......Hotels: Pierson, regular rates, $2; Warpole, Hudson.

Bury's Hall; seating capacity, 500; rental, one night $10, three $26; license, $2. Size of stage, 20x25.

URBANA, 8,000. R. R., Ind., Bloom. & West.; N. Y., Pa, & Ohio; Chic., St. Louis & Pitts. Bennett's Opera House, P. R. Bennett, Jr., manager; seating capacity, 960; rental, share only; license included. Size of stage, 28x48; size of proscenium opening, 18x24; height from stage to grooves, 15; height from stage to rigging loft, 22; depth under stage, 7; traps, 5; number sets scenery, 11; leader of orchestra, Prof. W. Small; stage carpenter, Wm. Yeasel; bill poster, Opera House; number of sheets can accommodate, 300; rates per sheet, 3½c.; theatrical teamster, Pat O'Gane. Newspapers: daily, Citizen, advertising rates, yearly contract; weekly, Gazette (Th), Democrat (Th.).....Hotels: Wean's, special rates, $1.25 to $2; Exchange, special rates, $1 25 to $2.

City Hall, S. J. Dixon, manager; seating capacity, 500; rental, one night $30, three $45; license included. Size of stage, 24x30; number sets scenery, 5.

URICHSVILLE, 3,700. R. R., Cleveland, Loraine & Wheeling; Pittsburg, Cin. & St. Louis. Central Hall, F. H. Mozerud, manager; seating capacity, 500; rental, one night $6; license, $3. Size of stage, 12x25; fair stock scenery; bill poster, M. Miles; theatrical teamster, Scott Dempster. Newspaper: Chronicle. Hotels: Central, regular rates, $2 (special also); United States.

VAN WERT, 5,000. R. R., Cin., Van Wert & Mich.; Pitts., Fort Wayne & Chic. Opera House, T. S. Gilliland, manager ; seating capacity, 700 ; rental, one night $10, three $25. Size of stage, 30x44; number sets scenery, 8 ; bill poster, McGaylord ; theatrical teamsters, Clippenger & Noble. Newspaper: daily, Bulletin ; weekly, Republican (Th.) Times (Fri.)....... Hotels : Van Wert, regular rates, $2 (special also) ; De Puy. Commercial.

Grand Opera House, L. R. Swineford, manager ; seating capacity, 600 ; rental, one night $12, three $28; license, $1.50; share also; number sets scenery, 8.

WAPAKONETA, 4,000. R. R., Cin., Ham. & Dayton. Dicken & Fisher's Hall, Marion Luce, manager; seating capacity 600 ; rental, one night $20, three $50 ; license, 20 tickets. Size of stage, 18x20; size of proscenium opening, 14x18 ; height from stage to grooves, 10 ; bill poster, Marion Luce ; number of sheets can accommodate, 200 ; rates per sheet, 4c. Newspapers : daily, Republican (Th.), advertising rates, 20c. per line ; Democrat (Th.), advertising rates, 20c. per line......Hotels : Henry, special rates, $1; Burnett, special rates, $1.

WARREN, 6,000. R. R , N. Y., Pa. & Ohio; Asht., Youngs. & Pitts.; Pitts., Clev. & Tol.; Painesville & Youngstown. Webb's Opera House, Lamb & Strong, managers; Brooks & Dickson, New York representatives; seating capacity, 600; rental, one night $24, three $45; share also; license, $1, and 10 tickets. Size of stage, 20x45; size of proscenium opening, 11x23; height from stage to grooves, 14; height from stage to rigging loft, 15; depth under stage, 3; traps, 1; number sets scenery, 6; leader of orchestra, A. Greator; bill poster, Lamb & Strong; number of sheets can accommodate, 150; rates per sheet, 4c ; theatrical teamster, M. D. Loveless. Newspapers, daily; Chronicle, advertising rates, per inch, $1; weekly; Chronicle (Wed.), Democrat (Fri.), Tribune (Tu.)   ...Hotels : Park, special rates, $1.50; Central, special rates, $1.25; Crescent, special rates, $1.25.

Opera House; seating capacity, 550; rental, one night, $15, three $35; license, $5. Size of stage, 17x23; number sets scenery, 6.

WASHINGTON, (Fayette Co.), 5,500. R. R., Panhandle; Toledo & St. Louis; Columbus & Midland; Ind., Bloomington & Western. Music Hall, H. B. Smith, manager; seating capacity, 750; rental, share only; license included. Size of stage, 20x28; height from stage to grooves, 11; height from stage to rigging loft, 18; depth under stage, 4; number sets scenery, 7; leader of orchestra, Ed. Burnett; stage carpenter, William Vincent; bill poster, H. W Smith; number of sheets can accommodate, 150 to 500; rates per sheet, 4c.; theatrical teamster, H. B Smith. Newspapers : Herald (Th.), advertising rates, 30c. per inch ; Register (Th.), advertising rates, 50c. per inch; Republican (Wed.), advertising rates, 50c. per inch   .Hotels : Cherry, regular rates, $2 (special also); Gardner, Arlington.

WAVERLY, 2,000. R. R., Ohio Southern; Scioto Valley. Emmett's Hall, James Emmett, manager; seating capacity, 550; rent or share. Size of stage, 30x50; full set scenery; bill poster, E. Rogers. Newspapers: Republican (Fri), Watchman (Tu.) .....Hotel: Emmett, regular rates, $2 (special also).

WELLINGTON, 2,600. R. R., Cleveland, Col., Cin. & Ind.; Wheeling & Lake Erie. Reninger's Hall; seating capacity, 500; rental, one night $10, three $25; share also. Size of stage, 30x48; fair stock scenery. Newspaper: Enterprise (Wed.).. ...Hotels: American, regular rates, $2 (special also); Wellington.

WELLSVILLE, 7,000. R. R., Cleveland & Pittsburg. Opera House; seating capacity, 850; Newspapers: Sun (Th.), Union (Fri.)......Hotel: Commercial, regular rates, $2 (special also).

WEST JEFFERSON, 1,000. R. R., Pittsburg, Cin. & St. Louis. Gregg's Opera House, Gregg & Hill, managers; seating capacity, 300; rental, one night $10, three $25; share also. Size of stage, 14x18; number sets scenery, 4; bill poster, Opera House......Hotels American, regular rates, $2 (special also); Mantle.

WILMINGTON, 3,500. R. R., Cin. & Columbus; Midland & Cin.; Muskingum Valley. City Hall, Wm. McMillan, manager; seating capacity, 1,000; rental, one night $15, three $35. Size of stage, 30x35; number sets scenery, 6; number sheets can accommodate, 150. Newspapers ; Journal (Tu.), Republican (Wed.), Democrat (Th.).. ..Hotels: Midland, special rates, $1.25 to $1.50; West, special rates, $1.25 to $1.50; Pierce, special rates, $1.25 to $1.50.

WOOSTER, 7,000. R. R., Pittsburg, **Ft. Wayne & Chic. Academy of Music, J. B. France,** manager; seating capacity, 800; rental, one **night $15 to $20.** three $35 to $50; share also; license included. Size of stage, 32x35; full set scenery; bill poster, J. J. France; theatrical teamster, **Charles Lawhead.** Newspapers: daily, News; weekly, Journal (Fri.), Republican (Th.)... ... ...Hotels: Archer, regular rates, $2 (special also); Central, regular rates, **$2 (special also);** American, Metropolitan.

Quimby Opera House; seating capacity, 800.

New Opera House.

XENIA, 10,000. R. R., Pitts., Cin. & St. L.; Tol., Cin. & St. L. Opera House, John A. Hivling, manager; seating capacity, 800; rental, $35 to $40, license included; share also. Size of stage, 32x35; depth under stage, 11; traps, 3; number sets scenery, 11; leader of orchestra, Professor C. A. Rustotter; scenic artist, W. W. Marshall; bill poster, Arthur Buckles; number of sheets can accommodate, 800; rates per sheet, 4c.; theatrical teamster, Davis Fifer. Newspapers: daily, Gazette, Torchlight; weekly, Republican (Tues.), News (Sat.); semi-weekly, Gazette (Tu. and Th.); Torchlight (Wed. and Sat.).....Hotels, Commercial, special rates, $1.50; St. George, special rates, $1.75; Depot, special rates, $1.75; **Barnet,** regular rates, $2 (special also).

YOUNGSTOWN, **26,000.** R. R., Ashtabula & Pitts.; Lake Shore & Mich. So.; N. Y., Pa. & Ohio, **Painesville & Youngstown; Pitts., Ft. W. & Chic.; Pitts. & Lake Erie.** Opera House, W. W. McKeown, manager; seating capacity, 1,600; share only. Size of stage, 95x75; height from stage to grooves, 20; height from stage to rigging loft, 42; depth under stage, 9; bill poster, S. C. Rook; theatrical teamster, M. Henkle. Newspapers: daily, News-Register; weekly, Vindicator (Fri.), Saturday Night, Sunday Morning..... Hotels: Tod, regular rates, $2 (special also); Morton, regular rates, $2 (special also); Miller.

Excelsior Hall, Thomas F. Hansard, manager; seating capacity, 1,000; rental, one night $15, three $35. Size of stage, 20x15; number sets scenery, 12.

ZANESVILLE, 20,000. R. R., Balt. & Ohio; Panhandle; Bel., Zanes. & Cin. Schultz Opera House, Schultz & Co., managers; seating capacity, 1,200; rental, share only; license, yearly. Size of stage, 35x66; size of proscenium opening, 37x31; height from stage to grooves, 20; height from stage to rigging loft, 55; depth under stage, 11; traps, 4; number sets scenery, 28; leader of orchestra, G. E. Gabest; scenic artist, E. T. Harvey; stage carpenter, Henry Cordes; bill poster, W. Jenkins; number of sheets can accommodate, 1,500; rates per sheet, 4c; theatrical teamster, John Crooks. Newspapers: daily, Courier, advertising rates, yearly contract; Signal, yearly contract; Times, yearly contract; weekly, News (Sun.), yearly contract.......Hotels: Clarendon, special rates, $1.50 to $2.50; Kirk, special rates, $1.50 to $2; Grand, special rates, $1 to $1.50; Clifton, special rates, $1 to $1.50.

Black's Music Hall, W. E. Guthrie, manager; seating capacity, 1,000; rental, one night $25, three $50; license included. Size of stage, 20x40; full set scenery.

Gold Hall, Schultz & Co., managers; seating capacity, 900; no scenery.

Odd Fellow's Hall; seating capacity, 600; no scenery.

OREGON.

ALBANY, 2,000. R. R., Oregon & California. Crawford's Hall, Wm. Crawford, manager; seating capacity, 200. Size of stage, 18x40; size of proscenium opening, 11x20; height from stage to grooves, 11; height from stage to rigging loft, 11; depth under stage, 3; bill poster, James Murray; theatrical teamster, J. R. Stewertson. Newspapers: weekly, Herald (Fri.), Democrat (Fri.). ,Hotels: Revere, regular rates, $1; American Exchange, regular rates, $1.

ASTORIA, 7,000. Reached by Oregon Railroad and Navigation Co.'s steamers. Occidental Hall, Carl Adler, manager; seating capacity, 600; rental, one night $30; license, $5. Size of stage, 32x33; number sets scenery, 9; bill poster, J. McCrea. Newspapers: daily, Astorian......Hotels: Occident, regular rates, $2.50 (special also); Parker.

BAKER CITY, 2,000. Rust's Hall, Henry Rust, manager; seating capacity, 700; rental, one night $15; license, $5; no scenery. Newspapers: daily, Sage Brush; semi-weekly, Tribune; weekly, Reveille (Wed.), Democrat (Wed.)......Hotels: Arlington, St. Lawrence.

DALLES, 4,000. R. R., Oregon R'y & Navigation Co. Dalles Opera House, Snipes & Kinersly, managers; seating capacity, '400; rental, one night $20, three $50; license, $6. Size of stage, 20x30; full set scenery; bill poster, O. Sandmen. Newspaper: Itemizer (Sat.). .Hotels: Parson's, Umatilla, Cosmopolitan.

EUGENE, 1,800. R. R., Oregon & California. Lane's Hall, James Lane, manager; seating capacity, 400; rental, one night, $20; license, $15. Size of stage, 30x20; number sets scenery, 6; bill poster, Wm. Callman. Newspapers: Guard (Sat.), Journal Sat.)...... Hotel: St. Charles, regular rates, $1.50 (special also).

INDEPENDENCE, 1,000. R. R., Oregon & California, Butler Opera House, J. M. Butler, manager; seating capacity, 500; rental, one night $8 to $15; license, $4. Size of stage, 35x25; number sets scenery, 6; bill poster, John McConley.. ...Hotel : Belt.

OREGON CITY, 1,800. R. R., Oregon & California. Opera Hall, Pope **& Co., managers;** rental, one night $15. Newspapers: Courier (Fri.), Enterprise (Th.).

PENDLETON, 2,000 R. R., Oregon R'y & Navigation Co. Liberty Hall, Jesse Tailing, manager; seating capacity, 500; rental, one night $20; license, $5. Size of stage, 26x30; fair stock scenery. Newspapers : semi-weekly, Oregonian; weekly, Tribune.....Hotel: Pendleton.

PORTLAND, 39,000. R. R., Oregon & California; Oregon R'y & Navigation Co. Haverly's **New** Market Theatre, F. W. Stoehbau, manager; seating capacity, 900 ; share only. Size of stage, 35x80; full set scenery; bill poster, John Williams. Newspapers: daily, Gazette, Telegram, Oregonian, Standard, **News.......**Hotels: Holton, regular rates, $3.50 (special also); Esmond, regular **rates,** $2 **to $4;** Clarendon, regular rates, $2 (special **also);** St. Charles.

Davis Music Hall, Wm. M. Davis, manager.

Ankernelg's Hall; seating capacity, 800.

Masonic Hall; seating capacity, 500.

SALEM, 5,000. R.R., Oregon **& California.** Reed's Opera House, C. E. Reed & Co., managers; seating capacity, 1,500; rental, one night $25; license, $3; **share also.** Size of stage, 40x60; full set scenery; bill **posters,** Taff & Skiff. Newspapers: daily, Talk, Statesman. Hotels : Chemeketa, **regular rates,** $2 (special also); Reed, Mansion Commercial.

Legislative Hall, seating capacity, **1,000.**

PENNSYLVANIA.

ALLENTOWN, 22,000. R. R., Central New Jersey; Lehigh Valley; Perkiomen; Phila. & Reading. Academy of Music, B. J. Hagenbuch, manager; seating capacity, 1,000; rental, one night $40, three $100; no license. Size of stage, 31½x60; size of proscenium opening, 21x29; height from stage to grooves, 16; height from stage to rigging loft, 21; depth **under** stage, 4; number sets scenery, 8; leader of orchestra, Lehman Ruhe; stage carpenter, A. W. Bertolet; bill poster, W. K. Ruhe; number of sheets can accommodate, 500; theatrical teamster, W. K. Ruhe. Newspapers : daily, Item, **Critic,** Chronicle... Hotels: Eagle, special rates, $1.25 to $1.50 ; Cross Keys, **special** rates, $1 to $1.25; American, special rates, $2.50.

ALTOONA, 24,000. R. R., Pennsylvania. Altoona City Opera House, Marriott & Kreider, managers; seating capacity, 1,200; rental, one night $50, three $180, license, $5. Size **of** stage, 35x30 ; number sets scenery, 11; bill poster, **J.** C. Kreider. Newspapers : daily, Call, Tribune, Times; weekly, Advance (Sat.), Radical (Th.) .... Hotels : Logan. Arlington, regular rates, $2 (special also); Globe, Central.

ARCHBALD, 3,000. R. R., Delaware & Hudson Canal Co. Swift Hall, J. J. Swift, **manager;** seating capacity, 350. Size of stage, 12x28......Hotels : Moyles, regular **rates, $2** (special also); Union, Mansion, Archbald.

ASHLAND, 10,000. R. R., Lehigh Valley, Philadelphia & Reading. Opera House, Theo. F. Barron, manager; seating capacity, 1,200; rental, one night $30; license included. Size of stage, 35x40; full set scenery; bill poster, Chas. B. Klingerman; theatrical teamsters, Stitzer & Livers. Newspapers: Advocate (Fri.), Messenger (Sat.), Record (Sat.)......
Hotels: Union, regular rates, $2 (special also). Locust Mountain, regular rates, $2 (special also).

Odd Fellows' Hall, Theo. F. Barron, manager; seating capacity, 600; rental, one night $15, three $35; license, $2; share also; Size of stage, 16x48; full set scenery.

BANGOR, 2,000. R. R., Bangor & Portland; Lehigh & Lackawanna. Bangor Opera House, J. Buzzard, manager; seating capacity, 500; rental, one night $15, three $35; license included; share also. Size of stage, 15x26; number sets scenery, 5; bill poster, E. Reah. Newspaper: Observer (Th.)...... Hotel: Broadway, regular rates, $2 (special also); Bangor, American, Garfield.

BEAVER FALLS, 10,000. R. R., Pitts., Ft. Wayne & Chic.; Pitts., & Lake Erie. Music Hall, C. B. Foster, manager; seating capacity, 900. Size of stage, 18x18; size of proscenium opening, 15x26; depth under stage, 4; number sets scenery, 4; stage carpenter, James Beaner; bill poster, Ed. Hassey, Newspapers: daily, Tribune, News, weekly, Globe (Fri.), Tribune (Fri.). Hotels: Central, special rates, $1; Merchants', special rates, $1.

BELLEFONTE, 5,000. R. R., Pennsylvania. Reynold's Opera House, John D. Sourbeck, manager; seating capacity, 800; rental, one night $30, three $50, share also; license, $3. Size of stage, 20x30; size of proscenium opening, 20x35; height from stage to rigging loft, 30; depth under stage, 5; traps, 1; number sets scenery, 6; leader of orchestra, Prof. A. Girod; bill poster, John D. Sourbeck; number of sheets can accommodate, 100; rates per sheet, 4c.; theatrical teamster, Jacob Barlet. Newspapers: daily, News, advertising rates, per inch, $4; weekly, Democrat (Th.), Watchman (Fri.), Republican (Wed.)......
Hotels: Brockerhoff, special rates, $1.25 to $1.50; Bush, special rates, $1.25 to $1.50.

BETHLEHEM, 20,000. R. R., Central N. J.; Lehigh Valley: Lehigh & Lacka.; Phila. & Reading. Grand Opera House (destroyed by fire October, 1884); bill poster, L. J. Schleppy; theatrical teamster, Al. Stein. Newspapers: daily, Times; weekly, Moravian (Wed.), ...Hotels. Eagle, regular rates, $2 (special also); Pacific, Sun, American.

Citizens' Hall; seating capacity, 650; rental, one night $10.

BLOOMSBURG, 5,000. R. R., Del., Lacka. & West; Phila. & Reading. Opera House, Wm. C. McKinney, manager; seating capacity, 800; rental, one night $30; share also; license, $2. Size of stage, 25x50; height from stage to grooves, 14; height from stage to rigging loft, 20; leader of orchestra, Thos. Wetherell; stage carpenter, R. D. Hagenbach; bill poster, R. D. Hagenbach; number of sheets can accommodate, 195; rates per sheet, 4c.; theatrical teamsters, Buckalew Bros. Newspapers: Columbian (Fri.), advertising rates, yearly contract; Republican (Th.), advertising rates, yearly contract. ......Hotels: Exchange, special rates, $1.50.

Cadman's Hall; seating capacity, 500.

Evans' Hall; seating capacity, 500.

BLOSSBURG, 5,000. R. R., Corn., Cow. & Ant.; Tioga. Opera House, Charles Fish, manager; seating capacity, 900; rental, one night $15, three $35. Size of stage, 14x30; size of proscenium opening, 14x40; depth under stage, 4; number sets scenery, 2; leader of orchestra, Chas. Wetheral; bill poster, Frederick Fish; number of sheets can accommodate, 400; rates per sheet, 4c.; theatrical teamster, Fred Fish. Newspapers: Register (Th.), advertising rates, per line, 10c......Hotels: United States, special rates, $1; Seymour, regular rates, $2 (special also).

BRADFORD, 20,000. R. R., Brad., Bor. & Kin; Brad., Eldred & C.; Erie, (Brad. Branch); Kendall & Eldred; Olean, Brad. & W.; Rochester & Pittsburg. Wagner Opera House, Wagner & Reis, managers; Brooks & Dickson, New York representatives; seating capacity, 1,000; rental, share only; license included. Size of stage, 30x50; size of proscenium opening, 24x20½; height from stage to grooves, 18; height from stage to rigging loft, 28; depth under stage, 7; traps, 6; number sets scenery, 30; leader of orchestra, J.

The News Letter.

EDITED BY D. DALZIEL.

PUBLISHED IN

CHICAGO AND NEW YORK.'

It is the LEADING DRAMATIC JOURNAL in America.

IT IS FILLED WITH

CRISP EDITORIALS,

FEARLESS CRITICISMS,

GOSSIPY PERSONALS.

It has TELEGRAPHIC CORRESPONDENCE from all points, and publishes each week

A CARTOON

IN COLORS OF A DRAMATIC CELEBRITY.

The NEWS LETTER is a correct record of the Dramatic Stage and should be read by everyone who visits the theatres.

Subscription, $4 per annum.
Advertising rates, 12½ cents per line.

D. DALZIEL,

44 W. 23d St., New York, N.Y.   87 Clark St., Chicago, Ill.

W. Jamison; stage carpenter, J. Blottenberger; bill posters, Wagner & Rels; number sheets can accommodate, 1,000; rates per sheet, 4c.; theatrical teamster, A. Arnold: Newspapers: daily, Era, advertising rates, yearly contract; Star, advertising rates, yearly contract; weekly, News (Sun.), advertising rates, yearly contract; Mail (Sun.); yearly contract...... .....Hotels: St. James, special rates, $1.50 to $2.50; Riddell, special rates, $1.50 to $2; Henderson, special rates, $1.50 to $2.

Orpheus Hall, George H. Johnson, manager.

Gem Theatre, M. J. Cain, manager.

BRADDOCK, 14,000. R. R., Baltimore & Ohio; Pittsburg & Lake Erie. Lytle's Opera House, George E. Cole, manager; seating capacity, 900; rental, one night $25, three $60; license $5; share also. Size of stage, 14x20; number sets scenery, 6; bill poster, Opera House; theatrical teamster, Wm. Sherwin. Newspapers: Herald (Sat.), Sun (Sat.), Times (Sat.)......Hotels: Central, regular rates, $2 (special also); Hays, Faucet.

BRISTOL, 5,500. R. R., Pennsylvania, (N. Y. Division). Opera House, J. Buzzard, manager; seating capacity, 500; full set scenery. Newspapers: Gazette (Th.), Observer (Sat.) ......Hotel: Closson's, regular rates, $2 (special also).

Cabeen's Hall; seating capacity, 325.

BROOKVILLE, 3,000. R. R., Allegheny Valley. Berstine's Opera Hall, George L. Sandt, manager; seating capacity, 600; rental, one night $10, three $25; license, $2. Size of stage, 30x16; number sets scenery, 4; bill poster, H. D. Frank; theatrical teamster, John Buhl. Newspapers: Democrat (Wed.), Jeffersonian (Wed.), Republican (Wed.)......Hotels: American, regular rates, $2 (special also); Central.

BUTLER, 4,000. R. R., Penna.; Pitts. & W.; Shenandoah & Allegheny. Butler Opera House, W. C. Thompson, manager; seating capacity, 600. Size of stage, 30x26; size of proscenium opening, 19x30; height from stage to grooves, 12; depth under stage, 11; number sets scenery, 5; bill poster, Opera House Co. Newspapers: daily, Times, advertising rates, special contract; weekly, Eagle (Tu.), advertising rates, special contract; Citizen (Wed.), Herald (Wed.)......Hotels: Willard's, Sourg, Vogeley.

CANTON, 1,400. R. R., Northern Central. Citizens' Hall, J. M. Fassett, manager; seating capacity, 400; rental, one night $8; license included. Size of stage, 17x22; size of proscenium opening, 12x18; height from stage to rigging loft, 13; depth under stage, 3; traps, 1; number sets scenery, 3; leader of orchestra, O. B. Westgate; bill poster, Billy Burns; theatrical teamster, Dick O'Donell. Newspaper: Sentinel (Fri.), advertising rates per inch, $1......Hotels: Commercial, special rates, $1 to $1.50; Canton, regular rates, $2; Central, Mountain View.

CARBONDALE, 10,000. R. R., Del. & Hud. Canal Co.; Erie (Jefferson Branch). Music Hall, John Nealon, manager; seating capacity, 800; rental, one night, $25; license, $3; Size of stage, 30x33; size of proscenium opening, 12x24; height from stage to grooves, 12; height from stage to rigging loft, 20; number sets scenery, 4; bill poster, J. O'Hearn. Newspapers: Advance (Sat.), Leader (Fri.).....Hotels: Harrison, American.

Nealon's Opera House, John Nealon, manager; seating capacity, 2,000; license, $7; full set scenery.

CARLISLE, 8,000. R. R., Cumberland Valley; Gettysburg & Harrisburg. Sentinel Opera House, W. H. Peffer, manager; seating capacity, 950; rental, one night $30; license, $2 to $10; share also. Size of stage, 20x54; full set scenery; bill poster, Opera House; theatrical teamster, Brett. Newspapers: daily, Sentinel; weekly, Volunteer (Wed.), Herald (Th.)......Hotels: Mansion, regular rates, $2 (special also); Florence, regular rates, $2 (special also).

Rheems' Hall.

CATAWISSA, 1,500. R. R., Pennsylvania, (P. & E. Division); Phila. & Reading. Masonic Hall, seating capacity, 400; no scenery. Newspaper: News Item (Th.)......Hotel: Susquehanna.

CHAMBERSBURG, 8,500. R. R., Cumberland Valley; Mont Alto; Western Maryland. Repository Hall, John P. Culbertson, manager; seating capacity, 500; rental, one night $10 to $25; license, $1.25 to $2.25. Size of stage, 30x35; number sets scenery, 9; bill

19

poster, Samuel Sellers. Newspapers : daily, Repository, Herald; weekly, Register (Fri.), Public Opinion (Sat.)..... Hotels: National, regular rates, $2 (special also); Montgomery, regular rates, $2 (special also); Union.

CHESTER, 2,500. R. R., Phila. & Reading; Phila., Wil. & Balt. **Holly** Tree Hall, George St. **Leger,** manager; seating capacity, **650;** rental, one night **$20** to **$30;** license **included.** Size of stage, 21x40; size of proscenium opening, 16x31½; height from stage to grooves, 12; height from stage to rigging loft, 17; depth under stage, 3½; number sets scenery, 7; **leader** of orchestra, William J Oglesby; bill posters, Hunter & Wheaton; number sheets can accommodate, 400; rates per sheet, 4c.; theatrical teamster, Edward Ryewell. Newspapers: daily; News, Times; advertising rates, special contract.... . Hotels : Brown's, special rates, $1.50; Beale, special rates, $1.50; Abbott's, special rates, $1.50; City, special rates, $1.50.

National Hall.

CLEARFIELD, 3,800. R. R., Pennsylvania. Pie's Opera House, R. **A. Campbell, manager;** seating capacity, 800; rental, one night $15; no license; fair stock scenery ; **bill poster,** R. L. Rollins. Newspapers : Citizen (Th.), Journal (Wed.), Republican (Wed.)........ Hotels: Leonard, regular rates, $2 (special also); Mansion, Allegheny.

COATSVILLE, 2,700. R. R., Pennsylvania; Wilmington & Northern. Market Hall, T. G. Hadley, manager; seating capacity, 700; rental, one night $15 ; license $2. Number sets scenery, 5; bill poster, George Baker. Newspapers : Union (Sat.), Times (Sat.)... ... Hotels: Stephenson, regular rates, $2 (special also); Vander.

COLUMBIA, 9,000. **R. R., Pennsylvania; Philadelphia & Reading.** Columbia Opera House. **J. H.** Zeamer, manager ; seating **capacity, 966 ;** rental, one night $25, license included. Size of stage, 28x30 ; full set scenery ; **bill** poster, E. Witter ; theatrical teamster, E. **Witter.** Newspapers: Courant (Th.), Herald (Wed.), Spy (Sat.)........Hotels: Franklin, **regular** rates, $2 (special also); Black's, regular rates, $2 (special also).

Odd Fellows' Hall; seating capacity, **300.**

CONNELLSVILLE, 11,000. R. R., Balt. & Ohio: Penn.; Pitts. & Lake Erie. Newmyer's Opera House, **Chas. W. Porter, manager; seating capacity,** 850; rental, share only; license yearly. **Size of stage, 40x40; size of proscenium opening,** 25x50; height from stage to grooves, 18; height **from stage to rigging** loft, 25; **depth under** stage, 5; number sets scenery, 12; leader **of orchestra,** B. Porter; stage carpenter, **Chas.** Stont; bill poster, George Critchfield; number of **sheets can** accommodate, 500; theatrical teamster, C. **B.** McCormick. Newspapers: **Courier** (Wed.); advertising **rates,** 50c. **per inch;** Monitor **(Fri.), 50c.** per inch.. ...**Hotel:** Smith, special rates, $1.25 to **$2.**

CONSHOHOCKEN, 5,500. R. R., Phila. **&** Reading. Washita Hall, Wm. Haywood, manager; seating capacity, 450; rental, **one** night $15, three $36; license included. Size of stage, 17x18; size of proscenium opening, 14x17; height from stage to grooves, 12; height from stage to rigging loft, 12; number sets scenery, 4; bill poster, H. C. Shevell. Newspaper: Recorder (Sat.)......Hotel: Montgomery, regular rates, $2 (special also).

CORRY, 9,000. R. R., Buff., N. Y. & Phila.; N. Y., Pa. & Ohio; Penn. (P. & E. division). **Corry** Opera House, O. E. Gleason, manager; seating capacity, 700 ; rent or share, license included. Size of stage, 30x40; number sets scenery, 12 ; bill **poster,** Henry Millard. Newspapers : daily, Herald; weekly, Telegraph (Fri.)......**Hotels:** St. James, regular rates, $2 (special also); Phœnix, St. Nicholas, Commercial.

Harmon Opera House, C. H. Bagley, manager; seating capacity, 600; rental, one night $25; **share also.** Size of stage, 30x50; number sets scenery, 10.

Wright's Opera House, **O. E.** Gleason, **manager; seating capacity, 900;** rental, one night, $25. Size of stage, 29x50.

DANVILLE, 10,000. **R. R.,** Del., Lack. **&** West.; Phila. **&** Reading. Danville Opera House, Frank C. Angle, manager; seating capacity, 1,200; rental, **one** night $40, three $110; share also; license included. Size of stage, 30x60 ; number sets scenery, 10; bill poster, W. E. Garrett. Newspapers: daily, Record, Sun; weekly, Intelligencer (Fri), American (Th.) ...Hotels: Montour, regular rates, $2 (special also); City, Union Hall.

DOYLESTOWN, 2,500. R. R., Phila. & Reading. Lenape Hall. A. H. Barber, manager; seating capacity, 800; rental, one night $15, license included. Size of stage, 28x40; number sets scenery, 5; bill poster, Myles Williams; theatrical teamster, Reading Express. Newspapers: Express & Reform (Tues.), Intelligencer (Sat.), Mirror (Sat.), Democrat (Tues.) .....Hotels: Purdy's, regular rates, $2 (special also); Fountain, Coldspring.

DU BOIS, 7,000. R. R., Rochester & Pittsburg; Alleghany Valley. Du Bois Opera House, Boyer & Hollister, managers; seating capacity, 940; rental, share only; license included. Size of stage, 30x48; size of proscenium opening, 16x25; height from stage to grooves, 11; height from stage to rigging loft, 20; depth under stage, 4; traps, 2; number sets scenery, 14; leader of orchestra, James Roscoe; bill poster, Opera House; number sheets can accommodate, 240; rates per sheet, 3c; theatrical teamster, Wm. Rumbarger. Newspapers: Courier (Wed.), advertising rates, per line, 5c.; Express (Wed.), advertising rates, per line, 5c......Hotels : Alpine, special rates, $1; Central, special rates, $1.25; National, special rates, $1.25.

Barr's Opera House, James McDonald, manager; seating capacity, 450.

DUKE'S CENTRE, 2,000. R. R. Kendall & Eldred; Bradford, Bordell & Kinzua. New Opera House. Hotel: Duke, regular rates, $2 (special also).

EAST BRADY, 1,500. R. R., Alleghany Valley. McGafferty's Opera House; seating capacity, 800......Hotel: Central, regular rates, $2 (special also).

EASTON, 25,000, (with surrounding towns). R. R., Lehigh Valley; Delaware, Lackawanna & West; New Jersey Central; Philadelphia & Reading; Pennsylvania. Able Opera House, Wm. M. Sholtz, manager; seating capacity, 1,500; rental, one night $60, three $150; share also; license included. Size of stage, 35x40; size of proscenium opening, 21x29; height from stage to grooves, 18; height from stage to rigging loft, 43; depth under stage, 10; traps, 5; number sets scenery, 20; stage carpenter, John Neubrand; bill poster, Opera House; number sheets can accommodate, 500 to 1,000; rates per sheet, 4c.; theatrical teamster, E. E. Hemingway. Newspapers: daily, Express, advertising rates per inch, 75c.; Free Press, advertising rates per inch, 75c.; Argus, advertising rates per inch, 75c.; weekly, Call (Sun.), advertising rates per inch, 50c......Hotels: United States, special rates, $2 to $2.50; Franklin, special rates, $2 to $2.25; Swan, special rates, $1 to $1.25.

Arion Theatre (variety), J. J. Magee, manager.

EAST STROUDSBURG, 5,500. R. R., Del., L. & W.; N. Y. & S. W. Academy of Music, Academy of Music Co., manager; seating capacity, 550; rental, one night $18, three $30; Size of stage, 23x30; size of proscenium opening, 15½x18; height from stage to grooves, 12; height from stage to rigging loft, 13; depth under stage, 4½; traps, 1; number sets scenery, 12; scenic artist, G. L. Stackhouse; stage carpenter, G. L. Stackhouse; bill poster, Academy of Music; number of sheets can accommodate, 100. Newspapers: Express (Th.), advertising rates, 10c. per line; Jeffersonian (Th.), advertising rates, 10c. per line; Democrat (Th.), advertising rates, 10c. per line......Hotels: Lackawanna, special rates, $1 to $1.50; Analomink, special rates, $1 to $1.50; Burnett, $2 to $2.50.

EDENBURG, 1,100. R. R., Pittsburg & Western. New Opera House, La Point & Ore, managers; seating capacity, 600. Newspapers: Freeman (Fri.), Herald (Fri.)...... Hotels: Edenburg, Wildman's, Opera.

ELDRED, 2,000. R. R., Bradford, Bordell & Kinzua; Brad., El. & Cuba; Buf., N. Y. & Phila.; Kendall & El. Wolcott Opera House, A. B. Rowley; seating capacity, 800; rental, one night $25; three $40; share also; license included. Size of stage, 30x48; size of proscenium opening, 16x22; height from stage to grooves, 12; height from stage to rigging loft, 20; depth under stage, 5; traps, 2; number sets scenery, 6; leader of orchestra, Grunman; scenic artist, Smith; stage carpenter, H. Kaufman; bill poster, B. F. Grunman; number of sheets can accommodate, 200; rates per sheet, 4c; theatrical teamster, F. Hall. Newspaper: Eagle (Fri.)......Hotels: Central, special rates, $1.25 to $150; Eldred, special rates, $1.25.

ERIE, 37,000. R. R., Lake Shore & Mich. So.; Erie & Pittsburg; Nickel Plate. Park Opera House, William H. Sell, manager; seating capacity, 1,675; rental, share only; license included. Size of stage, 36x82; size of proscenium opening, 39x36; height from stage to grooves, 18; height from stage to rigging loft, 52; depth under stage, 9; traps,

– THE –

NEW YORK MIRROR

A REFLEX OF THE DRAMATIC EVENTS OF THE WEEK.

HARRISON GREY FISKE, EDITOR.

Office of Publication   –   –   –   12 UNION SQUARE.

ADVERTISING RATES.

Measured by agate type measure, which equals 14 lines (in solid or display type) to the inch in depth.

Ordinary Advertisements, - - - - - - - - - - 20 *Cents Per Line*
Reading Notices, - - - - - - - - - - - - 30 *Cents Per Line*

On advertisements ordered for continued **insertions, and paid for** in advance, the following *discounts* will be allowed :

10 *per cent. on four insertions;*   15 *per cent. on eight insertions;*
20 *per cent. on thirteen insertions;*   •   25 *per cent. on twenty-six insertions.*

One column counted as 100 lines ; one-quarter page, 250 lines ; one-half page, 500 lines ; and one page, 1,000 lines.

PROFESSIONAL CARDS, 3 lines space, $3 PER QUARTER (13 insertions).
"   "   4 "   " $4 "   "   (13 "   ).
"   "   5 "   " $5 "   "   (13 "   ).
"   "   6 "   " $6 "   "   (13 "   ).

With proportionate charges for larger cards.
CARDS under heading " MANAGERS' DIRECTORY," same rates.
Matter in standing advertisements or professional cards changed as often as desired without extra charge.

SUBSCRIPTION RATES.

One Year, - - - - $4 00.   *Six Months,* - - - - - $2.00.

The **NEW YORK MIRROR** is published **every** Thursday at 12 Union Square, New York, and **is** for sale by all Newsdealers in the United States, Canada, and the principal **cities** of Europe. In sending remittances, make checks or drafts payable to *NEW YORK MIRROR*, and postoffice or money orders or registered letters to the

NEW YORK MIRROR,

STATION D.   NEW YORK P. O.

3; number sets scenery, 20; **leader of orchestra,** W. O. Mehl; scenic artist, H. N. Smith; stage carpenter, M. Scott; bill poster, W. J. Sell; **number of sheets can accommodate,** 2,000; rates per sheet, &c.; theatrical **teamster,** Erie Transfer Co. Newspapers : daily, Dispatch, Herald, Observer; weekly, Gazette (Sun.), Graphic (Sun.).. ...Hotels : Reed, special rates, $1.75; Moore, special rates, $1.50; Park, special rates, $1.25.

Music Hall; seating capacity, 700.

Academy of Music; seating capacity, 500.

FRANKLIN, 7,000. R. R., Schuylkill & Lehigh. Opera House, Hanna & Duffield, managers; seating capacity, 850; rental, **one night $30, license included.** Size of stage, 27x44; full set scenery; bill poster, E. Bradley; theatrical **teamster,** B. Moffat. Newspapers : daily, News; weekly, Citizen-Press (Th.); **Spectator** (Th.)......Hotels : Exchange, regular rates, $2 (special also); United States, regular **rates,** $2 (special also).

Court House; seating capacity, 1,000.

GERMANTOWN, 30,000. R. R., Pennsylvania. Parker's Hall, Joseph Parker, manager, seating capacity, 550; rental, one night $15, three $35; no license. Size of stage, 38x18; **number sets scenery,** 5; bill poster, John J. Holcomb......Hotel: Wayne.

Wilson Hall Opera House, Potter & Seymour, managers; seating capacity, 600.

GETTYSBURG, 3,000. R. R., Gettysburg & Harrisburg; Hanover Junc., Hanover & Gettysburg. McClellan Opera House; **seating capacity,** 650; rental, one night $15; license, $2.50; fair stock scenery; bill poster, M. Crilly; theatrical **teamster,** Charles Tait. Newspapers: Compiler (Tu.), Sentinel (Tu.) .....Hotels: Eagle, regular rates, $2 (special also); McClellan.

GIRARDVILLE, 2,700. R. R. Phila. & Reading. Lafferty's Hall; **seating capacity,** 300; fair stock **scenery.** Newspaper: Gazette (Sat.).. ..Hotel: Girard, regular rates, $2 (special also).

GLEN ROCK, 1,200. R. R., Northern Central. Item Hall, N. Z. Seitz, manager; seating capacity, 200; one night $5, three $9; license, $1. Size of stage, 13x21; no scenery. Newspaper: Item (Fri.).... .Hotels: Cold Spring, Fountain.

GREENSBURG, 5,000. R. R., Pennsylvania. Lomison Opera House, Dr. H. G. Lomison, manager; seating capacity, 1,000; rental, one night, $40, **three $100; share also.** Size of stage, 23x34; number sets scenery, 18; bill poster, G. G. Rudolf; theatrical **teamster,** James Milingle. Newspapers : daily, Press; weekly, Argus (Wed.), Tribune and Herald (Tues.).... .Hotels: Zimmerman, regular rate, $2 (special also); Dixon, Bovery, Berlin.

GREENVILLE, 5,000. R. R., Erie & Pittsburg; N. Y., Penn. & Ohio; Shenango & Allegheny. Laird's Opera House, J. F. Laird, manager; seating capacity, 1,000; rental, one night $25; three $50; license, $3; share also. Size of stage, 24x36; number sets scenery, 10; bill poster, James Garber; theatrical teamster, Reddy Smith. Newspapers: Argus (Th.), Progress (Sat.), News (Fri.),.....Hotels: National, regular rates, $2 (special also); Fell, regular rates, $2 (special also); Packard.

HANOVER, 3,000. R. R., Penn. (Fredericksburg Division); Hanover Junc., Hanover & Gettysburg. Central Hall, Malon H. Maille, manager; seating capacity, 600; rental, one night $8, three $18; no license; share also. Size of stage, 15x21; number sets scenery, 5; bill poster, J. H. Hanfman, theatrical teamster, Alex. Bitz. Newspapers: Citizen (Th.), Herald (Sat.), Spectator (Th.) Hotels: Central, regular rates, $2 (special also); Diller.

Concert Hall; seating capacity, 500.

HARRISBURG, 36,000. R. R., Penn.; Phil. & Reading; North. Central; Cumb. Valley Opera House, H. J. Steel, manager; seating capacity, 1,400; rental, one night $60, license included. Size of stage, 38x40; size of proscenium opening, 25x36; height from stage to grooves, 30; height from stage to rigging loft, 30; depth under stage, 7; traps, 1; number sets scenery, 14; stage carpenter, Wm. Dillon; bill poster, H. J. Steele; rates per sheet, 4c.; theatrical teamster, Wm. Neely Newspapers : daily, Patriot, Telegraph.....Hotels: United States, special rates, $1.50; Bolton, special rates, $1.75; Lochiel, regular rates, $2 (special also); Franklin, regular rates, $2 (special also).

Grand Opera House, Markly & Till, manager; seating capacity, 1,300; rental, one night $60, share also; license included. Size of stage, 36x90; number sets scenery, 16.

Masonic Hall.

HAWLEY, 5 000. **R. R.**, Penn. Coal Co.; Erie, (Honesdale Branch). Rodman's Hall, James T. Rodman, manager; seating capacity, 250; rental, one night $10, three $21, license, $5; share also. Size of stage, 16x24; no scenery; bill poster, manager of Hall; theatrical teamster, S. J. Sherret. Newspaper: Times (Fri). ...Hotels: Keystone; regular rates, $2 (special also); Eddy, Solone, Wayne.

Olnfalas Hall; seating capacity, 350.

HAZLETON, 8,000. R. R., Lehigh Valley Hazle Hall, John A. Barton, manager; **rental,** one night $15; license, $2.50. Newspapers : daily, Plain Speaker, Sentinel......Hotels : Central; regular rates, $2 (special **also)**; Hazleton, regular rates, $2 (special also).

HOLLIDAYSBURG, 5,000. R. R., Branch of Pennsylvania. Condron's Opera House, F. H. **Russ,** manager; **seating capacity, 5⁰0; rental, one night $15; license,** $2.50. Size of stage, 16x22; height from stage to grooves, 18; height from stage to rigging loft, 30; depth under stage, 4½; number sets scenery, 4; bill poster, **Harry Gardner; number** of sheets can accommodate, 130; **theatrical teamster,** Jacob Snyder. **Newspapers : Standard (Tu),** Register (Wed.)......Hotels: **American, regular rates, $2 (special also);** Logan.

Masonic Hall; seating capacity, 800.

HONESDALE, 10,000. R. R., Erie; Del. & Hudson Canal Co. New Opera House, Wm. **J.** Silverstone, manager; seating capacity, 660; rental, one night $20, three $75; license, **$3. Size of** stage, 24x22; size of proscenium opening, 18x20; height from stage to grooves, 12; depth under stage, 6; number sets scenery, 8; leader of orchestra, Eugene Haue and John Oldorf; scenic artist, J. Farrell; stage carpenter, Wm. J. Brown; bill poster, Wm. J. Silverstone and Adam J. Britenbaker; number sheets can accommodate, 125; rates per sheet, 4c; theatrical teamster, H. T. and J. H. Whitney. Newspapers: Citizen (Th.), advertising rates, special contract; Herald (Th.), special contract; Independent (Th.), special contract.   .Hotel: Allan, special rates,.$1.25; Ball, special rates, $1.25; Sliter, special rates, $1.25.

Liberty Hall, Fuller & Tracy, managers; seating capacity, 600; **rental,** one night $20; share also; license included Size of stage, 18x45; full set scenery.

HUNTINGDON, 4 000. R. R., Huntingdon & Broad **Top;** Penn. Penn Street Hall; seating capacity, 500; rental, one night $8, three $18; **no** license. Size of stage, 21 x40; number sets scenery, 6; bill poster, Gilbert Greenburg. Newspapers: semi-weekly, News; weekly, Globe (Th.), Journal (Fri), Monitor (Th.)......Hotels : Leister, regular rates, $2 (special **also)**; Miller, regular rates, $2 (special **also)**; Franklin.

Keystone Opera House, **J. C. Blair.**

HYDE PARK. R. R., Del., Lack. & West.; Central N. J. St. David's Hall, D. Jones, **manager; seating capacity, 750; rental, one night $25; license included. Size of stage, 30x37;** fair stock scenery.. ...Hotels: Herman, Wyoming, Luzerne.

INDIANA, 4,000. R. R., Pennsylvania. Armory Hall, John W. Sutton, manager; seating capacity, 350; rental, one night $10, **three** $20; license, $2. Size of stage, 17x24; size **of** proscenium opening, 12x22; height **from** stage to grooves, 13; number sets scenery, 7; leader of orchestra, J. Lisle Apple; bill poster, Harry Apple; rates per sheet, 2c.; theatrical teamster, W Brinkman. Newspapers Messenger (Wed.); Progress (Wed.); Times (Wed.)......Hotels : American, Indiana, Gompers, special rates, $1

IRWIN STATION, 1,5⁰0. R. R., Penn.; Youghiogheny. Kunkle's Opera House, J. Kunkle, **manager; seating capacity, 1,000. Size** of stage, 25x50; **full set** scenery. Newspaper: Chronicle (Sat.)......Hotel: Stewart; regular rates, $2 (special **also).**

Irwin Opera House, Wm. **Crookston, manager;** seating capacity, 500. Size of **stage, 16x22.**

JOHNSTOWN, 22 000. R. R., Baltimore & Ohio; Pennsylvania. Union Hall, Joseph Hamilton, manager; Brooks & Dickson, New York representatives; seating capacity, 1,000; rental, share only; license included. Size of stage, 40x26; height from stage to grooves, 24; height from stage to rigging loft, 28; depth under stage, 10; number sets scenery, 9; bill poster, Janitor Union Hall; theatrical teamsters, Mulligan & Patterson. Newspapers : daily, Tribune; weekly, Democrat (Wed.)......Hotels: Hulbert, special rates, $1.50; Merchants, special rates, $1 50.

Opera House, John Parke, manager; seating capacity, 1,000; rental, one night $25, three $60; license included. Size of stage, 33x24; number sets scenery, 5.

Turner Hall; seating capacity, 600.

KITTANNING, 2,600. R. R , Allegheny Valley. Kittanning Opera House, O. B. Hiner, manager; seating capacity, 800; rental, one night, $17, three $45; license, $2; fair stock scenery; bill poster, Charles Dugan; theatrical teamster, Alex. Gage. Newspapers: Sentinel (Th.), Republican (Wed.), Continental (Sat.), Times (Fri.), Free Press (Th.)..... Hotels: Reynolds, regular rates, $2 (special also); Dugand, Eagle, Walker, Cook.

Golden's Opera House.

LANCASTER, 30,000. R. R., Pennsylvania; Phila. & Reading. Fulton Opera House, B. Yecker, manager; seating capacity, 1,200; rental, one night $50, three $125; license included. Size of stage, 31x54; size of proscenium opening, 24x28; height from stage to grooves, 17; height from stage to rigging loft, 40; depth under stage, 7; traps, 1; number sets scenery, 24; scenic artist, Richert Farren; stage carpenter, Irwin R Rinehart; bill poster, B. Yecker; number sheets can accommodate, 2,000; rates per sheet, 4c; theatrical teamster, F. Brimmer. Newspapers: daily, Examiner, advertising rates per inch, 75c.; New Era, advertising rates per inch, 75c.; Intelligencer, advertising rates per inch, 75c.......Hotels: Stevens House, special rates, $2; Cooper's, special rates, $1.25 to $1.50; Grape, special rates, $1.25 to $1.50.

LATROBE, 2,400. R. R., Pennsylvania; Ligonier Valley. Showalter's New Opera House, John A. Showalter, manager; seating capacity, 1,000; rental, share only; license included. Size of stage, 18x47; size of proscenium opening, 17x25; height from stage to grooves, 13; height from stage to rigging loft, 20; depth under stage, 5; number sets scenery, 8; leader of orchestra, Prof. Harry Dunspaugh; stage carpenter, Thomas O'Brien; bill poster, Opera House; theatrical teamster, Gust Harris. Newspapers: daily, Greensburgh Press; weekly, Greensburgh Democrat (Wed.), Greensburgh Argus (Wed.), Greensburgh Tribune & Herald (Wed.), Latrobe Advance (Wed.)......Hotels: Parker's, special rates, $1.50 to $2; Quinliven's, special rates, $1.50 to $2; Clifford's, special rates. $1.50 to $2; Casey's, special rates, $1.50 to $2.

Young's Hall, E. H. Young, manager; seating capacity, 500; rental, one night $10; share also; license included. Size of stage, 16x40, no scenery

LEBANON, 11,000. R. R., Phila. & Reading; Pennsylvania. Fisher Hall, Geo. H. Spang, manager; seating capacity, 1,000; rental, one night, $25, license included. Size of stage, 47x22; size of proscenium opening, 20x24; height from stage to rigging loft, 28; depth under stage, 4; traps, 1; full set scenery; leader of orchestra, Pino; stage carpenter, C. Shirk; bill poster, G. H. Spang; rates per sheet, 4c.; theatrical teamster, D. Landermilch. Newspapers: daily, Advertiser, advertising rates, $1 per inch; Times, $1 per inch; News, $1 per inch... ..Hotels : Valley, special rates, $1.50; City, special rates, $1.50.

LEWISBURG, 4,200. R. R., Phila. & Reading; Pennsylvania (P. & E. Division). Music Hall, Wm. Jones, manager; seating capacity, 1,000; rental, one night $20, three $45; license, $3. Size of stage, 25x25; number sets scenery, 2; bill poster, Thomas Strickland; theatrical teamsters, Gibson & Blair.....Hotels: Cameron, regular rates, $2 (special also); American.

LEWISTOWN, 3,000. R. R, Pennsylvania. Town Hall, Chief Burgess, manager; seating capacity, 450; rental, one night $4, three $10; no scenery; bill poster, Charles Marks. Newspapers: Sentinel (Th.), Free Press (Th.), Gazette (Wed.)....Hotels : National, Coleman, regular rates, $2 (special also); Union, Ganville, Valley.

LOCK HAVEN, 10,000. R. R., Pennsylvania (P. & E. Div.); Bald Eagle Valley & Reading. Opera House, J. N. Farnsworth, manager; seating capacity, 900; rental, one night $25, three $50, license included; share also. Size of stage, 24x24; size of proscenium opening, 18x22; height from stage to grooves, 14; height from stage to rigging loft, 26; depth under stage, 4; traps, 2; number sets scenery, 9; leader of orchestra, John Daner; stage carpenter, D. Farnsworth; bill posters, Farnsworth Bros.; number sheets can accommodate, 600; rates per sheet, 4c.; theatrical teamster, A. H. Strayer. Newspapers: daily,

Express, advertising rates per inch, 75c; Democrat, per inch, 75c.. Hotels: United States, special rates, $1.25 to $1.50; Irvin, special rates, $2; Fallon, special rates, $2.

Academy of Music; seating capacity, 600.

Great Island Hall; **seating capacity, 500.**

MAHANOY CITY, 10,000. R. R., Phila. & Reading; Lehigh Valley Opera House, Const. **Metz,** manager; seating capacity, 800; rental, one night $25, three $60; license, $3; **share** also. Size of stage, 24x28; full set scenery; bill poster, Charles Hand; theatrical teamster, Adam Brown. Newspapers: tri-weekly, **Record**; weekly, Local (Sat.); Tribune (Sat.) ......Hotels: Merchants', Mansion, **Eagle, Central.**

City Hall; **seating capacity, 8X0; rental, one night $20.**

MANHEIM, 2,000. R. R., Phila. & Reading. Arndts' Hall, Henry Arndts, manager; seating capacity, **340**; rental, **one night** $5; **no license. Size of stage, 18x22; bill poster, L. H,** Gibble. Newspaper: Advertiser (Fri.) .....Hotels: Summey, regular rates, $2 (special also); **American,** Washington, Centennial, Black Horse.

MARIETTA, 5,000. R. R., Penn.; Phila. & Reading. Central Hall, John W. Rich, manager; seating capacity, 500; rental, one night $15, three $30; license included. Size **of** stage, 18x40; number sets scenery, 6; bill poster, John Naylor; theatrical teamster, Tony Sultzbach. Newspapers: Times (Sat.), Register (Sat.)..... Hotels: Broadway, special rates, $1; St. Johns, special rates, $1; Hauer, special rates, $1.

MARSTINSBURG, 1,500. R. R., Pennsylvania. Goetz Hall, E. D. Goetz, manager; seating capacity, 500; **rental, one night $10, three $17; no** license. Size of stage, 12x40; number sets scenery, 3; bill poster, C. G Houn. Newspaper: Independent (Sat.)..... **Hotels:** Globe, regular rates, $2 (special also); St. Cloud.

MAUCH CHUNK, 5,000. R. R, Central N. J.; Lehigh Valley. Concert Hall, Town Clerk, manager; seating capacity, 600 ; rental, one night $25; **license included.** Size of stage, 30x25 ; bill poster, Harry Albertson ; theatrical teamsters, Rex Brothers. Newspapers daily, Times ; weekly, Gazette (Th.), Democrat (Sat.) .....Hotels: Mansion, regular **rates, $2 (special also); American,** regular rates, $2 (special also).

Broadway **Music Hall, E. F. Burtolette, manager; seating capacity, 900; full set scenery.**

McKEESPORT, 12,000. R. R., Baltimore & Ohio ; Pgh. & Lake Erie ; Pennsylvania. White's Opera House, Jas. E. White, manager ; seating **capacity, 1 200 ; rental, share** only ; license, yearly Size of stage, 32x58 ; size of proscenium opening, 29x30; **height from stage to** grooves, 16 ; height from stage to rigging loft, 38 ; depth under stage, 14 ; **traps, 3** ; number sets scenery, 12 ; leader of orchestra, Prof. L. Zitterbart ; stage carpenter, Harry Gibson ; bill poster, A. C. Williamson ; number of sheets can accommodate, 400 ; rates per sheet, 4c. ; theatrical teamster, Peter Kinney. Newspapers: daily, Paragon, advertising rates, yearly contract ; Record, advertising rates, yearly **contract** ; Times, advertising rates, yearly contract ; News, advertising rates, yearly **contract;** weekly, Herald (Sun.), advertising rates, yearly contract......Hotels: National, **special rates, $1.50;** Wolfe, special rates, $1.25.

Turner's Hall, Skelley Brothers, managers ; seating capacity, 600 ; rental, one night, $25.

MEADVILLE, 12,000. R. R., N. Y., Penn. & Ohio; Meadville. **Library Hall, Charles E.** Richmond, manager; seating capacity, 700; rental, one night $30, **three $75; license, $3.** Size **of** stage, 20x16; leader of orchestra, Fred. Nichols; bill **poster, John** Paterson; Newspapers: daily, **News, Tribune,** Republican.......Hotels **: Commercial, Budd,** McHenry.

Opera House; **burned season of 1883-'84.**

Richmond Hall; **seating capacity, 300.**

MEDIA, 3,100. R. R., **Westchester & Phil. Gleave Hall, Henry** Green, manager; seating capacity, 325. Newspapers : **American (Wed.), Record (Sat.)**......Hotel : Charter, regular rates, $2 (special also).

MERCER, 3,000. R. R., Buff., N. Y. & Phil.; Shenango & Allegheny. Mercer Opera House; seating capacity, 650; rental, one night $25; license included. Size of stage, 26x53; full **set** scenery. Newspapers Despatch (Fri.), Republican Th.)......Hotel : St. Cloud, regular rates, $1.50 to $2 (special also).

MEYERSDALE, 2,000. R. R., Balt. & Ohio. Goodwill Hall; seating capacity, 600; rental, one night $5. Size of stage, 18x30; no scenery; theatrical teamster, Samuel Dehart. Newspaper: **Commercial (Fri.)**......Hotel: Jones, regular rates, $2 (special also).

MIDDLETOWN, 4,500. R. R., Pennsylvania. Young's Opera House, J. Young, manager; seating capacity, 350; rental, one night $12; license $1. Size of stage, 14x30; number sets scenery, 5. Newspapers: Journal (Th.), Press (Sat.)......Hotels: Railroad, regular rates, $2 (special also); Washington, Pennsylvania.

MIFFLINBURG, 1,600. R. R., Pennsylvania (P. & E. Div.) Sanky's Hall, Sanky, manager; seating capacity, 500; rental, one night $8 to $10; no license. Size of stage, 30x10; height from stage to rigging loft, 15. Newspaper: weekly, Telegraph (Wed.), advertising rates, 10c. per line......Hotel: Central, regular rates, $2 (special also).

MILLERSTOWN, 5,000. R. R., Pennsylvania. Millerstown Opera House, Dibble & Dougherty, managers; seating capacity, 600; rental, one night $35; license, $3. Number sets scenery, 8; bill poster, Fred Johnson. Newspaper: Review, Herald......Hotels: Central, regular rates, $2 (special also).

MILLERSVILLE, 1,500. R. R., Lancaster & Millersville. Union Hall, J. R. Pickel, sr., manager; seating capacity, 400; rental, one night $5; no license. Size of stage, 14x24; no scenery......Hotels: Black Horse, regular rates, $2 (special also); Swan.

MILTON, 5,000. R. R., Pennsylvania, Philadelphia & Reading. Opera House; seating capacity, 500; rental, one night $15; license, $3; number sets scenery, 1. Newspapers: Argus (Fri.), Economist (Sat.), Miltonian (Fri.)......Hotels: Riverside, regular rates, $2 (special also); Broadway.

Academy of Music, seating capacity, 1,000.

MONONGAHELA CITY, 4,000. R. R., Pennsylvania. School Hall, S. H. Williams, manager; seating capacity, 500; rental, one night $10 to $25; license, $4; no scenery. Newspapers: daily, Republican, weekly, Record (Th.).....Hotel: Miller, regular rates, $2 (special also).

MONTROSE, 2,800. R. R., Delaware, Lackawanna & Western; Montrose. Daniell's Hall, Frank Stevens, manager; seating capacity, 500; rental, one night $8; license, $2; share also. Size of stage, 14x32. Newspapers: Democrat (Fri.), Republican......Hotels: Tarbell, regular rates, $2 (special also); Montrose.

MOUNT CARMEL, 4,500. R. R., Pennsylvania; Phila. & Reading; Lehigh Valley. Grand Army Hall, Joe Gould, manager; seating capacity, 500; rental, one night $20, three $50, share also, license included. Size of stage, 30x40; size of proscenium opening, 12x16; from stage to grooves, 11½; depth under stage, 9; traps, 3; number sets scenery, 8; bill poster, Matt. Ward. Newspaper: News (Sat.)......Hotels: Mount Carmel, special rates, $1.50 to $1.75; National, special rates, $1.25 to $1.50; Commercial, $1.50 to $1.75.

MOUNT PLEASANT, 1,600. R. R., Balt. & Ohio. National Hall; seating capacity, 500. Newspaper: Journal (Tues.)......Hotel: National, regular rates, $2 (special also).

NANTICOKE, 7,000. R. R. Central New Jersey; Del., Lacka. & Western; Pennsylvania, (P. & E. Division). Broadway Hall, F. B. Crotzer, manager; seating capacity, 800; share only. Size of stage, 22x40; fair stock scenery; bill poster, J. D. Haines. Newspapers: Venture (Sat.), Sun (Fri.)......Hotel: Nanticoke, regular rates, $2 (special also).

NEW BRIGHTON, 7,000. R. R., Pittsburg & Lake Erie; Pitts., Ft. Wayne & Chic. Broadway Opera Hall, F. E. Merrick, manager; seating capacity, 600; rental, one night $30; license, $5. Size of stage, 20x25; number sets scenery, 10; bill poster, O'Farrer; theatrical teamster, James Edgar. Newspaper: daily, News......Hotel: Clyde, regular rates, $2 (special also).

NEW CASTLE, 14,000. R. R., Buff., N. Y. & Phila.; Erie & Pittsburg; Pittsburg & Lake Erie; Pittsburg, Clev. & Toledo; Pittsburg, Ft. Wayne & Chic.; Pittsburg & Western. Opera House, R. M. Allen, manager; seating capacity, 1,000; rental, share only; license, yearly. Size of stage, 35x65; size of proscenium opening, 30; height from stage to grooves, 20; height from stage to rigging loft, 28½; depth under stage, 4; traps, 3; number sets scenery, 11; leader of orchestra, Scott Kirk; scenic artist, Farres; stage car-

—— **SEASON 1884-5.** ——

5th Season in Texas.   *18th Annual Tour in U. S.*

STUTTZ'

CELEBRATED AND ONLY

TEXAS COMPANY.

FULL MILITARY SILVER HORN BAND AND OPERATIC ORCHESTRA,

Supporting America's Actor and Author,

J. G. STUTTZ

— AND —

THE PRO-VOKING SOUBRETTE. # E. ALMA STUTTZ. VIOLINIST.

PLAYING ONLY FIRST-CLASS PRODUCTIONS (BY *LADIES* AND *GEN-TLEMEN,* **AS** WELL AS *ARTISTS*), IN

COMEDY, FARCE, TRAGEDY AND MUSIC.

Opening for good artists at all times. Business enterprises receive prompt attention.
Address all communications :

J. G. STUTTZ, Manager and Proprietor.

Permanent address :   TEMPLE, TEX.

GOOD PAPER AND PLENTY OF IT AT ALL TIMES.

penter, R Donds; bill poster, Jacob Seigle; number of sheets can accommodate, 2,000; rates per sheet, 4c.; theatrical teamster, Sam Hazlip. Newspapers: daily, News, advertising rates, yearly contract; weekly, Courant (Fri.), Guard an (Fri.), Democrat (Th.) ......Hotels : Leslie, regular rates, $2.50 (special also); Central, regular rates $2 (special also); St. Cloud, Continental.

White's Hall; seating capacity, 450.

NEWPORT, 2,500. R. R., Pittsburg & Lake Erie; Pitt., Ft. Wayne & Chicago. Centennial Hall, Fletcher & Bosserman, managers; seating capacity, 400; rental, one night $5; license $1; number sets scenery, 2; bill poster, D. F. Demaree; theatrical teamster, Elias Beaumont. Newspapers: Ledger (Sat.), News (Sat.)......Hotels: Miller, regular rates, $2 (special also); Gault.

NORRISTOWN, 16,000. R. R., Philadelphia & Reading. Music Hall, Wallace Boyer, manager; seating capacity, 1,300; rental, one night $50 three $150, license included. Size of stage, 40x60; size of proscenium opening, 28x35; height from stage to grooves, 18; height from stage to rigging loft, 45; depth under stage, 15; traps, 3; number sets scenery, 22; leader of orchestra, John Harold; scenic artist, Richard Farren; stage carpenter, William McGay; bill poster, Wm. F. Koplin; number sheets can accommodate, 800; rates per sheet, 3c.; theatrical teamster, Humane Engine Co. Newspapers: daily, Herald, advertising rates per inch, $1; Times, advertising rates per inch, $1; weekly, Register (Tu.) Herald (Fri.)......Hotels: Hartranft, special rates, $1.50 to $2; Montgomery, special rates, $1.50 to $2; Rambo, special rates, $1.50 to $2; Windsor.

Odd Fellows Hall; seating capacity, 600.

NORTH EAST, 1,500. R. R., Lake Shore & Michigan South. Opera House, John Inglis manager; seating capacity, 600; rental, one night $15; license, $1; share also. Size of stage, 25x30; full set scenery; bill poster, Charles Plumby; theatrical teamster, Charles Plumby. Newspaper: Sun (Sat.)......Hotels: Haynes, regular rates, $2 (special also); Palace.

NORTHUMBERLAND, 2,200. R. R., Del., Lack. & West.; Phila. & Reading ; Penn., (P. & E. Division). Mertz Hall, John Laing, manager; seating capacity, 600 ; fair stock scenery. Newspaper : Press (Fri.)......Hotel: Van Kirk, regular rates, $2 (special also).

OIL CITY, 10,000. R. R., Alleghany Valley; Buff., N. Y. & Phila.; L. S., Mich. So.; N. Y., Pa. & Ohio. Grand Opera House, (burned Feb. 29, 1884). Newspapers : daily, Blizzard, Derrick......Hotels : Collins, regular rates, $2 (special also); Goodwin, regular rates, $2 (special also); Commercial.

OSCEOLA MILLS, 2,000. R. R., Pennsylvania. Heims Hall, George. E. Jones, manager; seating capacity, 400; rental, one night, $20, three $45; share also. Size of stage, 19x 25; number sets scenery, 4. Newspaper : Reveille (Fri.).....Hotels: Mountain, regular rates, $2, (special also); Lane, Osceola.

PARKER CITY, 3,200. R. R., Allegheny Valley; Pitts. & Western. Opera House, seating capacity, 600; rental, one night $30; license, $2; number sets scenery, $5; bill poster, W. Hollenback; theatrical teamster, E. J. Findley. Newspapers : Phœnix (Fri.)...... Hotels: Parker, regular rates, $2 (special also); Mead.

PETROLIA, 3,000. R. R., Pittsburg & Western. Opera House, T. Mason, manager; seating capacity, 600; rental, one night $25. Size of stage, 28x33; number sets scenery, 5; bill poster, D. W. Lerch; theatrical teamster, A. Cook. Newspaper : Record (Sat.)...... Hotels: Brunswick, regular rates, $2 (special also); Central, regular rates, $2 (special also); Opera Hotel.

PHILADELPHIA, 900,000. R. R., Camden & Atlantic; Camden, Gl. & Mt. E.; N. Y. & Phila., New Line; Pennsylvania (Amboy Division); Pennsylvania (New York Division); Pennsylvania (Pennsylvania Division); Baltimore & Ohio; Philadelphia & Atlantic City; Philadelphia & Reading; Philadelphia, N. & New York; Philadelphia, Wilmington & Baltimore; West Chester & Philadelphia; West Jersey. Academy of Music, Benjamin G. Owen, secretary; seating capacity, 3,000; rental, one night $175, three $325. Size of stage, 93x90; size of proscenium opening, 50x50 ; height from stage to grooves, 2?; height from stage to rigging loft, 72 ; depth under stage, 25 ; traps, 10 ;

number sets scenery, 100 ; scenic artist, **Russell Smith ; stage carpenter, Charles H.**
Higbee ; bill poster, Wm. Nagle, No. 504 Chestnut st.; **theatrical teamsters, Union Trans-**
fer Co., Ninth and Chestnut sts.; People's Express Co., **No. 936 Arch st. Newspapers,**
daily : Ledger, Press, Times, Record, Inquirer, North American, German Democrat,
Telegraph, Bulletin, Star, Chronicle-Herald, News, Item, Call......Hotels : St. Elmo,
special rates, $2 ; Plumer's, special rates, $2 ; Girard, special rates, $2.50 ; Washington,
special rates, $2.50 ; Continental, **$2.50 to $3** ; Bingham, special rates, $2.50 ; St. Cloud,
special rates, $3 ; Guy's (European **plan),** $1; Ashland, $6 to $9 per week; Mansion,
$8 to $9; London, $7 to $8.75.

Arch Street Theatre, Mrs. **John Drew, lessee; J. J.** Holmes, business manager; seating
capacity, 1,732; rental, share only. Size of stage, 45x67; size of proscenium opening,
35x35; height from stage to groves, 19½; height from stage to rigging loft, 42; depth
under stage, 10; traps, 3; full stock scenery; musical director, J. F. Zimmerman; scenic
artist, John B. Moran; stage carpenter, John Christie.

Haverly's Theatre (Broad st), W. H. Morton, manager. Devoted exclusively to the production of comic opera.

Walnut Street Theatre (oldest in America), J. Fleishman, manager; seating capacity, **1,621;**
share also. Size of stage, 63x38; height from stage to grooves, 20; height from stage to
rigging loft, 65; traps, 7; full stock scenery; musical director, W. E. Morgan; scenic
artists, Daniel L. Cremens & Sidney Baker; stage carpenter, John Penrose.

Chestnut Street Opera House, Nixon & Zimmerman, managers; seating capacity, 2,500;
share only; musical director, Theo. Bendy; scenic artist, J. Farren; stage carpenter,
Thos. Blackwood.

Chestnut Street Theatre, Nixon & Zimmerman, managers; seating capacity, 2,100.

National Theatre, T. F. Kelly, manager; seating capacity, 2,400. Size of stage, 75x80;
size of proscenium opening, 38x32; height from **stage** to grooves, 18; height from **stage**
to rigging loft, 54; depth under stage, 12; traps, **7;** full set scenery; musical director, **W.**
Hogan; scenic artist, W. J. Fetten; **stage** carpenter, James Pyle.

New Arch Street Opera House, John F. Gorman, manager; seating capacity, 1,000; **share**
also. Size of stage, 39x50; size of proscenium opentng, 37x29; height from stage **to**
grooves, 18; height from stage to rigging loft, 38; depth under stage, 9; traps, 6; **number**
sets scenery, 12; musical director, Paul Sentz; stage **carpenter,** Harry Palmer.

New Central **Theatre (variety), Gallagher & Gilmore, managers; seating** capacity, 2,000.

Eleventh Street Opera House, J. **L.** Carncross, manager; seating capacity, 900.

Bijou **Theatre, Adam** Forepaugh, manager (now museum).

Club Theatre (variety), Harry C. Bryant, manager; seating **capacity, 1,200.**

Horticultural Hall, Thomas A. Andrews, manager; seating capacity, **1,800.**

St. George's Hall, D. Drummond, manager; seating capacity, **800.**

Association Hall, 15th & Chestnut sts., Chas. H. Wevill, manager; seating capacity, 1,250;
rental, one night $75. Size of stage, 15x30.

PHILIPSBURGH, 3,200 R. R., Pennsylvania. Potter's Hall, Dr. Thomas Potter, manager;
seating capacity, 603; **rental, one** night $10, three $25; license, $1 to $3; **share also.**
Size of **stage, 20x30; number sets** scenery, 4; bill poster, Wm. Roberts. Newspapers:
Journal (Fri.), Record (Wed.)..... Hotels: Faulkner, regular rates, **$2** (special also);
Potter, Loyd.

PHŒNIXVILLE, 6,700. R. R., Phil. & Reading; Penn. Masonic **Hall,** John O. Oberholtzer,
manager; seating capacity, 600; rental, one night $15; license, **$1 to $6;** number sets scen-
ery, 5; theatrical teamster, H. Brower. **Newspapers: daily,** Independent; weekly, Messenger (Sat.)......Hotels: Phœnix, **regular rates, $2 (special also);** Washington, regu-
lar rates, $2 (special also); Mansion.

PITTSBURG, 200,000   R. R., **Baltimore & Ohio; Pennsylvania;** Cleveland & Pittsburg; Allegheny Valley; **Pittsburg & Lake Erie** ; Fort Wayne & Chicago;
Pittsburg, Cincinnati & St. **Lonis;** Pittsburg Southern. Library Hall, F. A.
Parke, manager; Brooks & Dickson, New **York** representatives; seating ca-
pacity, 1,400; **share** only. Size **of** stage, 40x80; size of proscenium opening, 38x40;
height from stage to grooves, 20; height from stage to rigging loft, 40; depth

COMPOSITE IRON WORKS CO.,

83 READE STREET, NEW YORK,

MANUFACTURERS OF

No. 1017.

FINE CHAIRS,

—FOR—

OPERA HOUSES, THEATRES & CHURCHES.

COMPOSITE IRON WORKS CO.,
83 READE ST., NEW YORK.

MANUFACTURERS OF

FINE CHAIRS,
For Opera Houses, Theatres and Churches.

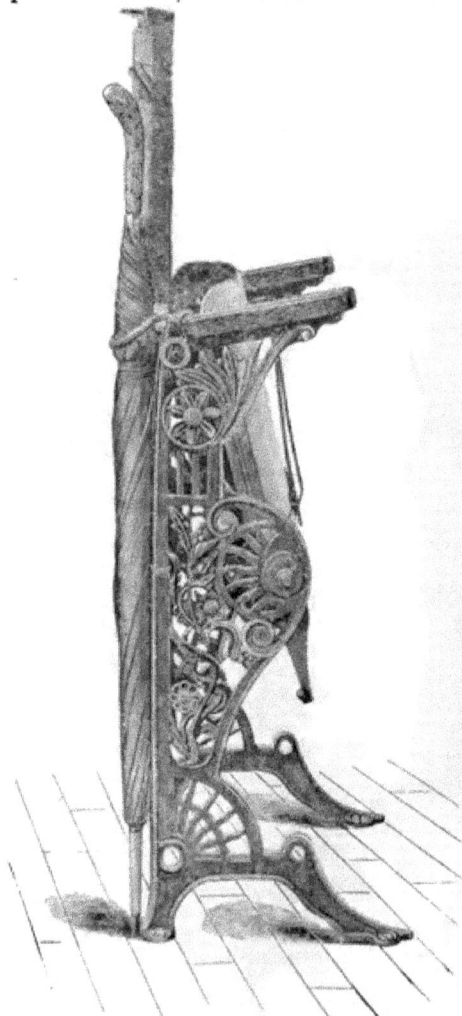

No. 1017.—Folded.

Our Chairs are are first class in every particular, and we have a variety of designs upholstered in Plush, Leather and Imitation Leather. Also a large line of perforated seat and back chairs.

under stage, 12; traps, 4; number sets scenery, 75; leader of orchestra, P. Weis; scenic artist, T. Carroll; stage carpenter, Chas. Crosby; bill posters, J. B. Murray & Co ; theatrical teamsters, Excelsior & Pittsburg Transfer Co. Newspapers: daily, Dispatch, Leader, Commercial Gazette, Times, Post, Chronicle, Telegraph, Mail......Hotels : Monongahela, Seventh Avenue, St. Charles, St. Claire, Hamilton, Central.

Opera House, John A. Ellsler, manager; seating capacity, 1,700; share only.

Harris' Mammoth Museum, William Chalet, manager; seating capacity, 1,500; share always, license included. Size of stage, 35x50; size of proscenium opening, 55x50; height from stage to grooves, 40; height from stage to rigging loft, 80; depth under stage, 4; traps, 2; number sets scenery, 15; leader of orchestra, Peter Schwartz; scenic artist, Nick Garland, stage carpenter, C. Luman; bill posters, Consolidated Co.

Williams' Academy of Music, H. W. Williams, manager.

People's Theatre, Geo. France, manager; seating capacity, 2,000.

Fifth Avenue Theatre; seating capacity, 1,600.

Henderson's Standard Theatre.

Lyceum Theatre.

Fourth Avenue Theatre.

PITTSTON, 20,000. R. R., Central N. J.: Del., Lack. & Western; Lehigh Valley. Music Hall, D. W. Evans, manager; seating capacity, 900; share only. Size of stage, 26x40; full set scenery; bill posters, Henry Armitage; theatrical teamster, Henry Armitage. Newspapers: daily, Gazette, Press ....Hotels. Farnham, regular rates, $2 (special also); Eagle, regular rates, $2 (special also).

Phoenix Hall; seating capacity, 600.

PLYMOUTH, 7,000. R. R., Del., Lack. & Western. Opera House, J. P. Smith & Son, managers; seating capacity, 1,200; rental, one night $25; license, $5; fair stock scenery; bill poster, Frank N. Girton. Newspapers: Record (Fri.), Star (Sat.)......Hotels : Parish, regular rates, $2 (special also); Frantz.

POTTSTOWN, 7,000. R. R., Phila. & Reading. Opera House; rental, one night, $30; three $90; bill poster, S. R. Bossert. Newspapers: daily, Ledger, Chronicle......Hotels : Farmers', regular rates, $2 (special also); Merchants', regular rates, $2 (special also); Madison.

Market Hall, W. O. Euchenbach, manager; seating capacity, 800; rental, one night $15: three $42; no license. Size of stage, 14x56; no scenery.

POTTSVILLE, 14,000. R. R., People's; Phila. & Reading. Academy of Music; Nathan Howser manager; seating capacity, 1,000; rental, one night $50; license included; share also. Size of stage, 28x64; height from stage to grooves, 16; height from stage to rigging loft, 45; depth under stage, 10; number sets scenery, 18; bill poster, Academy of Music; theatrical teamster, H. H. Stearns. Newspapers: daily, Chronicle, Journal...... Hotels: Pennsylvania, regular rates, $1.50 (special also); Merchants', regular rates, $2; Exchange, special rates, $1.25 to $1.50.

Mountain City Hall; seating capacity, 600.

Union Hall; seating capacity, 800.

READING, 50,000. R. R., Phila. & Reading; Schuyl. & Lehigh; Wil. & Nor.: Penna. Grand Opera House, Geo. M. Miller, manager; seating capacity, 1,200; rental, one night, $50; share also; license included. Size of stage, 34x60; size of proscenium opening, 22x28; height from stage to grooves, 15; height from stage to rigging loft, 32; depth under stage, 26; traps, 1; full set scenery; leader of orchestra, Wm. Koch; stage carpenters, H. Heath and J. Dickinson; bill poster, J. M. Schaeffer; number of sheets can accommodate, 2,600; rates per sheet, 4c.; theatrical teamster, T. Barto. Newspapers : daily, Times, advertising rates per line, 8c, to 21c.; Herald, advertising rates per line, 6c. to 19c.; News, advertising rates per line, 6c. to 20c.; Eagle, advertising rates per line, 6c. to 20c......Hotels : American, special rates, $1.50 to $2.50; Grand Central, special rates, $1.25 to $1.50, Merchants', special rates, $1 to $1.25; Keystone, $1.25 to $1.50.

Academy of Music, John D. Mishler, manager; Brooks & Dickson, New York representatives; seating capacity, 1,550; rental, one night $70. Size of stage, 31x50; size of proscenium opening, 38; number sets scenery, 24; **leader of** orchestra, **Will. H. Koch;** bill poster, James M. Schaeffer; number of sheets can accommodate, 8 000; **rates per sheet** 4c.; theatrical teamster, Tobias Barto.

Library Hall; seating capacity 800; **no scenery.**

Barlet & Schoch's Variety **Hall.**

Fairview Winter Theatre.

RENOVA, 3,600. R. R., Penn. (P. & D. Division). Association **Hall,** P. H. Sullivan, manager; seating capacity, 700; rental, one night $20; share also; number sets scenery, **5;** bill poster, manager of hall; theatrical teamster, M. O. Day. Newspaper: daily, News; weekly, Record (Th.)........Hotels: Renova, regular **rates,** $2 (special also); Revere.

REYNOLDSVILLE, 3,200. R. R., **Allegheny Valley. Reynolds Opera** House, Albert Reynolds, **manager; seating capacity, 400; rental, one night $15, three $30;** license, **$3;** share **also. Size of stage,25x36; number sets scenery,** 7. **Newspaper: Herald.... Hotels:** Belknap, **regular rates,** $2 (special also); Reynolds, Burns, **Ross, Central.**

RIDGWAY, 2,500. R. R., Penn. (P. & E. Division); Rochester & Pittsburg. Hyde Opera House, W. H. Hyde & Co., managers; seating capacity, 650; share only; license, **$2.** Size of stage, 22x32; number sets scenery, 10; bill poster, Opera House; theatrical teamster, Daniel Scribner. Newspapers: Advocate (Th.), Democrat (Th.)......Hotels: Hyde, regular rates, $2 (special also); McFarland, Ridgway.

SCOTTDALE, 5,500. **R. R., Pennsylvania.** Zearly & Poole's Hall, J. E. Farrer, manager; seating capacity, **400; share only. Size** of stage, 16x40; fair stock scenery, **bill poster,** Martin **Bishop. Newspapers: Independent** (Wed.), Tribune (Th.).. ...Hotels: **Scottdale,** Arlington, Broadway.

SCRANTON, 50,000. R. R., Del., Lack. & West.; **Phila.** & Reading; Del. & Hudson Canal **Co.;** Central of New Jersey. Academy of Music, **C.** H. Lindsay, manager; seating capacity, **1,500;** rental, share only. **Size of stage,** 35x60; size of proscenium opening, 30x **30;** height from stage **to grooves, 18; height from** stage to rigging loft, 42; depth under stage, 9; traps, 3; number sets scenery, 25; leader **of** orchestra, **Robt.** Banr; scenic artists, L. **W.** Seavey & L. H. Lempert; stage carpenter, Isaac Tice; bill poster, **W.** W. Murphy & Co.; number of sheets can accommodate, 3,000; rates per sheet, 4c.; theatrical teamster, W. W. Murphy. Newspapers: daily, Republican, advertising rates, yearly contract; **Times,** yearly contract; Truth, yearly contract......**Hotels:** Wyoming, special **rates, $1.50 to $2;** Lackawana Valley, $2; Forest House, **$1.50 to $2;** St. Charles, $1; **Susquehanna, $1;** Scranton (European plan).

Odd Fellows' Hall; seating capacity, 500.

Liederkranz Hall; seating capacity, 500.

SELINSGROVE, 1,500. R. R., Sunbury & Lewistown ; Penn. Town Hall, George R. Hendricks, manager; seating capacity, 600; rental, one night $8, three $20; no license. Size of stage, 16x20; height from stage **to** grooves, 20; height from stage to rigging loft, 18; depth under stage, 4; traps, 1; number sets scenery, 6; leader of orchestra, H. E. Richter; theatrical teamster, **George** Myers. Newspapers: Tribune, Times .. .. Hotels: Keystone, regular rates, $2 **(special** also); National, regular rates, $2 (special also); Riehl, regular rates, $2 (special also).

Odd Fellows' Hall, **J. M. Kreider, manager;** seating capacity, 550; **rental, one** night $5, share also; **no license. Size of stage, 16x38;** number sets scenery, **5.**

SHAMOKIN, 12,000. R. R., Phil. & Reading; Lehigh Valley; **Northern** Central, G. A. R. Opera House, J. F. Osler, manager; **seating capacity, 1,000; rental,** share only; license included. Size of stage, 26x47; size of proscenium opening, **18x23;** height from stage to grooves, 17; height from stage to rigging loft, 28; depth under stage, 12; number sets scenery, 10; leader **of** orchestra, John O'Connor; scenic artist, Joseph Dunklebergar; stage carpenter, H. Holshue; bill poster, D. S. Womer; **number** of sheets can accommodate, 400; rates per sheet, 3c.; theatrical teamster, W. **F.** Gilger. Newspapers: daily, **Times;** weekly, Herald (Th.), Sentinel (Sat.)......Hotels: City, special rates, $1.25; National, special rates, $2; Vanderbilt, special rates, $1.50 to $1.75; Windsor, special rates, $1.50 to $2.

Academy of Music, D. W. Friese, manager; seating capacity, 500; rental, **one** night, $20; **full set scenery,.**

SHARON, 6,000. R. R., N. Y., Pa. & Ohio; Erie & Pittsburg. Carver Opera House; seating capacity, 800; rental, one night $15; license, $5; **bill poster, Mounts.** Newspapers: daily, Eagle; weekly, Herald (Fri.)..... Hotels: Messer, regular rates, $2 (special also); **Carver, regular** rates, $2 (special also).

SHENANDOAH, 16,000. R. R., Lehigh Valley; Philadelphia & Reading. Ferguson's New Theatre, P. J. Ferguson, manager; seating capacity, 1,500; share only. Size of stage, 35x 50; size of proscenium opening, 25x30; height from stage to to grooves, 18; height from stage to rigging loft, 40; depth under stage, 8; traps; 3; number sets scenery, 15; stage carpenter, James Grossly; bill poster, Ed. Gibbons; number of sheets can accommodate, 400; rates per sheet, 4c.; theatrical teamster, apply to proprietor. Newspapers: daily, Herald, advertising rates, per inch, 25c.; Progress; weekly, Herald (Sat.), advertising rates, 50c. per line; News (Sun.), advertising rates, 50c. per line ...Hotels: Merchants', special rates, $1.50; Globe, regular rates $2 (special also); Washington, special rates, $1.25.

Robbins' Opera House, I. Robbins, manager; seating capacity, 1,000; rental, share only; Size of stage, 24x25; size of proscenium opening, 22x20; height from stage to rigging loft, 18; depth under stage, 8; full set scenery; leader of orchestra, Mr. Gay; stage carpenter, W. A. Elliott; bill poster, George W. Hossler; number of sheets can accommodate, 300; rates per sheet, 4c.

SLATINGTON, 2,800. R. R., Lehigh Valley; Schuylkill & Lehigh. Armory Hall, H. W. Hawkes, manager; seating capacity, 500; bill poster, J. E. Neff; theatrical teamster, J. E. Neff. Newspaper: News (Wed.)... ...Hotel: United States, regular rates, $2 (special also.)

SMITHPORT, 1,500. R. R., Buff., N. Y. & Philadelphia; Bradford, Bordell & Kinzua. Kittridge Opera House, C. F. Kittridge, manager; seating capacity, 500; rent or share; license, $1. Size of stage, 25x30; number sets scenery, 8; bill poster, Opera House. Newspapers: Miner (Fri.), Democrat (Fri.)........Hotels: Bennett, regular rates, $2 (special also); Grand Central, Wright

STROUDSBURG, 3,500. R. R., Del., Lack. & West; N. Y., Sus. & West. Williams Hall, A. C. Jansen, manager; seating capacity, 300; rental, one night $10; no license. Size of stage, 16x16; number sets scenery, 8. Newspapers: Jeffersonian (Th.), Democrat (Th.)......Hotels: Burnett, regular rates, $2 (special also); Washington, American, Indian Queen.

Academy of Music; seating capacity, 600; full set scenery.

ST. CLAIR, 6,000. R. R., Phil. & Reading. Walker's Hall, Daniel Walker, manager; seating capacity, 900; rental, one night $30; share also; license included. Size of stage, 18x20; number sets scenery, 4; bill poster, Daniel Walker, Jr., theatrical teamster, Daniel Walker, Jr. Newspaper: Splinters (Sat.)..... Hotels: Merchants', regular rates, $2 (special also); Marshall, Continental.

SUSQUEHANNAH, 5,000. R. R., Erie. Pope's Opera House, H. C. Lea, manager; seating capacity, 600; rental, one night, $8; license, $2 to $5. Size of stage, 15x25; number sets scenery, 15; bill poster, W. F. Forbes; theatrical teamster, H. Sellick. Newspapers: Journal (Sat.), Transcript (Sat.) Hotels: Starucca, regular rates, $2 (special also); Canawacta, Benson.

TAMAQUA, 6,000. R. R., Central New Jersey; Phil. & Reading. Seitzinger Hall, J. R. Seitzinger, manager; seating capacity, 500; rental, one night $15; license, $3. Size of stage, 22x28; fair stock scenery. Newspaper: Courier (Sat.)......Hotels: United States, regular rates, $2 (special also); Beard's, regular rates, $2 (special also); Columbia.

TIDIOUTE, 2,000. R. R., Buffalo, N. Y. & Phila. Grandian Opera House, N. J. Grandian, manager; seating capacity, 750; rental, one night $30, three $60; license, $3. Size of stage, 40x50; fair stock scenery; bill poster, Frank Lynch. Newspaper: News (Fri.)..... Hotels: National, regular rates, $2 (special also); Hale, Shaw.

TITUSVILLE, 10,000. R. R., Buffalo, N. Y. & Phil.; Dunkirk, Alleghany Val. & Pittsburg. Academy of Music, R. W. Barnsdall, manager; seating capacity, 700; rental, one night $30. Size of stage, 35x40; height from stage to grooves, 13; depth under stage, 3; bill

poster, R. W. Barnsdall; theatrical teamster, E. C. Brown. Newspapers: daily, Herald; weekly, World (Sun.)..... Hotels: Mansion, Brunswick, regular rates $2 (special also); Parshall, regular rates, $2 (special also).

Parshall Opera House, C. D. Goodsell, manager; seating capacity, 1,500; rental, one night $50; full set scenery.

TOWANDA, 5,000. R. R., Barclay; Lehigh Valley; State Line & Sullivan. Mercer Hall, D. Elsbree, manager; seating capacity, 600; rental, one night $20; license, $3 to $5. Size of stage, 25x40; number sets scenery, 4; bill poster, P. W. Pennypacker; theatrical teamster, Wm. Kerwin. Newspapers: daily, Review; weekly, Argus (Th.), Reporter (Th.).. Hotels: Ward, regular rates, $2 (special also); Elwell.

TREMONT, 3,000. R. R., Phil. & Reading. Union Hall, U. G. Batdorff, manager; seating capacity, 450; rental, one night $10; license, $2; bill poster, C. M. Adams. Newspaper: News (Th.)..... Hotels: National, regular rates, $2 (special also); Union, Tremont.

TUNKHANNOCK, 2,500. R. R., Lehigh Valley; Montrose. Pratt's Opera House, Frank H. Pratt, manager; seating capacity, 600; rental, share only. Size of stage, 20x47; size of proscenium opening, 20x23; height from stage to grooves, 14; depth under stage, 9; traps, 1; number sets scenery, 4; leader of orchestra, L. W. Emory; bill poster, Opera House; number sheets can accommodate, 75; rates per sheet, 4c.; theatrical teamster, J. M. Kelley. Newspapers: Democrat (Fri.), Republican (Fri.)......Hotels: Walls, Keeler, Packer.

TYRONE, 10,000. R. R., Pennsylvania. Conrad's Opera House, W. Fisk Conrad, manager; seating capacity, 900; rental, one night $40, three $100, license included. Size of stage, 25x50; number sets scenery, 11; bill poster, Opera House. Newspapers: Herald (Th.) Times (Tu.)......Hotels: Ward, regular rates, $2 (special also); Arlington, Eagle, Clearfield, City.

UNIONTOWN, 7,000. R. R., Baltimore & Ohio; Pennsylvania. Opera House, J. V. Thompson, manager; seating capacity, 1 000. Newspapers: Democrat (Tu.), Standard (Th.).........Hotels: McClelland, regular rates, $2 (special also); Clinton, regular rates, $2 (special also).

WARREN, 6,000. R. R., Phila. & Erie; Dunkirk, Allegheny Val. & Pitts.; Buff., N. Y. & Philadelphia. Library Hall, P. H. Carver, manager; seating capacity, 1,000 ; rental, share only; license included. Size of stage, 30x72; size of proscenium opening, 28x29; height from stage to grooves, 16; height from stage to rigging loft, 28; depth under stage, 11; traps, 3; number sets scenery, 11; leader of orchestra, T. Rieg; scenic artist, Wm. Fetters; stage carpenter, Emil Aman; bill poster, James Myers; number of sheets can accommodate, 600; theatrical teamster, Jacob Eysinger. Newspapers: daily, Times; weekly, Ledger (Fri.), Mail (Tu.).......Hotels: Carver (special rates) $2; Exchange (special rates) $1.50; Warren (special rates) $1.50.

Roscoe Hall: rental, one night $15; license included.

New Opera House.

WASHINGTON, 5,600. R. R., Balt. & Ohio. Town Hall, S. Hazzlit, manager; seating capacity, 800; rental, one night $10 to $15, three $25 to $30; license, included. Size of stage, 20x40; bill poster, Bunk White. Newspapers: daily, Reporter; weekly, Democrat (Wed.), Observer (Th.)......Hotels: Fulton, regular rates, $2 (special also); Anld, regular rates $2 (special also); Valentine.

WEATHERLY, 2,300. R. R., Lehigh Valley. Miller's Opera Hall, G. W. Miller, manager ; seating capacity, 550; rental, one night $15, three $30; license, $3; share also. Size of stage, 17x34; number sets scenery, 1. Newspaper: Herald (Sat.)......Hotels : Gilbert, regular rates, $2 (special also); Packer, Carbon, Verzl.

WELLSBORO, 3,500. R. R., Corning, Cowanesque & Antrim. Willcox Opera House, Geo. M. Covert, manager; seating capacity, 1,000; rental, one night $10 to $20; license $3 to $5; bill poster, G. M. Covert.

WEST BRIDGEWATER, 5,000 (with suburbs). R. R., Pittsburg & Lake Erie ; Cleveland & Pittsburgh; Pittsburgh, Ft. Wayne & Chicago. Hurst's Opera House, A. C. Hurst,

20

manager; seating capacity, 600; rent or share; size of proscenium opening, 21½. Size of stage, 30x21½; height from stage to grooves, 15; traps, 1; number sets scenery, 6; bill poster, Opera House; number sheets can accommodate, 200. Newspapers: daily, News and Argus.....Hotels: St. Cloud, special rates, $1 to $1.50; Summit, special rates, $1 to $1.50.

WESTCHESTER. 7,900. R. R., Penn.; Phil., Wil. & Balto. Horticultural Hall, W. D. Christman, manager; seating capacity, 1,200; rental, one night $25 to $30; license, $3 to $10; number sets scenery, 6; bill poster, David Townsend; theatrical teamster, Mifflin Smith. Newspapers: daily, News, Republican, Record......Hotels: Mansion, regular rates, $2 (special also); Green Tree, regular rates, $2 (special also).

Odd Fellows' Hall; seating capacity, 300.

WILKESBARRE, 30,000. R. R., Lehigh Valley; Penn. (P. & E. Division); Central N. J.; D. L. & W. Music Hall, M. H. Burgunder, manager; seating capacity, 1,200; rental, share only; license, yearly; Size of stage, 30x60; size of proscenium opening, 20x27; height from stage to grooves, 18; height from stage to rigging loft, 36; depth under stage, 5; traps. 6; number sets scenery, 10; leader of orchestra, Prof. Krebs; stage carpenter, Robert Spaulding; bill poster, A. F. Snyder; number of sheets can accommodate, 5,000; rates per sheet, 4c.; theatrical teamster, John F. Rainow. Newspapers: daily, Record, advertising rates, per inch, 75c.; Leader, per inch, 75c.; weekly, Newsdealer (Sun.), per inch, $1... ...Hotels: Bristol, special rates, $1.50; Luzerne, special rates, $2.00; Wyoming Valley, $2.50 to $3.

Garden City Hall, J. S. Hinds, manager; **seating capacity, 1,200; rent or share.** Size of stage, 18x20; full set scenery.

Atlantic Garden Theatre.

Myers' Opera House.

WILLIAMSPORT, 22,000. R. R., Pitts. & Erie; Nor. Cen.; Phila. & Reading; Cor., Cow. & Ant. Academy of Music, W. G. Elliott, manager; seating capacity, 1,100; rental, one night, $50; license, 1st $5, 2d $2.50; share also. Size of stage, 30x50; size of proscenium opening, 24x26; height from stage to grooves, 16; **height** from stage to rigging loft, 26; depth under stage, 8; full set scenery; leader of orchestra, V. Stofper; bill poster, W. G. Elliott; number of sheets can accommodate, 1,000; rates per sheet, 4c.; theatrical teamster, George Jackson. Newspapers: daily, Bulletin, advertising rates per inch, 75c.; Banner, advertising rates per inch, 75c.......Hotels: Hepburn's, special rates, $2.50; City, special rates, $2; Porter's, special rates, $1.50.

WRIGHTSVILLE. 1,700. R. R., Pennsylvania. Wrightsville Hall, G. K. Schumberger, manager. Newspaper: Star....Hotel: Leece's, regular rates, $2 (special also).

YORK, 20,000. R. R., Penna.; Northern Central. York Opera House, Adams & Dale, managers; seating capacity, 1,000; rental, share only; license included. Size of stage, 45x53; size of proscenium opening, 30x33; height from stage to grooves, 16; height from stage to rigging loft, 45; depth under stage, 8; traps, 3; number sets scenery, 16; leader of orchestra, Prof. Wecker; scenic artist, Richard Smith; stage carpenter, Alex. Shriver; bill poster, Alex. Shriver; number of sheets can accommodate, 1,000; theatrical teamster, N. C. R. W. Transfer Co. Newspapers: daily, Tribune, advertising rates, special contract; Age, advertising rates, special contract......Hotels: National, special rates, $2.50; Pennsylvania, special rates, $1.25; Central, special rates, $1.25; Washington, special rates, $1.

RHODE ISLAND.

BRISTOL, 6,500. R. R., Prov., Warren & Bristol. Town Hall, Trotter & Wardwell, managers; seating capacity, 815; rental, one night $15, no scenery. Bill poster, E. A. Fish. Newspaper: Phœnix (Sat.)......Hotels: Bristol, regular rates, $2 (special also); Church Street, State Street.

EAST GREENWICH, 3,600. R. R., New York, Providence & Boston. Odd Fellows' Hall, Will. E. Brown, manager; seating capacity, 400; rental, one night $10, three $24, license included. Size of stage, 14x19; size of proscenium opening, 13x21; height from stage to grooves. 13; depth under stage, 3; number sets scenery, 4; bill poster, Alfred A. Fry; number of sheets can accommodate, 200; rates per sheet, 4c.; theatrical teamster, Alfred A. Fry. Newspaper: Pendulum (Fri.), advertising rates, $1 per inch.. ...Hotels: Updyke, special rates, $1.50. Central, special rates, $1.50.

GREENWICH, 3,700. R. R., N. Y.,'Prov. & Boston. New Hall. S A. Slocum, manager. Size of stage, 40x54......Hotel: Updyke.

NEWPORT, 16,000. R R , Old Colony; Newport & Wickford. Opera House, Henry Bull, Jr., manager; seating capacity, 1,000; rental, one night $50; share also, license included. Size of stage, 45x55; width of proscenium opening, 29; height from stage to grooves, 15; height from stage to rigging loft, 26; depth under stage, 8; traps, 6; number sets scenery, full set; leader of orchestra, Wm. R. McQoown; stage carpenter, Chas. E. Thurston; bill poster, J. J. Flood, number of sheets can accommodate, 1,000; rates per sheet, 5c.; theatrical teamster, Wm. G. Peckham. Newspapers: daily, News, advertising rates, $1 per inch; weekly, Mercury (Sat.), advertising rates, $1 per inch. .....Hotels: United States, special rates, $1.50 to $1.75; Park, special rates, $1 25 to $1 50; Perry, special rates, $2.50

Casino Theatre

PAWTUCKET, 30,000. R. R. Boston & Providence; Providence & Worcester. Music Hall, Stephen F. Fisk, manager; seating capacity, 1,100; rental, one night $50, license included. Size of stage, 30x50; width of proscenium opening, 30; height from stage to grooves, 18; height from stage to rigging loft, 70; depth under stage, 10; traps, 3; number sets scenery, full set; bill poster, McMahon. Newspapers: Chronicle (Fri.), Sun (Wed.),.....Hotels: Benedict, regular rates, $2 to $2.5) (special also); Pawtucket, regular rates, $2 (special also).

Battery Hall, S. F. Fisk & Co., managers; seating capacity, 630; rental, one night $15, license included; share also. Size of stage, 17x21; number sets scenery, 8.

Opera House.

Varieties Theatre.

PHOENIX, 5,000. R. R , Branch of Providence & Stonington. Music Hall, James J. Smith, manager; rental, one night $10, three $20, license included. Size of stage, 14x32; size of proscenium opening, 14x14; height from stage to grooves, 10; height from stage to rigging loft, 16; depth under stage, 4; traps, 1; number sets scenery, 4. Newspaper: Pawtucket Valley Gleaner (Fri.),......Hotels: Phoenix, special rates, $1; Briggs', special rates, $1.

PROVIDENCE, 126,000. R. R., Boston & Prov.; N. Y., Prov. & Bos.; N, Y & N. E.; Prov. & Worcester; Prov., Warren & Fall River. Low's Grand Opera House, William H. Low, Jr., manager; seating capacity, 1,800; rental, one night $75, three $225; share also; license included. Size of stage, 31½x90; size of proscenium opening, 31x36; height from stage to grooves, 18; height from stage to rigging loft, 42; depth under stage, 9; full set scenery; leader of orchestra, Phillips; stage carpenter, Geo. Allen; bill poster, Cornell & Haskin; theatrical teamster, Hopkins Transfer Co., N. Hopkins. Newspapers: daily, Journal, advertising rates per inch, $1 first insertion; Star, $1 first insertion; Telegram, $1 first insertion; weekly, Sunday Despatch, $1 first insertion ... Hotels: Narragansett, special rates, $2.50; Dorrance, $2; City, $1.25 to $1.50; Aldrich, regular rates, $2; Central, $2; Freeman.

Providence Opera House, Geo. Hackett, manager; seating capacity, 1,500. Size of stage, 39x71; size of proscenium opening, 40x38; height from stage to grooves, 19; height from stage to rigging loft, 51; depth under stage, 12; traps of every kind; full set scenery; leader of orchestra, Fred, Von Olker; scenic artist, Geo. Johnson; stage carpenter, Jas. Nolan.

Sans Souci Garden, Wm. E. White, manager; seating capacity, 1,200; share only. Size of stage, 36x58; size of proscenium opening, 22x30; height from stage to grooves, 16; height from stage to rigging loft, 24; depth under stage, 14; traps, 3; number sets scenery, 12; leader of orchestra, W. Eugene White; scenic artist, H. L. Reid; stage carpenter, D. W. Marshall.

ESTABLISHED 1865.

C. B. DEMAREST,

MANUFACTURERS OF

IMPROVED TILTING BACK

Opera Chairs.

The mechanical construction of these chairs is the simplest it is possible to make. and, with great strength, make it impossible to get out of order.
Made in many different styles, and upholstered in any material to suit the purchaser.

STAGE HARDWARE.

A FULL LINE OF THE VERY BEST HARDWARE.
ORNAMENTAL BALCONY FRONTS.
BALCONY COLUMNS AND BRASS RAILINGS FOR BOXES.
STAGE CARPETS CUT AND FITTED TO ORDER.
CAMP STOOLS, MUSIC STANDS, UMBRELLA RACKS.
Send for prices on anything required.

FOUNDRY: BRIDGEPORT, CONN.

FACTORY, FIRST, GRAND and LITTLE WATER STS., BROOKLYN.
OFFICE, 257 FIRST ST., FOOT OF GRAND ST.. BROOKLYN, N. Y.

Infantry Hall, **Wm.** H. Teel, manager; rental, one night $60, three $150; share also; license included. Size of stage, 30x30; no scenery.

Academy of Music, Geo. H. Slade, manager; **seating capacity, 1,330; rental, one night** $30. **Size of stage,** 34x35; number sets scenery, 10.

Howard Hall; seating capacity, 1,000.

Dramatic Hall; seating capacity, 750.

People's Theatre.

Washington Varieties.

Theatre Comique.

WAKEFIELD, 850. R R., Narragansett Pier. **Wright's Opera House, Silas Wright,** manager. Newspaper: Times (Fri.)..... Hotel: **Donohue,** regular rates, $2 (special also).

WARREN, 4,000. R. R., Prov., **Warren & Bristol.** Armory Hall, F. E. Dana, manager; **seating capacity,** 400; rental, one **night** $12, **three** $30, license included. **Size of stage,** 15x18; **size of** proscenium opening, 10x18; **height from stage to grooves, 10; number sets scenery, 6; bill poster,** Wm. Carey; **rates per sheet, 4c ; theatrical teamster,** Samuel Munroe. Newspaper: **Gazette** (Fri.)......Hotels: **Cales,** special rates, $1.25; Fessenden, special **rates, $1.25.**

WESTERLY, 8,500. **R. R., N. Y.,** Prov. **& Boston.** Armory Hall, Eugene B. Pendleton, manager; seating capacity, 800; rental, **one night** $22, **three** $48, **license included.** Size of stage, 21x48; **size of** proscenium opening, 15x20; **traps, 1; leader of orchestra,** Wm. Yeager; **bill posters,** Edwin Maxson & **C. D. Lampson; theatrical teamster,** W. L. Bradford. Newspapers: Narragansett Weekly (Th.), **News** (Sat.)......Hotels: Dixon, regular rates, $2 to $2.50 (special also), Leonard, **regular rates, $2 (special also).**

WOONSOCKET, 20,000. R. R., N. Y. & New England ; **Providence & Worcester. Music** Hall, **T. S.** Luce, manager; seating capacity, 1,400; **rent or share; license, yearly. Size of stage,** 60x60; **size of** proscenium opening, 21x30; **height from stage to grooves, 16; height from stage to rigging loft,** 25; **depth under stage, 8; traps, 3; number sets scenery,** 17; **leader of orchestra,** R. Williams; **stage carpenter,** Wm. Wilson; **bill poster, John** Hackett; **number of sheets can accommodate, 1,800; rates per sheet, 5c.; theatrical teamster,** H. T. Wales. **Newspaper:** daily, Reporter........Hotels: Woonsocket, **special** rates, $1.50 to $1.75; Monument, special rates, $1.50 to $2.

Harris's Hall ; seating capacity, **1,100** ; rental, one night $25 to $35. **Size of stage,** 24x30 ; **number sets scenery, 1.**

SOUTH CAROLINA.

ABBEVILLE, 2,000. **R. R., Columbia** & Greenville. **Knox's Hall, J. Knox, manager ;** rental, one night $15 ; license, $5; no scenery ; bill poster, Mannal McKeller. **Newspapers :** Medium (Th.), Press and Banner (Wed.)........Hotels : **Branch,** regular rates, $2 (special also); Cater.

AIKEN, 2,000. R. R., South **Carolina.** Lyceum Hall, **S. Ott, agent; seating capacity, 500;** rental, one night $15, three $35; license, $5. Size of stage, **22x39; size of** proscenium opening, 10x19; height from stage to grooves, 11½; height from stage **to rigging loft,** 12; depth under stage, 6; number sets scenery, 3. Newspapers : Recorder (Tn.), advertising rates per inch, $1; Journal **and** Review (Wed.), per inch, $1.. ...Hotels : **Ashby, special rates, $1.50 to $2;** Busch, **special** rates, $1.50 to $2.

ANDERSON COURT HOUSE, 3,000. **R. R.,** Columbia & Greenville. Masonic Hall, J. **A. Brock,** managers; seating capacity, 500; rental, one night $10; **no** scenery; bill poster, **W. H. Thompson.** Newspapers: Intelligencer (Th.), Journal (Fri.)......Hotel: Waverly. **regular** rates, $2 (special also).

CAMDEN, 1,500. **R. R.,** South **Carolina.** Town Hall; seating capacity, 750. **Newspapers:** Journal (Th.), Gazette (Th.)......**Hotel:** De Kalb, regular rates, $2 (special also).

CHARLESTON, 38,000. R. R., Charleston & Sav.; Col. & Augusta; N. Eastern. Owens' Academy of Music, John E. Owens, manager; Brooks & Dickson New York representatives; seating capacity, 1,000; rental, one night $100, three $300, license included. Size of stage, 40x35; size of proscenium opening, 55x25; height from stage to grooves, 16; height from stage to rigging loft, 25; depth under stage, 6; traps, 3; number sets scenery, 15; musical director, C. Halls; bill poster, F. L. O'Neill; number sheets can accommodate, 1,200; rates per sheet, 4c.; theatrical teamsters, Picket & Jackson. Newspapers: daily, News & Courier, advertising rates per inch, $1.50; Mercury, per inch, $1.50... Hotels : Charleston, special rates, $3; Pavilion, special rates, $1.75 to $2.50; Waverly, special rates, $2 to $2.50.

German Freundschaftsbund Hall, Oskar Archel, manager; seating capacity, 700; rental, one night $30, three $75; license, $5. Size of stage, 25x46; number sets scenery, 4.

Hibernian Hall; seating capacity, 1,500,

CHESTER, 2,000. R. R., Charlotte, Columbia & Angusta. Coleman Hall, John K. Coleman, manager; seating capacity, 400; rental, one night $17; license included; fair stock scenery; bill poster, Thomas Lee. Newspapers: Bulletin (Fri.), Reporter (Th.)......Hotels : Nicholson, regular rates, $2 (special also); Central.

COLUMBIA, 15,000. R. R., South Carolina ; Greenville Columbia & Charlotte. Opera House, Eugene Cramer, manager; seating capacity, 800; rental, one night $60 ; share also; license included. Size of stage, 35x50 ; size of proscenium opening, height 26; height from stage to rigging loft, 46; depth under stage, 10; traps, 2 ; number sets scenery, 36; scenic artist, Eugene Cramer; stage carpenter, C. Dooley; bill poster, Clarence W. Taylor; number sheets can accommodate, 1,000; rates per sheet, 8c.; theatrical teamster, McKnight. Newspapers : daily, Register ; advertising rates per line, 25c.; Yeoman, advertising rates per line, 25c .....Hotels : Wright, special rates, $1 to $1.45; Grand Central, special rates, $1 to $1.75; Columbia, special rates, $1 to $1.75. Parker Hall; seating capacity, 450.

FLORENCE, 4,000. R. R., Cheraw & Darling.; Northeastern S. C.; Wilm., Col. & Aug. Barringer's Hall, J. L. Barringer, manager; seating capacity, 700; rental, one night, $10, three $30; license, $5. Size of stage, 15x25; size of proscenium opening, 12x25 ; height from stage to grooves, 11 ; height from stage to rigging loft, 12; depth under stage, 2; number sets scenery, 4; leader of orchestra, Frank Reimer ; bill poster, Chas. H. Barringer; number sheets can accommodate, 21. Newspapers: Times (Th.); advertising rates, $1 per inch......Hotels: Central, special rates, $1.25 ; Jacobi, regular rates, $2 (special also).

GAFFNEY CITY, 1,500. R. R., Atlantic & Charlotte Air Line. Wood's Hall, J. N. Wood, manager; seating capacity, 400. Size of stage, 16½x30; size of proscenium opening, 9x16. Newspaper: Carolinian (Wed.). ....Hotel: City.

GEORGETOWN, 2,600. R. R., Georgetown & Lanes. Walker's Hall, Le Grand G. Walker, manager; seating capacity, 500; rental, one night $25, three $60 ; share also ; license, $5. Size of stage, 20x36; size of proscenium opening, 9x28; height from stage to grooves, 12; height from stage to rigging loft, 20; depth under stage, 6; number sets scenery, 3; scenic artist, Eugene Cramer. Newspapers : weekly, Times (Sat.), Enquirer (Wed.) . ....Hotels : Georgetown, special rates, $1.50; Commercial, special rates, $1.50; Ponti, regular rates, $2 (special also).

GREENVILLE, 8,000. R. R., Columbia & Greenville; Richmond & Danville. Gilreath's Opera House, Gilreath & Cauble, managers; seating capacity, 800; rental, one night $50, three $125; share also; license included. Size of stage, 30x33; full set scenery; bill poster, Opera House. Newspapers : daily, News; weekly, Mountaineer (Wed.).. ... Hotels : Mansion, regular rates, $2 (special also); Exchange, regular rates, $2 (special also); Central, Commercial.

Clyde's Hall; seating capacity, 300.

NEWBERRY, 4,000. R. R., Columbia & Greenville. Opera House, W. L. Johnson, manager; seating capacity, 700; share only. Size of stage, 24x35; number sets scenery, 6; bill poster, George Boland. Newspaper : Herald (Th.), News (Fri.), Observer (Th.)...... Hotels: Newberry, regular rates, $2 (special also); Simmonds, Parker, Blease.

Thespian Hall, Schumpert & Johnson, managers; seating capacity, 350; rental, one night, $25, three $60; share also; license included. Size of stage, 22x30; number sets scenery, 5.

ROCK HILL, 1,000. R. R., Charlotte, Columbia & Augusta. Roddey's Hall, W. L. Roddey, manager; seating capacity, 600; fair stock scenery. Newspaper: Herald (Th.)........ Hotel: Globe.

SPARTANBURG, 6,000. R. R., Charlotte & Atlanta; Sp. & Union. Opera House, W. L. Johnson, manager; seating capacity, 600; rental, share only; license included. Size of stage, 21x47; size of proscenium opening, 19x24; height from stage to grooves, 14; height from stage to rigging loft, 21; depth under stage, 6; traps, 1; number sets scenery, 8; leader of orchestra, W. L. Johnson; bill poster, W. L. Johnson; number of sheets can accommodate, 150; rates per sheet, 4c. Newspapers: Herald (Wed.); advertising rates, $1 per inch; Spartan (Wed.), $1 per inch......Hotels: Merchant, special rates, $1.50 to $2; Windsor, special rates, $1.50 to $2; Central, special rates, $1 to $1.50. Court House; seating capacity, 200.

SUMTER, 3,000. R. R., Wilmington, Columbia & Augusta; Central of South Carolina. Music Hall, D. J. Auld; seating capacity, 600; rental, one night $25, three $65; share also; license included. Size of stage, 27x35; size of proscenium opening, 11x23; height from stage to grooves, 11; height from stage to rigging loft, 22; depth under stage, 4; number sets scenery, 7; bill poster, Mose Harrison; number of sheets can accommodate, 250; rates per sheet, 5c; theatrical teamster, Geo. F. Epperson. Newspapers: Advance (Sat.), advertising rates per inch, $1; Watchman and Southron, advertising rates per inch, $1......Hotel: Jervey House, special rates, $150.

UNION, 1,500. R. R., Spartansburg, Union & Columbia. Nicholson's, Wm. A. Nicholson, manager; seating capacity, 450; rental, one night $15, three $35; license, $5. Size of stage, 17x35; number sets scenery, 4. Newspaper: Times (Fri.)......Hotel: Union, regular rates,—— (special also).

WINNSBORO, 1,800. R. R., Charlotte, Columbia & Augusta. Thespian Hall, H. P. Miller, manager; rental, one night $10, three $18; license, $5; share also; bill poster, manager of Hall. Newspapers : tri-weekly, News and Herald......Hotels: Winnsboro, regular rates, $2 (special also); Brown's.

TENNESSEE.

BRISTOL, 9,000. R. R., East Tenn., Va. & Ga.; Norfolk & Western. Conway Hall; seating capacity, 400; rental, one night $10; no scenery; bill poster, Wm. Thomer. Newspapers: Courier (Th.), Reporter (Sat.)......Hotels: Virginia, regular rates, $2 (special also); Thomas', Nicklar.

Reynolds' Hall; seating capacity, 500.

BROWNSVILLE. 4,500. R. R., Louisville & Nashville. Mann's Opera House, M. L. Marrell, manager; seating capacity, 900; rental, one night $35, three $65; share also; license included. Size of stage, 25x50; number sets scenery, 6; bill poster, Opera House. Newspapers: Democrat (Fri.), States and Bee (Fri.)......Hotels: Exchange, regular rates, $2 (special also); Galt.

Lee Hall, Johnson & Winster, managers; seating capacity, 300; rental, one night $10.

CHATTANOOGA, 25,000. R. R., Nashville & Chattanooga; St. Louis, West. & Atlantic; East Tennessee, Virginia & Georgia; Memphis & Charleston; Alabama & Great Southern. James Hall, Stoops & Bro., managers; seating capacity, 900; rental, one night $50, three $125. Size of stage, 29x52; height from stage to grooves, 8; depth under stage, 4; bill poster, H. E. Stoops; number sheets can accommodate, 1,000; rates per sheet, 4c.; theatrical teamsters, L. J. Sharp & Co. Newspapers: daily, Times, advertising rates per inch, $2; Commercial, advertising rates per inch, $2......Hotels: Florentine, special rates, $1.50 to $2; Stanton, regular rates, $3 (special also); Read, regular rates, $3 (special also).

Poss Hall; seating capacity, 500.

CLARKSVILLE, 8,000. R. R., Louisville & Nashville. Elger's Opera House, James T. Wood, manager; seating capacity, 700; rental, one night $40, three $90; share also; license included. Size of stage, 30x50; size of proscenium opening, 19x27; height from stage to grooves, 15; height from stage to rigging loft, 21; depth under stage, 4; traps, 1; number sets scenery, 12; bill poster, Opera House; number of sheets can accommodate, 800; rates per sheet, 3c.; theatrical teamster, Opera House. Newspapers: semi-weekly, Tobacco Leaf (Tu. & Fri.) advertising rates per line, 7½c.; weekly, Chronicle (Sat.), Democrat (Fri.). ....Hotels: Franklin, special rates, $1.50 to $2; Washington.

Franklin Hall, A. B. Harrison, manager, seating capacity, 1,000; rental, one night $25; license, $13.75. Size of stage, 22x44; number sets scenery, 8.

CLEVELAND, 3,000. R. R. East Tenn., Va. & Ga. Opera House, Walter Cragmilis, manager; **seating capacity, 600; rental, one night $12;** license. $8.50; share also. **Size of stage, 42x25; number sets scenery, 3; bill poster, Opera House.** Newspapers: Banner (Fri.), Herald (Th.)......Hotels: Ocoll, regular rates, $2 (special also); Hatcher, Ocean.

COLUMBIA, 7,000. R. R., Louisville & Nashville; G. S.; Nashville & Florence; Duck River & N. G. Grand Opera House, E. P. Seary, manager; seating capacity, 856; rental, **one night $75, three $200;** share also; license included. Size of stage, 50x60; size of proscenium opening, 30x40; height from stage to grooves, 22; height from stage to rigging loft, 35; depth under stage, 12; traps, 3; number sets scenery, 14; leader of orchestra, E. Yoest; scenic artist, James S. Hutton; stage carpenter, George A. Dooley; bill poster, George A. Dooley; theatrical teamster, James Buchanan. Newspapers: Herald (Fri.), advertising rates, $1 per inch; Democrat (Th.), advertising rates, $1 per inch... ...Hotels: Bethel, special rates, $1.50; Guest, special rates, $1; Nelson, regular rates, $2 (special also).

Hamner's Hall; W. C. Sheppard, manager; seating capacity, 400; rental, one night $15; license, $19.25; share also. Size of stage, 18x20; number sets scenery, 5.

COVINGTON, 1,700. R. R., Chesapeake, Ohio & South Western. Covington Theatre, S. A. Smith, manager; seating capacity, 400; rental, one night $12, three $30; share also; license included. Size of stage, 16x24; size of proscenium opening, 13x16; height from stage to **rigging loft, 25;** depth under stage, 6; **leader** of orchestra, R. W. Sanford; stage carpenter, **C. McFadden**; bill poster, **C. McFadden**; theatrical teamster, Newton McFadden. **Newspaper:** Record (Fri.), advertising rates, **5c. to** 10c. per line.... ... Hotels Bledso, special rates, $1 to $2; Lockey, **special rates, $1 to $2; Mathe's,** special rates, $1 to $2.

South Street Hall, W. B. Hill, manager; seating capacity, 400; rental, one night $10, three $20; share also. Size of stage, 14x18; no scenery.

DYERSBURG, 1,600. R. R., Chesapeake, **Ohio** & South Western. Sawyer Hall, John Sawyer, manager; seating capacity 500; rental, one night $7. Size of stage, 16x40; number sets scenery, 5. Newspaper Gazette (Sat.)........Hotels: Sugg, regular rates, $2 (special also); Lenox.

FAYETTEVILLE, 2,500. R. R., Nashville, Chattanooga & St. Louis. Bright Hall, **Thos.** J. McGarory, manager; seating capacity, **400;** rental, one night $10; license, $13. **Size** of stage, 20x35; full set scenery. Newspapers: Express (Wed.), Observer (Th.)......... Hotels: Pettey, regular rates, $2 (special also); McElroy.

GALLATIN, 4,000. **R. R., Louisville & Nashville.** Tompkins Opera House, W. R. Tompkins, manager; seating capacity, 700; rent or share; license yearly. **Size** of stage, 27x48; full **set** scenery; ; bill poster, Lewis **Tompkins.** Newspaper: Examiner (Sat.), Tennessean (Sat.)......Hotels Sindle, regular rates, **$2** (special also), Sumner

Lucas Hall; seating capacity, **500; rental, one** night $15. Size of stage, 16x32; number sets scenery, 4.

HUMBOLDT, 2,300. R. R., Louisville & Nashville; Mobile & Ohio. Shaw's Hall, seating **capacity, 300; rental, one night $10, three $25; license,** $6. Size of stage, 12x29; no **scenery; bill poster, Richard Cross. Newspaper: Reporter (Sat.)......Hotels: Dunlop,** regular rates, **$2 (special also).**

JACKSON, 10,000. R. R., Illinois Central, Mobile & Ohio. Kings Opera House. Burned March 17, 1884. Bill posters, Jester & Co. Newspapers; Dispatch (Fri.), Tribune and Sun (Sat.).... ..Hotels: Robinson, regular rates, $2 (special also); Merchants, Lancaster, Cavnes.

Tomlin's Hall; seating capacity, 500.

KNOXVILLE, 25,000. R. R., East Tenn., Va. & Ga.; Louisville & Knoxville. Staub's Opera House, Fritz Staub, manager; seating capacity, 900; rental, one night $50, three $125, license included Size of stage, 30x50; size of proscenium opening, 28x27; height from stage to grooves, 11, height from stage to rigging loft, 23½; depth under stage, 5½; traps, 1 ; number sets scenery, 12; leader of orchestra, Chas. Cronch; bill poster, Jno. Holsey; number of sheets can accommodate, 300 to 500 ; rates per sheet, 3c.; theatrical teamsters, Wm. Bell & Bro. Newspapers : daily, Tribune, advertising rates, per inch, 50c.; Chronicle, advertising rates, per inch, 50c.... ..Hotels: Lamar, special rates, $1.50; Hattie, special rates, $2; Alpin, regular rates, $2 (special also).

LEBANON, 3,500. R. R., Nashville, Chattanooga & St. Louis. Masonic Hall, D. C. Williams, manager; seating capacity, 650; rent or share. Size of stage, 25x50; number sets scenery, 6; bill poster, manager of hall. Newspapers: Herald (Th.), Register (Th.)...... Hotels: Hardy, regular rates, $2 (special also); Union.

MEMPHIS, 34,000. R. R., Chesapeake, Ohio & S. W.; Kansas City, Spr. & M.; Louisville & Nashville; Mem. & Charleston; Mem. & Little Rock; Mississippi & Tenn. Leubrie Theatre, Frank Gray, manager; Brooks & Dickson, New York representatives; seating capacity, 1,200; rental, one night, $150. Size of stage, 45x57; height from stage to grooves, 20; height from stage to rigging loft, 40; depth under stage, 10½; bill poster, E. J. Norton; theatrical teamster, P. M. Patterson. Newspapers: daily, Appeal, Ledger, Avalanche, Scimeter ....Hotels : Peabody, special rates, $3; Clarendon, special rates, $3; Gaston.

Memphis Theatre; seating capacity, 1,500; rental, one night $125. Size of stage, 32x65; full set scenery.

Greenlaw Opera House; seating capacity, 800.

Assembly Hall, James Sutton & Co., managers; seating capacity, 500.

Hallenberg Hall.

People's Theatre.

MURFREESBORO, 5,000. R. R., Nashville, Chattanooga & St. Louis. Opera House, J. R. Osborne, manager; seating capacity, 1,000; rental, one night $50, three $100; share also. license included. Size of stage, 36x45; number sets scenery, 15. Newspaper: News (Fri.),.....Hotels: Miles, regular rates, $2; Reading.

NASHVILLE, 45,000. R. R., Louisville & Nashville; Nashville, Ch. & St. L. Masonic Theatre, J. O. Milson, manager; seating capacity, 900; rental, one night, $63; share also; license included. Size of stage, 34x56; height from stage to grooves, 15; height from stage to rigging loft, 20; depth under stage, 7; bill posters, Bentley & Clark; theatrical teamsters, Robertson & Cunningham. Newspapers: daily, American, Banner, World. ......Hotels: Maxwell, regular rates, $3 (special also); Scott, Commercial.

Grand Opera House, J. O. Milson, manager; seating capacity, 1,200; rental, one night $15; license included; share also. Size of stage, 58x58; height from stage to grooves, 18 ; height from stage to rigging loft, 35 ; depth under stage, 7 ; bill poster, Bentley & Clark; theatrical teamster, Robertson & Cunningham.

Buckingham Theatre (variety), Charles Redmond, manager; seating capacity, 800.

Odd Fellows Hall ; seating capacity, 400.

PULASKI, 3,500. R. R., Louisville & Nashville. Antoinette Hall, E. R. Sumpter, manager; seating capacity, 800; rental, one night $25, three $60; share also; license included. Size of stage, 35x50; number sets scenery, 6; bill poster, manager of hall. Newspaper: Citizen (Th.)......Hotels: St. Giles, regular rates, $2 (special also).

SHELBYVILLE, 4,500. R. R., Nashville, Chattanooga & St. Louis. Frierson's Hall, A. Frierson, manager; seating capacity, 400; rental, one night $6.50, three $17.50. Size of stage, 20x30; full sets scenery. Newspapers: Commercial (Fri.), Gazette (Th.)......Hotels: Evans, regular rates, $2 (special also); Barksdale.

JUST COMPLETED!

Garland Opera House,

J. P. GARLAND, - - Proprietor and Manager.

WACO, TEXAS.

POPULATION OF WACO, 12,000.

SEATING CAPACITY OF OPERA HOUSE, 1,000.

HANDSOMEST AND COSIEST IN TEXAS.

ELEGANT DRESSING ROOMS AND FINEST SCENERY,
HEATED WITH HOT AIR FURNACE AND COOLED WITH
STEAM BLOWERS.

Chairs Upholstered in Leather, with Tilting Backs and Largest Size.

EVERYTHING NEW, FIRST CLASS AND COMPLETE.

Opened in October 1884.

I BELONG TO NO CIRCUIT.   DO MY OWN BOOKING.

Waco is just half way between Austin and Fort Worth. Managers of attractions wishing dates or information in reference to Waco, should address all communications personally to the undersigned.

J. P. GARLAND, Proprietor and Manager

Garland Opera House, Waco, Texas.

SOMERVILLE, 2,000. R. R., Memphis & Charleston. Leach's Opera House, W. H. Leach, manager; seating capacity, 300; rental, one night $15. three $35; share also; license included. Size of stage, 18x24; number sets scenery, 8. Newspaper: Reporter and Falcon (Wed.)..... Hotels: Eagle, regular rates, $2 (special also); Weatherby.

UNION CITY, 1,000. R. R., Mobile & Ohio; Nashville, Chattanooga & St. Louis. Williams' Opera House, Theo. Williams, manager. Newspapers: Anchor (Fri.), Our Country (Fri.)......Hotels: Metropolitan, regular rates, $2 (special also); Southern

TEXAS.

AUSTIN, 10,000. R. R., Austin & N. W.; Houst. & Tex. Cent.; Inter. & Gt. Nor. Millet's Opera House, C. F. Millet, manager; seating capacity, 1,100; share only; license yearly. Size of stage, 42x60; height from stage to grooves, 16; height from stage to rigging loft, 25; depth under stage, 7; bill posters, Jas. Griffith & Co.; theatrical teamster. Monroe Miller. Newspapers: daily, Dispatch, Statesman......Hotels: Brunswick, special rates, $1.50 to $3; Avenue, special rates, $1.50 to $3: Raymond, special rates, $1.50 to $3; Southern.

Little's Opera House (variety), W. F. Little, manager.

Smith's Opera House.

BASTROP, 2,500. R. R., Colorado. Casino Hall, A. Schultze, manager; seating capacity, 300; rental, one night $15; license $2.50. Size of stage, 20x20; no scenery. Newspaper: Advertiser (Sat.)...... Hotels: Hoppe, regular rates, $2 (special also); Taylor.

BEAUMONT, 3,500. R. R., Texas & New Orleans; Sabine & East Texas. Crosby Opera House, John B. Goodhue, manager; seating capacity, 800; rental, share and rent; license, $4. Size of stage, 20x32; size of proscenium opening, 15x36; depth under stage, 7; traps, 1; number sets scenery, 7; stage carpenter, James Ory. Newspaper: Enterprise (Sat.), advertising rates per inch, $1......Hotel: Crosby, regular rates, $2 (special also).

BELTON, 4,000. R. R., Missouri Pacific, Gulf, Colorado & Santa Fe. Belton Opera House, Harry Fracker, manager; seating capacity, 750; rental, one night $25; license, $4; share also. Size of stage, 24x32; full set scenery; bill poster, Opera House. Newspapers: Journal (Th.), Reporter (Tu.)......Hotels: Avenue, regular rates, $2 (special also); City.

BONHAM, 3,000. R. R., Texas Pacific. Russell's Hall, J. R. Russell & Co., managers; seating capacity, 600; rental, one night $25; license, $4. Size of stage, 18x22; full set scenery; bill poster, Tom Benson. Newspapers: daily, Advocate; weekly, News (Fri.) ......Hotels: Burney, regular rates, $2 (special also); Crockct.

Alexandre Hall, C. S. Hewitt, manager; seating capacity, 300; license, $10. Size of stage, 12x25; number sets scenery, 2.

BREMOND, 1,700. R. R., Houston & Texas Central. Parr Hall, E. Parr, manager; seating capacity, 500; rental, one night $20, three $30 : license, $14. Size of stage, 16x18; fair stock scenery. Newspaper: Sentinel......Hotels: Bremond, regular rates, $2 (special also); Bryan.

BRENHAM, 5,000. R. R., Houston & Texas Central; Gulf, Colorado & Santa Fe. Grand Opera House, A. Simons, manager; seating capacity, 600; rental, one night $25, three $75; license, $10. Size of stage, 25x40; full set scenery; bill posters, Henderson & Williams. Newspapers: daily, Banner. Hotels : Central, regular rates, $2 (special also); McIntyre.

Eldridge's Hall, seating capacity, 400.

BRYAN, 5,000. R. R., Houston & Tex. Central. Tabor's Opera House, John Q. Tabor, manager; seating capacity, 450; rental, share only. Size of stage, 25x25; height from stage to rigging loft, 10; depth under stage, 3½; traps, 1; number sets scenery, 7; leader of orchestra, Ed. Khroli; bill poster, J. Q. Tabor; number of sheets can accommodate, 300. Newspapers: Pilot (Fri.), Enterprise (Wed.)......Hotels : Stoddard, special rates.

$1 to $1.50); Central, special rates, $1 to **$1.50**; **Walden,** special rates, $1 to $1.50; Washington.

Academy of Music; seating capacity, **400.**

CALVERT, 3,000.   R. R., Houston & Texas Central.   Casimir's Opera House, J. P. Casimer, manager; seating capacity, 500; rental, one night $20; license included.   Size of stage, 28x30; size of proscenium opening, 26x24; height from stage to grooves, 14; height from stage to rigging loft, 16; depth under stage, 3; traps, 1; number sets scenery, 5; scenic **artist,** L. Sals; bill poster, J. Abrams; rates per sheet, 4c.   Newspaper: Courier (Th.) ......**Hotels :** Park, special rates, $1.50; St. Charles, special rates, $1.50.

CLARKSVILLE, **2,800.   Texas & Pacific.   Opera House, T. S.** Rand, manager.   Newspapers: Standard (Fri.), **Times (Fri.)......**Hotels: **Donohoe, regular** rates, $2 (special also); **Stanley.**

City **Hall, Bailey &** Johnson, managers; seating capacity, 350; **rental, one** night $10, three $18; share also.   Size of stage, 16x25; full set scenery; bill posters, **managers** of hall.

CLEBURNE, 3,000.   R. R., Gulf, Colorado & Santa Fe.   Opera House, Charles Benton, manager; seating capacity, 1,000.   Size of stage, 20x20.   Newspapers: Chronicle (Fri.), Telegram (Wed.)......Hotel : Pennington, regular rates, $2 (special also).

Gaiety Music Hall (variety), C. Shacklett, manager.

COLUMBIA, 1,000.   **R. R.,** International & Gt. Northern; Columbia Opera House.   ..Hotel: **Payne,** regular rates, $2 (special also).

COLUMBUS, 3,000.   R. R., Galveston, Harrisburg & San Antonio.   Ilse's Hall, Henry Ilse, manager; seating capacity, 250; rental, one night, $15; license $10.   Size of stage, **16x** 20; number sets scenery, 3; bill poster, **Henry** Henderson.   Newspaper: Citizen (Th.) ..Hotels: Woolton, regular rates, $2 (special also); Thornton, Tooke.

CORSICANA, 5,000.   R. R., Houston & Texas Central; Texas & St. Louis.   Opera House, J. G. Campbell, manager ; seating capacity, 600; rental, one night $25 ; license, $10; share also.   Size of stage, 20x30; full set scenery; bill poster, Revare.   Newspapers: Courier (Sat.), Journal (Th.), Observer (Fri.), Messenger (Tu.)   Hotels: Commercial, regular rates, $2.50 to $3 (special also); Molloy, McKay.

Court House; seating capacity, 300.

CROCKETT, 4,000.   **R. R. International** & Great Northern.   **Crockett Opera House, W. B. Page, manager ;** seating capacity, 600; rental, one night **$25;** three, $62.50; license, **$7.50; share also.**   Size of stage, 22x50 ; number sets **scenery, 7.**   Newspaper: Patron **(Th.).......**Hotels : Hall, regular rates, $2 (special also).

Stubbfield's.

CUERO, 3,000.   R. R., Gulf, Western Texas & Pacific.   Turner Hall, C. Kosebiel, manager; seating capacity, 400;   rental, one night $25; three $60; license $4.   Size of stage, 20x30; full set scenery; bill poster, manager of hall.   Newspaper : Bulletin **(Fri.),** Star (Fri.)......Hotels : Muti, regular rates, $2 (special also); Steder, Gulf.

DALLAS, 37,000.   R. R., Hous. & Tex. Cen.; Tex. & Pac.; D. & W.; **G. T.;** Gulf., Col. & Santa Fe.; Mo. Pac.; Transcontinental.   Coliseum Theatre, Basco & De Beque, managers; 'seating capacity, 900; rental, one night $110, three $250; license included.   Size of stage, 45x30; size of proscenium opening, 21x20; height from stage **to** grooves, 17; height from stage to rigging loft, 36; depth under stage, 12; traps, 3; number sets scenery, **25;** leader of orchestra, George G. Stock; scenic artist, J. H. Connolly; stage carpenter, C. C. W. Dobins; bill poster, Walter Scott; number sheets can accommodate, 30; theatrical teamster, W. P. Siler.   Newspapers: daily, Herald, advertising rates per line, 20c.; Times, per line, 20c., weekly, Herald **(Sat.),** per line, 20c......Hotels: St. George, special rates, $1; Windsor, special rates, $2.

Opera House, Charles Benton, manager; seating capacity, 1,050; share only.   Size of stage, 40x35; size of proscenium opening, 40x30; height from stage to grooves, 22; height from stage to rigging loft, 80; depth under stage, 10; traps, 3; number sets scenery, 15; bill poster, Charles Benton; number sheets can accommodate, 1,000; rates per sheet, 3½c.

Craddock's Opera House, L. Craddock, manager; seating capacity, 600; rent or share; license, $4. Size of stage, 20x24; full set scenery.

Lyceum Theatre (variety).

DENISON, 11,000. R. R., Hous. & Texas Central; Mo. Pac. McDougall Opera House, J. B. McDougall, proprietor ; Fred. A. O'Maley, manager ; seating capacity, 1,200 ; rental, one night $65, three $100 ; license, $3.75 ; share also. Size of stage, 35x50 ; size of proscenium opening, 18x25 ; height from stage to grooves, 18 ; height from stage to rigging loft, 30 ; depth under stage, 5 ; traps, 3 ; number sets scenery, 20 ; leader of orchestra, W. A. **Everitt**; scenic artist, L. **Sala** ; stage carpenter, E. H. Glanding : bill poster, manager ; number of sheets can accommodate, 600 ; rates per sheet, 4c. ; theatrical teamster, T. Murphy. Newspapers: daily, Herald, News, advertising rates, $1.50 per inch ; Journal, advertising rates, $1.50 per inch ; weekly, Gazetcer (Sun.), advertising rates, $1 per inch........**Hotels:** McDougall, special rates, $1.75 to $2 ; Colonade.

DENTON, 4,900. R. R., Missouri Pacific. Opera House, Wm. J. Austin, manager. Newspaper : Chronicle **(Sat.)**......Hotel : Clyde, regular rates, $2 (special also).

EL PASO, 8,000. **R. R.,** Atchison, Topeka & Santa Fe; Mexican Central; Southern Pacific; Galveston. Harrisburg & San Antonio. National Theatre, N. S. Newland, manager ; seating capacity, 1,000 ; rental one night $75, three $175 ; share also. Size of stage, 24x30 ; number sets scenery, 8 ; bill poster, Harry Boyd. Newspapers : daily, Times ; semi-weekly, Lone Star; weekly. Herald **(Sun)**......Hotels; Central, Pierson, Windsor.

Pictorial Theatre (variety), Boyd & Swain, managers.

Coliseum Theatre.

FT. WORTH, 18,000. R. R., Mo. Pac. ; Tex. & Pac.; Houston & Tex. Cen. Opera House, Charles Benton, manager; seating capacity, 1,250; rental, share only. Size of stage, 35x 60; size of proscenium opening, 40x32; height from stage to grooves, 22; height from stage to rigging loft, 80; depth under stage, 9; traps, 1; number sets scenery, 12; bill poster, Charles Benton; number sheets can accommodate, 1,000; rates per sheet, 3½c.; theatrical teamsters, Kanfman & Dillon. Newspapers : daily, Gazette; advertising rates per inch, $2; Mail, advertising rates per inch, $1......Hotels : Pickwick, special rates, $2; Lindell, special rates, $1.50; Mansion, special rates, $1.50.

Evans' Hall, R. C. Evans, manager; seating capacity, 500; rental, one night $25, three $60; license, $10; fair stock scenery.

"My Theatre," George B. Holland, manager.

Theatre Comique.

GAINESVILLE, 5,000. R. R., Mo. Pac. Perry's Opera House, R. N. Brown, manager; seating capacity, 800; rental, one night $40; share also; license included. Size of stage, 30x49; full set scenery; bill poster, Jord Luper. Newspapers : daily, Hesperian, Independent... Hotels : Lindsay, regular rates $2 (special also); Laclede, regular rates $2 (special also).

GALVESTON. 30,000. **R. R.,** Gulf, Col. & S. Fe; Int. Gt. N.; Texas &'Mexican. Harmony Hall Theatre, Alt. **Wels,** manager; seating capacity, 900; rental, one night $50, three $125. Size of stage, 35x60; size of proscenium opening, 23x28; height from stage to grooves, 15½; height from stage to rigging loft, 33; depth under stage, 8; number sets scenery, 10. Newspapers: daily, Civilian, Reporter, News, Print... ..Hotels: Tremont, regular rates, $3 (special also); Girardin, regular rates, $3 (special also); Washington, regular rates, $2 (special also).

Tremont Opera House, Henry Greenwale, manager; seating capacity, 1,000; rental, one night $90; share also; full set scenery.

Grand Central Theatre, John **Bell, manager.**

Turner Hall; seating capacity, 800.

Casino Hall; seating capacity, 400.

GEORGETOWN, 2,700. R. R., International & Great Northern. Georgetown Opera House, **W. C.** Pfaeffle, manager; seating capacity, 600. Size of stage, 30x38; number sets scenery, 5; bill poster, Joe Richards. Newspaper: Record (Sat.)......Hotels; Slaton, special rates. $1.25 to $2; City, $1.25 to $2.

HEMPSTEAD, 2,500. R. R., Houston & Texas Central. Rankin's Hall, Henry L. Rankin, manager; seating capacity, 450; rental, one night $15, three $37.50; license, $3 to $5; number sets scenery, 2. Newspaper: Courier (Sat.).. ..Hotels: Sloan, regular rates, $2 (special also); Exchange, City.

HENDERSON, 1,600. R. R., International & Grt. Northern. Harris Hall, D. W. Bagley. manager; seating capacity, 200; rental, one night $15; number sets scenery, 8. Newspapers : News (Tu.), Times (Th.) ....Hotels: Southern, regular rates $2 (special also); Henderson.

HONEY GROVE, 2,000. **R. R., Texas & Pacific.** Opera House, Percy C. Cox, manager; seating capacity, 400; rental, **one night $15, three $35;** share also. Size of stage, 18x18; size of proscenium **opening, 14x22; height from** stage to grooves, 11; traps, **1:** number sets scenery, 8; **musical director,** Percy **C. Cox;** scenic artist, W. R. Burnett; **bill poster, W. R.** Burnett; rates per sheet, **4c.** Newspapers : Independent (Fri.), advertising rates per inch, 50c. to $1; Simon (Th.), per inch, 50c to **$1......**Hotels: Ligon, special rates, $1 to $1.50; Commercial, special rates, $1; Smith, special **rates, $1.**

Dramatic Hall, Jas. H. Robnett, manager; seating capacity, 250; rental, one night **$15;** license, $2.50. Size of stage, 18x28; no scenery.

HOUSTON, 30,000. R. R., Gal., Har. & San A.; Gulf, Col. & Santa Fe; Houston & Texas Central; Houston, E. & W. T.; International & Great Northern; Texas Western. Pillot's Opera House, J. E. Rielly, manager; seating capacity, 1,000; share only. Size of stage, 30x50; size of proscenium opening, 30x27; height from stage to grooves, 14½; height from stage to rigging loft, 20; depth under stage, 7; traps, 3; number sets scenery, 25; leader of orchestra, Al. Herb; stage carpenter, A. B. Wolf; **bill** poster, F. E. Rielly; theatrical teamster, J. C. Baldwin. Newspapers : **daily,** Post, Journal........Hotels : Capitol; special rates, $1.50; Hutchins, special rates, **$1.50;** Globe, special rates, $1.25; Tremont.

Gray's Opera House, L. E. Spencer, manager; seating capacity, 900; rental, one night $50, three $125; license, $10; share also. Size of stage, 35x83; number sets scenery, 20.

Turner Hall; seating capacity, 500.

HUNTSVILLE, 2,200. International & Great Western. **Huntsville Opera House, John K.** Wiley, manager; seating capacity, 600; rental, one night **$25; three $70.** Size of stage, 22x50; size of proscenium opening, 18x22; height from stage to grooves, **12; height from stage to** rigging loft, 14; depth under stage, **3;** number sets scenery, **6; bill poster, R. S.** Rabher. Newspaper : **Item** (Th.)....Hotel: **Cox,** special rates, **$1; Gibbs, regular rates, $2.50** (special **also).**

JEFFERSON, 8,000. R. R., Missouri Pacific; Texas & Pacific. Taylor's Opera House, John Hoban, manager; seating capacity, 500; rental, one night $35, license included. Size of stage, 20x22; bill poster, Opera House. Newspapers: daily, Jimpleente; weekly, Wide-Awake (Sat.)......Hotels: Excelsior, regular rates, $2 (special also); Brooks, Central.

Mardigras Hall; seating capacity, 1,000.

LA GRANGE, 1,500. R. R., Galveston, Harrisburg & San Antonio. La Grange Casino, H. Studemann, manager; seating capacity, 800; rental, one night $15. Size of stage, 18x20; number sets scenery, 3; bill poster, James Oakes. Newspapers: Journal (Th.), Slovan (Th.) .Hotels: Farquhar, regular rates, **$2** (special also); **Miller,** La Grange, Newmann.

LAMPASAS, 4,500. R. R., Gulf, Colorado & Santa Fe. Barnes Opera House, P. S. Jenkins, manager; seating capacity, 400; rental, one night $35 to $50; **share** also; license included. Size of stage, 25x32; size of proscenium opening, 12x20; height from stage to grooves, **12; height** from stage to rigging loft, 16; depth under stage, **3;** traps, 1; number sets scenery, **7;** bill poster, Opera House; number sheets can accommodate, 200; rates per sheet, 4c. Newspapers: daily, Dispatch, advertising rates per line, 7c.; weekly, Dispatch (Th.); Eagle (Fri.).. ...Hotels: Globe, special rates, $2; San Geronimo, special rates, $2; Park, special rates, $2.

Rubenstein's Opera House, A. R. Rubenstein, manager; seating capacity, 600; rental, one night $25, three $50; license, $3; share also. Size of stage, 25x40; number sets of scenery, 6.

LAREDO, 8,500. R. R., Mexican National; Rio Grande & Pecos. Laredo Opera House, J. C. Hart, manager; seating capacity, 1,000; rental, one night $30, three $75; license, $3; share also. Size of stage, 20x30; number sets scenery, 4; bill poster, Opera House. Newspapers: El Députado (Mon.), El Horizonte (Sat.), Times (Th.)... ...Hotels: Laredo, regular rates, $2.50 (special also): Wilson, Commercial.

City Hall; seating capacity, 700.

LONGVIEW, 3,000. R. R., International & Gt. Western; Texas & Pacific; Longview & Sabine Valley; Galveston, Sabine & St. Louis. Rempert Opera House, F. T. Rempert, manager; seating capacity, 400; rental, one night $25, three $60; license, $4; share also. Size of stage, 22x26; fair stock scenery; bill poster, Opera House. Newspapers: Democrat (Fri.), Surprise (Sat.), New Era (Sat.)......Hotel: Commercial, regular rates, $2 (special also); Central, Spencer.

Davis Hall, E. R. Davis, manager; seating capacity, 300; rental, one night $15, three $35; number sets scenery, 5.

LULING, 2,000. R. R., Galveston, Harrisburg & San Antonio. Bowers' Hall, G. T. Bowers, manager; seating capacity, 700; rental, one night $15, three $25; license, $3.50; share also. Size of stage, 16x40; number sets scenery, 3. Newspaper: Signal (Th.)...... Hotels: Thomas, regular rates, $2 (special also); Luling, Sunset.

MARSHALL, 7,500. R. R., Texas & Pacific. Mahone's Opera House, L. H. Norwood, manager; seating capacity, 1,000; rental, one night $25, three $60; license, $4.20; share also. Size of stage, 30x40; full set scenery; bill poster, Jim Johnson. Newspapers: tri-weekly, Herald; weekly, Messenger (Fri.)......Hotels: Capitol, regular rates, $2 to $2.50 (special also); King's.

McKINNEY, 3,500. R. R., Houston & Texas Central; Missouri Pacific. Shain's Opera House, Jesse Shain, manager; share only. Size of stage, 55x24; bill poster, Opera House. Newspapers: Black Waxy (Fri.), Democrat (Th.), Enquirer (Sat.)......Hotels: Foote, regular rates $2 (special also); McKinney.

MEXIA, 2,000. R. R., Houston & Tex. Central. Opera House, Hansen, Sorensen & Swinburn, managers; seating capacity, 500; rental, one night $25, three $60; license, $4. Size of stage, 22x50; number sets scenery, 6; bill poster, A. Denning; Newspapers: Ledger (Fri.). Hotels: McKay, regular rates, $2 (special also); Beckham, European.

MINEOLA, 3,000. R. R., Mo. Pacific; Tex. & Pacific; International & Great Northern. Caspary's Opera House, Julius A. Caspary, manager; seating capacity, 700; rental, one night $35, three $75; share also; license, $4. Size of stage, 20x25; size of proscenium opening, 12x30; height from stage to grooves, 12; height from stage to rigging loft, 14; number sets scenery, 6; leader of orchestra, E. D. Burress; scenic artist, G. T. Cofield; bill poster, G. T. Cofield; number of sheets can accommodate, 200; rates per sheet, 4; theatrical teamster, Mell Allen. Newspapers: Monitor (Sat.), advertising rates, $2 per inch. Hotels: McDaniel, special rates, $1.50; Boon Good, special rates, $2; Depot, special rates, $1.50.

NAVASOTA, 2,500. R. R., Houston & Texas Central; Gulf, Col. & Santa Fe. Smith's Opera House, P. A. Smith, manager; seating capacity, 600; rental, one night $25, three $50; share also. Size of stage, 22x47; size of proscenium opening, 12x20; height from stage to grooves, 13; height from stage to rigging loft, 23; depth under stage, 4; number sets scenery, 2; scenic artist, Le Mair. Newspaper: Tablet (Fri.), advertising rates, 10c. per line......Hotels: Exchange, special rates, $1.20; Camp's, special rates, $1.25; Geisel or Tirado, special rates, $1.50; Nixon, special rates, $1.

Miller's Hall, Miller Bros., managers; seating capacity, 300; rental, one night, $15; license, $7.50. Size of stage, 54x30; full set scenery.

PALESTINE, 4,500. R. R., International & Great Northern. Temple Opera House, Ozment & Sawyers, managers; seating capacity, 400; rental, share and rent. Size of stage, 36x28; size of proscenium opening, 14x18; height from stage to grooves, 11; height from stage to rigging loft, 6; depth under stage, 5; traps, 3; number sets scenery, 8; leader of orchestra, N. Back; stage carpenter, James Freedell; bill poster, C. B. Sawyers; number of sheets can accommodate, 500; rates per sheet, 4c.; theatrical teamster, Clint Bowden. Newspapers: Advocate (Wed.), advertising rates, $1.50 per inch; news (Fri.),

BLAKE OPERA HOUSE,

JOHN T. VAUGHAN,   -   -   -   MANAGER.

RACINE, WIS.

Population of Racine, 30,000; seating capacity of Opera House, 1,400

LIGHTED THROUGHOUT WITH ELECTRICITY.
Stage as Complete as Money can make it.
Twelve Handsomely-furnished Dressing-Rooms.
UNRIVALED in Decoration and Furnishing.
Supplied with Every Modern Improvement.
FINEST OPERA HOUSE IN THE WEST.

--- A ---

Limited Number of Attractions Played

AND

NONE BUT THE BEST.

Racine is a busy, manufacturing city, on the Chicago & North Western and Chicago, Milwaukee & St. Paul Railways, sixty-two miles from Chicago and twenty-three from Milwaukee, with a population given to liberal patronage of legitimate amusement enterprises.

(FOR DESCRIPTION SEE "THEATRE DIRECTORY—*Wisconsin*.")

advertising rates, $1 50 per inch ... Hotels: Watson, special rates, $1.25 to $1.50; International, special rates, $1.50 to $2; Sterne's, $2 to $2.50.

Palestine Market Hall; seating capacity, 400; rental, one night, $20; license, $10; fair stock scenery.

PARIS, 6,000. R. R., Texas & Pacific. **Babcock Opera House**, John H. Walker, manager; seating capacity, 1,000; rental, one night $75, three $185; share also. Size of stage, 25x45; size of proscenium opening, 14x28; height from stage to grooves, 12; height from stage to rigging loft, 6; depth under stage, 5; traps, 2; number sets scenery, 6; bill poster, J. F. Griner; number of sheets can accommodate, 300; rates per sheet, 4c.; theatrical teamsters; Paris Street Railway Co. Newspapers: North Texan (Fri.), Free Tongue (Th.)......Peterson, special rates, $1 50 to $1 75; Berke, special rates, $1 50

Paris Opera House, Bywater & Book, managers; seating capacity, 450; rental, one night $25, three $60; license, $10; share also. Size of stage, 15x35; fair stock scenery.

ROCKDALE, 3,000. R. R., International & Great Northern. Randle & Porter's Opera House, Randle & Porter, managers; seating capacity, 550; rental, one night $30, three $75; share also; license, $6. Size of stage, 20x30; size of proscenium opening, 12x20; height from stage to grooves, 10; depth under stage, 3; number sets scenery, 6; bill poster, Opera House. Newspaper: Messenger (Th.)......Hotels: Mundine, special rates, $1.25; Compton, special rates, $1,

SAN ANGELA, 1,500. Olympic Theatre, Billy Arlington, manager. Newspaper: Times-Enterprise (Th.)

SAN ANTONIO, 35,000. R. R., Galveston, Harris. & San Antonio; Southern Pacific; International & Great Northern. Turner Opera House, Tom W. Howard, manager; seating capacity, 1,000; rental, one night $50, three $150; license, $4; share also. Size of stage, 35x50; size of proscenium opening, 16x25; height from stage to grooves, 12; height from stage to rigging loft, 30; depth under stage, 6; traps, 2; number sets scenery, 4; leader of orchestra, Frank Hall; scenic artists, Cod & Mon; stage carpenter, Frank Hesse; bill poster, Tom W. Howard; number of sheets can accommodate, 2,500 to 3,000; rates per sheet, 4c.; theatrical teamster, John Draper. Newspapers: daily, Express, advertising rates per line, 10c.; Light, advertising rates per line, 10c.; Times, advertising rates per line, 10c......Hotels: Menger, special rates, $3; Maverick, special rates, $2; Vance, special rates, $1.50.

Casino Theatre; seating capacity, 700; rental, one night $35; license, $10. Size of stage, 20x30; full sets scenery.

Alamo Literary Hall; seating capacity, 500

Vaudeville Theatre, Hart & Martin, managers.

New Grand Opera House.

SHERMAN, 12,000. R. R., Houston & Tex. Cent.; Tex. & Pac. Sherman Opera House, C. W. Batsell, manager, seating capacity, 900; rental, one night $50, three $125; license, $3.75. Size of stage, 30x60; size of proscenium opening, 15x40; height from stage to grooves, 9; height from stage to rigging loft, 18; depth under stage, 7, traps, 1; number sets scenery, 12; stage carpenter, I. Lindsey; bill poster, C. W. Batsell. Newspaper: daily, Democrat, advertising rates, 50c. per inch; per line, 5c......Hotels: Binkly, regular rates, $2.50 (special also); Beiler, regular rates, $2.50 (special also).

SULPHUR SPRINGS, 3,500. R. R., Missouri Pacific. Sulphur Spring's Opera Hall. G. H. Wilson, manager; seating capacity, 400; rent or share; license, $3. Size of stage, 40x25; number sets scenery, 6; bill poster, manager of hall. Newspaper: Gazette (Th.)......Hotels: Whitworth, regular rates, $2 (special also); Sour Walls, City.

TEMPLE, 3,500. Gulf, Colorado & Santa Fe; Missouri Pacific. Brockham Theatre, B. M. Blythe, manager; seating capacity, 300; rental one night $10; license, $2. Size of stage, 12x25; number sets scenery, 4; bill posters, Shuttles & Griswell. Newspaper: Times (Sat.) .....Hotels: City, Temple.

McAlvey & Wortham's Hall; rental one night $20; share also. Size of stage, 25x30; full set scenery.

21

TERRELL, 3,700. R. R., Houston & Texas; Texas & Pacific. Clement's Opera House. Joseph Whomes, manager; seating capacity, 700; rental, one night, $17.50; share also. Size of stage, 25x50; number sets scenery, 8; bill poster, Opera House. Newspapers: Star (Sun.), Times (Fri.). ..Hotels : Terrell, regular rates, $2 (special also); City.

TEXARKANA, 6,000. R. R., St. Louis, Iron Mountain & Southern; Texas & Pacific. Ghio's Opera House, A. L. Ghio, manager; seating capacity, 1,000. Size of stage, 21x22; full set scenery; bill poster, James Doyle. Newspaper: daily, News........ Hotels: Bennefield, regular rates, $2 (special also); Marquand, regular rates, $2 (special also).

TYLER, 6,000. R. R., International & Great Northern; Texas & St. Louis. Albertson Opera House, Albertson Bros., managers; seating capacity, 800; rental, one night $40, three $100; license, $4; share also. Size of stage, 28x60; number sets scenery. 6 ; bill poster, Ben McFadden. Newspapers : daily, Courier; weekly, Reporter (Sat.)... Hotels : Ferguson, regular rates, $2 (special also); City.

City Hall, A. J. Swaum, manager; seating capacity. 400; rental, one night $5; license, $12.50; no scenery.

VICTORIA, 4,000. R. R., Gulf, West, Texas & Pacific; N. Y., Texas & Mexican. Casino Hall, Dr. Max Novitz, manager; seating capacity, 500; rental, one night $20, license, $3; fair stock scenery. Newspaper: Advocate (Sat.)......Hotels: Exchange, regular rates. $2 (special also); Thompson.

WACO, 13,000. R. R., Tex. & St. L.; Mo. Pa.; Houston & Tex. Central. Garland Opera House, J. P. Garland, manager [see p. 314]; seating capacity, 1,000; rental, share only; license included. Size of stage, 33x50; size of proscenium opening. 20x24; height from stage to grooves, 16; height from stage to rigging loft, 21½; depth under stage, 8; traps, 2; number sets scenery, 14; leader of orchestra, Prof. Daggett; scenic artists, Noxon, Albert & Toomey; stage carpenter, George Butler; bill poster, Louis Sternkorb; number of sheets can accommodate, 500; rates per sheet, 4c; theatrical teamster, Orand Brothers, Newspapers : daily, Day, Examiner.   Hotels : McClelland, special rates, $1.25 to $1.75; Pacific, special rates, $1.50 to $2.

McClelland Opera House, Sanford Johnson, manager.

Horse-Shoe Theatre, Holland & Bell, managers.

WAXAHATCHIE, 3,000. R. R., Houston & Texas Central. Waxahatchie Opera House. H. A. McMillan, manager; seating capacity, 450; license, $4; fair stock scenery; bill poster, Opera House. Newspapers: Enterprise (Fri.), Mirror (Wed.)......Hotel: Rogers' regular rates, $2 (special also).

WEATHERFORD, 5,000. R. R., Texas & Pacific. Weatherford Opera House, R. H. Font, manager; seating capacity, 900; rental, one night $35, three $75; license, $4. Size of stage, 25x62; number sets scenery, 10; bill poster, D. O. Haynes. Newspapers: Sun (Th.), Times (Sat.)... ...Hotels: Carson & Lewis', regular rates, $2 (special also); Mc-Fall's, Tennessee, City.

VERMONT.

BARRE, 2,500. R. R., Central Vt. Town Hall, L. F. Aldrich, manager; seating capacity, 600; rental, one night $12, three $25. Size of stage, 20x27; size of proscenium opening, 14x22; height from stage to grooves, 12; height from stage to rigging loft, 15; depth under stage, 3; traps, 1; number sets scenery, 3; stage carpenter, Frank Nichols; bill poster, Frank Nichols; theatrical teamster, McCrillis. Newspaper: Enterprise (Wed.)......Hotels: Octagon, special rates, $1; Gale's, regular rates, $2 (special also).

BELLOWS FALLS, 4,000. R. R., Central Vermont, (Rut. Div.); Cheshire, V. & Val.; Conn. Riv Union Hall, O. B. Arms, manager ; (Ed. Murphy, local sharing manager); seating capacity, 600; rental, one night, $15, three $40; share also; no license. Size of stage, 40x20; size of proscenium opening, 20x25; height from stage to grooves, 14; height from stage to rigging loft, 18; depth under stage, 3; traps, 1; number sets scenery, 6; bill posters, Ed. Murphy, T. F. Kinney; number sheets can accommodate, 250 ; rates per sheet, 4c.; theatrical teamster, Ed Murphy. Newspapers: Times (Th.), advertising rates $1 per inch; Transcript (Th.), advertising rates $1 per inch...... Hotel: Town, special rates, $1.50.

BENNINGTON, 6,000. R. R., Troy & Boston; Bennington & Rutland; Leebourn Springs. Free Library Hall, C. C. Kimball, manager; seating capacity, 500; rental, one night $12, three $30. Size of stage, 11x41; size of proscenium opening, 18: , height from stage to grooves, 13; depth under stage, 3½; number sets scenery, 5; leader of orchestra, R. O. Goldsmith; bill poster, R. O. Goldsmith; theatrical teamsters, J. H. Loring & Co. Newspapers: Banner (Th.), Reformer (Th.)......Hotels: Putnam, special rates, $1.50; Starkey, special rates, $1.50.

BRATTLEBORO, 6,000. R. R., Conn. River; New London Northern; Vermont Valley. Town Hall; seating capacity, 1,000; rental, one night $20, three $50. Size of stage, 25x27; number sets scenery, 4; bill poster, F. W. Green, jr. Newspapers: Phœnix (Fri.), Reformer (Fri.) ...Hotels: Brooks, regular rates, $2 (special also); Brattleboro, American.

Crosby Opera House, E. Crosby & Co., managers; seating capacity, 650; rental, one night $15 to $20; fair stock scenery.

BURLINGTON, 18,000. R. R., Central Vermont; Burlington & Lamoille. Howard's Opera House, K. B. Walker, manager; seating capacity, 1,200; rental, one night $75; three $200; share also. Size of stage, 74x33; size of proscenium opening, 20½x31½; height from stage to grooves, 20; height from stage to rigging loft, 31; depth under stage, 7½; traps, 2; number sets scenery, 10; leader of orchestra, Bert Waterman; scenic artist, Joseph Piggott; stage carpenter, C. Austin; bill poster, C. Saunders; number of sheets can accommodate, 300; rates per sheet, 4c., theatrical teamster, Wm. Lane. Newspapers: daily, Free Press, advertising rates per inch, $1; weekly, Clipper (Th.), advertising rates per inch, 75c ......Hotels: Ewart's, special rates, $1 to $1.50; Van Ness, special rates, $1.50 to $2; American, special rates, $1.25 to $2.

City Hall, L. J. Smith, manager; seating capacity, 1,200; rental, one night $20, three $45, license included. Size of stage, 22x26; full set scenery.

DANVILLE, 2,000. R. R., St. Johnsbury & Lake Champlain. Town Hall, Charles Ingalls, manager; seating capacity, 300; rental, one night $3, three $6. Size of stage, 10x16 depth under stage, 2; bill poster, Charles Ingalls. Newspaper: weekly, North Star...... Hotels: Elm, special rates, $1; Simmonds', special rates, $1.

HARTFORD, 3,000. R. R. Central Vermont; Woodstock. Pease's Hall, O. W. Pease, manager; seating capacity, 600; rental, one night $10, three $25. Size of stage, 22x20; number sets scenery, 6; leader of orchestra, H. C. Moore; newspapers: Landmark (Fri.); Sun (Fri.)......Hotel: Pease's, special rates, $1.25.

MANCHESTER, 2,000. R. R. Bennington & Rutland. Music Hall, F. H. Orvis, manager; seating capacity, 500; rental, one night $15, three $37.50; share also; no license. Size of stage, 20x30; full set scenery; bill posters, Walt & Hard. Newspaper: Journal (Th.)...... Hotels: Taconsit, regular rates, $2 (special also); Equinox, Manchester.

MILTON, 2,000. R. R. Central Vermont. Village Hall, C. B. Pratt, manager; seating capacity, 350; rental, one night $8, three $15. Size of stage, 12x30; size of proscenium opening, height 8½; depth under stage, 5; number sets scenery 1; leader of orchestra, C. A. Pratt; theatrical teamster, Joseph Perry......Hotels: Austin, special rates, $1, Elm Tree, special rates, $1.

MONTPELIER, 4,000. R. R. Central Vermont; Montpelier & Wells River. Capital Hall, J. J. Pratt, manager; seating capacity, 800; rental, one night $20, three $45. Size of stage, 30x25; size of proscenium opening 12x23; height from stage to grooves, 11½; height from stage to rigging loft, 14; depth under stage, 8; traps, 1; number sets scenery, 6 leader of orchestra, W. Hadley; stage carpenter, Will I. Pratt; bill poster, J. J. Pratt; number sheets can accommodate, 100; rates per sheet, 4c.; theatrical teamster, O. Shambo. Newspapers: Argus (Wed.), Watchman (Wed.)..... Hotels: Montpelier, special rates, $1.25; Pavilion, special rates, $1.50.

POULTNEY, 3,000. R. R., Delaware & Hudson Canal Co. Goodrich's Hall, R. W. Goodrich, manager; seating capacity, 600; rental, one night $15; no license. Size of stage,

30x40; number sets scenery, 8; bill poster, manager of hall; theatrical teamster, Jesse Howe. Newspaper: Journal (Fri.)......Hotels: Poultney, regular rates, $2 (special also); Beaman's, Brown's.

RUTLAND, 12,000. R. R., Benn. & Rutland; Central Vt.; Del. & Hud. Canal Co. Opera House; seating capacity, 900; rental, one night $40; share also. Size of stage, 25x54; height from stage to grooves, 17; height from stage to rigging loft, 17; depth under stage, 8; number sets scenery, 10; bill poster, M. P. Kingsley; theatrical teamster, R. Hubbard. Newspapers: daily, Herald; weekly, Courier (Wed.), Review (Fri), Standard (Fri.).....Hotels: Bates, regular rates, $2 (special also); Bardwell, regular rates, $2 (special also); Brunswick, regular rates, $2 (special also).

Town Hall, S. Hayward, manager; seating capacity, 1,000; rental, one night $15, three $30; license, $2 to $3. Size of stage, 15x30; no scenery.

SWANTON, 2,000. R. R , Central Vermont; St. Johnsburg & Lake Champlain. Bullard's Hall, H. H. Bullard, manager; seating capacity, 475; rental, one night $5; bill poster, Mort. Pierce. Newspapers: Courier (Sat.), Sentry (Th.) .....Hotels: Central, regular rates, $2 (special also); American.

ST. ALBANS, 8,000. R. R , Central Vt.; Missisquol. Waugh's Opera House, G. F. Huntington, manager; seating capacity, 700; share also; license included. Size of stage, 24x40; size of proscenium opening, 16½x24; height from stage to grooves, 11½; height from stage to rigging loft, 16½; depth under stage, 10; traps, 1; number sets scenery, 7; leader of orchestra, Calno Baker; stage carpenter, H. E. Moore; bill poster, H. E. Moore. Newspapers: daily, Messenger; weekly, Record (Sat.)......Hotels: Welden's, special rates, $1.50 to $2; American, $1.25 to $1.50.

Armory Hall, G. W. Barnes, manager; seating capacity, 600; rental, one night $15; no scenery.

ST. JOHNSBURG, 6,000. R. R., St. Johnsburg & Lake Champlain; Passumpsic. Town Hall, L. B. Flint, manager; seating capacity, 700; rental, one night $10; no license. Size of stage, 12x19; no scenery; bill poster, L. B. Flint; theatrical teamster, William Horn. Newspapers: Caledonian (Th.), Index (Th.)......Hotels: St. Johnsburg, regular rates, $2 (special also); Avenue.

Academy Hall; seating capacity, 1,100.

VERGENNES, 2,000. R. R., Central Vermont. Academy Hall, J. G. Hindes, manager; seating capacity, 400; rental, one night $10, three $20, license included; bill poster, John Karssaw; theatrical teamster, Louis Mott......Hotels: Stevens, American, Franklin.

School House Hall, J. G. Hindes, manager; seating capacity, 400; rental, one night $10; no scenery.

WINOOSKI, 4,000. R. R., Central Vermont. Corporation Hall, T. C. Kennedy, manager; seating capacity, 350; rental, one night $10, three $22.50. Size of stage, 20x15; number sets scenery, 1......Hotel: Stevens, regular rates, $2 (special also).

WINDSOR, 2,500. R. R., Central Vermont; Connecticut River. Town Hall, Chas. Sherman, manager; seating capacity, 535; rental, one night $20. Size of stage, 17x20; no scenery. Newspaper: Journal (Sat.)......Hotel: Windsor, regular rates, $2 (special also).

VIRGINIA.

ALEXANDRIA, 16,000. R. R., Virginia Midland; Washington, Ohio & Western ; Alexandria & Fredericksburg. Lannon's Opera House, J. M. Hill & Co., managers; seating capacity, 1,300; rental, one night $50, three $100; license included. Size of stage, 31x60; size of proscenium opening, 15x30, height from stage to grooves, 15; height from stage to rigging loft, 20; depth under stage, 5 ; number sets scenery, 8 ; leader of orchestra, Prof. Stein ; scenic artist, C. Lamb, of Washington. D. C.; stage carpenter, W. Gibson, bill posters, Summers & Allen ; number sheets can accommodate, 2,000 ; rates per sheet, &c.; theatrical teamster, Chas. Adams. Newspapers: Daily, Gazette; advertising rates per inch, $2; weekly, City Item (Sat.)........Hotels: Braddock, special rates, $1.25 to $1.50; Tontine, special rates, $1.50; Mansion.

Armory Hall, C. J. W. Summers, manager; seating capacity, 600; rental, one night $25, three $60; license, $7.25. Size of stage, 25x45; size of proscenium opening, 13x35; height from stage to grooves, 14; height from stage to rigging loft, 25; depth under stage, 4; traps, 1; number sets scenery, 4; scenic artist, C. Lamb.

BRISTOL, 4,000. R. R., Norfolk & Western; East., Tenn., Va. & Ga. Conway Hall, J. C. Conway, manager; seating capacity, 500; rental, one night $10; bill poster, Wm. Raider. **Newspaper: News (Tu.)**......Hotels: **Virginia**, Thomas.

CHARLOTTESVILLE, 5,500. R. R., Chesapeake & Ohio; Virginia Midland. Town Hall, seating capacity, 500; bill poster, Peter Diggs. Newspapers: Chronicle (Fri); Republican (Wed.)......Hotels: Central, regular rates, $2 (special also); Parish, regular rates, $2 (special also); Monticello.

CULPEPPER, 2,000. R. R., Virginia Midland. Academy of Music, C. J. Rixey, manager; seating capacity, 500; rental, one night $15, three $30; license, $6. Size of stage, 25x25; number sets scenery, 2; bill poster, John R. Williams; rates per sheet, 4c. Newspapers: Exponent (Fri.); Times (Fri)......Hotels: Waverly, regular rates, $1.50 (special also); Mrs. **Hicks.**

DANVILLE, 10,000. R. R., Richmond & Danville; Danville & New River; Danville, Markaville & S. Western. Pace's Opera House, J. E. Catlin, manager; seating capacity, 800; rental, one night $30, three $70; license, $9.25; share also. Size of stage, 14x25; full set scenery; bill poster: Opera House. Newspapers: daily, Register; weekly, Review (Sun.); Times (Fri.)......Hotels: Arlington, regular rates, $2 (special also); Windsor, regular rates, $2 (special also). Masonic Hall, seating capacity, 400.

FREDERICKSBURG, 5,500. R.R., Rich.,Fred. **& Potomac**; Potomac, Fredericksburg & Piedmont. Fredericksburg Hall; seating capacity, 500; rental, one night $25, three $60. Size of stage, 13x25; number sets scenery, 4; bill poster, W. T. Hicks. Newspaper: semi-weekly, News, True Standard, Star ..Hotel: Exchange, regular rates, $2 (special also).

GORDONSVILLE, 2,000. R. R., Chesapeake & Ohio; Virginia Midland. Opera House. Newspaper: Gazette (Wed.)... ...Hotels: St. Johns, regular rates, $2 (special also).

HAMPTON, 3,000. R. R., Chesapeake & Ohio. Soldiers' Home Theatre, Capt. P. F. Woodfin, manager; seating capacity, 900. Size of stage, 75x30; number sets scenery, 18; bill poster, manager of theatre. Newspaper: Monitor (Sat.)......Hotels: Barnes, regular rates, $2 (special also); Old Point, Hampton, Hygeia.

Greble Hall, J. Hefflefinger, manager; seating capacity, 500; rental, one night $10, three 18. Size of stage, 12x30; no scenery.

HARRISBURG, 3,000. R. R., Baltimore & Ohio. Masonic Hall, W. M. Rellenour, manager; seating capacity, 300; rental, one night $5; license $8; no scenery. Newspapers: Register (Th.), Spirit of the Valley (Sat.)......Hotels: Spottswood, regular rates, $2 (special also); Revere, regular rates, $2 (special also).

LEXINGTON, 3,500. R. R., Baltimore & Ohio; Richmond & Allegheny. Deaver's Opera House, T. H. Deaver, manager; seating capacity, 600; rental, one night $20, three $50, license included. Size of stage, 16x30; size of proscenium opening, 12x20; leader of orchestra, Joseph A. Penington. Newspapers: Gazette (Th.), Enterprise (Th.) .....Hotels: Horton, National, Campbell. Pettigrew.

LYNCHBURG, 23,000. R. R., New York & Western; Virginia Midland; Richmond & Allegheny. Opera House, J. H. Simpson, manager; seating capacity, 900; rental, one night $65, two $110. Size of stage, 30x36; size of proscenium opening, 25x34; height from stage to grooves, 18; height from stage to rigging loft, 40; traps, 3; number sets scenery, 10; stage carpenter, Sam'l Thurman; bill posters, Dunbar & Simpson; rates per sheet, 4c.; theatrical teamster, Wm. T. Clemmins. Newspapers: daily, News, Virginian, Advance. ......Hotels: Arlington, special rates, $1.50 to $2; Norvell, special rates, $1.50 to $2; Lynch, **Relay.**

Holcombe Hall, Wm. Bond, manager; seating capacity, 600; rental, one night, $20; license, $8. Size of stage, 18x25; full set scenery.

NORFOLK, 40,000. R. R., Norfolk Southern; Nor. & Va. Beach; Norfolk & Western; Old Dominion S. S. Co.; Bay Line Steamers. Van Wyck's Academy of Music, H. D. Van Wyck, manager; Brooks & Dickson, New York representatives; seating capacity, 1,350; rental, share only. Size of stage, 50x68; size of proscenium opening, 28x35; height from stage to grooves, 20; height from stage to rigging loft, 50; depth under stage, 8; traps, 7; number sets scenery, 15; musical director, Prof. Bergess; stage carpenter, Frank H. White; bill poster, S. Skelley; number sheets can accommodate, 2,000; rates per sheet, 4c.; theatrical teamster, Norfolk Transfer Co. Newspapers : daily, Landmark, advertising rates per inch, 75c; Virginian, per inch, 75c.; Ledger, per inch, 75c......Hotels : Atlantic, special rates, $1.75; Percell, special rates, $1.50; Manslon, $1.75.

Opera House; seating capacity, 1,500.

PETERSBURG, 23,000. R. R., Norfolk & Western; Petersburg; Richmond & Petersburg. Academy of Music; seating capacity, 700; bill poster, Cris. Quincy. Newspapers: daily, Index-Appeal, Mail.. ....Hotels: Newton, regular rates, $2.50 (special also); Jarrett's, regular rates, $4 (special also); Bollingbroke.

PORTSMOUTH, 14,000. R. R., Seabord & Roanoke; Str. to Baltimore. Oxford Hall, James Burke, manager; seating capacity, 700; rental, one night $25, three $60; share also; license, $3. Size of stage, 20x24; depth under stage, 4; number sets scenery, 4. Newspapers : daily, Times, Enterprise......Hotels : American, regular rates, $2 to $2.50 (special also); Ocean, Peabody.

RICHMOND, 80,000. R. R., Chesapeake & Ohio; Richmond & Allegheny; Richmond & Danville; Richmond & Petersburg; Richmond, Fred. & Pot. Richmond Theatre, Brooks & Dickson, New York representatives; seating capacity, 1,460; rental, one night $85 share also. Size of stage, 52x60; height from stage to grooves, 17½; height from stage to rigging loft, 80; depth under stage, 16; bill poster, Theatre; theatrical teamster, James Sweeny. Newspapers: daily, Dispatch, State, Whig......Hotels: Ford's, regular rates, $2.50 to $3 (special also) ; Exchange, regular rates, $2.50 to $3 (special also); Ballard's.

Virginia Opera House. R. B. Lyne, manager; seating capacity, 850; license, yearly. Size of stage, 25x60; full set scenery.

Mozart Hall, C. L. Seigel, manager; seating capacity, 850. Size of stage, 24x45.

Assembly Hall; seating capacity, 900; rental, one night $40.

Theatre Comique, Captain W. W. Putnam, manager.

STAUNTON, 8,500. R. R., Balt. & Ohio; Chesapeake & Ohio. Staunton Opera House, Robert Hill, manager; seating capacity, 1,086; rental, one night $25, three $55; license, $10.50. Size of stage, 24x30; number sets scenery, 7; bill poster, W. Glenn. Newspapers: daily, Dispatch, State, Whig. ....Hotels: Virginia, regular rates, $2 (special also); Kalarama, American.

Masonic Hall, Robert Hill, Jr., manager; seating capacity, 500; rental, one night $15, three $35; license, $10.50; share also.

WINCHESTER, 3,000. R. R., Balt. & Ohio. Court House Hall; seating capacity, 400; rental, one night $12; bill poster, Charles Pomate. Newspapers: News (Fri.), Times (Wed.)......Hotels: Taylor, regular rates, $2 (special also); Hart, regular rates, $2 (special also).

WEST VIRGINIA.

CHARLESTOWN, 6,000. R. R., Balt. & Ohio; Shenandoah Valley. Cotton Opera House, Albert Peyser, manager; seating capacity, 600; rental, one night $20. Size of stage, 18x30; number sets scenery, 7; bill poster, S. Beach. Newspapers: daily, Call; weekly, Gazette (Wed.)......Hotels: Hale, St. Albert, Madison.

CLARKSBURG, 3,500. R. R., Baltimore & Ohio; Clarksburg, Weston & Glenville. City Hall, Smith, Brown & Co., managers; seating capacity, 350; rental, one night, $15, three $30; no license. Newspapers : News (Sat.), Telegram (Sat.).. ..Hotels: Commercial, regular rates; $2 (special also); Walker, regular rates; $1.50 (special also); St. Charles.

FAIRMONT, 3,500. R. R., Baltimore & Ohio. Opera House, J. M. Lazzell, manager; seating capacity, 400; rental, one night $6, three $15; share also. Size of stage, 20x30; number sets scenery, 4. Newspapers: Index (Fri.), West Virginian (Fri)..... Hotels: Mountain City, regular rates; $2 (special also); Continental, Hough.

HUNTINGTON, 5,000. R. R., Chesapeake & Ohio. Harvey's Opera Hall, H. C. Harvey & Co., managers; seating capacity, 700; rental, one night $15, three $45; share also. Size of stage, 20x25; full set scenery; bill poster, Harry Potts. Newspapers: Advertiser, (Sat.), Argus (Th.), Commercial (Sat.). Hotels: Continental, regular rates; $2 (special also); Merchants'.

MARTINSBURG, 6,300. R. R., Balt. & Ohio; Cumberland Valley. Fuller's Hall, W. L. Fuller, manager; seating capacity, 850. Size of stage, 18x43; bill poster, Phil. Rhodes. Newspapers: Herald (Sat.); Independent (Sat.), Statesman (Th)......Hotels: St. Clair, regular rates, $2 (special also); Continental, regular rates, $2 (special also).

King Street Hall; seating capacity, 400.

NEW CUMBERLAND, 1,300. R. R., Cleveland & Pittsburgh. Town Hall, I. H. Atkinson, manager; seating capacity, 500; rental, one night $5, three $15. Size of stage, 15x30; number sets scenery, 2. Newspapers: Independent (Wed.)......Hotel: Virginia, regular rates, $2 (special also).

PARKERSBURG, 9,000. R. R., Balt. & Chicago; Cin., Wabash & Balt.; Ohio River. Academy of Music, Chas. P. Haney, manager; seating capacity, 900; rental, one night $50; share also. Size of stage, 30x42; number sets scenery, 20; bill poster, Thomas Huff. Newspapers: daily, Journal; weekly, Sentinel (Sat.), Standard (Fri.)..... Hotels: Central, regular rates, $2 (special also); Swan's, American.

Opera House, F. R. Rose, manager; seating capacity, 850; rental, one night $20, three $50; share also. Size of stage, 20x24; number sets scenery, 11.

Columbia Opera House, W. H. Wolfe, manager; seating capacity, 600; rental, one night $25; license, $20; share also; number sets scenery, 5.

VOLCANO, 2,500. R. R., Laurel, York & S. Hill. Volcano Music Hall, C. M. Magill, manager; seating capacity, 450; rental, one night $15. three $30; share also; no license. Size of stage, 17x25; number sets scenery, 3; bill poster, R. Williams. Newspaper: Walking Beam (Fri.)......Hotel: Silcott, regular rates, $1.50 (special also).

WHEELING, 35,000. R R., Balt. & Ohio; Cleve. & Pitts.; Ohio River; Panhandle; Pitts., Wash. & Cent. Ohio. Opera House, W.S. Foose, manager; seating capacity, 850; rental, one night $60, three $150. Size of stage, 25x60; size of proscenium opening, 30x30; height from stage to grooves, 18; height from stage to rigging loft, 36; depth under stage, 12; traps, 2; number sets scenery, 30; leader of orchestra, Louis Vaas; stage carpent r, Wm. Richardson; bill poster, Henry Shallcross; number of sheets can accommodate, 2,000; rates per sheet, 3c; theatrical teamster, Shallcross. Newspapers: daily, Register, Intelligencer.   .Hotels: McLure, regular rates, $2 to $3 (special also); St. James, regular rates, $2 to $3 (special also); Stanner, special rates, $1.50 to $2; Howell, special rates, $1 to $1.50.

Washington Hall, C. Y. Lucas, manager; seating capacity, 900; rental, one night $40. Size of stage, 35x52; full set scenery.

Academy of Music. Thos. B. Gill, manager.

WISCONSIN.

APPLETON, 1,200. R. R., Chic. & N. Western; Milwaukee & Northern; Mil., Lake Shore & Western. Appleton Opera House, E. A. Erb, manager; seating capacity, 900; rental, one night $40, three $100; share also; license yearly. Size of stage, 44x20; number sets scenery, 10; bill poster, Opera House. Newspapers: daily, Post; weekly, Crescent (Sat.), Wecker (Th)......Hotels: Waverly, regular rates, $2 (special also); Briggs, regular rates, $2 (special also); Appleton, Commercial, Avenue.

Bertschy Hall; seating capacity, 600.

AUGUSTA, 2,000. R. R., Chic., St. Paul, Min. & Omaha. Beebe's Hall, John F. Beebe, manager; seating capacity, 600; rental, one night, $8, three $18; license, $2; share also. Size of stage, 18x22; number sets scenery, 4; bill poster, manager of hall. Newspaper: Eagle (Sat.)... ...Hotels: Sheldon, regular rates, $2 (special also): Warren.

BARRABOO, 4,000. R. R., Chic. & N. Western. Free Congress Hall, J. Hawes, manager; seating capacity, 400; rental, one night $10; license, $2.50; bill poster, F. M. Lang. Newspapers: Bulletin (Fri.), Democrat (Sat.), Republic (Wed.)......Hotel: Sumner, regular rates, $2 (special also).

BEAVER DAM, 4,000. R. R., Chicago, Milwaukee & St. Paul. Concert Hall, Frank Doolittle, manager; seating capacity, 550. Newspapers: Argus (Th.), Citizen (Th.)..... Hotel: Clark, regular rates; $2 (special also).

BELOIT, 6,000. R. R., Chicago, Milwaukee & St. Panl; Chicago & Northwestern. Goodwin's Opera House, J. Goodwin, manager; seating capacity 850; rental, one night $20, three $45, license $5; share also. Size of stage, 26x56; number sets scenery, 9; bill poster, Robert Wilson. Newspapers: daily, Free Press; weekly, Outlook (Fri.)...... Hotels: Goodwin, regular rates: $2 (special also); Commercial, regular rates, $2 (special also).

Hanchett's Hall; seating capacity 600.

BERLIN, 5,000. R. R., Chicago, Milwaukee & St. Paul. Library Opera House, J. E. Williams, manager; seating capacity, 900; rental, share only. Size of stage, 35x40; size of proscenium opening, 18x25; height from stage to grooves, 12; depth under stage, 5; traps, 3; number sets scenery, 18; leader of orchestra, A. Crompton; scenic artist, C Buell; stage carpenter, John Hally; bill poster, Opera House; number of sheets can accommodate, 300; rates per sheet, 4c.; theatrical teamster, J. W. Jones. Newspapers daily, Journal, advertising rates per inch, 75c.; weekly, Conrant, (Tu.), Jonrnal, (Th.)...... Hotels: Belbi, special rates, $1 to $1.25; Dunham, special rates, $1 to $1.25; City, special rates, $1.

BLACK RIVER FALLS, 4,000. R. R., Chic., St. P., Minn. & Omaha. Opera House, W. R. O'Hearn, manager ; seating capacity, 500; rental, one night $15, license included : Size of stage, 18x35; number sets scenery, 6; bill poster, J. D. Hall. Newspapers: Banner (Fri.), Independent (Wed.)......Hotels: Merchants', regular rates, $2 (special also); Riverside, Freeman.

Freeman's Hall, Sam Freeman, manager; seating capacity, 600; rental, one night $15, three $30; license, $5. Size of stage, 14x25; number sets scenery, 3.

BOSCOBEL, 2,000. R. R., Chic., Mil. & St. Paul. Ruda's Hall, Ruda Bros., managers; seating capacity, 500; rental, one night $10; license $2. Size of stage, 16x20; number sets scenery, 4; bill poster, J. M. Dickerson. Newspaper: Dial (Tu.)... ...Hotel: Central, regular rates, $2 (special also).

BRANDON, 800. R. R., Chic., Mil. & St. Panl. Odd Fellows' Hall, Thos. Watson, manager; seating capacity, 400. Newspaper: Times (Th.).........Hotel: Ensign.

BRODHEAD, 1,800. R. R., Chicago, Milwaukee & St. Paul. Gambar's Hall. Newspaper: Independent (Fri).

BURLINGTON, 1,800. R. R., Chicago, Milwaukee & St. Paul. Teutonia Hall; seating capacity, 500; rental, one night $15, three $30; no license. Size of stage, 20x30; number sets scenery, 8; bill poster, Lorenz Stang. Newspapers: Free Press (Tu.), Standard (Sat.) Hotels: Jones, regular rates, $2 (special also); Merchants', Western Union.

CENTRALIA, 1,100. R. R., Chicago, Milwaukee & St. Paul; Green Bay, Winona & St. Paul. Garrison Hall, F. Garrison, manager; seating capacity, 350. Newspaper: Enterprise (Th).

CHILTON, 1,300. R. R., Milwaukee & Northern. Turner Hall, Henry Rollmann, manager; seating capacity, 250. Size of stage, 16x24 ; size of proscenium opening, 13x18 ; height from stage to grooves, 12; stage carpenter, Geo. Wippermann; bill poster, Archie Hume. Newspapers: Times (Sat.), News, (Wed.)... ...Hotel : Chilton, regular rates, $2 (special also).

CHIPPEWA FALLS, 6,000. R. R., Chic., Mil. & St. Paul ; Chic., St. P., Minn. & Omaha ; Wisconsin Central. Cobban's Opera House, S. C. Cobban, manager ; seating capacity, 1,000; rental, one night $35, three $70; license, $5; share also. Size of stage, 24x70; number sets scenery, 9. Newspapers : Independent (Th.), Herald (Fri.), Times (Wed.) .... Hotels : Stanley, regular rates, $2 (special also); Central, Riverside, Waterman.

Hook's Hall; **seating capacity, 400.**

CLINTON, 2,500. R. R., Chic., Mil. & St. Paul; Chic. & North Western. Wyman Opera House, Wm. Wyman, manager ; seating capacity, 1,100. Newspaper : Herald (Wed.). ....Hotel: Snyder, regular rates, $2 (special also).

Union Hall, Dickerman & Edwards, managers; seating capacity, 250.

COLUMBUS, 3,000. R. R., Chic., Mil. & St. Paul. Turner Hall, John Topp, manager; **seating capacity, 400;** bill poster, Will Shultz. Newspapers: Democrat (Fri.), Republican (Sat.)......Hotels: Fox, regular rates, $2 (special also); Meroin.

Opera House, **seating capacity, 250; rental, one night $8; license, $1.** Size of stage, 20x30.

DARLINGTON, 1,800. R. R., Chic., Mil. & St. Paul. Court House Hall, C. Vickers, manager; seating capacity, 350. Newspapers: Democrat (Th.), Republican (Fri.)......Hotel: Whitman, regular rates, $2 (special also).

DELAWARE, 2,000. R. R., Chic., Mil. & St. Paul. Harmony Hall, H. F. Sharp, manager; seating capacity, 500; rental, one night $10, three $20; license included. Size of stage, 21x40; depth under stage, 4; traps, 2; number sets scenery, 3; bill poster, Bert Webster. Newspapers: Enterprise (Wed.), Republican (Fri.)......Hotel: Delavan, regular rates, $2 (special also).

DE PERE, 4,000. R. R., Milwaukee & Northern; Chicago & Northwestern. Harmony Hall, P. R. Proctor, manager; seating capacity, 400; rental, one night $10, three $25; license, $2; share also. Size of stage, 30x30; size of proscenium opening, 11½x11½; height from stage to grooves, 14; depth under stage, 3½; traps, 1; number sets scenery, 4; theatrical teamster, Aug. Thiels, liveryman. Newspapers: Index (Wed.), News (Sat.) ......Hotels: Commercial, special rates, $1 to $1.50; Transit, special rates, $1 to $1.50.

California Hall, Henry Wattner, manager; seating capacity, 300, rental, one night $7; license, $2.50; share also. Size of stage, 12x18; number sets scenery, 2.

DODGEVILLE, 2,500. R. R., Chic. & N. Western. Spang's Opera House, S. S. Spang, manager; seating capacity, 500; rental, one night $10; license $2. Size of stage, 17x40; **full set scenery;** bill poster, L. Bancroft. Newspapers: Chronicle (Fri.), Sun (Fri.). Star (Fri.) .....Hotels: Marks, regular rates, $2 (special also); Wisconsin.

Court House, O. F. Blakely, manager; seating capacity, 400; rent or share. **Size of stage, 16x30; fair stock** scenery.

EAU CLAIRE, 12,000. R. R., Chic., Mil. & St. Paul; Chic., St. Paul, Minn. & Omaha; Chippewa Falls & Northern. Music Hall, J. Truax, manager; seating capacity, 800; rental, one night $25, three $60. Size of stage, 27x22; number sets scenery, 6; bill poster, J. Parrish. Newspapers: daily, Free Press, Leader......Hotels: Eau Claire, regular rates, $2.50 (special also); Galloway, regular rates, $2.50 (special also).

New Opera House.

FLORENCE, 4,500. R. R., Chic. & N. Western. Tully's Opera House, F. C. Tully, manager; seating capacity, 750; rental, one night $20; license, $5; share also. Size of stage, 21x30; number sets scenery, 7; **bill poster,** G. W. Dayton; theatrical teamster, G. W. Dayton; Newspaper: Mining News (Sat.)..... Hotels: Collins, regular rates, $2 (special also; Florence, Avenue, National.

FOND DU LAC, 18,000. R. R., Chic. & N. W.; Chic., Mil. & St. Paul; Wis. Cent. Grand Opera House, William Church, manager; seating capacity, 900; rental, one night $30, share also; license included. Size of stage, 30x48; size of proscenium opening, 27x23; height from stage to grooves, 20; height from stage to rigging loft, 48; depth under stage, 7; traps, 4; number sets scenery, 15; leader of orchestra, Prof. Hall; scenic artist, William Church; stage carpenter, Burt Pasko; bill poster, William Church & Co.; number of sheets can **accommodate,** 2,000; rates per sheet, 4c; theatrical teamster, J. C. Lowell. Newspapers:

daily, Reporter, advertising rates, per inch, $1; weekly, Journal (Th.). .... Hotels: Palmer, special rates, $1.50 to $2; American, $1.25 to $1.50; Lewis, special rates, $1.25 to $1.50.

Opera Hall; seating capacity, 800; rental, one night $15, three $37.50; license, $3 to $10. Size of stage, 20x30; number sets scenery, 6.

Armory Hall, **Swift & Arnold, managers;** seating capacity, 1,000. **Size of** stage, 23x50; number sets scenery, 6.

FORT ATKINSON, 2,500. **R. R., Chicago &** N. Western. City Hall, R. S. White, manager; **seating** capacity, **800; rental, one night $15,** three **$30; license, $3;** share also. Size of **stage, 26x44; number sets scenery,** 10; **bill** poster, J. W. Howard. Newspapers : Union (Fri.), Our Flag (Th.)...... Hotel: **Green Mountain,** regular rates, $2.50 **(special also); Higbee.**

FOX LAKE, 1,000. R. R., Chicago, Milwaukee & St. Paul. Odd Fellows' Hall, H. M. Germain, manager; seating capacity, 325; rental, one night $7, three $18; no license. Size of stage, 18x24; full set scenery; bill poster, manager of hall. Newspaper: Representative (Th.)...... Hotels : **Barron,** American.

GRAND RAPIDS, 3,000. R. R., Chicago, Milwaukee & St. Paul; Green Bay, Winona & St. Paul. Witters' Hall, D. & G. F. Witler, managers; seating capacity, 400; rental, one night $10, three $24; license $3. Size of stage, 15x30; fair stock scenery; bill poster. D. Huntington. Newspaper: Reporter (Th.)...... Hotels : Witler, regular rates, $2 (special also); **Central,** Grand Rapids.

GREEN BAY, 12,000. **R. R., C. & N. W.;** Milwaukee & Northern; **Wis. & Mich.; G. B., Winona & St.** Paul. Armory **Opera House,** Marshall Bros., managers; seating capacity, **700;** rental, one night, **$25;** three, **$60;** share also; license, **$3;** size of stage, 26x40; size of proscenium opening, 13x25; height from stage to grooves, 12½; height from stage **to** rigging loft, 8; depth under stage, 5; traps, 1; number sets scenery, 6; leader of orchestra, **C. T. Kimball;** scenic artist, T. B. Catlin; stage carpenter, C. A. Violet; bill poster, John Mallory; number of sheets can accommodate, 400; rates per sheet, 4c.; theatrical teamster, Tom Conch. Newspaper: daily, Gazette; advertising rates per inch, **25c. to** 75c. . Hotels: Cook's, special rates, $1.50 to $2; American, special rates, $1.50.

Klans' Hall, Chas. Klans, manager; seating capacity, 700; rental one night, $15; three, $35; share also; license, $2 to $5; size of stage, 25x40; number sets scenery, **8.**

HARTFORD, 2,700. R. R., Chic., Mil. & St. Paul. Turner Hall, A. Konrad, manager; seating capacity, 200. Newspaper: Press (Fri.)...... Hotel: Alton; regular rates, $2; (special also)

HUDSON, 3,000. R. R., Chic., **St.** Paul, Minn. & Omaha. Opera Hall, Wm. H. Crowe, manager; seating capacity, 600; rental, one night, $20; three, $50; share also; license included; size of stage, 20x53; number sets scenery, 9; bill poster, Albert Zaler. Newspapers: Star & Times (FrI.), Republican (Wed.)...... Hotels: Chapin Hall; regular rates, $2 (special also); Commercial, Central.

Music Hall, F. **D. Harding, manager; seating** capacity, 400; rental, one night, $10; license, $3 to $5.

JANESVILLE, 10,000. R. R., Chicago & Nor. West.; Chicago, Mil. **& St.** Paul. Myer's Opera House, Chas. E. Moseley, manager; seating capacity, 800. Size of stage, 32x44; size of proscenium opening, 30x24; height from stage to grooves, **17;** depth under stage, 8; traps, 2; number sets scenery, 14; leader of orchestra, Geo. Anderson; bill poster, W. W. Pierson; number of sheets can accommodate, 400; rates per sheet, 3c; theatrical teamster, H. Venable. Newspapers: daily, Gazette; Recorder. Hotels: Myers', special **rates,** $1.50 to $2; Grand, regular rates, $2 (special also).

Lappin's Music Hall, H. A. Doty, manager; seating capacity, 800; rental, one night $25, three $40; license, $2; share also. Size of stage, 24x24; number sets scenery, 13.

Janesville Theatre (variety), Wm. Hart, manager.

JEFFERSON, 2,500. R. R., Chicago & North Western. Stoppenbach's Opera House, Frank Stoppenbach, manager; seating capacity, 600; rental, one night $15, three $30; share also; license included. Size of stage, 30x48; number sets scenery, 8; bill poster; Opera House. **Newspaper:** Banner (Thurs.) Hotels: Jefferson, regular rates, $2 (special also); Sawyer.

KENOSHA, 7,000. R. R., Chic. & Northwestern; Chic., Mil. & St. Paul. Kimball Opera House. J. H. Kimball, manager; seating capacity, 700; rental, one night $16; three $36; license, twelve tickets. Size of stage, 25x40; number sets scenery, 8; bill poster, Becker. Newspapers: Courier (Th.), Telegraph (Fri.), Union (Th.) .....Hotels: Grant, regular rates, $2 (special also); American, regular rates, $2 (special also); City.

LA CROSSE, 20,000. R. R., Chic. & Northwestern, Chic., Mil. & St. Paul. La Crosse Opera House, H. Cramer, manager; seating capacity, 1,000; share and rent. Size of stage, 50; size of proscenium opening, 18x25; height from stage to rigging loft, 30; depth under stage, 10; traps, 2; number sets scenery, 12; bill poster, H. Cramer; number of sheets can accommodate, 1,000; rates per sheet, 4c.; theatrical teamster, D. Law. Newspapers: Chronicle, advertising rates per inch, 50c.; Republican, advertising rates per inch, 50c.......Hotels: International, special rates, $1.50; Cameron, regular rates, $3 (special also).

Germania Hall; seating capacity, 800.

Galberg's Hall; seating capacity, 500.

LAKE GENEVA, 2,500. R. R., Chicago & Northwestern. Ford's Opera House, Moore & Blake, managers; seating capacity, 550; rental, one night $15; three $40; share also, license included. Size of stage, 25x35; size of proscenium opening, 14x25; height from stage to grooves, 16; height from stage to rigging loft, 16½; depth under stage, 3½; traps, 1; number sets scenery, 3; bill poster, Elmer Chittenden; theatrical teamster, Dorkee & Son. Newspapers: Herald, (Fri.), News, (Th.), advertising rates, 1 line, 10 cents; 1 inch, 60 cents......Hotels, Lake, Whiting, Commercial.

LANCASTER, 1,500. R. R., Chicago & Northwestern. Hyde's Hall, A. E. Hyde, manager; seating capacity, 500; rental, one night $15, three $40; license, $1.50; share also. Size of stage, 25x40; number sets scenery, 9. Newspapers, Herald (Th.), Teller (Th.)......Hotels: Wright, Mansion, Lancaster, Horstman.

LISBON, 1,500. R. R., Chic., Mil. & St. Paul. Curtis Hall, Hurd & Nichols, managers; seating capacity, 350.

MADISON, 11,000. R. R., Chicago & North Western ; Chicago, Milwaukee & St. Paul. Hooley Opera House, Charles Pressentin, manager ; seating capacity, 800 ; rental, one night $30, three $75; license, $5. Size of stage, 30x50; size of proscenium opening, 28½ x30 ; height from stage to grooves, 15 ; height from stage to rigging loft, 21½ ; depth under stage, 4 ; traps, 1 ; number sets scenery, 4 ; leader of orchestra, John Lueders ; bill poster, Jack Reiner ; number of sheets can accommodate, 300 ; rates per sheet, 4c ; theatrical teamster, B. Jefferson. Newspapers : daily, State Journal, advertising rates, 50c. per inch ; Democrat, advertising rates, 50c. per inch ......Hotels: Park, special rates, $6; Vilas, regular rates, $2.50 (special also); Capital.

MANITOWOC, 7,000. R. R., Mil., Lake Shore & Western. Turner Hall, Chas. F. Fechter, manager ; seating capacity, 600; rental, one night $30, three $50 ; share also; license, $5. Size of stage, 40x30; size of proscenium opening, 20x20; depth under stage, 15; traps, 1; number sets scenery, 10 ; leader of orchestra, G. Bieling ; stage carpenter, C. Dahlman ; bill poster, Pat. Sullivan; rates per sheet, 4c.; theatrical teamster, E. Smith. Newspapers : Pilot (Th.), Tribune (Th.), Times (Tu) .....Hotels : Williams, special rates, $1.25; North Western, special rates, $1.25.

Stoeauskallpa Opera House, Janceck & Fisher, managers ; seating capacity, 800 ; rental, one night $20, three $50 ; license, $5 ; share also. Size of stage, 31x28 ; number sets scenery, 12.

MARINETTE, 3,000. R. R., Chic. & N. Western; Mil. & Northern. Stevenson Opera House. Newspapers : Eagle (Sat); North Star (Fri) .....Hotel: Dunlap, regular rates, $2 (special also).

MAUSTON, 1,200. R. R., Chic., Mil. & St. Paul. Opera House, G. Pennimat, manager; seating capacity, 500; rental, one night $10, three $25; license $3. Size of stage, 45x45; size of proscenium opening, 13x16; height from stage to grooves, 14; height from stage to rigging loft, 11; depth under stage, 2½; traps, 1; leader of orchestra, M. A. Rublee; theatrical teamster, L. Cass. Newspaper: Star, (Thurs.)......Hotel: Mauston, special rates, $1.25.

MAZOMANIE, 1,500.   R. R., Chic., Mil. & St. Paul.   **Schmitz's Hall, John A. Schmitz,** manager; seating capacity, 500.   **Newspaper: Sickle (Sat.).. ...Hotel: Carlisle, regular rates, $2** (special also).

MEDFORD, 800.   R. R., **Wisconsin Central.**   Music Hall, David McCartney, manager; seating capacity, 400; rental, **one** night $10, three $20; share also; no license.   Size of **stage,** 18x20; number sets **scenery,** 3; bill poster, Chas. **Anderson.**   Newspapers: **News (Sat.)......**Hotels: Forrest, Central, National.

MENASHA, 5,000.   R. R., Chicago & Northwestern; Milwaukee & Northern; Wisconsin **Central.**   Concordia **Hall, W. G. Merklin,** manager; seating capacity, 500; rental, one **night $15; three $35; license $5.   Size of** stage, 35x40; full set scenery; bill poster, W. Lansing.   **Newspapers: daily, News; weekly,** Press (Th.)   Hotel: National, regular **rates, $2 (special also).**

MENOMONEE, 5,000.   **R. R.,** Chicago, St. Paul, **Minn.** & Omaha.   **Concert** Hall, **David** Stovir, manager; seating capacity, 700; rent or share; license, **$5.   Size of** stage, 25x38; number sets scenery, 5; bill poster, manager of hall.   Newspapers: News (Sat.), **Times** (Fri.)......Hotels: Menomonee, regular rates, $2 (special also); Merchants'.

Grob's Hall, Fred Schmidt, manager; seating capacity, 600; rent or share.   Size of stage, 22x40; number sets scenery, 3.

MILWAUKEE, 152,000.   R. R., Milwaukee, Lake Shore & W.; Wisconsin Central; Chic. Mil. & St. Paul; Chicago & Nor. Western.   Deakin's Academy of Music, Henry Deakin, manager; seating capacity, 1,600; rental, one night $75 to $150, license included; share **also.**   Size of stage, 50x76; size of proscenium opening, 32x24; **height** from stage to grooves, 19½; height from stage to rigging loft, 48½; depth under stage, 8; all traps; complete stock scenery; musical director, H. **H.** Thiele; scenic artist, Otto Schmidt; **stage** carpenter, George Nitte; bill poster, H. **O.** Park; number of sheets can accommodate, 7,000; rates per sheet, 4c.; theatrical teamster, Davis' Omnibus Line.   Newspapers: daily, Sentinel, Wisconsin, Journal, Globe, Herald (Ger.), Der Seebote (Ger.), Freie Presse (Ger.), Germania (Ger.)......Hotels: Kirby, Plankinton, Axtel, St. Charles, Grand Central.

Grand Opera House, R. L. Marsh, manager; **Brooks & Dickson, New York representatives**; seating capacity, 1,700; rental, one night $100, **three $300, license included; share** also.   Size of stage, 40x80; size of proscenium opening, **33x30; height from stage to** grooves, 20; height from stage to rigging loft, 53; depth under stage, 9; traps, 7; number sets scenery, 30; musical director, Jos. Clander; scenic artists, **W. J.** Grimey **&** Kindt; stage carpenter, **W. Kindt;** bill poster, H. O. Parks; number of sheets can ac**commodate,** 3,500; rates per sheet, 2c. **to 4c.**

Cosmopolitan Dime Museum, J. E Warner, manager; seating capacity, 500.

Slensby's Vaudeville (variety).

MINERAL POINT, 3,000.   R. R., Chic., Milwaukee & St. Paul.   City Hall, Thos. S. Ansley, manager; seating capacity, 400; rental, one night $10, three $25, license included.   **Size** of stage, 12x18; full set scenery; theatrical teamster, Robert James.   Newspapers: Democrat (Fri.), Tribune (Th.)......Hotels : United States, regular **rates, $2** (special also); Globe, Wisconsin, Mineral Point, City.

MONROE, 4,500.   **R. R.,** Chic., Mil. & St. Paul.   Turner Hall, Robert Miller, manager; seating capacity, 1,000; rental, one night $12, three **$33;** license, $5.   Size of stage, 20x30; number sets scenery, **5.**   Newspapers: Gazette (Th.), Sentinel **(Wed.),** Sun (Sat.).... Hotels: United States, regular rates, $2 (special also); City, **Monroe,** Warefeald.

Chenoweth Hall, **S. M.** Hughes, manager; seating capacity, 500.

NECEDAH, 5,000.   R. R., Chic., **Mil. & St. Paul.**   Miner's Opera House, E. S. Miner, manager; seating capacity, 500.   Newspapers: Signal (Th.), Lumberman (Th.)......Hotel: Armstrong, regular rates, $2 (special also).

NEENAH, 4,500.   R. R., Chic. & N. Western; Milwaukee & Northern; Wisconsin Central.   Pettibone Hall, Alex. McNaughton, manager; seating capacity, 600; rental, one night $10; license, $2 to $5.   Size of stage, 24x40; number sets scenery, 3; bill poster, William Lansing.   Newspapers: daily, Times; weekly, Gazette (Sat.)......Hotel: Russell.

Schnetzen Hall, Wm. Kraeger, manager; seating capacity, 700; rental, one night, $15; license, $2; fair stock scenery.

NEILLSVILLE, 1,500. R. R., Chicago, St. Paul, Minn. & Omaha. Fireman's Hall, J. W. Hammer, manager; seating capacity, 500; rental, one night $15; license, $2; share also. Size of stage, 18x20; fair stock scenery. Newspapers: Press (Th.), Times (Tu.), Republican (Th.)......Hotel: O'Neill, regular rates, $2 (special also).

NEW LISBON, 1,500. R. R., Chicago, Milwaukee & St. Paul. Curtis Hall, C. D. Curtis, manager; seating capacity, 350; rental, one night $8 to $10, three $20 to $22; license, $2 to $5; share also. Size of stage, 12x30; fair stock scenery; bill poster, Geo. Stimatz. Newspaper: Argus (Th.)......Hotels: Crosby, regular rates, $2 (special also); Railway.

NEW LONDON, 2,200. R. R., Green Bay, Winona & St. Paul; Milwaukee, Lake Shore & Western. Cline's Hall, Jacobs & Co., managers; seating capacity, 300; rental, one night $5; license, $2; number sets scenery, 2; bill poster, J. G. Norman. Newspaper: Times (Sat.)......Hotels: New London, regular rates, $2 (special also); Angler.

OCONOMOWOC, 3,600. R. R., Chic., Mil. & St. Paul. Mamie Hall, A. L. Palmer, manager; seating capacity, 500; rental, one night $15, three $35, license included. Size of stage, 15x40; size of proscenium opening, 9x18; height from stage to rigging loft, 12; depth under stage, 3; number sets scenery, 6; bill poster, A. L. Palmer; number of sheets can accomodate, 150; rates per sheet, 4 cents; theatrical teamster, A. L. Palmer. Newspapers: Local (Fri.), Free Press (Sat.)......Hotels: Jones, special rates, $1.50; Draper, special rates, $2.

OCONTO, 4,700. R. R., Chic. & Northwestern; St. Paul, Eastern Grand Trunk. Music Hall, Chas. Hall, manager; seating capacity, 500; rental, one night $10, license $2.50 to $3; share also. Size of stage, 18x14; number sets scenery, 6; bill poster, George Heath. Newspapers: Enquirer (Sat.), Lumberman (Sat.), Reporter (Sat.)......Hotels: Beyer, regular rates, $2 (special also); Roth's.

OMRO, 2,500. R. R., Chic., Mil. & St. Paul. Putnam's Opera House, H. Putnam, manager; seating capacity, 800; rental, one night $15, three $35. Size of stage, 16x25; number sets scenery, 8; bill poster, H. J. Dickerson. Newspapers: Journal (Th.), Stalwart (Tu.) ....Hotel: Larrabee, regular rates, $2 (special also).

OSHKOSH, 16,000. R. R., Chic. & Northwestern; Chic., Mil. & St. Paul; Mil., Lake Shore & W.; Wisconsin Central. Opera House, R. L. Marsh, manager; seating capacity, 1,200; rent or share. Size of stage, 42x63; height from stage to grooves, 20; height from stage to rigging loft, 48; depth under stage, 9; number sets scenery, 18; bill poster, Henry Staraw. Newspapers: Times (Sat.), Telegraph (Fri.)......Hotels: Revere, regular rates, $2.50 (special also); Fremont, regular rates, $1.50 (special also).

Turner's Opera House, M. V. Kaas, manager; seating capacity, 800; rental, one night $25. Size of stage, 30x50; full set scenery.

Fraker Hall, C. D. Church, manager; seating capacity, 1,100; rental, one night $10 to $15, three $30; license, $2.50. Size of stage, 30x54; full set scenery.

PESHTIGO, 3,500. R. R., Chicago & Northwestern. Music Hall, J. B. Dawson, manager; seating capacity, 500; rental, one night $12; no license. Size of stage, 18x20; fair stock scenery. Newspapers: Eagle, North Star. Hotels: Duket, Gregg, Stewart.

PLATTEVILLE, 3,000. R. R., Chicago & Northwestern; Chicago, Milwaukee & St. Paul. Thomas Hall, W. J. Fanston, manager; seating capacity, 400; rental, one night $10, three $27; license, $3. Size of stage, 12x19; number sets scenery, 4; bill poster, T. Cordingly. Newspapers: Witness (Th.), Times (Wed.)......Hotels: Gates, regular rates, $2 (special also); Park.

PORTAGE, 6,000. R. R., Chic., Mil. & St. Paul; Wis. Central; Portage & Madison. Dullaghan's Opera House, John Dullaghan, Jr., manager; seating capacity, 850; rental, share only. Size of stage, 24x51; size of proscenium opening, 21x51; height from stage to grooves, 12; depth under stage, 3; traps, 3; number sets scenery, 18; leader of orchestra, Chas. Bliss; scenic artist, George Jewett; bill poster, Opera House; number of sheets can accommodate, 250; rates per sheet, 3c; theatrical teamster, M. Welsh. Newspapers: Democrat (Fri.); Register (Fri.); Wecker (Wed.)......Hotels: European, special rates $1.50; Corning, special rates, $2; Emder, special rates, $2.

Pettibone Hall, J. H. Merrill, manager; seating capacity, 600; license, $3 to $5; no scenery.

PRAIRIE **DU CHIEN, 3,000.   R. R., Chic., Mil.** & St. Paul.   Germania Hall, J. Geo
Schweizer, manager; seating capacity, 450; rental, one night $12, three $25; license, $3,
size of stage, 16x26; size of proscenium opening, 12½x18; height from stage to grooves,
11; height from stage to rigging loft, 12; depth under stage, **2; number** sets scenery, 7;
bill posters, C. H. Schweizer & Co., C. M. Hamilton; number **of** sheets can accommodate, 200; rates per sheet, 4c.; theatrical teamster, Frank Bitterle. Newspapers: Courier
(Sat.); Union (Thurs.)......Hotels: Commercial, special rates, $1.25 to $1.50; Williams',
regular **rates, $2 (special also).**

Music Hall, **J. Farnuhon, manager; seating capacity, 400; rental, one night, $5 to $10;
Size of stage, 18x22; number sets scenery, 1.**

RACINE, 20,000.   R. R., Chic., Mil. & St. Paul; Chic. & Northwestern.   Blake Opera
House (see page 329), J. T. Vaughn, manager; seating capacity, 1,250; rental, share only,
license included.   Size **of stage 38x66;** size of proscenium opening, 31x37; height from
stage to grooves, 20; height from stage to rigging loft, 56; depth under stage, 9; traps,
2; number **sets** scenery, 25; leader of orchestra, **Henry Schulte; stage carpenter Frank
B. Ward;** bill poster, Opera House; number of sheets can accommodate, 1,000; **rates per**
sheet, 4c.; theatrical teamster, Martin Throup. Newspapers: daily, Journal, **advertising rates,** yearly contract; Times, advertising rates, yearly contract; weekly, Advocate
(Th.), advertising rates, 50c. per inch; Correspondent (Fri.), advertising rates, 50c. per
inch; Folkets Avis (Wed.), advertising rates, 50c. per inch .....Hotels: Blake, special
rates, $1.50 to $2; Huggins', special rates, $1.50 to $2; Windsor, $1; Franklin, $1.

Turner Hall, F. Schneider, manager; seating capacity, 500; rental, one **night** $20, license,
$5; number sets scenery, 8.

REEDSBURY, 2,000.   R. R. Chic. & Northwestern.   Broot's Opera House, A. P. Ellinwood,
manager; seating capacity, 450; rental, **one night $10; license, $2.50.   Size of** stage, 16
x33; bill poster, manager of hall.   **Newspaper: Free Press (Th.)......**Hotels; Central,
regular rates, $2 (special also); Porter, **American.**

RIPON, 5,000.   R. R., Chic., Mil. **& St. Paul; Chic. & N. Western.**   Grand Opera House, **T.
D. Stone,** manager; seating capacity, **800; rental, one night $15, three** $30; license, $5;
share also.   Size of stage, 25x45; full set scenery; bill poster, Opera House. Newspapers:
Commonwealth (Fri.), Free Press (Th.)......**Hotel: Woods, regular rates, $2 (special**
also).

Opera Hall, O. W. Akin, manager; seating capacity, 1 000; rental, one **night $10, three $30;**
license, **$5.**   Size of stage, 22x28; number sets scenery, 7.

SHEBOYGAN, **8,000.**   R. R., Chic. & N. Western; Lake Shore & **Mich.** Southern.   Opera
House, **J. M.** Kohler, manager; seating capacity, 800; rental, one night $40; share also.
Size of stage, 38x50; full set scenery; bill poster, Edward Kempf; theatrical teamster,
H. Bessinger. Newspapers: Herald (Fri.), Times (Sat.)......Hotels: Pope, regular rates,
$2 (special also); Park, regular rates, $2 (special also).

SPARTA, 4,000.   R. R., Chic. & N. Western; Chic., Mil. & St. Paul.   Opera Hall, Ira **A.**
Hill, manager; seating capacity, 600; rental, one night $25; share also; license included.
Size of stage, 24x30; number sets scenery, 4; bill poster, A. Dunbar. Newspapers:
Herald (Tu.), Democrat (Sat.).....Hotel: Warner, regular rates, $2 **(special** also).

SHARON, 1,000.   R. R., Chicago & Northwestern.   Yates' Hall, James **M.** Yates, manager;
rental, one night $8, three $15; share also; no license.   Size **of** stage, 10x21; number
sets scenery, 2. Newspaper: semi-weekly, Reporter. Hotels: Central, regular rates, $2
(special also); Yates'.

SHULLSBURG, 1,100.   R. R., Chicago, Milwaukee & St. Paul.   **New** Opera House. News-
papers: Free Press (Fri.), Pick and Gad (Th.).   Hotels: Layfayette, regular rates, $2
(special also); City

STEVENS' POINT, 5,000.   R. R., Wisconsin Central; Green Bay, Winona & St. Paul.
McCulloch Hall, H. D. McCulloch, manager; seating capacity, 600; rental, one night
$10; license $3.   Size of stage, 16x32; number sets scenery, 5. Newspapers: Democrat
(Sat.), Journal (Sat.), Gazette (Wed.), Pinery (Fri.)......Hotels: Curran, regular rates;
$2.50 (special also); Mansion, Jacobs'.

STOUGHTON, 2,000. R. R., Chic., Mil. & St. Paul. Opera Hall, L. K. Luse, manager; seating capacity, 450; rental, one night $12. Size of stage, 20x44; number sets scenery, 4; bill poster, Wm. Lansing. Newspaper: Courier (Fri.), Hub (Tn.)......Hotel: Huston.

TOMAH, 1,500. R. R., Chic., Mil. & St. Paul. Opera Hall, Thos. McCaul, manager; seating capacity, 600. Newspapers: Monitor (Th.), Journal (Sat.)......Hotel: Sherman, regular rates, $2 (special also).

TREMPEALEAU, 1,200. R. R., Chic. & North Western; Green Bay, Winona & St. Paul. Healey's Hall, seating capacity, 200; rental, one night $6; license, $3 to $5. Size of stage, 12x16; no scenery; bill poster, B. F. Robinson. Newspaper: Sentinel (Th). .... Hotel : Milctor.

VIROQUA, 1,000. R. R., Chic., Mil. & St. Paul. Opera House, H. D. Williams, manager. Newspapers: Censor (Wed.), Leader (Fri.).......Hotel: Tremont, regular rates, $2 (special also).

WATERTOWN, 9,000. R. R., Chic., Mil. & St. Paul; Chic. & Nor. West. Turner Hall, Jacob Ditschler, manager; seating capacity, 900; rental, one night, $20, three, $50; share also; license, $3 to $5. Size of stage, 45x35; size proscenium opening, 14x22; height from stage to grooves, 16; height from stage to rigging loft, 21; depth under stage, 20; traps, 3; number sets scenery, full set; leader of orchestra, R. Hardeye; scenic artist, Louis Kind; stage carpenter, Hermann Bassler; bill poster, John McNulty; number of sheets can accommodate, 300; rates per sheet, 4c.; theatrical teamster, George Evans. Newspapers: Gazette (Fri.), Republican (Wed.)......Hotels: Commercial, special rates, $1.50; National, special rates, $1.25 to $1.50.

Music Hall; seating capacity, 400.

WAUKESHA, 5,000. R. R., Chic., Mil. & St. Paul. Carney's Opera House, Mrs. E. H. Carney, manager; seating capacity, 600; rental, one night $20, three $35; license, $3; share also. Size of stage, 24x30; number sets scenery, 5; bill poster, Henry Saltie. Newspapers: Freeman (Th.), Democrat (Sat.).......Hotels: American, regular rates, $2 (special also); Fountain, Exchange.

WAUPACA, 2,500. R. R., Wisconsin Central. Music Hall, Gilmore & Ware, managers; seating capacity, 400; rental, one night $8; license, $2 to $5; fair stock scenery; bill posters, managers of hall. Newspapers : Post (Th.), Republican (Fri.)......Hotels : Vosburg, regular rates, $2 (special also). Lems.

WAUPUN, 3,500. R. R., Chicago, Milwaukee & St. Paul. Butts' Opera Hall, Luther Butts, manager; seating capacity, 500; rental, one night $15, three $30. Size of stage, 24x32; number sets scenery, 9; bill poster, Fred Wilkes. Newspapers : Leader (Fri.), Times (Tu.).. .. Hotels : City, regular rates, $2 (special also); Shipman, Tyrrell.

WAUSAU, 8,000. R. R., Chicago, Milwaukee & St. Paul; Milwaukee, Lake Shore & Western. Grand Opera House, L. H. Wheeler, manager; seating capacity, 900; rental, one night $75; share also, license included. Size of stage, 32x59; number sets scenery, 14; bill poster, O. W. Dickson. Newspapers : daily, Central Wisconsin; weekly, Review (Mon.)......Hotels : Bell's, regular rates, $2 (special also); Riverside, Winkley, Lake Shore, City.

Music Hall, Schaible & Marquardt, managers; seating capacity, 500; rental, one night $15, three $35; license, $5; share also. Size of stage, 22x44; number sets scenery, 12.

Grand Central Theatre, Hyde Baughman, manager.

WHITEWATER, 4,600. R. R., Chic., Mil. & St. Paul. Bower's Hall, J. C. Bower, manager; seating capacity, 800 ; rental, one night $10 to $12 ; license, 2. Size of stage, 44x20 ; number sets scenery, 6 ; bill poster, G. W. Bower. Newspapers : Chronicle (Wed.), Register (Th.)......Hotels: Bower, regular rates, $2 (special also); Kinney.

WINNECONNE, 2,000. R. R., Chic., Mil. & St. Paul. Opera Hall, R. Harris, manager; seating capacity, 550; rental, one night $10, three $21; license, $5. Size of stage, 18x20; number sets scenery, 4; bill poster, E. R. Feavel. Newspaper : Enterprise (Sat.)......... Hotels: Lake View, regular rates, $2 (special also); Union, Farmers'.

TERRITORIES.

ARIZONA.

TOMBSTONE, 10,000. R. R., Southern Pacific. Crystal Palace Theatre ; seating capacity, 500 Newspapers: daily, Epitaph, Republican.

TUCSON, 10,000. R. R., Southern Pacific. Levern Hall, Bayerd & Schwartz, managers ; seating capacity, 300. Size of stage, 22x32 ; fair stock scenery. Newspapers : daily, Citizen, Star......Hotels: Cosmopolitan, Occidental, Palace.

DAKOTA.

ABERDEEN, 3,000. R. R., Chic., Mil. & St. Paul; Chic. & Nor. Western. Berry's Hall, Easton & McMasters, manager; seating capacity, 300; rental, one night $10, three $25; license, $5. Size of stage, 20x24; size **of** prosceninm opening, 12x20; depth under stage, 2½; leader **of orchestra, Frank Dille.** Newspapers: Pioneer (Th.), **rate,** 5c. per line; Republican **(Th.), rates, 5c. per line**......Hotels: Sherman, special rates, $1.50; Artesian, $1.50; **Park Place, $1.50.**

Tremont Hall, Bowman & Culbert, managers; seating capacity, 300.

BISMARCK, 5,000. **R. R.,** Northern **Pacific. Bismarck Athenæom, J. D.** Wakeman, manager; seating capacity, 1,000; rental, one night $40, **tbree $75; license, $5.** Size of stage, 32x34; size of prosceninm opening, 12x28; height **from stage to** rigging loft, 20; depth under stage, 8; **traps, 1; number sets** scenery, **7; leader of** orchestra, Ed. Brunsman. scenic artist, Robert Bannerman; **bill poster, Ed. Drumond;** number sheets can accommodate, 300; rates per sheet, 4½c.; theatrical teamster, **Dan Fowler.** Newspapers: daily, Tribune, Sentinel; weekly, Journal (Fri)......Hotels: **Sheridan,** special rates, $2.50; Merchants, special rates, $1.50; New Lamborn, special **rates, $3.**

Opera House, Samuel Whitney, manager; seating capacity, **300;** rental, one night $35, three **$75; share** also; no license. Size of stage, 14x17; number sets scenery, 3.

CANTON, 1,500. R. R., Chicago, Milwaukee & St. Paul. Bedford Hall, C. A. Bedford, manager; seating capacity, 350; rental; one night $10, three $25; license, $3. Size of stage, 25x32; size of prosceninm opening, 14x24; height from stage to grooves, 13; **depth** under stage, 5; number sets scenery, 3. Newspapers: Advocate (Th.), News (Fri.)...... Hotels : Harlan, special rates, $1.50; Merchants, special rates, $1.50.

CASTLETON, 1,000. **R. R., Northern** Pacific. Knight's Hall; fair stock scenery.

CHAMBERLAIN, 1,500. R. R., Chicago, Milwaukee & St. Paul. **Leslie's** Opera House, E. S. Burwell, manager; seating capacity, 500; rental, one night $15, three $25, license included. Size of stage, 14x22; size **of** prosceninm opening, 13x22, height from stage to grooves, 17; depth under stage, 3½; number sets scenery, **5.** Newspaper : Register (Th). ......Hotels: Brule, special rates, $1; Wright, special rates, **$1.**

DEADWOOD, 4,000. No railroad. Gem Theatre, Al. Swearlogen, manager.

Nye Opera House, John H. Rogers, manager. Newspapers daily, Pioneer, Times.

DELL RAPIDS, 1,000. R. R., Chic., Mil. & St. Paul. Collins Hall, **M. E. Collins, manager;** seating capacity, 300. Newspaper : Exponent (Th.).

FARGO, 12,000. R. R., Northern Pacific; St. Paul, Minn. & Manitoba. Fargo Opera House, A. S. Capehart, manager; seating capacity, 800; rental, one night $40; license included.

Size of stage, 22x24; full set scenery; bill poster, Geo. Miller. Newspapers: daily, Argus, Republican, Sun......Hotels: Continental, Headquarters.

Chapin Hall, J. B. Chapin, manager; seating capacity, 500; rental, one night $25 to $15 ; license, $5. Size of stage, 20x30; number sets scenery, 1.

Coliseum Theatre, B. P. Reynolds, manager.

FLANDREAU, 800. R. R., Chicago, Milwaukee & St. Paul. Court House, P. Clark, manager; seating capacity, 400. Newspapers: Herald (Fri.), Enterprise (Th.).

GRAND FORKS, 6,000. R. R., St. Paul, Minneapolis & Manitoba. Cline's Opera House, Mrs. Cline, manager; seating capacity, 500; fair stock scenery; bill poster, Frank L. Witt. Newspapers: daily, Herald, Plaindealer.....Hotel: Ingals.

Gatzian's Hall, H. Gatzian, manager; seating capacity, 270; rental, one night $10, three $25; license, $5. Size of stage, 18x26; height from stage to grooves, 10; depth under stage, 4; fair stock scenery.

JAMESTOWN, 3,500. R. R., Northern Pacific. Klaus' Hall, Chas. A. Klaus, manager; seating capacity, 600; rental, one night, $25; license, $5. Size of stage, 24x15; number sets scenery, 4; bill poster, J. F. Niemyer. Newspapers: daily, Capital, Alert.. ... Hotel: Grand Central.

MANDAN, 3,000. R. R., Northern Pacific. Opera House; license $2. Newspaper: daily, Pioneer; weekly, Times (Sat.)......Hotels: Merchants', Inter Ocean.

Emerson Institute, Tuttle & Wilson, managers; seating capacity, 300; rental, one night $25; license, $5; share also; fair stock scenery.

MITCHELL, 2,500. R. R., Chic. Mil. & St. Paul. Sullivan's Hall, J. H. Sullivan, manager; seating capacity, 300. Newspapers: daily, Republican; weekly, Mail (Th.)

RUNNING WATER, 1,200. R. R., Chic., Mil. & St. Paul. Turner Hall, B. Bade, manager; seating capacity, 500.

SCOTLAND, 1,500. R. R., Chic., Milwaukee & St. Paul. Campbell Hall, Campbell, manager; seating capacity, 350; rental, one night $5; license, $2; size of proscenium opening, 12x20. Newspaper: Citizen (Th.)

SIOUX FALLS, 6,000. R. R., Chic., Mil. & St. Paul; Chic., St. Paul, Minn. & Omaha. Germania Hall; seating capacity, 500; rent or share; full set scenery. Newspapers: daily, Press; weekly, Argus (Wed.), Leader (Th.)......Hotels: Merchants', Sherman, Phillips', Cataract, Central.

YANKTON, 5,000. R. R., Chic., Mil. & St. Paul. Turner Hall; seating capacity, 700; rental, one night $25, three $60, license included. Size of stage, 30x60; fair stock scenery; bill poster, John Rankin. Newspapers : daily, Press and Dakotian; weekly, Herald (Sat.)......Hotels: St. Charles, Smithsonian, Merchants', Jencks'.

Opera House.

IDAHO.

EAGLE ROCK, 600. R. R., Utah & Northern. Chamberlain Hall, D. F. Chamberlain, manager; seating capacity, 600; license, one night $25. Bill poster, D. F. Chamberlain.

HAILEY, 2,000. Hailey Theatre, H. D. Quanblell, manager ; seating capacity, 600 ; rental, one night $30; license, $3 ; share also. Size of stage, 20x40 ; number sets scenery, 1 ; bill poster, Myers. Newspapers: daily, News, Miner, Times .....Hotel: Merchant.

MONTANA.

BILLINGS. 2,000. R. R., Northern Pacific. Opera House; share only. Newspapers: daily, Herald; weekly, Post (Th.)......Hotel: Windsor.

Roller Skating Rink, W. Morgan Field, manager; seating capacity, 500; rental, one night $35; license, $1. Size of stage, 22x30.

BOZEMAN, 3,000. R. R., Northern Pacific. Palace Theatre, Oakwood & Mitchell, managers; seating capacity, 400. Size of stage, 24x24; number sets scenery, 3. Newspaper: Courier (Tb.)......Hotels: Laclede, North Pacific.

Chestnut's Hall, Col. Chestnut, manager; rental, one night $15; license, $1.

BUTTE CITY, 10 000. R. R., Union Pacific. Renshaw Opera House. Full set scenery; bill poster, John Simpson. Newspapers: daily, Inter-Mountain, Miner.

Theatre Comique (variety).

CLARK CITY, 1,200. R. R., Northern Pacific; Variety Hall; rental, one night $5; license $1......Hotel: Union.

DEER LODGE, 2,000. R. R., Union Pacific. Opera House, John O'Neil, manager; seating capacity, 400; rental, one night $20; fair stock scenery. Newspaper : North West (Fri.)

FORT BENTON, 1,500 R. R. Northern Pacific. Stocking's Hall, W. S Stocking, manager: seating capacity, 500; rental, one night $50. three $120. Size of stage, 25x40; fair stock scenery. Newspapers: daily, Record, River Press......Hotels: Pacific, Chotau, Grand Union.

GLENDIVE, 1,500. R. R., Northern Pacific. Helm's Opera House; license, $1 ; fair stock scenery; bill poster, D. Jordan. Newspapers: (Sat.)......Hotels: Merrill, Mercham's.

Camford & Raymond's Hall, W. H. Raymond manager ; seating capacity, 200 ; rental, one night $15; license, $1. Size of stage, 20x24.

HELENA, 5,000. R. R., Northern Pacific. Ming's Opera House, Francie Pope, manager: seating capacity, 800; rental, one night $50; license, $2.50; share also. Size of stage, 30x46; full set scenery; bill poster, Sam Alexandre. Newspapers: daily, Herald. Independent,....,Hotels: International, Cosmopolitan.

MILES CITY, 2,500. R. R., Northern Pacific. Park Theatre, W. E. Turner, manager : seating capacity, 300. Size of stage, 14x22; fair stock scenery. Newspapers : daily. Press, Journal......Hotels : Merchants, International, Grand Central.

MISSOULA, 1,500. R. R., Northern Pacific. Arthur House Hall, Arthur & Botteher, managers; seating capacity, 300; rental, one night $35, three $100; share also. Size of stage, 18x30 ; fair stock scenery. Newspapers : Times (Wed.), Missoulian (Fri.). .... Hotel: Arthur.

Town Hall; seating capacity, 300.

VIRGINIA CITY, 1,000. R. R., Utah & Northern. City Hall; seating capacity, 350; rental, one night $15; fair stock scenery. Newspaper: Madisonian (Sat.).

NEW MEXICO.

ALBUQUERQUE, 10,000. R. R., Atchison, Topeka & Santa Fe; Atlantic & Pacific. Grant's Opera House, H. E. Stoepel & Co., managers; seating capacity, 600; rental, one night $35, three $90; license, $3; share also. Size of stage, 25x30; size of proscenium opening, 18x22; height from stage to grooves, 15; depth under stage, 3; number sets scenery, 6; leader of orchestra, W. Stevers; stage carpenter, Johnson: bill poster, H. E. Stoepel & Co.; number of sheets can accommodate, 650; rates per sheet, 5c.; theatrical teamsters, W. L. Trimble & Co. Newspapers : daily, Journal, advertising rates, 10c. per line; Democrat, advertising rates, 10c. per line......Hotels; Armijo, special rates, $2 50 ; Girard, special rates, $2; Southern, special rates, $1.75.

LAS VEGAS, 8,000. R. R., Atchison, Topeka & Santa Fe. Ward & Tammie's Opera House, Ward & Tamme, managers; rent or share; license, $10. Size of stage, 20x30; number sets scenery, 15. Newspapers: daily, Gazette, Optic. Hotels: Depot, Sumner, St. Nicholas.

SANTA FE, 7,000. R. R., Atchison, Topeka & Santa Fe. Alhambra Theatre. Newspapers: daily, Review.

SILVER CITY, 3,000. R. R., Atchison, Topeka & Santa Fe. Centennial Theatre, John Emerson, manager; seating capacity, 700; full set scenery. Newspapers: daily, Citizen; weekly, Enterprise (Th.), Sentinel (Sat.)

UTAH.

BRIGHAM CITY, 2,000. R. R., Central Pacific; Union Pacific. Brigham Theatre; seating capacity, 500; rental, one night $15, license included. Size of stage, 20x30; fair stock scenery. Hotels: Jensens, Bordens.

LOGAN, 5,000. R. R., Union Pacific. Reese Opera House, David Reese, manager; seating capacity, 500; rental, one night $30, three $75; license, $5. Size of stage, 30x40; size of proscenium opening, 25x20; height from stage to grooves, 26; height from stage to rigging loft, 40; depth under stage, 3; number sets scenery, 10; leader of orchestra, Whalstrom; scenic artist, R. Kirkham; stage carpenter, John Wilson; bill poster, W. A. Crocket; number of sheets can accommodate, 500; theatrical teamster, H. Reese. Newspaper: semi-weekly, Journal........Hotels: Logan, special rates, $1.50; Coche Valley, special rates, $1.50; Hopkins, special rates. $1.50.

OGDEN CITY, 30,000. R. R., Union Pacific; Central Pacific; U. & N.; Denver & Rio Grande; Utah Central. Union Opera House, Paul F. Schaefer, manager; seating capacity, 700; rental, one night $25, share also, three $60; license, $3. Size of stage, 34x38; size of proscenium opening, 18x20; height from stage to grooves, 15; height from stage to rigging loft, 30 depth under stage, 3; traps, 1; number sets scenery, 12; leader of orchestra, L. W. Ford; scenic artist, Wm. Morris; stage carpenter, Wm. Morris; bill poster, P. F. Schaefer; number of sheets can accommodate, 350; rates per sheet, 4c.; theatrical teamster, John Hedlum. Newspapers: daily, Pilot, advertising rates per inch, 50c.; Herald, advertising rates per inch, 50c.... .. Hotels: Brown, special rates, $1.50 to $2; Chapman, special rates, $1.25 to $1.50; Depot, special rates, $1.25 to $1.50.

Minon Opera House; seating capacity, 800.

Woodmanser's Hall; seating capacity, 600.

PARK CITY, 3,000. R. R., Union Pacific. Opera Hall, Charles Shrelds, manager; seating capacity, 600; rental, one night $25; license $5; no scenery. Newspaper: Mining Record (Sat.)

PAYSON CITY, 2,500. R. R., Utah Central. Payson Opera House, James W. Memmott, manager; seating capacity 700; rental, one night $20 to $30, three $55 to $65; share also; license $2.50; size of stage, 30x46½; size of proscenium opening, 25x22; height from stage to grooves, 15; height from stage to rigging loft, 22; depth under stage, 10; traps 7; number sets scenery, 11, leader of orchestra, Wm. Clayson; stage carpenter, Martin Littlewood; bill posters, John E. Betts and Wm. C. Wightman; number of sheets can accommodate, 300; rates per sheet, 2½c. Newspapers: semi-weekly, Enquirer advertising rates, $2.50 per inch.

SALT LAKE CITY, 25,000. R. R., Union Pacific; Central Pacific; Denver & Rio Grande. Salt Lake Theatre, Caine & Clawson, managers; seating capacity, 1,850; rental, one night $75, three $200; share also; license included. Size of stage, 65x70; size of proscenium opening, 28x32; height from stage to grooves, 18; height from stage to rigging loft, 52; depth under stage, 11; traps, 5; number sets scenery, 25; leader of orchestra, Charles Thomas; scenic artist Henry C. Tryon; stage carpenter, James Evans; bill poster, Scott Anderson; number of sheets can accommodate, 750; rates per sheet, 3½c; theatrical teamsters, Mulloy & Paul. Newspapers: daily, Herald, advertising rates per inch, 50c; News, advertising rates per inch, 50c.; Tribune, advertising rates per inch, 50c........ Hotels: Valley, special rates, $1.50 to $2; Metropolitan, special rates, $1.50 to $2; Continental, special rates, $2.50 to $3.50.

Walker Opera House, D. McKinzie, manager.

WASHINGTON.

CHENEY, 1,400. R. R., Northern Pacific. Griswold's Opera House, W. W. Griswold, manager; seating capacity, 300; rental, one night $10; license, $5. Size of stage, 12x18; number sets scenery, 2; bill poster, Frank Newton. Newspaper: Tribune (Fri.). .....Hotel: Oakes.

DAYTON, 2,000. R. R., Oregon, Ry. & Navigat'on Co. Drake's Opera House, Will E. Peck, manager; seating capacity, 550; rental, one night $20; license, $5. Size of stage, 20x40; number sets scenery, 3; bill poster, Robert Drake. Newspaper: daily, Chronicle; weekly, Journal (Sat.)......Hotels: Columbia, Cameron.

OLYMPIA, 2,500. R. R., Olympia & Chehalis Valley. Columbia Hall, T. C. Van Epps. manager; seating capacity, 250; rental, one night $10; license, $10. Size of stage, 30x40; fair stock scenery; bill poster. Robert Mack. Newspapers: daily, Critic; weekly, Courier (Fri.), Transcript (Sat.)......Hotels: New England, Pacific, Carlton.

PORT TOWNSEND, 1,700. Good Templars' Hall, Daniel H. Hill, manager; seating capacity, 200; rental, one night $30; license, $2.50. Size of stage, 15x30; number sets scenery, 2; bill poster, Harry Barthrop. Newspaper: daily, Argus......Hotels: Cosmopolitan, St. Charles, Central.

SEATTLE, 12,000. R. R., Northern Pacific; Columbia & Puget Sound. Fry's Opera House, George R. Beede, manager; seating capacity, 1,300; rental, share only, license included, traps, 3; number sets scenery, 6; leader of orchestra, Taco Measdag. Newspapers: daily, Herald, advertising rates, yearly contract; Post Intelligencer, yearly contract......Hotels: Arlington, Occidental.

Standard Opera House, J. P. Howe, manager; seating capacity, 600; rent or share. Size of stage, 20x30; full set scenery.

TACOMA, 6,000. R. R., Northern Pacific. Alpha Opera House, Slaughter & Stier, managers; seating capacity, 700; rental, one night $30; license, $7. Size of stage of stage, 20x24; full set scenery; bill poster, James M. Janett. Newspapers: daily, Ledger. News....... Hotels: Halsted, Central, Tacoma.

WALLA WALLA, 6,000. R. R., Oregon Ry. & Navigation Co. City Hall; seating capacity, 600; rental, one night $10. Size of stage, 14x41; fair stock scenery ; bill poster, Jessup. Newspapers: daily, Journal, Statesman, Union........Hotels: St. Louis, Stine.

Stahl's Opera House, J. H. Stahl, manager; seating capacity, 500 ; rental, one night $17; license, $5. Size of stage, 20x20; fair stock scenery.

WYOMING.

CHEYENNE, 7,000. R. R., Union Pacific. Opera House, D. C. Rhodes and G. A. Guertin, managers ; seating capacity, 1,000; rental, one night $75, three $200 ; license included. Size of stage, 30x50; size of proscenium opening, 25x28; height from stage to grooves, 18; height from stage to rigging loft, 40; depth under stage, 12; traps, 3; number sets scenery, 15; leader of orchestra, Prof. Inman; bill poster, D. C. Rhodes; theatrical teamster, D. C. Rhodes. Newspapers: daily, Leader, Sun......Hotels Interocean, regular rates, $2.50; Dyer's, special rates, $1.75 to $2; Railroad House, special rates, $1.75 to $2; Metropolitan, special rates, $1.25 to $1.50.

Recreation Hall, Joslin & Arnold, managers; seating capacity, 500. Size of stage, 20x30.

EVANSTON, 1,600. R. R., Union Pacific. Downs' Theatre, J. P. Downs, manager; seating capacity, 300; rental, one night $35; share also; license included. Size of stage, 20x 25; number sets scenery, 6. Newspaper: Chieftain (Sat.) ....Hotels: Mountain Front, regular rates, $2.50 (special also); Ripen.

FORT STEELE, 500. R. R., Union Pacific. Fort Steele Theatre. Size of stage, 20x20; number sets scenery, 6.

LARAMIE, 3,500. R. R., Union Pacific. Ivenson's Hall; seating capacity, 500; rental, one night $25, three $50; share also. Size of stage, 20x24; fair stock scenery. Newspapers: daily, Boomerang; weekly, Sentinel (Sat.)......Hotels: Thornburg's, regular rates, $2 (special also); Laramie.

Blackburn's Hall; seating capacity, 500.

RAWLINS, 2,000. R. R., Union Pacific. Masonic Opera House. J. B. Adams, manager; seating capacity, 350; rental, one night $35; share also, license included Size of stage, 24x16; number sets scenery, 4; bill posters, Jackson & Adams. Newspaper: Journal (Sat.)......Hotels: Maxwell, regular rates, $2 (special also); Rawlins.

CANADA.

—

ARCADIA MINES (Londonderry, Nova Scotia) 5,000. R. R., Inter-Colonial. St. Bridget's Hall; seating capacity, 550; rental, one night $8, three $20, license included. Size of stage, 15x30; full set scenery. Newspapers: Sun, Guardian......Hotels: American, Waverly.

ACTONVALE (Quebec), 2,500. R. R., Grand Trunk; South Eastern. Town Hall; Charles Roscom, manager; seating capacity, 250; rental, one night $5, three $12. Size of stage, 19x24; theatrical teamster, Dolphis Lamontagne......Hotels: Windsor, special rates, $1 to $2; Richelieu, special rates, $1 to $2; South Easter, special rates, $1 to $2; Dominion, special rates, $1 to $2; Center, special rates, $1 to $2; Market, special rates, $1 to $2; Commercial, special rates, $1 to $2.

ALMONT (Ont.), 3,000. R. R., Canadian Pacific (E. Division). Music Hall, R. W. Haydon, manager; seating capacity, 450; rental, one night, $8; three, $18, share also; license $5. Size of stage, 30x15; depth under stage, 3; traps, 2; number sets scenery, 1; leader of orchestra, W. Scrimegour; bill poster, T. Ringrose. Newspapers: weekly, Gazette (Fri.); Times (Thurs.)......Hotels: Davis, Almonte.

BARRIE (Ont.), 5,000. R. R., Northern & North West. Town Hall, Town Clerk, manager; seating capacity, 700; rental, one night $12.50; three $30, license included. Size of stage, 20x45; traps, 2; bill poster, Charles Henry. Newspapers: Advance (Th.), Examiner (Th.), Gazette (Th.)......Hotels : Barrie, special rates, $1 : Queen's, special rates, $1.

BELEVILLE (Ont.) 20,000. R R., Grand Trunk; Mid. of Can. Opera House, Henry Tammadge, manager; seating capacity, 1,200; rental, one night $50, three $100; share also; license, $3. Size of stage, 58x37; size of proscenium opening, 29x29; height from stage to grooves, 18; height from stage to rigging loft, 34; depth under stage, 10; number sets scenery, 12; leader of orchestra, Professor Riggs; scenic artist, Richardson; stage carpenter, W. Wilkins; bill poster, Opera House; number of sheets can accommodate, 1,000; rates per sheet, 3c.; theatrical teamsters, Lake & Jenkins. Newspapers: daily, Ontario, intelligencer......Hotels: Defoe, special rates, $1.50; Queens, special rates, $1; Anglo-American, special rates, $1.

   Metropolitan Hall, J. R. Graham, manager; seating capacity, 650; rental, one night $10, three $25; full set scenery.

   City Hall, D. B. Robertson, manager; seating capacity, 600; rental, one night $15, three $35; license, $2.50.

BOWMANVILLE, (Ont.) 4,000. R R , Grand Trunk. Town Hall, R. Windatt, manager; seating capacity, 400; rental, one night $10, three $2.50; license included. Size of stage, 13x32; bill poster, G. D. Fletcher; theatrical teamster, William Glover. Newspapers: Sun (Th.), News (Fri.), Statesman (Fri.) Hotels: Raebottom, Alma, Arlington.

BROMPTON, (Ont.), 3,000. R. R., Grand Trunk & Canadian Pacific (Ont. Div.). Concert Hall, Town Clerk, manager; seating capacity, 500; rental, one **night $6**, three $12. Size of stage, 20x25; size of proscenium opening, height, **14. Newspapers:** Conservator. Times, Banner......Hotel: **Queen's.**

BRANTFORD (Ont.), **15,000. R. R.**, Grand Trunk. Stratford's Opera House, Jos. Stratford, manager; seating **capacity**, 1,000; rental, one night $50, three $100; share also, license included. Size of stage, 28x50; **full** set scenery; bill poster, Opera House. Newspapers: daily, Courier, Telegram, Expositor......Hotels: Kirby, regular rates, $2 (special also); American, Commercial.

Palmer's Hall; seating capacity, 600.

BRIGHTON, 2,000. R. R., Grand Trunk. Proctor's Hall, I. O. Proctor, manager; seating capacity, 400. **Size of stage, 12x25; size of proscenium opening, 18.** Newspaper: Ensign (Fri.)......**Hotel: Clark's.**

BROCKVILLE (Ont.), 9,000. R. R., Grand Trunk; Canadian & Pacific; U. & B. **Grand Opera House**, Geo. T. Fulpard, manager; seating capacity, 950; rental, one night $40, three $100. Size of stage, 18x36; size of proscenium opening, 24; traps. number sets scenery, 12; leader of orchestra, John Stinson; stage carpenter, John Bottum; bill poster, W. E. Toncks; number of sheets can accommodate, 800; rates per sheet, 2½c. Newspapers: daily, Times, Recorder... ..Hotels: Revere, special rates, $1.50; Grand Central, special rates, $1.50; St. Lawrence, **special** rates, $1.50.

Town Hall, Town Clerk, manager; seating capacity, **1,100; rent or share. Size of stage,** 16x30; full set scenery.

CHARLOTTETOWN (Prince Edward's Island), **12,000. R. R., Prince Edward's Island. Academy of Music,** W. Marsh, manager.

CHATHAM (Ont.), 10,000. R. R., Grand Trunk, **Erie & Huron.** Grand Opera House, Peter Rutherford, manager ; seating capacity, 1,200 ; rental, one night $50, three $150 ; share also ; license included. Size of stage, 32x40 ; size of proscenium opening, 27 ; height from stage to grooves, **16;** height from stage to rigging loft, 35; depth under stage, 3½; traps, 2 ; number sets **scenery**, 12 ; leader of orchestra, **Mr.** Callender ; stage carpenter, George White ; bill poster, **Wm.** Harding ; number of sheets can accommodate, 250 ; rates per sheet, 3c. Newspapers: tri-weekly, Planet, advertising rates, 8c. per line ; weekly, Banner (Wed.). Hotels: Garner, special rates, $1.25 to $1.50; Rankin, special rates, $1.25 to $1.50.

Bright's Opera House, J. C. Bright, manager; seating capacity, **1,200;** rental, one night $25, three $50; share also. Size of stage, 54x20; full set scenery.

Music Hall; seating capacity, 1,300.

CHATHAM (N.B.), 5,000. R.R., Intercolonial (Chatham Branch). Masonic Hall, T. F. Gillespie, **manager** ; seating capacity, 700 ; rental, one night $12, three $30 ; license, $3. Size of **stage**, 20x36 ; size of proscenium opening, 12x24 ; height from stage to grooves, 14 ; **depth** under stage, 7 ; traps, 1 ; **number** sets scenery, 6 ; leader of orchestra, John **Templeton** ; bill poster, William Tilett ; number of sheets can accommodate, 150 ; rates per sheet, 2c.; theatrical teamster, **Thos.** Fitzpatrick. Newspapers : semi-weekly, World (Wed. and Sat.); weekly, Advance (Wed.)......Hotels: Bowser's, special rates, $1 ; Metropolitan, special rates, 75c. to $1; Canada, special rates, 75c. to $1.

COBOURG (Ont.), 5,000. R.R., Grand Trunk. Victoria Opera House, Wm. H. Floyd, manager; seating capacity, 800; rental, one night **$19,** license included. Size of stage, 25x26; size of proscenium opening, 14x20; depth under stage, 4; traps, 1; number sets scenery, 3; bill poster, Dan Jeffrey; number sheets can accommodate, 140; rates per sheet, 2c.; theatrical teamster, James O'Neill. Newspapers: Sentinel-Star (Th.), advertising rates per inch, $1; World (Fri.), **advertising** rates per inch, **$1**......Hotels: Dunham, special rates, $1.25 to $1.50; Horton, special rates, $1; Queen's, special rates, $1.

COLLINGWOOD (Ont.), 5,000. R. R., Northern and North Western. Music Hall, Charles C. Lindsay; seating capacity, 700; rental, one night $10, three $20; share also; license, $3. **Size** of stage, 18x31; fair stock of scenery; bill poster, manager; number of sheets can accommodate, 150; rates per sheet, 3c.; theatrical teamster, George Eldon. Newspapers: Bulletin (Th.), advertising rates, 25c. per inch; Enterprise (Th.), 10c per line. ..... Hotels: Globe, special rates, $1; Central, special rates, $1 to $1.50.

CORNWALL (Ont.), 5,000. R. R., Grand Trunk. **Music Hall, Town Clerk, manager;** seating capacity, 800; rental, one night $25, license included. Size of stage, 28x47; number sets scenery, 6; bill poster, Geo. Durmo. **Newspapers:** Freeholder (Fri.), Gazette (Sat.).... , Hotels: American, Commercial, Ottawa.

New Opera House. •

EMERSON (Manitoba), 1,500. R. R., Canadian Pacific. **Emerson Opera House,** A. Russ- kopt, manager; seating capacity, 600; rental, one night $25; no license. Newspaper: In- ternational (Th.) ..... Hotel: Cardey.

FREDERICKSTON (New Brunswick), 7,000. R. R., New Brunswick. **City Hall,** M. S. Hall, manager; seating capacity, 600; rental, one night $10; license, $5. Size of stage, 16x21; no scenery; bill poster, Boyd Hamilton; theatrical teamster, Jas. Dorcus. News- papers: tri weekly, **Capital; semi-weekly, Reporter**......Hotels : Parker, Queen, Bayley, Waverly, Commercial.

St. Dunstan's Hall; seating capacity, 500.

GALT, (Ont.), 6,200. R. R., Can. Pac.; Grand Trunk. **Town Hall,** E. J. Wilkins, manager; seating capacity, 800; rental, one night $10, three $24. Size of stage, 16x30; size of proscenium opening, 12x22; depth under stage, 4; **number sets scenery, 1; leader of or-** chestra, Prof. Hindmarsh; bill poster, Israel Fisher; theatrical teamster, George Han- cock. Newspapers: Reformer (Th.), Reporter (Fri.) .....Hotels; Queen's, special rates, **50c. to $1;** Imperial, special rates, 50c. to $1.

GRAVENHURST, (Ont.), 2,000. R. R., **Nor.** & N. Western. **Town Hall, Town Clerk,** manager; **seating** capacity, 200; rental, one night $2.50. **Size of stage,** 18x30; size of proscenium opening, 11x13; depth under stage, 9; number **of sheets can accommodate,** 10. Newspaper Banner (Fri.).... , Hotels: Fraser's, special **rates, $1; Royal.**

GUELPH (Ont.) 12,000. R. R., Grand Trunk. **City Hall,** J. **Harvey, manager;** seating capacity, 1,500; rental one night $10, license included; full set scenery; bill poster, J. J. Sutton. Newspapers, daily, Herald, Advertiser......Hotels; Royal, regular rates, $1.50 (special also), Wellington, Western.

HALIFAX (N. S.)—including Dartmouth—70,000. R. R., Intercolonial; Boston & Maine; Windsor & Annapolis. Academy of Music, K. B. Clarke, manager; seating capacity, **1,100;** rental, one night, **$40; three** $120; **share also;** license, $10; size of stage, **33x39; size** of proscenium opening, 40x36; height from stage to grooves, 20; height from **stage** to rigging loft, 50; depth under stage, 20; full set of scenery; leader of orches- **tra, H.** Hagarty; stage carpenter, W. Whittaker; bill poster, C. Putnam; number of **sheets can** accommodate, 700; rates per sheet, 3c.; theatrical teamster, C. R. Barry. Newspapers: daily, Recorder, advertising rates, special contract; Herald, advertising rates, special contract; Chronicle, advertising rates, special contract; Mail and Citizen, adver- tising rates, special contract......Hotels; Halifax, special rates, $1.50 to $2; Inter- national, special rates, $1.25 to $1.75; Russell House, special rates, $1; Acadian, special rates.

Lyceum, John Delacy, manager; seating capacity, 750; rental one night $15; **three nights** $45; license, $5; share also; size of stage, 24x22; number sets scenery, 10.

HAMILTON, (Ont.), 40,000. R. R., Grand Trunk, Northern **& N.** Western. **Grand Opera** House, J. B. Spackman, manager; seating capacity, 1,200; rental, one night, $50 to $65, **license** included, share also. Size of stage, 35x50; height from stage to grooves, 18; height **from stage** to rigging loft, 18; depth under stage, 12; full set scenery; bill poster, P. J. **Culihane;** theatrical teamster, Jas. Reid. Newspapers: daily, Times, Spectator, Tribune. ......**Hotels:** Royal, special rates, $2; St. Nicholas, $1.25.

Mechanic's **Hall;** seating capacity, 1,200.

INGERSOLL, **(Ont.),** 6,000. R. R., Grand Trunk; Canada Pacific (Ontario Div.) Town Hall, seating capacity, 700. Newspapers; Reporter (Th.), Sun (Wed.). Hotels: Daly's, regular rates, $1.50 (special also); Atlantic, McMurray; Royal, Adair.

Music Hall; seating capacity, 500.

KINGSTON (Ont.), 15,000. **R. R., Grand** Trunk; King. & Pembroke. Martin's Opera House, W. C. Martin, manager; seating capacity, 1,054; share only. Size of stage, 32x 56; size of proscenium opening, 27x30; height from stage to grooves, 16; height from stage to rigging loft, 34; depth under stage, 10; number sets scenery, 18; leader of **or**chestra, Prof. Telymann; bill poster, Opera House; number of sheets can accommodate, 600; rates per sheet, **3c.**; theatrical teamsters, McCammon Bros. Newspapers: daily, Whig, advertising rates per line, 5c. to 10c.; News, advertising rates per line, 5c. **to** 10c...... Hotels: Burnett, special **rates, $1** to $1.25; British American, $1.25 to $1.50; City.   •

Opera House; **seating capacity, 1,200; rental, one** night $30. **Size of stage, 29x31.**

City Hall; **seating capacity, 1,400; rental, one night $20, license included.**

LINDSAY (Ont.), 6,000. **R. R., Grand** Trunk (Midland Division). **Bradborn's Opera House,** T. **E. Bradburn,** manager; seating capacity, 600; **rental, one night $20, three $50; share** also; **license** included. Size of stage, 39x26; size of proscenium **opening, 13x20;** height from **stage to grooves,** 14; height from stage to rigging loft, **15; depth under stage, 3;** number sets scenery, 11; leader of orchestra, J. Bates, Esq.; stage carpenter, **S. McGraw;** bill poster, manager of Opera House; number of sheets can accommodate, 550; rates per sheets, 3c; theatrical teamster, S. McGraw. Newspapers: Post (Fri.), Warder (Fri.) ...... Hotels: Benson, special rates, $1.25 to $1.50; Waters', 90c. to $1; Royal, 75c. to $1.

LONDON (Ont.), 30,000. **R. R.,** Grand Trunk. Grand Opera House, J. H. Davidson, manager; **seating** capacity, 1,200; rental, one night $75; three $200, license included; share also; full set **scenery;** leader of orchestra, Prof. Chadwick; stage carpenter, J. C. Bradley; bill poster, **Manville** & Brown; number **of** sheets can accommodate, 2,500; rates per sheet, 4c.; **theatrical** teamster, Manville & Brown. Newspapers: daily, Free Press, advertising rates, 10c. **per** line; Advertiser, advertising rates 10c. per **line.** ...... Hotels: Tecumseh, regular rate $2 to $3 (special also); Grigg, regular rate, $1.50 to $2 (special also); City, American.

Music Hall, Howard Clifton, manager; **seating capacity, 900;** full set scenery.

MENFORD (Ont.), 2,200. **R. R.,** Northern & North Western. **Town Hall,** James Cammar, manager; seating capacity, 350; rental, **one** night $5; **three $9. Size** of stage, 30x20. Newspapers: Mirror (Th.), Monitor (Fri.)...... Hotels: **Paul, special** rates, $1; Royal, special rate, $1; City, special rate, $1.

MONTREAL (Quebec), 165,000. **R. R** , Grand Trunk; South **Eastern; North Shore; Can. Pa**cific. **Crystal Palace Opera House, G. P.** Brown, **manager; seating** capacity, 3,000; rental, share only ; license, yearly. Size of stage, 50x20 ; size of proscenium opening, 25x30; height from stage to grooves, 14; height from stage **to** rigging loft, 18; depth under stage, 4½ ; traps, 1 ; number sets scenery, 20. Newspapers : daily, Gazette, Herald and Commercial Gazette, Post, Star, Witness.. ...Hotels : Windsor, regular rates, $3.50 (special also) ; St. Lawrence, regular rates, $3 to $3.50 (special also) ; Albion, regular rates, $1.50 to $2 (special also) ; Richelieu, regular rates, $2 to $3 (special also).

Academy of Music, Henry Thomas, manager; seating capacity, 1,835; rental, one night, $60, three $150, share also; license included. Size of stage, 34x48; full set scenery.

Nordheimer's Hall, A. & **L. Nordheimer,** managers; seating capacity, **1,000;** rental, one night $50; share also. Size of stage, 27x22; full set scenery.   •

Queen's Hall, Henry Thomas, manager; seating capacity, 1,200; rental, one night $50; share also, license included; no scenery

Mechanics' Hall, S. M. Sangum, manager; seating capacity, **£00;** rental, one night $25 to $35, license included. Size of stage, 28x30.

Albert Hall, De **Zouche & Co., managers;** seating capacity, 1,000.

Theatre Royal, seating capacity, 1,500.

Opera House, seating capacity, 1,500.

NEPANEE (Ont.), 3,600. R. R., Grand Trunk. Opera House, H. Empery, manager ; seating capacity, 600. Size of stage, 18x24. Newspapers Beaver (Sat.), Casket (Fri.), Express (Fri.), Standard (Sat.)......Hotels: Bursian, Hoffman, Campbell.

Symington's Opera Hall, Thos. Symington, manager; seating capacity, 800.

NEW WESTMINSTER (British Columbia), 3,500. Theatre Royal, C. N. Frew, manager; seating capacity, 300; rental, one night $25. Fair stock scenery. Newspapers : semi-weekly: Columbian, Guardian. Hotel : **Occident.**

NIAGARA FALLS (Ont.), 3,500. **R. R.,** Grand Trunk ; Michigan Central ; Erie ; West Shore ; Lehigh Valley. Town Hall, John **Robinson,** manager ; seating capacity, 450 ; rental, one night $8, three $15, license included. Size of stage, 12x18; size of proscenium opening, 25x18 ; height from stage to grooves, 11 ; number sets scenery, 5 ; bill poster, George Coulson ; theatrical teamster, Archie Moore. Newspaper: Review (Fri.)........ Hotels : American, regular rates, $2 (special **also**) ; Queen's Royal, regular rates, $2 (special also.)

ORANGEVILLE, (Ont.), 3,000. R. R., Toronto, Grey & Bruce; Canadian Pac., (Credit Val. Div.) Town Hall, F. Irwin, manager; seating capacity, 600; rental, one night $6. Size of stage, 15x18; proscenium opening, 17; no scenery; leader of orchestra, Eri Whaley; theatrical teamster, Joseph Lathwell. Newspapers: Sun (Th.), Advertiser (Fri.)......Hotels : Queens, Gordon House, Palslip House.

ORILLIA, (Ont.), 3,000. **R. R., Midland of Canada; Northern & North Western.** Music Hall, Frank Kean, **manager ; seating capacity,** 600; rental, one night $8, three $20. Size of stage, 16x21; **bill poster, J. J. Smith.** Newspapers : Packet (Fri), Times (Th.)........Hotels : **Russell, Orillia.**

Kennedy's Hall; seating capacity, **500; rental, one night §10.**

OSHAWA, (Ont.), 5,000. R. R., Grand Trunk. **Wilson's Music Hall.** John Wilson, manager ; seating capacity, 800; rental, one night **$10, license included.** Size of stage, 25x28; size of proscenium opening, 14x20; height from stage to grooves, 13; height from stage to rigging loft, 15; depth under stage, 4; traps, 1; number **sets scenery, 13; leader of orchestra, Anderson ; scenic artist, Morris & Toronto ; bill poster, Pattie ; number sheets** can accommodate, 500 ; rates per **sheet,** 3c. ; theatrical teamster, Mr. Thomas. Newspapers : Vindicator (Wed.), **Reformer (Fri).......**Hotels: American, Queens, Ontario, Commercial, Central.

OTTAWA (Ont.), 27,000. R. R., Canadian Pacific; Canada Atlantic. **Grand Opera House,** John Ferguson, manager; seating capacity, 1,300; share also. Size of **stage, 31x60** ; size of proscenium opening, 32; height from stage to grooves, 16; height from stage to rigging loft, 32; depth under stage, 10; traps, 3; number sets **scenery, 25; leader of orchestra,** A. Weakley; stage carpenter, T. Carl; bill poster, Alex **Jaques;** number sheets can accommodate, 500; rates per sheet, 3c.; theatrical teamster, **J. Wigmore.** Newspapers : daily, Citizen; advertising rates 5c. to 10c. per line; Free Press, advertising **rates** 5c. to 10c. per line......Hotels: Russell, special rates, $1.50 to $3; **Windsor,** special **rates,** $1.50 to $2; Grand Union, special rates, $1.50 to $2.

OWEN SOUND (Ont.), 4,000. **R. R , Canadian Pacific (Ontario Division).** Town Hall, A. J. pencer, manager ; seating **capacity, 700 ; rental, one night $10 ; no license.** Size of stage, 17x13, no scenery. **Newspapers : Advertiser (Th.), Times (Th.)......**Hotels : Albion, American, Queen's, Coulson.

Orangemen's Hall; seating capacity, 1,000.

PETERBOROUGH (Ont.), 10,000. R. R., Canadian Pacific **(Ontario Division); Midland of** Canada. Bradburn's Opera House, T. Bradburn, manager; **seating capacity, 1,000; rent** only. Size of stage, 30x40 ; fair stock scenery; bill poster, **E. C. Hill. Newspapers:** daily, Review; weekly, Examiner (Th.)......Hotels : Grand Central, Oriental, Choate.

PICTON (Ont.), 4,000. R. R., **Central Ontario.** Town Hall, seating **capacity, 500;** rental, one night $5, three $12; **number sets scenery, 3.** Newspapers: Gazette (Fri.), Times (Th.)......Hotels: Wilson. **Victoria, Mattashed.**

PORTAGE LA PRAIRE (Manitoba), 3,000. **R. R., Canada Pacific.** Town Hall, Town Clerk, manager; seating capacity, 400; **rental, one night $10** Size of Stage, 16x20; bill poster, Peter McPherson. Newspapers : **Liberal (Th.), Review (Fri.)......**Hotels: Grand Pacific, Lorne, Belleview, Queen's.

PORT ARTHUR (Ont.), 18,000. Prince **Arthur Theatre,** Geo. **Rankin, manager; seating** capacity, 600. Newspaper: Herald **(Th.) .....**Hotel: Queen's.

PORT HOPE (Ont.), 7,000.   R. R., Grand Trunk   Music Hall, F. Hobbs, manager ; seating capacity, 500; **rental,** one night, $10; share also.   Size of stage, 25x24; fair stock scenery; bill poster, manager of hall.   Newspapers: daily, Guide; weekly Times (Th.)... . Hotels: Queen's, **St.** Lawrence.

Town Hall; seating capacity, 350.

PRESCOTT, (Ont.), 3,500.   R. R., **Grand Trunk: St. Lawrence & Ottawa.   Victoria Hall,** B. White, manager; seating capacity, 900; **rental, $10.   Size of stage, 22x20; size of pro-**scenium, 12x22; height from stage to **grooves, 10; height from stage to rigging loft, 17;** depth under stage, 4; number sets **scenery, 4; bill poster, John Robinson; number sheets can accommodate, 400; rate per sheet, 3c.; theatrical teamster,** John Hollingsworth. Newspapers: Conservative Messenger (Fri.); advertising rates, 3c. to 10c. line; Telegraph, advertising rates, 3c. to 10c. line......Hotels: Daniele, special rates.

QUEBEC (Quebec), 65,000.   R. R., Grand **Trunk (south side); North Shore ; Quebec & Lake** St. John.   Victoria Hall, A. Lavigne, manager; seating capacity, **800; 'rental, one night,** $50; three $150.   *Size of stage, 31x24; size of proscenium opening, 18x30; depth under stage, 9; traps, 2; number sets scenery, 3; bill poster, Bernard Sewell; number of sheets can accommodate, 500; rates per sheet, 2c.   Newspapers : daily, Chronicle, advertising rates per line, 10c; Telegraph, advertising rates per line, 5c.; L'Evenement, advertising rates, 3c. per line; Le Canadien, advertising rates, 3c. per line; Le Electeur, advertising rates, 3c. per line... ...Hotels: St. Louis, special rates, $2; Mountain Hill, special rates, $1.25; Blanchard's, special rates, $1.

Music Hall; rental, **one night, $75, license included.**

Opera House; seating capacity, 1,100.

RIDGETOWN (Ont.), 4,000.   R. R., Michigan Central (Can. Division).   Porter's Opera House, Wm. Teetzel, manager; seating capacity, 800; rental, one night $30; three $60; share also.   Size of stage, 20x24; size of proscenium opening, 14 ; height from stage to grooves, 11½; height from stage to rigging **loft, 17; depth under stage, 3; traps, 2; num-ber sets scenery, 16; bill poster, Wm. Simpson; number of sheets can accommodate, 25;** rates per sheet, 3c; theatrical teamster, Sylvester **Potts.   Newspapers:** Plain Dealer (Wed.), advertising rates 10c. line; Standard (Wed.), **advertising rates, 10c. line......** Hotels: Grand Central, special rates $1; Benton.

SACKVILLE (N. B.), 1,500.   **R. R., Intercolonial, Junction N. B. & P. E.   Sackville Music** Hall, C. B. **Trueman,** manager ;   seating capacity, 600 ; **rental, one night $20.   Size of stage, 27x45 ;** size of **proscenium opening, 13x18 ;   height from stage to** grooves, 12 ; height from stage to rigging loft, 16 ;   theatrical **teamster, Chas. Scott.** Newspaper : Post (Tb.)......Hotels: Brunswick, special rates, $1.25 **to $2;** Temperance, special rates, $1 to $1.50; International.

ST. CATHARINES (Ont.), 20,000 (with suburbs).   R. R. St. Catharines' Opera House, H. S. Hunt, manager (see p. 100) ; seating capacity, 1,200 ; rental, one night $40, three $100; **share also,** license included.   Size of stage, 27x54 ;   size of proscenium opening, 30½x26½; height from stage to grooves, 20; height from stage to rigging loft, 26 ;   depth under stage, 7 ;   traps, 6 ;   number sets scenery, 15 ;   leader of orchestra, **Prof. Hyde ;** scenic artist, Baldwin ;   stage carpenter, **G. F.** Ledestrere ;   bill **poster,** Opera House ; number of sheets can accommodate, 600 ;   **rates** per sheet, 3c.;   **theatrical** teamster, W Sutton.   Newspapers :   daily, Journal, advertising rates, **yearly** contract ;   News, advertising **rates,** yearly contract......Hotels :   Welland, special rates, $1.25 to $1.50 ; Grand Central, special rates, $1 to $1.25.

ST. JOHNS (N. B.), 50,000.   R. R., **Grand** Southern; Intercolonial; New Brunswick; Internat. S. S. Co.   Mechanics' Institute, **C. C.** Parker, manager; **seating** capacity, 1,000; rental, one night $31.50; three $94.50; license, **$5; do not share; size of** stage. 28x54; height from stage **to** grooves, 15, depth under stage, 4; **full set scenery;** bill poster, Thos. Rogers.   Newspapers: daily, News, Sun, Globe, **Telegraph......Hotels:** Waverly, International, Park.

Dockrill Hall, J. B. Dockrill, **manager; seating capacity, 700.**

ST. JOHNS (Quebec), 6,000. R. R., **Grand Trunk; Central** Vermont.   **City Theatre, Roy Brothers, managers;** seating capacity, 500; rental, one night $10, three $22; **license, $5;**

share also; size of stage, 20x3); bill poster, Peter Sylvester; Newspapers: Advocate (Fri.) .....Hotels: United States, St. Johns.

Black's Opera House, Roy Brothers, managers.

ST. MARYS (Ontario), 5,000. R. R., Grand Trunk. Odd Fellows' Opera House, Wm. M. Lord, manager; seating capacity, 1,000. Newspapers: Argus, (Th.); Journal, (Th.)...... Hotels: Burley, regular rates, $1.50; special also; Ontario.

ST. THOMAS (Ontario), 12,000. R. R., Michigan Central; Grand Trunk; Credit Valley & London & Port Stanley. Opera House, Geo. F. Claus, manager; seating capacity, 900; rental, one night $25, three $60, license included. Size of stage, 18x46; size of proscenium opening, 36x32; height from stage to grooves, 11; height from stage to rigging loft, 22; depth under stage, 5; traps, 2, number sets scenery, 12; leader of orchestra, Prof. Symington; scenic artist, Adam Walthew; stage carpenter, H. Lendop; bill poster, D. Oxlay; number sheets can accommodate, 250, rates per sheet, 3c. Newspapers: daily, Times, advertising rates per line, 4c.; Journal, advertising rates per line, 4c..... Hotels: Grand Central, special rates, $1.50; Hutchinson, special rates, $1; Lisgar, special rates, $1; Dominion.

SARNIA (Ontario), 6,000. R. R., Grand Trunk. Town Hall, E. H. Johnston, manager; seating capacity, 650; rental, one night $11, three $23. Size of stage, 20x17; size of proscenium opening, 15x20; bill poster, Edward Hardway; number sheets can accommodate, 150; rates per sheet, 3c.; theatrical teamster, Morris Joy. Newspapers: Observer (Wed.), Canadian (Fri.), Sun (Sat.)......Hotels: Belchamber, Alexander, Chapman, McDonald.

SHERBROOKE (Quebec.) 8,350. R. R., Grand Trunk, Passumpsic; International; Quebec Central. City Hall, Wm. Griffith, manager; seating capacity, about 400; rental, one night $15; depth under stage, 4; leader of orchestra, Mr. Wilson; stage carpenter, Wm. Long; bill poster, Geo. McAndrews; rates per sheet, 3½c. Newspapers : Gazette (Fri.), Examiner (Fri.), Pionnier (Fri.), Progress de l'Est (Fri.) ......Hotels: Magog, Sherbrooke, Continental.

Town Hall; seating capacity, 500.

SOREL (Quebec.) 7,000 R. R., South Eastern; R. & Ont. Navigation Co. Town Hall, M. C. Blais, manager; seating capacity, 870; rental, one night $30, three $60. Size of stage, 30x12; size of proscenium opening, 18x26; height from stage to grooves, 16; depth under stage, 3½; traps, 4; number sets scenery, 12; stage carpenter, A. Allard; bill poster, F. Allard; number sheets can accommodate, 250; rates per sheet, 1c. Newspaper; News (Sat.).....Hotels: Pichi, special rates, $1.25; Richelieu, special rates, $1; Canada, special rates, $1.

STRATHROY (Ontario), 4,500. R. R., Grand Trunk. Albert Hall, Robert Richards, manager; seating capacity, 600; rental, one night, $15, share also; license included. Size of stage, 20x44; number sets scenery, 10; bill poster, John Frank. Newspapers : Age (Th.); Dispatch (Wed.)......Hotels : Revere, regular rates, $1.50 (special also); Queen, Praugley, Commercial, American.

Music Hall, Jas. Seaton, manager ; seating capacity, 700; rent or share.

TORONTO (Ont.). 93,000. R. R., Canadian Pacific (Ont. Div.); Mich. Central; Grand Trunk; Mid. of Can ; Nor. & N. W. Grand Opera House, O. B. Sheppard, manager; Brooks & Dickson, New York representatives; seating capacity, 1,650. Size of stage, 49x65; height from stage to grooves, 20; height from stage to rigging loft, 60; bill poster, William Tozer; theatrical teamsters, Toronto Baggage Transfer Co. Newspapers : daily, Canadian, News, Telegram, Globe, Mail, World..... Hotels: Rassin, regular rates, $2.50 to $3.50 (special also); Queen's, regular rates, $3 to $3.50 (special also); American, regular rates, $2 (special also).

People's Theatre, J. C. Conner, manager; seating capacity, 1,350; rental, share only, license included. Size of stage, 23½x46; size of proscenium opening, 18x22; height from stage to grooves, 18; height from stage to rigging loft, 33; depth under stage, 13; number sets scenery, 12; leader of orchestra, Ernest Morley; scenic artist, Geo. Morris; stage carpenter, Burress Raymond; bill posters, W. Foyer and H. Jackman, number of sheets can accommodate, 2,000; rates per sheet, 3 to 3½c.

Bijou Opera House, **J. C. Connor, manager; seating capacity, 1,200. Size of stage, 40x70;** height from stage **to grooves, 21; height from stage to rigging loft, 44;** depth under stage, 9.

Horticultural Hall; seating capacity, 3,000.

Royal Opera House; seating capacity, 1,400.

Shaftesbury **Hall; seating capacity, 1,100.**

TRENTON (Ontario) **4,000.   R. R., Central Ontario;** Grand Trunk. Purdy's Hall; seating capacity, 600; rental, one night $5; license, $2; fair stock scenery : bill poster, Scammerhorn. Newspapers: Courier (Th.), Advocate (Th.) .. ..Hotels: St. Lawrence Hall, Queen's.

TRURO **(Nova Scotia), 3,000.   R. R., Intercolonial.   Young Men's** Christian Association Hall; **seating capacity, 800; bill poster, John Pavoc**......Hotels: Victoria, Tremont, **Grand Central, Prince of Wales.**

Victoria Hall, Geo. Gunn, **manager; seating capacity, 400; rental, one** night $12; license, 4. Size of stage, **14x45;** no scenery.

VICTORIA (British Columbia), 8,000.   Philharmonic Hall, J. I. Hewlings, manager, seating capacity, 500; rental, one night $16; license, $5.   Size of stage, 23x23; number sets scenery, 5; bill poster, Hy. West. Newspapers: daily, Colonist, Standard .....Hotels: Oriental, Driard, Occidental.

WELLANS (Ont.), 3,000.   R. R., Michigan Central; Welland. Orient Hall, A. Williams, manager; seating capacity, 700; rental, one night $40, three $20; share also, license included.   Size of stage, 32x20; number sets scenery, 3; bill poster, Jos. Young. Newspapers: Farmer (Wed.), Telegraph (Fri.), Tribune (Fri.)......Hotels: Bender, Windsor, Welland, Queen's, Frazer, City.

WHITBY (Ont.), 3,500.   R. R., Grand Trunk; Midland of Canada. Town Hall, Thos. Huston, manager; seating capacity, 800; rental, one night, $12. Size of stage, 20x45; number sets scenery, 10; bill poster, Jos. Newberry. Newspapers: Chronicle (Fri.), Gazette (Fri.)......Hotels: Royal, Armstrong, American, British.

WINNIPEG (Manitoba), 65,000.   R. R., Canadian Pacific.   Princess Opera House, C. A Dunlap, manager; seating capacity, 1,300; rental, share only; license, $10. Size of stage, 73x38. Newspapers: daily, Free Press, Sun, Times......Hotels: Union, Grand.

City Hall, City Chamberlain, manager; seating capacity, 600; rental, three nights $60; fair stock scenery.

Standard Opera House, Reed & Co., managers.

WOODSTOCK (New Brunswick), 3,000.   R. R., New Brunswick.   Mechanics' Institute, Stephen B. Appleby, manager; seating capacity, 400 ; rental, one night $8. Newspapers: Sentinel (Sat), Press (Th.) .....Hotel: Cable.

MEXICO.

AGUAS CALIENTES, 35,000.   R. R., Mexican Central.   Theatre.

CHIHUAHUA, 25,000.   R. R., Mexican Central.   Theatre.

GUANAJUATO, 65,000.   R. R., Mexican Central.   Theatre.

LEON, 100,000.   R. R., Mexican Central   Theatre.

MEXICO CITY, 315,000.   R. R., Mexican National ; Mexican. Gran Teatro National; Teatro Principal.

ORIZABA, 35,000.   R. R., Mexican.   Theatre.

PUEBLO, 90,000.   R. R., Mexican.   Theatre.

QUERETARO, 45,000.   R. R., Mexican Central   Theatre.

VERA CRUZ, 25,000.   R. R., Mexican.   **Theatre.**

ZACAETCAS, 65,000.   **Theatre.**   ·

Dramatic and Musical Editors and Critics.

NEW YORK.

Tribune—Wm. Winter, dramatic; **H. E.** Khrebiel, musical.

Herald—Address Ed. Herald.

Times—Chas. A. Dithmar

World—A. C. Wheeler.

Sun—W. Laffau, dramatic; **G. Kobbe**, musical.

Journal—Chas. A. Byrne, dramatic; John Gilbert, musical.

Truth—J. **W. Keller.**

Post—**Mr. Towse.**

Telegram—Address Ed. Telegram.

Commercial Advertiser—Mr. Sheldon.

Mail and Express—J. M. Fleming.

News—**J. C.** Gallagher.

Graphic—Mr. Perkins.

Dial—**Geo. W. Horn**

Sunday Mercury—H. **L. Parker.**

Sunday Times—Chas. Smith.

Sunday Courier—Jerome Eddy.

Sunday Dispatch—John A. Harrington.

Mirror—H. G. Fiske.

Freund's Weekly—John C. Freund, dramatic; J. T. Quigg, musical.

Clipper—J. A. Fynes, dramatic; Geo. **W.** Keil, musical.

Dramatic News—J. W. Keller.

Dramatic Times—Charles A. **Byrne and** Leander Richardson.

The Judge—Geo. H. Jessup.

Puck—**B. B.** Valentine.

Staats Zeitung—Gustav Stein.

New **Yorker** Zeitung—L. Frank, dramatic; Herman Alexander.

New **Yorker Herald**—Same.

Courier des **Etats-Unis**—H. **Paulejenne.**

PHILADELPHIA.

Ledger—Robert McWade.

Press—M. P. Handy.

Times—J. H. Lambert.

Inquirer—L. Clarke Davis.

Record—M. M. Gillam.

North American—John M. **Perry.**

German Democrat, Herman Dieck.

Telegraph—W. H. Clark.

Bulletin—**L. Williamson.**

Star—C. **E. School.**

Chronicle-Herald—Edward T. Harvey

News—E. H. Nevin, Jr.

Item—H. Fitzgerald.

Call—Geo. D. Fox.

McClure's Times—Dr. Lambden.

Taggart's Times—Harry Taggart and L. Walazz.

Record—Wm. R. Lester.

Dispatch—William Anderson.

Sunday Press—W. B. Merrill.

Mercury—D Dealy.

Item—R Fitzgerald.

World—Hugh Mullen.

Transcript—Thomas Jackson.

Republic—J. W. Dunglison.

Mirror—J. F. Wallis

BROOKLYN.

Union—N. A. Clows.

Times—Chas. M. Skinner.

Free Press—Mr. Rohr.

CHICAGO.

Tribune—Edward McPhelim, dramatic; Chas. W. Britton, musical.

Times—Geo. M. McConnell.

The Inter-Ocean—Elwyn A. Barron, dramatic; **Charles E. Nixon, musical.**

Herald—F. D. Bogart. •

Journal—**W. K. Sullivan.**

Morning News—David Henderson, dramatic; Prof W. S. B. Mathews, musical.

Staats Zeitung—Paul Hardicke, dramatic; A. Simon, musical.

News Letter—D. **Dalziel**, dramatic; H. B Smith musical.

The Chicago World—Lee **Harris**, dramatic; E. H. Benton, musical.

The Indicator—Mrs. **O. L. Fox.**

Dunton's Spirit of **the Turf (weekly).—Miss** Dora A. Dunton

Skandinaven—F. S. **Anderson.**

Neue Freie Presse—Mr. Rorenegk.

Saturday Evening **Herald** (weekly)—L. B. Glover.

Swedish Tribune (weekly)—C. A. Melander.

Hemlandet (weekly)—Gustof W. Haliborn

BOSTON.

Herald—E. A. **Perry, dramatic;** F. P. **Bacon,** musical.

Globe—C. **W. Dyar.**

Traveller—J **W. Clarke.**

Advertiser—H. A. Clapp.

Journal—W. W. Clapp.

Transcript—F. **H.** Jenks, dramatic; W F Apthorpe, musical.

Post—G. **C. Burpee.**

Star—Wm. **O.** Haskell, jr.

Courier—J. F. Travers.

Times—H. Irving Dillenback.

Gazette—B. K. Woolf.

Express—Samuel M. Hobbs.

ST. LOUIS.

Globe-Democrat— Samuel A. **Cary**, **jr.**
Republican—Thos. E. Garrett.
Post-Dispatch—David L. Reed.
Westliche Post— E. D. Cargan.
Amerika—Carl Ungar.
Anzeiger des Westens— J. Schroers.
Chronicle—W. A. Beall.
Tribune (German)—Reinhold Deitzein.
Spectator (weekly)—Wilson Primm.
Critic (weekly)—D. Brugman.

BALTIMORE.

American—J. W. Shrieder and Chas. B. Clarke.
Day—Harry Wilson **and John V. Hood.**
Sun—N. E. Foard.
Evening News—Wm. P. Murray.
Telegram—Wm. J. Cook.
Item—Maurice Lobe.
Every Saturday—Chas. Coughy.

CINCINNATI.

Commercial-Gazette—Montgomery Phister, dramatic; James A. Homans, musical.
Enquirer—Al. Thayer, dramatic; Frank E. Tunnison, musical.
Times-Star— Henry **Miner**, dramatic; Wm. Butler, musical.
Penny Press—W. Ridenour.
Journal—Chas. McLean.
Volks-blatt—Mr. Markbreit.
Volksfreund—Mr. Puetch.

SAN FRANCISCO.

Morning Cali—Geo. Ed. Barnes.
Evening Bulletin—G. **B.** Densmore.
Alta California— W. **D. Walker.**
Chronicle—Peter Robertson.
Daily Examiner—Mrs. John M. Chretien.
Evening Post—Wm. Horace Wright.
The Figaro—John P. Bogardus, dramatic; Mary C. Bogardus, musical.
Daily Exchange—Will V. Walsh.
Daily Report—W. M. Bunker.
The Argonaut—Mrs. Mary Austin ("Betsy **B.**"), dramatic.
The Ingleside—Mrs. Frank Unger, dramatic; stage talk, H. D. Bigelow.
Le Courrier de San Francisco—Mons. **A.** Loiseau.
Le Petit Journal—Mons. A. Labadie.
Music **and** Drama—John C. Thrum.
California Journal—Otis von Ploennies.
The San Francisco—Wm. Eyre.
News Letter—Raoul Martinez.
Spirit of the Times—Alex. G. Abel, Jr.
Argus—W. F. A. Walker.
Democrat—Alex. **Von Hubn.**
Abend Post—Dr. B. Paulsen.
Sontagg's Gast—Chas. **Henfuer.**

CLEVELAND, O.

Leader—J. B. Wilson.
Herald—Maurice Weidenthal.
Penny Press—Maurice Perkins.
Plain Dealer—N. S. Cobleigh

Sentinel—**M.** Welfare.
Sun—F. A. Sanrying.
Voice—Mr. Burgess.

PITTSBURGH.

Commercial Gazette—F. F. Hudson.
Post—Park H. Walters.
Times—T. C. Keenan.
Leader—W. W. Clark.
Dispatch—
Chronicle—David Lowry
Telegraph—Geo. Martin.
Sunday Critic—Harry Brown.

BUFFALO, N. Y.

Morning **Express—L. G.** Chaffin.
Daily and Sunday **Courier and Evening** Republic—Simon Fleischman.
Evening Commercial—J. **R. Drake**, musical.
Sunday Times—John B. Sewell, jr., dramatic; O. H. Holt, musical.
Sunday and Evening News—No regular critic.
Evening Telegraph—No regular critic.

WASHINGTON, D. C.

Republican—W. D. Eaton.
Post—Wm. Splaine
Star—C. S. Noyes.
Critic—Frank Morgan.
Sunday Herald- J. N. Barritt.
Capital—Mr. Rheem.
Gazette—John Shaw.

LOUISVILLE, KY.

Courier-Journal—Harrison Robertson.
Commercial—S. H. Friedlander.
Post—Wm. **Finley.**
Anzeiger (Ger.)—C. **H. Cohen.**
Sunday Argus—L. Dinkelspiel.

DETROIT.

Post and Tribune—B. Frank Bower.
Free Press—Geo. **P.** Goodale.
Evening News—Charles F. May.
Michigan Volksblatt—Math. Kramer.
Abend Post—Augnet Marxhausen.
"Chaff"—Geo. M. Chester.
Every Saturday—Alice Cary.
Evening Journal—Lloyd Brezee.

MILWAUKEE.

Sentinel—A. Singwalt.
Evening Wisconsin—C. B. Harger.
Journal—L. W. Nierman.
Herald (Ger.)—Theo. Janssen.
Lee Bote (Ger.)—**Dr.** Knoster.
Freie Presse **(Ger.)**—Aug. Johnson.

PROVIDENCE.

Journal and **Bulletin—M. C. Day.**
Star—G. O. **Willard.**
Telegram **(evening** and Sunday)—O. M. Remington.
Sunday Transcript—Frank Moore.
Sunday Dispatch—R. S. Jones.

DRAMATIC.

Abbey, "Mam'zelle" Co.—Edgar Strakosch, manager.

Aldrich's "My Partner" Co.—Louis Aldrich, manager.

Alf Wyman Co.

"A Mountain Pink" Co. (Bella Moore).—C. A. Gregg, manager.

"A Mountain Pink" Co. (Laura E. Dainty).—E. A. Andreas, manager.

Atkinson Maude, Co.—Goodnow & Johnson, managers.

Atkinson, "Peck's Bad Boy" Co. No. 1.—Harry T. Wilson, manager.

Atkinson, "Peck's Bad Boy" Co. No. 2.

Baker & Farron Co.—F. C. Rust, business manager.

"Bandit King" Co.—Jas. H. Waldck, manager.

Bandmann's, Daniel, Co.

Barrett, Lawrence, Co.—Joseph Levy, manager.

Bartlett's "Rank and File" Co.—

Bayley, Eric, Co.—J. St, Maur, manager.

Beedle and Prindle's Pleasure Party—Johnnie Prindle, manager.

Berlin, Annie, Co.—Van Wyck & Mack, managers.

Bishop, C. B., Comedy Co.—Charles J. Bishop, manager.

Booth, Edwin, Co.—R. M. Field, manager.

Boston Theatre "Silver King" Co.—Eugene Tompkins, manager.

Boston Theatre "Youth" Co.—Eugene Tompkins, manager.

Boucicault, Dion, "Shaughraun" Co.

Boyd, Neilie, Co.—G. M. Welty, manager.

Broadway Theatre Co.—Walter Dudley, manager.

Brooks & Dickson's "In the Ranks" Co.

Brooks & Dickson's "La Charbonniere" Co.—James W. Morrissey, manager.

Brooks & Dickson's Ristori Co.

Brooks & Dickson's "Romany Rye," Co. A.—Sheldon Bateman, manager.

Brooks & Dickson's "Romany Rye," Co. B.

Brown, Lillian, Jollities Co.—Graham, Binford & Edwards, managers.

Buchanan Comedy Co.

"Bunch of Keys" Co., Flora Moore—Dudley McAdow, manager.

"Bunch of Keys" Co.—Frank Sanger, manager.

"Bunch of Keys" Co.—Bride & Frears, manager.

Burgess, Neil, "Vim" Co.—T. F. Reid, manager.

"Burr Oaks" Co., Walter Bentley—James Alexander, manager.

Byron, O. D., Co.—J. P. Johnson, manager.

"Called Back" Co.—J. H. Mallory & Co., managers.

Campbell, Bartley, "White Slave" Co.—Harry Kennedy, manager.

Campbell, Bartley, "Siberia" Co.—Thos. B. McDonough, manager.

Campbell, Bartley, "Separation" Co.—Phil. Simmons, manager.

Chanfrau, Mrs. F., S. Co.—C. W. Tayleure, manager.

Choate, Harry, Co.—Harry Choate, manager.

Claxton, Kate, Co.—Chas. A. Stevenson, manager.

Clayburgh's "Creole" Co.—Ed. Clayburgh, manager.

"Crimes of London" Co.—Chas. McDonald, manager.

Crossen, "Banker's Daughter" Co.—Jas. F. Crossen, manager.

Curtis, M. B., "Spot Cash" Co.—Frank Paul, manager.

Daly's "Vacation" Co.—

Davenport, Fanny, "Fedora" Co.—Edwin Price, manager.

"Alvin Joslin" Co.—C. L. Davis, manager.

"Devil's Auction" Co.—Gallagher, Gilmore & Gardner, managers.

Dickson's Sketch Club Co.—F. C. Hamilton, manager.

"Digby's Secretary" Co.—E. H. Gillette, manager.

Dixey-Rice "Adonis" Co.—E. E. Rice, manager.

Draper's "Uncle Tom" Co.—S. Draper, manager.

Earle Dramatic Co.—Graham Earle, manager.

Eliani, Lisetta, "Fun in a Boarding School" Co.—W. C. Cameron, manager.

Ellsler-Weston Co.—W. A. Edwards, business manager.

Emmet, J. K., "Fritz" Co.—P. H. Lehuen, manager.

Erwood & McCoy Surrey Theatre Co.

European Burlesque Co.

Evans, Lizzie, Co.—Chas. E. Callahan, manager.

Evans & Hoey, "Parlor Match" Co.—Harry Mahn, manager.

"Excelsior" Co.—Kiralfy Bros., managers.

Kytinge, Rose, Co.—Cyril Searl, manager.

23

"Falsely Accused" Co.

Florence, Mr. & Mrs. W. J. Co.

Ford's Metropolitan Dramatic Co.—Clint. G. Ford, manager.

Galley Slave Co.—Phil. Simmonds, manager.

C. A. Gardner's Karl Co.—T. C. Lombard, manager.

Goodwin, Nat., Co.—G. W. Floyd, manager.

Gotthold, Newton, Micaliz Co.—Chas. B. Griste, manager.

Grotesque Comedy Co.—John M. Hickey, manager.

Hanley, Dan's Tribulations Co.—M. W. Hanley, manager.

Hanlon Brothers Co.—John G. Magle, manager.

Harrigan & Hart's Travelling Co.—Harrigan & Hart, managers.

Harrison and Gourlay Co.—Samuel Harrison, manager; Robert Gourlay, business manager.

Herne's "Hearts of Oak."—James A. Herne.

Heege's "Peck's Bad Boy."—

"Her Atonement" Co.—Chapman & Sellers, managers.

Hewitt's Musettes.—

Hill's Theatre Co.—G. A. Hill, manager.

Holman, Miss Jennie, Co.—Otto Krause, manager.

"Hoop of Gold" Co.—Charles Hicks, manager.

Howorth's "Hibernica."—John Howorth, manager.

Howard Atheneum Co.—S. P. Coney, manager.

Irving, Henry—Marcus R. Meyer, American agent.

Ivanroff Co.—T. S. Wright, manager.

Jananschek—Ed. Taylor, manager.

Janish—H. J. Sargent, manager.

Jefferson, Joseph, Comedy Co.—H. S. Taylor, business manager.

Keane, Joseph H., Co.

Keene, T. W., Co.—W. R. Hayden, manager.

Kendall Dramatic Co.—H. A. Kendall, manager.

Kendall (Geo. and Lizzie) Co.—Geo. Kendall, manager.

Knight, Mr. and Mrs., Comedy Co.—Josh E. Ogden, manager.

"Kritenon Komedy."

Kroger, Jacques.

Lacy, "Planter's Wife" Co.—Harry Lacy, manager.

"Lights o' London" Co. (Eastern)—Shook & Collier, managers.

"Lights o' London" Co. (Western)—Shook & Collier, managers.

Little's "World" Co.—Geo. O. Morris, manager.

Lotta, Comedy Co.—Gus A. Pennoyer, manager.

"Lynwood" Co.—Williams & Tillotson, managers.

Maddern, Miss Minnie, Co.—Chas. Frohman, manager.

Madison Square "Hazel Kirke" Co.—Chas. Frohman, manager.

Madison Square "May Blossom" Co.—E. M. Roberts, manager.

Madison Square "Young Mrs. Winthrop" Co.—J. H. Mallory & Co., managers.

Madison Square "Private Secretary" Co.—Chas. Frohman, manager.

Madison Square "Private Secretary," No. 2 Co.—J. H. Mallory & Co., managers.

Murray's "Man Without a Country" Co.—Chas. E. Cooke, manager.

Mason & Morgan's "Uncle Tom" Co.—E. H. Lane, manager.

Mather, Miss Margaret, Co.—J. M. Hill, manager.

Mayo, Frank, "Nordeck" Co.—Sheridan Corbyn, manager.

McAuley's, Barney, Co.—B. D. Stevens, manager.

McNeil Family Concert Co.

McWade, Robert, Co.—Sam. M. Dawson, business manager.

"Ranch 10" Co.

Mestayer's We, Us & Co.—Wm. Mestayer, manager.

Mestayer's Tourists—Wm. Mestayer, manager.

Michael Strogoff Co.—Charles Andrews, manager.

Miln, George C., Co.—Francis B. Pardie, manager.

Miner's, Harry, "Silver King" Co. (No. 1)—J. H. Mack, manager.

Miner, Harry, "Silver King" Co. (No. 2)—J. H. Mack, manager.

Mitchell, Maggie, Comedy Co.—H. D. Paddock, manager.

O'Neill, Jas., "Monte Cristo" Co.—John Stetson, manager; N. D. Roberts, business manager.

Morris, Clara, Co.—Frank L. Goodwin, manager.

Morton & Bell's Strategists Co.

Mountcastle's, Miss Fanny, "Sea of Ice" Co.—Charles R. Thorpe, manager.

Maggs' Landing (Frances Bishop)—Matt Leland, manager.

Murphy, John S. "Kerry Gow" Co.

Murphy's, Joseph, Co., C. Wilkie, manager.

Nobles, Milton, Co.—

Nobody's Claim Co.—Rich & Harris, managers.

Norton, Mabel Co.—

Off to Egypt Co.—Augustus Pitou, manager.

Olcott, Lilian, Co.—Roland L. Tayleure, manager.

Only a Farmer's Daughter Co.—Chas. R. Gardiner, manager; Joseph Frank, business manager.

Only a Woman's Heart Co., Newton Beers'.—Charles R. Gardiner, manager; Jack Owen, business manager.

Owen, Garret N., Co.—Garrett N. Owen, manager.

Palmer, Miss Minnie, Comedy Co.—John R. Rogers, manager.

Patti Rosa Co.—Frank Irving, manager.

Pavements of Paris Co.—John Rickaby, manager.

Pickett's Great Southern Co.—A. St. J. Pickett, manager.

Power of Money Co.—George O. Morris, manager.

Putnam, Kate, Comedy Co.—

Queena Co.—Williams & Tillotson, managers.

Rag Baby Co.—Eugene Tompkins, manager.

Raymond, John T., Co.—

Redmond & Barry, "Midnight Marriage" Co.

Reed, Roland, "Cheek" Co.—Gus Mortimer, manager.

Rehan's "7-20-8" Co.—Arthur Rehan, manager.

Rhea Co.—A. B. Chase, manager.

Little Rhodes Co.—W. R. Ward, manager.

Ristori Co.—Brooks & Dickson, managers.

Robson & Crane Co.

Russell, Sol Smith—"Edgewood Folks" Co.

Saulbury's Troubadours—Frank Maeder, manager.

Sawtelle Comedy Co.—J. Al. Sawtelle, managers.

Scanlan, W. J., Co.—Mahn & Piton, managers.

Sedgewick, Miss Helen, "Silver Spur" Co.—E. F. Benton, manager.

"Seven Ravens" Co.—Poole & Gilmore, managers.

"Shadows of a Great City" Co.—Chas. Jefferson, manager.

W. E. Sheridan Co.

Shook & Collier's "Storm-beaten" Co. (Central).

Shook & Collier's "Storm-beaten" Co. (Western).

Shook & Collier's "Ruth Devotion" Co.

"Sieba" Co.—Kiralfy Bros., managers.

Silbon & Elliott's "Cupid" Co.—Harry W. Semon, manager.

Simon Comedy Co.—J. A. Simon, manager.

"Six Peas in a Pod" Co.—Oscar P. Sisson, manager.

Stafford-Foster Co.—Ed. Witting, manager.

Standard Dramatic Co.—E. E. Basye, manager.

Stanley, Miss Carrie, Co.—Charles B. Brown, manager.

Stevens, John A., "Unknown" Co.—John A. Stevens, manager.

"Strategists" Co.—Morton & Bell, managers.

Stutz Dramatic Co.—J. G. Stutz, manager.

Sully, Dan, "Corner Grocery" Co.

Swain, Carrie, Co.—Fred. G. Maeder, manager.

Sylvester, Miss Louise, "Freaks" Co.—Eugene Schultz, manager.

Tucker, Ethel, Co.

Two Johns Comedy Co.—P. Rice, manager.

Tavernier Comedy Co.—Knowlan Fraser, manager.

Thompson, Den, "Joshua Whitcomb" Co.—Denman Thompson, manager.

Thompson, Charlotte, Co.

Thorne, Edwin, "Black Flag" Co.—Robert Arthur, manager.

Ulmer, Lizzie May, Co.—George T. Ulmer, manager.

Vickers, Miss Mattie, Co.—C. S. Rogers, manager.

"Wages of Sin" Co.—E. B. Ludlow, manager.

Walker, Miss Ane, Co.—Phil. H. Irving, manager.

Wallack's Theatre Co.—Chas. Frohman, manager.

Wallick's "Bandit King" Co.—J. H. Wallick, manager.

Warde, Frederick, Co.—Harry F. Weed, manager.

Webber, "Nip and Tuck" Co.—Harry Webber, manager.

Welby, Miss Bertha, Co.—H. A. D'Arcy, manager.

"Well-Fed Dora" Co.

Wellaley & Sterling's "Danites," Co.—Wm. E. Sterling, manager.

Whitesides, Walker, Co.—Sam'l Keyser, manager.

Whitely's "Hidden Hand" Co.—Harry M. Clark, manager.

Williams, Gus, Co.—John J. Robb, manager.

Williams' "Birds of a Feather" Co.

Wood, N. S., Co.

Woodthorpe, Miss Georgia, Co.—James McNavin, manager.

Zanita Co.—Tompkins & Hill, managers.

OPERATIC AND MUSICAL.

Abbott, Emma, English Opera Co.

Bennett-Moulton Opera Co.—Moulton & Baker, managers.

Bijou Opera Co. ("Orpheus and Eurydice").—Miles & Barton, managers.

Boston Ideal Opera Co.

Carleton's English Opera Co.—Wm. Carleton, manager.

Abbie Carrington (Concerts).

Castleton, Kate.

Corinne Merrilmakers.

Fairweather Operatic Troubadours.

Ford's Opera Co.

Gaiety Opera Co.

Amy Gordon Opera Co.

Grau English Opera Co.—Robert Grau, manager.

Harris Opera Co.

Hewett's Musettes.

Holliwood Opera Co.

Johnson's Jubilee Singers.

Laurent, Henri.

Mapleson's Italian Opera Co. (Mme. Patti—Col. J. H. Mapleson, manager.

McCaul's Comic Opera Co.—John A. McCaul, manager.

McGibeny Family Concert Co.—Fred Pelham, manager.

Milan Opera Co.—Horace McVicker, manager

Norcross' Opera.

Oates, Miss Alice, **Opera Co.—Col. T. E.** Snelbaker, manager.

Rafael Joseffy.

Reeves' American Band.

Templeton, Miss Fay, Star **Comic Opera** Co—Jno. Templeton, manager.

Theo, Maurice.—Robert Grau.

Thompson's **Opera Co—W. A. Thompson,** manager; H. C. **Smart**, business manager.

Wilbur Opera **Co.—T. H. Mann, business** manager

VARIETY AND SPECIALTY.

Adamless Eden Co. No. 1—M. B. Leavitt, manager

Adamless Eden Co., No. 2.

Baylis and Kennedy, "Bright Lights"—Joe Baylis, manager.

Big Four Co.

Davene-Austin **Allied Attractions —J. C.** Patrick, manager.

Electric Flashes **of Fun.**

Fanny Herring.

Gibler Bros.' Show.

Hallen & Hart Co —Fred Hallen, manager.

Howard Athenæum Co.—Wm. Harris, manager.

Joyce-Carro'l-Crowley.

Kernell's New Enterprise Co.—H. **W. Wil-** liams, manager.

Leavitt's All-Star Specialty Co.

Montague's **"Dude" Co.**

Murphy & Mack Comedy **Co.--Mark L.** Townsend, manager.

Tony Pastor Co.—Tony Pastor, manager.

Rentfrow's Jolly Pathfinders —J. H. Rentfrow, manager

Rentz-Santley.

Rich & Harris Co.

Pat Rooney Co.

Siddons' Mastodons.—Wm. **Arnold**, manager.

Stanley's Mastodons.

Sullivan's Female Mastodons.

Agnes Wallace-Villa.—Sam. B. Villa, manager.

Wells & Castelotti's.

"Zozo, the Magic Queen" Co.—C. R. Gardner, manager.

MINSTREL.

Baird's.—J. W. Baird, manager.

Barlow-Wilson.—Harry J. Clapham, man- ager.

Carpenter's.

• **Calender's Colored Minstrels.**

Fulton's Juvenile Creoles.—Herman F. Greundler, manager.

Haverly's Mastodons.—Kit Clarke, mana- ger.

Heywood's **Mastodon's, P. W. Heywood,** manager.

Hi Henry's.—Hi Henry, manager.

Hills, Rice & Barton.

Hyde & Behman's—Richard Hyde, manager.

Original New Orleans—C. C. Pearl, manager.

San Francisco—Billy Birch, manager.

Skiff, **Gaylord** & Hicks—John C. Hicks, manager.

Star Minstrel and **Specialty Co.—Wm. H.** Sheriden, manager.

Thatcher, Primrose & West—Geo. **T.** Clapham, manager.

Wagner's, Cal—Cal Wagner, manager.

Wilber **& Ryan's —A. R.** Wilber, manager.

MISCELLANEOUS.

Bartholomew's **Equine Paradox—John** Mishler, manager.

Blitz's Show.

Prof Cromwell's Illustrated Art Lectures.

Misco "Humpty Dumpty" Co.—Alfred F. Misco, manager.

Tony Denier's "Humpty Dumpty" Co.— Geo. S. Sidney, manager.

Lovenburg, "Bell Ringers."

O'Connor, James Owen.

Wilmot Double Riders.

Routes of Harry Miner's Specialty Company.

1879.

September 1, Newark, N. J.
September 2, Yonkers, N. Y.
September 3, Newburg, N. Y.
September 4, Kingston, N. Y.
September 5, Poughkeepsie, N. Y.
September 6, Albany, N. Y.
September 9, Troy, N. Y.
September 10, Cohoes, N. Y.
September 11, Schenectady, N. Y.
September 12, Syracuse, N. Y.
September 13, Oswego, N. Y.
September 14, Utica, N. Y.
September 16, Auburn, N. Y.
September 17, Rochester, N. Y.
September 18, Rochester, N. Y.
September 19, Rochester, N. Y.
September 20, Buffalo, N. Y.
September 21, Buffalo, N. Y.
September 22, Dunkirk, N. Y.
September 23, Erie, Pa.
September 24, Sharon, Pa.
September 25, Newcastle, Pa.
September 26, Youngstown, O.
September 27, Cleveland, O.
September 29, Cleveland, O.
September 30, Sandusky, O.
October 1, Toledo, O.
October 2, Ann Arbor, Mich.
October 3, Detroit, Mich.
October 4, Detroit. Mich.
October 6, Port Huron, Mich.
October 7, Bay City, Mich.
October 8, East Saginaw, Mich.
October 9, Lansing, Mich.
October 10, Grand Rapids, Mich.
October 11, Jackson, Mich.
October 13, Chicago, Ill.
October 14, Chicago, Ill.
October 15, Chicago, Ill.
October 16, Chicago, Ill.
October 17, Chicago, Ill.
October 18, Chicago, Ill.
October 19, Chicago, Ill.
October 20, Racine, Wis.
October 21, Janesville, Wis.
October 22, Madison, Wis.
October 23, Milwaukee, Wis.
October 24, Milwaukee, Wis.
October 25, Milwaukee, Wis.
October 27, Joliet, Ill.

October 28, Bloomington, Ill.
October 29, Peoria, Ill.
October 30, Jacksonville, Ill.
October 31, Springfield, Ill.
November 1, Decatur, Ill.
November 2, St. Louis, Mo.
November 3, St. Louis, Mo.
November 4, St. Louis, Mo.
November 5, St. Louis Mo.
November 6, St. Louis, Mo.
November 7, St. Louis, Mo.
November 8, St. Louis, Mo.
November 10, Terre Haute, Ind.
November 11, Terre Haute, Ind.
November 12, Evansville, Ind.
November 13, Louisville, Ky.
November 14, Louisville, Ky.
November 15, Louisville, Ky.
November 17, Cincinnati, O.
November 18, Cincinnati, O.
November 19, Cincinnati, O.
November 20, Cincinnati, O.
November 21, Cincinnati, O.
November 22, Cincinnati, O.
November 23, Cincinnati, O.
November 24, Dayton, O.
November 25, Springfield, O.
November 26, Columbus, O.
November 27, Columbus, O.
November 28, Newark, O.
November 29, Zanesville, O.
December 1, Steubenville, O.
December 2, Wheeling, W. Va.
December 3, Wheeling, W. Va.
December 4, Pittsburgh, Pa.
December 5, Pittsburgh, Pa.
December 6, Pittsburgh, Pa.
December 8, Johnstown, Pa.
December 9, Altoona, Pa.
December 10, Lock Haven, Pa.
December 11, Williamsport, Pa.
December 12, Harrisburg, Pa.
December 13, Harrisburg, Pa.
December 15, Lancaster, Pa.
December 16, Reading, Pa.
December 17, Pottsville, Pa.
December 18, Mauch Chunk, Pa.
December 19, Pittston, Pa.
December 20, Scranton, Pa.
December 22, Wilkesbarre, Pa.
December 23, Allentown, Pa.

December 24, South Bethlehem, Pa.
December 25, Easton, Pa.
December 26, New Brunswick, Pa.
December 27, Trenton, N. J.
December 29, Philadelphia, Pa.
December 30, Philadelphia, Pa.
December 31, Philadelphia, Pa.
1880.
January 1, Philadelphia, Pa.
January 2, Philadelphia, Pa.
January 3, Philadelphia, Pa.
January 5, Stamford, Conn.
January 6, South Norwalk, Conn.
January 7, Danbury, Conn.
January 8, Bridgeport, Conn.
January 9, Waterbury, Conn.
January 10, New Haven, Conn.
January 12, Middletown, Conn.
January 13, Hartford, Conn.
January 14, Willimantic, Conn.
January 15, Norwich, Conn.
January 16, Providence, Conn.
January 17, Providence, Conn.
January 19, Newport, R. I.
January 20, New Bedford, Mass.
January 21, Taunton, Mass.
January 22, Brockton, Mass.
January 23, Chelsea, Mass.
January 24, Lynn, Mass.
January 26, Salem, Mass.
January 27, Gloucester, Mass.
January 28, Amesbury, Mass.
January 29, Portsmouth, N. H.
January 30, Biddeford, Me.
January 31, Portland, Me.
February 2, Bath, Me.
February 3, Gardiner, Me.
February 4, Augusta, Me.
February 5, Bangor, Me.
February 6, Bangor, Me.
February 7, Bangor, Me.
February 9, Lewiston, Me.
February 10, Portland, Me.
February 11, Manchester, N. H.
February 12, Concord, N. H.
February 13, Manchester, N. H.
February 14, Haverhill, Mass.
February 15, Lawrence, Mass.
February 17, Lowell, Mass.
February 18, Worcester, Mass.
February 19, Holyoke, Mass.
February 20, Springfield, Mass.
February 21, Pittsfield, Mass.
February 23, North Adams, Mass.
February 24, Albany, N. Y.
February 25, Binghamton, N. Y.
February 26, Owego, N. Y.
February 27, Ithaca, N. Y.
February 28, Elmira, N. Y.
March 1, Port Jervis, N. Y.
March 2, Middletown, N. Y.

March 3, Paterson, N. J.
March 4, Jersey City, N. J.
March 5, Jersey City, N. J.
March 6, Jersey City, N. J.
March 8, Philadelphia, Pa.
March 9, Philadelphia, Pa.
March 10, Philadelphia, Pa.
March 11, Philadelphia, Pa.
March 12, Philadelphia, Pa.
March 13, Philadelphia, Pa.
March 15, Brooklyn, N. Y.
March 16, Brooklyn, N. Y.
March 17, Brooklyn, N. Y.
March 18, Brooklyn, N. Y.
March 19, Brooklyn, N. Y.
March 20, Brooklyn, N. Y.
March 22, Williamsburg, N. Y.
March 23, Williamsburg, N. Y.
March 24, Williamsburg, N. Y.
March 25, Williamsburg, N. Y.
March 26, Williamsburg, N. Y.
March 27, Williamsburg, N. Y.
March 29, Newark, N. J.
March 30, Yonkers, N. Y.
March 31, Poughkeepsie, N. Y.
April 1, Kingston, N. Y.
April 3, Troy, N. Y.
April 4, Syracuse, N. Y.
April 5, Oswego, N. Y.
April 6, Watertown, N. Y.
April 7, Rome, N. Y.
April 8, Auburn, N. Y.
April 9, Rochester, N. Y.
April 10, Buffalo, N. Y.
April 12, Dunkirk, N. Y.
April 13, Erie, Pa.
April 14, Akron, O.
April 15, Toledo, O.
April 16, Ypsilanti, Mich.
April 17, Detroit, Mich.
April 17, Flint, Mich.
April 20, Bay City, Mich.
April 21, East Saginaw, Mich.
April 22, Lansing, Mich.
April 23, Grand Rapids, Mich.
April 24, Jackson, Mich.
April 26, Chicago, Ill.
April 27, Chicago, Ill.
April 28, Chicago, Ill.
April 29, Chicago, Ill.
April 30, Chicago, Ill.
May 1, Chicago, Ill.
May 2, Chicago, Ill.
May 3, Racine, Wis.
May 4, Janesville, Wis.
May 5, Madison, Wis.
May 6, Milwaukee, Wis.
May 7, Milwaukee, Wis.
May 8, Milwaukee, Wis.
May 10, Joliet, Ills.
May 11, Bloomington, Ills.

May 12. Peoria, Ills.
May 13, Jacksonville, Ills.
May 14, Springfield, Ills.
May 15, Decatur, Ills.
May 16, St. Louis, Mo.
May 17, St. Louis, Mo.
May 18, St. Louis, Mo.
May 19, St. Louis, Mo.
May 20, St. Louis, Mo.
May 21, St. Louis, Mo.
May 22, St. Louis, Mo.
May 24, Terre Haute, Ind.
May 25, Indianapolis, Ind.
May 26, Indianapolis, Ind.
May 27, Lafayette, Ind.
May 28, Logansport, Ind.
May 29, Richmond, Ind.
May 31. Cincinnati, O.
June 1, Cincinnati, O.
June 2, Cincinnati, O.
June 3, Cincinnati, O.
June 4, Cincinnati, O.
June 5, Cincinnati, O.
June 6, Cincinnati, O.

June 7, Springfield, O.
June 8, Columbus, O.
June 9, Newark, O.
June 10. Zanesville, O.
June 11, Steubenville, O
June 12, Wheeling, W. Va
June 14, Pittsburgh, Pa.
June 15, Pittsburgh, Pa.
June 16, Pittsburgh, Pa.
June 17, Pittsburgh, Pa.
June 18, Pittsburgh, Pa.
June 19, Pittsburgh, Pa.
June 21, Johnstown, Pa.
June 22, Altoona, Pa.
June 23, Reading, Pa.
June 24, Wilkesbarre, Pa.
June 25, Pittston, Pa.
June 26, Scranton, Pa.
June 28, Easton, Pa.
June 29, Trenton, N. J.
June 30, New Brunswick, N J
July 1. Elizabeth, N. J.
July 2 Harlem, N. Y.
July 3. Harlem, N. Y.

SEASON OF 1880–1881.

1880.
August 30, New York, N. Y.
August 31, New York, N. Y.
September 1, New York, N. Y.
September 2, New York, N Y
September 3, New York, N. Y.
September 4, New York, N. Y.
September 6, New York, N. Y.
September 7, New York, N. Y.
September 8, New York, N. Y.
September 9, New York, N. Y
September 10, New York, N. Y.
September 11, New York, N. Y.
September 13, Stamford, Conn.
September 14, Danbury, Conn.
September 15, S. Norwalk, Conn.
September 16, Bridgeport, Conn.
September 17, Waterbury, Conn.
September 18, New Haven, Conn.
September 20, Meriden, Conn.
September 21. Middleton, Conn
September 22, Hartford, Conn.
September 23, Springfield, Mass.
September 24, Worcester, Mass.
September 25, Woonsocket, R. I.
September 27, Providence, R. I.
September 28, Newport, R. I.
September 29. Fall River, Mass.
September 30, New Bedford, Mass.
October 1, Taunton, Mass.
October 2, Brockton, Mass.
October 4, Boston, Mass.
October 5, Boston, Mass.
October 6, Boston, Mass.

October 7, Boston, Mass.
October 8, Boston, Mass.
October 9, Boston, Mass.
October 11, Chelsea, Mass.
October 12, Salem, Mass.
October 13, Lowell, Mass.
October 14, Lawrence, Mass.
October 15, Haverhill, Mass.
October 16, Manchester, N. H.
October 18, Rochester, N. H.
October 19, Great Falls, N. H.
October 20, Dover, N. H.
October 21, Concord, N. H.
October 22, Nashua, N. H.
October 23, Greenfield, Mass.
October 25, Northampton, Mass.
October 26, Holyoke, Mass.
October 27, Westfield, Mass.
October 28, Pittsfield, Mass.
October 29, North Adams, Mass.
October 30, Albany, N. Y.
November 1, Albany, N. Y.
November 2, Albany, N. Y.
November 3, Albany, N. Y.
November 4, Albany, N. Y.
November 5, Albany, N. Y.
November 6, Albany, N. Y.
November 8, Buffalo, N. Y.
November 9, Buffalo, N. Y.
November 10, Buffalo, N. Y.
November 11, Buffalo, N. Y.
November 12, Buffalo, N. Y.
November 13, Buffalo, N. Y.
November 15, Port Huron, Mich.

November 16, Bay City, Mich.
November 17, E. Saginaw, Mich.
November 18, Jackson, Mich.
November 19, Grand Rapids, Mich.
November 20, Muskegon, Mich.
November 22, Chicago, Ill.
November 23, Chicago, Ill.
November 24, Chicago, Ill.
November 25, **Chicago**, Ill.
November 26, Chicago, Ill.
November 27, Chicago, Ill.
November 28, Chicago, Ill.
November 29, Cincinnati, O.
November 30, Cincinnati, O.
December 1, Cincinnati, O.
December 2, Cincinnati, O.
December 3, Cincinnati, O.
December 4, Cincinnati, O.
December 5, Cincinnati, O.
December 6, Troy, O.
December 7, Dayton, **O.**
December 8, Hamilton, O.
December 9, New Albany, Ind.
December 10, Louisville, Ky.
December 11, Louisville, Ky.
December 13, Evansville, Ind.
December 14, Evansville, Ind.
December 15, Henderson, Ky.
December 16, Hoppinsville, Ky.
December 17, Nashville, **Tenn.**
December 18, Nashville, **Tenn.**
December 20, Selma, Ala.
December 21, Montgomery, **Ala.**
December 22, Columbus, Ga.
December 23, Opelika, Ala.
December 25, Atlanta, Ga.
December 25, Atlanta, Ga.
December 27, Athens, Ga.
December 28, Augusta, Ga.
December 29, Augusta, Ga.
December 30, Macon, Ga.
December 31, Savannah, Ga.
1881
January 1, Savannah, Ga.
January 3, Charleston, S. C.
January 4, Charleston, S. C.
January 5, Columbia, S. C.
January 6, Charlotte, N. C.
January 7, Danville, Va.
January 8, Lynchburg, Va.
January 10, Petersburg, Va.
January 11, Richmond, Va.
January 12, Richmond, **Va.**
January 13, Portsmouth, **Va.**
January 14, Norfolk, Va.
January 15, Norfolk, Va.
January 17, Washington, D. C.
January 18, Washington, D. C.
January 19, Washington, D. C.
January 20, Washington, **D. C.**
January 21, **Washington, D. C.**

January 22, Washington, D. C.
January 24, Baltimore, Md.
January 25, Baltimore, Md.
January 26, Baltimore, Md.
January 27, Baltimore, Md.
January 28, Baltimore, Md.
January 29, Baltimore, Md.
January 31, Philadelphia, Pa.
February 1, Philadelphia, Pa.
February 2, Philadelphia, **Pa.**
February 3, Philadelphia, Pa.
February 4, Philadelphia, Pa.
February 5, Philadelphia, **Pa.**
February 7, Columbia, Pa.
February 8, Lancaster, **Pa.**
February 9, **Reading, Pa.**
February 10, Pittston, Pa.
February 11, Scranton, Pa.
February 12, Wilkesbarre, Pa.
February 14, Easton, Pa.
February 15, Trenton, N. J.
February 16, New Brunswick, N. J.
February 17, Newark, N. J.
February 18, Paterson, N. J.
February 19, Jersey City, N. J.
February 21, Brooklyn, N. Y.
February 22, Brooklyn, N. Y.
February 23, Brooklyn, N. Y.
February 24, Brooklyn, N. Y.
February 25, Brooklyn, N. Y.
February 26, Brooklyn, N. Y.
February 28, Yonkers, N. Y.
March 1, Kingston, N. Y.
March 2, **Poughkeepsie,** N. Y.
March 3, **Hudson, N. Y.**
March 4, **Albany, N. Y.**
March 5, **Troy, N. Y.**
March 7, **Utica, N. Y.**
March 8, Syracuse, N. Y.
March 9, **Auburn, N. Y.**
March 10, Rochester, N. Y.
March 11, Buffalo, N. Y.
March 12, Buffalo, N. Y.
March 14, Bradford, Pa.
March 15, Erie, Pa.
March 16, Titusville, **Pa.**
March 17, Oil City, Pa.
March 18, Meadville, **Pa.**
March 19, Sharon, Pa.
March 21, Youngstown, O.
March 22, Canton, O.
March 23, Massillon, O.
March 24, Cleveland, O.
March 25, Cleveland, O.
March 26, Cleveland, O.
March 28, Akron, O.
March 29, Akron, O.
March 30, **Urbana, O.**
March 31, Richmond, Ind.
April 1, **Kokomo,** Ind.
April 2, Indianapolis, Ind.

April 4, St. Louis, Mo.
April 5, St. Louis, Mo.
April 6, St. Louis, Mo.
April 7, St. Louis, Mo.
April 8, St. Louis, Mo.
April 9, St. Louis, Mo.
April 11, Springfield, Ills.
April 12, Quincy, Ills.
April 13, Keokuk, Iowa
April 14, Keokuk, Iowa
April 15, Davenport, Iowa
April 16, Rock Island, Ills.
April 18, Peoria, Ills.
April 19, Bloomington, Ills.
April 20, Danville, Ills.
April 21, Lafayette, Ind.
April 22, Logansport, Ind.
April 23, Logansport, Ind.
April 25, Fort Wayne, Ind.
April 26, Columbus, O.
April 27, Chillicothe, O.

April 28, Circleville, O.
April 29, Zanesville, O.
April 30, Wheeling, W. Va.
May 2, Pittsburgh, Pa.
May 3, Pittsburgh, Pa.
May 4, Pittsburgh, Pa.
May 5, Pittsburgh, Pa.
May 6, Pittsburgh, Pa.
May 7, Pittsburgh, Pa.
May 9, New Castle, Pa.
May 10, Oil City, Pa.
May 11, Jamestown, N. Y.
May 12, Bradford, Pa.
May 13, Duke's Centre, Pa.
May 14, Olean, N. Y.
May 16, Hornellsville, N. Y.
May 17, Corning, N. Y.
May 18, Elmira, N. Y.
May 19, Binghamton, N. Y.
May 20, Troy, N. Y.
May 21, Albany, N. Y.

SEASON OF 1881–1882.

1881
August 22, Boston, Mass.
August 23, Boston, Mass.
August 24, Boston, Mass.
August 25, Boston, Mass.
August 26, Boston, Mass.
August 27, Boston, Mass.
August 29, New York, N. Y.
August 30, New York, N. Y.
August 31, New York, N. Y.
September 1, New York, N. Y.
September 2, New York, N. Y.
September 3, New York, N. Y.
September 5, Harlem, N. Y.
September 6, Yonkers, N. Y.
September 7, Rondout, N. Y.
September 8, Poughkeepsie, N. Y.
September 9, Albany, N. Y.
September 10, Troy, N. Y.
September 12, Syracuse, N. Y.
September 13, Oswego, N. Y.
September 14, Utica, N. Y.
September 15, Auburn, N. Y.
September 16, Rochester, N. Y.
September 17, Rochester, N. Y.
September 19, Penn Yan, N. Y.
September 20, Canandaigua, N. Y.
September 21, Batavia, N. Y.
September 22, Buffalo, N. Y.
September 23, Buffalo, N. Y.
September 24, Buffalo, N. Y.
September 26, Hornellsville, N. Y.
September 27, Salamanca, N. Y.
September 28, Olean, N. Y.
September 29, Duke's Centre, Penn.
September 30, Bradford, Pa.

October 1, Bradford, Pa.
October 3, Dunkirk, N. Y.
October 4, Erie, Pa.
October 5, Corry, Pa.
October 6, Titusville, Pa.
October 7, Oil City, Pa.
October 8, Franklin, Pa.
October 10, New Castle, Pa.
October 11, Sharon, Pa.
October 12, Youngstown, O.
October 13, Akron, O.
October 14, Canton, O.
October 15, Sandusky, O.
October 17, Toledo, O.
October 18, Detroit. Mich.
October 19, Ypsilanti, Mich.
October 20, Ann Arbor, Mich.
October 21, Jackson, Mich.
October 22, Battle Creek, Mich.
October 24, Flint, Mich.
October 25, Bay City.
October 26, E. Saginaw, Mich.
October 27, Grand Rapids, Mich.
October 28, Grand Rapids, Mich.
October 29, Muskegon, Mich.
October 31, Chicago, Ill.
November 1, Chicago, Ill.
November 2, Chicago, Ill.
November 3, Chicago, Ill.
November 4, Chicago, Ill.
November 5, Chicago, Ill.
November 6, Chicago, Ill.
November 7, Milwaukee, Wis.
November 8, Milwaukee, Wis.
November 9, Milwaukee, Wis.
November 10, McGregor, Ia.

November 11, Dubuque, Ia.
November 12, Davenport, Ia.
November 14, Rock Island, Ill.
November 15, Ottawa, Ill.
November 16, Joliet, Ill.
November 17, Bloomington, Ill.
November 18, Decatur, Ill.
November 19, Springfield, Ill.
November 21, Jacksonville, **Ill.**
November 22, Peoria, Ill.
November 23, Galesburg, Ill.
November 24, Burlington, Ia.
November 25, Keokuk, **Ia.**
November 26, Quincy, Ill,
November 27, St. Louis, Mo.
November 28, St. Louis, Mo.
November 29, **St. Louis, Mo.**
November 30, St. Louis, Mo.
December 1, St. Louis, Mo.
December 2, St. Louis, Mo.
December 3, St. Louis, Mo.
December 5, Louisville, Ky.
December 6, Louisville, Ky.
December 7, Louisville, Ky.
December 8, Louisville, Ky.
December 9, Louisville, Ky.
December 10, Louisville, Ky.
December 11, Louisville, Ky.
December 12, Indianapolis, Ind.
December 13, Indianapolis, Ind.
December 14, Terre Haute, Ind.
December 15, Evansville, Ind.
December 16, Vincennes, Ind.
December 17, Crawfordsville, Ind.
December 19, Lafayette, Ind.
December 20, Logansport, Ind.
December 21, South Bend, Ind.
December 22, Fort Wayne, Ind.
December 23, Richmond, Ind.
December 24, Hamilton, O.
December 26, Cincinnati, O.
December 27, Cincinnati, O.
December 28, Cincinnati, O.
December 29, Cincinnati, O.
December 30, Cincinnati, O.
December 31, Cincinnati, O.
1882.
January 2, Dayton, O.
January **3,** Xenia, **O.**
January 4, Chillicothe, O.
January 5, Columbus, O.
January 6, Columbus, O.
January 7, Springfield, O.
January 9, Mt. Vernon, O.
January 10, Newark, O.
January 11, Zanesville, O.
January 12, Steubenville, O.
January 13, Wheeling, W. Va.
January 14, Wheeling, W. Va.
January 16, Pittsburgh, Pa.
January 17, Pittsburgh, Pa.
January 18, Pittsburgh, Pa.
January 19, Pittsburgh, Pa.
January 20, Pittsburgh, Pa.
January 21, Pittsburgh, Pa.

January 23, Cumberland, Md.
January 24, Hagerstown, Md.
January 25, Harrisburg, Pa.
January 26, Reading, Pa.
January 27, Lancaster, Pa.
January 28, Columbia, Pa.
January 30, Baltimore, Md.
January 31, Baltimore, Md.
February 1, Baltimore, Md.
February 2, Baltimore, Md.
February 3, Baltimore, Md.
February 4, Baltimore, Md.
February 6, Philadelphia, Pa.
February 7, Philadelphia, Pa.
February 8, Philadelphia, **Pa.**
February 9, Philadelphia, Pa.
February 10, Philadelphia, Pa.
February 11, Philadelphia, Pa.
February 13, Trenton, N. J.
February 14, New Brunswick, N. J.
February 15, Easton, Pa.
February 16, S. Bethlehem, Pa.
February **17,** Wilkesbarre, Pa.
February 18, Scranton, Pa.
February 20, Binghamton, N. Y.
February 21, Hornellsville, N. Y.
February 22, Corning, N. Y.
February 23, Elmira, N. Y.
February 24, Ithaca, **N. Y.**
February 25, Owego, **N. Y.**
February 27, Port Jervis, N. Y.
February 28, Middletown, N. Y.
March 1, Paterson, N. **J.**
March 2, Newark, **N. J.**
March 3, Newark, **N. J.**
March 4, Newark, **N. J.**
March 6, **Brooklyn, N. Y.**
March 7, Brooklyn, N. Y.
March 8, Brooklyn, N. Y.
March 9, Brooklyn, N. **Y.**
March 10, Brooklyn, N. Y.
March 11, Brooklyn, N. Y.
March 13, New York, N. Y.
March 14, New York, N. Y.
March 15, New York, N. Y.
March 16, New York, N. Y.
March **17,** New York, N. **Y.**
March 18, New York, N. **Y.**
March 20, Stamford, **Conn.**
March **21,** Danbury, **Conn.**
March 22, S. Norwalk, Conn.
March **23,** Bridgeport, Conn.
March **24,** Waterbury, Conn.
March 25, New Haven, Conn.
March 27, Middletown, Conn.
March 28, Hartford, Conn.
March 29, Springfield, Mass.
March 30, Worcester, Mass.
March 31, Woonsocket, R. I.
April 3, New York, N. Y.
April **4, New** York, N. Y.
April 5, **New** York, N. Y.
April 6, **New** York, N. Y.
April 7, **New** York, N. Y.
April **8, New** York, N. Y.

Time Differences, Population, Air-Line and Railroad Distances from New York to Fifty Cities.

CITIES.	STATES	TIME AT 12 O'CLOCK IN NEW YORK	POPULATION 1884.	AIR-LINE DISTANCE FROM N. Y. MILES.	RAIL'D DISTANCE FROM N. Y. MILES.
Albany	N. Y.	12.50 P. M.	100,000	136	142
Atlanta	Ga.	11.18 A. M.	50,000	745	894
Augusta	Ga.	11.27 A. M.	35,000	630	852
Baltimore	Md.	11.56 A. M.	400,000	155	187
Bangor	Me.	12.21 P. M.	20,000	386	458
Boston	Mass.	12.12 P. M.	400,000	165	214
Brooklyn	N. Y.	12.00 M.	700,000		
Buffalo	N. Y.	11.50 A. M.	270,000	295	422
Burlington	Vt.	12.03 P. M.	15,000	270	348
Charleston	S. C.	11.21 A. M.	58,000	600	807
Chicago	Ill.	11.06 A. M.	650,000	700	931
Cincinnati	O.	11.18 A. M.	300,000	545	757
Cleveland	O.	11.29 A. M.	220,100	390	598
Columbus	O.	11.24 A. M.	70,000	440	637
Concord	N. H.	12.10 P. M.	15,000	225	261
Denver	Col.	9.56 A. M.	50,000	1,700	1,971
Detroit	Mich.	11.24 A. M.	165,000	480	677
Dubuque	Iowa.	10.53 A. M.	30,000	885	1,178
Galveston	Tex.	10.37 A. M.	30,000	1,370	1,788
Hannibal	Mo.	10.55 A. M.	12,000	890	1,247
Hartford	Conn.	12.05 P. M.	42,000	105	110
Indianapolis	Ind.	11.12 A. M.	105,000	625	825
Kansas City	Mo.	10.37 A. M.	100,000	1,090	1,374
Little Rock	Ark.	10.47 A. M.	30,000	1,040	1,379
Louisville	Ky.	11.14 A. M.	140,000	625	867
Memphis	Tenn.	10.56 A. M.	34,000	925	1,244
Milwaukee	Wis.	11.04 A. M.	152,000	720	1,046
Minneapolis	Minn.	10.43 A. M.	100,000	1,021	1,381
Mobile	Ala.	11.04 A. M.	40,000	1,000	1,249
Nashville	Tenn.	11.09 A. M.	45,000	730	1,052
New Haven	Conn.	12.04 P. M.	70,000	66	74
New Orleans	La.	10.56 A. M.	300,000	1,120	1,389
New York	N. Y.	12.00 M.	1,300,000		
Omaha	Neb.	10.32 A. M.	60,000	1,135	1,414
Pensacola	Fla.	11.07 A. M.	7,000	945	1,325
Philadelphia	Penn.	11.55 A. M.	900,000	65	89
Pittsburg	Penn.	11.39 A. M.	200,000	300	444
Portland	Me.	12.15 P. M.	24,000	265	330
Providence	R. I.	12.10 P. M.	126,000	155	188
Quincy	Ill.	10.55 A. M.	42,000	800	1,224
Richmond	Va.	11.46 A. M.	80,000	270	349
St. Joseph	Mo.	10.38 A. M.	50,000	1,090	1,330
St. Louis	Mo.	10.55 A. M.	500,000	840	1,045
St. Paul	Minn.	10.38 A. M.	100,000	985	1,371
Salt Lake City	Utah.	9.28 A. M.	25,000	1,994	2,529
San Francisco	Cal.	8.46 A. M.	350,000	2,600	3,370
Savannah	Ga.	11.32 A. M.	40,000	680	951
Terre Haute	Ind.	11.06 A. M.	30,000	700	808
Vicksburg	Miss.	10.53 A. M.	16,000	1,055	1,397
Washington	D. C.	11.43 A. M.	200,000	190	228
Wilmington	N. C.	11.46 A. M.	50,000	490	597

DISTANCES AROUND THE WORLD.

	miles,		miles,
New York to San Francisco	3,350	Aden to Suez	1,308
San Francisco to Yokohama	4,764	Suez to Alexandria	1,290
Yokohama to Hong Kong	1,620	Alexandria to Marseilles	1,300
Hong Kong to Singapore	1,150	Marseilles to Paris	536
Singapore to Calcutta	1,200	Paris to London	376
Calcutta to Bombay	1,009	London to Liverpool	360
Bombay to Aden	1,664	Liverpool to New York	3,100

Total 23,172

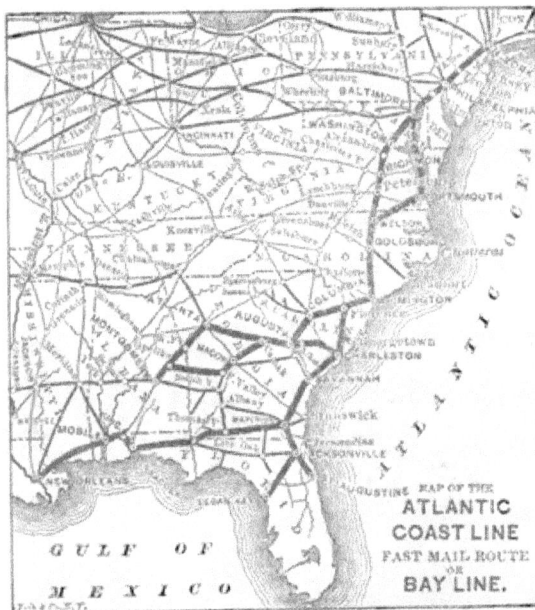

INDEX.

INDEX TO ADVERTISEMENTS.

www.ingramcontent.com/pod-product-compliance
Lightning Source LLC
Chambersburg PA
CBHW030905270326
41929CB00008B/581